The Gift of the Land
and the Fate of the Canaanites
in Jewish Thought

The Gift of the Land
and the Fate of the Canaanites
in Jewish Thought

Edited by Katell Berthelot,
Joseph E. David,
and

Marc Hirshman

OXFORD
UNIVERSITY PRESS

OXFORD
UNIVERSITY PRESS

Oxford University Press is a department of the University of Oxford.
It furthers the University's objective of excellence in research, scholarship,
and education by publishing worldwide.

Oxford   New York
Auckland   Cape Town   Dar es Salaam   Hong Kong   Karachi
Kuala Lumpur   Madrid   Melbourne   Mexico City   Nairobi
New Delhi   Shanghai   Taipei   Toronto

With offices in
Argentina   Austria   Brazil   Chile   Czech Republic   France   Greece
Guatemala   Hungary   Italy   Japan   Poland   Portugal   Singapore
South Korea   Switzerland   Thailand   Turkey   Ukraine   Vietnam

Oxford is a registered trademark of Oxford University Press
in the UK and certain other countries.

Published in the United States of America by
Oxford University Press
198 Madison Avenue, New York, NY 10016

Library of Congress Cataloging-in-Publication Data
The gift of the land and the fate of the Canaanites in Jewish thought / edited by Katell Berthelot,
Joseph E. David, and Marc Hirshman.
p cm
Includes index.
ISBN 978–0–19–995982–2 (pbk. : alk. paper)—ISBN 978–0–19–995980–8 (hardcover : alk. paper)
1. Jews—History.   2. Judaism—History.   3. Bible. Old testament—History and criticism.
I. Berthelot, Katell, editor.   II. David, Joseph E., editor.   III. Hirshman, Marc G., editor.
DS121.I75 2013
933'.004926—dc23
2013024479

1 3 5 7 9 8 6 4 2
Printed in the United States of America
on acid-free paper

{ CONTENTS }

{ LIST OF CONTRIBUTORS }

Baruch Alster, Givat Washington College, Israel.

Michael Avioz, Bar Ilan University, Israel.

Eyal Ben-Eliyahu, University of Haifa, Israel.

Katell Berthelot, CNRS/Aix–Marseille University, France.

Joseph E. David, Hebrew University of Jerusalem, Israel.

Paul Fenton, Paris IV—Sorbonne University, France.

Warren Zeev Harvey, Hebrew University of Jerusalem, Israel.

Annabel Herzog, Haifa University, Israel.

Marc Hirshman, Hebrew University of Jerusalem, Israel.

Yoram Jacobson, Tel Aviv University, Israel.

Menachem Kellner, Shalem College and the University of Haifa, Israel.

Menahem Kister, Hebrew University of Jerusalem, Israel.

Evyatar Marienberg, University of North Carolina, USA.

Matthias Morgenstern, University of Tübingen, Germany.

David Ohana, Ben Gurion University, Israel.

Meira Polliack, Tel Aviv University, Israel.

Ishay Rosen-Zvi, Tel Aviv University, Israel.

Avinoam Rosenak, Hebrew University of Jerusalem, and Van Leer Institute, Jerusalem Israel.

Dov Schwartz, Bar-Ilan University, Israel.

Nili Wazana, Hebrew University of Jerusalem, Israel.

Marzena Zawanowska, University of Warsaw, Poland.

{ LIST OF ABBREVIATIONS }

Secondary Sources

AB	Anchor Bible
ABD	*Anchor Bible Dictionary*
AGJU	Arbeiten zur Geschichte des antiken Judentums und des Urchristentums
AJSL	*American Journal of Semitic Languages and Literatures*
BDB	Brown, Francis, Samuel R. Driver, and Charles A. Briggs. *A Hebrew and English Lexicon of the Old Testament.* Oxford: Oxford University Press, 1907.
BibOr	Biblica et orientalia
BZAW	Beihefte zur Zeitschrift für die alttestamentliche Wissenschaft
CCSL	Corpus Christianorum: Series latina. Turnhout, 1953–
DJD	Discoveries in the Judaean Desert
DSD	*Dead Sea Discoveries*
FHJA	Holladay, C. H. *Fragments from Hellenistic Jewish Authors, Volume I: Historians.* Chico: Scholars Press, 1983.
GCS	Die Griechischen christlichen Schriftsteller der ersten [drei] Jahrhunderte
GLAJJ	*Greek and Latin Authors on Jews and Judaism*
HAT	Handbuch zum Alten Testament
HTR	*Harvard Theological Review*
ICC	International Critical Commentary
JECS	*Journal of Early Christian Studies*
JJS	*Journal of Jewish Studies*
JNES	*Journal of Near Eastern Studies*
JQR	*Jewish Quarterly Review*
JRE	*Journal of Religious Ethics*
JSJ	*Journal for the Study of Judaism in the Persian, Hellenistic, and Roman Period*
JSJS	Journal for the Study of Judaism Supplement Series
JSNT	*Journal for the Study of the New Testament*

JSOT	*Journal for the Study of the Old Testament*
JSOTSup	Journal for the Study of the Old Testament: Supplement Series
JSPSup	Journal for the Study of the Pseudepigrapha: Supplement Series
JSQ	*Jewish Studies Quarterly*
JSS	*Journal of Semitic Studies*
Jud.	*Judaica*
KAI	*Kanaanäische und aramäische Inschriften.* H. Donner and W. Röllig. 2d ed. Wiesbaden, 1966–1969
LCL	Loeb Classical Library
MGWJ	*Monatsschrift für Geschichte und Wissenschaft des Judentums*
MT	Masoretic Text
NICOT	New International Commentary on the Old Testament
OTL	Old Testament Library
PEQ	*Palestine Exploration Quarterly*
PG	Patrologia graeca [= Patrologiae cursus completus: Series graeca]. Edited by J.-P. Migne. 162 vols. Paris, 1857–1886
REJ	*Revue des études juives*
STDJ	Studies on the Texts of the Desert of Judah
StPatr	Studia Patristica
SVC	Supplements to Vigiliae Christianae
SVT	Studia in Veteris Testamenti
TDNT	*Theological Dictionary of the New Testament*
VT	*Vetus Testamentum*
VTSup	Vetus Testamentum Supplements
WUNT	Wissenschaftliche Untersuchungen zum Neuen Testament

Works by Josephus

Ant.	*Antiquitates judaicae*
B.J.	*Bellum judaicum*
C.Ap.	*Contra Apionem*

Works by Philo

Congr.	*De congressu eruditionis gratia*
Hypoth.	*Hypothetica*
Mos.	*De vita Mosis*

QG	*Quaestiones et solutiones in Genesin*
Spec.	*De specialibus legibus*
Somn.	*De somniis*

Miscellaneous Works

Praep. ev.	Eusebius, *Praeparatio evangelica*
Pol.	Plato, *Politicus*
Se	*Seʾelim*

Mishnah, Talmud, and Related Literature

Avod. Zar.	*Avodah Zarah*
B. Bat.	*Bava Batra*
B. Metzia	*Bava Metzia*
B. Qam.	*Bava Qamma*
Ber.	*Berakhot*
ʿEruv.	*ʿEruvin*
Git.	*Gittin*
Hul.	*Hullin*
Ketub.	*Ketubbot*
Maʿas. S.	*Maʿaser Sheni*
Meg.	*Megillah*
ʿOr.	*ʿOrlah*
Pesah.	*Pesahim*
Qidd.	*Qiddushin*
Sanh.	*Sanhedrin*
Shabb.	*Shabbat*
Shev.	*Sheviʿit*
Yad.	*Yadayim*

Other Rabbinic Works

MRI	*Mekhilta deRabbi Ishmael*
MRShY	*Mekhilta deRabbi Shimeʿon bar Yohaï*
PRK	*Pesikta deRav Kahana*
Rab. (e.g. Gen. Rab.)	*Rabbah* (+ biblical book)

Modern Jewish Works

IgM	*Iggerot Moshe*
SE	*Sefat Emet*

The Gift of the Land
and the Fate of the Canaanites
in Jewish Thought

Introduction

Katell Berthelot, Joseph David, and Marc Hirshman

Jewish thought over almost three millennia has reflected repeatedly on biblical legislation and historiography regarding the gift of the land of Israel and the fate of the Canaanites. It is stimulating to explore the Jewish intellectual efforts that have been invested over the millennia and the collection of the diverse approaches and interpretations presented here is extremely instructive. The scholars who joined us in this effort to depict Jewish reflection on this subject did so as part of their scholarly commitment to research Jewish thought in as objective a manner as possible. We hope that this volume will shed light on this important topic in the history of Judaism.

Most of the essays of this book were delivered in a conference convened jointly by the Centre de Recherche Français à Jérusalem (CNRS–MAEE), the Van Leer Jerusalem Institute, and the Yad Izhak Ben Zvi Institute for Research on the Land of Israel, to which we express our gratitude for their support, concerning both the organization of the conference and the publication of this volume. We were gratified by the participation of many of the leading scholars, comprising historians, philologians, and philosophers, whose areas of expertise cover antiquity through modern times. The program of the conference, which took place in Jerusalem on December 8–10, 2009, is appended at the end of this volume. At the reviewers' requests, we have added essays to give an even more comprehensive treatment of the subject. It is our conviction that these learned analyses of Jewish thinking on this subject will evince an appreciation of a religious tradition grappling with the moral and theological issues raised by its holy sources, while sustaining a firm belief in them. It is fascinating to follow the threads of the interpetations and arguments, polemics and apologetics as they are spun and re-spun over the millenia.

We have tried here to provide a sustained treatment of the various strategies and positions held in Jewish thought from biblical times through our own times. This volume is a comprehensive, though surely not exhaustive, analysis of major Jewish thinkers grappling with the biblical accounts of the gift of the land of Israel and the fate of its putative original inhabitants, the Canaanites.

Dwelling in the Land: Theological and Ethical Issues

The bitter fate of the Canaanites, as portrayed in some of the biblical sources, raises both ethical questions about the justification of the conquest of Canaan by Israel and theological questions about divine justice. Part I of this volume presents diverse approaches to these issues, from those suggested implicitly or explicitly in Scripture itself and on through modern times. The uneasiness felt by some committed readers of the Bible with these issues involves a clash of moral intuitions and commitments; the normative status of the Bible seemed to be inconsistent with some readers' ethical standards and theological principles. Coping with the tension between the prescripts of the texts and the morality of its addressees has led to the development of various interpretative strategies vis-à-vis what appeared to be problematic texts.

First, it must be recalled that there is a great deal of diversity within the biblical corpus itself, which reflects to some extent internal self-criticism. The disclosure of inner tensions among the biblical texts—the existence of counter-accounts, or what George Steiner termed "alternities,"[1] within the Bible itself—might then serve to soften or alleviate difficulties for some of the readers. Concerning the Book of Joshua, for example, Nili Wazana, in Chapter 1, shows that it contains more than one account of the Israelite conquest and the fate of the Canaanites. In the first account, the conquest consisted of a series of tribal, or individual, missions that eventually left Canaanite enclaves in peaceful coexistence alongside the settlements of the Israelites. In the other account, which corresponds to the dramatic promises given to the patriarchs, the conquest of the land is described in a spectacular way and in miraculous terms as a national task that was fully completed by the total expulsion of the Canaanites.

During the Second Temple period, when the biblical texts became more established and fixed, biblical rewriting and biblical commentary developed also as a strategy for coping with difficulties within the texts. In dealing with the theological and ethical issues connected with the Canaanites' fate, Jewish authors sometimes indulged in apologetics. Some scholars have argued that Josephus, for instance, refrained from formulating a "land-centered covenantal theology" out of apologetic concerns, in order to de-emphasize Jewish nationalistic trends. In Chapter 2, Michael Avioz challenges this scholarly assessment. The little weight Josephus gives to the "biblical land theology," Avioz argues, should not be taken as an expression of apologetics, but rather should be understood against the background of the varied accounts within the Bible itself.

Within the world of rabbinic literature, we actually hear voices of criticism and dissatisfaction with the biblical story of the conquest.[2] The rabbis not only envisaged the existence of the remaining Canaanites in the land of Israel, as Eyal Ben-Eliyahu shows (see below), but also held intensive discussions about the accurate meaning of the biblical imperative "and you shall destroy their name out of that place" (Deut 12:3). As the close reading by Ishay Rosen-Zvi in Chapter 3 reveals, the Tannaitic schools of Rabbi Ishmael and Rabbi Akiva debated the meaning of the biblical demand to destroy idols. The two schools were debating the question of whether the obligation is to destroy idols or rather to keep one's distance from them. Rosen-Zvi demonstrates the polemical efforts of the Mishnah to introduce a different ethics of idolatry in opposition to the biblical demand to destroy idols.

Menahem Kister, in Chapter 4, examines the fate of the Canaanites and the despoliation of the Egyptians as case studies to explore some apologetic debates originating in the Second Temple period and transformed in Late Antiquity and beyond. His deep and extensive analysis demonstrates how the theological-ethical problems rooted in the Bible were discussed in the Hellenistic and Roman periods, partly in response to Gentile accusations. However, he doubts that these debates developed in the specific context of the Hasmonean wars of territorial conquest, and he demonstrates that nothing in the sources themselves supports this hypothesis. Instead he suggests focusing on the interplay between biblical motifs and Second Temple apologetic motives against anti-Jewish indictments. His analysis of the Jewish traditions shows that the debate about the Canaanites and that about the despoliation of the Egyptians are closely intertwined, both as far as the sources of these traditions are concerned and the later texts that associate them; both attempt to cope exegetically with Gentile indictments that were based on biblical narratives—and probably also with some innate Jewish uneasiness. Finally, he demonstrates that many assertions in rabbinic literature transform earlier traditions, which emerged as early as the Second Temple period (documented, for example, in the *Book of Jubilees* and Philo), and that similar traditions are attested in early Christian literature, in various contexts (notably as part of anti-Gnostic polemics). The debates about the fate of the Canaanites and the despoliation of the Egyptians therefore represent remarkable cases of both continuity and transformation of apologetical exegetical traditions and motifs that operated for several centuries in different historical contexts.

Compared to the Mishnaic polemic discussions, post-talmudic reactions to the theological-ethical problems raised by the fate of the Canaanites seem to be much less audacious, and apologetics becomes again a prominent strategy for coming to terms with the textual difficulties. Thus medieval Jewish thinkers and commentators endeavored to bridge the ethical gap between their own moral senses and the biblical descriptions by their hermeneutical faculties and exegetical creativity.

In Chapter 5, Meira Polliack and Marzena Zawanowska examine the exegesis of Canaan's curse (Gen 9:25) by central Karaite thinkers of the "golden age" of this Jewish movement (tenth and eleventh centuries C.E.), in light of their scriptural ideology, individual moral principles, and Mu'tazilite theology. One of the intra-biblical accounts associates the Canaanites' fate with the curse that Noah had placed upon his grandson, Canaan (Gen 9:25). Accordingly, the settlement of the Israelites and the expulsion of the Canaanites are both justified in terms of cross-generational retributive justice. This reasoning contradicts the principles of Muʿtazilite theology. The justification of the Canaanites' expulsion thus provided the Karaites with the opportunity to discuss and elaborate on several topics, including divine retributive justice, the notion of freedom of choice, and the meaning of divine foresight. Polliack and Zawanowska trace the hermeneutical efforts of the Karaite school of exegesis (including Yaʿaqūb al-Qirqisānī, Yefet ben ʿElī, Yūsuf ibn Nūḥ, Abū al-Faraj Ḥārūn and Yeshuʿah ben Yehudah) in grappling with the biblical description, their individual solutions and their attempts to harmonize the biblical text with the rationalistic (Muʿtazili) worldview which formed part of their intellectual millieu and heritage.

Reflecting on medieval exegetical and halakhic developments concerning the Canaanites, Menachem Kellner, in Chapter 6, calls the reader's attention to the limits of apologetics. He points out that, despite the fact that medieval commentators acknowledged the hermeneutical potency at their hands, they did not always use those means to reduce, or to soften, the problem raised by the Deuteronomic command to eradicate the Canaanites. Kellner's analysis renews questions about the effectiveness of interpretation when confronting explicitly problematic texts within Scriptures. Living in peace with problematic texts brings puzzling questions of hermeneutics back to the forefront: the weight of the interpreter's values, motivations, and intentions; the objective constraints of interpretation; the independency of the text and its reader; and so on.

Through the case of the Canaanites, we contemplate the constitution of the notion of "otherness" in the religious imagination of Scripture-based societies. As such, the biblical relationship between Israel and Canaan in fact constitutes the fundamental categories of identity: us/them, self/other. Canaan, in that respect, designates the "other," whose conduct Israel is warned not to follow, whose idol Israel is commanded to destroy, and whose people Israel must dominate and kill. In Chapter 7, Joseph David describes the legal-theology of the thirteenth-century kabbalist and jurist Nahmanides (Moses b. Nahman, 1194–1270) and his attempt to construct a territorial notion of the halakhah. This innovative move revives biblical perceptions about the internal relatedness of law, land, and God, and corresponds to the Christian propaganda of the Crusades in his days. Interestingly, the territorial notion of the halakhah introduces new meanings to the self/other dichotomy, not on the basis of ethnic identity, but rather on the basis of territorial belongings. In that respect, the Canaanites' fate reflects the possible fate of any inhabitants who transgress the divine laws on God's land, be it the Jews or the Gentiles. This is perhaps the medieval meaning of the phrase "we have met the Canaanites and they are us."

Another strategy for coping with the ethical-theological problems of the Canaanites' fate is by de-historicizing the tension between Canaan and Israel and ascribing them spiritual meaning. Yoram Jacobson, in Chapter 8, in his analysis of the Sefat Emet, a late nineteenth-century work that shaped the theology of Gur Hasidism, identifies the two territorial belongings, the land of Canaan and the land of Israel, as representing two spiritual phases in the process of the redemption of reality. Inspired by the Zoharic Kabbalah and the thought of Maharal of Prague (Yehudah Loew b. Bezalel, 1520–1609) the Canaan-Israel juxtaposition comes to represent the theosophical dichotomies of natural/supernatural, impure/sanctified, unified/diverse, and so on. Within impure "nature," represented by the land of Canaan, there is hidden divine sanctity, represented by the land of Israel. The mission of the exiled people of Israel, therefore, is to open wide the locked gates of "nature," to expose the concealed sanctity, and to spread it over the entire world. By that, the sanctification of "nature" will turn all the world's territories into a holy land of Israel. Accordingly, the conquest of the land of Canaan was not an actual aggressive act, but rather an act by which the natural, impure, and fragmented conditions of reality were redeemed to become a supernatural, sanctified, and united order. This spiritualized interpretation not only escapes ethical and theological difficulties, but also redefines the relationship between Canaan and Israel as one of reciprocal cooperation within the divine plan and the cosmic order.

Identification with the Israelites' conquest against the Canaanites played a political role in various historical contexts. In the modern period, though, the issue of the fate of the Canaanites and of biblical texts that have recourse to violence in general became more problematic in a European context. Matthias Morgenstern, in Chapter 9, introduces us to nineteenth-century German-Jewish thinkers who found that the biblical accounts of the conquest of the land contrasted with their endeavors to portray Judaism as a tolerant, peaceful, and enlightened religion and their own unquestioned commitment and sense of belonging to Germany. Refering to biblical criticism, interclass struggles, historical materialism, and international law, each of the four analyzed thinkers—Heinrich Graetz (1817–1891), R. Samson Raphael Hirsch (1808–1888), Isaac Breuer (1883–1946), and his brother Raphael Breuer (1881–1932)—had to cope with the tension between biblical descriptions of the conquest and modern moral standards. Against the backdrop of their existential circumstances as a homeless minority in what they took to be an enlightened Europe and with an either implicit or explicit refusal to rely on apologetics, these orthodox authors focused their reactions on the morality of belonging and the ethical-theological statuses of "homeland," "fatherland," and "birthplace," rather than the Promised Land.

The Changing Uses of the Category "Canaanites"

Through the ages, and depending on the historical context, the category "Canaanite" has appeared to be astonishingly flexible. The chapters of Part II explore the changing uses of the category "Canaanite" and show that an essentialist understanding of the term should be proscribed. Katell Berthelot, in Chapter 10, shows that during the Second Temple period, apart from biblical quotations or the rewriting of biblical texts, Jewish literature hardly refers to the Canaanites. Moreover, a tendency toward anachronism can be observed, since many Jews writing in Greek refer to the land of Israel in biblical times using names that are contemporary, such as "Syria" or "Syrian Palestine." As a consequence, the ancient inhabitants of the land are sometimes called "Syrians," "Phoenicians," and so on. There are only two cases in which the name "Canaan" or "Canaanite" is used in connection with contemporary people living on the fringes of the land. First, the name appears in 1 Maccabees 9:37, where "one of the great nobles of Canaan" designates the father of a bride who is to marry one of the enemies of the Maccabean brothers Jonathan and Simon. Only one person is designated in such a way, and he is not personally involved in the fights between the Hasmoneans and their enemies. The second instance in which "Canaanite" is used corresponds to the passage in the Gospel of Matthew in which Jesus encounters a Syro-Phoenician woman whose daughter is possessed; in this case, the use of the adjective "Canaanite" certainly has a pejorative connotation and is meant to emphasize that Jesus extends God's grace to people who were antagonistic to Jews. In general, it appears that during the Second Temple period the category "Canaanites" was largely irrelevant as a means of reflecting on the Jews's relationship with the non-Jews in the land.

In Chapter 11, Eyal Ben-Eliyahu tackles the issue of the meaning of "Canaanites" in rabbinic literature, arguing that the Sages not only used the term "Canaanite" in connection with the ancient inhabitants of the land, by characterizing ancient cultic objects or places as "Amorite" or "Canaanite," for instance, but also considered that some descendants of the Canaanites still inhabited the land of Israel in their own time (the time of the Sages). Ezra 2:43–58, which mentions a man called "Sisera," is taken by the Sages as referring to some descendants of the Canaanites, who are even considered to hold lands. They constitute the category of the "taxpayers," which probably goes back to the biblical story of the Canaanites who were subjected to taxes by King Solomon. Through this story, the Sages were able to elaborate a halakhah that allowed the Canaanites to stay in the land, despite the explicit commandments not to let them do so, found in the Pentateuch. In contrast with the literature from the Second Temple period, rabbinic sources thus testify to the idea that it is possible that Canaanites may still be living among Jews.

A meaning of "Canaanites" partly estranged from its original biblical context can be found in medieval Jewish texts that deal with "Canaanite slaves," that is, non-Jewish slaves in Jewish households—a notion that goes back to rabbinic literature. Evyatar Marienberg, in Chapter 12, shows that in the Middle Ages, there were two ways of interpreting the notion of a "Canaanite slave": for some Jewish commentators, all non-Jewish slaves, regardless of their ethnic or geographical origin, were called "Canaanite"; for others, the term "Canaanite" designated the actual biological descendants of the biblical Canaanites, whether they were free or enslaved. The rabbinic story of the Canaanites who went to Africa was used in this context, but also was further developed, so that the African Canaanites were said to have reached Central Europe, where they eventually become the slaves of both the descendants of Shem and the descendants of Japhet, thus fulfilling the curse of Genesis 9. In Chapter 5 (in Part I), Meira Polliack and Marzena Zawanowska mention the fact that some Karaite exegetes solved the discrepancies between Genesis and Deuteronomy "by making a distinction between [the Canaanites] who remained in the land of Canaan and were to be erased and those who fled and were to become slaves." Karaite exegetes thus seem to have favored the idea that slaves in Jewish households in Europe were the descendants of the Canaanites who had fled, and not simply non-Jews.

Descendants of the Canaanites were thought to have inhabited not only Europe, but also North Africa. In Chapter 13, Paul Fenton shows that, from the Middle Ages onward, certain Arab historians came to identify the North African Berbers with the Middle Eastern Canaanites. No doubt influenced—at least in part—by rabbinic traditions which upheld that the Canaanites emigrated to Africa, their accounts are mixed with other legends that represent the Berbers as descendants of Goliath, hero of the Philistines. According to the famous historian Ibn Khaldun (fourteenth century), the Canaanites and the Philistines were all descendants of Ham, and the former helped the latter in their wars against the Israelites. The identification of the Berbers with the Philistines is also found in medieval Jewish sources; in later times, even the North African Jews originating from the Berber regions came themselves to be called Philistines! This again shows how traditions travel and evolve with the passing of time and according to the different contexts in which they are reformulated.

So far we have seen that the name "Canaanite" was mainly applied to peoples who were imagined to be descendants of the biblical ethnic group(s) designated as such (with the exception of the "Canaanite slaves," who could be non-Jews in general). In his study of the cultural-political movement of the "Young Hebrews" created by Yonatan Ratosh in the twentieth century, David Ohana, in Chapter 14, tackles a very different case, that of Jews called "Canaanites" by their adversaries, who then retained the name as a self-designation. They considered themselves "Hebrews" rather than Jews, connected first and foremost with the land of Canaan/Israel, not with Judaism (viewed as a Diaspora phenomenon), and they wanted to go back to the original relationship between the ancient people of Israel, the land of Canaan, and the Hebrew language. As part of the revival of the Hebrew nation, "Canaanism" also aimed at the Hebraization of the entire Middle East. David Ohana's chapter exposes the complexity of the Canaanite ideology (which extends beyond Ratosh's group), including its connections with the different streams of Zionism and with post-Zionism.

The Gift of the Land and the Fate of the Canaanites in the Modern Context of the Construction of the State of Israel

The chapters gathered in this third and last part of the book analyze the ways in which Zionism, both religious and secular, left-wing and right-wing, reflected on the new problems and the possible solutions linked to the encounter with the Arab population in Palestine and the construction of the modern state of Israel. Two major Jewish figures from the Diaspora, the American rabbi and legal thinker Moshe Feinstein and the French philosopher Emmanuel Levinas, who both reflected on the Jewish tradition and the modern state of Israel, are also included in these studies.

Dov Schwartz, in Chapter 15, deals with the connection of religious Zionism to biblical sources and with the question of whether acquaintance with force changed attitudes to the seven nations in religious-Zionist thought. When confronting secular-national arguments, religious Zionism has fluctuated between a religious-halakhic and a religious-spiritual approach. From a halakhic point of view, different views have been advocated. For Rabbi Reines, the founder of the Mizrahi (the religious faction within the Zionist movement), conquest is a means, whereas legal possession and settlement of the land are the end. The presence of other nations in Eretz Israel may therefore be accepted if those nations reject idolatry and acknowledge Jewish rule as legitimate. But for other rabbis—Rabbi Nussenbaum, for instance—the nations have to be gradually expelled. And for Rabbi Waldenberg, whose views are similar to those expressed in the *Sefer ha-Hinukh* (an anonymous commentary of the commandments written in thirteenth-century Spain), the destruction of the seven nations is an unambiguous command, leaving no room for leniency, which applies everywhere and at any time. However, Rabbi Waldenberg represents an exception; on the whole, most religious-Zionist views, be they militant or moderate, have endorsed the contextual approach, meaning that the destruction command is context-bound rather than absolute. From a haggadic perspective, on the other hand, the view that the seven nations had unlawfully settled a land that belonged to the children of Israel prevailed in the religious-Zionist movement, along with the notion of a mystical link between the people of Israel and the land.

The significance of the thought of Rabbi Reines (1839–1915) is also studied by Zeev Harvey in Chapter 16. Harvey argues that Rabbi Reines tried his best to sever all connections between modern political Zionism and the ancient Israelites' war of conquest against the Canaanites. Based on Nahmanides and Ribash (1326–1408), the position of Rabbi Reines was that it is a divine commandment to settle the land, in the present as in the past, but, in opposition to the time of Joshua and David, the settlement must be done only by peaceful means, such as purchasing land, for God has now forbidden conquest of the land "with a strong hand" (*b. Ketub.* 111a). One important authority who did follow Rabbi Reines's interpretation of the oath "not to storm the wall" was Rabbi Abraham Isaac Ha-Kohen Kook, the first Ashkenazi Chief Rabbi of Mandatory Palestine, for whom the settlement could be achieved only by peaceful means. Harvey argues that in religious Zionist circles today, however, the oath "not to storm the wall" is not usually understood according to the interpretation of Rabbi Reines and Rabbi Kook, but is considered anachronistic, irrelevant, and nonexistent, insofar as the nations have endorsed Jewish sovereignty in the land of Israel.

In Chapter 17, Avinoam Rosenak expounds in a detailed way the religious-Zionist doctrine of Rabbi Abraham Isaac Ha-Kohen Kook (1865–1935) and that of his disciples, challenging previous views, like those of Elie Holzer, who consider the disciples to have deviated from the pacific ideas of Rabbi Kook. Rosenak explores a theoretical matter concerning Rabbi Kook's complex attitude toward the inhabitants of biblical Canaan; the conquest of the land of Israel, past and present; and the potentially troublesome moral questions thereby raised. The article examines these issues on a number of levels. It examines Rabbi Kook's writings on the seizure of ancient Canaan from its inhabitants, his assessment of the morality of that action, and his view of the connection between the biblical conquest and contemporary historical events. The article notes two reactions on Rabbi Kook's part to the morality of war and the conquest of the land of Israel. His attitude with respect to the issue in the biblical period appears to be the polar opposite of his totally non-violent attitude in modern times. The gap between these reactions is evident and might well be taken as an internal inconsistency. Rosenak traces Rabbi Kook's dialectical logic, considers the complex attitude of academic scholarship toward these issues, and probes the ways in which Rabbi Kook's disciples have tried to apply his logic in the here and now—a context that Rabbi Kook did not know and could never have imagined.

With Baruch Alster's study, in Chapter 18, of the responsa of Rabbi Moshe Feinstein, we turn to a major figure of American Jewry. Focusing on a particular responsum of Rabbi Feinstein connected with the Israeli-Arab conflict, Baruch Alster shows that this strictly Orthodox rabbinic authority has in fact a very bold interpretation of the rabbinic teaching on "obligatory war" (*milhemet mitzvah*), such as the war against the seven nations and Amalek.

Rabbi Feinstein actually understands halakhah as effectively forbidding any current Jewish government to wage war (except in the case of a defensive war), implying that the prevention of war accomplished by a political agreement is a worthy goal in and of itself. By arguing that the kings of ancient Israel did not initiate a war against the Canaanites or against Amalek, and by requiring that before a declaration of war one must consult not only a High Court, but also a prophet, as well as the Urim and the Tummim, Rabbi Feinstein virtually cancels a biblical (and thus divine) commandment, without formally annulling it. According to Alster, he does so out of a desire, common in rabbinic literature, to see Jewish law as moral. The commandment to eradicate the seven nations or Amalek seems to be so morally problematic in Rabbi Feinstein's eyes that in this case he considers that God must manifest himself and clearly express— through a prophet as well as through the Urim and the Tummim—that such a war is undoubtedly his will. However, in this responsum Rabbi Feinstein presents his answer as a theoretical opinion, rather than a formal ruling with halakhic or practical consequences.

Finally, Annabel Herzog, in Chapter 19, tackles Levinas's reflection about the existence of the state of Israel, especially the contradiction between the idea that politics implies murder, the ethical imperative not to murder, and the necessity to be involved in politics in order to create a society that promotes universal justice, considered to be the core of the Torah. Levinas's reading of Numbers 13–14 (the exploration of the land of Canaan by the Hebrew emissaries) shows that the state must never be taken as an end in itself. It is a means to reach a higher goal, which consists in "care and responsibility for the other." Therefore "the state should be established not only for the sake of those who build it and fight for it, but also for the sake of the other—those who are not part of the political enterprise, those who lost everything, those who are defeated," including the Canaanites.

Notes

1. See George Steiner, *After Babel: Aspects of Language and Translation* (London: Oxford University, 1975), 222.

2. See for instance *Sifra* Qedoshim on Lev 20:24 and *y. Shevi'it* 6:1 (36c).

PART I

The Land: Theological and Ethical Issues

"Everything Was Fulfilled" versus "The Land That Yet Remains"

CONTRASTING CONCEPTIONS OF THE FULFILLMENT OF THE
PROMISE IN THE BOOK OF JOSHUA

Nili Wazana

Introduction

Biblical Israel perceived itself as a nation whose origins lay outside its land, and whose right to the land was founded upon an ancient divine promise.[1] This initial separation between people and land is one of the key features in the pentateuchal presentation of the formation of the triad God–people–land, the dominant theme of the majority of biblical writings.[2] In Priestly sources, the Promised Land is even named after its former inhabitants—"the land of Canaan" (e.g., Gen 17:8; Num 34:2)—thus representing this fundamental independence of people from land and vice versa.

The divine promise of the land is a central motif in the traditions of the Pentateuch, yet in the ten patriarchal promises concerning the land in Genesis, there is but a hint regarding the fate of the Canaanites, or addressing the question of why the former inhabitants are to lose their rights to the land.[3] It seems that the promissory texts that construct the quasi-legal right of the people to the land do not address the possibility of the rights of the autochthonous peoples to it.[4] The somewhat secondary excuse for the disinheritance of the former population of the land appears only in the account of the "covenant between the pieces," which alludes to the "iniquity of the Amorites" which must be completed before Israel may inherit the land (Gen 15:16). This concept is developed in non-promissory Priestly sources, such as Leviticus 18:24–29, or Deuteronomic texts alluding to the people before their entry to the land, which conclude in a fashion similar to Deuteronomy 9:5:

> It is not because of your virtues and your rectitude that you will be able to possess their country; but it is because of their wickedness that the Lord

> your God is dispossessing those nations before you, and in order to fulfill
> the oath that the Lord made to your fathers, Abraham, Isaac and Jacob.[5]

Thus, the iniquity of the former inhabitants of the land becomes a basis for
fulfilling the oath to the fathers, which initially needed no justification; at the
same time, this passage also provides a clue as to the reason for the eventual
expulsion from the land of the people of Israel themselves. In the pentateuchal
traditions, the Canaanites dwelling in the land are fated to be either gradually
expelled (Exod 23:27–32, 34:11) or, according to the Deuteronomic viewpoint,
proscribed and annihilated (Deut 7:2, 7:20–24). Yet for the details of how this
came about, we must turn to the historiographical texts that are set in the
period of the presumed entry of the Israelites into their Promised Land.[6]

An entire biblical book and a chapter in the following book describe the
realization and fulfillment of the promise of the land—that is, the book of
Joshua and Judges 1. Scholars have long pointed out the different conceptions of the inheritance of the land reflected in each of these sources: Joshua's
depiction of a heroic national and total *blitzkrieg*, resulting in complete ethnic
cleansing, versus Judges' account of tribal initiatives accompanied by some
successes (mainly by the tribe of Judah) and many failures, which resulted in
Israel's dwelling in the land alongside remaining Canaanites in Judges 1.[7]

The book of Joshua depicts the fulfillment of the promise of the land, beginning with Joshua's appointment as commander of the conquest and ending
with his death after the settlement of Israel in the land. The protagonist, Joshua,
is thus presented as the leader of the conquest par excellence in the book dedicated to the generation of the entry into the land. Yet a closer look reveals that
the different parts of the book do not offer a single, straightforward view of the
way that the land was conquered.

As a whole, the book of Joshua presents the process of inheritance in two
distinct stages—conquest followed by settlement. This is reflected foremost
through the general scheme of the book, which is very clear: First the land was
conquered in its entirety, and all its inhabitants killed (chapters 1–12, and in
particular 6–12), and then it was apportioned and settled by the tribes
(chapters 13–21).[8] The conquest of the entire land is depicted through four
schematic sweeping battles. The first two are mounted against individual
towns, Jericho in the east and Ai in the central area; the last two are sweeping
and "sudden" (פתאם, Josh 10:9, 11:70)[9] campaigns against coalitions of kings in
the southwest and in the north, which result in the complete overtaking of the
entire land and its population.

Like Judges 1, the second half of the book of Joshua presents a tribal, at
times even individual, point of view, versus the national outlook of the first
half. Each tribe receives its own territory, and each tribe deals with its lot. This
viewpoint is apparent even in the choice of literary actors characterizing each
part of the book. The story of the conquest in Joshua 1–12 presents Israel as

acting together, as one body under the leadership of Joshua who alone stands in the spotlight, heading the campaign. While non-Israelite characters such as Rahab or Adoni-zedek, king of Jerusalem, are given names and voices, Israelite individuals who play a role in events, such as the two spies sent by Joshua to Jericho (chapter 2), remain anonymous. The only story that presents another Israelite individual by name and tribal affinity in this part of the book is that of the antihero Achan, from the tribe of Judah, the exception that proves the rule. The moment that this sinner acts on his own initiative and violates the law of *herem* (חרם), all Israel suffers defeat (chapter 7). It seems that successful and total conquest can be achieved only when the people act as a whole, obedient to and united by one leader. In contrast, the second half of the book mentions many individuals by name; note, for example, Eleazar the priest, who is listed as a leader alongside and even preceding Joshua (14:1, 17:4, 19:21, 21:1), along with such individuals as Caleb, Achsah, Othniel (14:6–15, 15:13–19), and the daughters of Zelophehad (17:3–4), who take an active part in the conquest and settlement of their inheritance.

Besides the national versus tribal/individual orientation, there are also other differences within the book of Joshua itself in its depictions of the process of conquest and settlement and the resulting scope and success of this process, which may be summarized under the following three questions:

1. What is the relationship between the two stages of the inheritance, conquest and settlement—separate or contemporary?
2. What is the fate of the original inhabitants of the land—total annihilation or something else?
3. Did the Israelites succeed in conquering all the territory of the Promised Land, or did some of the territories of the Promised Land "remain"?

While the two last questions are related, they are not identical. Enclaves of foreign peoples within a conquered territory do not necessarily contradict the claim of a complete *territorial* takeover of that area, and land that remains unconquered is an issue by itself, whether it is inhabited by foreign people or not.

The Résumés That Recapitulate the Two Final Battles (Joshua 10:40, 11:16–20)

The model of conquest before settlement is given expression throughout the narrative of the first half of the book. In this part of the book, the Israelites do not settle the areas they overcome. During the preparatory stage and most of the conquest, they camp at Gilgal, the site where Israel had first encamped after having crossed the Jordan River (Josh 4:19–20). This thus far unidentified site, located in the territory of Benjamin somewhere between the Jordan River and Jericho on the threshold of the Promised Land (4:19–20, 5:9–10), is the bridgehead for the conquest campaigns (9:6, 10:6, 10:7, 10:9, 10:15, 10:43).[10] After each conquest, marked by annihilation of the conquered enemy, the entire people return to their base camp. Thus, conquest of the land is portrayed as a self-contained operation that does not "bleed over" into settlement.

Statements regarding the successful completion of this first stage—the conquest of the land—appear explicitly at the end of the two final episodes of the conquest narratives: the accounts of the campaigns against the southern and northern coalitions. Summing up the conquest of the southern country (which will later constitute the kingdom of Judah), the author claims: "Thus Joshua proscribed the whole country, the Negeb, the Shephelah and the slopes, with all their kings; he let none escape, but proscribed everything that breathed, as the Lord the God of Israel had commanded" (Josh 10:40). The total conquest of both territory and people is described without any reference to settlement, which has not yet begun.

In the second summary, set at the end of the account of the final battle against the northern coalition, a slight reservation is expressed in regard to the Gibeonites, a comment that is missing from the Septuagint, but the concept remains the same—a picture of total and complete conquest of both territory and population:

Joshua took the whole of this land: the hill country, the Negeb, the whole land of Goshen, the Shephelah, the Arabah, the hill country of Israel, and its low land, from Mount Halaq ascending to Seir, to Baal Gad in the valley of Lebanon at the foot of Mount Hermon. And he captured all those kings and executed them. *Apart from the Hivites who dwelt in Gibeon* not a single city made terms with the Israelites; all were taken in battle. For it was the Lord's doing to stiffen their hearts to give battle to Israel, in order that they might be proscribed without quarter and wiped out, as the Lord had commanded Moses. (Josh 11:16–20; emphasis added)

The second summary recounts both taking possession of the territory, using the root *lqh* (לקח) (11:16, 11:19), and the capture and proscription of the population, denoted by the roots *lkd* (לכד), *nkh* (נכה), *mwt* (מות; 11:17), *hrm* (חרם), and *shmd* (שמד) (11:20). It is followed by a final, abbreviated résumé commencing in the same language, and this time referring briefly to the successive process of settlement as well:

Joshua took the whole country, just as the Lord had promised Moses; and Joshua assigned it to Israel to share according to their tribal divisions [וַיִּתְּנָהּ יְהוֹשֻׁעַ לְנַחֲלָה לְיִשְׂרָאֵל כְּמַחְלְקֹתָם לְשִׁבְטֵיהֶם]; and the land had rest from war. (Josh 11:23)[11]

Thus the final appended summary reinforces the picture of the separation of the two processes, conquest and settlement, as implied in the former résumés and in the general organization of the book.

Conquest and Settlement according to the Second Half of the Book (Chapters 13–21)

The second part of Joshua deals with the distribution of the tribal portions, and it reflects a different conception from the first part of the book, in relation to the first two organizing questions. While the land was eventually conquered in its entirety, the relationship between the two stages of inheritance—conquest and settlement—is not necessarily the same as that which characterizes the first half of the book. In some cases the conquest of a specific area, a mere part of the whole land, is followed immediately by settlement, and there is no overall distinction between the two stages. This part of the book also presents a different picture regarding the fate of the inhabitants of the land. While the land was indeed conquered, foreign peoples remained in enclaves in parts of it, alongside the new Israelites.

The settlement of the tribes in the land is depicted as taking place in three stages.[12]

Stage 1: The first stage is a flashback to the days of Moses. While still in the Plains of Moab, Moses gave the tribes of Reuben, Gad, and half of Manasseh their land east of the Jordan.[13] This event is related in the book of Numbers and concludes with the lists of cities belonging to the tribes of Gad and Reuben (Num 32:33, 32:40); it is recalled in the book of Joshua and includes a detailed description of the territory of each tribe (13:8–32).

In the case of the two and a half trans-Jordanian tribes, the relationship between conquest and settlement is clear: Settlement followed directly upon the conquest of the territories; the tribes did not have to wait until the entire Promised Land was taken. Yet this situation had been made conditional by Moses, following the proposition of the tribes themselves (Num 32:16–24; see also Deut 3:18–20), and the condition was reinstated by Joshua (Josh 1:12–16; see also 4:12–13). Both leaders stipulated that the fighting men of the two and a half tribes needed to join the conquest of the Promised Land west of the Jordan River; only after its subjugation would they return to their children, wives, and the livestock they had left behind. As Samuel Loewenstamm argues, this reservation reflects the concept that "service in that army [i.e., participation in Joshua's conquest campaigns in the Promised Land] was the only reason that could justify the status of a tribe within the people of Israel,"[14] in other words, the pan-national war of conquest led by Joshua was deemed a formative and crucial stage in the making of the nation of Israel. Furthermore, this stipulation reflects the opinion that settlement before completion of conquest was seen as problematic indeed, as in need of special authorization. The story of the settlement of the two and a half eastern tribes reflects, therefore, the same concept of a two-stage process, that is, full conquest of the entire land before settlement, but allows an exception to the rule—the families of these eastern tribes are to be left behind, outside the "real" boundaries of the land, and not incidentally "in the fortified towns, because of the inhabitants of the land" (Num 32:17). Clearly the territories in trans-Jordan were not conquered in full before settlement, and the tribal portions there contained both people and land that remained unconquered. Since they dwelt in an area not initially part of the land that was promised, the persistence of non-Israelite inhabitants there should not surprise us.

Stage 2: The second stage involves the settlement of another group consisting of two and a half tribes, yet never designated as such (chapters 14–17). Although this tradition is connected, probably secondarily, to Gilgal (14:6),[15] it reflects a different concept of the process of inheritance than that of the first half of the book. The large tribes, Judah and the house of Joseph (Ephraim and the other half of Manasseh), receive their inheritance from representatives of the priestly (Eleazar), military (Joshua), and civilian (heads of the ancestral houses of the Israelite tribes) leadership, enumerated in this order. This three-tiered leadership structure is mentioned four times altogether in the second part of the book (14:1, 17:4, 19:51, 21:1), twice in introductory/summary passages (14:1, 19:51). Other passages, however, involve Joshua alone (14:6, 14:13 15:13, 17:14–18), a fact that points to the secondary nature of the concept of shared leadership. Yet Joshua does not act here as a military leader. His role is to allocate and define tribal or individual portions, *before* the completion or even the inception of the conquest of these territories.

There are many similarities, even parallels, between Judges 1 and this portrait of tribal and individual initiatives, intertwined with the descriptions of the two and a half western tribes' inheritances.[16] Yet though the two accounts share a non-unitary version of the conquest contrary to Joshua 1–12, the use of similar sources should not obscure the fact that they do not present the same process of conquest. Unlike the account in Judges 1, which contains no border descriptions or territorial definitions, Joshua's version of the settlement in 14–17 is an amalgam of descriptions of tribal portions alongside conquest accounts and other types of inheritance initiatives by individuals, some of which are of a non-military nature. I will illustrate this through an analysis of the literary components that make up the portrayal of the inheritance of this group of tribes: Judah, Ephraim, and western Manasseh.

First, eighty-five-year-old Caleb approaches Joshua at Gilgal, demanding that Joshua assign the hill country to him, in line with Moses' promise. His words emphasize his physical fitness: "I am strong today as on the day that Moses sent me, my strength is the same now as it was then, for battle and for activity" (14:11).[17] Caleb then dispossesses the Anakites who were in Hebron, after which it is stated that "the land had rest from war" (14:15).[18] Clearly this story is ignorant of the entire process of conquest conducted by Joshua, and Caleb confronts exactly the same situation as that observed earlier by the spies: The land is inhabited by Anakites living in great fortified cities (Num 13:22, 28; see also Josh 14:12).

This story precedes the description of the borders of Judah and may also be alluded to in Judges 1: "They gave Hebron to Caleb, as Moses had promised; and he drove the three Anakites out of there" (Judg 1:20). Caleb's achievement is mentioned again between the border description and the list of the Judahite towns:

> Caleb son of Jephunneh was given a portion among the Judahites, namely Kiriath-arba that is Hebron.... Caleb dislodged (וַיֹּרֶשׁ) from there the three Anakites: Sheshai, Ahiman and Talmai, descendants of Anak. (Josh 15:13–16)

In contradiction to the earlier explicit statement that after the dispossession of the Anakites the land had rest from war, Caleb now promises to give his daughter Achsah in marriage "to the man who attacks and captures Kiriath-sepher (Debir)" (15:16), and the lucky man is his kinsman, Othniel. The story ends when Achsah asks for and receives from her father a better tract of land, with water. It seems that this story is an elaborated version of the one preceding the description of the borders of Judah (14:6–15). This incident involving Caleb, Othniel, and Achsah is repeated in Judges 1. Here, however, it is the tribe of Judah that takes the initiative, and not Caleb the individual (Judg 1:10–15). It is the only tradition in Judges 1 that involves a non-military initiative; yet its inclusion in a chapter focusing otherwise only on military matters may be explained by its setting in a narrative framework that highlights the conquests of the tribe of Judah, the major protagonist of Judges 1.

At the end of the description of the Judahite lot according to its borders and town lists, a remark noting the tribe's failure to dispossess the inhabitants of Jerusalem explains why the Jebusites dwell in Jerusalem amidst the Judahites "to this day" (Josh 15:63). This statement is also paralleled in Judges 1, although this time the failure is attributed to the Benjaminites (Judg 1:21). Similarly, the two Josephite tribes, Ephraim and Manasseh, fail to dispossess some of the Canaanites within their territories. Thus Canaanites remain in Gezer, in the territory of Ephraim (16:10), although they perform forced labor. Like the Judahite failure, an account of this state of affairs is appended to the description of the tribes' borders in Joshua. Following the description of the borders of the tribe of Manasseh we learn that the conquest failures of this tribe were of a more complicated nature. According to Joshua, the tribe of Manasseh inherited regions within the territories of Issachar and Asher—Beth-shean, Ibleam, Dor, En-dor, Taanach, and Megiddo and their dependencies—that remained Canaanite. "When the Israelites became stronger they imposed tribute on the Canaanites; but they did not dispossess them" (17:13). The Ephraimite failure to capture Gezer appears in Judges 1:29, and information regarding the Manassite failures appears in Judges 1:27–28, where the alien enclaves are assigned, however, directly to Manasseh, rather than to the other tribes.

Prior to the description of the borders of Manasseh, we hear of another female initiative. The daughters of Zelophehad appear before Eleazar the priest, Joshua, and the chieftains, asking them to fulfill Moses' ruling to grant them a portion among their male kinsmen (17:3–6) as recounted in Numbers 27:1–11. This episode is not paralleled in Judges 1, presumably because it has nothing to do with the military takeover of the land.

The final episode of this kind of tribal initiative appears at the end of the recounting of the Josephite tribal inheritances. The Josephites complain to Joshua that they are too many for one portion and that the Canaanites who live in the valleys of Beth-shean and Jeezreel have iron chariots. Joshua acknowledges their claim and suggests they clear the forest for themselves in the land of the Perizzites and the Rephaim (17:14–18). Although this story is not repeated in Judges 1, there is a note concerning the Canaanites' iron chariots in that chapter. According to Judges 1, however, it is the Judahites who take possession of the hill country but are unable to dispossess the dwellers of the valley, "for they had iron chariots" (Judg 1:19). Since Judah is reported to have captured Gaza, Ashkelon, and Ekron and their territories (Judg 1:18), it is not clear which valley dwellers are indicated in this apologetic note. This note clearly makes more sense in the context of the conquests in the northern valleys of Megiddo and Beth-shean, which points to its secondary character in Judges (compare Josh 17:16 with Judg 1:19, 1:27).

In addition to their need to act in order to implement their settlements, another important characteristic of this group of the two and a half large tribes is that they did not receive their inheritances through a process of casting lots before the Lord. Although the Masoretic text categorizes the determination of their inheritances as like that of the remaining seven tribes—"The portion that fell by lot to the various clans" (Josh 15:1, 16:1, 17:1; compare 18:6, 8–10)[19]—the Greek version is to be preferred here. According to the Septuagint, they were assigned territories, but without mention of the casting of lots:

καὶ ἐγένετο τὰ ὅρια φυλῆς Ἰούδα / υἱῶν Ἰωσὴφ / υἱῶν Ἐφραὶμ / φυλῆς υἱῶν Μανασσῆ

[this is the border of the tribe of Judah / of the sons of Joseph / of the sons of Ephraim / of the tribe of the sons of Manasseh]. (15:1; 16:1, 5; 17:1)[20]

Dividing a conquered territory for inheritance was based on real customs, connected either to the issue of private inheritance,[21] or to the practice of dividing the spoils achieved in war among the victorious. In the book of Joel it is said that God will punish the nations and contend with them "over my very own people, Israel, which they scattered among the nations. For they divided my land among themselves and cast lots over my people"

(Joel 4:2–3; see also Isa 34:17; Mic 2:5; Obad 11). In the context of conquest and settlement, one can divide and allot a territory that is already in one's possession, like the distribution of land by lot (κλῆρος) among the Greek citizens of a colony.[22] But according to Joshua 14–17, Judah and the Josephite tribes were assigned territories *before* these territories were in Israelite hands; they had to actively take possession of their shares, and therefore the concept of lot was irrelevant for them.[23] Allocation rather than inheritance through the casting of lots is related to the fact that their portions had not yet been conquered. This is also reflected by the account in Judges 1. In that version of the conquest, the tribes inquire of the Lord who should go first to realize their allotment. The tribal territory is called "גורל" (Judg 1:3, twice), yet *goral* here means "estate." It does not indicate the process of allocation by lot.[24]

Thus, the allocation of territory is connected with a picture of gradual subjugation of the land and its peoples, whereas the conception of separation between the two stages of conquest and settlement is connected with that of dividing the land by lot, as the book of Numbers suggests:

> In the steppes of Moab, at the Jordan near Jericho the Lord spoke to Moses saying: Speak to the Israelite people and say to them: When you cross the Jordan into the land of Canaan, you shall dispossess all the inhabitants of the land....And you shall take possession of the land and settle in it [וְהוֹרַשְׁתֶּם אֶת-הָאָרֶץ וִישַׁבְתֶּם-בָּהּ], for I have assigned the land to you to possess. You shall apportion the land among yourselves by lot, clan by clan [וְהִתְנַחַלְתֶּם אֶת-הָאָרֶץ בְּגוֹרָל לְמִשְׁפְּחֹתֵיכֶם]. With larger groups increase the share, with smaller groups reduce the share. Wherever the lot falls for anyone, that shall be his. You shall have your portions according to your ancestral tribes. (Num 33:50–54)[25]

Division by lot is accordingly reserved for the next stage in the process of tribal inheritance (18:6), as well as for the allocation of the Levitical cities (Josh 21:4, 21:6, 21:10, 21:20), when the land is already in Israelite hands.

Joshua 14–17 thus reflects a process of conquest and settlement similar to Judges 1, yet without the Judahite penchant we find there. Another major difference between these passages is that while Judges 1 focuses only on the military aspect of the conquest-settlement process, the author of chapters 14–17 presents the settlement of the two and a half large tribes as involving the need to cope with difficulties of a diverse character. The challenges are indeed often military, as when local enemies possess superior technology or fortified towns, but they are also ecological or environmental, as when they must fight in dry or forested terrain. The story of the daughters of Zelophehad directs attention to an inner-Israelite legislative and governmental matter, arising due to a lack of male successors. These stories, as well as remarks about individual settlements or tribal failures, are intertwined with the description of borders and town lists in what seems like a deliberate order:

Joshua 14:6–15: Story of conquest initiative of Caleb in Hebron;

Joshua 15:1–12: The border description of the tribe of Judah;

Joshua 15:13–19: The capture and settlement of Hebron and Kiriath-sepher by Caleb and Othniel, and the initiative of Achsah, Caleb's daughter, for a tract of land with water;

Joshua 15:2–62: Town list of the tribe of Judah;

Joshua 15:63: Note on Judah's failure to capture Jerusalem, a Jebusite enclave;

Joshua 16:1–9: The Josephite portion: border description of the tribe of Ephraim;

Joshua 16:10: Note on Ephraim's failure to capture Gezer, hence a Canaanite enclave;

Joshua 17:1–2: The Manassite portion;

Joshua 17:3–6: A reference to the inheritance of the daughters of Zelophehad among their brothers;

Joshua 17:7–10: The border description of the tribe of Manasseh;

Joshua 17:11–13: Note on failure to capture towns allocated to Manasseh in the territories of the tribes of Issachar and Asher, Canaanite enclaves;

Joshua 17:14–18: The Josephites' query regarding military difficulties is answered with a suggestion to clear the forest for themselves.

The result is an intentional amalgam of genres—stories, geographical lists, and notes of military failures—that depicts a prolonged and complex settlement process undertaken by the two and a half major and central Israelite clans.

Stage 3: The third stage is connected to Shiloh in the territory of Ephraim (16:6), where the seven smaller tribes—Benjamin, Simeon, Zebulun, Issachar, Asher, Naphtali, and Dan—eventually receive their allotments (chapters 18–19). According to the text, "the land was now under their control" (והארץ נכבשה לפניהם 18:1), and there are no reports of alien enclaves within these tribal portions. How this state of affairs came about, we are not told. Was the land conquered through earthly means, or by divine miracle, or by a combination of both? In any case, it is clear that these tribes need not embark now on any conquest initiatives, whether tribal or national.[26] Yet they are depicted as "slack" (מתרפים 18:3) for failing to take the initiative in taking over their empty land; they are in need of the chastisement and encouragement of Joshua. He in fact sends them out to survey the land and divide it into seven parts; the tribal representatives then return to Joshua at Shiloh, who casts lots before the Lord to distribute the portions.

The silence on the subject of alien enclaves in the territories of the seven northern tribes is telling. Since Judges 1:30–33 tells us of such enclaves, located in the tribal shares of Zebulun, Asher, and Naphtali, their absence from the account in Joshua seems deliberate, reflecting this section's overall concept of how the land was inherited.

The organizing scheme of this part of the book points to the importance of Shiloh. At the initial stage, individuals and tribes need to do their parts toward the fulfillment of the promise through earthly efforts. The large central tribes have yet to conquer parts of their territories or to prepare them for habitation with varying degrees of success. It is only after Israel has made its way to Shiloh, in the territory of Ephraim (Josh 16:6), and set up the tent of meeting there that the third and final stage of settlement can begin: "The whole community of the Israelite people assembled at Shiloh, and set up the tent of meeting there. The land was now under their control" (18:1). Only after this human initiative can distribution and settlement—under God's control through complete conquest of the land followed by the casting of lots—begin.

Of the nine times that Shiloh is mentioned in the book of Joshua, six define it as the place of the casting of the lots and dividing of the land before the tent of meeting (18:1, 18:8, 18:9 [missing in the LXX], 18:10, 19:51, 21:2). The place of Shiloh in this scheme may point to the circles in which this material originated—the priests of Shiloh. The centrality of Shiloh to the distribution of the land is an organizing principle imposed upon material stemming from different sources. This can be seen from the stylistic differences between the descriptions of the inheritances of the southern tribes, Judah (including Simeon) and Benjamin on the one hand, and the inheritance of Ephraim and Manasseh on the other. The former use detailed reports of the territories on all four sides, together with town lists that are at variance with these reports, whereas the latter incorporate only border reports. Clearly the editor incorporated earlier, probably administrative documents, into a different ideological scheme that joined Judah with the Josephites in one group, and Simeon and Benjamin with five of the northern tribes—Zebulun, Issachar, Asher, Naphtali, and Dan—in another. As claimed by Shmuel Ahituv, Shiloh continued to exist throughout the Iron Age, and as the book of Jeremiah witnesses, the tradition that it served as God's first dwelling place in the land persisted until at least the end of the First Temple period (Jer 7:12, 7:14, 26:6, 26:9, 41:5).[27] It may well be that during the sixth century B.C.E., Shiloh was the source of the version of the conquest-settlement process dominating the second half of the book of Joshua.

The Résumés Following the Settlement (Chapters 21, 23)

A Deuteronomistic summary retelling the complete conquest of *the land* appears at the end of the chapters describing the settlement, and refers back to the promises to the forefathers:

> The Lord gave to Israel the whole land [כל הארץ] which He had sworn to their fathers that He would assign to them; they took possession of it and

settled in it [וַיִּרָשׁוּהָ וַיֵּשְׁבוּ בָהּ]. The Lord gave them rest on all sides, just as He
had promised to their fathers on oath. Not one man of all their enemies
withstood them; the Lord delivered all their enemies into their hands. Not
one of the good things which the Lord had promised to the House of Israel
was lacking. Everything was fulfilled. (Josh 21:41–43)

Here again we find expression of the idea that the land in its entirety was conquered. However, although the victory was complete, for "not one man of all
their enemies withstood them," the summary does not state that the population was entirely proscribed—in contrast to the earlier résumés that follow the
accounts of the two final battles (Josh 10:40, 11:16–20; see also the section "The
Résumés That Recapitulate the Two Final Battles [Joshua 10:40, 11:16–20]"
above).

Does the summary in Joshua 21 refer to the relationship between conquest
and settlement? The roots used in this case, yrsh (ירש) followed by yshb (ישב),
are absent from the earlier résumés. The root yrsh can denote both taking
possession of land (Lev 20:24; Num 21:24, 33:53), and dispossessing its native
peoples (Num 33:52, 33:55; Deut 2:12, 2:21).[28] While the phrase "they took
possession of it and settled in it" [וַיִּרָשׁוּהָ וַיֵּשְׁבוּ בָהּ] (Josh 21:41b) may express
sequential action—they took possession and then settled in it[29]—and thus fit
the pattern of separation we have noted in the first half of the book, it seems
that the two stages can also be contemporaneous, as in the Deuteronomistic
synopsis (2 Kgs 17:24) that follows the account of the downfall of the northern
kingdom. This passage describes the diametrically opposite case, when Israel
lost its land and was driven out of it to be replaced by other people:

The king of Assyria brought [people] from Babylon, Cuthah, Avva, Hamath,
and Sepharvaim, and he settled them in the towns of Samaria instead of
the Israelites. They took possession of Samaria and settled in its towns
[וַיִּרְשׁוּ אֶת-שֹׁמְרוֹן וַיֵּשְׁבוּ בְּעָרֶיהָ].

In this passage, the same pair of verbs is used, in the same order—yrsh followed by yshb—and the sequence of events is clear: The Israelites were driven
out of their land (2 Kgs 17:23), then other people were brought to the land to
inherit it by settling in Israel's towns. The same relationship between yrsh and
yshb could be noted, therefore, for this Deuteronomistic summary. It does not
emphasize the separation of the two processes of conquest and settlement, nor
does it make a claim of complete annihilation of the population of the land; it
asserts only total conquest of its territory: "The Lord gave to Israel the whole
land [כל הארץ] which He had sworn to their fathers that He would assign to
them" (Josh 21:41a).[30]

In discussing chapters 14–17, we noted that some of the former inhabitants of the land still dwelt among the tribes and had not been subjugated.
This refers to the native peoples that remained, and not to territory still

unconquered. The description of the tribal failures does not portray areas that were left outside of the tribal territories. The latter are connected and continuous. The same concept, of alien population enclaves left within Israel, is reflected in the Deuteronomistic farewell speech of Joshua, in chapter 23, in which he again claims that every good thing God had promised has been fulfilled (23:14, 23:15), reminding his followers yet again that "not a man has withstood you to this day" (23:9). Joshua always mentions the "nations that still remain" (הגוים הנשארים) in the plural form (23:4–5, 23:7, 23:12–13)[31] and points to the danger they pose due to religious pollution, forbidding "intermingling with these nations that are left among you" (23:7).

Although Joshua 23 does not specify precisely where the "nations that still remain" dwell, it is plausible that they reside in foreign enclaves *within* the territory of the tribal allotments (21:42, 23:1). An intimation of such a circumstance exists in 23:4, which locates these "nations that still remain" in the territory "from the Jordan to the Great Sea in the west." In this farewell speech then, the remaining peoples serve the same ideological role as the remaining Jebusites and Canaanites within the territories of the two and a half large tribes. It appears that this late Deuteronomistic stratum was well aware of the failures of conquest enumerated in the second half of the book.[32] The notion of separation between the two stages—conquest followed by settlement, intertwined with the notion of complete ethnic cleansing of the local population—reflected in the arrangement of the book as a whole, finds expression thus only in the first half of the book, reflected in the stories and in the conquest résumés.

It is noteworthy that even the persistence of the remaining peoples does not blemish the Deuteronomistic author's concept of complete fulfillment of the divine promise: "Acknowledge with all your heart and soul that not one of the good things that the Lord your God promised you has failed to happen; they have all come true for you. Not a single one has failed" (23:14). It is obvious that according to the farewell speech of Joshua, the complete conquest of the land is territorial in essence and does not encompass the total annihilation (or expulsion) of the former inhabitants of the land.

Other biblical texts offer various reasons for the phenomenon of the "remaining peoples." Two of the promise texts themselves touch upon this question. In the Deuteronomistic addition to the book of the covenant in Exodus 23, God promises:

> I will not drive them out before you in a single year lest the land become desolate and the wild beasts multiply to your hurt. I will drive them out before you little by little, until you have increased and possess the land. (Exod 23:29–30)[33]

This concept is repeated in Deuteronomy 7:22: "You will not be able to finish them at once, else the wild beasts would multiply to your hurt." Judges 2:21–23, continued in 3:4, states that the peoples were left in the land as a test for Israel, to see whether or not Israel would walk faithfully in the ways of the Lord (see also Judg 2:3). Immediately following this (Judg 3:1–2), another explanation is offered, interpreting the word לנסות not as a "test," but as "experience": God left the remaining peoples for "all the Israelites who had not known any of the wars of Canaan, so that succeeding generations of Israelites might be made to experience war." Whatever the reason, it is clear that the very concept of the remaining peoples was not deemed to contradict the fulfillment of the promise of the land. According to both parts of Joshua, the land was conquered in its entirety: For the first half of the book, this meant that its population was completely proscribed; for the second half, that foreign enclaves remained within the settled land.

"THE LAND THAT YET REMAINS" (JOSHUA 13:1–6)[34]

Wedged between the two major parts of the book, the complete conquest (1–12) and the settlement (13–23), a unique unit, different from both, was added. This surprising section, Joshua 13:1–6, features a divine appeal to the aging and not very successful Joshua to go ahead and give the land to Israel as an inheritance, even though it had *not* yet been conquered in its entirety: "And very much of the land still remains to be taken possession of" (13:1).[35] Unlike the concept of the "remaining peoples," always in plural, who are left in enclaves *within* the Israelite territories, the "remaining land" (הארץ הנשארת), in the singular, describes areas *bordering* on the conquered territory, to the south (13:2–3) and to the north (13:4–6). While the concept of the "remaining peoples" is compatible with a description of the promise fulfilled, in this passage God himself postpones the completion of the territorial conquest to a future, unspecified time (13:6).

Although this text mentions peoples who remain in the land ("all the inhabitants of the hill country…all the Sidonians, I Myself will dispossess those peoples for the Israelites"; 13:6), it refers mainly to the territorial aspect of the promise, rather than the ethnic one. There is no reference here to the religious problem of the remaining peoples, while the land is constantly referred to: "Much of the land still remained to be taken possession of. This is the land that still remains" (Josh 13:1–2); "you have only to apportion it [רק הפילה, "it" here translates a feminine singular demonstrative pronoun, which denotes the land] to Israel as an inheritance" (13:6).[36] The very combination "the remaining land" (הארץ הנשארת), unique to this document, is an innovation derived from the concept of the remaining peoples. From a semantic viewpoint the term "remaining peoples" fits well the meaning of the root *sh'r* (שאר) in the *niph'al*; in other contexts it appears in participial form and designates groups of people who remain after disaster, known sometimes as שארית. The concept that it is not native peoples, but the land itself, that survives the conquest, is innovative both linguistically and conceptually.

Contrary in outlook to both parts of the book of Joshua, the divine mandate in Joshua 13:1–6 constitutes an act of postponing the "expiration date" of the divine promise of the land.[37] This innovative concept probably answers an ideological need of the community of returnees in the Persian period, to validate their right to the land.[38] In so doing, it reverses the major organizing principle of the book of Joshua: It offers not a perfectionist viewpoint demanding total conquest of peoples and land followed by settlement (an impossible ideal to imitate), nor the model offered by the second half of the book, of complete territorial conquest, while admitting the continuing existence of enclaves of foreign peoples, but a realistic advocacy of temporary compromise—settlement within the limited but available territory, with a promise of total fulfillment in the future.

Conclusion

The book of Joshua touches upon one of the central issues of Israelite identity—the people's relationship to their land. It is not surprising, therefore, to find different conceptions and ideologies pertaining to that relationship within this not so large book, presented through a depiction of the people's past in one of their most crucial periods, the entry to the land.

Reconstructed chronologically, it appears that the second half of the book of Joshua contains the earliest portrayal of the process of the conquest and settlement. This Shiloh-oriented composition, formulated during the last decades of the First Temple period, depicts the process in two stages. In the first (Josh 14–17), the two and a half large central tribes, Judah, Ephraim, and Manasseh, engage in an active pursuit of their territorial allotments; address various military, environmental, and legal challenges; and complete their task by settling their territories to the full, while incorporating various foreign enclaves—conquest failures—within them. These tribes are initially assigned their territories by Joshua, and not via lot, perhaps according to tribal size (see 17:14, 17:17), before they have actually taken over the designated inheritances. Individuals or tribes initiate the settlement process, rather than a national unified body. While Joshua plays the role of a national leader who allocates the territories to tribes and individuals, the process of settlement is local in character. This stage is the closest to a realistically probable reconstruction of the historical process of the initiation of the first Israelite (or proto-Israelite, as some prefer to call them) settlements. Cumulative archaeological data show that between the thirteenth and eleventh centuries B.C.E. there was a dramatic shift of settlement patterns in the land of Israel. Rather than several large urban centers, a few hundred new small settlements appear in the area of the hill country. These egalitarian, unfortified hamlets, populating the less convenient settlement areas, exhibit the way in which the first Israelites dealt with the harsh ecological conditions.

Instead of a violent entry into a populated land, archaeology presents the first Israelite settlements as inhabiting a mostly empty territory.[39]

As the tribes reach Shiloh and erect there the "tent of meeting" as God's dwelling in the land, the narrative changes dramatically (Josh 18–19). The remaining seven tribes receive a portion from conquered territory and have only to send a mission of surveyors to write down its borders and then to receive their shares by lot. This section of the book, then, describes a process of conquest followed by settlement according to lot, fully successful in both geographic and ethnic terms, which is distinct from the process of intertwined conquest and settlement, totally successful geographically but not ethnically, described in the earlier chapters. According to this two-stage depiction of the entry to the land, the land was taken in its entirety, but Canaanite enclaves were left within the territories of the large two and a half large tribes, Judah and the house of Joseph. A late Deuteronomistic hand added the final résumés at the end of chapter 21, and in chapter 23, Joshua's farewell speech. While acknowledging the existence of "remaining peoples" in the land, this later writer still claims that everything was fulfilled, indicating that the promise to the patriarchs was understood as preeminently geographical rather than ethnic. The remaining peoples are at the center of various other biblical texts outside the book of Joshua, which constitute apologetic attempts to explain their continuing presence (see Exod 23:32–33; Deut 7:22–26; Judg 2:22, 3:4–6).[40] This part of Joshua does not intimate how the final conquest of these remaining peoples will eventually occur.

Perhaps in order to provide this missing story, the first part of the book focuses on the process of conquest alone. It takes the paradigm described for the seven smaller tribes, of total geographical and ethnic success followed by settlement by lot, and applies it to the entire land. According to this depiction of the entry to the land, there were *no* Canaanites left in the land by the time of its settlement. This Deuteronomistically oriented stratum was probably created from earlier traditions, more or less at the same period as the second half of the book, and as a Judean response to it.[41]

At a later stage, the community of returnees in the Persian period added the description of the "land that yet remains," wedged between the two parts of the book. According to this text the promise had not yet been fulfilled; there were large tracts of land left for later generations to possess. This passage does not itself offer a different depiction of the process of conquest and settlement; rather it delimits the notion of past geographic and ethnic conquest, extending the "expiration date" of the promise into an undetermined future.

Notes

1. For the concept of Israel's allochthonous origins, see Nili Wazana, "Natives, Immigrants and the Biblical Perception of Origins in Historical Times," *Tel-Aviv* 32, no. 2 (2005): 220–244.

2. Harry Orlinsky, "The Biblical Concept of the Land of Israel: Cornerstone of the Covenant between God and Israel," in *The Land of Israel: Jewish Perspectives*, ed. Lawrence A. Hoffman (Notre Dame, Ind.: University of Notre Dame Press, 1986), 27–64; Moshe Weinfeld, "The Covenantal Aspect of the Promise of the Land to Israel," in *The Promise of the Land: The Inheritance of the Land of Canaan by the Israelites*, Taubman Lectures in Jewish Studies 3 (Berkeley: University of California Press, 1993), 222–264.

3. See Gen 12:7, 13:14–17, 15:7, 15:18–21, 17:8, 24:7, 28:4, 28:13, 35:12, 48:4. For the argument placing the patriarchal promises in a late, unifying literary stratum, see John A. Emerton, "The Origin of the Promises to the Patriarchs in the Older Sources of the Book of Genesis," *VT* 32 (1982): 14–32.

4. For the resemblance of the language of the promissory texts to ancient legal terminology pertaining to transfers of land ownership, see David Daube, *Studies in Biblical Law* (Cambridge: Cambridge University Press, 1947), 26–39.

5. Biblical translations generally follow the NJPSV, with some modifications.

6. For the fate of the Canaanites according to the different pentateuchal traditions, see Weinfeld, "Expulsion, Dispossession, and Extermination of the Pre-Israelite Population in the Biblical Sources," in *The Promise of the Land*, 76–98; Baruch J. Schwartz, "Reexamining the Fate of the 'Canaanites' in the Torah Traditions," in *Sefer Moshe—The Moshe Weinfeld Jubilee Volume: Studies in the Bible and the Ancient Near East, Qumran, and Post-Biblical Judaism*, edited by Chaim Cohen, Avi Hurvitz, and Shalom M. Paul (Winona Lake, Ind.: Eisenbrauns, 2004), 151–170.

7. See *inter alia* G. Ernest Wright, "The Literary and Historical Problem of Joshua 10 and Judges 1," *JNES* 5, no. 2 (1946): 105; Norman K. Gottwald, *The Tribes of Yahweh: A Sociology of the Religion of Liberated Israel, 1250–1050 B.C.E.* (Maryknoll, N.Y.: Orbis, 1979), 163–175. For the pro-Judahite tendency of Judg 1, see Gottwald, *Tribes of Yahweh*, 174; and Roland de Vaux, *The Early History of Israel*, trans. David Smith (Philadelphia: Westminster, 1978), 805.

8. Yohanan Aharoni, "Joshua, Book of," *Encyclopaedia Judaica*, 2nd ed., vol. 11 (Detroit: Macmillan Reference, 2007), 445; Shmuel Ahituv, *Joshua: Introduction and Commentary* [in Hebrew] (Mikra Leyisrael, Tel-Aviv: Am Oved; Jerusalem: Hebrew University Magnes Press, 1995), 9; L. Daniel Hawk, *Joshua* (Collegeville, Minn.: Liturgical Press, 2000), 177–226. For slightly different divisions, see Martin Noth, *Das Buch Josua*, 2nd ed., HAT 7 (Tübingen: J. C. B. Mohr, 1953), 132–173; Robert G. Boling, *Joshua: A New Translation with Notes and Commentary*, AB 6 (Garden City, N.Y.: Doubleday, 1982), 319–470; Otto Eissfeldt, *The Old Testament: An Introduction*, trans. by P. Ackroyd (Oxford: Blackwell, 1966), 249; and Volkmar Fritz, *Das Buch Josua*, HAT 1.7 (Tübingen: J. C. B. Mohr [P. Siebeck], 1994), 139. The final chapters (Josh 22–24) offer closure to the issue of the settlement of the two and a half tribes east of the Jordan (22), as well as two separate speeches by Joshua (23, 24).

9. The surprise attack is a motif coloring the two final battles in similar hues; the word פתאם appears nowhere but these two instances in the entire historiographical corpus.

10. This has led to the opinion that the stories of the first two battles (at Jericho and Ai), as well as the first part of the battle against the southern coalition (Josh 10:1–15), are Benjaminite etiological legends, collected and handed down at the sanctuary of Gilgal. See Noth, *Josua*, 11–13; following Albrecht Alt, "Josua," in *Kleine Schriften zur Geschichte des Volkes Israel*, vol. 1 (Munich: Beck, [1936] 1953), 176–192; see also J. Alberto Soggin, *Joshua: A Commentary*, trans. R. A. Wilson, OTL (London: SCM, 1972), 7–14. Indeed the last, northern campaign does not mention the camp at Gilgal. Regardless of the question of the origin of the stories, the concept of a separate process of conquest underlying the first half of the book is clear.

11. The two résumés are separated by an addition dealing with the Anakites who remained in part of the land (Josh 11:21–22). For the secondary character of this passage regarding the Anakites, see Martin Noth, *The Deuteronomistic History*, trans. J. Doull et al., JSOTSup 15 (Sheffield: JSOT Press, 1981), 38–39; and Ahituv, *Joshua*, 187. For the nature of these verses as a "résumé on top of a résumé" (one following another), see Ahituv, *Joshua*, 188.

12. For this analysis, see Nili Wazana, All the Boundaries of the Land: The Promised Land in Biblical Thought in Light of the Ancient Near East, (Eisenbrauns: Winona Lake, Indiana, 2013), 244–246.

13. As is well known, the story in Num 32 refers to the tribes of Gad and Reuben only, with the half tribe of Manasseh added in a later comment (Num 32:33); whereas in Josh 1:12, 4:12, 13:15–33, the half tribe of Manasseh is an integral part of the trans-Jordanian tribes. See Samuel E. Loewenstamm, "The Settlement of Gad and Reuben as Related in Nu. 32:2–38—Background and Composition," in *From Babylon to Canaan* (Jerusalem: Hebrew University Magnes Press, 1992), 112–114.

14. Loewenstamm, "Settlement of Gad and Reuben," 117. He considers this condition to be secondary to the story of the initial settlement of the tribes of Gad and Reuben in the grazing land where they had left their livestock (Loewenstamm, "Settlement of Gad and Reuben," 116–130). Yet as he himself admits, the reconstruction of the initial story is conjectural, and I see no reason to separate the motif of conditional authorization from the apologetic story of the settlement of these tribes in trans-Jordan.

15. Soggin, *Joshua*, 171.

16. Soggin, *Joshua*, 13, lists the following: Josh 15:13–19 and Judg 1:11–15; Josh 15:63 and Judg 1:21; Josh 16:10 and Judg 1:29; Josh 17:11–13 and Judg 1:27–28; Josh 19:47 and Judg 1:34–35. To this we may add Josh 14:6–15 and Judg 1:20, and Josh 17:14–18 and Judg 1:19, 1:27.

17. The description of physical prowess, together with the use of the paired infinitives וְלָצֵאת וְלָבוֹא (literally, "to go out and come in"; למלחמה "for battle") all indicate Caleb's ability as a military leader. See, for example, the depiction of his younger kinsman, Othniel the Kenizzite, the first judge who "went out to war," ויצא למלחמה (Judg 3:10); or the depiction of the king demanded by the people, who was to "go out" before them and fight their battles (1 Sam 8:20); and in particular the description of David, who "went out and came in before the troops," (העם לפני ויבא ויצא 1 Samuel 18:13, 18:16). See Anton van der Lingen, "'Bw'-yṣ' ('To Go out and to Come in') as a Military Term," *VT* 42, no. 1 (1992): 62, who translates the phrase as "to command the army successfully." For the possibility of the existence of independent Calebite traditions perhaps originating in southern Hebron, for whose people Caleb was the eponymous ancestor, and their reworking in the various biblical literary strata, see James W. Flanagan, "History, Religion and Ideology: The Caleb Tradition," *Horizons* 3 (1976): 177–181, and the bibliography there.

18. This is a parallel tradition to the one appended to chapter 11, which ends in a similar way (11:21–23). See note 11 above.

19. Yehezkel Kaufmann, *SepherYehoshua* [The Book of Joshua; in Hebrew] (Jerusalem: Kiryat-Sepher, 1963), 172–174, 178.

20. A. Graeme Auld, *Joshua, Moses and the Land: Tetrateuch–Pentateuch–Hexateuch in a Generation since 1938* (Edinburgh: T & T Clark, 1980), 56. This version appears to be primary. The MT represents a secondary reworking, reflecting its conception that all nine and a half tribes received their heritage by lot—as the verse concluding this section explicitly states: "These are the portions assigned by lot to the tribes of Israel by the priest Eleazar,

Joshua son of Nun, and the heads of the ancestral houses, before the LORD at Shiloh, at the entrance of the Tent of Meeting" (Josh 19:51; see also Num 34:13, 34:16–18). See Wazana, *All the Boundaries of the Land*, 245 n. 6.

21. Shmuel Ahituv, "Land and Justice," in *Justice and Righteousness: Biblical Themes and Their Influence*, ed. Henning G. Reventlow and Yair Hoffman, JSOTSup 137 (Sheffield: JSOT Press, 1992), 25–27. He mentions the Middle Assyrian law determining that "the oldest son shall select and take one share, and for his second share he shall cast lots with his brothers" MAL B, §1; see Martha T. Roth, *Law Collections from Mesopotamia and Asia Minor*, 2nd ed., SBL Writings from the Ancient World 6 (Atlanta: Scholars Press, 1997), 176. Sirach speaks of leaving one's labors "to be divided by lot" (Sir 14:15). Perhaps the notion in the *Book of Jubilees* that the whole world was divided by lot between the three sons of Noah and then between their descendants is also a reflection of this inheritance custom (*Jub.* 8:9–9:15)

22. For the comparison of the tribal allotments in the Bible with the process of Greek colonization, see Weinfeld, "The Pattern of Israelite Settlement: A Comparison with the Pattern of Greek Colonization," in *The Promise of the Land*, 22–26; Ahituv, "Land and Justice," 24; and Ahituv, *Joshua*, 290.

23. Ahituv suggests that the fact that Judah and Joseph were the first to take their shares in the land, without reference to the lot, is "by virtue of their prime status in Israel, notwithstanding the fact that neither was the firstborn"; Ahituv, "Land and Justice," 26. While this is an interesting possibility, it does not explain why these tribes had to be active partners in the conquest in order to settle their territories, nor why they failed to conquer these portions in their entirety, leaving enclaves of foreign people in their midst.

24. The same meaning obtains in the compound בגורל נחלתם in Josh 14:2. See Ahituv, "Land and Justice," 17–18.

25. There are two initially conflicting principles at work here: division according to size, and division by lot (Soggin, *Joshua*, 169). According to Itamar Kislev, whereas in Num 26:53–56 the two principles are set polemically against each other, so that the division by lot succeeds and undermines the prior concept of division by size, in Num 33:54 the author *combines* the two principles. Kislev, however, does not note that the principle of division by lot requires taking possession of the land in its entirety prior to the settlement. It is thus clear why Num 26:53–56 does not mention the conquest of the land, while Num 33:54 depicts a process of taking possession of the land (והורשתם את הארץ וישבתם בה), followed by settlement as determined by lot (והתנחלתם את הארץ בגורל). Itamar Kislev, *On the Threshold of the Promised Land: The Account of the Preparations for Entering Canaan and the Formation of the Pentateuch* [in Hebrew]. Jerusalem: Magnes, 2013, 57–83.

26. The only exception is Dan, which has to go and conquer its northern territory (19:47). Yet this episode does not pertain to the original allotment in the Shephelah (19:40–46), and it is an addition to the story of settlement. This phrase (והארץ נכבשה לפניהם) appears only one other time in the Bible, in the story of the trans-Jordanian tribes (Num 32:22, 32:29); it refers here to the obligatory participation of the fighting men of the two and a half eastern tribes in the campaign west of the Jordan River. Cf. the Chronicler's use of a similar formula in the description of David's days (1 Chron 22:18).

27. Ahituv, *Joshua*, 22.

28. See BDB, 439. As is clear from Lev 20:23–24, taking possession of the land from its former inhabitants can mean driving them out of the land, rather than conscripting

them. On *yrsh* (ירש) as meaning both expulsion and extermination, see Moshe Weinfeld, "Expulsion, Dispossession, and Extermination of the Pre-Israelite Population in the Biblical Sources," in *The Promise of the Land*, 82–83 and n. 18. Norbert Lohfink defines *yrsh qal* as meaning that "by right of conquest one people or nation succeeds another in ruling over a territory." He says that this sense represents a specialized Deuteronomistic usage, yet Jan Joosten argues that the phrase existed as an independent legal term and was not invented by the Deuteronomists. See Norbert Lohfink, "ירש *yāraš*," in *Theological Dictionary of the Old Testament*, vol. 6, ed. G. Johannes Botterweck, and Helmer Ringgren, trans. John T. Willis (Grand Rapids, Mich.: Eerdmans, 1990), 371; and Jan Joosten, *People and Land in the Holiness Code: An Exegetical Study of the Ideational Framework of the Law in Leviticus 17–26*, VTSup 47 (Leiden: Brill, 1996), 187–189.

29. The verbs are connected via a *waw* of succession; see Paul Joüon, *A Grammar of Biblical Hebrew*, trans. and rev. by Takamitsu Muraoka, 2 vols., Subsidia biblica 14, no. 1–2 (Rome: Pontifical Biblical Institute, 1991; reprinted with corrections, 1993), §115c.

30. The Priestly source mentioned above, which employs the same two verbs in succession, וְהוֹרַשְׁתֶּם אֶת־הָאָרֶץ וִישַׁבְתֶּם־בָּהּ (Num 33:53a), does indicate a process of allotment that must follow the conquest: it is followed there by another sentence utilizing the root *nhl* (נחל), which thus indicates that the settlement is separate from the conquest (Num 33:54).

31. As is also known from other biblical texts (Exod 23:29–30; Deut 7:22; Judg 2:3, 2:21–23; 3:1).

32. Rudolf Smend, "Das Gesetz und die Völker," in *Probleme biblischer Theologie*, ed. Hans W. Wolff (Munich: Kaiser, 1971), 501, attributes chapter 23 to a late Deuteronomistic stratum.

33. For the Deuteronomistic nature of the epilogue to the Book of the Covenant (Exod 23:28–31) see Brevard S. Childs, *The Book of Exodus*, OTL (Philadelphia: Westminster, 1974), 486; Wazana, *All the Boundaries of the Land*, 98–99.

34. For this section, see Wazana, *All the Boundaries of the Land*, 207–239.

35. See Rudolf Smend, "Das uneroberte Land," in *Das Land Israel in biblischer Zeit*, Göttinger Theologische Arbeiten 25, ed. G. Strecker (Göttingen: Vandenhoeck & Ruprecht, 1983), 91–92.

36. As Moshe Greenberg pointed out, the root *npl* does not indicate the division of the land by lot, but the taking possession of it; see Moshe Greenberg, "The Terms נפל and הפיל in the Context of Inheritance," in *Ki Baruch Hu: Ancient Near Eastern, Biblical, and Judaic Studies in Honor of Baruch A. Levin*, ed. Robert Chazan, William H. Hallo, and Lawrence H. Schiffman (Winona Lake, Ind.: Eisenbrauns, 1999), 251–259.

37. Wazana, All the Boundaries of the Land, 231–239.

38. This tentative, relatively late dating of Josh 13:1–6 is based on the fact that only the Chronicler (1 Chron 13:5)—and perhaps the author of the elaboration in Judg 3:3 and the comments in Judg 1:36 (whose origin and date are uncertain)—takes note of it. This period posed new challenges to a populace that identified itself as the people of Israel and sought ways to cope with the enormous crisis created by the destruction of the First Temple and the exile. As Sara Japhet has demonstrated, ideas linked to the root *sh'r*—the "remnant [of the people] (שארית)" and those "remaining (הנשאר)"—played a significant role during this period; perhaps these concepts provided inspiration to the author of our document for his ideological and terminological innovation, "the land that yet remains." See Sara Japhet, "The Concept of the 'Remnant' in the Restoration Period," in *Das Manna fällt auch heute noch: Beiträge zur Geschichte und Theologie des Alten, Ersten Testaments: Festschrift für Erich Zenger*, Herders

biblische Studien 44, ed. Frank-Lothar Hossfeld and Ludger Schwienhorst-Schönberger (Freiburg: Herder, 2004), 340–361.

39. See, along broad lines, Amihai Mazar, "The Days of the Judges: Iron Age I," *Archaeology of the Land of the Bible, 10,000–586 B.C.E.*, ABRL (New York: Doubleday, 1990), 328–355.

40. The notation, "the peoples that still remain," in Joshua's farewell speech (Josh 23:4, 23:7, 23:12), points to the Israelites' disregard of God's will. In distinction from this formulation, Judges designates the nations as "the peoples that the LORD has left" (Judg 3:1), explaining the historical phenomenon of the continuing presence of the nations within the framework of an educational ethos: God left the nations for his own purposes: whether "to test Israel by them—to see whether they would walk in the ways of the LORD, as their fathers had done" (Judg 2:22; Judg 3:4); or "so that He might test by them all the Israelites who had not known any of the wars of Canaan, so that succeeding generations of Israelites might be made to experience war" (Judg 3:2; for a similar explanation using a different formula, see Exod 23:29–33).

41. The Judean provenance of Josh 1–12 is deduced not from the stories, which are of mainly Benjaminite origin, but from the concluding summaries after the two final battles (Josh 10:40–42, 11:16–20). The language of the résumé following the battle against the southern coalition describes the conquest of the future territory of the kingdom of Judah in the most hyperbolic terms: Joshua subdues the whole country (i.e., the territory of the kingdom of Judah) at a single stroke, "for the LORD, the God of Israel, fought for Israel" (v. 42; see also v. 14).

Bibliography

Aharoni, Yohanan. "Joshua, Book of." *Encyclopaedia Judaica*. 2nd ed. Vol. 11. Detroit: Macmillan Reference, [1972] 2007.

Ahituv, Shmuel. *Joshua: Introduction and Commentary* [in Hebrew]. Mikra Leyisrael, Tel-Aviv: Am Oved; Jerusalem: Hebrew University Magnes Press, 1995.

——. "Land and Justice." In *Justice and Righteousness: Biblical Themes and Their Influence*, edited by Henning G. Reventlow and Yair Hoffman, 11–28. JSOTSup 137. Sheffield: JSOT Press, 1992.

Alt, Albrecht. "Josua." *Kleine Schriften zur Geschichte des Volkes Israel*. Vol. 1, 176–192. Munich: Beck, [1936] 1953.

Auld, A. Graeme. *Joshua, Moses and the Land*. Edinburgh: T & T Clark, 1980.

Boling, Robert G. *Joshua: A New Translation with Notes and Commentary*. AB 6, Garden City, N.Y.: Doubleday, 1982.

Brown, Francis, Samuel R. Driver, and Charles A. Briggs. *A Hebrew and English Lexicon of the Old Testament*. Oxford: Oxford University Press, 1907.

Childs, Brevard S. *The Book of Exodus*. OTL. Philadelphia: Westminster, 1974.

Daube, David. *Studies in Biblical Law*. Cambridge: Cambridge University Press, 1947.

Eissfeldt, Otto. *The Old Testament: An Introduction*. Translated by P. Ackroyd (editor of 3rd ed. in German [1964]). Oxford: Blackwell, 1966.

Emerton, John A. "The Origin of the Promises to the Patriarchs in the Older Sources of the Book of Genesis." *Vetus Testamentum* 32 (1982): 14–32.

Flanagan, James W. "History, Religion and Ideology: The Caleb Tradition." *Horizons* 3 (1976): 175–185.

Fritz, Volkmar. *Das Buch Josua*. HAT 1.7. Tübingen: J. C. B. Mohr (P. Siebeck), 1994.

Gottwald, Norman K. *The Tribes of Yahweh: A Sociology of the Religion of Liberated Israel, 1250–1050 B.C.E.* Maryknoll, N.Y.: Orbis Books, 1979.

Greenberg, Moshe. "The Terms נפל and הפיל in the Context of Inheritance." In *Ki Baruch Hu: Ancient Near Eastern, Biblical, and Judaic Studies in Honor of Baruch A. Levin,* edited by Robert Chazan, William H. Hallo, and Lawrence H. Schiffman, 251–259. Winona Lake, Ind.: Eisenbrauns, 1999.

Hawk, L. Daniel. *Joshua.* Collegeville, Minn.: Liturgical Press, 2000.

Japhet, Sara. "The Concept of the 'Remnant' in the Restoration Period." In *Das Manna fällt auch heute noch,* edited by Frank-Lothar Hossfeld and Ludger Schwienhorst-Schönberger, 340–361. Freiburg: Herder, 2004.

Joosten, Jan. *People and Land in the Holiness Code: An Exegetical Study of the Ideational Framework of the Law in Leviticus 17–26.* VTSup 47. Leiden: Brill, 1996.

Joüon, Paul. *A Grammar of Biblical Hebrew.* Translated and revised by Takamitsu Muraoka. 2 vols. Subsidia biblica 14, no. 1–2. Rome: Pontifical Biblical Institute, 1991 [reprinted with corrections, 1993].

Kaufmann, Yehezkel. *Sepher Yehoshua* [*The Book of Joshua*; in Hebrew]. Jerusalem: Kiryat-Sepher, 1963.

Kislev, Itamar. *On the Threshold of the Promised Land: The Account of the Preparations for Entering Canaan and the Formation of the Pentateuch* [in Hebrew]. Jerusalem: Hebrew University Magnes Press, 2013.

Lingen, Anton van der. " 'Bw²-yṣ²' ('To Go out and to Come in') as a Military Term." *VT* 42, no. 1 (1992): 59–66.

Loewenstamm, Samuel E. "The Settlement of Gad and Reuben as Related in Nu. 32:2–38—Background and Composition." In *From Babylon to Canaan,* 109–130. Jerusalem: Hebrew University Magnes Press, 1992.

Lohfink, Norbert. "ירש yāraš." In *Theological Dictionary of the Old Testament,* edited by G. Johannes Botterweck and Helmer Ringgren, translated by John T. Willis, 368–396. Grand Rapids, Mich.: Eerdmans, 1990.

Mazar, Amihai. "The Days of the Judges: Iron Age I." *Archaeology of the Land of the Bible, 10,000–586 B.C.E.,* 328–355. New York: Doubleday, 1990.

Noth, Martin. *Das Buch Josua.* 2nd ed. HAT 7. Tübingen: J. C. B. Mohr, 1953.

Noth, Martin. *The Deuteronomistic History.* Translated by J. Doull et al. JSOTSup 15. Sheffield: JSOT Press, 1981.

Orlinsky, Harry. "The Biblical Concept of the Land of Israel: Cornerstone of the Covenant between God and Israel." In *The Land of Israel: Jewish Perspectives,* edited by Lawrence A. Hoffman, 27–64. Notre Dame, Ind.: University of Notre Dame Press, 1986.

Roth, Martha T. *Law Collections from Mesopotamia and Asia Minor.* 2nd ed. SBL Writings from the Ancient World 6. Atlanta: Scholars Press, 1997.

Schwartz, Baruch J. "Reexamining the Fate of the 'Canaanites' in the Torah Traditions." In *Sefer Moshe—The Moshe Weinfeld Jubilee Volume: Studies in the Bible and the Ancient Near East, Qumran, and Post-Biblical Judaism,* edited by Chaim Cohen, Avi Hurvitz, and Shalom M. Paul, 151–170. Winona Lake, Ind.: Eisenbrauns, 2004.

Smend, Rudolf. "Das Gesetz und die Völker." In *Probleme biblischer Theologie,* edited Hans W. Wolff, 494–595. Munich: Kaiser, 1971.

———. "Das uneroberte Land." In *Das Land Israel in biblischer Zeit,* Göttinger Theologische Arbeiten 25, edited by G. Strecker, 91–102. Göttingen: Vandenhoeck & Ruprecht, 1983.

Soggin, J. Alberto. *Joshua: A Commentary*. Translated by R. A. Wilson. OTL. London: SCM, 1972.

Vaux, Roland de. *The Early History of Israel*. Translated by David Smith. Philadelphia: Westminster, 1978.

Wazana, Nili. "Natives, Immigrants and the Biblical Perception of Origins in Historical Times." *Tel-Aviv* 32, no. 2 (2005): 220–244.

Wazana, Nili. *All the Boundaries of the Land: The Promised Land in Biblical Thought in Light of the Ancient Near East*. Winona Lake, Indiana: Eisenbrauns, 2013.

Weinfeld, Moshe. *The Promise of the Land: The Inheritance of the Land of Canaan by the Israelites*. Taubman Lectures in Jewish Studies 3. Berkeley: University of California Press, 1993.

Wright, G. Ernest. "The Literary and Historical Problem of Joshua 10 and Judges 1." *JNES* 5, no. 2 (1946): 105–114.

2

Josephus' Land Theology

A REAPPRAISAL

Michael Avioz

In his important monograph *The Territorial Dimension of Judaism*, William Davies writes: "The Land is so embedded in the heart of Judaism, the Torah, that—so its sources, worship, theology, and often its history attest—it is finally inseparable from it."[1] Similarly, Walter Brueggemann sees the theme of the land as "a central, if not the central theme of biblical faith."[2]

The land of Canaan was promised to the ancestors in the Pentateuch, and the promises are depicted as being fulfilled in the biblical books from Joshua to Kings.[3] In these books the people of Israel change their status twice from a landless to a landed people. The exile makes them landless again, but the return to Zion in the period of the Second Temple once more defines them as landed.[4]

Betsy Halpern-Amaru published a paper entitled "Land Theology in Josephus' *Jewish Antiquities*" in 1981,[5] arguing that Josephus downplayed the nationalist dimensions of a covenant theology that focused on the land. This conclusion is supported by a thorough examination of various citations from Josephus, mainly his *Antiquitates judaicae*.

This chapter seeks to reexamine the texts analyzed by Halpern-Amaru and to contest her conclusions regarding Josephus' land theology.[6]

Halpern-Amaru's Thesis

Halpern-Amaru analyzes "the development of land theology in Hellenistic literature through an examination of Josephus' *Jewish Antiquities*" and notices that the word ברית, or διαθήκη, is absent from Josephus' rewriting of the biblical sources that deal with the Promised Land.[7] In her opinion, Josephus has deleted the notion of a covenanted land because this would have been offensive to his Roman patrons, who had just reconquered that land. He does not want the land to be the main focus, given its significance for the revolutionary theology of the Zealots and the Sicarii, who both insisted that the land of Israel must be freed from foreign rule.

In the book of Genesis (Gen 15:18–21) there is a covenantal promise by God that Abraham's descendants will possess the land of Israel, whereas in Josephus (*Ant.* 1.185) there is merely a prediction that Abraham's descendants will vanquish the Canaanites and possess the land.

Halpern-Amaru also points to the fact that Josephus does not use the poetic attribute "land of milk and honey," but rather uses the general word γῆ, meaning "land." She claims that:

> Josephus ignored the theology of covenanted land because he did not want the land to be a focal point, as it was for Davidic messianism, with all its revolutionary implications in Josephus' day. Josephus feared and despised the messianism of the Zealots, and he structured his account of the Jewish origins and beliefs in such a way as to remove the theological basis for that messianism.

In conclusion, she argues that Josephus "simply does not portray the land as the heart of the Jewish experience. Instead, Judaism for Josephus is a religion of law, or virtue, of obedience to God's statutes."[8]

Critical Analysis

ALTERNATIVE EXPLANATIONS FOR THE OMISSIONS MADE BY JOSEPHUS

Several scholars have followed Halpern-Amaru's thesis and have cited her in their own studies. However, her explanations for the omissions of the so-called land theology from Josephus' rewriting of the biblical sources are not conclusive.

The omission of the word ברית from Josephus' rewriting of Genesis 17 seems to be connected to Josephus' ambiguous stance toward circumcision.[9] He does not emphasize this issue, in contrast to the rabbinic sources.[10] This is not the only place where the subject of circumcision is blurred; we find this to be the case in additional sources: He omits both the Shechemites' circumcision in Genesis 34 and the Israelites' circumcision in Joshua 5.

The word ברית appears in the biblical account of Isaac, Rebecca, and Abimelech, the king of Gerar, in Genesis 26. Josephus omitted this particular story, not because of its relation to the issue of land theology, but most likely for two other possible reasons: First, it contains a lie told by Isaac to Abimelech. Second, this story resembles the story of Abram and Sarai in Genesis 12 in a way that may have caused Josephus' audience to wonder how both Abram and Isaac could be involved in the same episode with the same scenario.[11]

Halpern-Amaru (p. 212) mentions also the omission of the biblical notion that the land has a particular nature and distinct qualities, a concept that was excluded by Josephus. However, one aspect of the land's nature is the link between incest and possession of the land, which appears twice in Leviticus: 18:25 and 20:21–24. Since one of Josephus' strategies is to avoid repetition, he mentions the prohibition of incest only in his rewriting of Leviticus 20 (*Ant.* 3.274–275). In addition, Josephus' omission of the phrase "the land of milk and honey" does not necessarily stem from a negative view of the land of Israel. Josephus may have not understood the exact meaning of this difficult phrase.[12] However, Josephus does designate the land of Israel in *Contra Apionem* 1.195 as beautiful and fertile. He also praises the fruitful soil of Jericho and Jerusalem (*Ant.* 5.77; *B. J.* 1.138; 4.459–475) and the fertility of the Galilee (*B. J.* 3.42). He describes the dates of Jericho; according to some interpreters, the honey in the phrase "milk and honey" is made of dates.[13]

Regarding the book of Deuteronomy, indeed the word ברית does appear here many times in reference to the covenant with the Fathers and the inheritance of the land, although Josephus repeatedly omitted it in his rendition (4:31, 7:9, 7:12, 8:18, 29:12).[14] The concept of ברית occurs also via the root שבע, or oath, in Deuteronomy 6:10, 6:18, 7:1, 8:1, 9:5, 10:11, 11:9, and 11:21.[15] Here, the reason for Josephus' omissions of references to land theology may be connected to the fact that Josephus is a historian, and the speeches of Moses, important as they may be, cannot be incorporated into a historian's account.[16]

As to the book of Joshua, Halpern-Amaru overlooked Josephus' rewriting of Joshua 7 in *Ant.* 5.38 ff., where he clearly mentions the divine promises given to Moses and to the people of Israel to inherit the land. In fact, in this passage, Josephus adds claims to Joshua's prayer before God, that are absent from the biblical story.

Josephus may have omitted references to the salvation oracles found in the Latter Prophets for the same reason. According to his conception, as a whole they do not contain significant historiographic material with the validity that is necessary for the authentic reconstruction of Israel's history. He did retain sections from Isaiah and Jeremiah when rewriting the book of Kings, since they fit nicely into his historical reconstruction of the period of the monarchy.[17] The book of Jeremiah was of great importance for Josephus, since he found in it ideas similar to his own concerning the need to accept the dominion of a foreign nation.[18] One also must not forget the fact that the Jewish ancestors are seldom mentioned in the Latter Prophets.[19] We cannot, therefore, expect Josephus to allude to these sources regarding the Promised Land theme.

BERITH AND ΔIαθHKH

It seems to me that Josephus did not necessarily avoid using διαθήκη due to his anti-messianic agenda, as Halpern-Amaru claimed.[20] In his article "διαθήκη" in the *Theological Dictionary of the New Testament*, J. Behm writes that "Aquila, Symmachus and Theodotion later substituted what seemed to them to be the

more literal *sunthēkē*."[21] Thus, it is not unreasonable to suppose that in choosing συνθήκη as the Greek equivalent of ברית, Josephus did not diverge from
the accepted rendition: it is the common translation for this word. The idea
that precedence in the establishment of the covenant belongs to God, and that
he exclusively imposes his covenant on man, was absent from the normative
Greek translation; hence the substitution of the term that prominently conveys
this idea. Thus, διαθήκη, like many other words, received a new meaning when
it became the vehicle of divine thought.[22]

Josephus does not use διαθήκη even for "the ark of covenant" (e.g., Josh 3:6,
3:8, 3:11, 3:14; *Ant.* 5.17), which is not by any means connected to the covenant
with the Fathers. Josephus does use the word "promise" (ἐπαγγελία) in *Ant.*
2.219, when speaking of the need to save Moses and not "dissolve God's promise"; he also cites this term in *Antiquitates judaicae* 2.275 and 5.39.

THE CONDITIONALITY OF THE PROMISES TO THE FATHERS

According to Halpern-Amaru, one of the changes that Josephus introduces
into the biblical record is that his "alliance structure makes acquisition of the
land conditional on morality and obedience, or even on the fortuitous swing
of God's rod."[23]

However, the conditionality of the land promises can hardly be assigned
to Josephus' own innovation. The promises to Abraham are conditional
according to Genesis 17–18 as well as Leviticus 26; Deuteronomy 5:30, 6:17,
9:4–6,[24] 11:17, 30:17–18; and in other occurrences in the Pentateuch and in the
Deuteronomistic history (Josh 23:13, 23:15, 23:16; 1 Kgs 9:7, 13:34, 14:15).

Therefore, even if we accept a radical dating of the Pentateuch to the days
of the Hasmoneans, one cannot deny that Josephus saw the conditional
rephrasing in the biblical text before him.[25] Biblical scholars are probably
familiar with Moshe Weinfeld's division of the biblical covenants into obligatory covenant and promissory covenant. In his view, the original promises to the Fathers were unconditional, and only in post-exilic times were
they transformed into conditional promises.[26] However, this differentiation
was challenged by certain scholars who hold that all biblical covenants are
conditional.[27]

Josephus could have used Ezekiel 33:25–26 as his source as well.[28] Ezekiel
claims in those verses that those who remained in the land of Israel after the
exile are not automatically defined as Abraham's heirs, since they do not match
the ideal of obedience to God.[29] Another possible source for Josephus may be
found in the book of Chronicles. In 1 Chronicles 16, the impression is that God
has done his part when he adhered to the promise with the Fathers. The people's duty is reiterated in 1 Chronicles 28:8: "And seek all the commandments
of Yahweh your God so that you may possess this good land and leave it as an
inheritance for your sons after you for ever." The Chronicler wishes to remind

his readers who came from exile that staying in God's land means adhering to his commandments.[30]

THE COMPLEXITY OF THE BIBLICAL LAND THEOLOGY

One of the problems with Halpern-Amaru's thesis is that it does not take into consideration the complexity of the biblical land theology. She refers at the beginning of her paper to the "classical biblical theology of land."[31] However, one should remember that there are many nuances and different theologies, and one need not present the covenant idea as the sole idea connected to the land theology. For instance, consider the differences between these assertions: Yahweh owns the land; the land was given to Israel as a gift; the occupation of the land will be achieved through military conquest rather than through a gift; fulfilling the commandments is a condition for receiving and possessing the land.[32]

This complexity enables Josephus, as well as other commentators, great flexibility in retelling the biblical version. One should not speak of "downplaying" or replacing ideas, but rather should use words like "choosing" or "stressing." Josephus was probably not far from the correct understanding of the biblical verbs ירש and נתן, which may denote military action in order to occupy the land (Deut 6:18–19).[33]

JOSEPHUS' ATTITUDE IN COMPARISON WITH HIS CONTEMPORARIES

Reading Halpern-Amaru's paper leads to the impression that Josephus is unique in affording little importance to the theology of the ברית. However, it seems that in the rabbinic literature the connection of the ברית with the Fathers and the acquisition of the land is also not stressed, as we might have expected. In fact, only in a few passages do the rabbis stress the historical right of the Jews for their land.

Interestingly, Halpern-Amaru expresses a similar opinion concerning this topic in the *Book of Jubilees*: There, too, she concludes that the author downplays the significance of the land.[34] However, James Scott rightly claimed that it is surely not the case in *Jubilees*, where "the Land obviously occupies a prominent position."[35] The concept of covenant is also very dominant in *Jubilees*. This book may serve as a contrast to the tone of the references to land and covenant in Josephus. Also, in *Jubilees*, Israel did not conquer a land that rightfully belonged to another nation; they were merely taking back territory that had been theirs all along.[36] The difference between Josephus and *Jubilees* is over the question of to whom the land originally belonged (see *Jub.* 8:11–9:15; 10:27–34). Josephus does not seem to know the "midrash" told by *Jubilees* about a

Canaanite who seized a land that did not belong to him. However, the *Book of Jubilees*, like Josephus, stresses, rather than land theology, the importance of observing the Torah as God's people.[37]

In this regard we may cite Katell Berthelot in her paper on the books of Maccabees.[38] She concludes that there is no necessary connection between the promises made to the Fathers or the memory of the conquest with Joshua and the Hasmonean wars and politics of conquest. Even 1 Maccabees 15:33–35, where Simon the high priest speaks of "the heritage of our fathers," does not necessarily imply a reference to the biblical promises found in the Pentateuch.

The notion that Israel is given the land conditionally also appears in the Temple Scroll from Qumran: צדק צדק תרדוף למען תחיה ובאתה וירשתה את הארץ אשר אנוכי נותן לכמה לרשתה כל הימים (LI 15–16).[39] In general, when compared with Josephus, there are many Qumran texts that deal with the different forms of the covenant.[40]

In the rabbinic literature we find the concept of the conditionality of the promises to the Fathers stated in the same way as it is in Josephus.[41] The idea of the covenanted land in fact gives way to the idea that the observance of the Torah is more important than the ancestral covenant.[42] Also important in this regard is the depiction of the land of Israel as a "land of milk and honey." It is important to note that the rabbis used this phrase only after the Bar-Kokhba revolt, so there is no reason to expect Josephus to use it frequently.[43]

Conclusion

In conclusion, I suggest that scholars not emphasize the absence of the word ברית in Josephus' writings, but rather give due attention to the element that he wanted to highlight: The connection between the Jewish people and the land of Israel may be maintained only through observance of God's commandments. One should not regard this formulation as a radical change of the biblical text by Josephus.[44] It is one thing to see a change in focus in Josephus, but it is another to conclude that he downplayed the significance of the land.

As I have shown elsewhere,[45] scholars tend too easily to adopt a simplistic solution with reference to Josephus' rewriting of the Bible. According to the prevailing view, the changes that Josephus introduced into the biblical text stem from the political, cultural, and historical circumstances in which Josephus found himself. I do not argue that this view is untenable, but rather suggest that we should first examine the possibility that the motive for his modifications is exegetical and determine whether they are based on a legitimate understanding of Scriptures. Only when we are convinced that this is not the appropriate explanation for the changes can we suggest alternative explanations.

Notes

* I wish to thank the Beit Shalom fund in Japan for their generous support of this research.

1. W. D. Davies, *The Territorial Dimension of Judaism*, 2nd ed. (Minneapolis: Fortress Press, 1991), 125. See also W. Brueggemann, *The Land: Place as Gift, Promise, and Challenge in Biblical Faith* (London: Society for Promoting Christian Knowledge, 1978), 3; M. Weinfeld, *The Promise of the Land: The Inheritance of the Land of Canaan by the Israelites* (Berkeley and Los Angeles: University of California Press, 1993), 183. G. von Rad, "The Promised Land and Yahweh's Land in the Hexateuch," in *The Problem of the Hexateuch and Other Essays*, trans. E. W. T. Dicken (New York: McGraw-Hill, 1966), 79–93, limited this assertion to the Hextateuch.

2. Brueggemann, *The Land*, 3.

3. P. R. Williamson, "Promise and Fulfilment: The Territorial Inheritance," in *The Land of Promise: Biblical, Theological and Contemporary Perspectives*, ed. P. Johnston and P. Walker (Downers Grove, Ill.: InterVarsity Press, 2000), 15; N. Wazana, *All the Boundaries of the Land: The Promised Land in Biblical Thought in Light of the Ancient Near East* [in Hebrew] (Jerusalem: Bialik Institute, 2007).

4. Definitions adopted from Brueggemann, *The Land*; and C. H. H. Scobie, *The Ways of Our God: An Approach to Biblical Theology* (Grand Rapids, Mich.: Eerdmans, 2003).

5. B. Halpern-Amaru, "Land Theology in Josephus' *Jewish Antiquities*," *JQR* 71 (1981): 201–229. Other versions of this article were published in Halpern-Amaru, "Land Theology in Philo and Josephus," in *The Land of Israel: Jewish Perspectives*, University of Notre Dame Centre for the Study of Judaism and Christianity in Antiquity, 6, ed. L. A. Hoffman (Notre Dame, Ind.: University of Notre Dame Press, 1986), 65–93; Halpern-Amaru, *Rewriting the Bible: Land and Covenant in Postbiblical Jewish Literature* (Valley Forge, Pa.: Trinity Press International, 1994). Halpern-Amaru's paper has won scholarly agreement from Josephus scholars such as P. Spilsbury, "God and Israel in Josephus: A Patron-client Relationship," in *Understanding Josephus: Seven Perspectives*, JSPS 32, ed. S. Mason (Sheffield, U.K.: Sheffield Academic Press, 1988), 172–191; P. Spilsbury, "Josephus," in *Justification and Variegated Nomism*, vol. 1, *The Complexities of Second Temple Judaism*, ed. D. A. Carson et al. Tübingen: Mohr Siebeck; Grand Rapids, Mich.: Baker Academic, 2001, 241–260; L. H. Feldman, "The Concept of Exile in Josephus," in *Judaism and Hellenism Reconsidered*, JSJS 107, ed. J. M. Scott (Leiden: Brill, 2006), 695–721; T. W. Franxman, Genesis and the "Jewish Antiquities" of Flavius Josephus, *BibOr*, 35 (Rome: Biblical Institute Press, 1979), 141; I. M. Gafni, *Land, Center and Diaspora: Jewish Constructs in Late Antiquity*, JSPS 21 (Sheffield, U.K.: Sheffield Academic Press, 1997), 62; J. M. G. Barclay, *Jews in the Mediterranean Diaspora from Alexander to Trajan (323 BCE–117 CE)* (Edinburgh: T & T Clark, 1996), 359; Z. Safrai and Ch. Safrai, "The Sanctity of the Land of Israel and Jerusalem: The Development of an Idea," in *Jews and Judaism in the Second Temple, Mishna and Talmud Period: Studies in Honor of Shmuel Safrai* [in Hebrew], ed. A. Oppenheimer et al. (Jerusalem: Yad Ben Zvi, 1993), 344–371.

6. I will not address here the question of the boundaries of the land of Israel. See B. Z. Rosenfeld, "Flavius Josephus and His Portrayal of the Coast (paralia) of Contemporary Roman Palestine: Geography and Ideology," *JQR* 91 (2000): 143–183; E. Ben Eliyahu, "National Identity and Territory: The Borders of the Land of Israel in the Consciousness of the People of the Second Temple and the Roman Byzantine Periods" [in Hebrew] PhD diss., Hebrew University, 2007. All translations of Josephus in this chapter are according to C. T. Begg,

Judean Antiquities Books 5–7: Translation and Commentary, Flavius Josephus: Translation and Commentary 4 (Leiden: Brill, 2005). I have also consulted H. St. J. Thackeray and R. Marcus, *Josephus Jewish Antiquities*, vol. 6, Loeb Classical Library (Cambridge, Mass.: Harvard University Press, 1934).

7. Halpern-Amaru, "Land Theology in Josephus' *Jewish Antiquities*," 202. Halpern-Amaru refers to several passages in *B.J.* as well, where the covenant with God is transformed into "ally terminology" (θεοῦ συμμαχία): *B.J.* 2.290; 5.366–369; 6.38–41.

8. Halpern-Amaru, "Land Theology in Josephus' *Jewish Antiquities*," 229.

9. See the references in M. Avioz, "Josephus' Portrait of Michal," *JSQ* 18 (2011): 1–18.

10. See the references in S. J. D. Cohen, *Why Aren't Jewish Women Circumcised? Gender and Covenant in Judaism* (Berkeley and Los Angeles: University of California Press, 2005); D. A. Bernat, *Sign of the Covenant: Circumcision in the Priestly Tradition* (Atlanta: SBL, 2009).

11. For the retelling of this story in Josephus, see Franxman, *Genesis*, 127–128.

12. On this phrase, see E. Levine, "The Land of Milk and Honey," *JSOT* 87 (2000): 43–57. He notes that interpreters through the ages have misunderstood this phrase.

13. S. Kottek, *Medicine and Hygiene in the Works of Flavius Josephus* (Leiden: Brill, 1994), 127; J. Kelhoffer, "John the Baptist's 'Wild Honey' and the Ambiguity of Certain References to 'Honey' in Antiquity," *Greek, Roman, and Byzantine Studies* 45 (2005): 59–73.

14. T. E. Fretheim, *Abraham: Trials of Family and Faith* (Columbia: University of South Carolina Press, 2007). On Josephus' use of the book of Deuteronomy, see David Lincicum, *Paul and the Early Jewish Encounter with Deuteronomy*, WUNT 2.284 (Tübingen: Mohr Siebeck, 2010), ch. 7.

15. S. Boorer, *The Promise of the Land as Oath: A Key to the Formation of the Pentateuch*, BZAW 205 (Berlin: de Gruyter, 1992), 112.

16. That does not mean, of course, that Josephus avoids retelling or even adding speeches. He usually adds "commander speeches" that the leader delivers before battles. See J. W. van Henten, "Commonplaces in Herod's Commander Speech in Josephus' A. J. 15.127–146," in *Josephus and Jewish History in Flavian Rome and Beyond*, JSJS 104, ed. G. Lembi and J. Sievers (Leiden: Brill, 2005), 183–206. In any case, speeches are usually found in *Ant.* 11–20 and in *B.J.* See Pere Villalba i Varneda, *The Historical Method of Flavius Josephus* (Leiden: Brill, 1986), 92.

17. S. Schwartz, *Josephus and Judaean Politics* (Leiden: Brill, 1990), 46–47. Cf. L. H. Feldman, *Josephus and Modern Scholarship* (Berlin: de Gruyter, 1984), 942: "the shift in Josephus may be due to the fact that he is primarily a historian and hence focuses on Abraham, for example, as a historical figure, rather than on theological issues."

18. See R. Gray, *Prophetic Figures in Late Second Temple Jewish Palestine: The Evidence from Josephus* (Oxford: Oxford University Press, 1993), and the literature cited there.

19. H. D. Preuss, *Old Testament Theology*, 2 vols., trans. L. G. Perdue (Louisville, Ky.: Westminster John Knox, 1995), 2:14.

20. André Paul suggests that Josephus was polemical and anti-Christian ("Flavius Josephus' 'Antiquities of the Jews': an Anti-Christian Manifesto," *New Testament Studies* 31 [1985], 473–480). Schreckenberg thinks that Paul's view is unconvincing. See H. Schreckenberg, "The Works of Josephus and the Early Christian Church," in *Josephus, Judaism, and Christianity*, ed. L. H. Feldman and G. Hata (Leiden: Brill, 1987), 323 n. 11. Cf. Spilsbury, "God and Israel," 174–175 n. 2. Josephus does use the word διαθήκη in *Ant.* 17.3, 248 and *B.J.* 2.20 with the meaning of "will."

21. J. Behm, "διαθήκη," *Theological Dictionary of the New Testament* 2 (Grand Rapids, Mich.: Eerdmans, 1964), 126. See the extensive discussion of S. E. Murray, "The Concept of *diatheke* in the Letter to the Hebrews," *Concordia Theological Quarterly* 66 (2002): 41–60.

22. L. Berkhof, *Systematic Theology* (Grand Rapids, Mich.: Eerdmans, 1949), 262–263. Cf. A. E. Abbott, *Christ's Miracles of Feeding* (Cambridge: University Press; New York: Putnam, 1915), 148; A. M. Schwemer, "Zum Verhältnis von Diatheke und Nomos in den Schriften der jüdischen Diaspora Ägyptens in hellenistisch-römischer Zeit," in *Bund und Tora: zur theologischen Begriffsgeschichte in alttestamentlicher, frühjüdischer und urchristlicher Tradition*, ed. Friedrich Avemarie und Hermann Lichtenberger (Tübingen: J. C. B. Mohr [Paul Siebeck], 1996), 67–109.

23. Halpern-Amaru, "Land Theology in Josephus' *Jewish Antiquities*," 211.

24. P. C. Craigie, *Deuteronomy*, NICOT (Grand Rapids, Mich.: Eerdmans, 1976), 193, writes that there are two concepts in Deut 9: one that sees the gift of the land as deriving from God's grace, and the other as seeing the continuous possession of the land by the Israelites as contingent upon their obedience to God's laws.

25. J. Milgrom, *Leviticus 23–27: A New Translation and Introduction and Commentary*, AB 3B (New York: Doubleday, 2001), 2340. See also I. Joosten, *People and Land in the Holiness Code: An Exegetical Study of the Ideational Framework of the Law in Leviticus 17–26* (Leiden: Brill, 1996), 110–112; H. E. von Waldow, "Israel and Her Land: Some Theological Considerations," in *A Light unto My Path: Old Testament Studies in Honor of Jacob M. Myers*, ed. Howard N. Bream et al. (Philadelphia, Pa.: Temple University Press, 1974), 493–508; H. M. Orlinsky, "The Biblical Concept of the Land of Israel: Cornerstone of the Covenant between God and Israel," in *The Land of Israel: Jewish Perspectives*, ed. L. A. Hoffman (Notre Dame, Ind.: University of Notre Dame Press, 1986), 46.

26. See also E. Noort, "'Land' in the Deuteronomistic Tradition: Genesis 15—The Historical and Theological Necessity of a Diachronic Approach," in *Synchronic or Diachronic? A Debate on Method in Old Testament Exegesis*, ed. J. C. de Moor (Leiden: Brill, 1995), 137.

27. M. Haran, "The Berit 'Covenant': Its Nature and Ceremonial Background," in *Tehilla le-Moshe: Biblical and Judaic Studies in Honor of Moshe Greenberg*, ed. M. Cogan et al. (Winona Lake, Ind.: Eisenbrauns, 1997), 203–219; Milgrom, *Leviticus 23–27*, 2340.

28. On the use of Ezekiel by Josephus, see C. T. Begg, "The 'Classical Prophets' in Josephus' *Antiquities*," in *The Place Is Too Small for Us: The Israelite Prophets in Recent Scholarship*, ed. R. P. Gordon (Winona Lake, Ind.: Eisenbrauns, 1995), 561.

29. M. Fishbane, *Biblical Interpretation in Ancient Israel* (Oxford: Clarendon, 1985), 419–420.

30. See M. Shipp, "'Remember His Covenant Forever': A Study of the Chronicler's Use of the Psalms," *ResQ* 35 (1993): 29–39. For the conditionality of the promises in post-biblical sources, see C. H. Cosgrove, *The Cross and the Spirit: A Study in the Argument and Theology of Galatians* (Macon, Ga.: Mercer University Press, 1988), 96–98. For the use of the book of Chronicles in Josephus' writings, see E. Ben Zvi, *History, Literature, and Theology in the Book of Chronicles*, Bible World (London: Equinox, 2006), 256–259.

31. Halpern-Amaru, "Land Theology in Josephus' *Jewish Antiquities*," 205.

32. See Boorer, *Promise of the Land*, 65; von Waldow, "Israel and Her Land"; Joosten, *People and Land*, 174–175.

33. For details, see M. Weinfeld, *Deuteronomy and the Deuteronomic School* (Oxford: Clarendon, 1972), 177, 315, 342. See also P. D. Miller, *Deuteronomy* (Interpretation; Louisville, 1996), 45–46. On Josephus' adaptation of the Deuteronomistic attitude toward covenant, see J. R. Wisdom, *Blessing for the Nations and the Curse of the Law: Paul's Citation of Genesis and Deuteronomy in Gal 3.8–10* (Tübingen: Mohr Siebeck, 2001), 117–124.

34. B. Halpern-Amaru, "Exile and Return in Jubilees," in *Exile: Old Testament, Jewish, and Christian Conceptions*, JSJS 56, ed. J. M. Scott (Leiden: Brill, 1997), 143–144.

35. J. Scott, *On Earth as in Heaven: The Restoration of Sacred Time and Sacred Space in the Book of Jubilees*, JSJS 91 (Leiden: Brill, 2005), 162.

36. Scott, *Sacred Time and Sacred Space*, 177; D. Mendels, *The Land of Israel as a Political Concept in Hasmonean Literature: Recourse to History in Second Century B.C. Claims to the Holy Land* (Tübingen: J. C. B. Mohr, 1987), 57–88.

37. E. J. Christiansen, *The Covenant in Judaism and Paul: A Study of Ritual; Boundaries as Identity Markers*, AGJU, 27 (Leiden: Brill, 1995), 82–85; J. C. VanderKam, "'Putting Them in their Place': Geography as an Evaluative Tool," in *From Revelation to Canon: Studies in the Hebrew Bible and Second Temple Literature*, ed. J. C. VanderKam (Leiden: Brill, 2000), 476–499.

38. K. Berthelot, "The Biblical Conquest of the Promised Land and the Hasmonaean Wars according to 1 and 2 Maccabees," in *The Books of the Maccabees: History, Theology, Ideology*, JSJS 118, ed. G. G. Xeravits and J. Zsengellér (Leiden: Brill, 2007), 45–60.

39. L. H. Schiffman, "Israel," in *Encyclopedia of the Dead Sea Scrolls*, ed. L. H. Schiffman and J. C. VanderKam (New York: Oxford University Press, 2001), 1:390.

40. See for instance T. R. Blanton, *Constructing a New Covenant: Discursive Strategies in the Damascus Document and Second Corinthians*, WUNT 2, Reihe 233 (Tübingen: Mohr Siebeck, 2007).

41. P. E. Sanders, *Paul and Palestinian Judaism: A Comparison of Patterns of Religion* (London: SCM Press, 1977), 189, and the rabbinic sources cited at note 39 there.

42. A. Goshen-Gottstein, "The Covenant with the Fathers and the Inheritance of the Land—Between Biblical Theology and Rabbinic Thought" [in Hebrew], *Daat* 35 (1995): 5–28.

43. See Gafni, *Land, Center and Diaspora*, 62–63.

44. Cf. A. Kasher, *Josephus Flavius "Against Apion": A New Hebrew Translation with Introduction and Commentary*, 2 vols. (Jerusalem: Zalman Shazar Center, 1996), 1:41–42.

45. M. Avioz, "Josephus' Rewriting of 1 Samuel 25," *JJS* 59 (2008): 73–85; M. Avioz, "Saul as a Just Judge in Josephus' *Antiquities of the Jews*," in *Perspectives in Hebrew Scriptures V: Comprising the Contents of Journal of Hebrew Scriptures*, vol. 8, ed. E. Ben Zvi (Piscataway, N.J.: Gorgias Press, 2009), 391–400.

Bibliography

Abbott, E. A. *Christ's Miracles of Feeding*. Cambridge: University Press; New York: Putnam, 1915.

Avioz, M. "Josephus' Rewriting of 1 Samuel 25." *JJS* 59 (2008): 73–85.

———. "Saul as a Just Judge in Josephus' Antiquities of the Jews." In *Perspectives in Hebrew Scriptures V: Comprising the Contents of Journal of Hebrew Scriptures*, vol. 8, edited by E. Ben Zvi, 391–400. Piscataway, N. J.: Gorgias Press, 2009.

Avioz, M. "Josephus' Portrait of Michal." *JSQ* 18 (2011): 1–18.

Barclay, J. M. G. *Jews in the Mediterranean Diaspora from Alexander to Trajan (323 BCE–117 CE)*. Edinburgh: T & T Clark, 1996.

Begg, C. T. "The 'Classical Prophets' in Josephus' *Antiquities*." In *The Place Is Too Small for Us: The Israelite Prophets in Recent Scholarship*, edited by R. P. Gordon, 547–562. Winona Lake, Ind.: Eisenbrauns, 1995.

——. *Judean Antiquities Books 5–7: Translation and Commentary*. Flavius Josephus: Translation and Commentary 4. Leiden: Brill, 2005.

Behm, J. "διαθήκη." *TDNT*. Vol. 2, 124–129. Grand Rapids, Mich.: Eerdmans, 1964.

Ben Eliyahu, E. "National Identity and Territory: The Borders of the Land of Israel in the Consciousness of the People of the Second Temple and the Roman Byzantine Periods" [in Hebrew]. PhD diss., Hebrew University, 2007.

Ben Zvi, E. *History, Literature, and Theology in the Book of Chronicles*. Bible World. London: Equinox, 2006.

Berkhof, L. *Systematic Theology*. Grand Rapids, Mich.: Eerdmans, 1949.

Berthelot, K. "The Biblical Conquest of the Promised Land and the Hasmonean Wars according to 1 and 2 Maccabees." In *The Books of the Maccabees: History, Theology, Ideology*, JSJS 118, edited by G. G. Xeravits and J. Zsengellér, 45–60. Leiden: Brill, 2007.

Blanton, T. R. *Constructing a New Covenant: Discursive Strategies in the Damascus Document and Second Corinthians*. WUNT 2, Reihe 233. Tübingen: Mohr Siebeck, 2007.

Boorer, S. *The Promise of the Land as Oath: A Key to the Formation of the Pentateuch*. BZAW 205. Berlin: de Gruyter, 1992.

Brown, A. M. "The Concept of Inheritance in the Old Testament." PhD diss., Columbia University, 1965.

Brueggemann, W. *The Land: Place as Gift, Promise, and Challenge in Biblical Faith*. London: Society for Promoting Christian Knowledge, 1978.

Christiansen, E. J. *The Covenant in Judaism and Paul: A Study of Ritual; Boundaries as Identity Markers*. AGJU 27. Leiden: Brill, 1995.

Colautti, F. M. *Passover in the Works of Josephus*. JSJS 75. Leiden: Brill, 2002.

Cosgrove, C. H. *The Cross and the Spirit: A Study in the Argument and Theology of Galatians*. Macon, Ga.: Mercer University Press, 1988.

Craigie, P. C. *Deuteronomy*. NICOT. Grand Rapids, Mich.: Eerdmans, 1976.

Davies, W. D. *The Territorial Dimension of Judaism*. 2nd ed. Minneapolis: Fortress, 1991.

Feldman, L. H. *Josephus and Modern Scholarship*. Berlin: de Gruyter, 1984.

——. "The Concept of Exile in Josephus." In *Exile: Old Testament, Jewish, and Christian Conceptions*, JSJS, 56, edited by J. M. Scott, 145–172. Leiden: Brill, 1997.

Feldman, L. H. "Prophets and Prophecy in Josephus." In *Prophets, Prophecy, and Prophetic Texts in Second Temple Judaism*, Library of Hebrew Bible/Old Testament Studies, 427, edited by M. H. Floyd and R. D. Haak, 210–239. London: T & T Clark, 2006.

Fishbane, M. *Biblical Interpretation in Ancient Israel*. Oxford: Clarendon, 1985.

Franxman, T. W. *Genesis and the "Jewish Antiquities" of Flavius Josephus*. BibOr, 35. Rome: Biblical Institute Press, 1979.

Fretheim, T. E. *Abraham: Trials of Family and Faith*. Columbia: University of South Carolina Press, 2007.

Gafni, I. M. *Land, Center and Diaspora: Jewish Constructs in Late Antiquity*. JSPSup 21. Sheffield: Sheffield Academic Press, 1997.

Goshen-Gottstein, A. "The Covenant with the Fathers and the Inheritance of the Land— Between Biblical Theology and Rabbinic Thought" [in Hebrew]. *Daat* 35 (1995): 5–28.

Gray, R. *Prophetic Figures in Late Second Temple Jewish Palestine: The Evidence from Josephus*. Oxford: Oxford University Press, 1993.

Halpern-Amaru, B. *Rewriting the Bible: Land and Covenant in Postbiblical Jewish Literature.* Valley Forge, Pa.: Trinity International, 1994.

Halpern-Amaru, B. "Exile and Return in *Jubilees.*" In *Exile: Old Testament, Jewish, and Christian Conceptions,* JSJS 56, edited by J. M. Scott, 127–144. Leiden: Brill, 1997.

——. "Land Theology in Josephus' *Jewish Antiquities.*" *JQR* 71 (1981): 201–229.

——. "Land Theology in Philo and Josephus." In *The Land of Israel: Jewish Perspectives,* University of Notre Dame Centre for the Study of Judaism and Christianity in Antiquity, 6, edited by L. A. Hoffman, 65–93. Notre Dame, Ind.: University of Notre Dame Press, 1986.

Hannah, Darrell D. "Isaiah within Judaism of the Second Temple Period." In *Isaiah in the New Testament,* New Testament and the Scriptures of Israel, edited by S. Moyise and M. J. J. Menken, 7–33. London: T & T Clark, 2005.

Haran, M. "The Berit 'Covenant': Its Nature and Ceremonial Background." In *Tehilla le-Moshe: Biblical and Judaic Studies in Honor of Moshe Greenberg,* edited by M. Cogan et al., 203–219. Winona Lake, Ind.: Eisenbrauns, 1997.

Heinemann, I. "The Relationship between the Jewish People and Their Land in Hellenistic Jewish Literature" [in Hebrew]. *Zion* 13–14 (1948–1949): 1–9.

Joosten, I. *People and Land in the Holiness Code: An Exegetical Study of the Ideational Framework of the Law in Leviticus 17–26.* Leiden: Brill, 1996.

Kasher, A. *Josephus Flavius against Apion: A New Hebrew Translation with Introduction and Commentary.* 2 vols. Jerusalem: Zalman Shazar Center, 1996.

Kelhoffer, J. "John the Baptist's 'Wild Honey' and the Ambiguity of Certain References to 'Honey' in Antiquity." *Greek, Roman, and Byzantine Studies* 45 (2005): 59–73.

Kottek, S. S. *Medicine and Hygiene in the Works of Flavius Josephus.* Leiden: Brill, 1994.

Levine, E. "The Land of Milk and Honey." *JSOT* 87 (2000): 43–57.

Levy, Y. "A Territorial Dispute in the Land of Israel in Ancient Times" [in Hebrew]. In *Olamot Nifgashim* [Studies in Jewish Hellenism], 60–78. Jerusalem: Mossad Bialik, 1960.

Lincicum. *David, Paul and the Early Jewish Encounter with Deuteronomy.* WUNT 2.284. Tübingen: Mohr Siebeck, 2010.

Manning, Gary T., Jr. *Echoes of a Prophet: The Use of Ezekiel in the Gospel of John and in Literature of the Second Temple Period.* JSNTSup 270. London: T & T Clark, 2004.

Mendels, D. *The Land of Israel as a Political Concept in Hasmonean Literature: Recourse to History in Second Century B.C. Claims to the Holy Land.* Tübingen: Mohr, 1987.

Milgrom, J. *Leviticus 23–27: A New Translation and Introduction and Commentary.* AB 3B. New York: Doubleday, 2001.

Miller, P. D. *Deuteronomy* (Interpretation). Louisville: John Knox, 1996.

Murray, S. E. "The Concept of *diatheke* in the Letter to the Hebrews," *Concordia Theological Quarterly* 66 (2002): 41–60.

Noort, E. "'Land' in the Deuteronomistic Tradition: Genesis 15; The Historical and Theological Necessity of a Diachronic Approach." In *Synchronic or Diachronic? A Debate on Method in Old Testament Exegesis,* edited by J. C. de Moor, 129–144. Leiden: Brill, 1995.

Orlinsky, H. M. "The Biblical Concept of the Land of Israel: Cornerstone of the Covenant between God and Israel." In *The Land of Israel: Jewish Perspectives,* edited by Lawrence A. Hoffman, 27–64. Notre Dame, Ind.: University of Notre Dame Press, 1986.

Paul, A. "Flavius Josephus' *Antiquities of the Jews*: An Anti-Christian Manifesto." *New Testament Studies* 31 (1985): 473–480.

Preuss, H. D. *Old Testament Theology.* 2 vols. Translated by L. G. Perdue. Louisville, Ky.: Westminster John Knox, 1995.

Rad, G. von. "The Promised Land and Yahweh's Land in the Hexateuch." In *The Problem of the Hexateuch and Other Essays,* translated by E. W. T. Dicken, 79–93. New York: McGraw-Hill, 1966.

Rosenfeld, B. Z. "Flavius Josephus and His Portrayal of the Coast (paralia) of Contemporary Roman Palestine: Geography and Ideology." *JQR* 91 (2000): 143–183.

Safrai, Z., and Ch. Safrai. "The Sanctity of the Land of Israel and Jerusalem: The Development of an Idea" [in Hebrew]. In *Jews and Judaism in the Second Temple, Mishna and Talmud Period-Studies in Honor of Shmuel Safrai,* edited by A. Oppenheimer et al., 344–371. Jerusalem: Yad Ben Zvi, 1993.

Sanders, E. P. *Paul and Palestinian Judaism: A Comparison of Patterns of Religion.* London: SCM Press, 1977.

Schiffman, L. H. "Israel." In *Encyclopedia of the Dead Sea Scrolls,* vol. 1, edited by L. H. Schiffman and J. C. VanderKam, 388–391. New York: Oxford University Press, 2001.

Schreckenberg, H. "The Works of Josephus and the Early Christian Church." In *Josephus, Judaism, and Christianity,* edited by L. H. Feldman and G. Hata, 315–324. Leiden: Brill, 1987.

Schwartz, S. *Josephus and Judaean Politics.* Leiden: Brill, 1990.

Schwemer, A. M. "Zum Verhältnis von Diatheke und Nomos in den Schriften der jüdischen Diaspora Ägyptens in hellenistisch-römischer Zeit." In *Bund und Tora: Zur theologischen Begriffsgeschichte in alttestamentlicher, frühjüdischer und urchristlicher Tradition,* edited by Friedrich Avemarie und Hermann Lichtenberger, 67–109. Tübingen: J. C. B. Mohr Paul Siebeck, 1996.

Scobie, C. H. H. *The Ways of Our God: An Approach to Biblical Theology.* Grand Rapids, Mich.: Eerdmans, 2003.

Scott, J. *On Earth as in Heaven: The Restoration of Sacred Time and Sacred Space in the Book of Jubilees.* JSJ 91. Leiden: Brill, 2005.

Shipp, M. "'Remember His Covenant Forever': A Study of the Chronicler's Use of the Psalms." *ResQ* 35 (1993): 29–39.

Shochat, A. "The Views of Josephus on the Future of Israel and its Land" [in Hebrew]. In *Yerushalayim,* vol. 1, Review for Erez-Israel Research Dedicated to Isaias Press, edited by M. Ish Shalom et al., 43–50. Jerusalem: Mosad Ha-Rav Kook, 1953.

Spilsbury, P. "God and Israel in Josephus: A Patron-Client Relationship." In *Understanding Josephus: Seven Perspectives,* JSPS 32, edited by S. Mason, 172–191. Sheffield: Sheffield Academic Press, 1988.

Spilsbury, P. "Josephus." In *Justification and Variegated Nomism.* Vol. 1. *The Complexities of Second Temple Judaism,* edited by D. A. Carson et al., 241–260. Tübingen: Mohr Siebeck; Grand Rapids, Mich.: Baker Academic, 2001.

St. J. Thackeray, H., and R. Marcus. *Josephus Jewish Antiquities.* Vol. 6. Loeb Classical Library. Cambridge, Mass.: Harvard University Press, 1934.

VanderKam, J. C. "'Putting Them in Their Place': Geography as an Evaluative Tool." In *From Revelation to Canon: Studies in the Hebrew Bible and Second Temple Literature,* edited by J. C. VanderKam, 476–499. Leiden: Brill, 2000.

Van Henten, J. W. "Commonplaces in Herod's Commander Speech in Josephus' *A. J.* 15.127–146." In *Josephus and Jewish History in Flavian Rome and Beyond,* JSJSup 104, edited by G. Lembi and J. Sievers, 183–206. Leiden: Brill, 2005.

Varenda, Pere Villalba I. *The Historical Method of Flavius Josephus*. Leiden: Brill. 1986.

Von Waldow, H. E. "Israel and Her Land: Some Theological Considerations," In *A Light unto My Path: Old Testament Studies in Honor of Jacob M. Myers*, edited by Howard N. Bream, et al., 493–508. Philadelphia: Temple University Press, 1974.

Wazana, N. *All the Boundaries of the Land: The Promised Land in Biblical Thought in Light of the Ancient Near East* [in Hebrew]. Jerusalem: Bialik Institute, 2007.

Weinfeld, M. *From Joshua to Josiah: Turning Points in the History of Israel from the Conquest of the Land until the Fall of Judah* [in Hebrew]. Jerusalem: Magnes Press, 1992.

Weinfeld, M. *The Promise of the Land: The Inheritance of the Land of Canaan by the Israelites*. Berkeley and Los Angeles: University of California Press, 1993.

Williamson, P. R. "Promise and Fulfilment: The Territorial Inheritance." In *The Land of Promise: Biblical, Theological and Contemporary Perspectives*, edited by P. Johnston and P. Walker, 15–34. Downers Grove, Ill.: InterVarsity Press, 2000.

Wisdom, J. R. *Blessing for the Nations and the Curse of the Law: Paul's Citation of Genesis and Deuteronomy in Gal 3.8–10*. Tübingen: Mohr Siebeck, 2001.

3

Rereading *herem*

DESTRUCTION OF IDOLATRY IN TANNAITIC LITERATURE

Ishay Rosen-Zvi

The biblical God is a jealous God, and his jealousy is manifest first and foremost in his unwillingness to bear the presence of other gods and their statues, and in the demand, which appears several times in the Bible, to be jealous for him and to do away with all images.[1] Mishnah *Avodah Zarah*, however, presents an entirely different picture, in which the obligation to destroy idols is replaced by an imperative to keep away from idols and to derive no benefit from them. Scholars attempted to locate the roots of the great chasm between the biblical and Second Temple ethic of idolatry, on the one hand, and that of the Mishnah, on the other. There were those who wished to see it as a concession grounded in simple political weaknesses,[2] or an economic move designed to facilitate adequate commerce.[3] Others saw it as an ideological sea-change that set the stage for "coexistence with the enemy,"[4] and even as a theological understanding that there is no point in destroying idols when those who worship them are not cognizant of their futility.[5]

In this chapter I will demonstrate that the biblical imperative to destroy idols is not entirely absent from the Mishnah but can be found between the lines. A careful reading of these clues will help reconstruct a wide-ranging polemic over this imperative, grounded in the Tannaitic midrashim and reflected in the Mishnah. Exposing this polemic will allow a better understanding of the exact move made in the Mishnah and will shed new light on the alternative it presents to biblical zealotry. Beyond the question discussed by many scholars, of the motivation for the rabbinic reform, it is important to understand the precise nature of the alternative the rabbis offered to the biblical model and the exegetical moves that allowed for the transformation of biblical annihilation to the rabbinic avoidance of idols.

The case through which this issue is examined here is the biblical concept of the *herem* (חרם). Originally, *herem* designates anything that is consecrated to God, and therefore out of bounds for profane use. However, in some cases this status brings about an obligation to destroy the *herem* (expressed by the

derived imperative: החרם).[6] In Deuteronomy the term applies specifically to
the inhabitants of Canaan (Deut 7:2, 20:17; cf. Josh 6:17). According to the
Deuteronomist, the dangers posed by the Canaanites lay first and foremost
in the anxiety that contact with them will bring the Israelites to adopt their
gods and their worship. It is thus not an accident that the two main places
in which the command of *herem* appears regard idolatry—Deuteronomy 7
regarding the Canaanite gods and Deuteronomy 13 regarding a subverted city
(עיר הנדחת);[7] in both cases, it is connected to a total destruction of the enemy
and their property.[8] The analysis of the Tannaitic homilies on these verses will
shed light on the rabbinic revision of the biblical ideology of the total destruction of the Canaanites and their gods.

My claim will be developed in two stages. In the first half of the chapter,
I will expose a central polemic between the Tannaitic schools of Rabbi Akiva
and Rabbi Ishmael regarding the obligation to destroy idolatry, as reflected
in the parallel homilies of *Sifre* and *Mekhilta Deuteronomy* to Deuteronomy
12:1–3. The *Mekhilta* to these verses has been preserved in Genizah fragments,
and they reflect a conception substantially different from that of the *Sifre*. In
the second half of the chapter, I will analyze the Mishnah's view on the matter as laid out in Mishnah *Avodah Zarah*, chapters 3–4. I will claim that the
Mishnah does not disregard the imperative to destroy idolatry, but rather conducts a subtle polemic against it, using sophisticated hermeneutic techniques
to limit it. The Mishnah is debating the Ishmaelian approach explicated in the
first half of the chapter.

The second part of the chapter focuses especially on the verses cited in
Mishnah *Avodah Zarah*, which have not been until now part of the scholarly
discourse about the tractate. I would claim that the homilies in the tractate are
segments of this polemic and—among other techniques—do so by reinterpreting the term *herem*, which is used in its biblical source to denote the imperative
to totally destroy objects. I will therefore argue that Mishnah *Avodah Zarah* is
an attempt to offer a systematic alternative to the Deuteronomic commandment
to destroy idols which was accepted in the school of R. Ishmael at face value.

The Homilies in Mishnah *Avodah Zarah* 3:3–4

Mishnah *Avodah Zarah* (3:4) tells a famous story about Rabban Gamaliel and
Proklos, son of Phlaslos, at Aphrodite's bath. Scholars produced much literature about this story,[9] but most of it focused solely on R. Gamaliel's answer and
overlooked the important innovation that appears already in Proklos's question: "Proklos b. Phlaslos asked R. Gamaliel, as he was bathing at the bathhouse of Aphrodite. He said: your Torah says *and none of the herem shall cling
to your hand*; why therefore are you bathing in the bath of Aphrodite?" Proklos
quotes Deuteronomy 13:18, which discusses *'Ir Hanidahat*, a city in which the

majority of the populace worshipped foreign idols. The citation of this verse in Proklos's question looks simple, but in fact is based on a hidden homily: The words "and none of the *herem* shall cling to your hand" are interpreted as an obligation to distance oneself from the statue (and thus the surrounding bathhouse). Such an interpretation may seem quite innocent, but it is not the only possible legal reading of the verse. An alternative reading is indeed attested already in the previous Mishnah unit (3:3), which reads:

> If one finds utensils with the shape of the sun, or the shape of the moon, or the shape of the dragon, he should take them to the Dead Sea. R. Simon b. Gamaliel says: [if they are found] on the dignified [utensils]—[then] they are forbidden, [but] on the common [utensils]—they are permitted.[10] R. Jose says: he should file them down and scatter [the dust] to the wind or throw [the whole utensil] into the sea. They told him: it, too, becomes fertilizer, [and is forbidden], as it says *and none of the herem shall cling to your hands.*

R. Jose offers two techniques for handling utensils with forbidden shapes on them: filing them down or throwing them into the sea (the entire vessel, for dust is not "thrown," מטיל). The Sages (worried from the possible usage of the forbidden dust, שחקים), disagree with the first method, approving only the alternative: throwing the whole vessel into the sea. The entire Mishnah offers various methods of destruction, which should be discussed in detail,[11] but I would like to focus on the common fact that all are actions that are focused on the vessel itself (and the forbidden shape that it holds).

Toward the end of the Mishnah, the Sages buttress their objection to filing down the shape and throwing the dust into the wind with the same verse from Deuteronomy 13:18, which Proklos cites in the very next Mishnah unit: "and none of the *herem* shall cling to your hand." The full meaning of this prooftext is uncovered in a *baraita*, found in the Tosefta and both Talmuds,[12] in which R. Jose presents a list of biblical precedents to support his opinion that there is no need for the total destruction of the vessel and that filing the forbidden shape is enough, but they are all refuted by the Sages. This *baraita* clarifies that the Mishnah should be viewed against the backdrop of the biblical commandment to destroy idolatry and that the dispute is about the possible manners of implementing this commandment.

Thus, two successive *mishnayot* present two very different readings of the same biblical verse: In one, *herem* should be destroyed; in the other, it should just be kept at a distance. In both cases, *herem* is a prohibition, but according to Proklos, the prohibition means keeping away from the statue and not acting upon it, as in the previous Mishnah unit. This is why Proklos asks "Why are you bathing in the bath?" and not "Why are you not destroying the bath or the idol?" In fact, this alternative reading of the biblical verse seems to be the very reason that the story about Aphrodite's bath is juxtaposed to the dispute in Mishnah 3:3.

This difference becomes even clearer when Proklos's question is compared to the question of the elders in Rome, at the end of the "Laws of Idols," in Mishnah 4:7. The elders there ask: "If [God] does not will an idol to exist, why does he not cancel it [מבטלה]?" The meaning of "cancel" here is undoubtedly "destroy," as becomes clear in the Sage's response: "He should destroy his world for the mindless?" (יאבד עולמו מפני השוטין?).[13] Proklos, on the other hand, does not discuss the statue at all and instead focuses on the alleged prohibition to use the bath. R. Gamaliel and Proklos may be at odds over whether the bath is permitted or not, as scholars emphasized, but they both agree that *herem* is not to be destroyed, but simply kept at a distance. In light of the dispute in the previous Mishnah unit, and the dialogue with the elders in Rome in Mishnah 4:7, such interpretation is far from being trivial.[14]

The Mishnaic rereading of the biblical imperative to destroy idols as nothing more than a prohibition to enjoy it—as seen in the narrative of Aphrodite's bath—is not limited to the case of *herem* but appears in various other contexts. Thus, in the next Mishnah unit (3:5), R. Jose the Galilean infers from Deuteronomy 12:2—"their gods on the mountains"—that "the mountains are not their gods." The Mishnah uses this homily to teach that "gentiles who worship the mountains . . . they are permitted and [only] what is on them is forbidden." The Mishnah then asks about the case of *asherah*, a sacred tree, which is forbidden, although the same verse, which says "on the mountains," also says "under the tree," and thus one could infer that the tree itself, just like the mountain itself, is not forbidden. The Mishnah clarifies the difference: "For [in the case of *asherah*] human hands intervened [יש בו תפיסת יד אדם], and any human intervention creates a prohibition." A similar discussion is found in *Sifre Deuteronomy* 60, with a slight change (using "blemish," פסול, instead of "prohibition," אסור). In *Mekhilta Deuteronomy*, however, the homily appears in a profoundly different manner:

> *You shall surely destroy*—this should be understood as including the mountains and the hills and the oceans and the rivers and the deserts, but scripture says "*and you shall break* etc." the altars and high places and groves of v. 3—these were singled out to teach that just as these are unique, since they are a product of human intervention, and they must be destroyed, anything that is a product of idolatrous intervention *must be destroyed*.

Mishnah, *Sifre*, and *Mekhilta* all single out "human intervention" as being the source of the problem, therefore distinguishing man-made idols from natural objects. But the *Mekhilta* is different on two counts. The first is the exegetical basis of the homily: Mishnah and *Sifre* adduce the law from the word "on," an inference that characterizes R. Akiva's school, while the *Mekhilta* uses a *middah* typical of the school of R. Ishmael. It is the second difference, however, that is mostly significant in our context: While Mishnah and *Sifre* use the homily to decide the *prohibition* of various idolatrous objects, the *Mekhilta* uses it to apply the *obligation to destroy* them. The biblical statement, "You shall surely destroy" (אבד תאבדון), is read as "prohibition" or "blemish" in the Mishnah and *Sifre*, while the *Mekhilta* maintains the simple reading: "destroy and annihilate" (כלה ואבד).

Both the *herem* from Deuteronomy 13 and the obligation of destruction from Deuteronomy 12 are thus reread by the Mishnah as mere prohibitions. This reading is far from being self-evident, and we have indeed seen competing readings in other sources. *Herem* was read in another way in the Mishnah itself (in fact, in the preceding Mishnah unit), while אבד תאבדון was interpreted differently in the parallel *Mekhilta*. This second case deserves further attention. Chapter 12 in the book of Deuteronomy presents one of the most severe and comprehensive descriptions of the obligation to destroy idols in the Bible:

> You shall surely destroy all the places where the peoples worshipped, those peoples which you are displacing, their gods, on the high mountains, and the hills, and under every green tree. And you shall splinter their altars and break their monoliths, and burn their *asherim*, and uproot the statues of their gods, and you shall remove their names from that place. (Deut 12:2–3)

These verses are expounded in *Sifre* 60–61, but this source adds very little to our discussion since most of the homilies there parallel our Mishnah and are probably dependent on it. However, we have another Midrash on these verses, a Genizah fragment of the Ishmaelian *Mekhilta* to Deuteronomy,[15] and the homilies there are much more elaborate and radical. A comparison of these homilies shows that the difference we have discussed above between the prohibition espoused by the Mishnah and *Sifre* and the obligation to destroy appearing in the *Mekhilta* is not an isolated case but rather part of a systematic dispute between the corpora. Let us skim through some examples.

SIFRE VERSUS MEKHILTA

a. Deuteronomy 12:3 reads: "And you shall splinter their altars." The *Mekhilta* expounds:

> I understand [or hear: שומע אני] [from this] that he should splinter them and leave them, therefore the verse adds [תלמוד לומר], *break their monoliths*. I understand [from this] that he should break them and leave them, the verse adds *and their asherot burn with fire*. I understand [from this] that he should burn and leave them, the verse adds *uproot the statues of their gods*. I understand [from this] that he should uproot and leave them, the verse adds *destroy their name from that place*, a destruction of annihilation [אבידת כלאה]. Annihilate and obliterate and burn and destroy and remove from the world.

This homily reads the multiple verbs in the verse, demanding that various forms of idols be destroyed, as a sequence of instructions directed at the same object. As a result, all forms of destruction in the verse are applicable to all forms of idols. *Sifre* has no such homily, and instead forms the mirror image of the *Mekhilta*: "You have splintered the altar? Leave it. You have broken the monolith? Leave it." The *Sifre* here is definitely closer to the plain meaning of Scripture, which uses different verbs for each object: break the monoliths, splinter the altars, burn the *asherot*, and so on. In fact, the *Sifre*'s reading is exactly the one that the *Mekhilta*'s homily rejects in its *Talmud Lomar* inferences. Moreover, the language used by the *Sifre*'s homily, "leave it" (הנח לו/לה), is atypical and looks like a direct polemic against the more active reading of the *Mekhilta*, commanding one to "annihilate and obliterate and burn and destroy and remove from the world." Thus the two tendencies are pitted against each other in both midrashim.

b. *Mekhilta of R. Ishmael, Pasha* expounds the verse "and I will perform wonders on all of the gods of Egypt," thus: "They will rot, they will become disjointed, they will be uprooted, they will burn." This annihilation is here ascribed to God himself, but it seems as but a reflection of the laws of destruction of idolatry according to the school of R. Ishmael, laws demanding that various forms of destruction be applied to the same object.

Furthermore, *Mekhilta Deuteronomy* continues and cites a Mishnaic source that is not included in our Mishnah, and thus may be an Ishmaelian Mishnah: "From here they said: whatever can be burned—burn. And what cannot be burned, file down and throw into the wind or throw into the sea or rub against the ground until it disappears." According to this source, "file down and throw into the wind or throw into the sea" is not a special *halakhah* for vessels, as is Mishnah *Avodah Zarah* 3:3 cited above, but is an imperative for all idols.[16]

c. *Sifre* 60 expounds Deuteronomy 12:3 thus: "A tree originally planted for idolatry is forbidden, as it says *and their* asherim *you shall burn in fire*." Here, as above, the imperative of destruction (burning) is supplanted in the homily with a prohibition. The source for this prohibition is Mishnah *Avodah Zarah* 3:7, to which the *Sifre* only adds prooftexts. In *Mekhilta Deuteronomy* cited above, however, the verse is read as an obligation to completely destroy the idol: "*Break their monoliths*. I understand that he should break them and leave them, the verse says *and their* asherot *burn with fire*." As we have already seen, this homily reads the obligation to burn as applying to all forms of idolatry, not only *asherah*. In order to understand this radical interpretive move, we should notice that Deuteronomy 12, demanding burning for an *asherah*, contradicts other verses, which demand that they be chopped down (Exod 34:13; Deut 7:5). *Sifre Deuteronomy* indeed mandates chopping for the *asherah* in one place: "R. Eliezer says, how do we know that the chopper of the *asherah* should uproot it as well? The verse says: destroy their name." The *Mekhilta* also uses the verses demanding the chopping of the *asherah* as proof that the tree itself must be destroyed, and not just what is under it: "*And under every green tree*—but not every green tree [itself]? [Therefore] the verse adds: *and their* asherim *you shall chop down*, adding also these [מכל מקום]." Both midrashim read the verses requiring that the *asherot* be chopped down at face value, while reinterpreting the contradictory verse in Deuteronomy 12. However, while the *Sifre* rereads it as referring to *prohibition*; *Mekhilta* reads it plainly as an imperative to burn, but applies it to idols in general rather than to *asherah* specifically. This difference reflects, once again, the more stringent demands of destruction of idolatry in the *Mekhilta*.

d. The *Mekhilta* expounds the words *you shall surely destroy* (אבד תאבדון) thus: "And why, if he destroyed them once, should he destroy them many times? The verse says 'surely destroy', in the words of R. Akiva. And why even if he destroyed them in one place, they should be destroyed in all places? The verse says 'surely destroy'. R. Ishmael says 'all of the days that you live on the earth, you shall surely destroy'." The two Sages are not disputing a point of law here, but only of prooftext. Both Sages agree that idols should be destroyed "as many times as it takes," but R. Akiva expounds the double verb here, as is his habit, while R. Ishmael adduces the law from the joining of the end of the previous verse ("all of the days") with the current one. Thus in the *Mekhilta*, "all Sages agree" that idols must be destroyed. However, in the *Sifre*, the words are adduced very differently: "From where do you say that if he pruned an *asherah* and it grew out, even ten times, that he must prune it? The verse says: *you shall surely destroy*." Although this homily, too, adduces the need to act several times to eradicate idolatry, and corresponds to R. Akiva's homily in the *Mekhilta* in both its technique (reading a double verb to signify double action) and style ("even ten times," "many times"), the substance of the homilies is quite different. The *Sifre* does not discuss an obligation to eradicate idols in general, but only to prune the new shoots that grew since the tree was consecrated as an *asherah*, with accordance to the ruling of Mishnah 3:7 ("he should remove what grew anew," נוטל מה שהחליף). Since the view of R. Akiva in the *Mekhilta* has a parallel in neither the Mishnah nor the *Sifre*, and the latter even presents a different homily for the verse, it is not improbable that the *Mekhilta* reshaped R. Akiva's homily, and in fact the entire dispute, to reflect its view that idols must be completely destroyed. Indeed, it is not uncommon in Tannaitic midrash that the words of Sages of the opposing school are framed in the terminology and methods characteristic of the school in which the midrash is formed.[17]

e. At the beginning of the *Mekhilta* we find this homily: "*You shall surely destroy*: The verse is applicable [only] after conquest and settlement." Later, the *Mekhilta* elaborates:

All the places where they worshipped etc. I understand [from this that] even out of the Land, the verse says: *those that you conquer*—Peoples [סיוג] whom you conquer, you may destroy their idols." A similar homily appears in *Sifre*

61: "Is it possible that you are commanded to pursue them outside the land? The verse says *and you shall destroy their name from that place*—In the Land of Israel you are commanded to pursue them, and you are not commanded to pursue them outside of the Land.

Both homilies are based on the tension between the beginning of the verse, which requires that "all places of worship" be destroyed, and its end, which restricts the commandment to those peoples whom "you are conquering." But while *Sifre* is categorical in its restriction of pursuit to the land of Israel, *Mekhilta* presents it as a matter of political expediency, and so the restriction is to the *peoples* who are to be conquered, not to the land per se. Such a view, keeping the demand to destruct idolatry in accordance with political situation, appears one more time in the *Mekhilta*, in a statement cited in the name of R. Yohanan b. Zakai:

> Do not rush to break the *bemai* of the gentiles, lest you build it with your own hands, lest you break one of brick and they tell you to make it of stone, of stone and they tell you to make it of wood. And scripture also says: *and with this the iniquity of Jacob shall be atoned for* (Isa 27:9).

While the *Sifre* follows here the Deuteronomistic ideology that limits the need to destroy idolatry to the Holy Land, the *Mekhilta* knows only of political restrictions but does not know of limitations in principle to the destruction imperative. Note also that the *Sifre* speaks generally about "pursuing" (לרדוף) while the *Mekhilta* specifically about "destroying" (לאבד).

A far-reaching dispute between the schools, on whether certain *mitzvot* became binding upon Israel immediately when they entered the land or only after "conquest and settlement," is recorded in several homilies. The midrashic techniques that elicited these different responses have been studied in depth, but their practical meaning remains a riddle. Thus, Menahem Kahana, in his dissertation, wonders "why the Sages saw a need to debate the 'historical' question when exactly each mitzvah became binding upon Israel" and hesitantly suggests that "relevant questions of the time" may have a role in the discussion. Our matter is exactly such a "relevant question." The same "conquest" (ירושה) that seemingly appears in one homily as a solely "historical" academic issue ("The verse is applicable [only] after conquest and settlement," ירושה וישיבה) appears later as a directive: "Those peoples whom you conquer [יורשים אותם], you may destroy their gods."

This dispute uncovered above regarding Deuteronomy 12:2–3 may explain other homilies as well. One example is the discussion of the sin offering in Numbers 15, read by the school of R. Ishmael as directed specifically for one sin—idolatry.[18] Another one is the difference between the two *Mekhiltas* on Exodus 20, regarding the prohibition on the creation of images and sculptures. *Mekhilta de-Rabbi Ishmael* Bahodesh 6 (p. 225) explains the great length in which the verse details all the various images that one should avoid creating ("of what is in the heavens above and on the earth below and in the water under the earth"), noting that "scripture pursued the evil *yetzer* so far, so as not to give it room to find a pretext of permission." E. E. Urbach suggested that this homily may be conducting a polemic with other, more lenient, views regarding the prohibition to make images.[19] I would suggest that it is directed against the school of R. Akiva, whose lenient views may indeed be seen as a "pretext of permission."

The position of the school of R. Ishmael, which demands total destruction of idolatry, is not only closer to a simple reading of Scripture, but also to traditional attitudes reflected in Second Temple literature. Various episodes related by Josephus and others[20] show that this was not only a theoretical position, and that idolatry was indeed destroyed when possible.[21] The Akivan homilies are thus a deviation from both practical and interpretive earlier traditions. It is thus necessary to dig deeper for a new, revolutionary, position. In order to do so, we must turn back to the laws of images in Mishnah *Avodah Zarah*, chapters 3 and 4.

The Mishnah of "All Images"

In his work on Mishnah *Avodah Zarah*, Moshe Halbertal claimed that the basic innovativeness of the Mishnah lays in its complete disregard for the obligation to destroy idols, an obligation that is most basic in the Bible.[22] Our analysis above, however, reveals a somewhat different picture. The Mishnah does not "disregard" the imperative of destruction; rather, it contains a latent polemic against this imperative. This polemic was recovered in the narrative on Aphrodite's bath and can be further exemplified from the homilies appearing in the next Mishnah units (3:4–5). The word אלהיהן, "their gods," is expounded in a pair of *mishnayot* in chapter 3. Mishnah *Avodah Zarah* 3:4 expounds Deuteronomy 7:25 ("the statues of their gods you shall burn in fire")[23] and comments: "Those which are treated[24] like gods are forbidden, but those which are not treated like gods are permitted." Mishnah 3:5 expounds Deuteronomy 12:2 and reads: "Gentiles who worship mountains and hills, they are permitted, and what is on them is forbidden ... *their gods on the mountains*, but the mountains are not their gods." The first homily, though not necessarily attributable to R. Gamaliel, is another Mishnaic answer to Proklos, limiting the prohibition on derivation of benefit from statues only to dignified ones (excluding those standing in the bathhouse). The second homily is attributed to R. Jose, and distinguishes between objects *on* the mountains, which are forbidden, and the mountains themselves, which are not. The two homilies share a hermeneutic move, which though barely noticeable is in fact crucial. Both read the verses, which, in context, command to destroy idols, as referring merely to prohibition of taking advantage from them. Note especially the transformation in the first case between the language of the verse—"the statues of their gods you shall burn in fire"—and the language of the homily: "Those which are treated like gods are *forbidden*." Since we have already seen that both verses are read according to their plain meaning in *Mekhilta* Deuteronomy from the school of R. Ishmael, we can view them as a Mishnaic polemic against this view, similar to the polemic found in the *Sifre*.

In the case of the *herem* verses, the picture in more complicated, for the debate appears in the Mishnah itself. While Proklos read *herem* as a mere prohibition, the preceding Mishnah read it as plain destruction. The two *mishnayot* may not be in agreement, as indeed suggested by G. Blidstein in his dissertation.[25] But the context of the two *mishnayot* are markedly different: Mishnah 3 discusses only utensils that are in a person's hand (thus the Mishnah emphasizes that the issue raises only "if one finds utensils," המוצא כלים, but not with those that are on the market). Mishnah 4, on the other hand, is about statues in public areas (such as the public bath); it is only in this last context that destruction is supplanted by prohibition. The combination of these two *mishnayot* thus indicates that destruction is limited to items that one owns, while in the public sphere it is substituted by an obligation to distance oneself from the prohibited item. This is apparent also in the different attitude of the Mishnah to the distinction made in these two Mishnah units. Both R. Gamaliel in 3:4 and his son Simon in 3:3 distinguish between cultic and non-cultic contexts,[26] but the Mishnah chooses to end its argument with R. Gamaliel's opinion (thus accepting it), while refuting that of R. Simon, his son. The distinction is thus accepted in the public sphere while being rejected in the private one.

Such hierarchy between the public and the private, between what is under one's control and what is not, also accounts for the structure of chapters 3–4 in the Mishnah. Chapter 3 begins with the prohibition of statues, both whole (3:1) and broken (3:2), as well as the images on vessels (3:3). The discussion then moves to the prohibition of mountains (3:5), houses (3:6–7), *asherot* (3:7–10), and stones (4:1–2), and lastly, grove and bathhouse (4:3). The motion is thus from defined and delimited idols and idolatrous utensils to their surrounding zones: mountains, buildings, trees. This order is further evidence of the Mishnaic attempt to distinguish between different spheres, limiting the biblical *herem* command only to the most personal sphere of המוצא כלים. It is thus not surprising that these chapters end with the laws of cancellation of idolatry (ביטול, 4:5–7), which are a functional alternative to the biblical imperative of destruction.[27]

This reading shows that while scholarship focused on R. Gamaliel's far-reaching distinction between forbidden and permitted arenas, the more significant move is essentially present already in Proklos's question, which disregards the obligation to destroy the *herem* and discusses the prohibition inherent in it alone. Proklos's stance, moreover, is typical of the Mishnaic rulings in these two chapters in general. Its attribution to Proklos, a foreigner, in a debate with R. Gamaliel, should thus be read as a determination of the limits of the discourse. The whole debate is limited to questions of prohibition—which statues one should distance oneself from and which not—not the imperative to destroy idols.[28]

Homilies that read the *herem* verses in Deuteronomy 7 as a mere obligation to keep idols at a distance appear in the Mishnah in several other places.[29] Thus Mishnah 1:8 introduces Deuteronomy 7:25 as a prooftext that idols may not be placed in homes rented to Gentiles ("and you shall not bring an abomination into your home"). Mishnah 3:6 reads Deuteronomy 7:27 as support for the ruling that idols render impurity ("you shall wholly abhor it," שקץ תשקצנו). Deuteronomy 7:25 is cited in Mishnah 3:5 as a proof for the rule that hills and mountains are not made forbidden by worship. The innovativeness of these homilies is revealed when they are compared to the homily on *herem* in 3:3, which reads it in its simple meaning as "destruction." Furthermore, in light of the homilies from *Mekhilta Deuteronomy* discussed above, we can identify the target of the Mishnah's polemic—the school of R. Ishmael.

Various scholars read R. Gamaliel's position as an expression of a second-century leniency, and contrasted it with more stringent, earlier opinions.[30] Our discussion demands a double correction of this image: (1) The leniency of Raban Gamliel is but one component of a much larger move in these chapters in Mishnah *Avodah Zarah;* and (2) the adversaries of this move are not only older traditions but the contemporaneous school of R. Ishmael. The basic move of the Mishnah—rereading the commandment to destroy idols as mere prohibition—limited the biblical *herem* to items held in a person's hand alone. The basic Mishnaic innovation thus lays not in Raban Gamliel's answer to Proklos, but in the whole framework of the debate between them: One requires absolute abstinence from idolatrous surroundings, while another allows leniency in certain contexts; none, however, requires that idols be banished from the land or the earth.

Some wished to reduce the Mishnah's stance to economics or politics,[31] but the comparison with R. Ishmael's school makes such reductionist explanations unlikely. Considerations of *realpolitik* appear in that school also, for only peoples "whom you conquer" may be subjected to destruction of idols. The school of R. Akiva goes much further. The dispute is not about their own time, when the "hand of Israel is not strong," but about the most basic aspiration, and the perception of space lying behind it. Mishnah *Avodah Zarah* and *Sifre* Deuteronomy, unlike the *Mekhilta*, contain no vision for a future time in which idols shall be destroyed again. This concession requires a different understanding of the reality surrounding the Sages. Those who are interested in destruction, delaying them only for practical reasons, are different from those who gave up this option completely. Only the second attitude encourages the formation of alternative strategies to cope with a public arena full of a pagan presence,[32] strategies that occupy these chapters in Mishnah *Avodah Zarah.*

Notes

1. An earlier version of this paper was published in Hebrew in *Reshit: Studies in Judaism* 1 (2009): 91–115. This version is focused more on the ideological side of the matter. On textual and philological matters, references will be made to the Hebrew version.

2. See S. Schwartz, "Gamliel in Aphrodite's Bath," in *The Talmud Yerushalmi and Graeco-Roman Culture*, ed. P. Schaefer (Tübingen: Mohr Siebeck, 1998), 203–217. This concept was woven into a larger framework in his *Imperialism and Jewish Society 200 BCE to 640 CE* (Princeton, N.J.: Princeton University Press, 2001), 165–174.

3. See Efraim E. Urbach, "The Laws of Idolatry and the Archaeological and Historical Reality of the Second and Third Centuries," in *From the World of the Sages* (Jerusalem: Magnes, 1987), 125–178.

4. M. Halbertal, "Coexisting with the Enemy: Jews and Pagans in the Mishnah," in *Tolerance and Intolerance in Early Judaism and Christianity*, ed. G. Stanton and G. Strounsa (Cambridge: Cambridge University Press, 1988), 158–172. Halbertal claims that the Mishnah constructs a neutral space that is not determined by any particular identity, in which persons of different cultures and religions can live together: "The concept of neutrality, so essential to the enlightenment concept of tolerance, was present, in my opinion, already in the Mishnah" (p. 163). The story of Rabban Gamaliel in the bathhouse exemplifies this idea for Halbertal in the clearest manner (p. 166).

5. N. Zohar, "Idolatry and Its Nullification," *Sidra* 17 (2001–2002): 63–77. For an analysis and critique of this approach, see Y. Furstenberg, "Nullification of Idolatry: The Sages in Dialogue with Idolatry under the Roman Empire," *Reshit* 1 (2009): 117–144.

6. See S. A. Lowenstamm, "Herem" [in Hebrew], *Biblical Encyclopedia* (Jerusalem: Mossad Bialik, 1964), 3:290–292.

7. While chapter 13 does not mention idols explicitly, the rabbis read verse 18, "and none of the Herem shall cling to your hand," as referring to idols, apparently through a comparison with the verses in Deut 7.

8. Cf. the same command but without the term *herem* in Exod 24:12–16.

9. See G. (Y.) Blidstein, "Studies in Tractate Avoda Zara Chapter 1 and the Approach of the Sages to the Creation of Images" [in Hebrew], PhD diss., Yeshiva University, 1968, 280–284; I. Friedheim, "The Story of Rabban Gamaliel in the Bathhouse of Aphrodite in Acco: A Study in Palestinian Realia" [in Hebrew], *Kathedra* 105 (2003): 7–32; A. Wasserstein, "Rabban Gamaliel and Proclus of Naucratis" [in Hebrew], *Zion* 45 (1980): 257–267; M. Jacobs, "Romische Thermenkultur in Spiegel des Talmud Yerushalmi," in *The Talmud Yerushalmi and Graeco-Roman Culture*, ed. P. Schaefer (Tübingen: Mohr Siebeck, 1998), 219–311; Schwartz, "Gamliel," 203–217; A. Yadin, "Rabban Gamaliel, Aphrodite's Bath, and the Question of Pagan Monotheism," *JQR* 96 (2006): 149–179. I am not interested here in the story itself, its plausibility or the realia it reflects, but just its place in the Mishnah.

10. That is, objects used for adornment versus functional articles, especially those used for drinking, as explicated in the Tosefta ad loc.

11. What, for example, is the difference between R. Jose's "the sea," and the Sages' "the Dead Sea"?

12. *T. Avod. Zar.* 4:4; *y. Avod. Zar.* 3:3, 42c; *b. Avod. Zar.* 42a. Although the baraita in the Tosefta appears in the context of one who "conducts commerce at a fair [יריד] of gentiles," it is obviously connected to our Mishnah, rather than to the laws concerning produces sold at a fair, regarding which R. Jose is more stringent.

13. See Zohar, "Idolatry," 70.

14. In contrast to a scholarly tendency to see "the rabbis" in general, without distinguishing between schools or approaches, as supplanting destruction with prohibition. See, e.g., Schwartz, "Gamaliel," 212; I. Stern, "Images in Halakha in Talmudic Times" [in Hebrew] *Zion* 61 (1996): 403–413, 404; M. Haran, *The Biblical Collection* [in Hebrew] (Jerusalem: Magness 1996), 1:279–280; Z. Grossmark, "The Laws of Idolatry Regarding Jewelry as a Mirror of Jewish-Gentile Relations in Palestine in Talmudic Times" [in Hebrew], in *Jews and Gentiles in Palestine in the Times of the Second Temple, the Mishnah and the Talmud*, ed. A. Oppenheimer et al. (Jerusalem: Zalman Shazar Center 2003), 2.

15. The fragment was published first by Solomon Schechter, printed in David Zvi Hoffmann's *Midrash Tannaim* (Berlin: 1898), 58–62, and then reread and republished by M. Y. Kahana, *Geniza Fragments of the Halakhic Midrashim* [in Hebrew] (Jerusalem: Magnes 2005), 347–348. The latter was the source consulted and cited in this paper. Note that these fragments are the only explicit source that can be used to compare the approaches of both schools to the prohibition of idolatry. There are no fragments of the Akivan *Mekhilta de RASHBI* to Exod 20:4–5 (the homilies in ed. Epstein-Melammed, [Jerusalem: Mekitze Nirdamim, 1955], 147–148, are reconstructed from the thirteenth-century Yemenite *Midrash Hagadol*). There is no *Mekhilta of Rabbi Ishmael* to Exod 34:13–14 (and probably no *Mekhilta* of Rabbi Shimon either; see M. Kahana, "The Halakhic Midrashim," in *The Literature of the Sages, Part 2* (*CRINT IV*), ed. S. Safrai et al. [Assen: Van Gorcum 2006], 3–105, 75). There is no *Sifre* on Deut 4:16–16 or 7:5, and there probably was no *Mekhilta* either; Hoffmann reconstructs none and see Kahana, "Halakhic Midrashim," 100.

16. The homily does not quite match the law introduced by *mikan amru*: the law required that the object be destroyed "properly," whereas the homily requires that many destructive actions be performed on the same object consecutively. As is common in Rabbi Ishmael's midrashim, there are several discrepancies in this segment between homilies and *mikan amru* that follow them. See Rosen Zvi, "Surely Destroy," 97–98, n. 30.

17. See Kahana, "Halakhic Midrashim," 35–36.

18. *Sifre Numbers* 112 (ed. Horowitz, p. 121) and *b. Hor.* 8. On the Ishmaelian view that "I am the Lord" and "Thou shall have no other gods" are one commandment regarding idolatry, see B. Schwartz, "We Heard 'I Am' and 'Thou Shall Have No' from the Almighty," in *The Bible in the Mirror of Its Exegetes: The Sarah Kamin Memorial Volume*, ed. S. Yefet (Jerusalem: Magnes, 1994), 170–197. Cf. A. Shemesh, *Punishment and Sin: From the Bible to Rabbinic Literature* (Jerusalem: Magnes, 2003), 94, and in Rosen-Zvi, "Surely Destroy," 100.

19. See Urbach, "Laws," 154.

20. See Josephus' description of the Jews' protest at Herod's introduction of Roman trophies to the theater in Jerusalem (*Ant.* 15.275–279), as well as their willingness to die rather than let Roman soldiers enter with Caesar's effigies to Jerusalem (*Ant.* 18.55–59; *B.J.* 169–174). Cf. a similar story in Philo, *Legat.* 299–305. (For the relationship between these two stories,

see D. Schwartz, "Josephus and Philo on Pontius Pilate," in *Flavius Josephus: A Historian of Palestine*, ed. U. Rappoport [Jerusalem: Zalman Shazar Center 1983], 217–236). Cf. also the martyrdom of Judah of Zippori and Matthias b. Margalit, who broke the golden eagle Herod placed over the temple gates, a narrative that Josephus relates quite sympathetically (*Ant.* 17.149–167, *B.J.* 1.648–655). See also Josephus' *Vita* 65, in which he relates his own mission to destroy the palace of Herod Antipas, which was decorated with images of animals.

21. This was the situation in both the Maccabean Wars (1 Macc 5:68), and in the Kitos War, which was contemporary with the Sages of Yavneh. See G. Alon, *A History of the Jews in the Land of Israel in the Talmudic Period* [in Hebrew] (Tel Aviv: Hakibbutz Hameuhad 1959), 1:139–240; V. (A.) Tcherikover, *The Jews in Egypt in the Hellenistic Period in Light of Papyrology* (Jerusalem: Magnes, 1963), 177; S. Appelbaum, *Jews and Greeks in Ancient Cyrene* (Jerusalem: Mossad Bialik 1969), 235–237.

22. Halbertal, "Coexisting," 163.

23. The Mishnah only quotes "their gods," but the parallel in *t.* 6:6 quotes "the statues of their gods [the Printed edition alone adds *you shall burn in fire*]—those which are treated like gods are forbidden." This quote suits both Deut 7:25 ("you shall burn in fire") and 12:3 ("you shall uproot"). However, the verse indicated seems to be the former rather than the latter, since the context of the homily is the *herem*, which only appears there.

24. The Mishnah (but not the parallel Tosefta) may be referring here in fact to the statue itself, which "acts" (נוהג) like a god.

25. Blidstein, "Studies," 15, 25–27.

26. Most scholars attribute this story—though without definite proof—to Rabban Gamaliel of Yavneh (see the references cited in Wasserstein, "Rabban Gamaliel," 260–261, n. 9, cf. M. Hirshman, *Torah for the Entire World* [in Hebrew] [Tel Aviv: Hakibbutz Hameuhad, 1999], 158: "most literary evidence of dialogs between Sages and gentiles in Tannaitic compilations were connected to the house of the patriarch and the character of Rabban Gamaliel of Yavneh in particular." Wasserstein, "Rabban Gamaliel," suggests that the character in question is R. Gamaliel the son of R. Judah the Patriarch, but his claim that it is not plausible that Rabban Gamaliel of Yavneh would sit in a bathhouse in Akko and converse with a Gentile only one generation after the destruction is far from convincing.

27. On these laws, see Zohar, "Idolatry."

28. Undoubtedly, the purpose of having a Gentile represent the more stringent approach is to indicate that the more lenient approach is to be adopted. However, as we have seen, Proklos's approach is also supported by other places in the Mishnah. Presenting the question as the subject of a debate between a Sage and a Gentile achieves thus a double effect: on the one hand, the more stringent approach presented by the Gentile is rejected, and on the other hand, the framework of the debate is presented as agreed upon by everyone—including Gentiles. (See the suggestion of Azzan Yadin, "Rabban Gamaliel," 166–167, that Proklos here is not a pagan who wishes to taunt the Sages, as in the story of the Sages in Rome, *m. Avod. Zar.* 4:7, but a philosopher who believes that the gods should not be represented by images.)

29. The printed editions of the Mishnah cite only the beginnings of the verses, for brevity's sake, but the MSS quote the verses in full, including the word *herem*.

30. See the summary in L. Feldman, *Josephus and Modern Scholarship (1937–1980)* (Berlin: De Gruyter, 1984), 512–515.

31. See the literature in nn. 2–3 above.

32. On such strategies, see I. Rosen-Zvi, "Blessings as Mapping: Structure and Content in Mishnahh *Berakhot* Chapter 9" [in Hebrew], *Hebrew Union College Annual* 79 (2009): 1–24.

Bibliography

Alon, G. *A History of the Jews in the Land of Israel in the Talmudic Period* [in Hebrew]. Tel Aviv: Hakibbutz Hameuhad, 1959.

Appelbaum, S. *Jews and Greeks in Ancient Cyrene*. Jerusalem: Mossad Bialik, 1969.

Blidstein, G. (Y.) "Studies in Tractate Avoda Zara Chapter 1 and the Approach of the Sages to the Creation of Images" [in Hebrew]. PhD diss., Yeshiva University, 1968.

Feldman, L. *Josephus and Modern Scholarship (1937–1980)*. Berlin: De Gruyter, 1984.

Friedheim, I. "The Story of Rabban Gamaliel in the Bathhouse of Aphrodite in Acco: A Study in Palestinian Realia" [in Hebrew]. *Kathedra* 105 (2003): 7–32.

Furstenburg, Y. "Nullification of Idolatry: The Sages in Dialogue with Idolatry under the Roman Empire." *Reshit* 1 (2009): 117–144.

Grossmark, Z. "The Laws of Idolatry Regarding Jewelry as a Mirror of Jewish-Gentile Relations in Palestine in Talmudic Times" [in Hebrew]. In *Jews and Gentiles in Palestine in the Times of the Second Temple, the Mishnah and the Talmud*, edited by A. Oppenheimer et al., 1–8. Jerusalem: Zalman Shazar Center, 2003.

Gur-arie, Hagar. "Rabbinic Derashot on the Biblical Laws of Ban and Expulsion of the Canaanites" [Hebrew], .PhD Thesis, University of Haifa 2007.

Halbertal, M. "Coexisting with the Enemy: Jews and Pagans in the Mishnah." In *Tolerance and Intolerance in Early Judaism and Christianity*, edited by G. Stanton and G. Strounsa, 158–172. Cambridge: Cambridge University Press, 1988.

Haran, M. *The Biblical Collection* [in Hebrew]. Jerusalem: Magnes, 1996.

Hirshman, M. *Torah for the Entire World* [in Hebrew]. Tel Aviv: Hakibbutz Hameuchad, 1999.

Jacobs, M. "Romische Thermenkultur in Spiegel des Talmud Yerushalmi." In *The Talmud Yerushalmi and Graeco-Roman Culture*, edited by P. Schaefer, 219–311. Tübingen: Mohr Siebeck, 1998.

Kahana, M. *Geniza Fragments of the Halakhic Midrashim* [in Hebrew]. Jerusalem: Magnes, 2005.

Kahana, M. "The Halakhic Midrashim." In *The Literature of the Sages, Part 2 (CRINT IV)*, edited by S. Safrai et al., 3–105. Assen: Van Gorcum, 2006.

Lowenstamm, S. A. "Herem" [in Hebrew]. *Biblical Encyclopedia*, 3:290–292. Jerusalem, Mossad Bialik 1964.

Rosen-Zvi, I. "Blessings as Mapping: Structure and Content in Mishnah Berakhot Chapter 9" [in Hebrew]. *Hebrew Union College Annual* 79 (2009): 1–24.

Schwartz, B. "We Heard 'I Am' and 'Thou Shall Have No' from the Almighty." In *The Bible in the Mirror of Its Exegetes: The Sarah Kamin Memorial Volume*, edited by S. Yefet, 170–197. Jerusalem: Magnes, 1994.

Schwartz, D. "Josephus and Philo on Pontius Pilate." In *Flavius Josephus: A Historian of Palestine*, edited by U. Rappoport, 217–236. Jerusalem: Zalman Shazar Center, 1983.

Schwartz, S. "Gamliel in Aphrodite's Bath." In *The Talmud Yerushalmi and Graeco-Roman Culture*, edited by P. Schaefer, 203–217. Tübingen: Mohr Siebeck, 1998.

Schwartz, S. *Imperialism and Jewish Society 200 BCE to 640 CE*. Princeton, N.J.: Princeton University Press, 2001.

Shemesh, A. *Punishment and Sin: From the Bible to Rabbinic Literature*. Jerusalem: Magnes, 2003.

Stern, I. "Images in Halakha in Talmudic Times" [in Hebrew]. *Zion* 61 (1996): 403–413.

Tcherikover, V. (A.) *The Jews in Egypt in the Hellenistic Period in Light of Papyrology*. Jerusalem: Magnes, 1963.

Urbach, Efraim E. "The Laws of Idolatry and the Archaeological and Historical Reality of the Second and Third Centuries." In *From the World of the Sages*, 125–178. Jerusalem: Magness Press, 1987.

Wasserstein, A. "Rabban Gamaliel and Proklos of Naucratis" [in Hebrew]. *Zion* 45 (1980): 257–267.

Yadin, A. "Rabban Gamliel, Aphrodite's Bath, and the Question of Pagan Monotheism." *JQR* 96 (2006): 149–179.

Zohar, N. "Idolatry and Its Nullification." *Sidra* 17 (2001-2002): 63–77.

The Fate of the Canaanites and the Despoliation of the Egyptians

POLEMICS AMONG JEWS, PAGANS, CHRISTIANS, AND GNOSTICS: MOTIFS AND MOTIVES

Menahem Kister

This chapter discusses the treatment in Second Temple and rabbinic literature of the complex theme of the conquest of Canaan by the Israelites and the fate of the Canaanites, against the background of the biblical material, on the one hand, and contemporaneous non-Jewish arguments, on the other hand.* In this particular instance, we can see how the later traditions elaborate upon biblical motifs and offer exegesis, theological views, and apologetic attitudes. The despoliation of Egypt, which will be discussed in the second section of the chapter, is a similar apologetic challenge to ancient Judaism, and there are many features of similarity between the handling of the two themes. In both cases, there is a remarkable continuum from ancient sources to compositions of late antiquity and the Middle Ages. The vitality of ancient traditions may be demonstrated in both themes. Both are, according to Jewish sources, responses to pagan indictments, and both became arguments of Gnostics against the God of the Law, which are answered by Christians. They raise important questions concerning pagan anti-Jewish accusations, the relationship between pagan and gnostic attitudes, the relationship between the Jewish and the Christian responses and their different foci, as well as other profound questions related to the history of religious ideas and the contact between particular religious groups, especially Jews and Gnostics. I do not attempt to provide a definitive solution to these problems, but the data brought forth here might offer a new perspective for viewing such complex problems. I will first trace the various motifs reflected in the traditions and will then examine the motives to which these traditions owe their emergence, paying attention to their function in the dialogue or polemic with opponents.

My starting point is the rabbinic tradition found in *Genesis Rabbah* 61:7.[1] This text raises and responds to arguments against the Jewish possession of the land and the despoliation of Egypt by the Israelites:

"And unto the sons of the concubines that Abraham had, Abraham gave gifts" (Gen 25:6).

[A] In the days of Alexander of Macedon the Ishmaelites came to dispute the birthright with Israel and they were accompanied by two evil families, the Canaanites and the Egyptians. "Who shall go to plead against them?" it was asked. Said Gevihah b. Qosem: "I will go and plead against them." "Take heed not to let the land be legally declared their property," they cautioned him.…

[B] Said the Ishmaelites: "We are the claimants, and we base our claims on their own Torah: It is written: 'but he shall acknowledge the firstborn, the son of the hated' (Deut 21:17) and Ishmael was a firstborn." Said Gevihah b. Qosem: "Your majesty, cannot a man do as he wishes with his sons?" "Yes," replied he. "Then," pursued he, "surely it is written 'And Abraham gave all that he had unto Isaac' (Gen 25:5). But where is the legal deed [attesting to it]?" He replied: "'And unto the sons of the concubines that Abraham had, Abraham gave gifts' (Gen 25:6)."[2]

[C] The Canaanites then pleaded: "We base our suit against them on their own Torah. It is everywhere written 'the land of Canaan'—then let them return our country to us." Said he [Gevihah]: "Your majesty! Cannot a man do as he wishes with his slave?" "Yes," replied he. "Then surely it is written 'a slave of slaves shall he [Canaan] be to his brethren' (Gen 9:25), hence they are now our slaves." Thereupon they fled in shame.

[D] Then said the Egyptians: "We base our suit against them on their own Torah. Six-hundred-thousand left us, laden with silver and gold utensils, as it is written 'and they despoiled the Egyptians' (Exod 12:36)—let them return our silver and gold to us." Said Gevihah b. Qosem: "Your majesty! Six-hundred-thousand men served them two-hundred-and-ten years, of whom some were silversmiths and some goldsmiths. Let them pay us [for their labor] at the rate of a dinar per day." Thereupon mathematicians calculated [what was owed for their labor], and they had not reached a hundred years before Egypt was found to be [forfeit for the sum due] to the treasury, and so they departed in shame.[3]

In the context of this chapter, we are mainly interested in sections C and D. The plaintiffs in this imaginary scene are the Canaanites, according to *Genesis Rabbah*. In a parallel tradition (*b. Sanh.* 91a), they are "the Africans" (i.e., the inhabitants of North Africa). This reflects a well-known tradition, which will be discussed at length later, that the inhabitants of the land emigrated from Canaan to North Africa. An analysis of the tradition reveals, however, that originally it was about "Canaanites" rather than "Africans."[4]

The Land of Canaan

The land of Canaan was promised by God to the patriarchs. The fate of the Canaanites, its former inhabitants, was depicted differently in various traditions of the Bible.[5] It is worthwhile to observe at the outset that the ways in which this problem is addressed in the different biblical strata do not seem to be a reaction to a specific political situation or claim; rather, as far as I can judge, these various biblical formulations seem to arise from internal motivations alone. This observation will be of some significance later, when apologetic motives for the solutions of the same problem in the Second Temple period and later will be considered together with the internal motives, some of which are a heritage of biblical thinking. The Canaanites were expelled, or—according to other passages—exterminated (either by God, in a supernatural way, or by the Israelites themselves, with God's help).[6] According to Genesis 15:16, the promise of the land cannot be realized in Abraham's lifetime; Abraham's descendants will inherit the land only "in the fourth generation, for the iniquity of the Amorites is not yet complete." The iniquity of the inhabitants of the land of Canaan is mentioned in several passages (e.g., Lev 20:22–24; Deut 9:4–5) as justifying their being uprooted, and, by extension, also predicting a similar fate for Israelites who commit iniquity in the land.[7] According to some biblical passages, the case of the conquest of the land of Canaan by the Israelites and of the fate of its original inhabitants is similar to other historical cases in which new inhabitants took the place of autochthonous peoples (see, for example, Amos 9:7,[8] and especially Deut 2:10–12, 2:20–22).[9] Noah's curse of Canaan is an etiology for the inferiority of the Canaanites and their enslavement,[10] albeit not for their being driven out of the land: "Cursed be Canaan, a slave of slaves shall he be to his brothers. . . . Blessed be the Lord, God of Shem, and let Canaan be his slave [עבד למו]. God enlarge Japhet['s lot] and let him dwell[11] in the tents of Shem, and let Canaan be his [or their][12] slave [עבד למו]" (Gen 9:25–27).

SOME INTERPRETATIONS TO CANAAN'S CURSE

In the Second Temple period, the curse of Canaan became a justification for the uprooting of the Canaanites.[13] Thus we read in a work found at Qumran:

ויקץ נוח מיינו וידע את אשר עשה לו בנו הקטן ויומר ארור כנען עבד עבדים יהיה לאחיו ולוא קלל את חם
כי אם בנו כי ברך אל את בני נוח ובאהלי שם ישכון, ארץ נתן לאברהם אהבו

And Noah awoke from his wine and knew what his youngest son had done to him. And he said: "Cursed be Canaan! A slave of slaves shall he be to his brothers." But he did not curse Ham, but his [Ham's] son, because God blessed the sons of Noah, and in the tents of Shem may He dwell, [the] Land He gave to Abraham his friend.[14]

Canaan's curse (Gen 9:25) is juxtaposed here with 2 Chronicles 20:7: "You, our God, drove away [הורשת] the inhabitants of this land from before [מלפני] Your people Israel, and gave it forever to the descendants of Abraham Your friend [אהבך]."[15] The land was transferred by God from the cursed Canaan to God's friend, Abraham, a descendant of Shem. Whereas the Chronicler gives no justification for the replacement of the Canaanites, 4Q252 seeks to justify it by Canaan's curse. Philo writes very similarly concerning Canaan's curse in a comment on the verse "Ham was the father of Canaan" (Gen 9:19):

> It may be that [Scripture] foretells…that He [God] will take away the land of the Canaanites after many generations and *give it* to the chosen and god-beloved race.[16]

The similarity between the two passages, one in Hebrew and composed in Palestine and the other in Greek and written by a Hellenistic Jew, is indeed striking. Josephus also considers Noah's curse of Canaan as the reason for the destruction of the Canaanites.[17] It is therefore evident that Genesis 9:25–27 was a significant, even central, passage for explaining Israel's inheritance of the land and the destruction of the Canaanites. In 4Q252 the emphasis is on the words "let him [God] dwell in the tents of Shem" (Gen 9:27).[18] The same verses are used as a nuanced legal argument in the rabbinic tradition with which we are dealing here.[19] This argument might be a refinement of the usages of these verses in sources of the Second Temple period.[20]

CANAAN'S TWO CURSES IN THE BOOK OF JUBILEES

The *Book of Jubilees* deals with the destruction of the Canaanites in a number of passages. Abraham warns Jacob[21] not to marry a Canaanite woman, "for through Ham's sin Canaan erred, and all of his descendants and all of his (people) who remain will be destroyed from the earth" (*Jub.* 22:20–21).[22] The scene in Genesis 9 is once again of central importance for the destruction of Canaan, but the emphasis is on its being uprooted in the Day of Judgment rather than on the Israelite conquest of the land or any historical conquest. In another passage, however, similar phraseology is used for the destruction of the Amorites in trans-Jordanian territories by the Israelites: "they no longer have life on earth" (*Jub.* 29:11). The original inhabitants of these territories, the Refaim, were destroyed by God because of their wickedness, and the Amorites settled in their place (*Jub.* 29:9–11; based on Deut 3:13 and Deut 2:20–21); the Amorites in their turn "no longer have life on earth" because "today [i.e., in Moses' time] there is no nation that has completed all their sins" (*Jub.* 29:11); this seems to be an allusion to Genesis 15:16 ("for the sin of the Amorites is not yet complete").[23]

Unlike these passages, the main passage justifying the Israelites' inheritance of the land and the dispossession of the Canaanites uses an original argument, not drawn from the Bible. A detailed analysis of the passage may be instructive. The *Book of Jubilees* has a long narrative concerning the division of the earth by Noah between his three sons and the division of inheritance between Noah's descendants.[24] The relevant passage reads:

> (9:1) Ham divided [his share] among his sons. There emerged a first share for Cush to the east; to the west of him [one] for Egypt; to the west of him [a share] for Put; to the west of him [a share] for Canaan; and to the west of him was the sea. (10:29) When Canaan saw that the land of the Lebanon as far as the stream of Egypt was very beautiful, he did not go to his hereditary land to the west of the sea.... (10:30) His father Ham and his brothers Cush and Mitzraim said to him ... (10:31) Do not settle in Shem's residence.... (10:32) You *are* cursed and *will be* cursed[25] by all of Noah's children[26] through the curse by which we obligated ourselves with an oath before the holy judge and before our father Noah. (10:33) But he did not listen to them. He settled in the land of Lebanon—from Hamath to the entrance of Egypt—he and his sons until the present. (10:34) For this reason that land was named the Land of Canaan.

The following notes are worthy of consideration:

a. Canaan should have settled in North Africa, where there was a Punic (i.e., Phoenician, Canaanite) population at the time of the composition of the *Book of Jubilees*. If Canaan and his sons settled in Phoenicia and Palestine, how is the Phoenician settlement in North Africa to be explained? The answer must have been that the Canaanites emigrated there (or fled there) when the Israelites conquered the land of Canaan.[27] There was nothing wrong in conquering the land and expelling its inhabitants, this tradition explains, for the emigration of the Canaanites to Africa was simply an act of repatriation.[28] Thus the *Book of Jubilees* contains the most ancient (if implicit) evidence for a new interpretation of the book of Joshua.

b. The wording "for this reason that land was named the land of Canaan" proves that the name of the land in the Bible, "the land of Canaan," posed a problem, because it could imply Canaan's ownership of it; the solution of the *Book of Jubilees* is that the land is called "the land of Canaan" not because it *belonged* to Canaan, but rather because the Canaanites *unlawfully* settled in it. The argument from the name of the land, "the land of Canaan," to which the *Book of Jubilees* responds is precisely the argument found in the rabbinic tradition cited at the outset of this article (*Gen. Rab.* 61:7) in the name of the Canaanite plaintiffs.[29]

c. The *Book of Jubilees* makes it clear that Canaan settled unlawfully in Phoenicia and Palestine because this territory was "very beautiful," much better than the one allotted to him in Africa.

d. It has been observed that a medieval haggadic collection, *Midrash Haggadah*, is similar to the tradition of the *Book of Jubilees*. According to this source,

> When the Holy one, blessed be He, divided the world among them, Noah made his three sons swear [החרים] that none of them would enter the territory of the other. And the Seven nations passed through the land of Israel and transgressed the oath [החרם]. Therefore the Holy One, blessed be He, commanded "You shall utterly destroy them" [החרם תחרימו; Deut 7:2].[30]

I think it is quite likely that the word for "oath" in the Hebrew original of the *Book of Jubilees* was *herem*.[31] Thus the annihilation (*herem*; verb: *heherim*) to which the Canaanites were doomed, according to the Torah, could be justified as a measure-for-measure punishment, as in this medieval haggadic passage.[32]

e. When Canaan does not settle in his inheritance, his brothers say: "Do not dwell in the dwelling of Shem" (10:31). These words probably allude to the words "God enlarge Japhet and *let him dwell in the tents of Shem*, and let Canaan be his [or their] slave" (Gen 9:27). Indeed Japhet dwelled, according to the *Book of Jubilees*, in Shem's residence: Madai, a descendant of Japhet asked to settle near Elam, in the share of Shem (*Jub.* 10:35–36).[33] According to *this* interpretation the words "let *him* dwell in the tents of Shem" apply not to God, but rather to Japhet![34]

Elsewhere in the *Book of Jubilees* we read: "Noah was very happy that this share had emerged (by lot) for Shem and his children. He recalled everything that he said in prophecy in his mouth, for he said: 'May the Lord, the God of Shem, be blessed, and may the Lord dwell in the dwellings of Shem'" (8:17–18, see also 8:20); here the words "let him dwell" unequivocally refer to God. Two interpretations were combined in the *Book of Jubilees* (one reading "him" as referring to God, the other as referring to Japhet).[35] Noah's blessing is considered a prophecy in the latter passage. The transformation of a curse into a prophecy is attested already in the Hebrew Bible: Joshua's curse (Josh 6:26) is interpreted as prophecy (1 Kgs 16:34).[36] Similarly, blessings of the patriarchs are conceived of as words of prophecy elsewhere in the *Book of Jubilees* (25:13, 31:12).

Now, the tradition of *Jubilees* 10:31 (if indeed it alludes to Gen 9:27) might be best interpreted under the assumption that Noah's curse was in fact a prophecy that Canaan would dwell *illegitimately* in Shem's residence and that harsh consequences would follow this transgression.

THE MIGRATION OF THE CANAANITES TO AFRICA

The story implied in the *Book of Jubilees*, namely that the Canaanites emigrated to North Africa when Israel conquered and inhabited the land, is mentioned in Tannaitic works. Thus we read in the Tannaitic midrash *Mekhilta de-Rabbi Ishmael*:

> [A] "And when the Lord brings you into the Land of Canaan" (Exod 13:11). Canaan merited that the land should be called by his name. What did Canaan [i.e., the Canaanites] do? As soon as Canaan heard that Israel was about to enter the Land, he moved away from before them [עמד ופינה מפניהם]. God said to him: You have moved away from before My children; I, in turn, will call the Land by your name and will grant you a land as good as your country [אף אני אקרא את הארץ על שמך ואתן לך ארץ יפה כארצך];[37] and which is this? Africa [אפריקין].
>
> [B] Likewise it says: "And Canaan begat Zidon his first-born and Heth" (Gen 10:15), and it is written: "And the children of Heth answered Abraham, saying unto him: 'Hear us my lord, [you are God's prince among us; bury your dead in the choicest of our sepulchres] (Gen 23:6). God then said to them: You have shown respect towards My beloved [Abraham; אתם כבדתם את ידידי]. I, in turn, will call the Land by your name and grant you a land as good as your country.[38] And which is it? Africa.[39]

According to this passage, the Canaanites moved away from their land voluntarily so that Israel would settle in it. The Canaanites settled in Africa (i.e., in the Punic territories of North Africa), this being the territory given to them by God as a fair substitute at the time of Joshua. Unlike the *Book of Jubilees*, this tradition does not imply that their *original* lot was in Africa; rather, it implies that they were willing to evacuate their own land for Israel. We shall see that a strikingly similar tradition occurs in one of Philo's works. In contradistinction to the *Book of Jubilees*, where Canaan's lot in Africa is worse than the good land that he unlawfully inhabited, in the midrash discussed here, Africa is described as a land that is as good as the land of Israel.[40] The justification of the name of the land—"the land of Canaan"—is central for this passage no less than for the *Book of Jubilees* and the rabbinic story on Gevihah ben Qosem in *Gen. Rab.* 61:7, cited at the beginning of this chapter;[41] in the *Mekhilta* and its parallels, this name of the land is considered a reward for the Canaanites' *forfeiture* of their land.

One of the components shared by the two traditions is the notion, expressed explicitly in the *Mekhilta* and implicitly in the *Book of Jubilees*, that the Canaanites left the land for Africa—that is, the Punic settlements in North Africa and especially Carthage[42]—in Joshua's time. Interestingly, a similar synchronism exists in a passage of Apion cited by Josephus:

> Apion, however, the surest authority of all, precisely dates the exodus in the seventh Olympiad, and in the first year of the Olympiad, the year in which, according to him, the Phoenicians founded Carthage.[43]

Now, according to Apion's chronology, the year of the Exodus from Egypt is also the year of the conquest of Canaan:

> "After six days' march,"[44] he says, "they developed tumors in the groin, and that is why, after safely reaching the country now called Judaea, they rested on the seventh day[45] and called the day *sabbaton*."[46]

Compare also Tacitus: "They then marched six days continuously, and on the seventh *seized a country, expelling the former inhabitants*."[47]

To be sure, there is no indication that Apion blamed the Jews for the expulsion of the Phoenician population. I do not contend that Apion made such an accusation, or even that he considered the foundation of Carthage a consequence of the conquest of Canaan;[48] this notwithstanding, the synchronism is evident, and it dovetails the Jewish sources (from the *Book of Jubilees* to rabbinic sources) concerning the emigration of Canaanites from the land of Canaan to North Africa due to the same event.

As has been noted long ago,[49] a similar account is known from a passage of Procopius (sixth century C.E.) in his *History of the Wars*:

> When the Hebrews had withdrawn from Egypt and had come near the boundaries of Palestine...by displaying a valour greater than that natural to a man, [they] gained the possession of the land. And after overthrowing all the nations he [Joshua] easily won the cities, and he seemed to be altogether invincible. Now at that time the whole country along the sea from Sidon as far as the boundaries of Egypt was called Phoenicia. And one king in ancient times held sway over it, as is agreed by all who have written the earliest accounts of the Phoenicians. In that country there dwelt very populous tribes, the Gergashites and the Jebusites and some others[50] with other names by which they are called in the history of the Hebrews. Now when these nations saw the invading general was an irresistible prodigy, they emigrated from their ancestral homes and made their ways to Egypt, which adjoined their country. And...they proceeded to Libya. And they established numerous cities and took possession of the whole of Libya as far as the pillars of Heracles, and there they have lived even up to my time, using the Phoenician tongue. They also built a fortress in Numidia, where now is the city called Tigisis. In that place are two columns made of white stone near by the great spring, having Phoenician letters cut in them which say in the Phoenician tongue: "We are they who fled from the face of Joshua, the robber, son of Nun." [Ἡμεῖς ἐσμεν οἱ φυγόντες ἀπὸ προσώπου Ἰησοῦ τοῦ λῃστοῦ υἱοῦ Ναυῆ.][51]

The last sentence is by all probability an imaginative reading of an ancient unintelligible inscription.[52] The Semitism[53] ἀπὸ προσώπου (Hebrew, מפני, "from before") in the alleged text of this inscription has been noted. Could it be due to pagans of Punic origin who "read" the inscription in this manner?[54]

Be it as it may, according to this narrative the Phoenicians who reached North Africa were not refugees of war, but rather emigrants who evacuated the land because they realized the superiority of Joshua, and yet they did not do so quite willingly: Joshua is referred to as "the robber."

THEOLOGICAL JUSTIFICATION

A similar accusation of the Jewish people as "a nation of robbers" occurs in a well-known passage of *Genesis Rabbah* 1:2:

> Rabbi Joshua of Sikhnin [ca. fourth century C.E.] said in the name of Rabbi Levi [ca. fourth century C.E.]: "He has recounted to His people the power of His works, to grant them the inheritance of the nations" (Ps 111:6)—Why did the Holy One, blessed be He, reveal to Israel what was created on the first day, and on the second day, and on the third day? So that the nations of the world might not taunt Israel [מונים את ישראל] and say to them: "You are a nation of robbers [אומה שלבזחות]!" Israel can retort: "And do you not hold yours as a spoil, for surely 'the Caphtorim that came forth out of Caphtor, destroyed them, and dwelt in their stead' (Deut 2:23)!" The whole world belongs to God. When He wished, He gave it to you, and when He wished He took it from you and gave it to us.[55]

The accusation of the "nations of the world" is met by two different Jewish answers in this short passage. The first is a mundane one: There is nothing unique in Israel's case. Deuteronomy 2:23 does imply this answer. The second is a theological one: God is the sovereign of the world, and he grants lands to peoples according to his absolute will. The midrash borrows legal terminology for theological purposes.[56] There is no explicit reference here to the iniquity of the Canaanites; God's sovereignty is sufficient for explaining His acts. The accusation of the Gentiles is clearly aimed at the Jews, not at their God; God's responsibility for the expulsion of the Canaanites is part of the Jewish *response* to the Gentile accusation. We shall return to this fundamental observation.

Treating the Torah as "the Law," ὁ Νόμος, motivated several reactions to the question of why the Torah began with the *story* of creation. The question is already treated by Philo.[57] Especially instructive, however, is the solution to this question offered by Acacius of Caesarea (fourth century C.E.); according to him, the Giver of the Law began by describing creation in order to show the people who are required to keep God's laws that he is not the god of one nation, but rather the creator of the whole universe.[58] For the Jewish rabbi, God's deeds, as well as his Law, are always oriented toward his people, while the Christian father stresses universalistic concepts and plays down God's relations to one people. The contrast between the two explanations is striking. They were offered in Palestine in about the same time (fourth century C.E.) and probably reflect some Jewish-Christian discourse and debate.

POSSIBLE MOTIVES FOR APOLOGETIC MOTIFS

What is the cultural background for the apologetic motifs discerned thus far? Hans (Yohanan) Lewy wrote an erudite and insightful article on this subject.[59] He underscored the apologetic dimension of the various passages in Second Temple literature and in rabbinic writings[60] and suggested an actual historical and cultural context for the apologetic motifs: The tradition of the contest concerning the land, in which Alexander the Great was allegedly the judge, reflects, according to Lewy, an actual territorial struggle between the Phoenicians and the Jews concerning the ownership of Phoenician territories conquered by the Hasmoneans. Hellenized Phoenicians led the contest, and Hellenized Jews, represented by the *Book of Jubilees*, responded to the argument.[61] The Phoenicians, in their dispute with the Jews, used the canonical writings of the latter, as Homer and other canonical writings were used in the Hellenistic world as proof in various political disputes, for conquest by force was not considered legitimate in the Hellenistic world.

It seems, however, that Lewy's brilliant and influential suggestion cannot be accepted. First of all, the occurrence of this motif in the *Book of Jubilees* does not speak for Lewy's theory. The *Book of Jubilees* cannot be considered as written by "Hellenized Jews," as argued by Lewy, who had accepted Schürer's position that it was written at the end of the Hasmonean kingdom.[62] The date of the book's composition is disputed: Some scholars maintain that it was written at the beginning of the Maccabean revolt, or even prior to it; others argue that the book was written during the Hasmonean kingdom, several decades after the revolt (I tend toward the later dating). However, even if a later date is preferred, it seems to me implausible to assume that the narrative of the *Book of Jubilees* is a reaction to Phoenician accusations against the Hasmoneans' conquests of territories under Phoenician influence (if its date is earlier, the argument becomes untenable). Moreover, it seems that the passage in the *Book of Jubilees* reflects older traditions, which must be taken as antedating it.[63] It should also be mentioned that the *Genesis Apocryphon*[64] shares with the *Book of Jubilees* not only the tradition of the allotment of Noah's sons, but also the insistence that Canaan is a usurper and that the land is in the lot of Shem.[65] Another Aramaic apocryphon apparently alludes to the seizure of the land from the sons of Shem by the sons of Ham.[66] Second,[67] it should be noted that there is no clear correlation between the Hellenistic accounts of the conquest of Canaan and of the Hasmonean conquests. The writers cited by Lewy[68] do not draw a line of similarity between those conquered by the Hasmoneans and the Canaanites. Strabo, who accused the Hasmoneans of "seizing the property of others," did not accuse Moses or his successors of anything similar;[69] on the contrary, they are described as having a friendly relationship with the few inhabitants of the land.[70] Diodorus,[71] while accusing the Jews since Moses of having "misanthropic and lawless" customs and describing the ancestors of the Jews as lepers, apparently did not mention any claim of robbery of the land of the Canaanites. Tacitus's account of the Jewish people and their history included a very brief statement that the lepers expelled from Egypt "seized a country, expelling its former inhabitants,"[72] but he does not accuse the Hasmoneans of seizing other peoples' land. It has been suggested that anti-Jewish descriptions (by Lysimachus of Alexandria) of the Jews as destroying temples on their way to Judaea may be explained as reflecting the destruction of pagan temples by the Hasmoneans,[73] but even if this were the case, the description does not refer to the conquest of Canaan as such. In the sources collected in Stern's book *Greek and Latin Authors on Jews and Judaism*, I have not succeeded in finding any evidence for connecting the accusations against the conquerors of Canaan with the Hasmoneans. It is, of course, quite possible that there were those who connected the seizing of Canaan with the conquest of the Hasmoneans, but such a connection is far from self-evident, nor is it necessarily the origin of the apologetic argument in the *Book of Jubilees* and elsewhere. Third, Lewy's argument that conquest by force was not considered legitimate was recently challenged by Israel Shatzman.[74]

A different Hasmonean background has also been suggested. According to Philip Alexander, "the powerful anti-Canaanite thrust of this section, coupled with the assertion of the right of Shem's descendants to the 'land of Canaan,' should surely be seen as a propaganda for the territorial expansion of the Hasmonean state."[75] Israel Shatzman has suggested[76] that the issue at stake in the *Book of Jubilees* was "an exhortation to take control of Eretz Israel, unjustly usurped by 'Canaan,' that is, the nations roundabout Judaea....it is possible to regard the polemic as part of a Jewish debate on the merits, dangers and religious justification of the expansionist wars."[77] This suggestion seems to me unlikely. There is no clue that "Canaan" should mean "the nations *around* Judaea"; it refers to a specific ethnicity—Phoenicians. An existing tradition asserting that the Phoenician colonies in Northern Africa were settled in the land allotted to Canaan is reflected in the book, as we have seen. While Shatzman is certainly right that the account in the *Book of Jubilees* makes sense only if one considers the whole land as the Jewish homeland, such a notion is not necessarily connected to the Hasmonean kingdom;[78] it could well have emerged centuries earlier.[79] In contrast to Shatzman, I do not find compelling evidence that the Hasmoneans considered their wars as analogous to Joshua's conquest, and that the biblical law of *herem* was considered as applicable to the Gentile inhabitants of the land. In 1 Maccabees, a work that comes closest to Hasmonean ideology, there are very few allusions to the nations of Canaan or to Joshua.[80] It also does not account for the apologetic overtones of this passage in the *Book of Jubilees*. Francis Schmidt and Daniel Machiela[81] have suggested that the concern of the *Book of Jubilees* is Hellenism, but this does not explain most of the details concerning the fate of the Canaanites.

OTHER ANTI-JEWISH INDICTMENTS IN GENESIS RABBAH

After this long but necessary detour, let us return to *Genesis Rabbah* 1:2. The wording of this passage—"So that the nations of the world might not taunt Israel and say to them: 'You are a nation of…'"—occurs in two other passages of the same composition:

[A] Rabbi Hama b. Rabbi Hanina said: … Why are there miserable and poor people among them [the nations of the world]? So that they might not taunt Israel and say to them [שלא יהו מונים את ישראל ואומרים להם]: "You are a nation of miserable and poor people" [לא אומה שלדווים ושלסחופים אתם?!]… Rabbi Samuel b. Nahman said: … Why are there people with scabs among the nations of the world? So that they might not taunt Israel and say to them: "You are a nation of lepers" [לא אומה שלמצורעים אתם?!].[82]

[B] Rabbi Shim'on ben Yohai said: … So that they [the nations of the world] might not taunt Israel and say to them [שלא יהו מונים את ישראל ואומרים להם]: "You are a nation of exiles and wanderers" [לא אומה שלגולים אתם ושלמטטליטלים?!].[83]

Although the Sages to whom these utterances are ascribed belong to different generations (*Gen. Rab.* 1:2 and [A] are supposedly uttered by Amoraim, while [B] is attributed to a Tanna), the wording of the three passages of *Genesis Rabbah* is strikingly similar. All three passages refer to vilification and maligning of the Jewish nation.[84] The allegation in *Genesis Rabbah* 88:1 that the Israelites who left Egypt were lepers is well documented in the Gentile writings and probably originated in Egypt.[85] We may also note that the passage from Procopius's *Wars* (sixth century C.E.), discussed at length by Lewy, testifies to a tradition far removed both in place and time from Phoenicia and the second century B.C.E.[86]

PHILO'S EVIDENCE

Indeed, we have ancient circumstantial evidence that the issue at stake was the scornful and hostile attitude toward the Jews by pagans.[87] A passage in Philo's treatise *Hypothetica* reads:

Which alternative do you prefer? Were they still superior in the number of their fighting men though they had fared so ill to the end, still strong and with weapons in their hand, and did they then take the land by force, defeating the combined Syrians and Phoenicians when fighting in their own country? Or shall we suppose that they were unwarlike and feeble, quite few in numbers and destitute of warlike equipment, but won the respect of their opponents who voluntarily surrendered their land to them and that as a direct consequence they shortly afterwards built their temple and established everything else needed for religion and worship? This would clearly show that they were acknowledged as dearly beloved of God even by their enemies. For those whose land they suddenly invaded with the intention of taking it from them were necessarily their enemies.[88]

This is a fragment of an apologetic work of Philo, "that wishes to meet the hostile criticism of the Gentiles."[89] The passage confronts the defamation of the Jews as cowards, on the one hand, and as robbers, on the other hand. This double defamation can be reconstructed also in an apologetic passage of Josephus: "Nor, again, did our forefathers, like some others, have recourse to *robbery* [ληστεία] or to military schemes of aggrandizement, although their country contained myriads of *courageous men*."[90] The apologetic nature of this passage of Philo's *Hypothetica* is evident. It probably answers an indictment of the Jews. This conclusion neatly dovetails with the later passages in *Genesis Rabbah* 1:2, where a defamation of the Jews is at stake, and it fits Procopius' account.

A striking parallel to Philo's remarkable narrative occurs also in the *Mekhilta de-Rabbi Ishmael* cited above (in the section "The Migration of the Canaanites to Africa").[91] According to this narrative, the Canaanites evacuated the land voluntarily in order to let Israel settle there. Interestingly, Philo's wording, that the Israelites "won the *respect* of their opponents…acknowledged as *dearly beloved of God* even by their enemies," is strikingly similar to the wording of unit B in the *Mekhilta*, "You have shown respect toward My beloved" (but this unit refers to Abraham).[92] Be that as it may, Philo's evidence proves that the rabbinic material is not the product of the post–70 C.E. period.[93]

ACCUSING GOD: FROM PAGAN TO GNOSTIC ACCUSATION

In the dispute between the Jews and other ethnic groups before Alexander the Great, according to *Genesis Rabbah* 61:7, the Canaanites' indictment of the Jews for the illegal seizure of their land is adjoined to the Egyptians' accusation concerning the goods that had been illegally taken from Egypt by the Israelites.[94] As we shall see below, both are ethnic defamations of the Jews.

In the first centuries of the common era, similar accusations against the God of the Law are found in patristic writers.[95] Thus Mani (third century C.E.) says, according to Epiphanius (fourth century C.E.):

Some "good" God of the Law! He spoiled Egyptians, expelled the Amorites, Gilgashites[96] and other nations, and gave their land to the children of Israel. If He said, "thou shalt not covet," how could He give them that which belong to others [τὰ ἀλλότρια]?[97]

Here also the two accusations are juxtaposed, but, unlike the midrash, the God of Israel is accused rather than His people. Early Christian literature had to answer this challenge of the "heretics." Epiphanius, using a tradition ultimately derived from early Jewish retorts to the Gentile claims, says: "The ignoramus [Mani] did not know that they *took their own land back, which was seized from them*," and here follows a paraphrase of the tradition of the *Book of Jubilees*.[98]

The argument continues along the same lines: While Mani's argument is virtually the same as the pagan accusations of the "nations of the world" in *Genesis Rabbah* 1:2 and the putative Phoenician inscription of Procopius, Epiphanius invokes Jewish counterarguments. Another accusation of "robbery" related to the Israelite conquest is made, according to a tradition in the Babylonian Talmud, by a heretic, *min*, who had read in Balaam's *pinax* that he had been killed by "Phinehas the robber" (פנחס ליסטאה; *b. Sanh.* 106b).[99] This tradition, like that of Procopius, attests to the existence of counter-histories to the biblical account, perhaps originated by Gnostics and pagans, respectively.

Most of the midrashim, as we have seen, are concerned with the problem of why the Israelites seized the land of the Canaanites. This seems to indicate that the rabbis felt obliged to answer the ethnic defamation brought forth by pagans, while they did not feel threatened by Gnostic arguments (assuming that they knew them). Such a conclusion, even though it is limited to a specific tradition, is significant for assessing the cultural world of the Sages. Below we shall see that the same applies to another case, namely the despoliation of Egypt.

Yet there is an ancient source, a dialogue between the Israelites and their God, in which the problem is presented as a theological one. In the *Sifra*, a Tannaitic midrash to Leviticus, we read:

> "[But I said to you: you will inherit their land,] and I shall give it to you to inherit it" (Lev 20:24)—I shall give it [the land] to you as an eternal inheritance. You [pl.] might say: Can You give us only that which belongs to another? [God would say]: In truth it is yours! It is indeed the portion of Shem, and you are Shem's sons, and they are the sons of Ham. What [were] they doing in it? They were the guardians of the place until you came.[100]

The argument "Can You give us only that which belongs to another?" is rather similar to Mani's argument, "How could God give them that which belong[s] to others?" Yet it is not put in the mouth of Gentiles or *minim*,[101] but rather it is presented as a hypothetical question of *pious* Jews put forward to God. God's answer is basically similar to that of the *Book of Jubilees*. The Canaanites, however, are accused neither of trespassing (as in the *Book of Jubilees*) nor of committing any of the moral sins that are mentioned explicitly in the preceding verse in Leviticus (Lev 20:23), a verse that gives a very good ethical reason for the uprooting of the Canaanites. A deep feeling of uneasiness concerning the inheritance of the land of Canaan is reflected in this passage, and the solution ready at hand in the biblical text does not alleviate it. The Canaanites are described here merely as "the guardians of the place" for Israel.[102] It may well be that this problem bothered some Jews. The option of a polemic between Jews and non-Jews and the option of an internal Jewish problem are not mutually exclusive; claims of non-Jews could occupy the Jews themselves. The tone of the passage sounds apologetic, but there is no indication in the text that this was part of an polemic with some other group.

Indeed, as early as the *Wisdom of Solomon* (Egypt, not later than the first century C.E.) the problem is posed in theological terms:

> The ancient inhabitants of Your holy land, who were hateful to You for their loathsome practices…it was Your will to destroy at the hand of our forefathers.…Yet these too You spared as being men, and sent wasps.…Judging them gradually You gave them space for repentance, not unaware that their seed was evil, and their viciousness innate, and that their mode of thought would in no way vary to the end of time, for their race was accursed from the very first.…Who shall say to You, "What have You done?" or shall take issue with Your decisions? Who shall bring charge against You for having destroyed nations of Your own making?…Your might is the source of justice, and it is Your mastery over all which causes You to spare all.[103]

The reason given for the destruction of the Canaanites is their wickedness, as stated in Leviticus 20,[104] while Canaan's curse in Genesis 9:25–27 is conceived as derived from their moral degeneracy: "Their seed was evil and their viciousness innate." We have seen (above, in the section "Two Curses in the Book of Jubilees") that Canaan's curse was employed as a reason for the destruction of the Canaanites, both in the Second Temple period and in rabbinic literature. In the light of these passages, it seems that the allusion to Genesis 9:25–27 in the *Wisdom of Solomon* is but a peculiar use of Canaan's curse. According to this passage, however, the Canaanites were not uprooted *because* Canaan had been cursed; rather, Canaan's curse signifies his evil nature and his inability to repent.[105]

Unlike Rabbi Levi's saying in *Genesis Rabbah* 1:2 cited above in the section "Theological Justification", God's sovereignty over the world, a central idea in this passage, is not perceived in the *Wisdom of Solomon* as sufficient for justifying his destruction of the Canaanites.[106] The author of this work is clearly bothered about God's justice. Was this passage motivated solely by innate theological uneasiness, or was it also responding to pagan accusations against the Jews and their God? It is difficult to decide. In either case, the Gnostic argument might have seized on the argument to which the *Wisdom of Solomon* responds.

I contended above that in rabbinic passages, pagans argue against the Jews, and the character of their argument is ethnic rather than theological. In a late midrash, what is clearly at stake is God's justice in the light of an apparently polemical context, in which the older arguments against the Jews receive a new twist:

[A] You might say: The H[oly One] treated the Canaanites unjustly when He gave them into the hand of I[srael] and gave Israel their land. God forbid that He would have treated them unjustly, "Far be it from God to do evil, from the Almighty to do wrong" (Job 34:10).

[B] The Canaanites are slaves to Is[rael], as it says: "And he said: Cursed be Canaan, a slave of slaves shall he be to his brothers. And he said: Blessed be the Lord, God of Shem, and let Canaan be his slave." If a slave acquires possess[ions], [the slave] belongs to whom, and the possessions belong to whom? Therefore He gave them into the hand of Is[rael] and gave Israel their land.

[C] Furthermore, [they were wicked], and for this they were doomed to be destroyed, as it says: "but on account of the wickedness of these nations, the Lord will drive them out from before you, to accomplish what He swore to your forefathers" (Deut 9:5).[107]

The first solution (unit B), based on Genesis 9:27, is the one we met in the contest before Alexander. The wording of our midrash suits the Babylonian Talmud (*Sanh.* 91a). The second solution (unit C), that the Canaanites were destroyed because of their iniquity, is derived from biblical verses such as Leviticus 20:22–24 cited in this midrash. As we have seen, the two arguments were combined to defend God's righteousness as early as the *Wisdom of Solomon*. (Needless to say, there is no dependence of the late midrash on the *Wisdom of Solomon!*) This late midrash certainly reflects the theological dimension of the argument; however, its time and cultural setting are unknown. As we shall see below, the apologetic arguments concerning the despoliation of Egypt in the Exodus present a somewhat similar, but more persuasive, case.

THE TRADITION OF THE BOOK OF JUBILEES IN CHRISTIAN LITERATURE

As has been noted above, the tradition of the *Book of Jubilees* was used by several Christian writers, such as the Pseudo-Clementines[108] and Epiphanius.[109] The latter, who uses it to combat the Manicheans, probably came across a Jewish tradition similar to, but not identical with, the one in the *Book of Jubilees*. According to Epiphanius, Noah cast the lots between his descendants in Rhinocorura. This is how נחל מצרים is rendered in the Septuagint to Isaiah 27:12; it is identified as modern al-'Arish, situated on the border between the land and Egypt, נחל מצרים, the "River of Egypt."[110] The meaning of the word *nahalah* in Hebrew is "inheritance."[111] Moreover, this tradition is based not only on a Hebrew wordplay, but also on an interpretation of Ezekiel 48:28–29, according to the Masoretic Text:

(28) The boundary shall run from Tamar to the waters of Merivat Qadesh [to] *Nahalah*[112] on the Great sea. (29) This is the land which you shall allot *from Nahalah* [מנחלה][113] to the tribes of Israel.

The peculiar reading מנחלה in the Masoretic Text in this context must have been interpreted to mean that Nahalah is where the tribes of Israel will be allotted their territories in the future. According to Epiphanius, it is in this very same place that Noah allotted the territories of his descendants (and divided between Shem and Ham). This tradition is in all likelihood Jewish, but it does not occur in the *Book of Jubilees*.[114] It would therefore not be implausible to suggest that Epiphanius's tradition, close as it is to the *Book of Jubilees*, is not derived from it.

The tradition of the *Book of Jubilees* was used as an anti-Jewish argument in a dialogue between a Christian and a Jew. In the *Dialogue between Timothy and Aquila* we read:[115]

> *The Christian said*: Abraham himself, having seen before in the Spirit the one who would come from him in flesh, swore by him the [slave] who was in charge of his house that he would not take a Canaanite wife for Isaac (Gen 24:2–3), but Isaac and Jacob will bless him.
>
> *The Jew said*: ... Speak accurately about the commandment of Abraham which was given with an oath (ibid.). ...
>
> *The Christian said*: Abraham, being urged on by the Lord God, was angry with the sons and daughters of the Canaanites for two reasons, for the Lord was saying to him: "This is pleasing before me." And everything that was not pleasing to the Lord, Abraham hated [A] ... Canaan, the son of Ham, transgressed the commandment of his father, and the oath, for Noah has made them swear. Canaan had this sin: He seized the land of his brother, Shem. For the land of Canaan belonged to the lot of Shem. ... Canaan ... rose up and overpowered Shem and took his land. And God was saying to Abraham: "The sins of the Amorites are not yet complete" (Gen 15:16). For God is waiting and will at some time return the land to Shem and release their curse. But they did not understand. [B] This is the second curse of the sons of Ham. For the first curse was given by Noah, when Ham saw the nakedness of his father. ... he cursed him saying: "Cursed be Ham. ..." (Gen 9:25).[116] ... Ham had these two curses.[117] [C] And because of these (curses) he caused his sons and daughters to pass through the fire to demons.
>
> Because Abraham knew these things, he did not want to take a wife for Isaac from the Canaanite daughters, so that his seed would not mix with these evil people.[118]

"The Christian" gives two reasons for Abraham's prohibition that Isaac would marry a Canaanite (sections A and B); Section C is, in fact, a third reason to avoid intermingling with the Canaanites, as it is written: "When ... you dispossess them and dwell in their land, *take heed that you be not ensnared to follow them* ... for every abominable thing which the Lord hates they have done to their gods; for they even *burn their sons and daughters in the fire* to their gods" (Deut 12:29–31). Section C, then, is only a remnant of a much more elaborated argument, which was not well handled by the author of the *Dialogue* as we have it. This demonstrates that the passage depends on a more detailed discussion.

The detailed explanation is based on a source similar to (and plausibly drawing on) the *Book of Jubilees*, probably through mediating source(s). The function of the argument is not explicitly defined, but apparently in the Christian-Jewish debate its aim was to give a specific reason for Abraham's reluctance to intermarry with the Canaanites: It does not imply, as a Jew might argue, that the "holy seed" should not intermingle with the Gentiles; the prohibition to marry the Canaanites was because they specifically were cursed. This is not said in so many words in the *Dialogue*, but is apparently the underlying issue behind it, either in an earlier form of the *Dialogue of Timothy and Aquila*[119] or in another *adversus Judaeos* text that was a source of the *Dialogue*.

NON-APOLOGETIC USAGE OF THE JEWISH TRADITIONS

Some passages in the midrash literature use the same building blocks of apologetic midrashim in a non-apologetic system. Thus we shall investigate *Tanhuma Numbers, Masse'e* 11–12, on the words "[When you enter the land of Canaan,] this is the land that will fall for you as an inheritance" (Num 34:2). A comparison of the two alternative interpretations suggested in *Tanhuma Numbers* to the passage cited above (see the section "Possible Motives for Apologetic Motifs") in *Genesis Rabbah* 1:2 is instructive (see Table 4.1).

TABLE 4.1

Genesis Rabbah 1:2	*Tanhuma Numbers*, Masse'e 11–12[120]
He has recounted to His people the power of His works, to grant them the inheritance of the nations (Ps 111:6)—Why did the Holy One, blessed be He, reveal to Israel what was created on the first day, and on the second day, and on the third day?	[12] ["This is the land that will fall for you as an inheritance"]—this is what Scripture says (elsewhere): *He has recounted to His people the power of His works, to grant them the inheritance of the nations* (Ps 111:6)—the Holy One, blessed be He, said: I could have created for you a new land, but in order to show you my power I shall dispossess your enemies from before you and shall give you their land.
So that the nations of the world might not taunt Israel and say to them: "You are a nation of robbers!" Israel can retort: ... *The whole world belongs to God.* When He wished, He gave it to you, and when He wished He took it from you and gave it to us.	[11] "This is the land that will fall for you as an inheritance"—the land is intended for *you*.... The Holy One, blessed be He, said: *The Land* [ארץ] *is mine as it is written,* "*The whole earth* [הארץ] *is the Lord's*" (Ps 24:1), and Israel are mine... it is best that I will inherit. My land [ארצי] to My slaves, my own to my own [שלי לשלי].

The *Tanhuma* passage ignores the designation of the land in Numbers 34:2 as "the land of Canaan," and discloses no apologetic features. Its tone is very different from *Genesis Rabbah*, although the two midrashic passages use the same building blocks. The emphasis that the whole earth belongs to God suits very well the apologetic argument in *Genesis Rabbah*, that God could give the earth to whomever He wished. Plausibly, an apologetic argument was twisted into a non-apologetic one. Psalm 111:6 also functions as a non-apologetic proof text, in contradistinction to its function in *Genesis Rabbah* 1:2. The *Tanhuma* passage may therefore serve as an example for a post-apologetic reworking of earlier material.

The apologetic tradition was alive well into the Middle Ages, and it is well represented in the first sentence in Rashi's commentary to the Torah.[121]

The Despoliation of Egypt and the Fate of the Canaanites: Two Interrelated Apologetic Challenges

JUSTIFICATION OF THE JEWS AND THEIR GOD

In the passage of *Genesis Rabbah* cited at the outset of this article, the Canaanites, the Ishmaelites, and the Egyptians are portrayed as plaintiffs against the Jews in Alexander's court. Whereas the Canaanites and the Ishmaelites have legal claims for the ownership of the land of Israel (not "territorial claims" in the precise sense of this expression), the Egyptians' claim is financial: They argue that the Jews should give them back the silver and gold that the Israelites took with them when they left Egypt. The Jewish answer was that whatever was taken by the Israelites was a compensation for many years of slavery. A thorough investigation of this theme is out of place in the present context;[122] as we shall see, however, it gives an additional dimension to the problem with which this article is concerned.

The dominant Jewish argument is known from the *Book of Jubilees*: Prince Mastema, the evil angel, was bound so that he could not accuse the Israelites for requesting utensils and clothing from the Egyptians "so that they could plunder the Egyptians in return for the fact that they were made to work when they enslaved them by force" (*Jub.* 48:18).[123] The *Book of Jubilees* envisages an accusation against the Jews by the national angel of the Egyptians, and thus presents its own apologetic position to such accusations (either real or putative).[124] The same justification is found in the *Wisdom of Solomon* (10:17),[125] in a fragment of the *Exagoge* of Ezekiel the tragedian (lines 162–166)[126] and in Philo:[127]

> They took with them much spoil [λεία]...and they did this not in avarice [φιλοχρηματία], or, as one might say, in accusation [ὡς ἄν τις κατηγορῶν εἴποι], in covetousness of what belonged to others [τῶν ἀλλοτρίων ἐπιθυμία].... Whether one regard it as...the acceptance of payment [μισθός] long kept back...or as an act of war, the claim under the law of the victor to take their enemies' goods[128]—in either case, their action was right.[129]

Philo's apologetic utterances are again (like in the case of Canaan's owner-ship of the land) circumstantial evidence of an indictment against the Jews. Whoever used this argument could not expect the Jews to return the wealth that had been taken by their forefathers a little before the Exodus; the purpose was rather defamation of the Jews for their avarice and their covetousness of what belongs to others, an "anti-Semitic" portrayal of the characteristic traits of the Jewish people.[130] Interestingly, the pagans' claims against the Jews con-cerning the Exodus from Egypt do not criticize their forefathers for making off with their neighbor's goods (although some pagan authors try to malign the Jews in other ways), with the exception of the report of "the Memphians" cited by the Jewish writer Artapanus (second century B.C.E.).[131] Pompeius Trogus (first century B.C.E.–first century C.E., preserved only in an epitome composed in the third century C.E.) blames them for stealing the Egyptian *sacra*[132] but not the property of their Egyptian neighbors, and this has nothing to do with Philo's apologetic argument.[133] Artapanus and Philo imply that such an accusation did exist in their time. Was it directly based on the biblical text, "based on the Jews' own Law," as it is put in the tradition in *Genesis Rabbah* 61:7 (and its parallels)? This is not *necessarily* the case—the biblical account *could* possibly have been known from hearsay—but the possibility that the opponents based their attack on the biblical text cannot be excluded: Claims against the details of Jewish Scriptures, otherwise scarcely known to us in this period, were known to Philo.[134] To return now to the issue of the ownership of the land of Canaan, the ancient argument (attributed to the Canaanites in *Gen. Rab.* 61:7 and answered as early as the *Book of Jubilees*) that the land was called "the land of Canaan" is also apparently based on the biblical text, although this detail might have been known to Gentiles not from reading the biblical text itself.[135]

   In the case of the despoliation of Egypt, as in the case of the Canaanites, the *Jews* are accused, not their God; the argument in both cases is in the ethnic, not the theological realm. The Manichean argument cited by Epiphanius is strikingly similar: "He [God] spoiled the Egyptians, expelled the Amorites.... and gave their land to the children of Israel. If He said, 'thou shalt not covet,' how could He give them that which belong[s] to others ｛ ἀ ἀλ ὁρια]?"[136] The despoliation of Egypt and the conquest of Canaan are juxtaposed here, as they are in *Genesis Rabbah* 61:7, and the wording of the accusation is strikingly reminiscent of Philo's passage, but the indictment is not against the Jews but rather against the God of the Law, that is, the God of Israel. The Gnostics, Marcionites, and the Manicheans continue in this case the pagan arguments, while transforming the ethnic accusations against the Jews into theological ones against God, whereas the Church Fathers use the Jewish counterarguments.[137] It was noted by Israel Lévi that Tertullian (ca. third century C.E.) had recourse to a haggadah quite similar to the one in *Genesis Rabbah* as an answer to Marcionite claims against the God of the Old Testament.[138] Tertullian concludes: "If, therefore, the case of the Hebrews be a good one, the Creator's case, that is His commandment, must be likely a good one."[139]

In the Middle Ages, by the time the Gnostic threat had disappeared, Christian accusations of the Israelites as thieves and cheats were heard once again,[140] as one may infer from the polemic of Rashbam (Rabbi Shmuʿel ben Meir, twelfth century C.E.) against such arguments.[141] Although this passage is far beyond the chronological boundaries of the present article, it illustrates the dynamics of exegesis of the biblical verses, moving between ethnic anti-Jewish accusations, on the one hand, and the need to defend the Hebrew Bible and its heroes, on the other hand.[142]

As stated above, the Jews in antiquity scarcely reacted to the Gnostic allegations against God concerning the despoliation of Egypt.[143] A similar dynamic can be detected also in the case of the Jewish justification of the conquest of Canaan.

A MEDIEVAL COMPILATION AND ITS ANCIENT ORIGINS

Only in a late midrashic source, preserved in a medieval Yemenite commentary on the Torah compiled by Yaʿakov ben Mansur al-Bihani in the sixteenth century C.E.,[144] do we find the Gentiles condemning God for his command to take the Egyptians' property. Scholars have noted ancient material in other late midrashic compilations from Yemen.[145] The following passage, however, has not been discussed in scholarship. It reads:[146]

[A] A Gentile entered [a Jewish school] and found the students reading: "each woman shall ask of her neighbour" (Exod 3:22). He said to them: "Your God is a robber, for He said: '[and I will give this people favor in the sight of the Egyptians], and when you go, you shall not go empty, but each woman shall ask of her neighbor.... you shall despoil the Egyptians'" (Exod 3:21).

[B] One of the students responded: "It is not as you think. It is because the Egyptians enslaved the Israelites more than a hundred years, and did not give them their payment. Therefore the Israelites took their payment immediately, and they took only a little of their payment."

[C] Said the Gentile: "This would have been known [i.e., justified] had the Egyptians enslaved the Israelites, but it was only Pharaoh who enslaved them, while the Israelites took the money of all of the Egyptians."

[D] A second student responded: "No, the Egyptians had slaughtered numberless Israelites. The Israelites took but a little of the [compensation money] for their [slaughtered] sons."

[E] Said the Gentile: "Only Pharaoh commanded killing [the sons of the Israelites]. Why were the other Egyptians punished for his sin?"

[F] The third student responded: "You know that Joseph had gathered all the money in Egypt, and he had been the king of the Egyptians, and they had been his slaves, and their land and their money had belonged to him, as it is written, '[Buy us and our land for food] and we with our land' etc.[147] (Gen 47:19), and we are first in Joseph's heritage."

[G] Said the Gentile: "The Israelites took also the money that Joseph did not allow [them] to take, that is the money of the priests of Egypt, as it is written, 'only the land of the priests he did not buy'" (Gen 47:22).

[H] The fourth student responded: "No, because the Egyptians are our slaves, as it is written, 'The sons of Ham: Cush, Egypt, Put and Canaan' (Gen 10:6); and it is said, 'a slave of slaves shall he [Canaan] be to his brethren.' For this reason it was allowed to us that we take all their money, for whatever a slave possesses is the possession of his master."

[I] The Gentile then admitted: "Your God is just and your Torah is just."

Clearly the argument against the justice of the God of the Law is typically Gnostic. The argument is well-known from the writings of the Church Fathers, as are some of the responses to the Gentile in this passage. Some of the arguments put forward in responses to the arguments of the Gentile are known to us from rabbinic literature (the compensation for the slavery [unit B], that the money took by the Israelites had been gathered by Joseph [unit F]; *b. Pesah.* 119a). Other arguments are hitherto known only from patristic literature (although their origin might well be Jewish). The argument that Pharaoh alone is guilty, and there was no justification to take the money of all the Egyptians (units C and E) is known from Theodoret of Cyrus (fifth century C.E.), who struggles with Gnostic arguments:

> There are those who find fault with God's command that the Hebrews ask the Egyptians for gold and silver vessels.... Since the Lord God wanted them to receive some recompense for their labors, He ordered them to do this. No one should think it unfair that, though it was Pharaoh who wronged the people, payment was required of the Egyptians. They had also participated in this injustice by imitating the cruelty of their king.[148]

The wording "the Israelites took but a little of the [compensation] money for their [slaughtered] sons" (unit D) is almost literally Tertullian's wording: "It was plainly less than their due which He commanded to be exacted. The Egyptians ought to have given back to the Hebrews also [compensation money for] their children."[149] The citation of Genesis 47:19 (unit F) is reminiscent of Irenaeus's words, "the Egyptians were debtors to the [Jewish] people, not alone as to property, but also as to their very lives, because of the kindness of the patriarch Joseph in former times."[150]

The concluding argument (unit H) is evidently borrowed from the rabbinic argument in the debate about the Canaanites' possession of Canaan; according to this passage the cursed person is Ham rather than Canaan, and therefore the argument could be applied to the Egyptians. This passage therefore demonstrates the connection between the traditions related to the two apologetic problems, the fate of the Canaanites and the despoliation of Egypt.

This passage, found in a late Yemenite compilation, preserves some intriguing, even unique, exegetical and polemical features. It is a striking example for the preservation of ancient material in late works.

THEOLOGICAL JUSTIFICATION

Another justification of the despoliation of Egypt, found in a sermon of Gregory of Nazianzus, (fourth century C.E.), is that all silver and gold belong to God:

> It [the wealth] isn't theirs. They plundered it, they seized it [ἐσύλησαν, ἥρπασαν] from the One who said, "Silver is mine and so is gold" (Haggai 2:9) and "I will give it to whomever I wish" (Dan 4:22). Yesterday it was theirs for so it was permitted. Today the Lord takes it and gives it to you [σοὶ προσάγει καὶ δίδωσιν] who are using it well and with a view towards salvation.[151]

This is strikingly reminiscent of the Jewish argument concerning Canaan in *Genesis Rabbah* 1:2:[152] "Israel can retort: 'And do you not hold yours as a spoil...the whole world belongs to God. When He wished, He gave it to you, and when He wished He took it from you and gave it to us.'"[153] Gregory uses this theological argument in juxtaposition to the legal argument of the "fair wages."

There are clear lines of similarity between the two themes, concerning the dispossession of the Canaanites and concerning the despoliation of Egypt. Most of the material in rabbinic literature concerning these two themes is not a product of *beth ha-midrash*;[154] rather, it is by and large the heritage of Second Temple Judaism. Many of the traditions are of an apologetic nature, and they respond to anti-Jewish claims, although a component of internal uneasiness is also likely. The two accusations of the Jews (concerning Canaan and Egypt) are juxtaposed in Jewish literature, as well as in early Christian literature. Moreover, there is a clear resemblance between the two accusations and between the responses to them. In both cases, the anti-Jewish indictment was inherited by the Gnostics to attack the God of the Law, while Jewish arguments were adopted by patristic writings answering them, but only late Jewish material may be considered as dealing with Gnostic claims.

NON-APOLOGETIC USAGE

As we have seen above (see the section "A Medieval Compilation and Its Ancient Origins"), in the case of the conquest of Canaan, there are statements in rabbinic literature that are not apologetic at all. This is also true in reference to the despoliation of Egypt. Some Sages thought that the taking of Egyptian property was a compelling divine commandment, and therefore Moses and

Aaron would have committed an inconceivable transgression had they not participated in it. They took, therefore, Egyptian property that had been deposited with them.[155] The triumphalist and utterly non-apologetic character of this statement is evident. According to another Tannaitic midrash on Exodus 12:36, whose apologetic tone is clear, the Egyptians gave the Israelites their property "against their will," (וישאילום.....—היו משאילים אותם על כרחם), that is, against the will of the Israelites.[156] The Babylonian Talmud, however, cites a similar midrash on the same word in Exodus 12:36: "They [the Egyptians] gave them [their property] against their will." The Talmud discusses the meaning of this utterance: Was the property given against the will of the Egyptians, or was it given against the will of the Israelites, because they did not to want to have too much burden on their way?[157] An apologetic statement was interpreted in an utterly non-apologetic manner.

Conclusion

This chapter has dealt mainly with the Jewish arguments concerning the fate of the Canaanites according to the literature of the Second Temple period and rabbinic literature (and also, to a limited extent, early Christian writings). While the problem is rooted in the biblical period as an internal theological-ethical theme, in the Hellenistic and Roman period it was raised again, this time in the context of Gentile accusations and Jewish apologetics. The Sages of these periods, of course, knew the reasons given in the Bible for the uprooting of the Canaanites and made use of them, but other reasons, different from those recorded in the Bible, were suggested, and those were mingled with some elaborations of tendencies that already occur in the Bible. The similarity of the various traditions, Hebrew and Greek, Palestinian and Jewish-Hellenistic, rabbinic, pre-rabbinic, and Christian, is striking. The main arguments continue for a period of over a thousand years, from the second century B.C.E. into the Middle Ages. The formative period of these traditions, as of many others, was the Second Temple period; later sources transmit the ancient traditions. It was not out of methodological negligence, but due to this striking continuity, that the passages cited in the present article were cited not in a chronological order, but according to theme and argument; quite often, a later source enables us to understand the full dimensions of an earlier one.

What was the essential motivation for the emergence of these apologetic arguments concerning the Canaanites' ownership of the land? Most scholars have concluded that it was the Hasmonean conquests of territories within what was historically Eretz Israel that stand behind the emergence of this motif. This, however, seems unlikely. Although it is not impossible to imagine that those conquests had some connection to the accusations discussed in this chapter, there is no evidence of such a connection in the passages in which these accusations appear. Such a starting point therefore seems doubtful. Rather, the context in which this motif appears—in Philo, rabbinic literature, and possibly also Procopius—leads us in a different direction: the defamation of the Jews as taking hold of what had not been theirs. It is not surprising, then, that the accusation of the Israelites' dispossession of the Canaanites is related several times and in several ways to a similar indictment, namely the theme of the taking of Egyptian property, known as the despoliation of Egypt. Unlike the dispossession of the Canaanites, the Israelites' taking of their neighbors' goods is not given any explicit justification in the Bible. No apologetic argument was apparently required for it in biblical times; in the Hellenistic and Roman period, however, a justification was needed, and there emerged the various apologetic arguments seen above. The subject at stake is ostensibly judicial, namely, by what legal right did the Israelites take with them the property of the Egyptians? Clearly, this problem is similar to the problem of the Israelite claim of ownership of the land of Canaan. The apparently legal claim of the Egyptians was invoked only as a means to defame the character of the Jews; this may be true as well of the claim regarding the Canaanites, at least at the end of the Second Temple period (Philo) and later. If this is the background to the argument of the *Book of Jubilees*, then it is one of the earliest attestations of such a debate, a Gentile accusation and a Jewish response, at this early date.

The indictment of stealing the Egyptians' property is based on an inversion of the biblical story. It may be inferred from the various sources that the biblical name of Eretz Israel, "the land of Canaan," was a Gentile argument with which the Jews had to cope. Pagans could know that the territory of the Jews was named Canaan, but it seems that the argument was also that the Jews themselves call it by this name, and since it was not used by contemporary Jews, it may well be that the pagans refer to the Bible. Anti-Jewish polemics based on the Bible are quite atypical before the emergence of Christianity; I suggest, however, that the existence of such arguments may be inferred from Philo's writings. Yet it might be argued that not only the title "the land of Canaan" but also the biblical description of the despoliation of Egypt could be known to Gentiles not by any access to the Bible itself, but rather by consulting Jewish informants. Both polemics demonstrate once again how partial and fragmentary our knowledge is of anti-Jewish allegations: In the case of the Canaan indictment there is good evidence from Jewish sources that the polemic endured for hundreds of years, and yet the evidence for its existence is merely circumstantial. Inversion of biblical stories is well known from Gnosticism, and one wonders whether it might be a continuation of pagan anti-Jewish readings of biblical passages.

In both cases—Canaan and the despoliation of Egypt—it seems that Marcionites and Manicheans made use of the pagan anti-Jewish arguments, turning them against the God of the Law, while the Christian responses are based on Jewish arguments. Some of the Jewish arguments might have been known to the Church Fathers through Philo and the *Book of Jubilees* or writers using them, while other arguments are probably derived from other Jewish sources, using at least partly Jewish oral traditions, some of which are recorded in rabbinic literature. In at least one instance, an argument borrowed, probably indirectly, from the *Book of Jubilees* (or a similar source) was used by Christians against the Jews, displaying once again the kaleidoscopic nature of notions and traditions when transferred from one religious context to another in antiquity. Interestingly, while rabbinic traditions deal with allegations against the Jews, they do not mention such allegations against the God of the Jews, that is, the Gnostic allegations that troubled Christian authorities at the same period. Only in medieval midrashic works do we find responses to such allegations, both concerning the ownership of Canaan and the despoliation of Egypt; in the latter case there are striking affinities to responses given by several Church Fathers that are, in all likelihood, of Jewish origin.

In this chapter we have seen how biblical heritage, exegesis of biblical passages, aggadic and midrashic motifs, polemics with other groups, and ideology and theology are intertwined; how passages of various sources illuminate each other and may be interpreted correctly only when scrutinized together; and how a thorough analysis of one passage (*Gen. Rab.* 61:7) leads to drawing the contours of a much larger picture.

Notes

* The first part of this chapter is an elaboration of my presentation at the conference held in Jerusalem on August 12, 2009. Only after I had finished writing the article in its final form, in December 2011, did I see the most recent articles by Katell Berthelot: "The Original Sin of the Canaanites," in The "Other" in Second Temple Judaism: Essays in Honor of John J. Collins, ed. D. Harlow et al. (Grand Rapids, Mich.: Eerdmans, 2011), 49–66; and "The Canaanites Who 'Trusted in God': An Original Interpretation of the Fate of the Canaanites in Rabbinic Literature," *JJS* 62 (2011): 233–261. The reader will benefit from consulting these articles.

1. *Genesis Rabbah* is often thought to have been compiled in the fifth century C.E. The parallels in the scholion to *Megillat Ta'anit* and in the Babylonian Talmud (see below) seem to indicate that this unit is Tannaitic (first through early third centuries C.E.).

2. The verse "and unto the sons of the concubines (that Abraham had) Abraham gave gifts" refers to the sons of Qeturah. This led the Babylonian Talmud (*b. Sanh.* 91a, according to most versions; see the next note concerning the variant readings of this passage) to add "the sons of Qeturah" as plaintiffs. It is not clear to whom the plural form of the word "concubines" in the biblical text refers. Gevihah ben Qosem assumes, according to *Genesis Rabbah*, that it refers to Hagar, and that Ishmael is one of "the sons of the concubines." *Jub.* 20:11–12, in retelling Gen 25:6, explicitly mentions Ishmael, together with the sons of Qeturah, as being sent away by Abraham, who gave everything to Isaac.

3. *Gen. Rab.* 61:7 (ed. Theodor-Albeck, 666–669); the English translation is based on H. Friedman, *Midrash Rabbah: Genesis* (London: Soncino, 1951), 2:545–547. Parallels to the story in rabbinic literature *b. Sanh.* 91a; the scholia to *Megillat Ta'anit* (V. Noam, *Megillat*

Ta'anit: Versions, Interpretations, History, with a Critical Edition [Jerusalem: Yad Ben Zvi, 2003], 70–77, 141–147, 198–205). *Scholion P* of *Megillat Ta'anit* does not include the dispute with the Egyptians. The reason for this could be technical. The dispute with the Egyptians, however, is missing in a Genizah fragment of the Babylonian Talmud and occurs either after the dispute with the Africans (i.e., Canaanites) or after the dispute with the Ishmaelites; in one manuscript it was copied in the margin (see Noam, *Megillat Ta'anit*, 143, 145). Noam rightly inferred from these data that this pericope may well be a secondary addition in the Talmud (Noam, *Megillat Ta'anit*, 201).

4. According to the Talmud, the Jews, who had a limited amount of food because of the *Shemitah* year, ate the crops of their opponents, who fled and deserted them; this does not make sense in North Africa (where the *shemitah* would not be observed), but is perfectly intelligible if the plaintiffs are "the Canaanites"; see M. M. Kasher, *Torah Shelemah* [in Hebrew] (New York: 1948, repr. Jerusalem: Beth Torah Shelemah, 1992), 12, 44 n. 569; H. Z. Hirschberg, *History of the Jews in North Africa* (Leiden: Brill, 1974), 1:44; M. Kister, "Metamorphoses of Aggadic Traditions" [in Hebrew] *Tarbiz* 60 (1991): 220.

5. M. Weinfeld, *The Promise of the Land: The Inheritance of Canaan by the Israelites* (Berkeley and Los Angeles: University of California, 1993). See also B. J. Schwartz, "Reexamining the Fate of the Canaanites in the Torah Traditions," in *Sefer Moshe: The Moshe Weinfeld Jubilee Volume*, ed. C. Cohen, A. Hurvitz, and S. M. Paul (Winona Lake, Ind.: Eisenbrauns, 2004), 151–170.

6. M. Weinfeld, "The Ban of the Canaanites in the Biblical Codes and Its Historical Development," in *History and Traditions of Early Israel: Studies Presented to Eduard Nielsen*, ed. A. Lemaire and B. Otzen (Leiden: Brill, 1993; SVT 50), 142–160. See Amos 2:9; the total annihilation of the Canaanites seems to have been carried out, according to this verse, by God himself. See also the traditions concerning the mysterious צרעה in Exod 23:28, Deut 7:20, and Josh 24:12.

7. Weinfeld, *Promise of the Land*, 76–96.

8. See S. M. Paul, *Amos: A Commentary on the Book of Amos* (Minneapolis: Fortress, 1991; Hermeneia), 282–284.

9. J. H. Tigay, *The JPS Torah Commentary: Deuteronomy* (Philadelphia: JPS, 1996), 27, 29.

10. See, e.g., J. Skinner, *Genesis* (Edinburgh: T & T Clark, 1994; ICC), 186; I. L. Seeligmann, "Aetiological Elements in Biblical Historiography" [in Hebrew], *Zion* 26 (1961): 156. Note that Canaan was punished for inappropriate behavior related to sexual licentiousness, which is the sin of the Canaanites according to Lev 18:3, 18:24, 18:27.

11. Hebrew: וישכן. The word may refer either to Japhet or to God; see commentaries. See also below in the section "Canaan's Two Curses in the Book of Jubilees".

12. The word למו in v. 26 could also be interpreted in the plural, as referring to "his brothers" (v. 25), but this is somewhat awkward, because the preceding words refer only to Shem, and thus a singular form would be expected. A solution to the various problems of this verse (textual, linguistic, and contextual) is of course far beyond the scope of this chapter. I mention this problem because it is significant for the understanding of post-biblical passages (see below, n. 19).

13. A major reason for that is apparently that the fate of the Canaanites is seldom described in the Bible as servitude. While this is not a valid objection for interpreting the plain text of the Bible, it could certainly motivate post-biblical exegetes. The centrality of this passage in the present context is striking (see also below n. 103 for the use made of it in the *Wisdom of Solomon*). It is possible that in one text of the Second Temple period Noah's curse

was interpreted as referring to the enslavement of the Gibeonites; Joshua says, according to this text: וה[נ]ה נתתיו עבד ע]בדים ליש[ראל (4Q522 9 ii, 11, according to the reading of E. Qimron, *The Dead Sea Scrolls: The Hebrew Writings* [in Hebrew; Jerusalem: Yad Ben Zvi, 2013], 2.76), but the reconstruction עבד עבדים "slave of slaves" is conjectural, and hence the relation of this passage to Noah's curse is tentative).

14. 4Q252 II 5–8; see G. J. Brooke, "252. 4QCommentary on Genesis A," *Qumran Cave 4.XVII: Parabiblical Texts, Part 3* (Oxford: Clarendon Press, 1996; DJD 22), 198.

15. Brooke, "252," 200.

16. Philo, QG 2.65; see R. Marcus, *Questions and Answers on Genesis Translated from the Ancient Armenian Version of the Original Greek* (London: William Heinemann, 1953; LCL), 156.

17. Josephus, *A.J.*, 1.139–142 (trans. H. St. J. Thackeray, *Josephus in Nine Volumes*, vol. 4, *Jewish Antiquities, Books I–IV* [London: W. Heinemann, 1930; LCL], 67–69). See also L. H. Feldman, *Judaean Antiquities 1–4: Translation and Commentary* (Leiden: Brill, 2000), 50–51, who draws attention to Philo and to rabbinic literature.

18. For a suggestion concerning the main motif(s) of the anthology of para-biblical passages in 4Q252, see M. Kister, "Notes on Some New Texts from Qumran," *JSS* 44 (1993): 287–289.

19. The basic argument is that the land, as well as every possession of the Canaanites, belongs to Israel because of Canaan's status of slavery. According to the tradition in *Megillat Ta'anit*, however (see above, n. 3), the Canaanites are the servants of Alexander the Great. This is not sheer flattery, but a reading of the words ויהי כנען עבד למו as referring to Japhet, or to both Shem and Japhet (see above, n. 12).

20. It is not impossible that such an argument was employed as early as the Second Temple period, although it is hitherto unattested. A similar legal emphasis is found in unit B, which deals with the legal status of Ishmael and his rights as a firstborn. A passage of the *Book of Jubilees* is motivated by a similar problem, namely the legal status of Esau, which is solved in a similar legal manner; it makes Esau say: "I sold (it) to Jacob; I gave my birthright to Jacob. It is to be given to him. I will say absolutely nothing about it because it belongs to him" (36:14). The phrase "I will say nothing about it" is a legal formulation meaning "I have no further claims"; for the usage of the word *dibber* for "suing" see, for instance, 1 Kgs 3:22; for formulae similar to the one in the *Book of Jubilees* such as דין ודברים אין לי בנכסיך, *m. Ketub.* 9:1 (reflecting the Aramaic legal expression מלין לאיתי [=לא איתי] לי; דין ודבב] לי, Se 8a:12–13 (A. Yardeni, 'Nahal Se'elim' Documents [Beer Sheva: Ben Gurion University, 1995], 103). It should be noted, however, that the *Book of Jubilees* is interested in the legally binding announcement concerning the transfer of the firstborn rights and the property that accompanies them from Esau to Jacob, whereas the tradition in *Genesis Rabbah* is interested in the legal aspect of the transfer of these rights and possessions from Ishmael to Isaac.

21. *Jub.* 20:4: "Because the descendants of Canaan will be uprooted from the earth."

22. Compare C. Werman, "The Attitude towards Gentiles in the Book of Jubilees and Qumran Literature Compared with Early Tannaitic Halakha and Contemporary Pseudepigrapha" [in Hebrew] (PhD diss., Hebrew University of Jerusalem, 1995), 215–221.

23. Mendels (*Land of Israel*, 69) considers these verses as pointing to a specific historical constellation. I view them as elaborations of biblical motifs that were important for the *Book of Jubilees* on the ideological level.

24. See J. C. VanderKam, "Putting Them in Their Place: Geography as an Evaluative Tool," in *Pursuing the Text: Studies in Honor of Ben Zion Wacholder*, ed. J. C. Reeves and J. Kampen (Sheffield, U.K.: Sheffield Academic Press, 1994; JSOTS 184), 46–69. A close parallel for the

94   The Land: Theological and Ethical Issues

division of the earth among Noah's sons exists in the *Genesis Apocryphon* (the lines concerning Canaan have not been preserved, but much space is dedicated to the division of the earth, and elsewhere Canaan's trespass is mentioned in another context, see below, n. 65); see D. A. Machiela, "Each to His Own Inheritance: Geography as an Evaluative Tool in the Genesis Apocryphon," *DSD* 15 (2008): 50–66.

25. See below, n. 117.

26. VanderKam translates the phrase as "more than all of Noah's children," as does Wintermute (O. S. Wintermute, "Jubilees," in *Old Testament Pseudepigrapha*, ed. J. H. Charlesworth, 2:77). However, Noah's children are not cursed; it seems therefore that the word *emk^welomu* means "by all" (Hebrew: *mikkol*) rather than "more than."

27. Y. Gutman, *The Beginnings of Jewish-Hellenistic Literature* [in Hebrew] (Jerusalem: Mosad Bialik, 1963), 138–143.

28. According to the Pseudo-Clementines, *Recognitions* (1.31), Abraham's ancestors were expelled from the land by force; therefore "God promised him that those districts should be restored rather than given to them" (1.32 [*Die Pseudoklementinen:II: Recognitiones in Rufins Übersetzung*, ed. B. Rehm, GCS 51 (Berlin: Akademie-Verlag, 1965), 26–27]). This explains why, according to the Bible, Terah, Abraham's father, began the journey from Ur to Canaan (Gen 11:31, although this verse is not explicitly mentioned). The *Book of Jubilees* does not give this explanation or hint at it, nor does it mention an expulsion of Shem's descendants from the land. For the passage in the *Pseudo-Clementines* and the interpretation of the *Book of Jubilees*, see R. H. Charles, *The Book of Jubilees: Translated from the Editor's Ethiopic Text and Edited, with Introduction, Notes, and Indices* (London: A & C Black, 1902), 84; J. M. Scott, *Geography in Early Judaism and Christianity: The Book of Jubilees* (Cambridge: Cambridge University, 2002), 97–107 (I am not convinced by the thesis of this chapter). See also below, n. 66.

29. The name "land of Canaan" should not have bothered the Jewish reader unless there was a claim that this name indicated legal ownership; otherwise it would naturally be interpreted as "the land of the Canaanites," who inhabited it before the Israelites (and were uprooted because of their moral behavior).

30. *Midrash Aggadah*, ed. Buber, 1.26: נח החרים בשעה שחלק הקב"ה את הארץ לשלשת בניו שלא יהא אחד סרחה יכ" ה"בקה הוצ רכיפל, סרחה לע ורבעו לארשי ץראו ורבע וייממע 'זו וריבח סוחתל סנכנ סהמ "תחרימם. J. M. Scott, *Geography in Early Judaism*, 39; D. Mendels, *The Land of Israel as a Political Concept in Hasmonean Literature* (Tübingen: Mohr Siebeck, 1987), 65 n. 21. This source can scarcely be attributed to the "sages" (of the talmudic period); it is a medieval compilation of haggadic material, a product of the school of Rabbi Moshe ha-Darshan. This school drew mainly on rabbinic midrashim, but also used ancient sources, derived from the literature of the Second Temple period, either in its original language or in translation (for references to previous discussions of this matter, see M. Kister, "Ancient Material in Pirqe de-Rabbi Eli'ezer: Basilides, Qumran, the Book of Jubilees," in *'Go Out and Study the Land' (Judges 18:2): Archaeological, Historical and Textual Studies in Honor of Hanan Eshel*, ed. A. M. Maier, J. Magness, and L. H. Schiffman (Leiden: Brill, 2011), 69–93.

31. According to *1 Enoch* 6:5–6 Mount Hermon received its name from the oath of the watchers (*'irim*), [ו]אחרמן. 4QEn^a, J. T. Milik, *The Books of Enoch* (Oxford: Clarendon Press, 1976), 150.

32. There is a tension in the tradition, if it is reconstructed correctly, between the emigration of the Canaanites and their annihilation.

33. See VanderKam, "Putting Them in Their Place," 62.

34. Early Christian writers understood that the story of Madai is based on this interpretation of Gen 9:27; see Charles's note to *Jub.* 10:35 from Diodore of Antioch (fourth century C.E.; R. H. Charles, *The Book of Jubilees*, 85).

35. The combination of two interpretative traditions is a well-known phenomenon in the *Book of Jubilees*. For instance, the word אור in the geographical name Ur Kasdim is interpreted as referring to Ur the son of Kesed (*Jub.* 11:1) and also as meaning "fire" (12:12).

36. See also 4Q175, 21–30.

37. Lauterbach prefers the reading ואתן לך ארץ יפה בארצך which he translates: "and will give you a goodly land in your own country"; J. Z. Lauterbach, *Mekilta de-Rabbi Ishmael* (Philadelphia: JPS, 1961), 158–159. Lauterbach interprets "your own country" as Africa, the original homeland of the Canaanites. This reading, however, is implausible: According to this text God granted the Canaanites *another* land as a *reward* for their benevolent deed. Moreover, the parallel in the *Tosefta* and in the Palestinian Talmud prove the originality of the reading ארץ כארצך / כארצכם (see below, n. 39).

38. According to a parallel tradition in the *Sifra* and in the Tannaitic midrash on Leviticus, *Mekhilta de-ʿArayot*, whose text is incorporated into the *Sifra*, the Canaanites' respect toward Abraham granted them forty-seven additional years in their land, in spite of their wicked deeds (*Sifra*, Ahare Mot, parasha 9, 3–7 [ed. Weiss, 85c]).

39. *MRI* Pisha 18 (ed. Horovitz and Rabin 69–70). The translation is based on Lauterbach, *Mekilta*, with several alterations. According to a parallel tradition in *t. Shabb.* 7:25 (ed. Lieberman, 29), Rabban Shimʿon ben Gamaliel states that the Amorites "had faith in God and went to Africa, and God gave them a land as good as theirs [ארץ שיפה כארצם], and the land of Israel was called by their name." The Canaanites were replaced in this tradition by "the Amorites," but the land is called "the land of the Amorites" only very seldom, whereas "the land of Canaan" is the usual name of the land in the Bible, and the latter name needed a justification as early as the second century B.C.E. (*Jubilees*). Therefore, it seems that the wording of the *Tosefta* is secondary in comparison with the text of the *Mekhilta*. According to the *Tosefta*, the Amorites "had faith in God," which also seems a more elaborate form of the tradition. An Amoraic form of this tradition occurs in the Palestinian Talmud (*y. Sheviʿit* 6:1 [36c]; *Lev. Rab.* 17:6 [ed. Margulies, 386]) in the name of the Amora Rabbi Shemuel bar Nahman (late third century B.C.E.):

> Joshua sent three proclamations to the (inhabitants of) the land of Israel before the Israelites entered the land: "Whoever wishes to leave, let him leave; whoever wishes to make peace, let him make peace; whoever wants to fight, let him fight." The Girgashites left and had faith in God and went to Africa; "until I come and take you away to a land as good as your land" (2 Kgs 18:32 = Isa 36:17), this is Africa; the Gibeonites made peace, as it is written, "how the inhabitants of Israel made peace with Israel" (Josh 10:1); the thirty-one kings (Josh 12:24) made war and were defeated.

The phrase "to a land as good as their land" (*Mekhilta*) was erroneously taken in these traditions as an allusion to a biblical verse (2 Kgs 18:32) that is irrelevant in this context (however, it does validate the reading כארצכם; see n. 37). According to the Babylonian Talmud (*b. Sanh.* 94a), Mar Zutra said that the Israelites of the Northern Kingdom were expelled by the Assyrians to Africa; this is clearly the result of the secondary wording of the Palestinian Talmud: While in the tradition of the Palestinian Talmud, Ravshake's words are used because of some flaw of transmission, in the Babylonian Talmud it is inferred from them that the

Assyrians had expelled the ten tribes to Africa. The Canaanites who went to Africa, according to this tradition, are the Girgashites, because they are almost never mentioned in the wars with the inhabitants of Canaan (Josh 3:10, 9:1, 12:8; Judg 3:5; they are mentioned, however, in Josh 24:11). The statement of Rabbi Shemuel bar Nahman revolutionarily reformulates the biblical narrative of the conquest of the land. The limitation of the annihilation of the Canaanites is found also in Tannaitic sources (t. Sotah 8:7; cf. Tosafot b. Sotah 35b s.v. לרבות; Maimonides, Mishneh Torah, Hilkhot Melakhim 6:5). See S. Lieberman, Tosefta ki-Fshutah Sotah [in Hebrew] (New York: Jewish Theological Seminary, 1973), 702; M. Weinfeld, Promise of the Land, 210–213; the bold re-interpretation of the story of the Gibeonites is even more intriguing (cf. Tosafot b. Git. 46a s.v. כיון; Weinfeld, Promise of the Land, 211–213). See also M. D. Herr, "Peace in Rabbinic Thinking" [in Hebrew], in Peace according to Jewish Sources: Lectures in the President's Residence (Jerusalem: President's Residence, 1997), 23–39.

40. Cf. Strabo, Geogr. 16.2.36: "He [Moses] took possession of the place, since it was not a place that would be looked on with envy, nor yet one for which anyone would make a serious fight" (M. Stern, Greek and Latin Authors on Jews and Judaism [Jerusalem: Israel Academy of Sciences and Humanities, 1976], 1:295, 300.

41. A similar sensitivity to this appellation of the land occurs elsewhere in rabbinic literature. According to anonymous Sages (רבנין) in an Amoraic midrash, the name "land of Canaan" was given to the land in order to convey a moral message: As Canaan was inflicted because of Ham's sin, so is the land inflicted because of Israel's sins; according to another anonymous statement, it was called "the land of Canaan" because all its inhabitants were merchants (Lev. Rab. 17:5; ed. Margulies, 383). Both interpretations detach the name "the land of Canaan" from any ethnic identity.

42. Lauterbach, Mekilta de-Rabbi Ishma'el, 107 n. 1. See also S. I. Rapoport, 'Erech Millin [in Hebrew] (Prague: M. I. Landau, 1852), s.v. אפריקא I, 184–185 (this entry includes a number of pioneering observations, alongside some curious speculations); L. Ginzberg, Legends of the Jews (Philadelphia: JPS, 1968), 6:177 n. 34.

43. Josephus, C. Ap. 2.17 (trans. H. St. J. Thackeray, LCL); M. Stern, Greek and Latin Authors, 1:395–97. See Barclay's commentary: "Although Josephus does not reveal it, Apion apparently reflected a triple correlation between the founding of Rome, the founding of Carthage and the Exodus from Egypt. We have to suppose this had some symbolic significance for Apion… [implying] future hostility between Judaeans and Rome" (J. M. G. Barclay, Josephus: Against Apion; Translation and Commentary [Leiden: Brill, 2007], 178 n. 59). This, however, is mere speculation, and the context in which this sentence was written by Apion is a matter of conjecture.

44. See Stern, Greek and Latin Authors, 2:36.

45. Note that according to the Jewish chronology, the Israelites marched seven days before the crossing of the sea, which is celebrated by the second holiday of Pesah; see, e.g., Ezekiel the Tragedian's Exagoge: "But when at last you enter your own land, take heed that from the morn on which you fled from Egypt and did journey seven days, from that same morn, so many days a year you eat unleavened bread and serve your God" (167–171; trans. R. G. Robertson in Old Testament Pseudepigrapha, 2:815; see also H. Jacobson, The Exagoge of Ezekiel [Cambridge: Cambridge University, 1983] 125–126; C. R. Holladay, Fragments from Hellenistic Jewish Authors [Atlanta: Scholars Press, 1989], 2:380–381; Seder 'Olam Rabbah, chapter 5). Ezekiel's wording is based on Exod 13:5: "And when the Lord brings you into the land of the Canaanites, the Hittites, the Amorites, the Hivites and the Jebusites.... Seven days

[LXX: six days] you shall eat unleavened bread and on the seventh day there shall be a feast to the Lord." According to the Jewish material, then, the Israelites marched six or seven days on their way from Egypt, and on the seventh day they were relieved, and this has to be celebrated when they enter their land (after conquering the autochthonous inhabitants of that land). It cannot be ruled out, perhaps, that Gentiles in Alexandria and elsewhere erroneously interpreted a Jewish tradition referring to the seven days of Passover as an etiology for the Sabbath.

46. *C. Ap.* 2.21 (see Barclay, *Josephus: Against Apion*, 179); see also 2.25.

47. Tacitus, *Hist.* 5.3.2 (Stern, *Greek and Latin Authors*, 2:18, 25).

48. See Stern, *Greek and Latin Authors*, 1:397, 1:385 on the chronology.

49. Rappaport, *Erekh Millin*, 185.

50. For the particular mention of the Girgashites see above, n. 39.

51. H. B. Dewing, trans., *Procopius: History of the Wars, Book III–IV* (London: W. Heinemann, 1916; LCL), 2:287–289.

52. Most scholars take the text of the ancient inscription to be an imaginative "reading" of Procopius or his source(s), and rightly so; see P. C. Schmitz, "Procopius' Phoenician Inscriptions: Never Lost, Not Found," *PEQ* 139 (2007): 99–104. I thank Prof. Israel Shatzman for drawing my attention to this article. See also most recently: O. Amitay, "Procopius of Caesarea and the Girgashite Diaspora," *JSP* 20 (2011): 257–276. This article gives a helpful survey of primary sources and scholarship; the possibility entertained there, that the name of Joshua in this inscription has something to do with his Greek namesake, Jesus, seems to me quite unlikely. I thank Dr. Katell Berthelot for drawing my attention to this article.

53. This expression was already noted by Lewy. He considered it "a Hebraism known to Procopius and his readers from the Septuagint" (Lewy, "Rechtsstreit," 99 n. 4).

54. An alternative suggestion is that the alleged text of the inscription is influenced by the style of Christian chronographers, who in their turn developed the tradition of the *Book of Jubilees*, and of passages of the Hebrew Bible (Schmitz, "Procopius Phoenician Inscriptions," 101; see Georgios Synkellos, *Chronography*, ed. A. Mosshammer [Leipzig: Teubner, 1984], 50; English translation: W. Adler and P. Tuffin, *The Chronography of George Synkellos* [Oxford: Oxford University, 2002], 65). Schmitz's suggestion, that the inscription is dependent on Christian chronographers, does not easily account for the word "robber" in it; as we shall presently see, the accusation of "robbery" is by no means unique to Procopius, and I do not think (unlike Schmitz) that the word was added by him. On the other hand, the Semitic preposition מפני (and also expressions like נס מפני, literally: "fled from the face") is common enough not to be necessarily an indication of dependence between texts.

55. *Gen. Rab.* 1:2, ed. Theodor, p. 4. This midrash has a parallel in *Tanhuma Buber Genesis, Bereshit* 11 (ed. Buber, 7): "Rabbi Isaac said: the Torah should have commenced with [the passage] 'this month is for you...'" [Exod 12:2; the first commandment of the Torah]. Why then does it commence with 'At the beginning...' [Gen 1:1], to announce the power of His might [כח גבורתו], as it is said 'He has recounted to His people the power of His works, to grant them the inheritance of the nations' [Ps 111:6]." The first lemma in the Torah commentary by Rashi has a similar midrash, probably taken from some version of the *Tanhuma* literature, which had a closer parallel to the passage cited from *Gen. Rab.* The passage in Rashi's commentary reads: "The Torah should have commenced with 'this month is for you...' [Exod 12:2]... Why does it commence with 'In the beginning?' Because [of what is implied by the verse] 'He has recounted to His people the power of His works, to grant them the inheritance of the nations' [Ps 111:6]; for if the nations of the world should say to Israel, 'You are robbers [ליסטים אתם], for

you conquered [by force] the lands of the seven nations [of Canaan],' they [Israel] will reply, 'The entire earth belongs to the Holy One, blessed be He [כל הארץ של הקב"ה היא]; He created it and gave it to whomever He deemed proper. When He wished, He gave it to them, and when He wished, He took it away from them and gave it to us.'" For possible (doubtful) motives for opening Rashi's commentary with this passage see E. Touitou, "The Historical Background of Rashi's Commentary on Genesis 1–5" [in Hebrew], in *Rashi Studies*, ed. Z. A. Steinfeld (Ramat-Gan: Bar Ilan, 1993), 101–102. The Christian parallel discussed in Touitou's article seems to me rather remote. For another parallel in the *Tanhuma* literature, see below. 157.

56. J. C. Greenfield, "Našu-Nadanu and Its Cognates," in *Al Kanfei Yonah: Collected Studies of Jonas Greenfield on Semitic Philology* (Jerusalem: Magnes, 2001), 724; M. Kister, "Some Early Jewish and Christian Exegetical Problems and the Dynamics of Monotheism," *JSJ* 37 (2006): 553–563.

57. Philo, *Opif.*, §§1–3.

58. R. Devreesse, *Les anciens commentateurs grecs de l'Octateuque et des Rois: Fragments tirés des chaînes* (Vatican City: Biblioteca apostolica vaticana, 1959), 106.

59. H. Lewy, "Ein Rechtsstreit um den Boden Palästinas im Altertum," *MGWJ* 77 (1933): 84–99, 172–180. This article enjoyed great influence also in its Hebrew version: J. H. Levy, *Studies in Jewish Hellenism* (עולמות נפגשים) (Jerusalem: Mosad Bialik, 1969), 60–78.

60. Compare: V. Aptowizer, "Les premiers possesseurs de Canaan: Légendes apologétiques exégétiques," *REJ* 82 (1926): 275–286.

61. Lewy, "Rechtsstreit," 173–174, 180.

62 . Lewy, "Rechtsstreit," 95.

63 . This is clear enough, I think, when one compares the *Book of Jubilees* with other traditions, which have much in common but are not derived from the former.

64. Recently it has been suggested that the *Genesis Apocryphon* was a source of the *Book of Jubilees* (M. Segal, "The Literary Relationship between the *Genesis Apocryphon* and *Jubilees*: The Chronology of Abram and Sarai's Descent to Egypt," *Aramaic Studies* 8 [2010]: 71–88); for a contradicting view, however, see J. L. Kugel, "Which Is Older, *Jubilees* or the *Genesis Apocryphon*? An Exegetical Approach," in *The Dead Sea Scrolls and Contemporary Culture*, ed. A. D. Roitman et al., *STDJ* 93 (Leiden: Brill, 2011), 257–294. See also C. Werman, "The Book of Jubilees and Its Aramaic Sources" [in Hebrew], *Meghillot* 8–9 (2010): 135–154.

65. This seems to underlie 14:14–18 as well as 19:12–13, where the land of Israel is called "our land" in the mouth of Abraham (in contrast to "the land of Ham"); see D. A. Machiela, *The Dead Sea Genesis Apocryphon*, *STDJ* 79 (Leiden: Brill, 2009), 98–99, 92, 133.

66. בני חם לבני שם (4Q529 1 7 (4Q529 17); see E. Puech, *Qumrân grotte 4.XXII: Textes araméens première partie*, DJD 31 (Oxford: Clarendon Press, 2001), 4 (Puech's restoration [בין] בני שם לבני חם seems to me unlikely; the meaning is more plausibly that the sons of Ham captured or expelled [see above, n. 28] the sons of Shem).

67. I. Shatzman, "The Hasmoneans in Greco-Roman Historiography" [in Hebrew], *Zion* 57 (1992): 5–64.

68. Lewy, "Rechtsstreit," 94.

69. Strabo, or rather his source, idealizes Moses, and contrasts him with the Hasmonean "tyrants"; see B. Bar-Kochva, *The Image of the Jews in Greek Literature* (Berkeley and Los Angeles: University of California Press, 2010), 391–397.

70. Stern, *Greek and Latin Authors*, 1:295, 300, 306; Bar-Kochva, *Image of the Jews*, 376–379.

71. Stern, *Greek and Latin Authors*, 1:182–183.

72. Tacitus, *Hist.* 5.3.2 (Stern, *Greek and Latin Authors*, 281).

73. Bar-Kochva, *Image of the Jews*, 333–337; for a thorough analysis of Lysimachus's account of the Exodus story see Bar-Kochva, *Image of the Jews*, 306–337.

74. Shatzman contends this in a forthcoming work. I am grateful to him for showing me the relevant passages prior to its publication.

75. P. S. Alexander, "Retelling the Old Testament," in *It Is Written: Scripture Citing Scripture; Essays in Honour of Barnabas Lindars* (Cambridge: Cambridge University, 1988), 102–103. In a note (118 n. 3) Alexander says: "The author of Jubilees may also have in mind the accusation, well attested at a later date, that the Jews were 'brigands' who had stolen the land of others," and he refers to the works of Bacher, Lewy, and Hirschberg. See also VanderKam's assertion: "The way in which *Jubilees* formulates the Canaanite usurpation makes one believe that when the book was written the issue of who owned Canaan was debated" (J. C. VanderKam, "Putting Them in Their Place," 67–69; for his attitude to former scholarship see 68, n. 46). See also O. Amitay, "The Story of Gviha Ben-Psisa and Alexander the Great," *JSP* 16 (2006): 61–74; the author contends that "Alexander" in the tradition cited in full at the beginning of this chapter, *Gen. Rab.* 61:7 and parallels, reflects the historical figure of Pompey, and that Hasmonean conquests are referred to. His argument, "The story takes for granted that Eretz Israel is already under Jewish rule.... The legitimacy of [the Jewish] sovereignty over the land is under attack" (65), is not convincing: According to the story, the Canaanites proclaimed their ownership of the whole territory called Eretz Israel by the Jews and thus can scarcely be related to any specific historical constellation. The accusations in the presence of Alexander the Great reflect, as we have seen, arguments with which the Jews struggled in the Second Temple period, and it is therefore not necessary that the contest of Jews and Canaanites before a Gentile king using the Torah as evidence reflects any historical event at all.

76. I. Shatzman, "Jews and Gentiles from Judas Maccabaeus to John Hyrcanus according to Contemporary Jewish Sources," in *Studies in Josephus and the Varieties of Ancient Judaism: Louis H. Feldman Jubilee Volume*, ed. S. J. D. Cohen and J. J. Schwartz (Leiden: Brill, 2007), 237–270.

77. Shatzman, "Jews and Gentiles," 264–265; see also 270.

78. Even if, as I personally tend to believe, the *Book of Jubilees* was composed in the Hasmonean kingdom.

79. S. Japhet, The Ideology of the Book of Chronicles and Its Place in Biblical Thought [in Hebrew] (Jerusalem: Bialik Institute, 1977), 303–309.

80. See also the detailed discussion of Katell Berthelot, "The Biblical Conquest of the Promised Land and the Hasmonaean Wars according to *1* and *2 Maccabees*," in *The Books of the Maccabees: History, Theology, Ideology*, ed. G. G. Xeravitz and J. Zsengellér, JSJS 118 (Leiden: Brill, 2007), 45–60.

81. Francis Schmidt has written: "The *Jubilees* sect, by thus modifying the Table of Nations... demanded of its adversaries that they hold strictly to their fathers' promises, under the threat of a curse, while reminding them of the absolute prominence of Shem's descendants over the descendants of Japhet or Ham" ("Jewish Representations of the Inhabited Earth during the Hellenistic and Roman Periods," in *Greece and Rome in Eretz Israel*, ed. A. Kasher, U. Rappaport, and G. Fuks [Jerusalem: Yad Ben-Zvi and Israel Exploration Society, 1990], 131–134). None of Japhet's offspring, however, committed such a trespass according to the *Book of Jubilees!* Schmidt's suggestion was followed and modified by Machiela: "It seems likely that Jubilees is also making a claim on the land vis-à-vis foreign occupation.... The Greeks may

be the target of such a claim...against those modern Canaanites, the Greeks, who possess the audacity to usurp a land not their own in explicit contradiction to divine mandate" (Machiela, *The Dead Sea Genesis Apocryphon*, 120); this is, however, what we do not find in the *Genesis Apocryphon*: assertions against Japhet's conquest of the land.

82. *Gen. Rab.* 88:1 (ed. Theodor-Albeck, 1077–1078).

83. *Gen. Rab.* 95, according to MS Vatican 30 (ed. Theodor-Albeck, 1234).

84. The expression occurs also in other midrashim: in *Song Rab.* 4:12 the nations taunt Israel by saying that the Israelites were the children of Egyptians (who raped the Israelite women; see also a parallel in a *Yelamdenu* passage, in J. Mann and I. Sonne, *The Bible as Read and Preached in the Old Synagogue* [Cincinnati, Ohio: Hebrew Union College, 1996], Hebrew section 164). This is a defamation of the Jews as bastards in a type of counter-history similar to other "anti-Semitic" narratives (for the narrative that those who left Egypt at the time of the Exodus were in fact Egyptians see, e.g., Manetho and Chairemon [Josephus, *C. Ap.* 1.233, 1.289, 1.305]), but the point these authors make is different). While the formula discussed here is used in *Gen. Rab.* for arguments of Gentiles aimed at defaming the Jewish people ethnically, in midrashim later to *Gen. Rab.* (*PRK*, Shor o kesev, 7 [ed. Mandelboim, 157]; *Song Rab.* 1:6:3, 8:9:2; *Lam. Rab.* 3:7) it is used *mainly* to express the Christian views that the Jews were idol worshippers by nature (exemplified by the golden calf episode) and that they have been abandoned by God.

85. Thus Manetho, Chairemon, Lysimachus (Josephus, *C. Ap.*, 1.233, 1.289, 1.305) and others. See Bar-Kochva, *Image of the Jews*, 327, 364. The notion that those who left Egypt at the time of the Exodus were lepers, and that Moses himself was infected by leprosy, was known to the rabbis, who responded to it implicitly. Thus we read that Pharaoh was a leper (*Exod. Rab.* 1:34) and that his daughter, who had been infected by leprosy, was cured from it when she took Moses out of the Nile (*Tanhuma Exodus*, Shemot 7). A rabbinic interpretation of Exod 4:6 (where the mention of leprosy was omitted as early as the LXX) takes pains to assert that Moses was not a leper (*Exod. Rab.* 3:13); the same verse is interpreted symbolically as implying that the Egyptians were impure and defiled Israel (*Tanhuma Exodus*, Shemot 23; *Exod. Rab.* 3:13), quite contrary to the allegations of the above-mentioned writers that the Jews were expelled from Egypt because they had been impure and had defiled Egypt. These midrashic statements (most of which happen to belong to the postclassical *Tanhuma* literature) are probably reactions to the anti-Jewish pagan narrative; this is also the case of *Gen. Rab.* 88:1, discussed here.

86. Taking into account the occurrence of this tradition in the *Book of Jubilees* and *Genesis Rabbah*, it may scarcely be considered "a product of the propaganda of Greek and Hellenized Poeni in Africa, who sought to defame the Jews when these began to arrive in increasing numbers" (Hirschberg, *History of the Jews in North Africa*, 46).

87. It is not impossible, of course, that such accusations had, under some historical circumstances, territorial dimensions and that they were raised by Hellenized Phoenicians (as suggested by Lewy), but this is no more than a guess, and the present data do not lead me in this direction.

88. Philo, *Hypoth.* 6:6–7.

89. This is the wording of F. H. Colson, *Philo in Ten Volumes* (London: William Heinemann, 1941), 9:408 (concerning our subject he writes: "I find it difficult to understand the motive of Philo in this treatment of the story," 9:409). David Rokeah, in his Hebrew translation of the *Hypothetica* (*Philo of Alexandria: Writings* [in Hebrew], ed. S. Daniel-Nataf [Jerusalem: Israel Academy of Sciences and Humanities, 1986], 158 n. 7), refers to Lewy's article.

90. Josephus, *C. Ap.* 1.62; see Barclay, *Josephus: Against Apion*, 44. For Apollonius Molon's accusation of Jewish cowardice, see also Bar-Kochva, *Image of the Jews*, 492–496.

91. See Weinfeld, *Promise of the Land*, 210, and his conclusion: "In this case there are clear overlappings between the rabbinic literature and the Jewish-Hellenistic writings of the Second Temple period. One should therefore view the rabbinic traditions as rooted in the ideological reality of the first century C.E." (Weinfeld, *Promise of the Land*, 213 n. 66). Katell Berthelot has shown the different strategies in Philo's writings concerning the conquest of Canaan and the fate of the Canaanites (K. Berthelot, "Philo of Alexandria and the Conquest of Canaan," *JSJ* 38 [2007]: 39–59.) She introduces a parallel from Strabo's account of the conquest of the land, a parallel that seems to me less impressive than the tradition of the *Mekhilta*. Philo apparently is less "original and personal" than it might seem; plausibly, he makes use of an already existing tradition.

92. I do not conclude from the similarity of wording of Philo and the midrash that either is dependent on the other. If it is not a coincidence (and it does not seem to me to be so), it is to be explained as a tradition common to Philo and the rabbis (or their predecessors).

93. Contrast Shatzman, who draws a clear line between the *Book of Jubilees* and later traditions ("Jews and Gentiles," 264).

94. Concerning the pericope of the dispute with the Egyptians, see above, n. 3.

95. Lewy mentions this passage *en passant* in a footnote; see Lewy, "Rechtsstreit," 96 n. 3.

96. Note that this particular nation is mentioned here; see above, nn. 39, 50.

97. Epiphanius, *Pan.* 66, 83, ed. K. Holl, GCS 37 (Berlin: Akademie Verlag, 1985), 124; F. Williams, trans., *The Panarion of Epiphanius of Salamis: Books II and III* (Leiden: Brill, 1994), 302.

98. David Rokeah has stressed "the transmutation of the pagan-Jewish polemic into a pagan-Christian one" (D. Rokeah, "Jews and Their Law (Torah) in the Pagan-Christian Polemic in the Roman Empire" [in Hebrew], *Tarbiz* 40 (1971): 471; D. Rokeah, *Jews, Pagans and Christians in Conflict* [Jerusalem: Magnes, 1982], esp. 211). For a discussion of a case study in which a Jewish-pagan debate concerning resurrection was used for inter-Christian debates, see also M. Kister, "Allegorical Interpretations of Biblical Narratives in Jewish Palestine, Philo and Origen: Some Test Cases," in *New Approaches to the Study of Biblical Interpretation in Judaism of the Second Temple Period and in Early Christianity: Proceedings of the Eleventh International Symposium of the Orion Center for the Study of the Dead Sea Scrolls and Associated Literature, Jointly Sponsored by the Hebrew University Center for the Study of Christianity, 9–11 January, 2007*, ed. G. A. Anderson, D. Satran, and R. C. Clements (Leiden: Brill, 2013; STDJ 106 forthcoming).

99. Rapoport and Bacher note the similarity in wording between Procopius's "inscription" and Balaam's "*pinax*" (Rapoport *Erech Millin*, s.v. אפריקא, 184; W. Bacher, "The Supposed Inscription upon 'Joshua the Robber' [Illustrated from Jewish Sources]," *JQR* O.S. 3 [1891]: 354–357). They also noted that "Robbery" is the indictment of the "nations of the world" in *Gen. Rab.* 1:2 and the *Tanhuma* (above, n. 55).

100. *Sifra, Mekhilta de-ʿArayot*, Qedoshim, on Lev 20:24 (ed. Weiss, 93c).

101. The *Sifra* was composed some decades prior to Mani's activity. It consists of much earlier material.

102. This may be inferred from Exod 23:29, where it is stated that the Canaanites will not be expelled immediately so that the land will not become desolate. Note that a tradition (probably of Jewish origin) recorded by Epiphanius regards the Samaritans as "guardians

of the land"; they were brought to the land so that it does not become desolate after the ten tribes had been exiled (Epiphanius, *De Gemmis: The Old Georgian Version and the Fragments of the Armenian Version*, ed. R. P. Blake [London: Christophers, 1934], 189). This is clearly an explanation of the name שמרים, which the Samaritans gave to their own group. While the Samaritans considered themselves ancestors of Joseph and understood the name as meaning the (real) *observers* of the Torah (this explanation is also recorded by Epiphanius in the same sentence) or guardians of the holy place, the explanation of the name as "guardians of the land" (for the ten tribes) stresses the foreign origin of the Samaritans and their temporary presence in the land.

103. Wis 12:3–18.

104. K. Berthelot, "'Ils jettent au feu leurs fils et leurs filles pour leurs dieux': Une justification humaniste du massacre des Cananéens dans les textes juifs anciens?" *RB* 112 (2005): 161–191, esp. 174–182.

105. God does not uproot the Canaanites immediately in order to give the Canaanites a chance to repent (compare Exod 23:29). Similarly, according to a Tannaitic passage, the Israelites addressed the Canaanites before capturing the land, saying: "If you repent, we will accept you" (*t. Sotah* 8:7; ed. Lieberman, 205). See Weinfeld, *Promise of the Land*, 211.

106. See Winston, *Wisdom of Solomon*, 242; Kister, "Some Early Jewish and Christian Exegetical Problems," 553–563, esp. 559–561.

107. L. Ginzberg, *Ginze Schechter* (New York: Jewish Theological Seminary, 1928), 1:151–152.

108. See note 28.

109. W. Adler, "The Origins of the Proto-Heresies: Fragments from a Chronicle in the First Book of Epiphanius' Panarion," *JTS* 41 (1990): 472–501, esp. 488–501. Adler suggests that the source for this tradition is the early Christian chronographer Julius Africanus.

110. See S. E. Loewenstamm, s.v. נחל מצרים, *Encyclopedia Biblica* [in Hebrew] (Jerusalem: Bialik Institute, 1968), 813–814.

111. Adler, "The Origins of the Proto-Heresies," 496: "The Rhinocorura tradition is developed from the Greek rendering of Isa 27:12...evidently associating the word נחל with the Hebrew word נחלה (Gr. κλῆρος). Epiphanius even identifies Rhinocorura as the site where Noah divided the earth." It could be inferred from this sentence, but it is not explicitly stated by Adler, that the tradition could emerge only in Hebrew (if my following suggestion is correct, it emerged from a midrashic reading of the MT), and therefore is likely to be of Jewish origin.

112. LXX: καὶ ὕδατος Μαριμωθ Καδης κληρονομία[ς]; similarly *Targum Jonathan* (אחסנא) and the Peshitta (יורתנה) as well as Vulgate "hereditas." Modern interpreters consider נחלה in v. 28 to be a place name and identify it with נחל מצרים, Wadi Al-'Arish; see, e.g., D. I. Block, *The Book of Ezekiel: Chapters 25–48* (Grand Rapids, Mich.: 1998; NICOT), 720 (see also 717).

113. LXX: ἣν βαλεῖτε ἐν κλήρῳ ταῖς φυλαῖς Ισραηλ; similarly *Targum Jonathan* (דתפלגון באחסנא) and the Peshitta (דתפלגון ירתותה).

114. The problem of the border of the land of Canaan should be discussed elsewhere: Is it "the brooke of Egypt," Wadi al-'Arish, as in Epiphanius, or the Nile, as in *Jub.* 8:22 and the *Genesis Apocryphon* (1QGenAp 19:12–13; see also Gen 15:18; 1 Chr 13:5)? And how is it related to *Jub.* 10:29?

115. The dialogue in its present form is probably from the fifth or sixth century C.E. It draws, however, on much older material, some of it shared with passages in Epiphanius.

According to some scholars, the dialogue is based on earlier forms of it; see J. Z. Pastis, "Dating the Dialogue of Timothy and Aquila: Revisiting the Earlier *Vorlage* Hypothesis," *HTR* 95 (2002): 169–195; L. Lahey, "The Dialogue of Timothy and Aquila: Critical Greek Text and English Translation of the Short Recension with an Introduction Including a Source-critical Study," PhD diss., Cambridge University, 2000.

116. The biblical text reads "Canaan," which is more appropriate in the context of the dialogue, both in this sentence and in the sentences omitted in this citation. A grave error of transmission seems to have occurred at this point.

117. Compare the two curses in the *Book of Jubilees* (discussed above) and especially the wording "You *are* cursed and *will be* cursed" (*Jub.* 10:32); this wording may well be interpreted as referring to two distinct curses of Ham.

118. *Dialogue of Timothy and Aquila* 31.3–16, according to W. Varner, *Ancient Jewish-Christian Dialogues: Athanasius and Zacchaeus, Simon and Theophilus, Timothy and Aquila; Introduction, Texts and Translations* (Lewiston, N.Y.: Edwin Mellen, 2004), 210–213.

119. See above, n. 115.

120. I changed the order of the midrashic units to facilitate comparison with *Gen. Rab.*

121. See above, n. 55.

122. See P. F. Beatrice, "The Treasures of the Egyptians: A Chapter in the History of Patristic Exegesis and Late Antique Culture," *StPatr* 39 (2006): 159–183; J. S. Allen, *The Despoliation of Egypt in Pre-Rabbinic, Rabbinic, and Patristic Traditions*, SVC 92 (Leiden: Brill, 2008). For a different point of view, see G. J. Blidstein, "The Despoliation of Egypt in Rabbinic Literature" [in Hebrew], in *Studies in Halakhic and Aggadic Thought* (Beer-Sheva: Ben Gurion University, 2004), 11–23. Blidstein is certainly right that several traditions in rabbinic literature are not apologetic, but to my mind there is an apologetic component in many rabbinic traditions concerning this subject.

123. The similarity in wording between Exod 3:21 and Deut 15:13 may be noted. If the two verses are read together, the property of the Egyptians taken by the Israelites is only a fair grant given to them as to every freed slave. It is doubtful, however, whether the resemblance between the two verses had an important role in the emergence of the post-biblical arguments: Not only are the verses not explicitly connected, the Egyptian property is not described in the terms of a grant given to slaves after the legitimate period of slavery has ended.

124. The *Book of Jubilees* does not mention that it was God who commanded the Israelites to take the Egyptians' property with them.

125. D. Winston, *The Wisdom of Solomon* (New York: Doubleday, 1979; AB), 220.

126. C. R. Holladay, *Fragments from Hellenistic Jewish Authors*, 2:381; Jacobson, *Exagoge*, 126–127.

127. The *Wisdom of Solomon*, the *Exagoge*, and Philo are Jewish-Hellenistic sources, probably written in Egypt. The struggle with the problem in the *Book of Jubilees* clearly indicates that it was not exclusive to Hellenistic Judaism, or to Egypt, as one could have thought.

128. This may well have been influenced by the usage of σκυλεύω, the Greek verb in which Hebrew נצל is rendered (Exod 3:22, 12:36). This verb could have military connotation in Greek. In the LXX the verb renders words derived from the Hebrew roots בז and שלל. (See also the Hebrew usage in 2 Chr 20:25.) In the Peshitta to Exod 12:36, Hebrew נצל is rendered חלץ ("to take spoil, seize"). The common rabbinic term ביזת מצרים could be based on a similar interpretation of a military victory (compare: Blidstein, "Despoliation," 13), and perhaps even on a similar interpretation of Exod 3:22, 12:36, although interestingly

such a military interpretation does not occur either in the midrashim or in the targumim (it should be noted that the rendering of נצל in the Peshitta to Exod 3:22 agrees in meaning with the targumim).

129. Philo, *Moses* 1.141–142 (trans. F. H. Colson, *Philo in an English Translation* [London: William Heinemann, 1935] 4.349, with some modifications).

130. In this context it is found also in Haman's "anti-Semitic" accusations of the Jews in *Esther Rabbah* 7:13. As has been noted (Amitay, "The Story of Gviha," 69 n. 32; Allen, *Despoliation*, 277), a similar "juristic" case was raised quite recently: The Egyptian jurist, Dr. Nabil Hilmi, Dean of the Faculty of Law at the University of Zaqaziq, prepared in August 2003 a lawsuit against "all the Jews of the world." According to Dr. Hilmi, "this theft...fits the morals and the character of the Jews" (for an interview with Dr. Hilmi, see the online site of *MEMRI*, August 22, 2003, special dispatch no. 556). According to another site, Alan Dershowitz, a Harvard law professor who is a Jew, said that such a suit "invites a countersuit from the Jews....[It] could also be calculated in trillions of dollars and would expose the oppressive life the Jews had under the Egyptian slavery" (ReligionNewsBlog.com, August 29, 2003). While one might suspect that Dershowitz *could have* access to the rabbinic story, this is most probably not the case with the Egyptian jurist, who developed it on the basis of the biblical account. The two jurists formulated their claims in legal terms, but there is no question that anti-Jewish propaganda is the only thing at stake here.

131. Artapanus (apud Clement of Alexandria, *Stromata* 1.36; C.R. Holladay, *Fragments from Hellenistic Jewish Authors* ([Atlanta: Scholars Press, 1983], 1:224, 242 n. 113. For an overview of the Gentile accounts of the "expulsion from Egypt" in antiquity, see P. Schäfer, *Judeophobia* (Cambridge, Mass.: Harvard University, 1997), 15–33. I do not agree with Allen's assertion that "Josephus' argument, as well as many other pre-rabbinic interpretations, depend upon the ignorance of the reader," whereas the rabbis "were aware that their opponents knew the Hebrew Scriptures too well to be fooled" (Allen, *Despoliation*, 176). Josephus writes that the Egyptians "honored the Hebrews with gifts, some in order that they might depart more swiftly, others from neighborly relations with them" (*Ant.* 2.314). Josephus here combines two biblical interpretations: giving gifts to the Israelites "in order that they might depart more swiftly" is based on reading Exod 12:33 together with Exod 12:35; the "neighborly relations" mentioned by Josephus are an interpretation of Exod 12:36 on the basis of Exod 3:22 (and 11:2) where the neighborly relations are emphasized (compare *MRShY* on Exod 12:36, ed. Epstein and Melamed, 31 lines 6–7). Josephus' account is thus based on subtle exegetical considerations similar to the exegetical solutions in rabbinic midrash combined with an apologetic tendency. On the other hand, it is unclear how well the opponents of the rabbis knew the Bible. The only thing that can be said is that the matter was seriously treated both by Josephus and by the rabbis. See also J. L. Kugel, *Traditions of the Bible* (Cambridge Mass.: Harvard University Press, 1998), 554–555.

132. M. Stern, Greek and Latin Authors on Jews and Judaism, 1:335, 337.

133. Contrast Winston, *Wisdom of Solomon*, 220; Allen, *Despoliation*, 99; and others.

134. Philo, *Abr.* 178–199: "But quarrelsome critics who misconstrue everything and have a way of valuing censure above praise do not think Abraham's action [sacrificing Isaac] great and wonderful. They say that many other persons...have given their children, some to be sacrificed for their country to serve as a price to redeem it from wars or drought or excessive rainfall or pestilence, others for the sake of what was held to be piety"; *Conf.* 2: "Persons who cherish a dislike of the institutions of our fathers and make it their constant study to

denounce and decry the Laws…say: 'See, your so-called holy books contain also myths, which you regularly deride' "; *QG* 3.3: "But I am not unaware that all such things give occasion to idle calumniators to reject the Sacred Writings and to talk nonsense about them"; *QG* 1.53: "Some may ridicule the text when they consider the cheapness of the apparel of tunics, as being unworthy of the touch of such a creator." The first three citations criticize and undermine the authority of the biblical text by tools of "comparative religion"; I do not think such an attitude can be attributed to Philo's "Jewish colleagues" who had interpreted the Torah critically and "had gone too far in the research in Philo's eyes" only, as suggested by Maren Niehoff concerning the passage in the *Confusion of Tongues* (M. Niehoff, *Jewish Exegesis and Homeric Scholarship in Alexandria* [Cambridge: Cambridge University, 2011], 77–94; the words quoted are on p. 92). These passages demonstrate that Philo had to face a critical and *negative* reading of the biblical text that probably had been put down in writing (*Conf.* 14). I do not know who these critics were. (Were they Pagans who took the trouble to read passages of the Pentateuch? Jewish apostates? When did they flourish?)

135. For the question regarding the extent to which the Bible was known (directly or indirectly) to the pagans prior to the emergence of Christianity, see, e.g., M. Amit, "Worlds Which Did Not Meet," in *The Jews in the Hellenistic-Roman World: Studies in Memory of Menahem Stern* [in Hebrew], ed. I. M. Gafni, A. Oppenheimer, and D. R. Schwartz (Jerusalem: Zalman Shazar Center and the Historical Society of Israel, 1996), 260–267; J. G. Cook, *The Interpretation of the Old Testament in Greco-Roman Paganism* (Tübingen: Mohr Siebeck, 2004); P. W. van der Horst, "Did the Gentiles Know Who Abraham Was?" in *Abraham, the Nations and the Hagarites*, ed. M. Goodman et al. (Leiden: Brill, 2010), 61–75.

136. Above, n. 97.

137. According to a haggadah in the Babylonian Talmud (*Ber.* 9a–b, in the name of the Palestinian *Amora* Rabbi Yanai), the Israelites did not desire the Egyptians' money, and it was God who asked them to take it in order to fulfill His promise to Abraham. This tradition denies Israel's covetousness by putting all the responsibility for Egypt's despoliation on God; this demonstrates that, at least for the author of this haggadah, the main challenge was ethnic rather than theological.

138. I. Lévi, "La dispute entre les Egyptiens et les Juifs devant Alexandre: Echo des polémiques antijuives à Alexandrie," *REJ* 63 (1912): 211–215. In this passage, Tertullian drew mainly, or solely, on a rabbinic tradition similar to the one in *Gen. Rab.* 61:7. As happens quite often, the church fathers' use of the tradition demonstrates that the tradition is earlier than the works in which it is recorded in rabbinic literature.

139. *Marc.* 2.20.4 (*Tertullianis Opera:1*, ed. A. Kroymann, CCSL 1 [Turnholt: Typographi Brepols, 1964], 498). The translation is based on A. Roberts and J. Donaldson (eds.), *Ante-Nicene Fathers* (repr. Grand Rapids, Mich.: Eerdmans, 1985), 3:313.

140. Concerning a similar anti-Jewish argument of Christians, see D. Berger, "On the Morality of the Patriarchs in Jewish Polemic and Exegesis," in *Understanding Scripture: Explorations of Jewish and Christian Traditions of Interpretation*, ed. C. Thoma and M. Wyschogrod (New York: Paulist Press, 1987), 49–62. I thank D. R. Schwartz for drawing my attention to this article.

141. Rashbam's commentary to Exod 3:22.

142. According to Berger ("On the Morality," 49–50), the "surprising Christian willingness to criticize Jacob as a means of attacking his descendants" is "consequently absent from

major Christian works....On the medieval street, then, Christians did not shrink from such attacks on Jews and their forebears."

143. The significant distinction between anti-Jewish claims and Gnostic arguments, and the fact that the latter are not met by rabbinic midrashim, was overlooked by Allen in his discussion of the midrashic literature (e.g., Allen writes concerning a midrash that "it would have been inappropriate and ineffective for direct confrontation with the Gnostics" [Allen, *Despoliation*, 162–163]; "If the Egyptians were seeking repayment for their lost valuables, this line of argumentation could be effective. It would not, however, completely answer the original charges made by the Gnostics and anti-Jews, in terms of the question of the morality of the biblical exodus narrative" [Allen, *Despoliation*, 165]; the midrashim are not addressed to "anti-Semitic/Gnostic challengers" [Allen, *Despoliation*, 176]).

144. MS Rab. 1652 (Mic 4906) in the Jewish Theological Seminary, commenting on Exod 12:36. It has been noted that this compilation used earlier ones (M. Kahana, "The Yemenite Midrashim and Their Use of Halachic Midrashim," *Proceedings of the World Congress of Jewish Studies, Jerusalem, August 16–24, 1989, Division C*, vol. 1, *Jewish Thought and Literature* [in Hebrew] [Jerusalem: World Union of Jewish Studies, 1990], 33). Although most of the commentary is not original, I have not found the source of the passage discussed in this chapter.

145. S. Lieberman, *Yemenite Midrashim* [in Hebrew], 2nd ed. (Jerusalem: Wahrmann Books, 1970).

146. The passage was copied in M. M. Kasher, *Torah Shelemah* [in Hebrew], 12.44 n. 569.

147. The verse reads, however, "and we with our land will be slaves to *Pharaoh*." The prooftext cannot be easily explained.

148. Theodoret of Cyrus, *The Questions on the Octateuch*, ed. J. F. Petruccione and R. C. Hill (Washington, D.C.: Catholic University of America, 2007), 260–263 (Questions to Exodus, xxiii).

149. *Marc.* 2.20.4; see above, n. 138.

150. Irenaeus's brief statement and the statement of the Amora Shemuel in *b. Pesah.* 119a clarify each other, yet the two arguments are not identical. Section F combines the two arguments.

151. Gregory of Nazianzus, *Oratio in S. Pascha* 45.20 (PG 36, 652B), translation according to Allen, *Despoliation*, 265. Gregory continues: "We should acquire for ourselves friends from unrighteous mammon, in order that whenever we are in need, we might receive back at the time of judgment (Luke 16:9)." This is another line of argumentation, which follows the allegorical interpretation of Irenaeus (the affinity with the latter has been noted by Allen, *Despoliation*, 266).

152. Rabbi Levi, to whom this saying is attributed, flourished about a hundred years before Gregory of Nazianzus.

153. For a discussion of the background to this saying, see above n. 55.

154. Contrast Allen, *Despoliation*, 176–177.

155. *MRShY* Exod 12:36 (ed. Epstein and Melamed, 32), which should be interpreted according to *Midrash ha-Gadol* Exod 11:3 (ed. Margulies, 163), which is probably also derived from a lost section of this *Mekhilta*.

156. *MRShY* Exod 12:36 (ed. Epstein and Melamed, 31).

157. *b. Ber.* 9b.

Bibliography

Adler, W. "The Origins of the Proto-Heresies: Fragments from a Chronicle in the First Book of Epiphanius' Panarion." *JTS* 41 (1990): 472–501.

Alexander, P. S. "Retelling the Old Testament." In *It Is Written: Scripture Citing Scripture; Essays in Honour of Barnabas Lindars*, edited by D.A. Carson and H.G.M. Williamson, 99–121. Cambridge: Cambridge University, 1988.

Allen, J. S. *The Despoliation of Egypt in Pre-Rabbinic, Rabbinic, and Patristic Traditions*. SVC 92. Leiden: Brill, 2008.

Amit, M. "Worlds Which Did Not Meet." In *The Jews in the Hellenistic-Roman World: Studies in Memory of Menahem Stern* [in Hebrew], edited by I. M. Gafni, A. Oppenheimer, and D. R. Schwartz, 260–267. Jerusalem: Zalman Shazar Center and the Historical Society of Israel, 1996.

Amitay, O. "The Story of Gviha Ben-Psisa and Alexander the Great." *JSP* 16 (2006): 61–74.

———. "Procopius of Caesarea and the Girgashite Diaspora." *JSP* 20 (2011): 257–276.

Aptowizer, V. "Les premiers possesseurs de Canaan: Légendes apologétiques exégétiques." *REJ* 82 (1926): 275–286.

Bacher, W. "The Supposed Inscription upon 'Joshua the Robber' (Illustrated from Jewish Sources)." *JQR* O.S. 3 (1891): 354–357.

Barclay, J. M. G. *Josephus: Against Apion; Translation and Commentary*. Leiden: Brill, 2007.

Bar-Kochva, B. *The Image of the Jews in Greek Literature*. Berkeley and Los Angeles: University of California, 2010.

Beatrice, P. F. "The Treasures of the Egyptians: A Chapter in the History of Patristic Exegesis and Late Antique Culture." *StPatr* 39 (2006): 159–183.

Berger, D. "On the Morality of the Patriarchs in Jewish Polemic and Exegesis." In *Understanding Scripture: Explorations of Jewish and Christian Traditions of Interpretation*, edited by C. Thoma and M. Wyschogrod, 49–62. New York: Paulist Press, 1987.

Berthelot, K. "Philo of Alexandria and the Conquest of Canaan." *JSJ* 38 (2007): 39–59.

———. "The Biblical Conquest of the Promised Land and the Hasmonaean Wars according to 1 and 2 *Maccabees*." In *The Books of the Maccabees: History, Theology, Ideology*, edited by G. G. Xeravitz and J. Zsengellér, 45–60. JSJS 118. Leiden: Brill, 2007.

———. "The Canaanites Who 'Trusted in God': An Original Interpretation of the Fate of the Canaanites in Rabbinic Literature." *JJS* 62 (2011): 233–261.

———. " 'Ils jettent au feu leurs fils et leurs filles pour leurs dieux': Une justification humaniste du massacre des Cananéens dans les textes juifs anciens?" *RB* 112 (2005): 161–191.

———. "The Original Sin of the Canaanites." In *The "Other" in Second Temple Judaism: Essays in Honor of John J. Collins*, edited by D. Harlow et al., 49–66. Grand Rapids, Mich.: Eerdmans, 2011.

Blidstein, G. J. "The Despoliation of Egypt in Rabbinic Literature" [in Hebrew]. In: idem, *Studies in Halakhic and Aggadic Thought*, 11–23. Beer-Sheva: Ben Gurion University, 2004.

Block, D. I. *The Book of Ezekiel: Chapters 25–48*. NICOT. Grand Rapids, Mich., 1998.

Brooke, G. J. "252. 4QCommentary on Genesis A." *Qumran Cave 4.XVII: Parabiblical Texts, Part 3*, 185–207. DJD 22. Oxford: Clarendon Press, 1996.

Charles, R. H. *The Book of Jubilees: Translated from the Editor's Ethiopic Text and Edited, with Introduction, Notes, and Indices*. London: A & C Black, 1902.

Colson, F. H., trans. *Philo in an English Translation*. London: William Heinemann, 1935.

——. *Philo in Ten Volumes*. London: William Heinemann, 1941.

Cook, J. G. *The Interpretation of the Old Testament in Greco-Roman Paganism*. Tübingen: Mohr Siebeck, 2004.

Devreesse, R. *Les anciens commentateurs grecs de l'Octateuque et de Rois: Fragments tirés des chaînes*. Vatican city: Biblioteca apostolica vaticana, 1959.

Dewing, H. B., trans. *Procopius: History of the Wars, Book III–IV*. LCL. London: W. Heinemann, 1916.

Epiphanius. *De Gemmis: The Old Georgian Version and the Fragments of the Armenian Version*. Edited by R. P. Blake. London: Christophers, 1934.

——. *Panarion*. Edited by K. Holl. GCS 37. Berlin: Akademie Verlag, 1985.

Feldman, L. H. *Judaean Antiquities 1–4: Translation and Commentary*. Leiden: Brill, 2000.

Friedman, H. *Midrash Rabbah: Genesis*. London: Soncino, 1951.

Ginzberg, L. *Ginze Schechter*. New York: Jewish Theological Seminary, 1928.

——. *Legends of the Jews*. Philadelphia: JPS, 1968.

Greenfield, J. C. "Našu-Nadanu and Its Cognates." In *Al Kanfei Yonah: Collected Studies of Jonas Greenfield on Semitic Philology*, 720–724. Jerusalem: Magnes, 2001.

Gutman, Y. *The Beginnings of Jewish-Hellenistic Literature* [in Hebrew]. Jerusalem: Mosad Bialik, 1963.

Herr, M. D. "Peace in Rabbinic Thinking" [in Hebrew]. In *Peace according to Jewish Sources: Lectures in the President's Residence*. Jerusalem: President's Residence, 1997.

Hirschberg, H. Z. *History of the Jews in North Africa*. Leiden: Brill, 1974.

Holladay, C. R. *Fragments from Hellenistic Jewish Authors*. Atlanta: Scholars Press, 1989.

Horst, P. W. van der. "Did the Gentiles Know Who Abraham Was?" In *Abraham, the Nations and the Hagarites*, edited by M. Goodman et al., 61–75. Leiden: Brill, 2010.

Jacobson, H. *The Exagoge of Ezekiel*. Cambridge: Cambridge University, 1983.

Japhet, S. *The Ideology of the Book of Chronicles and Its Place in Biblical Thought* [in Hebrew]. Jerusalem: Bialik Institute, 1977.

Kahana, M. "The Yemenite Midrashim and Their Use of Halachic Midrashim." *Proceedings of the World Congress of Jewish Studies, Jerusalem, August 16–24, 1989, Division C*. Vol. 1. *Jewish Thought and Literature* [in Hebrew], 31–38. Jerusalem: World Union of Jewish Studies, 1990.

Kasher, M. M. *Torah Shelemah* [in Hebrew]. New York: 1948. Reprint, Jerusalem: Beth Torah Slelemah, 1992.

Kister, M. "Metamorphoses of Aggadic Traditions" [in Hebrew]. *Tarbiz* 60 (1991): 179–224.

——. "Notes on Some New Texts from Qumran." *JSS* 44 (1993): 287–289.

——. "Some Early Jewish and Christian Exegetical Problems and the Dynamics of Monotheism." *JSJ* 37 (2006): 553–563.

——. "Ancient Material in Pirqe de-Rabbi Eliʿezer: Basilides, Qumran, the Book of Jubilees." In *'Go Out and Study the Land': Judges 18:2; Archaeological, Historical and Textual Studies in Honor of Hanan Eshel*, edited by A. M. Maier, J. Magness, and L. H. Schiffman, 69–93. Leiden: Brill, 2011.

——. "Allegorical Interpretations of Biblical Narratives in Jewish Palestine, Philo and Origen: Some Test Cases." In *New Approaches to the Study of Biblical Interpretation in Judaism of the Second Temple Period and in Early Christianity: Proceedings of the Eleventh International Symposium of the Orion Center for the Study of the Dead Sea Scrolls and Associated Literature, Jointly Sponsored by the Hebrew University Center for* the Study of Christianity, 9–11 January, 2007, edited by G. A. Anderson, D. Satran, and R. C. Clements. STDJ 106, Leiden: Brill, 2013.

Kroymann, A., ed. *Tertullianis Opera:1*. CCSL 1. Turnholt: Typographi Brepols, 1964.

Kugel, J. L. *Traditions of the Bible*. Cambridge, Mass.: Harvard University Press, 1998.

——. "Which Is Older, *Jubilees* or the *Genesis Apocryphon*? An Exegetical Approach." In *The Dead Sea Scrolls and Contemporary Culture*, edited by A. D. Roitman et al., 257–294. STDJ 93. Leiden: Brill, 2011.

Lahey, L. "The Dialogue of Timothy and Aquila: Critical Greek Text and English Translation of the Short Recension with an Introduction Including a Source-critical Study." PhD diss., Cambridge University, 2000.

Lauterbach, J. Z. *Mekilta de-Rabbi Ishmael*. Philadelphia: JPS, 1961.

Lévi, I. "La dispute entre les Egyptiens et les Juifs devant Alexandre: Echo des polémiques antijuives à Alexandrie." *REJ* 63 (1912): 211–215.

Lewy, H. "Ein Rechtsstreit um den Boden Palästinas im Altertum." *MGWJ* 77 (1933): 84–99, 172–180.

——. *Studies in Jewish Hellenism* (עולמות נפגשים). Jerusalem: Mosad Bialik, 1969, 60–78.

Lieberman, S. *Yemenite Midrashim* [in Hebrew]. 2nd ed. Jerusalem: Wahrmann Books, 1970.

——. *Tosefta ki-Fshutah Sotah*. New York: Jewish Theological Seminary, 1973.

Loewenstamm, S. E. נחל מצרים [in Hebrew]. *Encyclopedia Biblica*, 5:813–814. Jerusalem: Bialik Institute, 1968.

Machiela, D. A. "Each to His Own Inheritance: Geography as an Evaluative Tool in the Genesis Apocryphon." *DSD* 15 (2008): 50–66.

——. *The Dead Sea Genesis Apocryphon*. STDJ 79. Leiden: Brill, 2009.

Mann, J., and I. Sonne. *The Bible as Read and Preached in the Old Synagogue*. Cincinnati, Ohio: Hebrew Union College, 1996.

Marcus, R. *Questions and Answers on Genesis Translated from the Ancient Armenian Version of the Original Greek*. LCL. London: William Heinemann, 1953.

Mendels, D. *The Land of Israel as a Political Concept in Hasmonean Literature*. Tübingen: Mohr Siebeck, 1987.

Milik, J. T. *The Books of Enoch*. Oxford: Clarendon Press, 1976.

Niehoff, M. *Jewish Exegesis and Homeric Scholarship in Alexandria*. Cambridge: Cambridge University, 2011.

Noam, V. *Megillat Ta'anit: Versions, Interpretations, History, with a Critical Edition*. Jerusalem: Yad Ben Zvi, 2003.

Pastis, J. Z. "Dating the Dialogue of Timothy and Aquila: Revisiting the Earlier Vorlage Hypothesis." *HTR* 95 (2002): 169–195.

Paul, S. M. *Amos: A Commentary on the Book of Amos*. Minneapolis: Fortress, 1991; Hermeneia.

Puech, E. *Qumrân grotte 4.XXII: Textes araméens première partie*. DJD 31. Oxford: Clarendon Press, 2001.

Rapoport, S. I. *'Erech Millin* [in Hebrew]. Prague: M. I. Landau, 1852.

Rehm, B. *Die Pseudoklementinen II: Recognitiones in Rufins Übersetzung*. GCS 51. Berlin: Akademie-Verlag, 1965.

Roberts, A., and J. Donaldson, eds. *Ante-Nicene Fathers*. Grand Rapids, Mich.: Eerdmans, 1985.

Rokeah, D. "Jews and Their Law (Torah) in the Pagan-Christian Polemic in the Roman Empire" [in Hebrew]. *Tarbiz* 40 (1971): 462–471.

——. *Jews, Pagans and Christians in Conflict*. Jerusalem: Magnes, 1982.

——. *Philo of Alexandria: Writings* [in Hebrew]. Edited by S. Daniel-Nataf. Jerusalem: Israel Academy of Sciences and Humanities, 1986.

Schäfer, P. *Judeophobia*. Cambridge, Mass.: Harvard University, 1997.

Schmidt, Francis. "Jewish Representations of the Inhabited Earth during the Hellenistic and Roman Periods." In *Greece and Rome in Eretz Israel*, edited by A. Kasher, U. Rappaport, and G. Fuchs, 119–134. Jerusalem: Yad Ben-Zvi and Israel Exploration Society, 1990.

Schmitz, P. C. "Procopius' Phoenician Inscriptions: Never Lost, Not Found." *PEQ* 139 (2007): 99–104.

Schwartz, B. J. "Reexamining the Fate of the Canaanites in the Torah Traditions." In *Sefer Moshe: The Moshe Weinfeld Jubilee Volume*, edited by C. Cohen, A. Hurvitz, and S. M. Paul, 151–170. Winona Lake, Ind.: Eisenbrauns, 2004.

Scott, J. M. *Geography in Early Judaism and Christianity: The Book of Jubilees*. Cambridge: Cambridge University, 2002.

Seeligmann, I. L. "Aetiological Elements in Biblical Historiography" [in Hebrew]. *Zion* 26 (1961): 141–169.

Segal, M. "The Literary Relationship between the Genesis Apocryphon and Jubilees: The Chronology of Abram and Sarai's Descent to Egypt." *Aramaic Studies* 8 (2010): 71–88.

Shatzman, I. "The Hasmoneans in Greco-Roman Historiography" [in Hebrew]. *Zion* 57 (1992): 5–64.

——. "Jews and Gentiles from Judas Maccabaeus to John Hyrcanus according to Contemporary Jewish Sources." In *Studies in Josephus and the Varieties of Ancient Judaism: Lois H. Feldman Jubilee Volume*, edited by S. J. D. Cohen and J. J. Schwartz, 237–270. Leiden: Brill, 2007.

Skinner, J. *Genesis*. ICC. Edinburgh: T & T Clark, 1994.

Stern, M. *Greek and Latin Authors on Jews and Judaism*. Jerusalem: Israel Academy of Sciences and Humanities, 1976.

Synkellos, G. *Chronography*. Edited by A. Mosshammer. Leipzig: Teubner, 1984. English translation by W. Adler and P. Tuffin, *The Chronography of George Synkellos*. Oxford: Oxford University, 2002.

Thackeray, H. St. J., trans. *Josephus in Nine Volumes*. Vol. 4. *Jewish Antiquities, Books I–IV*. LCL. London: W. Heinemann, 1930.

Theodoret of Cyrus. *The Questions on the Octateuch*, edited by J. F. Petruccione and R. C. Hill. Washington, D.C.: Catholic University of America, 2007.

Tigay, J. H. *The JPS Torah Commentary: Deuteronomy*. Philadelphia: JPS, 1996.

Touitou, E. "The Historical Background of Rashi's Commentary on Genesis 1–5" [in Hebrew]. In *Rashi Studies*, edited by Z. A. Steinfeld, 97–105. Ramat-Gan: Bar Ilan, 1993.

VanderKam, J. C. "Putting Them in Their Place: Geography as an Evaluative Tool." In *Pursuing the Text: Studies in Honor of Ben Zion Wacholder*, edited by J. C. Reeves and J. Kampen, 46–69. JSOTS 184. Sheffield, U.K.: Sheffield Academic Press, 1994.

Varner, W. *Ancient Jewish-Christian Dialogues: Athanasius and Zacchaeus, Simon and Theophilus, Timothy and Aquila; Introduction, Texts and Translations*. Lewiston, N.Y.: Edwin Mellen, 2004.

——. *The Promise of the Land: The Inheritance of Canaan by the Israelites*. Berkeley and Los Angeles: University of California, 1993.

——. "The Attitude towards Gentiles in the Book of Jubilees and Qumran Literature Compared with Early Tannaitic Halakha and Contemporary Pseudepigrapha" [in Hebrew]. PhD diss., Hebrew University of Jerusalem, 1995.

Werman, C. "The Book of Jubilees and Its Aramaic Sources" [in Hebrew]. *Meghillot* 8–9 (2010): 135–154.

——. "The Ban of the Canaanites in the Biblical Codes and Its Historical Development." In *History and Traditions of Early Israel: Studies Presented to Eduard Nielsen*, edited by A. Lemaire and B. Otzen, 142–160. SVT 50. Leiden: Brill, 1993.

Williams, F., trans. *The Panarion of Epiphanius of Salamis: Books II and III*. Leiden: Brill, 1994.

Winston, D. *The Wisdom of Solomon*. AB. New York: Doubleday, 1979.

Wintermute, O. S. "Jubilees." In *Old Testament Pseudepigrapha*, edited by J. H. Charlesworth, 2:35–142. Garden City, N.Y.: Doubleday, 1983.

Yardeni, A. *Nahal Se'elim Documents*. Beer Sheva: Ben Gurion University, 1995.

"God Would Not Give the Land, but to the Obedient" Medieval Karaite Responses to the Curse of Canaan (Genesis 9:25)

Meira Polliack and Marzena Zawanowska

Introduction

The curse of Canaan in Genesis 9:25 and its wider episode (verses 18–28) form an interpretive crux in the history of Jewish Bible exegesis, encompassing several textual and theological difficulties, the most salient among them being the placing of the curse upon Canaan rather than Ham.[1] In the major exegetical works of the Karaite Jews, who commented on this verse during the tenth to the eleventh centuries C.E., the problem of divine justice received special attention. The Karaites, as Jewish scripturalists, rejected the sanctified status of received tradition (Jewish Oral Law) and concentrated their intellectual efforts on expounding the Hebrew Bible anew for the purpose of legal (halakhic) derivation. To this end they introduced sophisticated linguistic, contextual, and literary tools that were meant to ground the explanation of a biblical verse or passage in revealed Scripture alone, and to exclude what they saw as homiletic ("extra-biblical") expositions of the biblical text based on midrashic tradition.[2]

Since the time of Saʿadyah Gaon (d. 942) adherence to the Islamic system of rationalist religious thought known as *kalam*, and especially to the Muʿtazilite school of *kalam*, had become a hallmark of Jewish thinkers in the East at large, most notably during the tenth to eleventh centuries, though the Jewish reception of Muʿtazilite theology was not limited to this period alone. The Karaite intellectuals had a dominant voice in its internalization by the Jews. Among the leading principles of Muʿtazilite *kalam* were the primacy of reason and the autonomy of human agents in explaining the nature of God and the world. Ideas concerning God's omniscience, justice, and man's ability to determine good and evil through reason—as opposed to predetermination—permeate the exegetical writings of tenth-century Karaites such as Yaʿqub al-Qirqisani and Yefet ben ʿEli. Their discussions of various biblical passages often point to a *kalamic* backdrop and reflect a Muʿtazilite consciousness or worldview, even though they do not always employ detailed Muʿtazilite argumentation or consistently use its explicit terminology in their running commentaries on the Bible.³ The full-fledged theological engagement with Muʿtazilite *kalam* may be found in the non-exegetical treatises of their contemporary Yusuf al-Basir, and eleventh century Karaites such as Yeshuʿah ben Yehudah and Levi ben Yefet.⁴

In this chapter, the story of the curse of Canaan serves as a point of departure for presenting the varied views of prominent Karaite commentators on Genesis 9:18–28, including Yaʿqub al-Qirqisani, Yefet ben ʿEli, Yusuf ibn Nuh (as preserved in an abridgement compiled by Abu al-Faraj Harun, and known as the *Talkhis*), and Yeshuʿah ben Yehudah.⁵ The comparative analysis is arranged according to seven leading thematic-exegetical questions, while in each category the exegetical responses are presented in chronological order, commencing with al-Qirqisani (first half of the tenth century) and ending with Yeshuʿah (mid-eleventh century).

Within this theological milieu, the first question—which became central to the Karaites' deliberations over Genesis 9:25 and the story of the curse of Canaan at large—is why Canaan was cursed by Noah when it was Ham, Canaan's father, who actually committed the sin, or, put differently, whether God was just in punishing the progeny for a sin committed by its progenitor (section 1). The fragmented portions that have survived of Saʿadyah Gaon's commentary on Genesis suggest that he, too, as the major Rabbanite *mutakallim* of this period, was troubled by this question.⁶

Second, the issue of free moral choice, a known Muʿtazilite tenet, is raised, since if it was this very curse that led the Canaanites to sinful and punishable deeds, then what was their degree of free will in exercising moral judgment, and how could God be just in predestining them to such a fate? (section 2).⁷

Third, God's omniscience, as opposed to the limits of human knowledge, was also a focus of concern for these exegetes: If the curse was visited upon Canaan on account of the presaged sinful behavior of his offspring, the Canaanite people, how could Noah know about it? The concept of prophetic knowledge as developed in Muʿtazilite *kalam* is brought to bear in this respect also on the Karaite discussions of Noah in the wider narrative of the curse (section 3).⁸

The fourth question concerns aspects of inner contradiction in the biblical text, which also disturbed the Karaite exegetes for whom intelligibility and consistency were a central feature of the divine will and hence of the divinely originated biblical text. Thus the question of how Noah's curse of Canaan, his grandson, could be reconciled with God's blessing invested upon Noah and all of his sons, including Ham, the father of Canaan, immediately after the flood and shortly preceding the curse (Gen 9:1, 9:9) troubled the Karaite commentators since it implied an apparent inconsistency in God's actions and words, as preserved in Scripture (section 4). Another apparent inner contradiction exists between Noah's curse of Canaan and the dooming of his offspring to slavery (Gen 9:25), on the one hand, and the divine instruction to expel (Exod 23:28–33) and completely eradicate the Canaanites (Deut 20:16–18), on the other hand (section 5).

The overall analysis leads to a discussion of the divine conditions for dwelling in the Holy Land (section 6). In this context, the question of ethnic as opposed to ethical categories by which the Canaanites are discussed is also addressed (section 7). It will be shown that while some of these Karaite exegetes upheld the idea of a strict ethnic differentiation between Israel's faithful forefathers and the Canaanite "others," some were more inclined to apply general criteria of moral behavior and values, which they associated with wider religious customs and beliefs, such as monotheism or polytheism that characterized the Israelites and the Canaanites, historically.

1. Why Was Canaan Cursed instead of Ham?

A universal question that many Bible exegetes face in interpreting the wider story of the curse of Canaan in Genesis 9:18–29 is why Canaan was cursed in the first place (verse 25: *arur kena'an 'eved 'avadim yihyeh le-ehaw*), when it was actually Ham, Canaan's father, who witnessed Noah's nakedness (verse 22) and did not take pains to cover it, as did his brothers, Shem and Japhet (verse 23).[9] Should the sin of the father be visited upon the son, when even the Bible itself is ambiguous concerning such a "collective" form of punishment?[10] And even if it were Canaan who committed an offense against Noah, should his offspring be punished because of what he did? In response to this complex exegetical conundrum the Karaite commentators provided diverse explanations.

1.1 YA'QUB AL-QIRQISANI

According to al-Qirqisani, it is not improbable that it was Canaan, rather than Ham, who performed the vile deed against Noah, his grandfather: To wit, he witnessed Noah's nakedness, and he may even have committed some sexual offense, to which al-Qirqisani alludes in another place:[11]

> We say that there is no indication that Canaan was not present at the time of the curse.... It is indicated by the beginning of the story, where it is said: *And Ham, the father of Canaan, saw* [Gen 9:22] and it says *And Ham is the father of Canaan* [Gen 9:18].[12] [Scripture] would not have mentioned that he [i.e., Ham] was his [i.e., Canaan's] father, unless [Canaan] had [already] been present [i.e., in the scene].... Similarly, the statement *And Ham, the father of*

Canaan, saw [Gen 9:22] indicates the presence of Canaan [i.e., in the scene].
This statement necessitates that at that very moment Canaan had done a
reprehensible deed, deserving [*istahaqa bihi*] the curse. Scripture alludes
to that, when it says [*And Noah awoke from his wine,*] *and knew what his
youngest son had done unto him* [Gen 9:24]. For as far as Ham is concerned,
he was not his [i.e., Noah's] youngest son, but the middle [son], whereas
Canaan was the youngest of Ham's children, as it is said: *And the sons of
Ham: Cush, and Mitzraim, and Put, and Canaan* [Gen 10:6].[13]

Al-Qirqisani's solution to the interpretive crux is to present Canaan as justly
cursed on account of his own deed. He bases this solution on what he perceives
as textual evidence within the passage, namely, the repetitive presentation of
Ham as Canaan's father in verses 18 and 22. Such information is deemed by
al-Qirqisani to be relevant to the scene as a whole, for if Canaan was not present therein, what could be the narrative purpose of his twice being evoked by
name? Further evidence is found in the wording *beno ha-qatan* ("his youngest
son") used in describing Noah's awakening consciousness. Such wording can
only befit Canaan's status among Noah's extended family.

While the textual argumentation is compelling, al-Qirqisani's theological
argumentation is inconsistent in that it is not carried over to the Canaanites as
a nation, for if Canaan was punished on account of his own deed, why should
his future progeny carry his curse? Should they not be judged according to
their own transgressions alone? As will be shown below (see sections 2.1, 3.1,
and 4.1), to escape this pitfall, al-Qirqisani—just like Yefet—speculates that
Noah might have been informed through revelation about their future behavior and he cursed them in advance of it.

1.2 YEFET BEN ʿELI

Whereas al-Qirqisani suggests that it is probable that Canaan's presence and
action in the scene makes him the worthy subject of Noah's curse, Yefet's interpretation turns this probability into a certainty. He firmly admits that at the
time of Noah's curse, Canaan had already been born and that he was definitely punished by the curse on account of his own deed. In his view, however,
Canaan was punished not because of what he did to his grandfather, Noah.
In the scriptural passage under discussion it was clearly Ham, contends Yefet,
who committed an offense against his father, Noah. Canaan is justifiably the
one to be cursed, nonetheless, on account of all the transgressions that he
merely commenced to commit at that time, and which find their continuation
in the abominable and sinful behavior of his offspring, the Canaanites:

Next [Scripture] informs [us] that he [i.e., Noah] cursed Canaan. This
indicates that Canaan had already been born and [that] he was not cursed
because of a deed [that] he had done in that instant. Rather, [Noah] cursed

him [i.e., Canaan] for the initiation of his [sinful] deeds, meaning the deeds of the seven nations who exceeded all bounds in abominations, and hence had necessitated by God their annihilation at the hand of Israel. [Noah] alluded to this meaning in his wording: *Cursed be Canaan* [*a slave of slaves shall he be unto his brothers*] [Gen 9:25].[14]

Yefet is reluctant to depart from the literal sense of the passage, which clearly describes Ham as the one who saw Noah's nakedness and hence as the subject of the sentence (verse 22). Yet, in order to avoid the possibility, also deriving from a literal reading of the passage, that an unjust punishment was inflicted upon Canaan, Yefet argues that Canaan also sinned, in some other unspecified manner.[15] Consequently, the offense he committed at the time of Noah—be what it may—was merely a prelude, an initiation of future forms of abominable behavior perpetrated by his offspring, the Canaanites, who well deserved to be punished. His interpretation hinges on the poetic style of Noah's Hebrew curse, which may be understood as referring to Canaan impersonally (as a collective) and is expressed in a present continuous-future tense (**arur Kena'an** 'eved 'avadim **yihyeh** le-ehaw; emphasis added).

As will be demonstrated further below (see sections 6.2 and 7), Yefet upholds that divine retribution—in the form of punishment or reward—cannot be dependent on the behavior of one's ancestors. By the same token, he puts in relief the role of human free will and emphasizes the full responsibility of each individual for his own lot.[16] Divine punishment is thus just and unbiased, measured according to individual deed.

1.3 AUTHORS OF THE *TALKHIS*: YUSUF IBN NUH AND ABU AL-FARAJ HARUN

The two great Karaite grammarians, authors of the *Talkhis*, were of opinion that the interpretive crux is best solved by rendering verse 25 not as a declarative sentence containing a "live curse"—namely, a performative speech act—but rather as a descriptive utterance that conveys information that Noah received through revelation concerning the future behavior of Ham's offspring, the Canaanites. The information about the future misfortune of his children was meant to punish Ham, by causing him to feel grief and pain over their prospective lot:[17]

And he said: *Cursed be Canaan* [Gen 9:25] is not a proclamation [du'a] made by Noah concerning Canaan, since crime was perpetrated by his [i.e., Canaan's] father, Ham, and not by him [i.e., Canaan]. Rather, it is an account [akhbar] of what [Noah] knew through revelation ['alimahu bi-al-wahi] about his [i.e., Canaan's future] misfortune, in order to fill his father, Ham, with that [i.e., knowledge] and [thereby] trouble his heart.[18]

Similarly to Yefet—but in distinction from al-Qirqisani, who allowed for the possibility that it was Canaan who committed the sin against his father, Noah—the *Talkhis* is of the opinion that it was Ham whose transgression is related in this biblical passage. Having stuck to the literal meaning of the text, the authors of the *Talkhis* still endeavored to explain the just aspect of Noah's focusing on Canaan in his so-called curse. In doing so, they were even more determined than Yefet to reject any possibility of an offense committed by Canaan, since there is no mention of it in the text. Their ingenuous solution was syntactic in nature: They transformed verse 25 from a declarative sentence, proclaiming Noah's curse of Canaan, into a descriptive sentence, containing Noah's (prophetic) description of Canaan's future misbehavior (Canaan functions accordingly as a collective name for the Canaanite peoples). Noah's description, as explained in the *Talkhis*, was intended as a punishment to Ham, not to Canaan, since the foreknowledge it conferred upon him caused Ham to grieve over the future of his offspring.

1.4 YESHU'AH BEN YEHUDAH

In his solution to the interpretive problem, Yeshu'ah concurs with some other Karaite exegetes of Jerusalem in rejecting the possibility that Canaan rather than Ham committed the sin. Nevertheless, he, too, cannot accept that Canaan could have been cursed instead of his father, Ham, and is the first among our exegetes to formulate this problem as a clear exegetical question ("it has been asked: How is it that the father sins yet the son is cursed?"). Neither is Yeshu'ah ready to accept that Canaan was in some way present in the scene (see al-Qirqisani and to a certain extent Yefet, sections 1.1 and 1.2 above). In taking up the direction of the authors of the *Talkhis*, Yeshu'ah provides a refined grammatical explanation of the verse, suggesting that it has a missing syntactical part:

> [Concerning] *And he said: Cursed be Canaan* [Gen 9:25] it has been asked: "How is it that the father sins yet the son is cursed?" One of the [deceased] sages, may God have mercy on him, responded that it is possible to interpret it via completion [*taqdirihi*] as "Cursed be the father of Canaan" and [the Hebrew word] *avi* [meaning "father of"] has been elided [*ikhtasara*], [just] as in another place [the word] *akhi* [meaning "brother"] is elided, as it is said *and Elhanan the son of Jaare-oregim the Beth-lehemite slew Goliath the Gittite* [2 Sam 21:19], whereas in another version [*nuskhah*] containing this report in Chronicles it says *and Elhanan the son of Jair slew Lahmi the brother of Goliath the Gittite* [1 Chr 20:5].[19]

In pursuing his individual syntactical direction—which he nonetheless attributes to another Karaite scholar—Yeshu'ah makes a deft attempt to solve the textual difficulty by means of a grammatical reconstruction of the verse.[20]

Unlike the authors of the *Talkhis*, he does not choose to transform the mood of the verse. His solution involves the semantic notion of elision (*ikhtisar*), which is amply used by Arab and Karaite grammarians (like Yusuf ibn Nuh) to explain a missing element within the sentence structure, especially within a construct state, which is assumed by the speaker or author. The exegete's "reconstruction" of this element is sometimes called *taqdir*.[21] For the medieval Jewish grammarians, the missing element, it is important to point out, is part of the language structure of biblical Hebrew, and is not the result of a mistake in the transmission or copying of the biblical text. In support of this interpretation, Yeshu'ah provides a fascinating parallel example, in his view, of the existence of the elided and full structures in the case of the same report (*khabar*) contained in the different version (*nuskhah*) *et goliath* versus *et akhi goliath* found in the books of Samuel and Chronicles, respectively.[22] Yeshu'ah's explanation, corroborated by a textual analogy from another biblical passage wherein the same grammatical phenomenon may be witnessed, is meant to confirm that it was actually Ham, and not Canaan, who served as the direct subject of Noah's just curse. Nevertheless, Yeshu'ah is aware that Ham was cursed in relation to Canaan, his offspring. For this reason he also accepts (see sections 2.2 and 3.4 below), that the saying *cursed be Canaan* (Gen 9:25) is a report (*akhbar*) about the decline of the progeny of Canaan. Hence, in this wider reading of the passage he builds directly on the solution offered by the *Talkhis*.

All of the aforementioned Karaite commentators provide different exegetical responses in order to resolve the exegetical problem, namely, how is it that the father sins yet the son is cursed? Their skillful solutions have a common motive—their theological and ethical concern with the apparent injustice of the curse. They do not suggest a historical solution of the kind that in biblical times the visitation of a parent's punishment upon the child may have been considered a just form of divine retribution, as expressed in some scriptural passages.[23] The idea that the Bible may give expression to an ideology that has changed over time—even within the biblical period itself, not to mention later periods, would have been largely alien to these medieval exegetes' conception of it as a revealed and innately truthful text. As such, Scripture had to be shown to reflect theological consistency in the expression it gives to God's justice and logic.

Whereas the Karaites' exegetical motivation is in this sense extra-textual and uniform, their exegetical solutions are textually based, in that they apply strict grammatical and contextual tools in their extrapolation of this passage. Their varied solutions are generated within the hermeneutic boundaries set by the Karaite exegetical school in the study of the meaning of the biblical text.[24] No midrashic homily is employed in uncovering, as it were, this meaning, or smoothing out the problematic aspects of the verse, by filling in the gap through additional (extra-biblical) "data" regarding the biblical characters.[25]

The syntax, literary style, and immediate context of the biblical verse are the criteria employed by the Karaites exegetes in solving the crux.[26] Nonetheless, their motives and basic questions stem from their fundamental conviction as theologians (*mutakallimun*) that it is morally unjust, and thus unbefitting a just God to curse a child because of a sin committed by his father.

2. The Problem of Divine Justice: God's Foreknowledge and Predetermination

Some Karaite authors tried to solve the problem of Canaan's apparently unjust punishment by suggesting that the curse was laid upon his offspring in advance, due to God's foreknowledge of the sins that these descendants were to commit in the future. Nevertheless, if we admit that the progeny of the initial perpetrator were punished by a curse because of their future offenses, there arises yet another moral question, whether it is just to punish someone in advance, before he has actually committed the sin. Furthermore, under such circumstances, the curse itself might be conceived as a partial cause for the subsequent transgressions of the Canaanites, in that it was their unjust and lowly positioning that engendered, as in a vicious circle, the perpetration of further wrongs.[27] In other words, the curse could have inevitably and irrevocably doomed the offspring of Canaan, denying them the exercise of free will in their moral choices and thus predetermining their fate. Objection to predestination was a basic tenet of the Mu'tazilite conception of divine justice (*'adl*), and as such was shared by Jewish (Karaite and Rabbanite) as well as Christian religious philosophers (*mutakallimun*) of the Islamic milieu.[28]

2.1 YAʿQUB AL-QIRQISANI

Al-Qirqisani deals with this question by evoking the concept of divine omniscience and God's foreknowledge, as follows:

> As for [someone] who rejects [the idea of] cursing the absent [person], this is not reprehensible if it comes from [the One] from whom nothing of what will happen is concealed. Since the Creator, the Almighty and Sublime, knows all things prior to [their] coming into being, and informs His holy men of these things through prophecy is not objectionable to them to censure someone who must be censured, before it [i.e., the sin] occurs as well as to curse him, and likewise to praise [the one] who needs to be praised and [deserves] blessing.[29]

In this passage, God's omniscience, yet another of his distinctive attributes in Muslim *kalam*, though not specific to Muʿtazili *kalam*, serves al-Qirqisani to ward off the possibility that God doomed Canaan's fate in advance of his future sinful actions. Al-Qirqisani speculates that since God knows exactly what will happen, He can inform his chosen ones about the course of events through the medium of prophecy (*nubuwah*), and therefore, if they curse someone, their curse is justifiable on the basis of the foreknowledge to which they have been made privy by the Almighty.[30]

2.2 YESHUʿAH BEN YEHUDAH

Yeshuʿah is reluctant to accept the somewhat schematic answer provided by al-Qirqisani. His primary conviction, similarly to Yefet's, is that divine punishment should be administered not only individually, to each according to his own sins, but also not prior to when the sin is actually committed. For if we assume that God knows ahead of time about the future sins of every man and woman, then it would also be possible to argue that these sins are, at least to some extent, determined by God's foreknowledge and that Canaan's offspring became sinful as a result of the curse. In order to avoid this circular argumentation, Yeshuʿah insists on determining cause and effect, in that God's punishment must proceed from Canaan's sins. Since these had not yet been committed, then the verse cannot be understood as an actual curse, but rather, as a descriptive report regarding Canaan's future:

> It is possible that the father [i.e., Ham] is being punished by what will happen to the son [i.e., Canaan], and his heart hurts because of what he is informed about his [i.e., the son's misfortunate] state. Later, the child will be tested through what occurs to him and punished for his [own] disobedience, for the cursing of Canaan entails his [future] disobedience. And if it is asked: "Is it permissible to curse someone who will deserve the curse [only] when he disobeys [in the future], before it [i.e., the actual deed] is accomplished or before he is disobedient?" The answer is that the saying *cursed be Canaan* [Gen 9:25] is a report [*akhbar*] about the blighting that will occur in regard to the progeny of Canaan, who was the source of [various] tribes.[31]

Yeshuʿah cannot refrain from contemplating the text through the prism of his own moral sense, by which God's deeds must conform to an abstract and universal ideal of goodness and cannot be deemed as good merely by the fact of His performance of them. Yeshuʿah's deliberations differ from al-Qirqisani's unbiased argument for God's foreknowledge, which leaves no place for doubts about God's judgment. In this respect, he is more of a religious skeptic than al-Qirqisani, and, as a result, his deliberations are more dialectic. He accepts the principle of divine justice as well as God's foreknowledge. Nevertheless, he underlines the problematic nature of the curse put on Canaan as one that casts a shadow on the future of his offspring, whose disobedience becomes its necessary sequel. Yeshuʿah's solution, namely, that Noah's statement was not a proclaimed curse but a descriptive report, echoes the syntactic transformation found in the *Talkhis* (see section 1.3 above). This brings us to a related problem, namely, how could Noah know what the future held for Cannan's offspring?

3. The Problem of Human Knowledge: Noah's Source of Information

The limits of human knowledge also pose a concern in relation to Noah's description in the passage. For even if we assume, at least *pro tem*, that Ham's punishment for what he had done to his father consisted, among other things, of being informed by Noah about the future misfortune of his offspring, which would result from their sinful behavior over time, and even if we accept that Canaan was punished on account of his accumulative sins[32]—still the question remains: How could the drunken Noah possibly know about what happened to him or be capable of divining the future transgressions of the Canaanites? Moreover, Scripture is silent about his receiving any information from God in this respect. The Karaite exegetes found invariable ways to solve this matter, as follows.

3.1 YAʿQUB AL-QIRQISANI

Al-Qirqisani is prepared to admit the exegetical possibility that Canaan may not have committed the sin. In such a case, Noah's cursing is justified on account of his foreknowledge of the future sinful behavior of Canaan's offspring, the Canaanites, which was revealed to Noah through prophecy:

> And it [i.e., this verse] may have another meaning, which is that if it is true that Canaan was absent [i.e., when Noah pronounced the curse] and that he did not commit an offense at that time, then it is possible that it was revealed to Noah, may peace be upon him, through prophecy that the most heretic among the children of Ham, the most wicked [in their] manners and the most abhorrent [in their] abominations and breaking of the forbidden customs of the Holy Land, would be the seven nations, [with regard to] whom God, the Almighty and Sublime, commanded, that absolutely[33] not one of them shall be spared, and [that] their repentance shall not be accepted and [that] they shall not enter the religion [i.e., be able to become Israelites]. All of them are the children of Canaan. So Noah, may peace be upon him, cursed them [i.e., the children of Canaan], when their ways [i.e., in the future] were explained to him through prophecy.[34]

In this comment, al-Qirqisani gives expression to his severe conception of divine justice, wherein God commands the total annihilation of the seven nations (i.e., the Canaanites) as a collective punishment for their sins, leaving no space for individual repentance. Interestingly, al-Qirqisani does not

exclude the possibility that some of them may wish to repent, but he emphasizes that even if it were so, God commanded that "their repentance shall not
be accepted." In this sense, he diminishes the role of moral responsibility of
individuals for their own fate; God seems not merely to know, but also—at
least to a certain extant—to plan ahead, who will deserve to be destroyed
("not one of them shall be spared"), leaving no choice of amendment through
conversion ("they shall not enter the religion"). The divine decision is irrevocable, and, in the case of these seven nations, it is not dependent on human
repentance.

This stance is strikingly opposed to Yefet's often expressed conviction that
God accords to everyone a chance to repent and that if one repents, his repentance will be accepted and he will be delivered, as found, for instance, in his
commentary on Genesis 18:21:

> If someone were to say: "What is the reason why God made this mat-
> ter [i.e., the destruction of Sodom and Gomorrah along with their inhab-
> itants] dependent on the entering of the messengers to them?" It will be
> said to him that out of compassion for his servants, the Creator, Almighty
> and Sublime, warns them when they exaggerate in terms of offenses, and
> informs them that the time limit [al-ajal][35] has already approached, so that
> it be an argument for them [to repent]. If they comprehend and return from
> their offenses, the punishment will not fall upon them. Yet, if they do not
> return [from sin], the punishment will fall upon them.[36] To the people of
> the generation of the flood [God] had granted a long time limit, that is one
> hundred and twenty years.[37] [In addition], when the time limit elapsed, and
> they did not repent, He granted them a short time limit, that is a period of
> seven days.[38] Yet, when they did not return, He destroyed them. As far as
> the inhabitants of Nineveh are concerned, He granted them [a respite of]
> forty days,[39] and they returned to God, so the trial did not fall upon them.
> [As for] these inhabitants of Sodom, God granted them a respite [of] twenty
> five years, but they did not repent. Rather, they exceeded all bounds [in their
> sins] and multiplied the offenses. [Nonetheless], when the time came, He
> granted them [a short term] concurrent with the coming of the messengers
> to them. Had they repented, [God] would not have destroyed them.[40]

According to this passage, Yefet is of the opinion—which he grounds on
various scriptural reports—that everyone, even the worse sinners, whether
Israelites or non-Israelites, are warned and given a chance to repent. Moreover,
after a divine warning, the sinner is granted a respite to have enough time to
think things over and repent. If he repents, he is delivered. Thus, in the end,
the deliverance is dependent on human actions, as Yefet in fact admits overtly
elsewhere.[41]

3.2 YEFET BEN ʿELI

While pondering the question of how Noah could know about what would happen in the future, Yefet accepts al-Qirqisani's basic solution, namely, that it was through divine revelation. Nevertheless, he goes into greater detail in describing the information God provided Noah. Accordingly, Noah was informed about Ham's deed but also about two other matters, namely, the future sinful behavior of the Canaanites and the future special status of the Israelites. The latter would become the worshippers of God, and would be chosen by Him to be His priests and to abide in His Temple, to witness His signs and miracles, to enjoy the divine presence (*shekhinah*), as well as to receive the Torah and the gift of prophecy:[42]

> [Scripture] informs [us] that when Noah woke up from his wine, he knew what Ham had done. It is not unlikely that God granted him this knowledge, for in this pericope[43] three matters are reported [i.e., what Ham had done to him, Canaan's subsequent sinful behavior, the future special status of the Israelites] which indicate that he undoubtedly knew this through divine revelation.[44]

Yefet infers from the broader context of the story that Noah was informed about various issues regarding Israel's future through divine revelation (*wahi*).[45] These serve Yefet as proof that Noah also received a revelation that informed him *inter alia* of what had happened to him during his drunken spell. This type of reasoning is employed similarly to a gap-filling midrash on the part of Yefet, for nowhere in the biblical passage is Noah literally described as owning to such a revelation from God.[46] Yefet infers that various information was revealed to him mainly in order to justify Noah's placing of the curse on Canaan even though Ham, according to Yefet (see section 2.2 above) was clearly the one who performed the sin.

In this manner Yefet adopts al-Qirqisani's solution—divine revelation—as a means of explaining Noah's decision to curse Canaan, yet he tries to connect it to the wider (literary) context of the Noah story at large, in which Noah does receive, at various stages, divine instruction from God. Without such a solution the only possible option is to admit that Noah made a mistake as a result of his drunkenness and cursed the wrong person. This may be an option inferred by the biblical narrative, yet it is not one that can be reconciled with a just God whose created world is run according to an intelligible plan and not haphazardly and who chooses His human agents (Noah) on the basis of their overall merit and worthiness. The possibility of a mistake, which renders Noah's curse a haphazard one, even though effective, is therefore unfathomable to al-Qirqisani and to Yefet. In order to avoid this possibility al-Qirqisani prefers the exegetical option that identifies Canaan as guilty of the sin related in Genesis 9:25 (see section 1.1 above).

Yefet, on the other hand, who cannot accept this exegetical possibility due to lack of direct evidence in the text as to Canaan's actual presence in the scene has to find a more winding literary route through which to prove that Noah nonetheless acted justly and knowledgeably in dooming Canaan and his seed to slavery.

3.3 AUTHORS OF THE *TALKHIS*: YUSUF IBN NUH AND ABU AL-FARAJ HARUN

The *Talkhis* is in agreement with other Karaite commentators of the time that in this passage Noah must have received some information through revelation. Yet, its authors emphasize that in this way, Noah learned about what Ham had done to him, rather than about the future behavior of his progeny:

> (As for) the statement (*And Noah awoke from his wine,) and knew what his youngest son had done unto him* (Gen 9:24), it is not precluded that he knew about that (i.e., what had occurred to him) through revelation.[47]

Whereas Yefet broadened the range of information provided to Noah through revelation in order to ground Noah's insights—despite drunkenness—within his wider portrayal in the pericope, the authors of the *Talkhis* narrow this revelation to one detail only, namely, to what had happened to Noah, when he had been drunk. They stick to the literal meaning of the specific passage on the curse, which indeed refers to Noah's retrospective "knowledge" of what had been done to him by his "youngest son," despite his drunkenness (Gen 9:25). Their solution explains how Noah came to know this fact alone. The difference in regard to the scope of Noah's revelation results from the difference in the *Talkhis*'s answer to the question of why Noah cursed Canaan in the first place. As shown above (see section 1.3) the *Talkhis* authors consider the curse to be a descriptive rather than a declarative statement on Noah's part. Hence if there was no curse to begin with, Noah did not need to receive specific divine revelation as to Canaan's future misdeeds that would justify such a curse. The only thing that Noah knew, which he could not have learned in any other way than revelation, was what was done to him while he was unconsciously drunk.

3.4 YESHUʿAH BEN YEHUDAH

Similarly to al-Qirqisani and Yefet, Yeshuʿah also allows for the possibility that Noah learned about the future behavior of his offspring through revelation. The idea of revelation not only filled in the narrative gap as to how Noah knew about what had occurred to him when he had been drunk, but it also rendered the cursing and punishment of Ham and Canaan justifiable and well deserved. Since in Yeshuʿa's view the phraseology of the curse elides the element *avi*, meaning "the father of (Canaan),"[48] he, too, has to focus on the insight that led Noah to curse Ham as Canaan's father:

> It is likely that the statement *and he knew* [Gen 9:24] [means] through revelation. The revelation also included [information about] what Ham will deserve for this abomination as well as what would happen to Shem and Japhet. And he [i.e., Noah] said, beginning with Ham, *Cursed be Canaan* [Gen 9:25].[49]

Yeshu'ah's explanation hinges on the same reference to Noah's knowledge (Gen 9:24) that preoccupies the *Talkhis*. He nevertheless adds the wider theological reasoning, akin to al-Qirqisani's and Yefet's readings of the curse. Accordingly, Noah was informed through revelation about three things: (1) what happened to him when he was drunk; (2) what will be the punishment inflicted on Ham for his offense; and (3) what will happen to his two other sons and their progeny. Furthermore, he specifies that the punishment of Ham consists of him being informed about his progeny's future subservience.[50]

Thus, despite the fact that there is no explicit mention of a revelation made to Noah in the curse passage, the Karaite exegetes appear to hold a consensus that Noah acquired some knowledge about the events that occurred when he was drunk through divine revelation. They differ only with regard to the extent of this knowledge, and especially as to what further information, if at all, this revelation contained, in their explanations regarding Noah's subsequent actions.

As Mu'tazilite theologians and devout interpreters, none of them allows for the possibility that the biblical narrative is deliberately portraying Noah as humanly flawed, flippantly fixing his curse upon Canaan rather than Ham while awakening from drunkenness, and uttering a mistaken curse, which, like a mistaken blessing, once made cannot be revoked. Moreover, the possible irony of the biblical narrative in presenting Canaan's destiny as a stroke of bad luck, as that of one who finds himself in the wrong place at the wrong time, is also beyond the boundaries of these exegetes' reading of the Bible, which does not focus on its dramatic (imaginative) power.[51]

4. The Problem of Inner Contradiction: The Blessing of Ham versus the Curse of Canaan

The above-cited discussions focus on theoretical problems, which, though connected to the text of the curse of Canaan (Gen 9:18–28), are engendered by theological ("extra-textual") considerations, as well as by the need to fill in what are perceived as informational gaps within the biblical account. Nevertheless, there are also a number of contextual ("inner-textual") problems in this scriptural passage, which were spotted and addressed by the medieval Karaite exegetes. They involve two kinds of incongruities, namely those apparent within this particular scriptural pericope and those that arise from its juxtaposition with other biblical passages.

According to the immediate biblical context, right after the flood, *God blessed Noah and all his sons* (Gen 9:1, 9:9). Thus there is an apparent contradiction between the initial divine blessing made to all of Noah's offspring and the subsequent curse of one of their representatives. *Nota bene* the blessing of Ham might provide a convenient excuse to justify why Canaan was the one to be cursed instead of his father, Ham, for a deed he did not commit, since God had previously invested Ham with a blessing (see sections 4.1 and 4.2 below). Nonetheless, the question remains of how it is possible that anyone of Noah's blessed offspring should be cursed at all, in contradiction to an earlier scriptural statement. Furthermore, from a theological perspective, too, if God knows everything in advance, why would He bless Ham in the first place, knowing that his offspring would sin? At least two of the Karaite commentators surveyed above felt compelled to address this contextual and theological problem.

4.1 YAʿQUB AL-QIRQISANI

As we have seen, al-Qirqisani admits that it is not improbable that Ham was the one who had sinned. Nonetheless, Noah cursed Canaan, instead of Ham, precisely because of the divine blessing, which prevented him from putting a curse on someone who had previously been blessed by God.[52]

> Others say that [Noah] cursed Canaan, and did not curse Ham, because God blessed Noah and his sons, so it was impossible to curse the one whom God blessed.[53]

Allowing for this possibility might return al-Qirqisani to square one, to wit, is it just to punish the progeny because of the transgression committed by its progenitor? In order to avoid this theological pitfall, al-Qirqisani provides another, more likely explanation in his view, according to which divine blessings and curses are never general, but refer to specific individuals, who most deserve them:

> Therefore [Noah] singled them out [i.e., the children of Canaan] in the curse, excluding the rest of his [i.e., Ham's] children, of whom [he knew that] this would not be [their] way, for Scripture permitted the entrance of Egyptians in the religion [i.e., their conversion and becoming Israelites] and their marriage, when it said *thou shalt not abhor an Egyptian* [Deut 23:8] etc. Thus, his [i.e., Noah's] curse of Canaan was not their curse [i.e., the Egyptians and other children of Ham, apart from Canaan], since from all of his [i.e., Ham's] children, [Canaan] deserved it [i.e., the curse] most. Had [Noah] cursed them, the curse would be applied to the worse of his children,

and [to the one] who is most deserving of it than the others, for it would be impossible to afflict [with it someone], who was the most obedient among them, especially taking into account [that] God blessed Noah and his sons in what preceded, as it is said *And God blessed Noah and his sons* [Gen 9:1]. So Noah did not act contrary to the earlier blessing, but afflicted with the curse the one [offspring] of whom he knew would deserve it. Joshua did the same when he cursed the Gibeonites [and said] *Now therefore ye are cursed* [Josh 9:23]....Moreover, this story is similar to the story, [wherein] God forbade the children of Israel to travel in the land of Edom. For [God] had said *for I will not give thee of his land for a possession* [Deut 2:9] and He had said *Thou shalt not abhor an Edomite* [Deut 23:8]. Next, He singled out some of the children of Esau, to wit Amalek, and commanded their eradication, as it is said *That thou shalt blot out the remembrance of Amalek* [Deut 25:19]. It [was] so, because from [all of] the children of Esau, they [i.e., the Amalekites] deserved that [most], [just] as from [all of] the children of Ham, Canaan deserved the curse [most].[54]

In al-Qirqisani's view, Noah's curse, apparently sanctioned by God, was very precise and selective. By the same token, it constituted a kind of specifying "annex" to the initial blessing administered by God to Noah's offspring in general.[55] To prove his claim, al-Qirqisani brings various quotations from other scriptural passages, containing similar specifying verses.

4.2 YEFET BEN ʿELI

Like al-Qirqisani, though in a more resolute way, Yefet expresses the opinion that Noah would not curse someone blessed by God, and therefore it was Canaan whom he cursed. Yet, as we have seen above (see section 1.2), Canaan was not cursed without a reason:

> [Noah] did not deem [it proper] to curse him [i.e., Ham], since God had blessed him together with all his brothers. Therefore he made his [i.e., Ham's] punishment over [what] he had done into a token unto him of the high rank of Shem and Japheth and of the curse of Canaan as well as the decrease in the rank of his children.[56]

In this passage, Yefet admits that Ham was not free from blame. As we remember, according to Yefet, Canaan was punished by curse not because of what he did at that moment to his grandfather, Noah, but on account of the sinful deeds that he merely commenced to perform at that time, which will find their continuation in the transgressions perpetrated by his progeny. For it was Ham, who, according to Yefet's literal reading of this passage, committed an offence against Noah (see section 1.2 above). Yet, Noah could not have cursed him as punishment for this offense since it would have undermined God's previous blessing. Therefore, Ham's punishment consisted of being informed about the misfortune that will occur to his offspring and about the fact that despite the blessing, they will not be as distinguished as the progeny of Shem and Japheth.[57] A distinct feature of Yefet's comment on this pericope is that without distorting the literal sense of Scripture—Ham is the object of the curse—he endeavors to provide a cohesive explanation which, at the same time, concords with his moral sensibility.

5. The Lot of the Canaanites: Slavery or Eradication?

The contextual difficulties regarding the curse of Canaan are not limited to inconsistencies found within the immediate pericope but are also apparent in the broader scriptural account. Such are the apparent discrepancies between the curse as pronounced by Noah in the book of Genesis and the severe prescriptions concerning Canaan as formulated in the books of Exodus and Deuteronomy. These presented a problem in biblical exegesis at large and especially in the contextual reading of the medieval Judaeo-Arabic exegetes,[58] for how could the Canaanites become slaves, if they are to be eradicated? While commenting on this passage, two of our Karaite exegetes found it appropriate to address this cross-textual problem.

5.1 YEFET BEN ʿELI

Yefet skillfully solves the aforementioned exegetical crux by drawing on the data provided in the interpreted passage and on his wider knowledge of the biblical background. He suggests a simple solution: Some of the descendants of Canaan were killed, whereas others escaped, and those who escaped were to become slaves. Thus, he manages to avoid defying the literal meaning of this verse, by proposing a harmonizing interpretation of the apparent contradiction, which seems to rely on a form of specification or narrowing-down (takhsis) of a general category, without invoking extra textual arguments.[59]

> The statement and let Canaan be [their servant] [Gen 9:26] refers to the remaining children of Canaan, who escaped from the Israelites. [Scripture] informs [us] that they will become a servant of servants [Gen 9:25] to the rest of the children of Ham, that is to Mitzraim [i.e., Egypt], Cush, Put. It means that when they [i.e., the children of Canaan] escaped from the Israelites, some of them spread in these countries. And some of them spread in the countries of the children of Shem, that is in the countries of Elam, Asshur, Lud, and Aram [Gen 10:22] and in the land of the subdivisions of the tribes of Arpachshad, others than the Land of Israel, from which the Master of the Universe expelled them. Similarly, some of them dispersed in the land of Japheth and became slaves to them [i.e., the children of Japheth].[60]

As opposed to al-Qirqisani, according to whom all the Canaanites should be killed and "not one of them shall be spared" (see section 3.1 above), Yefet proposes a more lenient vision of divine justice, by admitting that the prescription to eradicate the seven nations does not refer to all of the descendants of Canaan but only to those who remained in the land of Israel. The Canaanites, who according to the biblical account had previously populated that land, were allowed to escape from it without being eradicated, and those who did so became slaves, in accordance with Noah's curse. By advancing a more lenient interpretation of God's prescriptions concerning the Canaanites, Yefet comes across as more respectful of the literal meaning of the scriptural passage under discussion, which reads *"and let Canaan be their servant"* (Gen 9:26).

5.2 YESHUʿAH BEN YEHUDAH

Yeshuʿah also identifies the discrepancy in the biblical accounts of the fate of the Canaanites. His explanation is based, like Yefet's, on the immediate and related biblical passages, yet his solution differs from Yefet's: While only the Canaanites that remained in the land of Israel were eradicated, those who fled the land became dispersed and fell into decline:

> God, the Sublime, had brought about the eradication of some of them [i.e., the Canaanites], prior to the Israelites' entry to the Land. Next, He sent them the hornet [Exod 23:28]. Then Israel killed some of them, whereas many [others] were dispersed between the lands whence they fled from the Israelites to the west countries. And they became slaves to Cush and Mitzraim [i.e., Egypt] and, at times, also to the children of Shem[61] and to the children of Japheth, for the hand of Greece and others was raised from the children of Japheth, as the hand of Ashur and others was raised from the children of Shem in the [former] countries of the Canaanites. And [the expression] *a slave of slaves shall he be* [Gen 9:25] is a hyperbole [*mubalagah*][62] of their fall and decline, [just] as [the expression] "the king of kings" is a hyperbole of elevation.[63]

In Yeshuʿah's view, what appear as contradictory fates, annihilation and slavery, may be reconciled—the former befalling a segment of Canaan's descendants who remained in the land and the latter pertaining to those who fled the land. Yeshuʿah perceives the expression *slave of slaves* as a rhetorical trope (*mubalagah*), which typically expresses exaggeration in biblical Hebrew. This original interpretation affects Yeshuʿah's overall reading of the passage, which also contends that Noah's words should be construed as a descriptive report, not an actual curse (see section 1.3 above). In such a reading, Noah is describing to Ham the Canaanites' fate as one of future decline, rather than actual slavery. This interpretation lessens the severity of the Canaanites' predicament and minimizes the harshness of their punishment. Through the use of linguistic and grammatical tools, it diminishes the apparent cruelty and unjust character of Canaan's curse, first since it is an elided form of expression—the subject of the curse is clearly Ham (see section 1.4 above). Second, even then, it is not an actual curse, but a descriptive report made by Noah to Ham, the father of Canaan, regarding the fate of his progeny (see section 2.2 above). Third, this fate—at least in regard to those Canaanites who fled the Land of Israel—does not specify actual but rather a more general dependency on other nations. In effect, says Yeshu'ah, some Canaanites were annihilated, but many fled and were dispersed from their original land and made to live among other nations. It is this general state of decline that is presaged by Noah's report and which serves as an adequate punishment for Ham's deed. Moreover, the state of decline in itself is not vested upon the Canaanites due to the sin of their forefather; rather, it is the result of their own accumulative sins over time, of which Ham is being made aware, in advance, as part of his punishment.

6. Who Should Inherit the Holy Land?

The last moral issue on which our commentators focus is the right of dwelling in the Holy Land and taking it into possession. First, is this right dependent on a predetermined divine plan—in the sense of God deciding ahead of time who should dwell where and who should be eradicated—and so may be deemed unconditional, or is it dependent on the fulfillment of certain conditions? Second, if there are such conditions, are they determined by ethnic origin (i.e., Canaanites versus Israelites) or by religious-ethical values (i.e., polytheists versus monotheists)?

6.1 YA'QUB AL-QIRQISANI

The Bible provides narrative detail, according to al-Qirqisani, when this detail is necessary or vital to the understanding of the divinely revealed Law (namely, the commandments [furud], be they positive or negative). The purpose of any religious person is to live in accordance with the will of God, by obeying His commandments. In order to do so accurately, however, the person needs to know in detail the exact provenance of each and every nation:

> Therefore, God obliged[64] us [in Scripture] to do various things concerning the matter of [distinct] nations and people. For there are those whom He obliged us to eradicate completely, including their children and women, like the seven nations. And there are those whom He commanded us to invite into peace, and [only] if they do not respond, we [should] kill [all] the adult men, and [God] asked us to spare [their] wives and [their] children. And there are those, who were permitted to enter the religion [i.e., convert and

became Israelites] and He authorized us to marry them, after three generations, like the Egyptians and the Edomites, and other examples of what [God] imposed on us with regard to the rest of nations. Therefore it is absolutely vital to determine the lineage of every nation and people in order to obey to what we were commanded concerning these people, not others.[65]

In the opinion of al-Qirqisani, Scripture is not only conceived as a repository of God's commandments, but also as a kind of guidebook for their proper fulfillment. Accordingly, the divine instructions regarding the seven nations of Canaan were of the binding (unrelenting) type, wherein there is no room for deliberation, since they must be obeyed. It was only in order that they be obeyed correctly that the Bible includes a narrative explanation as to who were the Canaanites. According to this conception, individual responsibility is overshadowed by God's ultimate plan of justice, which in the case of the seven nations gives precedence to a collective form of responsibility (see section 3.1 above).

6.2 YEFET BEN ʿELI

Yefet is reluctant to express views on the collective (and/or preplanned) dimension of divine justice akin to those advocated by al-Qirqisani.[66] In his Bible commentaries he often emphasizes that every individual is responsible for his own deeds. This tenet is also apparent in Yefet's argument that although the punishment of Ham consisted of his being informed about what would happen to his children, the children themselves will be punished on account of their *own* sins:

In this story [Scripture] informs [us] [about] the degradation of Canaan and [about] the decrease of his rank [below the rank of] the rest of the children of Noah. Moreover, it mentions the distinction of the children of Shem. The purpose of mentioning Canaan and what will happen to him was to cause pain to the heart of Ham in requital of his deed....It resembles [Nathan's] words [directed] to David, may peace be upon him, *Now therefore, the sword shall never depart from thy house* [2 Sam 12:10]. For we should not believe that his [i.e., Ham's] children will be killed because of him [i.e., Ham], but rather they will be killed because of their [own] deeds, as Ahaziah and Amaziah and Jehoiachim and the children of Zedekiah were killed because of their [own] deeds. God caused pain to his [i.e., Ham's] heart as a token of that. Similarly, He informs the righteous about what will happen to their obedient children, so that they [may] rejoice by it.[67]

Yefet goes to great lengths in order to convince the reader that every (biblical) individual is responsible for his own deeds and that although God is omniscient and knows ahead what will happen, He does not predetermine individual fate by deciding that someone's repentance cannot be accepted (see section 3.1 above). Even the land of Israel is not irrevocably "destined" to be handed over to the Israelites or unconditionally promised to them. Rather, the children of Israel have to deserve the land and gain it by their own merits. For sure, these merits are dependent on their belief in God and obedience to Him.

In Yefet's view, therefore, the divine promise of the land, as it is described in the Bible, is conditional and does not depend on Israel's ethnic origin as a "chosen people" but rather on their moral behavior.[68] This reading can be reconciled with the ideology expressed in certain biblical books, especially Deuteronomy and Kings, in which Israel's presence in the land (or their exile from it) is dependent on religious-moral behavior.[69] In this respect, Yefet's reading is hardly paralleled by the other Karaite exegetes of the tenth and eleventh centuries. In another place, while commenting on Genesis 15:8, he expounds it further:

> Someone may ask, and say: "What does it mean that [Scripture says] *and he believed in the Lord* [Gen 15:6] with regard to the first saying, which is an imprecise promise [of offspring], without [Abram] having asked *whereby shall I know*, whereas, regarding this promise [of the land] he asked: *whereby shall I know* [Gen 15:8]." The answer to this [question] is that, when the promise is about the great number of offspring, God sometimes does similar [things] to the unbelievers. Yet, [with regard to] the handing over of the land, **God would not give it, but to the obedient**. It was possible that Abram's offspring would be obedient, but it was [equally] possible that they would disobey, and would not **deserve it** [i.e., the land]. So God's words: *Unto thy seed will I give this land* [Gen 12:7] would [only be fulfilled], "if [your offspring] are obedient to Me." Thus [Abram's] words *whereby shall I know* mean: "I want to know for certain that I will inherit it [i.e., the land]. For if I made certain of that, I would know that my offspring would, most certainly, be obedient." Therefore he said in the first statement *And he believed in the Lord* [Gen 15:6], whereas in the second [statement] *whereby shall I know*.[70]

By so stressing the ethical-religious aspect of inheritance, and identifying religious obedience (*ta'ah*) as a necessary condition, a prerequisite for dwelling in the Holy Land and possessing it, Yefet accords to human beings an important role in shaping the course of human history and makes them fully responsible for their own fate. Even God's threats to the sinners and promises to His chosen people are not unconditional, but depend on free decisions and actions of individual human agents.[71] In this, Yefet differs from other Karaite commentators of the period, especially from al-Qirqisani, who appears to put more stress on God's control over history, in that He irrevocably commands in His Scripture the complete eradication of certain nations as a collective punishment for their sins. Yefet, on the other hand, emphasizes the role of individual human beings, and the children of Israel among them, as having their own share in shaping history and wielding influence upon their fate by their own deeds.[72]

The ultimate purpose of human history, in Yefet's view, is that everyone, irrespective of his or her ethnic origin, will come to an understanding of divine truth, as revealed in the Torah, and convert or repent. He formulates this idea explicitly in his comment *ad* Numbers 24:17:

> The third meaning [of the word "star"] is the light which the people of the world will see from their darkness in the matters of their religions, and they will return to the truth, for the Torah is being compared to the light, as it is said *For the commandment is a lamp, and the teaching is light* [Prov 6:23]. And [Scripture] [also] compared the Messiah to the light, as it is said *I will also give thee for a light of the nations, [that My salvation may be unto the end of the earth]* [Isa 49:6]. Moreover, they will cease afflictions and wars which were between them and in this [respect] they will resemble someone who went out of the darkness to the light.[73]

In Yefet's opinion, the truth—to wit, the Jewish religion in its Karaite version, based on the Hebrew Bible—will in the end shine through. For the time being, the ignorance and deficiency of human intellect (symbolized by darkness) prevents certain people from seeing the truth (symbolized by light). Yet, Yefet is convinced that one day all humanity ("people of the world") will understand that the Torah is the unique repository of truth–the Truth–and having realized that, they will convert to Judaism (in its Karaite version). Such being, in the exegete's view, the final purpose of human history, his vision of it appears more universal (and messianic) than that proposed by other Karaites of this peod, espriecially al-Qirqisani.

6.3 AUTHORS OF THE *TALKHIS:* YUSUF IBN NUH AND ABU AL-FARAJ HARUN

The interpretation found in the *Talkhis* resembles the one proposed by al-Qirqisani in that it also seems to stress the importance of God's decisions. The authors of the commentary do not overtly proclaim in this context that the "future misfortune" of Canaan's offspring is justified by their own reprehensible moral behavior, deserving such a punishment, and hence God's decisions take on a more arbitrary dimension in their explanation:

> [About the statement] *And he said: Blessed be the LORD, the God of Shem; and let Canaan be their servant* [Gen 9:26] it is said [that] God, the God of Shem and his children, who made the children of Canaan slaves to them [i.e., to Shem and his children], is thank-worthy, meaning that He, the Sublime, is thank-worthy for what He decided in terms of the decrease in the rank

of the children of Canaan [that is to be] below the rank of the children of
Shem, so that they [i.e., the children of Canaan] become slaves to them [i.e.,
to the children of Shem], for He, the Almighty and Sublime, is just in what
He decided in this respect.[74]

Hence, God made an irrevocable decision as to what would be the lot of the
offspring of Canaan and that of the offspring of Shem. This decision, moreover, does not seem to be dependent, in the *Talkhis*'s view, on human actions.
The only thing that human beings can do is to thank the creator and praise
Him for what He decides.

6.4 YESHUʿAH BEN YEHUDAH

Unlike Yefet, Yeshuʿah diminishes the role of individual responsibility of human
agents by admitting that the curse of Canaan, which preceded the disobedience
of his offspring, has in some ways determined the fate of the Canaanite peoples
("for the cursing of Canaan *entails* his [future] disobedience," see section 2.2
above, emphasis added). Thus, Yeshuʿah's initial concern for divine justice, which
does not allow the punishment by a curse of someone who did not commit the
sin (see sections 1.3 and 1.4 above), appears to admit to the idea that the punishment of children may form part of the punishment of the sin committed by
their father ("The revelation also included [information about] *what Ham will
deserve for his abominations*," see section 3.4 above, emphasis added). Moreover,
Yeshuʿah puts in relief God's role as the sovereign ruler of human history. It is
He who "brought about the eradication of some of them (i.e., the Canaanites),"
who "sent them the hornet" and who, at the end of the day, caused their fall and
decline (see section 5.2 above). Nevertheless, his interpretation finds other ways,
as we have shown above, to lessen the severity of the Canaanites' predicament
and to minimize the harshness of the divine verdict visited upon them (see section 5.2). This would suggest that he was affected, in part, by Yefet's overall stance
on the ethical preconditioning of the land's inheritance.

7. The Canaanites as a Reference Point to Ethnic versus Ethic Criteria in Distinguishing the True Believer

Most of the Karaite commentators discussed in this chapter appear to agree
that, according to the Bible, ethnic divisions between peoples may, to a certain extent, determine their fate. In the view of some of these exegetes, God
explained this to the believers in His Scripture, so that they could fulfill His
specific commandments regarding these people (see section 6.1 above).

Against this background, Yefet's attitude toward "others" appears to stand
out as much more lenient, depending, after all, on individual responsibility,

irrespectively of ethnic origin. It is therefore important to clarify who the Canaanites were in his view. In this context, it is instructive to quote Yefet's commentary on Genesis 12:8, wherein he emphasizes Abraham's missionary activity upon his arrival in the land of Canaan:

> Two interpretations are said about [the fact that Scripture] adds here *And [Abram] called upon the name of the Lord*: [1] The one is that he called for the religion, and summoned people [to come] to him. [2] The other is that he called [God] [in prayer][75] with gratefulness and exultation.[76]

The emphasis put by Yefet on the missionary activity of the forefathers (*nota bene* attested also in the *Talkhis*), gives the impression that he perceived other nations, including the Canaanites, as potential proselytes to the monotheistic (Abrahamic) faith and not as peoples unconditionally doomed to eradication in advance by an irrevocable divine decree.[77] Such a view also accords with Yefet's generally more open and inclusive conception of the "children of Israel" and, as a result, of Karaite Judaism as a community ready to accept new members, irrespective of their ethnic origins.

This conception finds expression in Yefet's introduction to the book of Job, where he overtly admits that people from other communities might also exhibit a most righteous belief in one God, like Job, who, Yefet emphasizes, was not an Israelite (i.e., "from the worm of Jacob"), according to his biblical portrayal, and yet is the ideal representative of righteous faith. The unique difference, in Yefet's view, between the Israelites and the non-Israelites in this respect is quantitative rather than qualitative: Whereas in the case of the Israelite community all of its members—or at least most of them—are righteous believers, in the case of other communities the righteous monotheists are but isolated individuals.[78] Accordingly, the line of demarcation that divides between the faithful forefathers and "the others" seems to run, in his opinion, along what he conceived as ethical values, being dependent upon righteousness, faith in one God and obedience to His commandments, rather than encoded ethnic bounds.

A similar open and welcoming attitude to "others," which attaches value to what Yefet conceived as moral ideals rather than ethnic affiliation, is echoed in his comment on Psalm 1:1, wherein he explains that Scripture says *Happy is the man* and does not say "Happy is the nation" for three reasons, the first being

> to include therein everyone, whom God should wish [to include] from one of the nations, before the prophet [i.e., Moses], may peace be upon him, as well as after him. Therefore, it does not say "Happy is the nation" or "Happy is the people," which would be specified to Israel alone.[79]

Thus, the community of the "happy man," the virtuous, the righteous, is not ethnically limited to the children of Israel but encompasses all those who believe in the God of Israel, are obedient to His laws, and refrain from sin.

Religious-moral behavior, and not ethnic affiliation, is the criterion for their inclusion in God's blessing.

In the same vein, Yefet interprets Habakuk 3:3: "*And the earth is full of His praise*: means among Israel and (among) all those from the rest of the nations, who are monotheists (*muwahhid*)."[80] Accordingly, "otherness" is a feature by which also Israelites may be defined (*zar*), provided that they worship something other than God ('*avodah zarah*). Interestingly, if they do so, in Yefet's view, as expressed explicitly elsewhere, they become "like the seven nations."[81] Thus, in Yefet's understanding of the Bible, the ethnic divide between Israelites and Canaanites is superseded by strictly ethical-religious values.

Conclusions

The story of the curse of Canaan in Genesis 9 as explored by the Karaite exegetes aroused theological and moral difficulties, especially with regard to divine justice. They also identified in it certain contradictions, within the pericope itself (the blessing of Ham *versus* the curse of some of his offspring) and the wider biblical context (Were the Canaanites doomed to be slaves or to be eradicated?). These exegetes also engaged in reader-response gap-filling, since the story is silent concerning some important information (How did Noah know what happened to him when he was drunk, and how could he know what would be the future fate of his progeny?). As a cross-section of various exegetical cruxes, the story constitutes a case study in analyzing the medieval Karaites' varied approaches to the questions of the fate of Canaanites and Israel's inheritance of the Holy Land.

The ethical-theological problem of the curse of Canaan (sections 1 and 2). The Karaite exegetes gave different responses to the question of why Canaan was cursed: Because it was he who had committed the sin against Noah; because he had committed some other transgressions; he was not cursed at all, but Noah simply informed him about the future behavior of his offspring, the Canaanites, which was meant to grieve him, and this grief served as a punishment for his deed; the curse actually referred to Ham, but there is a missing syntactical part in this verse (i.e., "the father of" [*avi*]). It has been shown that the common denominator behind these diverse interpretations is the concern with divine justice, a paramount Mu'tazilite tenet whose general influence is apparent in the exegetical discussions.

God's omniscience and the prophetic revelation to Noah (section 3). How could Noah know about what had happened to him, as well as what would be the future lot of his offspring? All the exegetes are in agreement that he was informed through prophecy. Nevertheless, they differ in determining the nature of the information that Noah received: He was informed only of what had happened to him when he had been drunk, or perhaps also about the future elevation of the progeny of Shem and Japhet and the degradation of the progeny of Canaan, the son of Ham.

The textual discrepancies within the story of Noah (section 4). The previous blessing of Noah and all of his children (Ham, Shem, and Japhet) versus the subsequent curse of Canaan the son of Ham finds different exegetical responses: Ham could not be cursed because of the previous blessing and that is why Canaan, his son, was cursed; the blessing was general, whereas the curse was specific and relative: the offspring of Canaan was not to be as elevated as the progeny of Shem and Japhet.

The textual discrepancies within the broader biblical context (section 5). Some of the exegetes solve the discrepancies between Genesis and Deuteronomy by making a distinction between those who remained in the land of Canaan and were to be erased and those who fled and were to become slaves.

The problem of Canaanites and the inheritance of the Holy Land (sections 6 and 7). Regarding the conditions for dwelling in the Holy Land and inheriting it, most of the Karaite commentators seem to contend that God determines inheritance, in that He is the one who made the decision (namely, to punish the Canaanites for their sins by complete eradication); the only thing that his believers can do is to be grateful to Him for His resolutions and to attempt to contribute to the proper execution of His will by fulfilling His commandments, and by doing so, deserve the inheritance. As opposed to this dominant interpretive tradition, Yefet's interpretation poses inheritance to be strictly conditional upon behavior and hence dependent on individual conduct in respect of religiously conceived ethics, to wit, the belief in one God and obedience to His law. Everyone, including the Canaanites, may be a potential proselyte to the true monotheistic faith. The ultimate end of human history is that all humanity accepts the truth, that is, God's Torah, converts (nonbelievers), or repents (sinning believers).

A chronological scrutinizing of all these distinct responses to the problematic passage suggests a gradual development of textual consciousness in the works of these Karaite commentators, who, over time, appear to be more and more concerned with the "plain" or "apparent" meaning of the scriptural passage, attempting to adhere to it in their exegesis as much as possible. This concern, however, is invariably tilted by the extra-textual, theological-ethical considerations, apparently of overriding importance, relating to the concept of divine justice. Some commentators employ the concept of God's foreknowledge to prove that His decisions are always just. Others are inclined to approve of collective responsibility of certain nations for the sins of their members, even if not all individuals equally participate in their commitment.

Against this background, Yefet's Bible commentaries are exceptional in that they display a much more lenient, and thus inclusive, attitude toward "others," leaving the door open for those of them who wish to convert or repent. Thereby he emphasizes individual responsibility in determining one's fate, at least in terms of divine compensation, as completely independent of ethnic origin.

Finally, all of the commentators try to prove that textual discrepancies are but apparent, by providing harmonizing (contextually based) interpretations of seemingly contradicting biblical statements, though they each do so in their own way.

Notes

1. For pre-medieval ponderings of such questions, including what was the precise nature of Ham's transgression, see, for example, *Gen. Rab.* 36:7–8; *b. Sanh.* 70a. We would like to express our heartfelt gratitude to Gregor Schwarb, for his helpful comments regarding the Jewish reception of Mu'tazilite theology and other aspects of this paper. This publication was prepared within the framework of the DFG-DIP grant project (2013 -2017) entitled Biblia Arabica: The Bible in Arabic among Jews, Christians and Muslims (Project Investigators: Camilla Adang, Meira Polliack, Sabine Schmidtke).

2. For detailed works on the development and leading principles of Karaite exegesis in the Islamic milieu, see Daniel Frank, *Search Scripture Well, Karaite Exegetes and the Origins of the Jewish Bible Commentary in the Islamic East*, Études sur le judaïsme médiéval 29 (Leiden: Brill, 2004); Meira Polliack, "Major Trends in Karaite Biblical Exegesis in the Tenth and Eleventh Centuries," in *A Guide to Karaite Studies: An Introduction to Literary Sources of Medieval and Modern Karaite Judaism*, ed. Meira Polliack (Leiden: Brill, 2003), 363–413; Meira Polliack, "Historicizing Prophetic Literature: Yefet ben 'Eli's Commentary on Hosea and Its Relationship to al-Qumisi's *Pitron*," in *Pesher Nahum: Texts and Studies in Jewish History and Literature from Antiquity through the Middle Ages presented to Norman Golb*, eds. J. L. Kraemer and Michael G. Wechsler (Chicago: University of Chicago Press, 2011), 153–190; Gregor Schwarb, "Capturing the Meaning of God's Speech: The Relevance of *usul al-fiqh* to an Understanding of *usul al-tafsir* in Jewish and Muslim *kalam*," in *A Word Fitly Spoken: Studies in Mediaeval Exegesis of the Hebrew Bible and the Qur'an Presented to Haggai Ben-Shammai*, eds. Meir M. Bar-Asher, Simon Hopkins, Sarah Stroumsa, and Bruno Chiesa (Jerusalem: Ben-Zvi Institute for the History of Jewish Communities in the East, Yad Izhaq Ben-Zvi and the Hebrew University of Jerusalem, 2007), 111–156.

3. For the study of Mu'tazilite thought and the use of its terminology and concepts in the works of Ya'qub al-Qirqisani and Yefet ben 'Eli, see especially Haggai Ben-Shammai, *The Doctrines of Religious Thought of Abu Yusuf Ya'qub al-Qirqisani and Yefet ben 'Eli* [in Hebrew], 2 vols. (PhD diss., Hebrew University of Jerusalem, 1977). For the overall assessment that Yefet displayed a negative attitude toward the Mu'tazila, see Ben-Shammai, *Abu Yusuf Ya'qub al-Qirqisani and Yefet ben 'Eli*, 2:xliii. See also Michael Wechsler, *The Arabic Translation and Commentary of Yefet ben 'Eli the Karaite on the Book of Esther*, Karaite Texts and Studies, vol. 1, Études sur le judaïsme médiéval 36 (Leiden: Brill, 2008), 40–58. For an example of Mu'tazilite terminology as used within the Karaite exegetical debate, see below, n. 77. For an example of Yefet's selective use of Islamic exegetical terminology, see Marzena Zawanowska, "Islamic Exegetical Terms in Yefet ben 'Eli's Commentaries on the Holy Scriptures," Journal of Jewish Studies 64 (2013): 1–20. For a detailed review of scholarly studies devoted to Yefet, see Marzena Zawanowska, "Review of Scholarly Research on Yefet and His Works," *Revue des études juives* 173 (1/2) (2014), forthcoming.

4. For studies on the adoption of Mu'tazilism theology and its typical foci into medieval Jewish and especially Karaite thought, see Camilla Adang, Sabine Schmidtke, David Sklare, eds., *A Common Rationality: Mu'tazilism in Islam and Judaism* (Würzburg: Ergon Verlag Würzburg, 2007), especially 11–20, 157–216, 229–296, 377–462; Haggai Ben-Shammai, "Kalam in Medieval Jewish Philosophy," in *History of Jewish Philosophy*, eds. Daniel H. Frank and O. Leaman (Leiden: Brill, 1997), 115–148; Haggai Ben-Shammai, "Major Trends in Karaite Philosophy and Polemics," in *A Guide to Karaite Studies: An Introduction to Literary Sources of Medieval and Modern Karaite Judaism*, ed. Meira Polliack (Leiden: Brill 2003), 339–362; Wilfred Madelung and Sabine Schmidtke, *Rational Theology in Interfaith Communication, Abu l-Husayn al-Basri's Mu'tazili Theology among the Karaites in the Fatimid Age* (Leiden: Brill, 2006); Colette Sirat, *A History of Jewish Philosophy in the Middle Ages* (Cambridge: Cambridge University Press and Maison des Sciences de l'Homme, 1985), 15–56; Gregor Schwarb, "Kalam," in *Encyclopedia of Jews in the Islamic World*, 4 vols., eds. Norman Stillman et al. (Leiden: Brill, 2009), 3:91–98.

5. It appears that no commentaries on this passage by Daniel al-Qumisi, Sahl ibn Masliah, Salmon ben Yeruhim, David ben Bo'az, or 'Ali ibn Sulayman have been identified/found yet. We express our gratitude to the Center for the Study of Judaeo-Arabic Literature and Culture at the Ben-Zvi Institute and especially to its director, Dr. David Sklare, for granting Dr. Zawanowska the opportunity to study "working editions" of Karaite Bible commentaries compiled and stored at the center.

6. On Sa'ayah's exposition of this verse, which has several features in common with that of Yeshu'ah ben Yehudah, see below, n. 20. It should also be pointed out that the commentary by Samuel ben Hofni Gaon is an important (but often implicit) reference point for the Jerusalem Karaites. All in all, the Karaite tradition of scriptural exegesis was not separatist or isolationist. Nevertheless, a detailed analysis of medieval Judaeo-Arabic Rabbanite exegesis on this verse lies beyond the scope of this chapter.

7. Questions concerning free will and predestination were raised in ancient Jewish sources, as in the known interpretive crux in Exod 10:1, where God admits "toughening" Pharaoh's heart in his refusal to release the Israelites. (See, e.g., chapters 1–14 in *Midrash Shemot Rabbah*, ed. Avigdor Shinan (Jerusalem: Dvir, 1984), 257 (section 13.3) and n. 31 therein). Nevertheless, the philosophical couching of such questions becomes apparent in Jewish Bible exegesis from the time of the Jews' encounter with Islamic *kalam*, see Haggai Ben-Shammai, *Abu Yusuf Ya'qub al-Qirqisani and Yefet ben 'Eli*, 1:101–111; Meira Polliack, "Major Trends in Karaite Biblical Exegesis," 339–348; George Vajda, *Deux commentaires karaïtes sur l'Ecclésiaste*, Études sur le judaïsme médiéval 12 (Leiden: Brill, 1971), 121–138.

8. On the Karaite theories of prophecy and the adoption of Mu'tazilite tenets, see Haggai Ben-Shammai, *Abu Yusuf Ya'qub al-Qirqisani and Yefet ben 'Eli*, 1:268, 277; 2:173–174, 232–233; Colette Sirat, *Les théories des visions surnaturelle dans la pensée juive du Moyen Age*, Études sur le judaïsme médiéval (Leiden: Brill, 1969), 40–60. See also Meira Polliack and Eliezer Schlossberg, "Historical-literary, Rhetorical and Redactional Methods of Interpretation in Yefet ben Eli's Introduction to the Minor Prophets," in *Exegesis and Grammar in Medieval Karaite Texts*, ed. Geoffrey Khan (Oxford: Oxford University Press, 2001), 1–39; Meira Polliack and Eliezer Schlossberg, *Commentary of Yefet ben 'Eli the Karaite on the Book of Hosea* [in Hebrew] (Ramat Gan: Bar Ilan University Press, 2009), 14 n. 23.

9. The question of "inherited" guilt, blame, and punishment was addressed in Jewish and Muslim *kalam* treatises of the time (*atfal al-mushrikin*). For a short version of such,

see Manekdim Sheshdiv, *Ta'liq Sharh al-Usul al-Khamsa*, ed. 'Abd al-Karim 'Uthman (Cairo: Maktabat Wahba, 1996), 477.

10. On the idea of "corporate personality" punishment in the Hebrew Bible, such as that visited upon the children of the offender, and the prophetic polemic against it, see Exod 20:5; Jer 31:28; Ezek 18. For a detailed study, see, e.g., Gordon H. Matties, *Ezekiel 18 and the Rhetoric of Moral Discourse* (Atlanta: Scholars Press, 1990).

11. Qirqisani mentions the opinion of those who think there might have been a sexual act involved in the scene beyond the mere witnessing of Noah's nakedness. He quotes specifically from *b. Sanh.* 70a where the sages debate Ham's sexual mutilation or violation of Noah on the basis of the analogy with the form וירא in the story of Dinah and Shechem (Gen 34:2). Nevertheless, he finds this explanation unlikely in the context of this passage: קלנא קד זעם קום
אנה קד כאן הנאך בטיה גיר אלנטֹר והו פעל וקע מנה ואן קר׳ וירא נטֹיר קר׳ וראה את ערותה והי תראה את ערותו אלדֹי
ליס הו נטֹר פקט בל הו פעל וקע לקר׳ ערות אחותו גלה. ואעתלו בקר׳ וידע את אשר עשה לו בנו הקטן פאכֹבר באן קד כאן
הנאך פעל גיר אלנטֹר תבינה נח וראי אתֹארה ענד מא אנתבה פלענה לדלך. See Ms. Russian National Library in St. Petersburg, Firkovitch Judaeo-Arabic collection (RNL Yevr.-Arab.) I: 4529, fol. 17b.

12. Our translations of citations from the Hebrew Bible are based on the King James Version (JPS, 1917) with slight modifications when necessary.

13. וירא קֹצה אול פי יקול אנה אנא דֹלך עלי דיל...מוגֹודא יכן לֹם אללענה וקת וקם אן יקם לם אלדליל אן פנקול
חם אבי כנען וירא חם חיתֹ כאן מוגֹודא...ומתֹל דלך קר׳ וירא חם אבי כנען אלא אנה אבו דֹכר פלם כנען. אבי הוא וחם ויקול כנען אבי
ורמזֹ אללענה. בה אסתחק מדֹמום פעל חאל נפס פי תלך לכנען כאן יכון קד לכנען אן אלקול מן הדֹא גֹב. ונגֹד כנען וגֹד עלי אלדאל
וכנען ופוט ומצרים כוש חם ובני לקר׳ חם בני (Ms. RNL Yevr.-Arab. I: 4529, fol. 18b). אצגר כאן כנען ולכן אלואסט אלא כאן ואנמא אלצגיר אבנה יכן פלם וחם. הקטן. בנו לו עשה אשר את וידע קר׳ אלכתאב מן דֹלך

14. ואנמא. ללוקת. פעלה כאן מן גֹהֵ פעל כנען ילען ולם ולד קד כנען אן עלי דֹלך פדל כנאען. לען אנה ערף תֹם
כנען ארור בקולה ישיר אלמעני הדֹא ואלי ישראל. יד עלי See Ms. RNL Yevr.-Arab. (SP IOS) B222, fol. 54b. אלהלאך אללה ענד מוגֹבו פאסתֹ אלתועבאת פעל פי אסרפו אלדֹין גֹים שבעה פעל אעני אפעאלה מן יסתאנף למא לענה

15. On the limits of Yefet's literalistic approach, see Marzena Zawanowska, *The Arabic Translation and Commentary of Yefet ben 'Eli on the Abraham Narratives (Genesis 11:10–25:18)*. Karaite Texts and Studies, vol. 4. Études sur le judaïsme médiéval 46 (Leiden: Brill, 2012), 155–188; Marzena Zawanowska, "In the Border-Land of Literalism: Interpretative Alterations of Scripture in Medieval Karaite Translations of the Bible into Arabic," *Journal for Intellectual History of the Islamicate World* 1 (2013): 179–202.

16. For the discussion of these subjects as addressed by the adherents of the Mu'tazilite *kalam*, see, e.g., Sophia Vasalou, *Moral Agents and Their Deserts: The Character of Mu'tazilite Ethics* (Princeton, N.J.: Princeton University Press, 2008).

17. For a similar idea (of punishing the father by informing him about the future misfortune of his children) expressed by Yefet, see below, n. 67. It is also found in the commentary of Yeshu'ah, see below, n. 31.

18. ויאמר ארור כנען מן נח דעא עלי כנען אד אללגֹנאיֹה עליה כאנת מן אביה חם לא מנה. ואנמא הו אלכבאר.
קלבה ויצדע חם בדֹלך מן אבאה ליגם חאלה סו מן באלוחי עלמה במא (Mss. SP RNL Yevr.-Arab. I: 1754, fols. 249b–250a; SP RNL Yevr.-Arab. I: 4785, fols. 49b–50a).

19. ויאמר ארור כנען קד יקאל כיף יבֹטי אלאב פילען אלאבן. פאגֹאב בעֹץ אלשיוך׳ רחמה אללה באנה יגֹח אן
גלית את הלחמי בית אורגים ידי בן אלחנן ויך כקר׳ אחי אכֹר מוצֹע פי אכֹתצר כמא אבי אכֹתצר ואנה כנען אבי ארור תקדירה
הגתי אחי לחמי את יעיר בן אלחנן ויך הימים דברי פי אלכֹבר להדֹא אלמתאׂמנה אלאכֹברֹ אלנסכֹה פי וקאל הגתי. גלית אחי לחם את
(Ms. RNL Yevr.-Arab. I: 3204, fol. 53a).

20. In his Arabic translation of Noah's curse (Gen 9:25) Sa'adyah also employs the addition *abu* before Canaan, suggesting that Noah cursed Ham, who was called "the father of

Canaan," *abu Canaan* (וקאל מלעון אבו כנעאן). This is also how Saʿadyah translates "and Ham was the father of Canaan" in Gen 9:18: "and Ham was called the father of Canaan" (וכאן חם יכנא אבא כנעאן). See the editions by J. Derenbourg, *Oeuvres complètes de r. Saadia ben Iosef Al-Fayyoûmî: Version arabe du Pentateuque* (Paris: Ernest Leroux, 1893), 16, and Yoseph Qafih, *Peyrushey Rabbenu Saʿadyah Gaon ʿal ha-Torah* (Jerusalem: Mossad Harav Kook, 1984), 31. Saʿadyah explains the verse in line with his translation in his surviving (fragmented) commentary on Genesis. See Moshe Zucker, *Saadya's Commentary on Genesis* [in Hebrew] (New York: Jewish Theological Seminary of America, 1984), 109–110, 351–353.

21. In the early tenth-century grammatical work of the Karaite Ibn Nuh the Arabic term employed for elision of words from a verse is *ikhtisar*, especially with regard to the anomalous occurrence of a construct form, which is often explained as the result of the elision of the noun to which it is conjoined, and which should be supplied when translating the text. The "absent" noun is called *kalima mukhtasara* or *kalima mudmara*. On these concepts as employed in the Qurʾan exegesis, see Michael C. Carter, "Elision," and Michael C. Carter and Kees Versteegh, "*ʾIdmar*" in *Encyclopedia of Arabic Language and Linguistics* (Leiden: Brill, 2006), 2:16–18, 300–302. On the use of *ikhtisar* by Ibn Nuh, see Geoffrey Khan, *The Early Karaite Tradition of Hebrew Grammatical Thought, Including a Critical Edition, Translation and Analysis of the Diqduq of Abu Yaʿqub Yusuf ibn Nuḥ on the Hagiographa*, Studies in Semitic Languages and Linguistics 32 (Leiden: Brill, 2000), 48–50, 128, 147–131. On the hermeneutical term *taqdir*, as used in Judaeo-Arabic and Islamic exegesis, to refer to the methodology of exegesis as well as to grammatical difficulties in biblical verses, see Hadassa Shy, "Taqdir and Its Counterparts in Mediaeval Judaeo-Arabic," in *Genizah Research after Ninety Years: The Case of Judaeo-Arabic*, eds. Joshua Blau and Stefan C. Reif (Cambridge: Cambridge University Press, 1992), 144–154.

22. In his surviving commentary on the passage, Saʿadyah Gaon also refers to other examples of elision of *ben* and *akhi* (including 2 Sam 21:19) in biblical syntax. See Moshe Zucker, *Saadya's Commentary on Genesis*, 353, who also refers to David Kimhi's commentary on 2 Sam 21:19. Nevertheless, Saʿadyah uses the Arabic term *idmar* ("hidden element," see also above, n. 20) and not *taqdir* in referring to this feature. In discussing his examples, Saʿadyah does not refer to the existence of a parallel version (*nuskhah*) of the same story as Yeshuʿah does in relation to Samuel and Chronicles. On the function of *khabar* in the Karaite's theory of biblical composition, see Meira Polliack, "*Qisas wa-akhbar jarata*: Karaite Distinctions of Biblical Genre in the Work of the Biblical Mudawwin," in *The Semitic Languages of Jewish Intellectual Production*, Memorial volume for Dr. Friedrich Niessen, eds. M. A. Gallego and J. P. Monferrer-Sala. Cambridge Genizah Studies Series (Leiden: Brill, forthcoming).

23. On the biblical stance on deferred and corporate retribution, see above, n. 10.

24. On the belief shared by some medieval Karaite exegetes that Scripture has one true meaning, whereas the multiplicity of opinions in exegesis reflects the imperfections of human intellect, which ponders different interpretations in quest of the ultimate truth, see Haggai Ben-Shammai, "Between Ananites and Karaites: Observations on Early Medieval Jewish Sectarianism," *Studies in Muslim-Jewish Relations* 1 (1993): 19–29, especially 23; Haggai Ben-Shammai, "Return to Scriptures in Ancient and Medieval Jewish Sectarianism and in Early Islam," in *Les retours aux Ecritures: Fondamentalismes présents et passés*, eds. E. Patlagean and A. Le Boulluec (Louvain-Paris: Peeters, 1993), 319–339, especially 329; Daniel Frank, "The Limits of Karaite Scripturalism: Problems in Narrative Exegesis," in *A Word Fitly Spoken: Studies*

in Mediaeval Exegesis of the Hebrew Bible, and the Qur'an, eds. Meir M. Bar-Asher, Simon Hopkins, Sarah Stroumsa, and Bruno Chiesa (Jerusalem: Yad Izhak Ben-Zvi, 2007), 41–82, especially 51–55; Meira Polliack, *The Karaite Tradition of Arabic Bible Translation: A Linguistic and Exegetical Study of Karaite Translations of the Pentateuch from the Tenth and Eleventh Centuries C.E.* Études sur le judaïsme médiéval 17 (Leiden: Brill, 1997), 24, n. 5; Meira Polliack, "Major Trends in Karaite Biblical Exegesis," 372–388; Zawanowska, *The Arabic Translation and Commentary of Yefet ben 'Eli on the Abraham Narratives (Genesis 11:10–25:18)*, 67–69.

25. Such as Ham's alleged sexual misconduct, as discussed in *b. Sanh.* 70a.

26. See also Sa'adyah's similar refraining from midrashic-typed gap-filling and his preference of a grammatical and contextual gap-filling measure through the insertion of *abu* into his translation of Gen 9:25 (see, for example, above, n. 20).

27. On the concepts of divine promise and thread (*al-wa'd wa l-wa'id*) as well as balance (*al-muwazana*) and repentance (*al-tawba*) in the thought of later Karaite exegetes and thinkers, see Georges Vajda (ed.), *Al-Kitab al-Muhtawi de Yusuf al-Basir: Texte, traduction et commentaire par Georges Vajda*, edited by David R. Blumenthal, Études sur le judaïsme médiéval 12 (Leiden: Brill, 1985), 546–632 (chap. 37–40); Wolfgang von Abel (ed.), *Das Buch der Unterscheidung von Yusuf Al-Basir, übersetzt und eingeleitet von Wolfgang von Abel* (Freiburg: Herder Verlag, 2005); David Sklare (ed.), *Kitab al-Ni'ma by Levi ben Yefet*, in *A Common Rationality: Mu'tazilism in Islam and Judaism*, eds. Camilla Adang, Sabine Schmidtke, and David Sklare (Würzburg: Ergon, 2007), 157–216.

28. See above, n. 3.

29. פאמא מן אנכר לענה אלמעדום פאן דלך גיר מנכר אדֿא כאן דלך ממן לא יכסא עליה מא יריד אן יכן. פאדֿא כאן אלבארי גל ועז עאלמא בגֿמיע אלאשיא קבל וקוע כונהא ועלם אוליאה דלך באלנבוﾃ לם ינכר מנהם דֿם מן יגֿב עליה אלדֿם קבל כונה ולענה וכדֿלך מדֿ מן יגֿב לה אלמדח ותבריכה. (Ms. RNL Yevr.-Arab. I: 4529, fol. 19a).

30. For a similar idea (of God sharing His knowledge with the righteous), see below, n. 67.

31. וקד יגֿוז אן יעאקב אלאב במא יגֿרי עלי אלאבן ויולם קלבה במא יערֿף בה מן חאלה. תֿם קד יכון אלולד במא יגֿרי עליה ממתחנא וקד יכון מעאקבא לכונה עאציא ולען כנעו יקתצֿי עציאנה. פאן קיל פהל יסוג לען מן יסתחק אללען אלֿא עצֿא מן קבל אן יוגֿד או מן קבל אן יעצֿי. פכֿא אלגֿואב אן קי' ארור כנעו הו אכֿבאר במא יכון מן אלארירﾃ פֿי דֿריה כנעו אלדֿי כאן אצלא לקבאיל. (Ms. RNL Yevr.-Arab. I: 3204, fol. 53a). See, for example, above, n. 18.

32. See, for example, above, n. 27.

33. On such meaning of Arabic *battatan*, see Joshua Blau, *A Dictionary of Mediaeval Judaeo-Arabic Texts* [in Hebrew] (Jerusalem: Academy of the Hebrew Language, the Israel Academy of Sciences and Humanities, 2006), 30a; Hans Wehr, *A Dictionary of Modern Written Arabic (Arabic-English)* (Urbana, Ill., and Ithaca, N.Y.: Spoken Languages Services 1994), 51.

34. ופי דלך מעני אבֿר והו אנה לו צח אן כנעו כאן מעדומא ואנה לם יכן לה גֿרם פי דלך אלחאל פיגֿוﾄ פֿינֿו אן יכון נח ע'. א' אנכשׁף לה באלנבוﾃ אן אכפר אולאד חם וארדֿאהם מדֿהבא ואקבחהם פעלא ללפואחש ואלפרוגֿ אלחראם מן מגֿארי אלארﾑ אלמקדסﾃ הם אלסבעﾃ שעוב אלדֿין אמר אללה עז וגֿל אן לא יסתבקי מנהם אחדא בתה ולא תקבל להם תובﾏ. ולא ידֿלֿון פי אלדֿין והם גֿמיעא בני כנען. פלענהם נח ע' א' למא תבין לה מן מדֿהבהם פי אלנבוﾃ. (Ms. RNL Yevr.-Arab. I: 4529, fol. 18b). For the following part of this passage, see below, n. 54.

35. Other possible translations of *al-ajal* are "appointed time" and "time of death." The phrase refers to the predetermined life span of humans, which constitutes a classical topic in Islamic *kalam*. It is usually discussed in relation to God's foreknowledge and in relation to the question of whether it is mere abstract knowledge or whether it determines the fate of humans. See Haggai Ben-Shammai, "Kalam in Medieval Jewish Philosophy," 115–148, especially 133; Daniel Gimaret, "Mu'tazila," in *Encyclopaedia of Islam*, new edition, 12 vols., eds.

H. A. R. Gibb et al. (Leiden: Brill, 1960–2002), fasc. 127–128, 7:783–793. Cf. also Vajda (ed.), *Al-Kitab*, 582–592 (chap. 40).

36. Yefet's theodicy in this passage as a whole also seems to echo the qurʾanic statements that God never punishes a city by destruction, without sending a messenger to its inhabitants, in order to warn them and dissuade them from their sins (e.g., Sura 28:59).

37. See, for example, Gen 6:3.

38. See, for example, Gen 7:10.

39. See, for example, Jonah 3:4.

40. פאן קאל איש אלמעני פי אן גֹעל אללה הֹדא אלבאב אלבאב מנוט בדכֹול אלרסל אליהם. יקאל לה אן מן שפקֹה.
אלבֹאבֹל גֹל וגֹלאלה עלי עבאדהֹ ינדֹרהם ענד מא אסראפהם פי אלמעאצי ויערפהם אן אלאגֹל קד דנא ליכון דֹלך חגֹה
עליהם. פאן הם אנתבהו ורגֹעו מן מעאציהם לם יחל בהם אלעקובהֹ. ואן לם ירגֹעו חלת בהם אלעקובהֹ. וכמא אגֹל לאהל
דור המבול אגֹל טויל והו קֹ' כֹ' סנהֹ. פלמא אנקצֹא אלאגֹל ולם יתובו אגֹלהם אגֹל קציר והו מדהֹ דֹ איאם. פענד מא לם
ירגֹעו אהלכהם. ואמא אהל נינוה פאנה אגֹלהם מֹ יומא פתאבו אלי אללה ולם יחל בהם אלבלא. פהאולי אהל סדם אמהל
עליהם אללה כֹ' הֹ' סנהֹ ולם יתובו בל אסרפו וחאדו פי אלמעאצי. פענד מא גֹא אלוקֹת אגֹלהם במקדאר מא ימרון אליהם
אהלכהם ואלא תאבו פאן ואלא. אלרסל. (Ms. SP IOS B222, fols. 176b–177a). For the sake of comparison, while commenting on this passage the authors of the *Talkhis* focus on counting how long the sins of the inhabitants of Sodom and Gomorrah actually did last. See Ms. SP RNL Yevr.-Arab. I: 4785, fol. 77b.

41. See, e.g., Yefet's comment *ad* Dan 4:26–27, in David Samuel Margoliouth, *A Commentary on the Book of Daniel by Yefet ibn Ali the Karaite* (Oxford: Anecdota Oxoniensia, 1889), 23 (Eng.), ٥٠ (Ar.).

42. תֹם דֹכר מא אסתחק שם ויפת עלי פעולהמא פאבْתْדَי בשם לאנה אכבר ואגֹל מרתבהֹ. פקאל ברוך יֹ אלהי.
שם ולם יקל ברוך שם למעני והו אנה לו קאל ברוך שם לْכَאן אן יכון מברך פי כֹתרהֹ אלנסל או כֹתרהֹ אלנעם או סעהֹ
אלארץ פקאל ברוך יֹ אלהי שם ופי מנה מעאני גֹלילה. אחדהא אנהם יכונו עבאד אללה מתֹל אברהם יצחק ויעקב חרעו
ואדֹא כאנו עבאד אללה הו אכבר שרף להם דניא ואכֹרה. ואלבֹ' אנה אוקע אסם רב אלעאלמין עליה דון גירה לישאיר בה
אלי אבْתْהار אללה באברהם חרעו מן סאיר אלאמם. ואיצֹא ישיר בה אלי פעל אלאתת ואלמפתים ואלנבואהֹ ואלכהונהֹ
ואלמקדש ואלכבוד ואלתורה מע סאיר אלמעאני אלمليحة אלْגֹليلה אלדֹי פצّל אללה בהא לישראל וכלהא תחת קולה להם והייתי
לכם לאלהים ואתם תהיו לי לעם [ויקרא כו:יב]. פערّف רב אלעאלמין מא יכון מן אולאד שם פלדֹלך קאל ברוך יֹ אלהי שם
(Ms. SP IOS B222, fols. 55a–b).

43. Yefet seems to be referring to the wider pericope (*parashah*) of Noah (Gen 6:9–11:32) in which Noah receives divine revelations.

44. ערף אן נח ענד מא אסתיקֹץֹ מן אלסכר עלם מא פעלה חם. והֹדא אלעלם ליס הו בّעيد אן אללה אעלמהֹ.
לאנה קד אכבר פי הֹדא אלפצל בגֹ' אשיא תדל עלי אנה עלם דֹלך בוחי לא שך פיה. (Ms. SP IOS B222, fol. 54a).

45. On this concept, see, e.g., Ben-Shammai, "On *mudawwin*—the Editor of the Books of the Bible in Judaeo-Arabic Exegesis" [in Hebrew], in *Rishonim ve-Achronim: Studies in Jewish History presented to Avraham Grossman*, eds. Joseph Hacker, Benjamin Z. Kedar, Joseph Kaplan (Jerusalem: Zalman Shazar Center for Jewish History, 2009), 73–110.

46. On Yefet's tendency to make use of "midrashic" expansions, see Frank, "The Limits"; Ilana Sasson, *Methods and Approach in Yefet ben ʿEli al-Basri's Translation and Commentary on the Book of Proverbs* (PhD diss., New York: Jewish Theological Seminary, 2010), 115–128; Miriam Goldstein, "The Beginnings of the Transition from Derash to Peshat as Exemplified in Yefet ben Eli's comment on Psa. 44:24," in *Exegesis and Grammar in Medieval Karaite Texts*, ed. Geoffrey Khan (Oxford: Oxford University Press, 2001), 41–64. See also Miriam Goldstein, "The Structural Function of Biblical Superfluity in the Exegesis of the Karaite Yusuf ibn Nuh" [in Hebrew], *Sefunot* 8, no. 23 (2003): 337–349. On Yeshuʿah's tendency to employ such "extra-textual" additions also in his translation of the Pentateuch, see Meira Polliack, "Alternate Renderings

and Additions in Yeshu'ah ben Yehudah's Arabic Translation of the Pentateuch," *JQR*, n.s., 84 (1994): 209–226. See also Yeshu'ah's discussion above (section 1.4). On the Karaite conception of biblical "gap creation" in the narrative span, see Meira Polliack, "Major Trends in Karaite Biblical Exegesis," 403–410; Meira Polliack, "The Unseen Joints of the Text: On the Medieval Judaeo-Arabic Concept of Elision (*IHTIṢĀR*) and its Gap-filling Functions in Biblical Interpretation," in *Words, Ideas, Worlds in the Hebrew Bible – The Yairah Amit Festschrift*, eds. A. Brenner and F. H. Polak (Sheffield: Sheffield Phoenix Press, 2012), 179–205.

47. קו' וידע את אשר עשה לו בנו הקטן לא ימתנע אנה עלם דלך עלי טריק אלוחי. (Mss. SP RNL Yevr.-Arab. I: 1754, fols. 248b–249a; SP RNL Yevr.-Arab. I: 4785, fol. 49a).

48. See above, n. 19, and n. 31.

49. קולה וידע יקרב אנה בוחי ותצמן אלוחי איצא מא אסתחקה חם עלי הדא אלמנכר ותצמן איצא מא יכון מן כבר. שם ויפת. פקאל מבתדיא בחם ארור כנען. (Ms. RNL Yevr.-Arab. I: 3204, fol. 53a).

50. See above, n. 18.

51. On the biblical worldview that distinguishes humans as limited and flawed by their very nature when compared to God, see, for instance, Robert Alter, *The Art of Biblical Narrative* (New York: Basic Books, 1981). The notion that a curse or a blessing, once uttered, whether intentionally or by mistake, is irrevocable is an underlying theme in the book of Genesis; see, for example, the stories of Isaac's unconscious blessing of Jacob (Gen 27) and Jacob's unconscious cursing of Rachel (Gen 31:32).

52. See, for example, *Gen. Rab.* 36:7. A similar explanation was already put forward in a Qumran text commenting upon Genesis (4Q252, col. II, frag. 1 and 3, ll. 5–8). We are thankful to Katell Berthelot for drawing our attention to these parallels.

53. וקאל אלברון אנה אנמא לען כנען ולם ילען חם לאן אללה ברך נח ובניה פלם יסתגיז אן ילען מן קד ברכה אללה. (Ms. RNL Yevr.-Arab. I: 4529, fol. 18a).

54. פלדלך כצהם באללענה דון סאיר ולדהם אלדי ליס הדה סבילהם אד כאן אלכתאב קד אכאז אדכֹאל אלמצריין פי אלדין ומזאוגתהם אד קאל לא תתעב מצרי וג'. וכאנה לענתה לכנען ליס הי לענה להם אד כאן הו אלחקיקי בהא מן סאיר ולדה. אד לו כאן לענתה לכאנה אללענה מנצרפה אל אשר אולאדה ומן הו אחק בהא מן גירה אד כאן לא יגֹד אן ילחק מן אטאע מנהם וכאצה מע מא תקדם מן ברכֹה אללה לנח ולבניה לקו' ויברך אלהים את נח ואת בניו. פלם יסתעמל נח מנאקצֹה מא תקדם מן אלברכֹה בל צרף אללענה אלי מן עלם אנה הו אחק בהא. ומֹל דלך גֹעל יהושע פי לענתה ללגבעונים לקו' ועתה ארורים אתם....והדה אלקצֹה נטיר לקצֹה מנע אללה לבני אסראיל מן אלסלוך פי ארצֹ אדום. וקו' כי לא אתן לך מארצו ירושה וקו' לא תתעב אדומי. תם כֹין בעץֹ ולד עשו והם עמלק באן אמר באבאדתהם לקו' תמחה את זכר עמלק. ודלך לאסתחקאקהם דלך מן בין ולד עשו כמא כמא אסתחק כנען אללענה מן בין ולד חם. (Ms. RNL Yevr.-Arab. I: 4529, fols. 18b–19a). For the previous part of this passage, see above, n. 34.

55. For the differentiation between general and particular expressions ('umum versus khusus) in Scripture as an example of Karaite adoption of Islamic hermeneutic, formed on the model of Mu'tazilite *usul al-fiqh*, as well as for al-Qirqisani's use of this terminology, see Gregor Schwarb, "Meaning of God's Speech," 120.

56. ולם ירי אן ילענה אן ילען לאן אללה קד ברכה פי גֹמלֹה אבותה פגֹעל עקובתה עלי פעלה אלעאלמֹה לה שרף שם. ויפת ולענה כנען ונקף מרתבה אולאדה. (Ms. SP IOS B222, fols. 56b). For the rest of this passage, see below, n. 67.

57. See above, n. 18.

58. On common traits in Rabbanite and Karaite Judaeo-Arabic exegesis, see Meira Polliack, "Concepts of Scripture among the Jews of the Medieval Islamic World," in *Jewish Concepts of Scripture: A Comparative Introduction*, ed. Benjamin D. Sommer (New York: New York University Press, 2012), 80–101. See also Mordechai Cohen, "Bible Exegesis: Rabbanite," in

Encyclopedia of Jews in the Islamic World, 5 vols., eds. Norman Stillman et al. (Leiden: Brill, 2009), 1:442–457.

59. We thank Gregor Schwarb for drawing our attention to the parallels between the exegetical solutions proposed by Yefet (and also Yeshuʿah; see section 5.2) and the concept of *takhsis al-umum* in *usul al-fiqh*. See, for example, above, n. 55

60. וקולה ויהי כנען יריד בה בקיהֿ אולאד כנען אלדֿין הרבו מן קדאם ישראל. פערף אנהם יצירו עבד עבדים לסאיר אולאד חם יעני מצרים כוש פוט. ומעניה אנהם למא הרבו מן קדאם ישראל תפרק בעצֿהם פי הדֿה אלבלדאן. ובעצֿהם תפרקו פי בלד בני אעני פי בלד עילם ואשור ולוד וארם ופי אראצֿי אפכֿאדֿ ארפכשד גיר ארץ ישראל אלדֿי טרדהם רב אלעאלמין מן קדאמהם. וכדֿלך תפרק בעצֿהם פי בלד יפת פצארו עבדים להם. (Ms. SP IOS B222, fols. 54b–55a).

61. According to the Ms.: "the children of Sheth"—most probably *lapsus calami*.

62. *Mubalagah* and *iblag* are terms used in Arabic and Judaeo-Arabic poetic works (such as Moshe ibn Ezra's *Kitab al-Muḥaḍarah wal-Mudhakarah*) in referring to the poetic trope of hyperbole, namely, exaggeration. See, for example, Joseph Dana, *Poetics of Medieval Hebrew Literature according to Moshe ibn Ezra* [in Hebrew] (Tel-Aviv: Dvir, 1982), 26–32, 159–161. Moshe ibn Ezra singles out the prophetic genre in this respect. See A. S. Halkin's edition of *Moses ben Yaʾakov ibn Ezra, Kitab al-Muḥaḍarah wal-Mudhakarah*, Liber Discussionis et Commemorationis (Poetica Hebraica) (Jerusalem: Mekize Nirdamim, 1975), 265–267 (chapter 16, fol. 137b).

63. ואללה תעׄ תולי מחק בעצֿהם קבל דכׄול ישראל אלי אלארצֿ. תֿם בעתֿ פיהם אלצֿרעהֿ תֿם קתל ישראל מנהם מן קתלו ותפרק כתֿיר מנהם פי אלאראצֿין ענד הרבהם מן קדאם ישראל אלי בלאד אלגרב וצאר עבﬞדיﬞא לכוש ומצרים ולבני שתֿ [!] פי אוקאת ולבני יפת איצֿא לאן קד עלת יד יון וגירה מן אולאד יפת כמא עלת יד אשור וגירה מן בני שם עלי בלאד אלכנעאניין. ומעני עבד עבדים הו אלמבאלגהֿ פי נזולהם ואנחטאטהם כמא יקתצֿי מלך מלכים מבאלגﬞה פי אלרפעהֿ. (Ms. RNL Yevr.-Arab. I: 3204, fols. 53a–b).

64. See, for example, Joshua Blau, *A Dictionary of Mediaeval Judaeo-Arabic Texts*, 421.

65. והו אן אללה קד תעבדנא באשיא מכֿתלפהֿ מן אמר אלאמם ואלשעוב פמנהא מן תעבדנא בקתלהם באסרהם מעﬞ אטפאלהם וחרמהם. ודֿלך מתֿל שבעה גוים. ומנהם מן אמרנא באן נדעוהם אלי אלמסאלמהﬞ פאן לם יגֿיבון קתלנא אלרגֿאל אלבﬞאלגין ואסתבקינא אלנסא ואלאטפﬞאל. ומנהם מן אגֿאז אדכֿאלהם פי אלדין ותזוגֿהם בעד גֿ אגֿיאל. ודֿלך מתֿל אלמצרין ואלאדומיין וגיר דֿלך ממא אפתרﬞץ פי סאיר אלאמם. פלמא כאן דֿלך כדﬞלך לם יכן בד מן תערﬞיף אנסאב כל אמﬞהﬞ ושעב לנמתﬞל פי כל קום במא אמרנא דון גירהם. (Ms. RNL Yevr.-Arab. I: 4529, fol. 20a).

66. On the Muʿtazilite adherence to free will, and the concepts of *qudra* and *daʿi*, their mutual relations and fine tuning, see Richard M. Frank, "The Autonomy of the Human Agent in the Teaching ʿAbd al-Ǧabbar," *Le Muséon* 95 (1982): 323–355; Daniel Gimaret, "Théories de l'acte humain en théologie musulmane," *Études musulmanes* 24 (Paris: Librairie Philosophique; Leuven: Editors Peeters, 1980); Wilferd Madelung, "The Late Muʿtazila and Determinism: The Philosophers's Trap," in *Yád-Náma in Memoria di Alessandro Bausani*, eds. B. Scarcia Amoretti and L. Rostagno, 2 vols. (Rome: Islamistica Ed., 1991), 1:245–257. We are grateful to Sabine Schmidtke for clarifying to us the overall Muʿtazilite stance in rejecting pre-determination and drawing our attention to these works. Apart from the Muʿtazilite influence on Yefet's (and other Karaite) stances toward the Canaanites' free will, their exegetical debates may also have been informed by the rabbinic debates on the integration of man's free will and the ways of Providence as reflected in Rabbi Akiva's aphorism (*m. Avot* 3:15) הכל צפוי והרשות נתונה ("everything is seen and freedom of choice is given"), on which see Ephraim E. Urbach, *The Sages, Their Concepts and Beliefs*, trans. Israel Abrahams (Jerusalem: Magness Press, 1979), 256–285.

67. פערﬞף פי הדֿה אלקצֿהﬞ דֿל כנען ונקץ מרתבתה ען סאיר אולאד בני נח. ודֿכר שרף שם ויפת ואכאן אלקצד פי דֿכר כנען ומא יכון מנה ליוצֿע בה קלב חם גֿזא פעלה.....והדֿא נטיר קולה לדוד עﬞ אלסלﬞ ועתה לא תסור חרב מביתך עד עולם.

ולים יניז נעתקד אנה יקתל אולאדה מן גהתה בל יקתלהם מן גהה אפעאלהם כמא קתל אחזיה ואמציה ויהויקים ואולאד
צדקיה מן גהה אפעאלהם. ואנגמא אוגע אללה קלבה באעלאמה דלך. וכדלך יבשר אלצאלחין במא יכן מן אולאדהם
אלטאיעין ליסרון בה (Ms. SP IOS B222, fols. 56b–57a). For the elided part of the text, see above,
n. 56. On the idea that God informs the sinner of his fate in advance, see above, n. 29.

68. That the granting of special position by God and the gift of prophecy to Israel neces-
sitates (*yastahiq*) obedience (*taʿah*) is also made clear in Yefet's comment on Joel 3:2, see
Lawrence Marwick, *Retribution and Redemption: Yefet Ben ʿEli on the Minor Prophets; A Lost
Work of Lawrence Marwick* (n.p., 2003), 27.

69. See especially Deut 28–30; 2 Kings 17.

70. ולעל סאיל יסל פיקול איש אלמעני פי אנה האמין ביّ אנה האמין ביّ אלקול אלאול והו ועד מרסל ולם יקל במה אדע ופי הדא
אלועד קאל במא אדע אלנّואב פי דלך הו אנה למא כאן כאן אלועד בכתהّ אלנסל קד יפעל אללה נטירה מע אלכפאר וכאן
תסלם אלארץ ליס יעטיהא אללה אלא לטאיע וכאן אברם וגّה אן יכון נסלה טאיעא וגّה אנה יעצי פלא יסתחקהא פיכון
אטועני אלא הזאת הארץ את אתן לורעך אללה קול (Ms. SP IOS B 222, fols. 121b–122a). The emphasis in
translation is ours.

71. See, for example, Yefet's comment on Deut 24:9: פנכת בלעם פי הדה אלאיה אצול אלמואעיד
להם אללה שרטהא אלّדי אלגלילה. ("In this verse, Balʿam summarized primary lofty promises that
God, the Sublime, *stipulated to them*"; emphasis ours). See Tzvi Avni, "Balaam's Poetic Verses
in the Commentary of Yefet ben ʿEli the Karaite" [in Hebrew], *Sefunot* 8, no. 23 (2003): 370–
457, especially 406 (Ar.), 442 (Heb.). Characteristically, Yefet does not say here "the promises
that God, the Sublime, promised us," but "the promises that God, the Sublime, *stipulated to
us*" (emphasis ours). For an additional example in which Yefet emphasizes that the covenant
between God and Israel is conditional (שרט), see his comment *ad* Amos 2:5 in Marwick,
Retribution and Redemption, 53.

72. For Yefet stressing the importance of obedience, see especially his commentary on
the Song of Songs. See Joseph Alobaidi, *Old Jewish Commentaries on the Song of Songs I
(Bible in History). The Commentary of Yefet ben Eli* (Bern, New York: Peter Lang, 2010). For
another example of Yefet stating that for deliverance one has to deserve it and that it is not
unconditional and will not come without repentance, see Yefet's comment *ad* Dan 12:9 in
Margoliouth, *Commentary on the Book of Daniel*, 81 (Engl.), ١٥٠ (Ar.).

73. See, e.g., Yefet's comment *ad* Deut 24:17: ואלמעני אלתّאכّלה הו מע' אלצّיא אלّדי יתפרג אהל
אלעאלם מן טّלמתהם פי אמור דיאנתהם פירגّעון אלי אלחק לאן אלתורה ממתّלה באלנור כמא קאל כי נר מצוה ותורה
אור ומתّל אלמסיח באלנור כמא קאל ונתיך לאור גוים ואיצّא אנהם יתפרגו מן אלשדאיד ואלחרוב אלّדי כאנת בינהם
פיכון מתّלהם פי דלך מתّל מן כרג מן טّלמה אלי נור (See Avni, "Balaam's Poetic Verses," 413 (Ar.), 448 (Heb.).

74. ויאמר ברוך ייّ אלהי שם ויהי כנען עבד למו. יקאל משכור אללה אלّאה [= אלה] שם ואולאדה אלّדי סבב
אולאד כנען עבידّא להם יעני [= יעّ] אנה תעאלי משכור פימא חכם בה מן חטיט רתבהّ אולאד כנען ען רתבהّ אולאד שם
ויّ וגّ' [= ע' וגّ'] עّ אדלّא פימא חכם בה מן דלך .חתי צארו עבידّא להם לאנה עז וגّל [= ע' וגّ'] עّ אדלّא פימא חכם בה מן דלך (Mss. SP RNL Yevr.-Arab. I: 1754,
fols. 250a–b; SP RNL Yevr.-Arab. I: 4785, fol. 50a). Versions that diverge from the second ms.
are are provided in square brackets.

75. On various meanings of the Ar. root *daʿawa*, see Joshua Blau, *Dictionary of Mediaeval
Judaeo-Arabic Texts*, 215; Hans Wehr, Dictionary of Modern Written Arabic, 326–328.

76. וקאל ההנא ויקרא בשם ייّ קיל פיה תפסירין. אחדהמא אנה נאדא באלّדין ואסתהדיّא באלנّאס אליה. ואלב' אנה
דעי באלשכר ואלתהליל (Ms. SP IOS B222, fols. 85a–b).

77. Rabbinic midrash also emphasizes the missionary activities of Abraham and ascer-
tains that every place wherein Abraham erected an altar was "a centre for his missionary activities"; see Louis Ginzberg, *The Legends of the Jews*, 6 vols. (Philadelphia: Jewish Publication
Society, 1937), especially 1:219. See, for example, *Gen. Rab.* 39:16: ויקרא בשם ח' מלמד שהקריא בשמו
של הקבّ"ה בפי כל בריה ד"א ויקרא התחיל מגייר גרים ולהכניסם תחת כנפי השכינה ("*And called upon the name*

of the Lord: With prayer. Another interpretation of *And called*: He began to make converts.")
The English translation follows H. Freedman and Maurice Simon, *Midrash Rabbah*, 10 vols.
(London: Soncino Press, 1961), 1:325. For further bibliography, see Ginzberg, *Legends of the
Jews*, 1:219, 5:220, n. 61. Similar comments regarding Abraham's missionary activity are found
in the *Talkhis*: ויעתד משם ענד מא תגׄלא אליה אלוקאר ובשרה בתסלים אלארץׄ לנסלה קוי קלבה ואטמאן מן
אלכנענים ואכׄד פי תנקל ותטאף אלארץׄ ובנא אלמדׄבח ואסתדעי אלנאס אלי אלעדל ואלתוחיד כקו ויבן שם מד׳(בח) ליהי
ויקרא בשם יהי ("When the Glory appeared unto him [i.e., Abram] and announced to him the
handing over of the land to his offspring, his heart strengthened and felt secured of the Canaanites, so he commenced to move and travel about the land. Moreover, he built an altar and summoned people to justice and monotheism [*al-'adl wa al-tawhid*], as it is said *and he built there an
altar unto the Lord, and called upon the name of the Lord* [Gen 12:8]."] (Ms. SP RNL Yevr.-Arab.
I: 4785, fols. 55a-b). This last remark made by the *Talkhis* constitutes an example of the adoption
of typical Muʿtazilite terminology within a distinctively exegetical Karaite work (see our comments above and n. 3). In contradistinction to these Jerusalem Karaite sources, al-Qirqisani
does not mention Abraham's missionary activity while commenting on this verse, but rather
he again puts the emphasis on divine planning, and on how history will develop: ויעתד משם
ההרה מקדם לבית אל ובנא הנאך איצׄא מדׄבחא וכל דׄלך באמר אללה גׄל תׄנאוה ולאנהא קבלה וכמא ערפה מן אלמוצׄע
אלמכׄתארהׄ אלתי ירידו אולאדה יעבדו אללה פיהא וכדׄלך הר המוריה אלדׄי הו ירושלים ובנא איצׄא מדׄבחא׳ תׄאלתׄא פי
חברון ודׄלך פי אלוני ממרא לקו׳ ויאהל אברם ויבא וישב באלוני ממרא אשר בחברון ויבן שם מזבח ליהי וקד וגׄדנא פי
אלאׄתׄאר אלכתׄאביהׄ אנה קד כאן פי חברון מוצׄע עבאדהׄ אללה אד׳ יקול אבשלום אלכה נא ואשלם את נדרי אשר נדרתי
ליהי בחברון ("*And he removed from thence unto the mountain on the east of Beth-el* [Gen 12:8],
and also there he built an altar. All that [he did] at God's command, great be His glory, and
because [these places] [were meant to be] the places of worship, and as [God] informed him
about the chosen places, in which his descendants would worship God. Similarly, the mount
of Moriah, which is [in] Jerusalem. Moreover, he built a third altar in Hebron, and that is [the
one] by the Oaks of Moreh, as it is said *And Abram moved his tent, and came and dwelt by the
Oaks of Mamre, which are in Hebron, and built there an altar unto the Lord* [Gen 13:18]. We
have found in the scriptural tradition [i.e., testimony] that there was in Hebron a place for
the worship of God, since Absalom says *I pray thee, let me go and pay my vow, which I have
vowed unto the LORD, in Hebron* [2 Sam 15:7]."]) (Ms. SP RNL Yevr.-Arab. I: 4529, fol. 27a).
See also Bruno Chiesa and Wilfrid Lockwood, "Al-Qirqisani's Newly-found Commentary on
the Pentateuch: The Commentary on Gen. 12," *Henoch* 14 (1992): 153–180, especially 164 (Ar.),
173–174 (Eng.). On the missionary and messianic zeal of the Mourners of Zion, namely, the
Karaites of the tenth century who called for the return to the Holy Land, see Yoram Erder,
"The Mourners of Zion: The Karaites in Jerusalem of the Tenth and Eleventh Centuries," in
Guide to Karaite Studies, ed. Meira Polliack, 213–235. This may partly explain the Jerusalem
Karaites' disparity with al-Qirqisani on the question of Abraham and the Canaanites, as well
as the wider issues involved.

78. See Haider Abbas Hussain, *Yefet ben Ali's Commentary on the Hebrew Text of the Book
of Job I–X* (PhD diss., University of St. Andrews, 1986), 4 (Ar.), xiii, xv (discussion). See also
Joshua Blau, *Judaeo-Arabic Literature: Selected Texts* [in Hebrew] (Jerusalem: Magnes Press,
1980), 73–86, especially 79, but also 80; Haggai Ben-Shammai, *The Arabic Commentary of
Yefet ben ʿEli on the Book of Job 1–5* [in Hebrew] (MA thesis, Hebrew University, 1972), 11 (Ar.),
12 (Heb.).

79. ופי קול אשרי האיש ולם יקל אשרי הגוי גׄ׳ מעאני אחדהא הו לידכׄל פי דׄלך כל מן אראד אללה בה מן אחאד
See Jean אלאמם קבל אלרסול עׄ׳ה ובעדה פלדׄלך לם יקל אשרי הגוי ולא אשרי העם אלדׄי יבתׄן בישראל דון גירהם
Joseph Léandre Bargès, *Excerpta ex R. Yapheth ben Heli commentariis in Psalmos Davidis regis*

et prophetae (Paris: Lutetle Parisiorum [prostat apud B. Duprat], Instituti Imperialis Gallicani Bibliopolam, 1846), 15–16 (Ar.), 75 (Lat.). In a similar vein, in his comment *ad* Joel 4:16 ("but the LORD will be a refuge unto His people [*'amo*], and a stronghold to the children of Israel"), Yefet explains that the Hebrew term *'amo*, meaning "unto His people" is used in addition to the expression "to the children of Israel," so as to include in it also the converts (*gerim*). See Marwick, *Retribution and Redemption*, 16.

80. ותהלתו מלאה הארץ יריד בה פימא בין ישראל וכל מא כאן מוחד מן סאיר אלאמם. See Ofer Livne-Kafri, "The Commentary on Habakkuk 1–3 by the Karaite Yefet ben 'Eli al-Basri" [in Hebrew], *Sefunot* 6, no. 21 (1993): 73–113, especially 90 (Ar.), 107 (Heb.). For a discussion of Jewish notions on the universality of the Torah in the East during the tenth and eleventh centuries, see David Sklare, "Are the Gentiles Obligated to Observe the Torah?" in *Be'erot Yitzhak: Studies in Memory of Isadore Twersky*, ed. Jay M. Harris (Cambridge, Mass: Harvard University Press, 2005), 311–346. Nevertheless, Yefet's open stance toward "the other" in these passages does not make his view of Islam favorable. On the contrary, among the Karaite exegetes he expresses a staunch negative stance toward Islam as a religion, see Yoram Erder, "The Attitude of the Karaite Yefet ben 'Eli to Islam in the Light of His Interpretation of Psalm 14:53" [in Hebrew], *Michael* 14 (1997): 29–49; Moshe Sokolow, "The Negation of Muslim Sovereignty over the Land of Israel in Two Karaite Commentaries of the Tenth Century" [in Hebrew], *Shalem* 3 (1981): 309–318. It appears that his exegesis in the above-quoted passages is meant to openly encourage converts to Karaite Judaism and in this sense is in line with the proselytizing activities of the Jerusalem Karaites in general.

81. See Yefet's comment on Hos 5:7 in Meira Polliack and Eliezer Schlossberg, *Commentary of Yefet ben 'Eli the Karaite on the Book of Hosea* [in Hebrew] (Ramat Gan: Bar Ilan University Press, 2009), 179 (Ar.), 325–326 (Heb.). Cf. also Philip Birnbaum, *The Arabic Commentary of Yefet ben 'Ali the Karaite on the Book of Hosea, Edited from Eight Manuscripts and Provided with a Critical Notes and an Introduction* (Philadelphia: Dropsie College for Hebrew and Cognate Learning, 1942), 83.

Bibliography

Abel, Wolfgang von, ed. *Das Buch der Unterscheidung von Yusuf Al-Basir, übersetzt und eingeleitet von Wolfgang von Abel*. Freiburg: Herder Verlag, 2005.

Adang, Camilla, Sabine Schmidtke, and David Sklare, eds. *A Common Rationality: Mu'tazilism in Islam and Judaism*. Würzburg: Ergon Verlag Würzburg, 2007.

Alobaidi, Joseph. *Old Jewish Commentaries on the Song of Songs I (Bible in History). The Commentary of Yefet ben Eli*. Bern, New York: Peter Lang, 2010.

Alter, Robert. *The Art of Biblical Narrative*. New York: Basic Books, 1981.

Avni, Tzvi. "Balaam's Poetic Verses in the Commentary of Yefet ben 'Eli the Karaite" [in Hebrew]. *Sefunot* 8, no. 23 (2003): 370–457.

Ben-Shammai, Haggai. "On *mudawwin*—the Editor of the Books of the Bible in Judaeo-Arabic Exegesis" [in Hebrew]. In *Rishonim ve-Achronim: Studies in Jewish History Presented to Avraham Grossman*, edited by Joseph Hacker, Benjamin Z. Kedar, Joseph Kaplan, 73–110. Jerusalem: Zalman Shazar Center for Jewish History, 2009.

——. "Major Trends in Karaite Philosophy and Polemics." In *A Guide to Karaite Studies: An Introduction to Literary Sources of Medieval and Modern Karaite Judaism*, edited by Meira Polliack, 339–362. Leiden: Brill 2003.

——. "Kalam in Medieval Jewish Philosophy." In *History of Jewish Philosophy*, edited by Daniel H. Frank and O. Leaman, 115–148. Leiden: Brill, 1997.

——. "Between Ananites and Karaites: Observations on Early Medieval Jewish Sectarianism." *Studies in Muslim-Jewish Relations* 1 (1993): 19–29.

——. "Return to Scriptures in Ancient and Medieval Jewish Sectarianism and in Early Islam." In *Les retours aux Ecritures: Fondamentalismes présents et passés*, edited by E. Patlagean and A. Le Boulluec, 319–339. Louvain-Paris: Peeters, 1993.

——. *The Doctrines of Religious Thought of Abu Yusuf Ya'qub al-Qirqisani and Yefet ben 'Eli* [in Hebrew]. 2 vols. PhD diss., Hebrew University of Jerusalem, 1977.

——. *The Arabic Commentary of Yefet ben 'Eli on the Book of Job 1–5* [in Hebrew]. MA thesis, Hebrew University, 1972.

Birnbaum, Philip. *The Arabic Commentary of Yefet ben 'Ali the Karaite on the Book of Hosea, Edited from Eight Manuscripts and Provided with a Critical Notes and an Introduction*. Philadelphia: Dropsie College for Hebrew and Cognate Learning, 1942.

Blau, Joshua. *A Dictionary of Mediaeval Judaeo-Arabic Texts* [in Hebrew]. Jerusalem: Academy of the Hebrew Language, the Israel Academy of Sciences and Humanities, 2006.

——. *Judaeo-Arabic Literature: Selected Texts* [in Hebrew]. Jerusalem: Magnes Press, 1980.

Carter, Michael C. "Elision." In *Encyclopedia of Arabic Language and Linguistics*, 5 vols., edited by Kees Versteegh, Mushira Eid, Alaa Elgibali, Manfred Woidich and Andrzej Zaborski, 2:16–18. Leiden: Brill, 2006.

Carter, Michael C., and Kees Versteegh, "*'Idmar*." In *Encyclopedia of Arabic Language and Linguistics*, 5 vols., edited by Kees Versteegh, Mushira Eid, Alaa Elgibali, Manfred Woidich and Andrzej Zaborski, 2:300–302. Leiden: Brill, 2006.

Cohen, Mordechai, "Bible Exegesis: Rabbanite." In *Encyclopedia of Jews in the Islamic World*, 5 vols., edited by Norman Stillman et al., 1:442–457. Leiden: Brill, 2009.

Dana, Joseph. *Poetics of Medieval Hebrew Literature according to Moshe ibn Ezra* [in Hebrew]. Tel-Aviv: Dvir, 1982.

Derenbourg, J. *Oeuvres complètes de r. Saadia ben Iosef Al-Fayyoûmî: Version arabe du Pentateuque*. Paris: Ernest Leroux, 1893.

Erder, Yoram. "The Mourners of Zion: The Karaites in Jerusalem of the Tenth and Eleventh Centuries." In *A Guide to Karaite Studies: An Introduction to Literary Sources of Medieval and Modern Karaite Judaism*, edited by Meira Polliack, 363–413. Leiden: Brill, 2003.

——. "The Attitude of the Karaite Yefet ben 'Eli to Islam in the Light of His Interpretation of Psalm 14:53" [in Hebrew]. *Michael* 14 (1997): 29–49.

Frank, Daniel. "The Limits of Karaite Scripturalism: Problems in Narrative Exegesis." In *A Word Fitly Spoken: Studies in Mediaeval Exegesis of the Hebrew Bible, and the Qur'an*, edited by Meir M. Bar-Asher, Simon Hopkins, Sarah Stroumsa, and Bruno Chiesa, 41–82. Jerusalem: Yad Izhak Ben-Zvi, 2007.

——. *Search Scripture Well, Karaite Exegetes and the Origins of the Jewish Bible Commentary in the Islamic East*. Études sur le judaïsme médiéval 29. Leiden: Brill, 2004.

Frank, Richard M. "The Autonomy of the Human Agent in the Teaching of 'Abd al- Ğabbar." *Le Muséon* 95 (1982): 323–355.

Freedman, H., and Maurice Simon, trans. *Midrash Rabbah*. 10 vols. London: Soncino Press, 1961.

Gimaret, Daniel. "Mu'tazila." In *Encyclopaedia of Islam*, new edition, 12 vols., edited by Gibb H.A.R. et al., fasc. 127–128, 7: 783–793. Leiden: Brill, 1960–2002.

——. "Théories de l'acte humain en théologie musulmane." *Études musulmanes* 24. Paris: Librairie Philosophique; Leuven: Editors Peeters, 1980.

Ginzberg, Louis. *The Legends of the Jews*, 6 vols. Philadelphia: Jewish Publication Society, 1937.

Goldstein, Miriam. "The Structural Function of Biblical Superfluity in the Exegesis of the Karaite Yusuf ibn Nuh" [in Hebrew]. *Sefunot* 8, no. 23 (2003): 337–349.

——. "The Beginnings of the Transition from Derash to Peshat as Exemplified in Yefet ben Eli's Comment on Psa. 44:24." In *Exegesis and Grammar in Medieval Karaite Texts*, edited by Geoffrey Khan, 41–64. Oxford: Oxford University Press, 2001.

Halkin, A. S., ed. *Moses ben Ya'akov ibn Ezra, Kitab al-Muḥaḍarah wal-Mudhakarah. Liber Discussionis et Commemorationis (Poetica Hebraica)*. Jerusalem: Mekize Nirdamim, 1975.

Hussain, Haider Abbas. *Yefet ben Ali's Commentary on the Hebrew Text of the Book of Job I–X*. PhD diss., University of St. Andrews, 1986.

Khan, Geoffrey. *The Early Karaite Tradition of Hebrew Grammatical Thought, Including a Critical Edition, Translation and Analysis of the Diqduq of Abu Ya'qub Yusuf ibn Nuh on the Hagiographa*. Studies in Semitic Languages and Linguistics 32. Leiden: Brill, 2000.

Léandre Bargès, Jean Joseph. *Excerpta ex R. Yapheth ben Heli commentariis in Psalmos Davidis regis et prophetae*. Paris: Lutetle Parisiorum (prostat apud B. Duprat), Instituti Imperialis Gallicani Bibliopolam, 1846.

Livne-Kafri, Ofer. "The Commentary on Habakkuk 1–3 by the Karaite Yefet ben 'Eli al-Basri" [in Hebrew]. *Sefunot* 6, no. 21 (1993): 73–113.

Madelung, Wilferd. "The Late Mu'tazila and Determinism: The Philosophers's Trap." In *Yád-Náma in Memoria di Alessandro Bausani*, 2 vols. edited by B. Scarcia Amoretti and L. Rostagno, 1:245–257. Rome: Islamistica Ed., 1991.

Madelung, Wilfred, and Sabine Schmidtke. *Rational Theology in Interfaith Communication, Abu l-Husayn al-Basri's Mu'tazili Theology among the Karaites in the Fatimid Age*. Leiden: Brill, 2006.

Margoliouth, David Samuel. *A Commentary on the Book of Daniel by Yefet ibn Ali the Karaite*. Oxford: Anecdota Oxoniensia, 1889.

Marwick, Lawrence. *Retribution and Redemption: Yefet Ben 'Eli on the Minor Prophets; A Lost Work of Lawrence Marwick*. n.p., 2003.

Matties, Gordon H. *Ezekiel 18 and the Rhetoric of Moral Discourse*. Atlanta: Scholars Press, 1990.

Polliack, Meira. "*Qisas wa-akhbar jarata*: Karaite Distinctions of Biblical Genre in the Work of the Biblical Mudawwin." In: *The Semitic Languages of Jewish Intellectual Production*, Memorial volume for Dr. Friedrich Niessen edited by M.A. Gallego and J. P. Monferrer-Sala. Cambridge Genizah Studies Series. Leiden: Brill, forthcoming.

——. "The Unseen Joints of the Text: On the Medieval Judaeo-Arabic Concept of Elision (*IHTIṢĀR*) and its Gap-filling Functions in Biblical Interpretation." In: *Words, Ideas, Worlds in the Hebrew Bible – The Yairah Amit Festschrift*, edited by A. Brenner and F. H. Polak. Sheffield: Sheffield Phoenix Press, 2012, 179–205.

——. "Concepts of Scripture among the Jews of the Medieval Islamic World." In *Jewish Concepts of Scripture: A Comparative Introduction*, edited by Benjamin D. Sommer, 80–101. New York: New York University Press, 2012.

——. "Historicizing Prophetic Literature: Yefet ben 'Eli's Commentary on Hosea and Its Relationship to al-Qumisi's *Pitron*." In *Pesher Nahum: Texts and Studies in Jewish History and Literature from Antiquity through the Middle Ages presented to Norman Golb*, edited by J. L. Kraemer and Michael G. Wechsler, 153–190. Chicago: University of Chicago Press, 2011.

——. "Major Trends in Karaite Biblical Exegesis in the Tenth and Eleventh Centuries." In *A Guide to Karaite Studies: An Introduction to Literary Sources of Medieval and Modern Karaite Judaism*, edited by Meira Polliack, 363–413. Leiden: Brill, 2003.

——. *The Karaite Tradition of Arabic Bible Translation: A Linguistic and Exegetical Study of Karaite Translations of the Pentateuch from the Tenth and Eleventh Centuries C.E.* Études sur le judaïsme médiéval 17. Leiden: Brill, 1997.

——. "Alternate Renderings and Additions in Yeshu'ah ben Yehudah's Arabic Translation of the Pentateuch." *JQR*, n.s., 84 (1994): 209–226.

Polliack, Meira, and Eliezer Schlossberg. *Commentary of Yefet ben 'Eli the Karaite on the Book of Hosea* [in Hebrew]. Ramat Gan: Bar Ilan University Press, 2009.

——. "Historical-literary, Rhetorical and Redactional Methods of Interpretation in Yefet ben Eli's Introduction to the Minor Prophets." In *Exegesis and Grammar in Medieval Karaite Texts*, edited by Geoffrey Khan, 1–39. Oxford: Oxford University Press, 2001.

Qafih, Yoseph. *Peyrushey Rabbenu Sa'adyah Gaon 'al ha-Torah* [in Hebrew]. Jerusalem: Mossad Harav Kook, 1984.

Sasson, Ilana. *Methods and Approach in Yefet ben 'Eli al-Basri's Translation and Commentary on the Book of Proverbs*. PhD diss., Jewish Theological Seminary, 2010.

Schwarb, Gregor. "Kalam." In *Encyclopedia of Jews in the Islamic World*, 5 vols. 3, edited by Norman Stillman et al., 3:91–98. Leiden: Brill, 2009.

——. "Capturing the Meaning of God's Speech: The Relevance of *usul al-fiqh* to an Understanding of *usul al-tafsir* in Jewish and Muslim *kalam*." In *A Word Fitly Spoken: Studies in Mediaeval Exegesis of the Hebrew Bible and the Qur'an Presented to Haggai Ben-Shammai*, edited by Meir M. Bar-Asher, Simon Hopkins, Sarah Stroumsa, and Bruno Chiesa, 111–156. Jerusalem: Ben-Zvi Institute for the History of Jewish Communities in the East, Yad Izhaq Ben-Zvi and the Hebrew University of Jerusalem, 2007.

Sheshdiv, Manekdim. *Ta'liq Sharh al-Usul al-Khamsa*. Edited by 'Abd al-Karim 'Uthman. Cairo: Maktabat Wahba, 1996.

Shinan, Avigdor, ed. *Midrash Shemot Rabbah*. Jerusalem: Dvir, 1984.

Shy, Hadassa. "Taqdir and Its Counterparts in Mediaeval Judaeo-Arabic." In *Genizah Research after Ninety Years: The Case of Judaeo-Arabic*, edited by Joshua Blau and Stefan C. Reif, 144–154. Cambridge: Cambridge University Press, 1992.

Sirat, Colette. *A History of Jewish Philosophy in the Middle Ages*. Cambridge: Cambridge University Press and Maison des Sciences de l'Homme, 1985.

——. *Les théories des visions surnaturelle dans la pensée juive du Moyen Age*. Études sur le judaïsme médiéval 1. Leiden: Brill, 1969.

Sklare, David, ed. *Kitab al-Ni'ma by Levi ben Yefet*. In *A Common Rationality: Mu'tazilism in Islam and Judaism*, edited by Camilla Adang, Sabine Schmidtke, and David Sklare, 157–216. Würzburg: Ergon, 2007.

——. "Are the Gentiles Obligated to Observe the Torah?" In *Be'erot Yitzhak: Studies in Memory of Isadore Twersky*, edited by Jay M. Harris, 311–346. Cambridge, Mass.: Harvard University Press, 2005.

Sokolow, Moshe. "The Negation of Muslim Sovereignty over the Land of Israel in Two Karaite Commentaries of the Tenth Century" [in Hebrew]. *Shalem* 3 (1981): 309–318.

Urbach, Ephraim E. *The Sages, Their Concepts and Beliefs*. Translated by Israel Abrahams. Jerusalem: Magness Press, 1979.

Vajda, Georges, *Al-Kitab al-Muhtawi de Yusuf al-Basir: Texte, traduction et commentaire par Georges Vajda*. Edited by David R. Blumenthal. Études sur le judaïsme médiéval 12. Leiden: Brill, 1985.

——. *Deux commentaires karaïtes sur l'Ecclésiaste*. Études sur le judaïsme médiéval 4. Leiden: Brill, 1971.

Vasalou, Sophia. *Moral Agents and Their Deserts: The Character of Mu'tazilite Ethics*. Princeton, N.J.: Princeton University Press, 2008.

Wechsler, Michael. *The Arabic Translation and Commentary of Yefet ben 'Eli the Karaite on the Book of Esther*. Karaite Texts and Studies, vol. 1. Études sur le judaïsme medieval 36. Leiden: Brill, 2008.

Wehr, Hans. *A Dictionary of Modern Written Arabic (Arabic-English)*. Urbana, Ill., and Ithaca, N.Y.: Spoken Languages Services, 1994.

Zawanowska, Marzena. "Review of Scholarly Research on Yefet and His Works," *Revue des études juives* 173 (1/2) (2014), forthcoming.

——. "Islamic Exegetical Terms in Yefet ben 'Eli's Commentaries on the Holy Scriptures," *Journal of Jewish Studies* 64 (2013): 306–325.

——. "In the Border-Land of Literalism: Interpretative Alterations of Scripture in Medieval Karaite Translations of the Bible into Arabic," *Journal for Intellectual History of the Islamicate World* 1 (2013): 179–202.

——. *The Arabic Translation and Commentary of Yefet ben 'Eli on the Abraham Narratives (Genesis 11:10–25:18)*. Karaite Texts and Studies, vol. 4. Études sur le judaïsme médiéval 46. Leiden: Brill, 2012.

Zucker, Moshe. *Saadya's Commentary on Genesis* [in Hebrew]. New York: Jewish Theological Seminary of America, 1984.

{ 6 }

And Yet, the Texts Remain

THE PROBLEM OF THE COMMAND TO DESTROY THE CANAANITES

Menachem Kellner

The "vengeful God of the Old Testament" has for generations been unfavorably compared with the "loving God of the New Testament." Of late, a group of writers whom I like to call "evangelical atheists" have taken up the cudgels. Read, for example, what Richard Dawkins has to say about the God of Abraham, Isaac, and Jacob:

> The God of the Old Testament is arguably the most unpleasant character in all fiction: jealous and proud of it, a petty, unjust, unforgiving control-freak; a vindictive, blood-thirsty ethnic cleanser, a misogynistic, homophobic, racist, infanticidal, genocidal, filicidal, pestilential, megalomaniacal, sado-masochistic, capriciously malevolent bully.[1]

When confronted with screeds such as these, one typical Jewish response is to point out that Judaism is not a fundamentalist religion and that it reads the Hebrew Bible (not the "Old Testament!") through the lenses of rabbinic texts that greatly modify the apparent ferocity of the Bible.[2] That may be called the official response of Jews. For most Jews, however, the immediate response is one of amazement: That is hardly the God to whom religious Jews of whatever persuasion turn in prayer! This is, I think, an important point: Dawkins's God is simply unrecognizable to believing Jews because of what Judaism itself has taught them. Diaspora Jews the world over, for example, know that one takes a drop out of the Passover wine cup with the mention of each of the ten plagues, out of sympathy with the suffering of the Egyptians.[3]

True enough, but the biblical texts remain holy, revered, and a permanent challenge for those who pray to a loving God, not a vengeful and bloodthirsty one.[4] Focusing on the Pentateuch alone, and on God's relationship with the people called chosen, and on just one book of the Pentateuch, the "Glorious Book of Numbers" as Mary Douglas called it,[5] we find a horrifying string of very unloving passages. Thus, in Numbers 14, God seeks to wipe out the Jewish people (as in Exod 32—in both cases, God wanted to wipe out the

Israelites and begin the whole story anew with the descendants of Moses[6]); in Numbers 17, over fourteen thousand complaining Jews are killed in a plague; in Numbers 21, a great multitude were killed by venomous snakes sent by God; twenty-four thousand more died in the plague following upon the whoring after the Midianites in Numbers 25 (and the leaders of the sinning were apparently killed by exposure, thus condemned to a slow and miserable death). The Canaanite nations are repeatedly promised extermination in the "Glorious Book of Numbers" (and elsewhere), and in Numbers 31, Moses waxes wroth with the Israelite army for failing to kill all the Midianite men, women who were not virgins, and all male children.

Jews read these passages every summer in the synagogue and, it is safe to say, pay almost no attention to them. Why is that? In the final analysis, I am more interested here in raising a "Jewish" question than in asking scholarly and historical questions of the texts. How do we as Jews handle texts that prescribe the destruction of the Canaanites?[7] On the one hand, the answer is clear. Thanks to the writings of the rabbinic Sages, we do not focus on these texts, we read them in a very nonliteral fashion, we say that they are no longer applicable—in other words, we background them, turn them into backdrop noise, into static, as it where, and foreground other texts. But the texts remain, and not only in Christian (or evangelical atheist) depictions of the jealous, warlike God of the "Old Testament." There is sadly no dearth of contemporary rabbis who want to use these texts in order to instruct Israelis how to deal with their enemies.[8]

Let us remember that it is the God whom we revere, in whose love we are secure and by which we feel sustained ("With great love have you loved us, O Lord" we repeat every morning before reciting the Shma), who condemned *all* of humanity (save a tiny remnant) to death in Noah's flood, who subjected Abraham (characterized as God's lover in Isa 41:8) and his son to exquisite mental torture in the Akedah, who wiped out the firstborn of the Egyptians (children and animals, as well as adults), who urged the Levites to slay their fellows after the golden calf—and these are the people God loves! Repeated promises of destruction of the seven Canaanite nations (which the book of Joshua claims were actually carried out—against the evidence of the book itself[9]) round out this picture.

We as Jews are so used to reading the Torah through the eyes of rabbinic Sages that looking at it in a "Protestant/Fundamentalist" fashion as I have done here can be a shocking experience since God appears cruel—not the God whom Jews typically address as "Our Father in Heaven" (or, in Yiddish, as *tateh ziseh*, "sweet father").

Why are these texts so shocking? With Abraham, we are convinced that the Judge of all the world does only justice. The Torah itself has taught us to be shocked.

Rabbinic texts, as is well-known, moderate many of the Bible's more bloodthirsty passages, forcing them into the framework of rabbinic jurisprudence.

Perhaps the clearest example of this is provided by the many rabbinic passages that turn King David from a womanizer and cruel warrior into a subtle rabbinic exegete and decisor.[10] For the rabbis, David as author of Psalms was in the foreground, while David as described in the books of Samuel remained far in the background. We find a similar approach in the texts that teach that not all of God's attributes are fit for imitation. Thus (*Deut. Rab.*, Shofetim 5):

> R. Hama son of R. Hanina further said: What means the text: *You shall walk after the Lord your God* (Deut 13:5)? Is it, then, possible for a human being to walk after the *Shekhinah* [divine presence]? Has it not been said: *For the Lord your God is a devouring fire* (Deut 4:24)? But [the meaning is] to walk after the attributes of the Holy One, blessed be He. As He clothes the naked, for it is written: *And the Lord God made for Adam and for his wife coats of skin, and clothed them* (Gen 3:21) so do you also clothe the naked. The Holy One, blessed be He, visited the sick, for it is written: *And the Lord appeared to him by the oaks of Mamre* (Gen 18:1), so do you also visit the sick. The Holy One, blessed be He, comforted mourners, for it is written: *And it came to pass after the death of Abraham, that God blessed Isaac his son* (Gen 25:11), so do you also comfort mourners. The Holy one, blessed be He, buried the dead, for it is written: *And He buried him in the valley* (Deut 34:6), so do you also bury the dead.

It is apparent that the author of this passage wanted to preserve the idea of imitating God, and also wanted to limit those attributes of God that humans are to imitate. After all, God is not only characterized as *a devouring fire*, but also as a "jealous" God of vengeance (Exod 20:4, 34:14; Deut 4:24, 5:8, 6:15). R. Hama son of R. Hanina wanted to be sure that no one thought it appropriate to imitate *that* divine attribute![11]

And Yet, the Texts Remain

Turning to the Middle Ages, I searched for halakhic and exegetical responses to what I take as the challenge posed by the Torah's violent teachings. Building on rabbinic precedents (on which, see the relevant chapters in this volume[12]), Maimonides adds important qualifications of his own, and sets the parameters for much subsequent discussion.

In "Laws of Kings and Their Wars" 5.1, we read:

> The primary war which the king wages is a *milhemet mitzvah*. What is a *milhemet mitzvah*? It includes the war against the Seven Nations, that against Amalek.

Milhemet mitzvah is usually translated as "obligatory war," but the connotation of the expression in Jewish contexts is wider. It is not only a *mitzvah*, a commandment, to wage this war, but it is also a *mitzvah*, a good deed to do so. This is so much the case—at least with respect to Amalek—that Maimonides opens his "Laws of Kings" with the following statement:

> Three commandments—to be carried out on entering the Land [of Israel]—were enjoined upon Israel: to appoint a king, as it is said, *You shall in any way set him king over you* (Deut 17:15);[13] to destroy the seed of Amalek, as it is said: *You shall blot out the remembrance of Amalek* (Deut 25:19); and to build the sanctuary, as it is said: *Even unto His habitation shall you seek, and there you shall come* (Deut 12:5). The appointment of a king precedes the war with Amalek, as it is said: *The Lord sent me to anoint you to be king over His people…Now go and smite Amalek* (1 Sam 15:1,3). The destruction of the seed of Amalek precedes the erection of the sanctuary, as it is written: *And it came to pass, when the king dwelled in his house, and the Lord had given him rest from all his enemies round about, that the king said to Nathan the prophet:…I dwell in a house of cedar but the ark of God dwells within curtains* (2 Sam 7:1–2).[14]

Maimonides emphasizes the point in the fourth paragraph of "Laws of Kings," 5:

> It is a positive command to destroy the Seven Nations, as it is said (Deut 20:17): *But you shall utterly destroy them.* If one does not put to death any of them that fall into one's power, one transgresses a negative command, as it is said (Deut 20:16): *You shall save alive nothing that breathes.* But their memory has long since perished.

On the one hand, we are told that the commandment to destroy the seven nations has a negative corollary: Failing to put any one of them to death when we have the power to do so constitutes the violation of a negative commandment. On the other hand, we are immediately told that fulfilling these commandments, positive and negative both, is no longer possible: "But their memory has long since perished." The commandments remain on the books, as it were, but their application becomes moot. Is this the beginning of an attempt by Maimonides to modify the ferocity of the biblical law?

Paragraph 6.1 gives one reason to think so. There Maimonides states (and, as we shall see below, when we get to Nahmanides' disagreement with Rashi, this is not a standard position):

> No war is made against any person before peace offers are made. This obtains both for an optional war and a *milhemet mitzvah.*

Suddenly the wars against the seven nations and even Amalek take on a different hue: War is never the preferred option. War is no longer a *mitzvah* in the sense of good deed, but an unfortunate consequence of idolatrous intransigence. War is indeed declared against the seven nations and Amalek, but they are given the opportunity to submit. If they submit to Israel, their lives are spared. What constitutes submission? Agreement to abide by the seven Noahide laws and to pay a tax to the Israelite authorities as a sign of their suzerainty.

There are two Maimonidean innovations here: Peace must be offered to the Canaanites and Amalekites before going to war against them,[15] and part of their acceptance of peace terms involves the acceptance of the seven Noahide commandments.[16] That these decisions are innovations is made abundantly clear by Maimonides' irascible glossator, Rabbi Abraham ben David of Posquieres (Rabad), and subsequent commentators. Rabad rejects the exegesis of verses that Maimonides offers by way of justifying his decisions as *shibbush*, or blunder.[17]

Maimonides' insistence on acceptance of the seven Noahide commandments is not, to put it mildly, universally accepted by other decisors.[18] It probably reflects what I take to be his (unstated) view that the ultimate point of Israelite warfare is the spread of monotheism, or, at the very least, the extirpation of idolatry and its attendant horrors. Be that as it may, it is clear that the obligatory wars against the Canaanite nations and Amalek are wars against practices and principles, not against ethnicities.[19]

What happens if the enemy does not accept all the conditions demanded of them? To our ears, the answer is horrifying; to medieval ears, one assumes, much less so:

> VI.4: If they refuse to accept the offer of peace, or if they accept the offer of peace but not the seven commandments, war is made with them; all adult males are put to death; all their money and little ones are taken as plunder, but no woman or minor is slayed.

In biblical terms, "all adult males" usually means all men eligible for military service, and that would appear to be Maimonides' point here. Such men are put to the sword, but the women and children are spared for a life of servitude. But this "merciful" approach only obtains with respect to non-obligatory wars:

> This applies to an optional war, that is a war against any other nation; but in a war against the seven nations or against Amalek, if these refuse to accept the terms of peace, none of them is spared... Whence do we derive that the [above-cited] command refers only to those who refuse to accept the terms of peace? Because it is written (Josh 11:19–20): *There was not a city which made peace with the Children of Israel, save the Hivites, the inhabitants of Gibeon; they took all in battle. For it was of the Lord to harden their hearts, to come against Israel in battle, that they might be utterly destroyed.* We infer therefrom that the offer of peace had been made, but they did not accept it.

It is Rabad's claim that Maimonides' decisions in these cases reflect determinations of his own, as opposed to standard received tradition.

In Maimonides' hands, wars of extermination against national enemies become wars against barbaric individuals in defense of civilization. But even recast in these terms, such wars offend our sensibilities: Men, women, and children, combatants and not, all are to be slayed. No quarter is to be given, none is spared. For Maimonides, the applicability of the biblical texts may have been circumscribed, but the texts remain, and they remain a challenge to Jews whose moral intuitions have been framed by those teachings of Judaism that emphasize that all human beings are created in the image of God and that all human beings will ultimately worship God out of a stance of spiritual equality.

And Yet, the Texts Remain

Apologists for Judaism, myself among them, often cite Maimonides' words, "but their memory has long since perished" as proof that he sought to historicize and thus render null and void the laws concerning the utter wiping out of the seven Canaanite nations (and Amalek). The second and third paragraphs in the following passage, from Maimonides' *Book of Commandments*, do not refute this apologetic approach, but make it harder to sustain:[20]

POSITIVE COMMANDMENT 187—The Law of the Seven Nations

By this injunction we are commanded to exterminate the Seven Nations that inhabited the land of Canaan, because they constituted the root and very foundation of idolatry. This injunction is contained in His words (exalted be He), *You shall utterly destroy them* (Deut 20:17). It is explained in many texts that the object was to safeguard us from imitating their heresy.[21] There are many passages in Scripture which strongly urge and exhort us to exterminate them, and war against them is obligatory.

This paragraph introduces Maimonides' explanation (later to inform his above-cited decisions in "Laws of Kings") that the war against the seven nations has nothing to do with racial wars of extermination or ethnic cleansing as understood today and is more akin to Christian persecution of the Jews in the Middle Ages (in which the object of the persecution was to bring about the conversion of the Jews to Christianity) than to the Nazi persecution of the Jews in the Holocaust (in which the object of the persecution was the eradication of the Jew as Jew, with no reference to what the Jew might have done or believed).[22] Small comfort, perhaps, but not unimportant in the context of what I am trying to do here.

The object of the wars of extermination to be waged against the seven Canaanite nations is not against the Canaanites themselves, but against their ideas (and, of course, the actions that follow from those ideas). The moment they are willing to give up those ideas, war against them ceases. What is wrong with their ideas? For Maimonides the answer is straightforward: Idolatry is the single most important mistake a person can make. The Jews are charged with the obligation to eradicate idolatry, in order to make the spread of truth possible. But there is another issue here as well, one central to the Jewish opposition to idolatry. Fairly or not,[23] Jewish texts see a deep and unbreakable link between idolatry and the worst forms of brutality and sexual immorality. The prophets of Israel made this the central focus of their attacks on idolatry, and the rabbis of the Talmud were certainly aware of it.[24]

An indication of how central this point is to Jewish conceptions of idolatry may be found in the reasoning of R. Menachem ha-Meiri (1249–ca. 1310). Meiri reasoned as follows: Idolaters are morally corrupt. My Christian neighbors are not morally corrupt. Ergo, they are not idolaters.[25] Be that as it may, what we have shown to this point is that Maimonides' position vis-à-vis the seven nations, while hardly one to meet with our approval, obviates the need to destroy the Canaanites, and, given medieval realities, is far less bloodthirsty than it might appear to be at first glance.

Fine and good, but the next paragraph of positive commandment 187 introduces a wrinkle that can only upset anyone seeking to find in Maimonides support for Jews today whose moral sensibilities—framed, as I have been suggesting, by Judaism itself—gag at the laws concerning the seven nations and Amalek. Maimonides takes up the question of the applicability of the laws concerning the seven nations:

> One might think that this commandment is not binding for all time, seeing that the Seven Nations have long ceased to exist; but that opinion will be entertained only by one who has not grasped the distinction between commandments which are binding for all time and those which are not. A commandment which has been completely fulfilled by the attainment of its object, but to the fulfillment of which no definite time limit has been attached, cannot be said not to be binding for all time, because it is binding in every generation in which there is a possibility of its fulfillment. If the Lord completely destroys and exterminates the Amalekites—and may this come to pass speedily in our days, in accordance with His promise (exalted be He), *For I will utterly blot out the remembrance of Amalek* (Exod 17:14)—shall we then say that the injunction *you shall blot out the remembrance of Amalek* (Deut 25:19) is not binding for all time? We cannot say so; the injunction is binding for all time, as long as descendants of Amalek exist, they must be exterminated. Similarly in the case of the Seven Nations, their destruction and extermination is binding upon us, and the war against them is obligatory: We are commanded to root them out and pursue them throughout all generations until they are destroyed completely. Thus we did until their destruction was completed by David, and this remnant was scattered and intermingled with the other nations, so that no trace of them remains. But although they have disappeared, it does not follow that the commandment

to exterminate them is not binding for all time, just as we cannot say that the war against Amalek is not binding for all time, even after they have been consumed and destroyed. No special condition of time or place is attached to this commandment, as is the case with those commandments specially designed for the desert or for Egypt. On the contrary, it applies to those on whom it is imposed, and they must fulfill it so long as [any of those against whom it is directed] exists.

Generally speaking, it is proper for you to understand and discern the difference between a commandment and the occasion for it. A commandment may be binding for all time, and yet the occasion [for its fulfillment] may be lacking at a particular time; but the lack of occasion does not make it a commandment which is not binding for all time. A commandment ceases to be binding for all time when the contrary is true: When, that is, it was at one time our duty in certain conditions to perform a certain act or carry out a certain ordinance, but this is not our duty today, although these conditions still obtain. An example is the case of the aged Levite, who was disqualified for service in the desert, but is qualified among us today, as is explained in its proper place. You should understand this principle and lay it to heart.

The apologetic approach to this long passage from the *Book of Commandments* (and it is very likely the correct approach as well) is to maintain that Maimonides' interest here is threefold: to explain why the commandment to eradicate the seven nations is counted as one of the 613 commandments of the Torah, even if it is no longer applicable; to maintain the integrity of the body of Jewish law; and to keep the fight against idolatry (and its associated brutality) in the forefront of Jewish consciousness.

The first point is primarily technical: Maimonides is counting and explaining the 613 commandments of the Torah—he cannot simply leave out one that is explicitly stated as a commandment in the Torah and is regarded as such by rabbinic tradition. The second point relates to a broader issue in Maimonides' thought. He explains many of the Torah's commandments historically. This opens him to the objection that once the historical reason for a commandment no longer obtains, perhaps there is no point in observing the commandment? This argument has been raised repeatedly against Maimonides, and there can be little doubt that he was sensitive to it.[26] Maimonides clearly distinguished between the reason that a law was given, and the reason to obey it.[27] That distinction lies behind his argument here. The last point relates to an issue emphasized by Kenneth Seeskin in his book, *No Other Gods*:[28] Idolatry is a constant threat to humankind.

Be this last point as it may, Maimonides' approach to the question of how and when to prosecute war against the seven nations became dominant in the Middle Ages. This becomes clear in the commentary of Nahmanides to Deuteronomy 20:10 ("When you draw near to a city to fight against it, then proclaim peace toward it").[29] Nahmanides opens his commentary, as is wont, by quoting Rashi:

> "Scripture is speaking of a[n] optional war [rather than an obligatory war, such as the invasion of the seven nations of Canaan], as it is expressly stated in this section, *Thus shall you do to all the cities which are very far off from you* (Deut 20:15)." This is Rashi's language. Rashi wrote this based on the *Sifre* where it is taught: "Scripture is speaking of a[n] optional war."[30]

Rashi's point here is to limit the applicability of the verse, which mandates making an offer of peace before opening hostilities, to nations "very far off from thee," and not to the seven nations of Canaan.

Nahmanides, following Maimonides, differs from Rashi's position:

> But the intent of our Rabbis with reference to this verse [before us, was not to say that the requirement of proclaiming peace applies exclusively to optional, but not to obligatory, wars; rather, their teaching in the *Sifre*] refers only to the later section wherein there is a differentiation between the two kinds of wars [i.e., in verses 13–14 declaring that if the enemy insists on war, then only the men are to be killed, but the women and children are to be spared—that law applies only to a[n] optional but not to an obligatory war]. But the call for peace applies even to an obligatory war. It requires us to offer peace-terms even to the Seven Nations [of Canaan], for Moses proclaimed peace to Sihon, king of the Amorites, and he would not have transgressed both the positive and negative commandments in this section: *But you shall utterly destroy them* (Deut 20:17), and *you shall save alive nothing that breathes* (Deut 20:16).[31] Rather, the difference between them [i.e., obligatory and optional wars] is when the enemy does not make peace and continues to make war. Then, in the case of the *cities which are very far off* (Deut 20:15), Scripture commanded us to smite every male thereof (Deut 20:13) and keep alive the women and male children, but in *the cities of these people* (Deut 20:16) [i.e., the seven nations of Canaan in the event they refuse the call to peace], it commanded us to destroy even the women and children.

Nahmanides continues his argument with Rashi by citing additional rabbinic texts:

> And so did our Rabbis say in the Midrash of *Eileh Hadevarim Rabbah*, and it is found also in *Tanhuma*[32] and the Gemara Yerushalmi:[33] "Rabbi Shmuel the son of Rabbi Nahmani said: Joshua the son of Nun fulfilled the laws of this section. What did Joshua do? Wherever he went to conquer, he would send a proclamation in which he wrote: 'He who wishes to make peace let him come forward and make peace; he who wishes to leave, let him leave, and he who wishes to make war, let him make war.' The Girgashite left. With the Gibeonites who made peace, Joshua made peace. The thirty-one kings

who came to wage war[34]—the Holy One, Blessed be He, cast them down etc."
And so indeed Scripture states with reference to all cities [including those
of the seven nations], *There was not a city that made peace with the children
of Israel, save the Hivites the inhabitants of Gibeon; they took all in battle. For
it was of the Eternal to harden their hearts, to come against Israel in battle,
that they might be utterly destroyed.*[35] Obviously, if they had wanted to make
peace, the Israelites would have made peace with them.

Just as Maimonides had reasoned directly from the biblical text, so does
Nahmanides here, using different texts. Had they explicit and authoritative
rabbinic texts on which to rely, it is more than likely that they would have
cited them.

But there remain severities that apply only in the case of the seven nations:

It appears that regarding the terms of peace, there were differences
[between what was offered *the very far off* cities and what was offered the
seven nations], for, with reference to the distant cities, we ask that they
make peace and become tributary to us and serve, but, regarding *the cities
of these peoples* [the seven nations] we demand[36] of them peace, tribute and
service, on the condition that they agree not to worship idols. Scripture
does not mention it in this section, because concerning idolators, it has
already given the prohibition, *They shall not dwell in your Land, lest they
make you sin against Me, for you will serve their gods* (Exod 23:33). It is
possible that we must inform them only of the peace offer, tribute and
service; after they are subject to us, we tell them that we execute judgment
upon idols and their worshippers, whether individuals or the community.
Similarly, that which is stated here, *That they teach you not to do after all
their abominations* (Deut 20:18), and with reference to it the Rabbis said
in the *Sifre*,[37] "But if they repent [of their idol-worship] they are not to be
killed"—this refers to the Seven Nations.[38] The "repentance" is that they
accept upon themselves the seven commandments in which "the sons of
Noah" were commanded, but not that they must convert to become righteous proselytes.

There are a number of interesting implications in this text. Once again, as in
Maimonides, the objection to the seven nations is not to what they are, but
to what they preach and practice. Second, it turns out that they are not to
be treated any more harshly than any other idolatrous nation: Idolatry is not
permitted in the land of Israel, to any one, Canaanite or not. Third, and to
me most interesting and suggestive, Nahmanides speaks of the possibility of
(and, one assumes, would welcome) repentance on the part of the Canaanite
nations. Repentance in Judaism implies many things, one of which is a return
to a pristine beginning point. Thus, since Canaanite idolaters have the option
of repenting, that means that they cannot be seen in any sense as essentially

evil, and their little children, who have not yet been corrupted by their societies, must be seen as wholly innocent.

Indeed, Nahmanides reverts to his argument with Rashi to emphasize this point:

> Now, in Tractate *Sotah* (38b) the Rabbis have said that "they [i.e., the Israelites upon coming into the Land] inscribed the Torah upon stones in seventy languages and that, below, they wrote, *That they teach you not to do* (Deut 20:18). However, [we deduce,] if the peoples were to repent, the Israelites would accept them." Rashi explained this text as follows: "[This verse was written upon the stones below] to inform the nations that dwelled outside the border of the Land of Israel that they [i.e., the Israelites] were not commanded to destroy [populations] except for those [the seven nations] that dwell within the borders in order that they [the Canaanites] should not teach them their perverted practices. But as to those who dwell outside [the boundaries] we tell them, 'If you repent, we accept you.' Those who dwell within the Land we do not accept because their repentance was due to fear." This is the language of the Rabbi [Rashi]. But it is not correct, for it was with reference to *the cities of these peoples that the Eternal your God gives you for an inheritance* (Deut 20:16)—it was of them that he said *that they teach you not* (Deut 20:18) thus indicating that if they do repent [thereby negating the fear that they may *teach you*] they are not to be slayed. Similarly He said of them, *They shall not dwell in your Land, lest they make you sin against Me, for you will serve their gods* (Exod 23:33), which indicates that if they abandon their gods they are permitted to dwell there.

Rashi is unwilling to accept the repentance of members of the seven Canaanite nations, since he doubts that their repentance will be sincere. Nahmanides rejects this claim and (at least by implication) deduces from the fact that the Torah was inscribed upon stones (stelae?)[39] in seventy languages that all idolatrous nations of the world—including the seven Canaanite nations—are invited to repent their idolatry. Where Rashi sees a warning, Nahmanides appears to see an invitation.

Nahmanides supports his opposition to Rashi with a further bit of independent textual interpretation:

> This is the project of Solomon concerning which it is written, *And this is the account of the levy which King Solomon raised; to build the House of the Eternal, and his own house, and Millo, and the wall of Jerusalem, etc.* (1 Kgs 9:15). *All the people that were left of the Amorites, the Hittites, the Peruzites, the Hivites, and the Jebusites, who were not of the Children of Israel; even their children that were left after them in the Land, whom the children of Israel were not able utterly to destroy, of them did Solomon raise a levy of bondservants, unto this day. But of the children of Israel did Solomon make*

no bondservants (1 Kgs 9:20–22). This project he did in accordance with the Law,[40] for they accepted the observance of the seven commandments upon themselves. Now it is clear that since Solomon was able to draft them as his laborers, he had power over them and he could have destroyed them, except that it was permissible to let them live, as we have written.

Solomon would not have violated the commandment of the Torah had it indeed insisted upon the eradication of all the seven Canaanite nations under all circumstances. That a God-fearing king like Solomon enslaved the remnants of the seven nations instead of killing them all, when he obviously had power over them, proves that killing them is only mandated if they refuse to repent their idolatry and accept upon themselves the other six Noahide commandments.

Again, Nahmanides' position is unlikely to appeal to a modern conscience, but it surely represents an important step in that direction, especially against the background of medieval realities, of which he was all too personally aware.

The following points should be emphasized here:

- One must offer peace before beginning even an obligatory war, including one prosecuted against any of the seven nations.
- If the seven nations do not accept the offer of peace (which involves their *dhimmi*-like status), then they must be exterminated.
- In the case of the seven nations, acceptance of the offer of peace must include the renunciation of idolatry (although, Nahmanides says, this may not have to be made known to them originally).
- Nahmanides emphasizes that the whole point of the war against the seven nations is to extirpate idolatry. Thus, if individuals from the seven nations repent, they are not to be killed. Repentance in their case means acceptance of the seven Noahide laws, not full conversion to Judaism.

And Yet, the Texts Remain

The only medieval exegete I have found who seems explicitly alive to the moral difficulty posed by the commandment to wipe out the seven nations, including the murder of little babies, was Nahmanides' "grand-student," Bahya ben Asher (thirteenth century),[41] but his "solution" leaves much to be desired.[42] Here follow portions of his commentary on Deuteronomy 20:10. Bahya, following his master Nahmanides, begins by quoting Rashi in order to disagree with him:

It is only with respect to a[n] optional war that Scripture speaks with reference to peace overtures, but with respect to the obligatory war of the Seven Nations, no peace overture is made—thus did Rashi interpret this verse. But Scripture speaks generally, *When you draw near unto a city* [*to fight against it, then proclaim peace unto it*]. Surely this implies every city, and every war, and one is to make peace overtures whether in a[n] optional war or in an obligatory war, with the exception of the Ammonites and the Moabites, about whom Scripture wrote explicitly: *You shall never concern yourself with their welfare or benefit* [*so long as you live*] (Deut 23:7). But even with respect to the Ammonites and Moabites, even though no offer of peace is made, if they of their volition consented, they are accepted, to teach you how great is the power of peace.[43]

Bahya follows Nahmanides in rejecting Rashi but uses a different argument to do so. I leave it to others to decide if there is any significance to that fact.

He then turns to his own interpretation of the verse.

This passage warns Israel not to wage war on any nation in the world without first offering peace: This is true both of an optional war with any of the nations, and of an obligatory war with the seven nations. If they consented and accepted upon themselves the seven Noahide commandments and the king's levy, not a single one of them is to be put to death, as it is written: "If it responds peaceably and lets you in, all the people present there shall serve you at forced labor" (Deut 20:11). By "levy" is meant that they be ready to do the king's work, both with their bodies and with their wealth, such as building walls and strengthening fortresses, building the king's palace, and so on, as it says:

This was the purpose of the forced labor which Solomon imposed: *It was to build the House of the Lord, his own palace, the Millo, and the wall of Jerusalem... and all of Solomon's garrison towns* (1 Kgs 9:15, 19). But if they did not consent, or even if they consented but refused to accept the seven Noahide commandments, then all the adult males are to be put to death, as it says: *If it does not surrender to you, but would join battle with you, you shall lay siege to it, and when the Lord your God delivers it into your hand, you shall put all its males to the sword* (Deut 20:12–13)—but not the children and women, as it says: [*You may, however, take as your booty,*] *the women, the children,* [*the livestock and everything in the town...*] (Deut 20:14)—this refers to male children.[44] But in the case of an obligatory war, such as that of the Seven Nations and Amalek, all are to be slayed.

This is the meaning of:

In the towns of the latter peoples, which the Lord your God is giving you as a heritage, you shall not let a soul remain alive (Deut 20:16)—only in this case are you commanded to kill them all, even women and children.

Bahya moderates the ferocity of the commandments in question by seeking to mitigate the overt meaning of the biblical texts. Peace is to be offered to all. He makes no exception here for the seven Canaanite nations or even for

Amalek: Israel may not wage war on anyone without first offering peace. Only when the peace overtures are rejected is war to be waged, and then, in most wars, women and children are to be spared. It is only in the case of Amalek and the seven Canaanite nations—if they reject peace offers—that total war is waged, and women and children are also put to death. In the final analysis, Bahya's position does not differ from that of Nahmanides, but he goes to the trouble of finding new arguments and texts to support it, thus strengthening the position he shares with Nahmanides.

This shared position is harsh, but no harsher than what the Allies did to Dresden, Tokyo, Hiroshima, and Nagasaki. And it is certainly much less harsh than what many Crusader bands did to the Jews of Europe and of Jerusalem. I make these comments not in order to criticize the Allies or in order to approve of Rabbenu Bahya's positions, but in order to remind the reader to judge him by the standards of his time, not ours.

On what grounds do I say that Rabbenu Bahya's prescriptions are harsh? He himself draws attention to the harshness of his claims and in so doing demonstrates a measure of sensitivity that I have not found in other contemporary Jewish writers:

> If your heart should ache[45] saying: In this we act violently[46] against children who have not sinned against us, behold, it is the law of heaven and the decree of Scripture.[47] Furthermore, since the Holy One, blessed be He, uproots their power from above, it is as if what we do to them below counts for nothing, as the Sages expounded (*Sanhedrin* 96b): "You have slayed a dead people, you have burned a Temple already burned, you have ground flour already ground."[48] There is no violence in this, and it is not considered killing, since they are already as if dead. Further, if they are not considered as already dead, there is no violence in killing the children, branches of the root of rebellion, *that fierce, impetuous nation* (Hab 1:6)[49] since there is no doubt but that they will continue in the ways of their fathers, [*You shall not act thus towards the Lord your God,*] *for they perform for their gods every abhorrent act that the Lord detests* (Deut 12:31) and Israel will learn from them, as is mentioned in this passage: *Lest they lead you into doing all the abhorrent things* [*that they have done for their gods and you stand guilty before the Lord your God*] (Deut 20:18).

It seems obvious to me that when an author brings a series of reasons for an action with which he or she is clearly uncomfortable, it means that none of the reasons is really satisfactory. Be that as it may, it is clear that Bahya ben Asher is in a quandary. The Torah commands that we do things that he finds morally repugnant, at least *ab initio*.

Our author continues struggling with the text:

> Lest you say, "when they grow up, they might[50] enter the covenant[51] and repent, go forth and learn[52] who permits shedding their blood—the Lord,

Who knows that they will not repent.[53] And thus did Isaiah of blessed memory say explicitly: *Prepare a slaughtering block for his sons because of the guilt of his father. Let them not arise to posses the earth! Then the world's face shall be covered with towns* (Isa 14:21). And thus, if we allowed them to live, behold, their lives would be the cause of much greater damage than the damage involved in their killing, and it is reasonable that a person do a small amount of damage in order to forestall much greater damage; thus, the good-hearted and intelligent person[54] will jump off a roof to save himself from [greater] danger,[55] or will amputate an arm or a leg or another limb to save his body, or will drink something as bitter as wormwood in order to eject illness from him and in so doing does not do violence to himself; rather he acts with loving-kindness towards himself by keeping himself alive. In that a person can behave thusly towards himself and it is impossible to convict him thereby of violence, it is all the more so not violence when done to others.[56] It is for this reason that the Torah permitting killing children, doing a small amount of damage while saving the world from much greater damage which would have occurred had they lived. There is no violence in this, but will be seen to be rational by one who examines the issue.

This text is particularly horrifying to anyone living in Israel—the same argument is often used by Palestinian murderers of Jewish children, who, they say, will grow up to become Israeli soldiers and are therefore fair game. Rabbenu Bahya is not the problem here. Given medieval realities, and the policies of Christian and Muslim polities toward their Jewish subjects, one can actually admire the fact that he thought it necessary to find excuses for the biblical commands. The problem for Judaism today is that Rabbenu Bahya is read as an authority on moral matters whose positions represent normative Jewish teaching vis-à-vis Gentiles to this very day.[57]

Returning to Bahya's text, we find him immediately seeking to modify the harshness of the position he has just excused:

When Scripture permitted[58] the killing of all the women and children, it is only in a case where they refused to consent; but if they consented then all the nations are equivalent in connection with the issue of peace, even the Seven Nations, for it is written in the book of Joshua: *Apart from the Hivites who dwelt in Gibeon, not a single city consented to the Israelites; all were taken in battle. For it was the Lord's doing to stiffen their hearts to give battle to Israel in order that they might be proscribed without quarter and wiped out, as the Lord had commanded Moses* (Josh 11:19–20). From this it follows that Joshua made peace overtures to them, which they rejected. And so we have learned in the *Sifri*:[59] "Joshua sent three letters before he entered the Land. In the first, he wrote to them: 'All who wish to consent should come and consent.' He wrote again: 'All who wish to leave should leave.' He wrote again: 'All who wish to wage war against us should wage war.'" In the Jerusalem Talmud it is written: "The Gibeonites consented, the Girgashites left, and thirty-one kings waged war."[60]

Bahya's discussion closes, then, by subtly reworking the biblical text to *permit*, as opposed to *command*, the killing of women and children and by emphasizing that peace overtures are to be extended to all peoples, "even the Seven Nations."

Zeev Harvey drew my attention to another passage in Rabbenu Bahya's commentary, a passage that shows how very alive he was to the issue raised in this chapter. In his exegesis of Genesis 32:8, Bahya teaches that it behooves the Jews, when dealing with the descendants of Esau (among whom we find Amalek in Gen 36:12), to follow in the footsteps of the patriarch Jacob and to approach all nations descended from Esau with presents and prayer; he rejects war as an option in (as I understand him) the pre-messianic world.

In terms of making the biblical texts accord with the values of much of rabbinic teaching and of making them accord with many of our moral intuitions today, Bahya takes us about as far as the medievals will go—and even he justifies the slaughter of innocents in certain restricted circumstances.

And So, the Texts Remain

Another thirteenth-century work, the *Hinnukh*,[61] also wrestles with the moral issues raised by the command of destroying the seven nations, although the positions it espouses (in commandment 425) are hardly likely to rest softly on the consciences of readers of this chapter.

Like those who preceded him, the author of the *Hinnukh* offers as a reason for the obligation of wiping out the seven nations their connection to idolatry. He then raises a question that had not been raised by earlier writers: If they were going to be destroyed, why did God create them in the first place? He offers a number of reasons:

- When originally created, the seven nations could have chosen to be good—like all human beings, they can choose between good and evil. It was their choice to become evil.
- Alternatively, it might be offered that they were evil all the time, but had one opportune time.[62]
- A third possibility is that one decent person descended from them, and for that reason they were created.
- A fourth possibility is that they were created as an object lesson for other human beings.
- A final possibility is that they were created so that they could build cities and plant gardens and vineyards for the Jews.

The *Hinnukh* concludes its discussion of our issue by emphasizing that, even though the seven nations no longer exist, if one finds a person belonging to them, one is obligated to kill that person. That is the direction in which he chooses to take Maimonides' argument, cited above, that the commandment has not lost its force, even though the seven nations have long since disappeared.

By speaking in terms of "repentance," Nahmanides and Rabbenu Bahya implicitly move the focus of the discussion from the seven nations as corporate entities to the individuals who make up those entities. Isaac Abravanel (1437–1508) uses that focus to explain why only adult males are to be killed in a "regular" war (Deut 20:13): Only adult males can make peace, and only adult males (not women, not children, not animals) can be held accountable if Jewish peace overtures are rejected. But in the case of the seven nations, if peace overtures are rejected, then all must be eradicated. "Let this not be considered cruelty, anger, nor quickness to anger," Abravanel explains, "because the Torah makes clear that the reason for this commandment is: *Lest they lead you into doing all the abhorrent things [that they have done for their gods and you stand guilty before the Lord your God] (Deut 20:18)*." In other words, continuing the line established much earlier, Abravanel makes it clear that there is nothing "ethnic" (in modern terms) about the war against the seven nations; it is purely ideological. But, like all the other authorities I have found after Bahya, he ignores the moral challenge of killing non-combatants with which Bahya ben Asher struggled.

In the continuation of his discussion, Abravanel draws some interesting distinctions between combatants and non-combatants and the chivalrous behavior expected of soldiers vis-à-vis women (and uses it to explain Alexander the Great's refusal to make war on the Amazons!), but despite this, he justifies the extermination of the seven nations if they refuse to make peace "for the reason which I mentioned."[63]

Because of the way in which the Talmudic rabbis read many of the biblical texts that lie at the heart of our discussion, Jews find those texts troubling. One sermonic response to this is to say that Judaism, as a religion, is not "fundamentalist" and that just as we are not meant to think that "an eye for an eye" means anything other than monetary compensation, so we are not meant to think that the Torah really means for us engage in brutal wars against idolaters—rather, these biblical commands are expressions of how abominable idolatry (and its related practices) are in the eyes of the Lord. Further, just as Jacob never really lied to his father, so David did not really sin.

From my perspective, the problem with this approach is that it does not get us very far. The medieval texts we have surveyed show that figures such as Maimonides, Nahmanides, Gersonides, Rabbenu Bahya ben Asher, and Abravanel all, following the Sages, moderate the biblical texts, but do not come close to modern sensibilities concerning targeting non-combatants (especially children), the wholesale slaughter of prisoners, and the imposing through force of one's own ideology.

Unless one is simply willing to say that the Torah reflects a primitive moral-ity,[64] we are stuck with a religious/moral problem: The texts remain. The fact that talmudic texts wrestle with these problems and propose a variety of solu-tions is comforting, but the original texts remain.

Even Bahya's exegesis leaves us with the obligation to murder the infant children of unregenerate idolaters. Reverting to Maimonides may place us in a somewhat better position. As Eugene Korn points out,

> Once the criterion for the object of the biblical commandment becomes behavioral, it is a small logical step to restrict the determination of Canaanite and Amalekite identity to individuals, not nations or collectivities. Further, the category would apply only to informed adult individuals bearing legal responsibility for their decisions who by principle promote violence to undermine the foundations of civilized society. In other words, the only objects of the genocide *mitzvah* are individual aggressors committed to destroying the foundations of the social order.

On Korn's reading of Maimonides, then, the biblical imposition of total destruction on Canaanite or Amalekite children becomes moot—it cannot be applied.[65]

But Still the Texts Remain

Two more steps might be taken. All civilized nations today pay at least lip service to the idea that great efforts must be made to avoid harm to non-combatants.[66] Is it possible that Judaism might demand less of its adherents today? The Talmud (*Sanh.* 59a) teaches that there is nothing forbidden to an idolater that is permitted to a Jew.[67] If we are to succeed in truly providing a Jewish reading of the biblical texts underlying our discussion here, we have no choice but to follow this talmudic idea and maintain that what was mandated by the text of the Torah, even as modified by our medieval teachers, may have been permis-sible to them, but is forbidden to us—and this we learn from the highest ideals (if all too rarely the actual practice) of the nations.

To my mind, however, a more satisfying way of approaching our issue is to focus on an idea driven home to me time and again by my late teacher, Steven S. Schwarzschild. Maimonides brings his *Mishneh Torah* to a close with two chapters on the messianic era. The last paragraph of that discussion, and thus of the *Mishneh Torah* as a whole, describes the world when the messianic pro-cess reaches its completion:

> Then there will be[68] neither famine nor war, neither jealousy nor strife. Good things will be abundant, and delicacies as common as dust. The one preoccupation of the whole world will be only to know the Lord. Hence

[they][69] will be very wise, knowing things now unknown and will apprehend knowledge of their Creator to the utmost capacity of the human mind,[70] as it is written: *For the land[71] shall be full of the knowledge of the Lord, as the waters cover the sea[72]* (Isa 11:9).[73]

Wisdom, apprehension, and knowledge, cannot be achieved by war, only by study. The whole world can become preoccupied with the knowledge of the Lord only if war is replaced by teaching. To the extent that it is rational for ends to determine means, then the only way to bring about the fulfillment of the messianic redemption, at least as it is understood by Maimonides, is to make the study of true Torah (which includes *ma'aseh bereshit*, physics, and *ma'aseh merkavah*, metaphysics) our aim, and not wars of extermination. The texts will remain, not as any sort of ideal, but as a permanent reminder of the dangers of idolatry: replacing God with humans or human artifacts. Judaism calls on us to look forward to the messiah, and not backward to Amalek and the Canaanite nations.[74]

Notes

1. Richard Dawkins, *The God Delusion* (Boston: Houghton Mifflin, 2006), 31. See also Regina Schwartz, *The Curse of Cain: The Violent Legacy of Monotheism* (Chicago: University of Chicago Press, 1997). For a useful and insightful correction to Schwartz's approach, see Joel S. Kaminsky, *Yet I Loved Jacob: Reclaiming the Biblical Concept of Election* (Nashville: Abingdon, 2007).

2. In a polemical vein, Jews are also tempted to point out that it is odd to call a God who causes his only begotten son to die a horrible death, a God of love.

3. For a text often cited as a source for this custom, see *Sanh.* 39b and parallels; see also, Joseph Heinemann, "'The Work of My Hands Is Being Drowned in the Sea…'" [in Hebrew] *Bar Ilan Annual* 7–8 (1970): 80–84. I specified Diaspora Jews, since no Israeli Jew I ever met (and I conduct informal surveys every Passover) was familiar with this explanation for the custom.

4. And, as I will note below, it remains a source enthusiastically mined by contemporaries who have no reservations about the violence endorsed by the literal text of the Torah. For a critique of some of these, see Yitzchak Blau, "Ploughshares into Swords: Contemporary Religious Zionists and Moral Restraints," *Tradition* 34 (2000): 39–60. With particular reference to the texts examined here, see Dov Schwartz, "The Conquest of the Land and the Attitude Towards the Nations Living in It: Approaches in Religious Zionist Thought" [in Hebrew], *Cathedra* 141 (2011): 75–104.

5. Mary Douglas, "Glorious Book of Numbers," *JSQ* 1 (1993–94): 194–216.

6. Who, interestingly, play no role in the Pentateuch or in subsequent Jewish history.

7. I am attempting to do here something similar to what Leon Roth did in his classic essay, "Moralization and Demoralization in Jewish Ethics," *Judaism* 2 (Fall 1962): 291–302; reprinted in *Is There a Jewish Philosophy?* (London: Littman Littman Library of Jewish Civilization, 1999), 128–143. Also relevant, methodologically, is Hermann Cohen, *Religion out of the Sources of Judaism.*

8. Relevant to this is the fact that it is a staple of prominent (if not necessarily dominant) elements of Haredi thought that the Nazi Holocaust was God's measured and restrained punishment for the sins of Enlightenment and emancipation. When challenged on this conception of God, some Haredi spokesmen reply (and I have heard this myself from leading figures in that camp, usually thought of as moderates) that, given the history recounted in the Torah, it should come as no surprise that God punishes sin severely. This "fire and brimstone" view of God has moved of late into the religious Zionist camp in Israel as well. For one example, see the article by Yehudah Yifrah in the *Makor Rishon, Sabbath Supplement* (Sept 3, 2010), 23. See further below, note 57.

9. The book of Joshua describes a gradual and incomplete conquest. The Sages of the Talmud were well aware of this, and even claim that the prophet Jeremiah was descended from Canaanites who remained. See *Pesikta de-Rav Kahana* 13.5. On the book of Joshua, see Chapter 1 by Nili Wazana in the present book.

10. For a subtle study of these passages, one which suggests that the rabbis may have been covertly seeking to criticize rather than exonerate David, see James Diamond, "King David of the Sages: Rabbinic Rehabilitation or Ironic Parody?" *Prooftexts* 27 (2007): 373–426.

11. For important comments *on imitatio Dei* in Judaism, see Steven S. Schwarzschild, *The Pursuit of the Ideal: The Jewish Writings of Steven Schwarzschild*, ed. Menachem Kellner. (Albany: SUNY Press, 1990), 137–161.

12. Norman Lamm, "Amalek and the Seven Nations: A Case of Law vs. Morality," in *War and Peace in the Jewish Tradition*, ed. Lawrence Schiffman and Joel B. Wolowelsky (New York: Yeshiva University Press, 2004), 201–238. In addition to the texts and studies cited there, see also *Midrash Tanhuma, Zav* 3, in which God accedes to Moses' decision not to slaughter innocent Amorites. My thanks to Eugene Korn for drawing this text to my attention.

13. On Maimonides' decision to read this verse as a commandment, see Ya'akov Blidstein, *Ekronot Mediniim bi-Mishnat ha-Rambam* [in Hebrew], 2nd ed. (Ramat-Gan: Bar Ilan University Press, 2001), 21–24.

14. I cite the translation of Abraham M. Hershman, *Book of Judges* (New Haven, Conn.: Yale University Press, 1949), emended.

15. Norman Lamm comments that Maimonides' decision that peace must be offered even to Amalek and the seven Canaanite nations "is a bold ruling" for which Lamm "can find no clear precedent in earlier Talmudic literature." See p. 213 in Lamm, "Amalek and the Seven Nations." Already in *y. Shev.* 6.1, 6.36c and in *Lev. Rab.* 14.34, however, one finds the idea that peace was offered to the Canaanites.

16. On the Noahide commandments, see David Novak, *The Image of the Non-Jew in Judaism: An Historical and Constructive Study of the Noahide Laws* (New York: Edwin Mellen Press, 1983).

17. For an illuminating discussion of many of these issues, see Eugene Korn, "Moralization in Jewish Law: Genocide, Divine Commands and Rabbinic Reasoning," *Edah Journal* 5, no. 2 (2006): 11 pages. An expanded Hebrew version of that article is about to appear in the journal *Akdamot 18 (2007): 41–54* under the title "*Genocide, Zav Elohi, ve-Hanmakah Hilkhatit*" [in Hebrew].

18. But, as we shall see below, it did not take long for it to become the normative position. See Shlomo Goren, *Meshiv Milhamah* (Jerusalem: Ha-Idra Rabbah, 1983), 153; cited by Eugene Korn in his Hebrew article, note 35. This is the place to thank Prof. Korn for sending me galleys of his article.

19. On this point, compare Josef Stern, "Maimonides on Amalek, Self-Corrective Mechanisms, and the War against Idolatry," in *Judaism and Modernity: The Religious Philosophy of David Hartman*, ed. Jonathan Malino (Aldershot: Ashgate, 2004), 359–392. On p. 362 Stern notes that Maimonides' ruling that peace must be offered even to Amalek "radically transforms the biblical injunction, by qualifying, or conditionalizing the absolute and unconditional commandment to exterminate Amalek. It also suggests that it is only when Amalekite descendents act like their ancestor that they are considered the Amalek that Israel is scripturally commanded to exterminate. Like Maimonides' explanation in the *Guide*, this ruling focuses the evil of Amalek on the impropriety of its behavior rather than on a property of its person." Maimonides' view here is consistent with his overall claim that all human beings are created in the image of God, and that what distinguishes them is nothing built-in, as it were, but the principles they adopt and the practices they perform—software, not hardware, in the felicitous words of my friend Daniel J. Lasker. For support of this interpretation of Maimonides, see Kellner, *Maimonides on Judaism and the Jewish People* (Albany: SUNY Press, 1991) and Kellner, *Science in the Bet Midrash: Studies in Maimonides* (Boston: Academic Studies Press, 2010), chs. 16–20. For background to Lasker's distinction, see Daniel J. Lasker, "Proselyte Judaism, Christianity, and Islam in the Thought of Judah Halevi," *JQR* 81 (1990): 75–91.

20. I quote from the translation of Charles B. Chavel, *Book of Commandments*, 2 vols. (London: Soncino, 1967). Nahmanides wrote critical glosses on the *Book of Commandments*; he has no gloss on this passage.

21. Arabic: *min kufrhum*.

22. Tattooing numbers on the arms of concentration camp inmates was not only bureaucratically efficient, but emphasized that the Jews so treated were interchangeable nonentities.

23. See Jon Levenson, *Sinai and Zion: An Entry into the Hebrew Bible* (Minneapolis: Winston, 1985).

24. That is the reason they did not think that idolaters in their day were "good old-fashioned" idolaters, but only engaged in customary practices. See, for example, *Avod. Zar.* 2a and *Hul.* 13b and the discussion in Jacob Katz, *Exclusiveness and Tolerance: Jewish-Gentile Relations in Medieval and Modern Times* (New York: Schocken, 1962), 24–36.

25. On Meiri, see Moshe Halbertal, *Bein Torah Le-Hokhmah: R. Menachem Ha-Meiri U-Ba'alei Ha-Halakhah Ha-Maimuniim Be-Provanz* [in Hebrew] (Jerusalem: Magnes, 2000).

26. See Abraham P. Socher, *The Radical Enlightenment of Solomon Maimon: Judaism, Heresy and Philosophy* (Stanford, Calif.: Stanford University Press, 2006), 82–84.

27. Menachem Kellner, *Maimonides' Confrontation with Mysticism* (Oxford: Littman Library of Jewish Civilization, 2006), 239 n.

28. Kenneth Seeskin, *No Other Gods: The Modern Struggle against Idolatry* (New York: Behrman House, 1995).

29. I cite the translation of Charles B. Chavel, *Ramban (Nachmanides), Commentary on the Torah* (New York: Shilo, 1976), 5:238–241. Explanatory material in square brackets is Chavel's.

30. *Sifra*, Shofetim 199.

31. Here we see Nahmanides' explicit dependence upon Maimonides.

32. *Midrash Tanhuma*, Shofetim 18.

33. *y. Shev.* 6.

34. Josh 12:9–24.

35. Josh 11:19.

36. Hebrew: *nishal*; Chavel translates this, literally, as "request"; my translation more accurately reflects the sense of the passage.

37. *Sifra*, Shofetim 202.

38. Interestingly, Rashi also cites this passage from the *Sifra* in his commentary on verse 18; according to the Bar Ilan Responsa Project and the DBS Taklitor Torani, Nahmanides and Rashi are the only early authorities (*rishonim*) who cite it anywhere. It is entirely possible that Maimonides did not cite it because he also read it the way Rashi did.

39. Compare Meiri, *Bet ha-Behirah* to *Sotah* 36a on these stelae and on the issue of repentance.

40. Hebrew: *ke-torah 'asa'an*.

41. Rabbenu Bahya was the student of R. Shlomo ben Aderet (Rashba), who in turn was a student of Nahmanides.

42. In his commentary to Deut 20:10, Gersonides (1288–1344) taught that those of the seven nations which do not accept offer of peace, subservient status, and fulfillment of the Noahide laws, are to be exterminated to the last child. In the edition of *Ya'akov Levi* (Jerusalem: Mossad ha-Rav Kook, 2000), the text is found on p. 189.

43. This expression occurs several times in *Midrash Tanhuma*, as a quick search in any rabbinic database will show.

44. Who are thus not to be killed.

45. Literally: "itch." In his article in this volume Zeev Harvey translates as follows: "If your heart hesitates, saying that we thus do unjust violence…"

46. *Hamas*; the sin of the generation of the Flood; see Gen 6:11.

47. Against which no protest can be made.

48. In this passage a heavenly voice tells Nebuchadnezzar to take no pride in his victory over the Jews, as it had been determined from Above: "His mind was now elated [with his triumph], when a voice came forth from Heaven saying to him, 'You have slayed a dead people, you have burned a Temple already burned, you have ground flour already ground, as it is written, *Take the millstones, and grind meal: Uncover your locks, make bare the leg, uncover the thigh, pass over the rivers* [Isa 47:2]—not 'wheat' but meal [already ground] is said."

49. "For lo, I am raising up the Chaldeans, that fierce impetuous nation, who crosses the earth's wide spaces to sieze homes not their own."

50. Literally: "will."

51. I assume that means that they accept the seven Noahide commandments, not that they convert to Judaism.

52. A common rabbinic expression, best known from the Passover haggadah.

53. Bahya seems untroubled by the implications this has for the questions of freedom of the will and punishment before the crime.

54. *Ish nilbav u-maskil*—I do not really know what the expression means.

55. Images of 9/11 spring to mind here, even though they are not, of course, relevant to the issue at hand.

56. That is, if one sacrifices someone else's limb to save that person.

57. Sadly, while I write these words (August 2010) a controversy swirls around a despicable book, *Torat ha-Melekh: Dinei Nefashot bein Yisrael le-'Amim*, by Yitshak Shapira and Yosef Elitsur (Yitshar: Yeshivat 'Od Yosef Hai, 2010), which uses this very text of Rabbenu Bahya to justify the killing of innocent and non-threatening Palestinian children if it is "clear"

that they will grow up to harm the Jews (pp. 206–207). The authors of this book do not have to pretend that Palestinians are Canaanites or Amalekites to make their point; it is enough for them that they are Gentiles seen as threatening. Their use of Rabbenu Bahya here is thus actually an abuse of his text, not a use of it.

58. This language is surprising and illuminates, I submit, Rabbenu Bahya's state of mind, since Scripture does not *permit* this killing, it commands it!

59. Maimonides quotes this passage in "Laws of Kings," 6.5, which, on linguistic grounds, appears to be Bahya's source. The original source is in the sixth chapter of *y. Shev.* 36c, not the *Sifri*. It is also cited by Nahmanides (above).

60. Bahya seems to have confused his sources; this passage is the continuation of the text sourced in the previous note.

61. There is no scholarly consensus over the identity of the author of this work, but it seems to have originated in the circle of the Rashba.

62. *She'at kosher*; apparently they were created because God knew that at some point they would do something worthwhile.

63. Abravanel on Deut 20:10 in the edition of Avishai Shotland (Jerusalem: Horev, 1999), 318; the reference to Alexander and the Amazons is on p. 320.

64. This is, in effect, the position of Rabbi Abraham Isaac Kook, although I have no doubt he would have squirmed at the way I phrased it. For discussion, see David Shatz, "'From the Depths I Have Called to You': Jewish Reflections on September 11th and Contemporary Terrorism," in Shatz, *Jewish Thought in Dialogue: Essays on Thinkers, Theologies, and Moral Theories* (Boston: Academic Studies Press, 2009), 268. The source Shatz cites is *Iggerot ha-Reayah*, vol. 1 (Jerusalem: Mossad haRav Kook, 1985), #89, p. 100. There Rabbi Kook offers a series of explanations for why the Torah called for such brutal warfare: When all its neighbors were *wolves of the wilderness* (Hab 1:8 and Zeph 3:3) (Radak interprets: "wolves of the evening"), Israel had to fight as they did, or face extermination. Further, cruelty was necessary to put fear into the enemies of Israel so as to bring humanity (in the future) to what it ought to be, without forcing the hour. Further, the Torah sought to bring humanity to humaneness out of love and generosity, not because it was so commanded. Furthermore, the issue was handed over to the courts to determine the moral character of each form of idolatry: They were not all to be treated alike.

This passage of Rav Kook's is popular with Orthodox rabbis seeking a solution to the challenge of violent biblical texts. See, for example, Shalom Carmy, "The Origin of Nations and the Shadow of Violence: Theological Perspectives on Canaan and Amalek," in *War and Peace in the Jewish Tradition*, ed. by Lawrence Schiffman and Joel B. Wolowelsky (New York: Yeshiva University Press, 2004), 169–170 and Hayyim Angel, *Creating Space between Peshat and Derash: A Collection of Studies on Tanakh* (Jersey City: Ktav, Hayyim, 2011). On page 82 Angel quotes Carmy quoting Rav Kook.

65. Two articles by Ya'akov Blidstein appear to offer indirect support to Korn. In analyses of the rape of Dinah and its aftermath, Blidstein shows how Maimonides seeks to turn the biblical account in the direction of personal responsibility. See "The Case of Shechem: Collective Punishment and Contemporary Halakhic Thought" [in Hebrew], *Et ha-Da'at* 1 (1997): 49–55; and "The Case of Shechem: Maimonides' Normative Reading" [in Hebrew], in *Sefer Yizhak England*, ed. D. Barak-Erez (Ramat-Gan: Bar-Ilan University Press, 2009), 375–387.

66. The nearly worldwide acceptance (at least in principle) of these ideals is the work of a Jew, René Cassin, the moving force behind the UN's "Universal Declaration of Human Rights."

67. My thanks to Eugene Korn for directing me to this and other sources.

68. Hebrew: *lo yihiyeh sham*. This Arabism calls to mind the very first paragraph of the *Mishneh Torah*, a text addressed to all human beings.

69. On the textual issues here, see Simon-Raymond Schwarzfuchs, "Les lois royales de Maïmonide," *REJ* 111 (1951–1952): 63–86. On pp. 81–82 Schwarzfuchs shows that many printed editions and manuscripts add the word "Israel" here. Yohai Makbili has it in the first printing of his edition (Haifa: Yeshivat Or Veshua, 2006), with a note that Sheilat excludes the word from his text (*Ha-Rambam ha-Meduyak*). The word was excluded in subsequent editions. On literary grounds alone, it appears clear that the word is an emendation since the prooftext from Isaiah speaks of the entire earth. See also the next note.

70. On this expression, and many of the issues raised here, see Aviezer Ravitzky, "'To the Utmost of Human Capacity': Maimonides on the Days of the Messiah," in *Perspectives on Maimonides: Philosophical and Historical Studies*, ed. Joel Kraemer (Oxford: Littman Library of Jewish Civilization, 1991), 221–256. It must be recalled that in this context the intellectual perfection to which Maimonides refers here is relative, not absolute. Human beings, even in the messianic era, achieve intellectual perfection to different degrees. When Maimonides says here that humans will come to know God *kifi koah ha-adam*, he means, to translate him literally, "according to human abilities" and not "according to human ability." The latter reading would involve a miraculous change in human nature.

71. On the question of what this land is (and for more on the textual issues), see Blidstein, *Ekronot Mediniim*, 246 n. 56. Ridbaz to "Kings," 12.1 understands the term as referring only to the Land of Israel. Maimonides' use of the verse in *Guide* 3.11 would seem to preclude Ridbaz's reading. The text there reads:

If there were knowledge, whose relation to the human form is like that of the faculty of sight to the eye, they would refrain from doing any harm to themselves and to others. For through cognition of the truth, enmity and hatred are removed and the inflicting of harm by people on one another is abolished. It holds out this promise, saying, *The wolf shall dwell with the lamb, the leopard shall lie down with the kid*, and so on. *And the sucking child shall play*, and so on (Isa 11:6–8). Then it gives the reason for this, saying that the cause of the abolition of these enmities, these discords, and these tyrannies, will be the knowledge that men will then have concerning the true reality of the deity. For it says: *They shall not hurt nor destroy in all My holy mountain; for the earth shall be full of the knowledge of the Lord, as the waters cover the sea* (Isa 11:9). Know this.

Zeev Harvey has pointed out (to my chagrin, since I thought that I had hit upon this idea myself) that this chapter of the *Guide* is a kind of poetic and philosophical rendition of the last paragraph of the *Mishneh Torah*, glossing it in the way Maimonides meant it to be read. See pp. 23–24 in Harvey, "Averroes, Maimonides, and the Virtuous State," in *Iyyunim bi-Sugyot Philosophiot…Likhvod Shlomo Pines* (Jerusalem: Israel Academy of Sciences, 1992), 19–31. Pushing Harvey's insight one step further, I think that the next chapter in the *Guide* also glosses the last paragraph in the *Mishneh Torah*.

72. The verse from Isaiah recalls Gen 6:13. I am tempted to say that just as that verse surely relates to humans simpliciter, and not to Jews, Maimonides uses the parallel verse from Isaiah in the same way. The prophet is surely alluding to the difference between the messianic and

antediluvian eras through the use of the expression *ki malah ha-aretz*; it is a safe bet that if I noticed it, Maimonides certainly did.

73. Rabbi Jeffrey Bienenfeld pointed out to me (modestly claiming that the idea was not his, but it is from him I heard it, so I shall cite it in his name, and, perhaps, bring the redemption that much closer) that the meaning of the word "sea" here is "seabed" and that just as water spreads to cover every part of any enclosure in which it is placed, seeping into every nook and cranny (as anyone who has had plumbing problems knows), so too will the knowledge of God extend to and seep into every nook and cranny of the world, and, hence, into the hearts of all human beings. For extensive discussion of this text, see Menachem Kellner, "Maimonides' *True Religion*—for Jews, or All Humanity?" *Meorot* [*Edah Journal*] 7, no. 1 (2008) http://www.yctorah.org/content/view/436/10/, reprinted in Kellner, *Science in the Bet Midrash*, 291–319.

74. For a similar approach, see Zeev Harvey's discussion of Rabbi Reines in Chapter 16 of this volume. Prof. Harvey kindly showed me an advance copy of his article. I here record my thanks to him and to Eugene Korn and to James Diamond for many helpful suggestions, and to Avram Montag for his incisive (and insightful) criticism of an earlier draft of this essay. Raphi Jospe and Rivka Kellner were generous in helping me with some tricky translation questions.

Bibliography

Abravanel, Isaac. *Perush ʿal ha-Torah.* Edited by Avishai Shotland. Jerusalem: Horev, 1999.

Angel, Hayyim. *Creating Space between Peshat and Derash: A Collection of Studies on Tanakh.* Jersey City: Ktav, Hayyim 2011.

Blau, Yitzchak. "Ploughshares into Swords: Contemporary Religious Zionists and Moral Restraints." *Tradition* 34 (2000): 39–60.

Blidstein, Yaʿakov. "The Case of Shechem: Maimonides' Normative Reading" [in Hebrew]. In *Sefer Yizhak Englard*, edited by D. Barak-Erez, 375–387. Ramat-Gan: Bar-Ilan University Press, 2009.

——. *Ekronot Mediniim bi-Mishnat ha-Rambam.* 2nd ed. Ramat-Gan: Bar Ilan University Press, 2001.

——. "The Case of Shechem: Collective Punishment and Contemporary Halakhic Thought" [in Hebrew]. *Et ha-Daʿat* 1 (1997): 49–55.

Carmy, Shalom. "The Origin of Nations and the Shadow of Violence: Theological Perspectives on Canaan and Amalek." In *War and Peace in the Jewish Tradition*, edited by Lawrence Schiffman and Joel B. Wolowelsky, 163–199. New York: Yeshiva University Press, 2004.

Dawkins, Richard. *The God Delusion.* Boston: Houghton Mifflin, 2006.

Diamond, James. "King David of the Sages: Rabbinic Rehabilitation or Ironic Parody?" *Prooftexts* 27 (2007): 373–426.

Douglas, Mary. "The Glorious Book of Numbers." *JSQ* 1 (1993–94): 194–216.

Gersonides. *Perush al ha-Torah.* Edited by Yaʿakov Levi. Jerusalem: Mossad ha-Rav Kook, 2000.

Goren, Shlomo. *Meshiv Milhamah.* Jerusalem: Ha-Idra Rabbah, 1983.

Halbertal, Moshe. *Bein Torah Le-Hokhmah: R. Menachem Ha-Meiri U-Baʿalei Ha-Halakhah Ha-Maimuniim Be-Provanz.* Jerusalem: Magnes, 2000.

Harvey, Zeev. "Averroes, Maimonides, and the Virtuous State." In *Iyyunim bi-Sugyot Philosophiot…Likhvod Shlomo Pines*, 19–31. Jerusalem: Israel Academy of Sciences, 1992.

Heinemann, Joseph. "'The Work of My Hands Is Being Drowned in the Sea...'" [in Hebrew]. *Bar Ilan Annual* 7–8 (1970): 80–84.

Kaminsky, Joel S. *Yet I Loved Jacob: Reclaiming the Biblical Concept of Election.* Nashville: Abingdon, 2007.

Katz, Jacob. *Exclusiveness and Tolerance: Jewish-Gentile Relations in Medieval and Modern Times.* New York: Schocken, 1962.

Kellner, Menachem. *Science in the Bet Midrash: Studies in Maimonides.* Boston: Academic Studies Press, 2010.

——. "Maimonides' *True Religion*—for Jews, or All Humanity?" *Meorot [Edah Journal]* 7, no. 1 (2008). http://www.yctorah.org/content/view/436/10/.

——. *Maimonides' Confrontation with Mysticism.* Oxford: Littman Library of Jewish Civilization, 2006.

——. *Maimonides on Judaism and the Jewish People.* Albany: State University of New York Press, 1991.

Kook, Abraham Isaac. *Iggerot.* Vol. 1. Jerusalem: Mossad ha-Rav Kook, 1985.

Korn, Eugene. "Moralization in Jewish Law: Genocide, Divine Commands and Rabbinic Reasoning." *Edah Journal* 5, no. 2 (2006): 11 pages. [An expanded Hebrew version of that article is about to appear in the journal *Akdamot 18 (2007): 41–54* under the title "*Genocide, Zav Elohi, ve-Hanmakah Hilkhatit.*"]

Lamm, Norman. "Amalek and the Seven Nations: A Case of Law vs. Morality." In *War and Peace in the Jewish Tradition*, edited by Lawrence Schiffman and Joel B. Wolowelsky, 201–238. New York: Yeshiva University Press, 2004.

Lasker, Daniel J. "Proselyte Judaism, Christianity, and Islam in the Thought of Judah Halevi." *JQR* 81 (1990): 75–91.

Levenson, Jon. *Sinai and Zion: An Entry into the Hebrew Bible.* Minneapolis: Winston, 1985.

Maimonides, Moses. *Book of Commandments.* Translated by Charles B. Chavel. London: Soncino, 1967.

——. *Book of Judges.* Translated by Abraham M. Hershman. New Haven, Conn.: Yale University Press, 1949.

Nahmanides, Moses. *Ramban (Nachmanides), Commentary on the Torah.* Translated by Charles B. Chavel. New York: Shilo, 1976.

Novak, David. *The Image of the Non-Jew in Judaism: An Historical and Constructive Study of the Noahide Laws.* New York: Edwin Mellen Press, 1983.

Ravitzky, Aviezer. "'To the Utmost of Human Capacity': Maimonides on the Days of the Messiah." In *Perspectives on Maimonides: Philosophical and Historical Studies*, edited by Joel Kraemer, 221–256. Oxford: Littman Library of Jewish Civilization, 1991.

Roth, Leon. "Moralization and Demoralization in Jewish Ethics." *Judaism* 2 (Fall 1962): 291–302. Reprinted in *Is There a Jewish Philosophy*, 128–143. London: Littman Littman Library of Jewish Civilization, 1999.

Schwartz, Dov. "The Conquest of the Land and the Attitude Towards the Nations Living in It: Approaches in Religious Zionist Thought" [in Hebrew]. *Cathedra* 141 (2011): 75–104.

Schwartz, Regina. *The Curse of Cain: The Violent Legacy of Monotheism.* Chicago: University of Chicago Press, 1997.

Schwarzfuchs, Simon-Raymond. "Les lois royales de Maïmonide." *REJ* 111 (1951–1952): 63–86.

Schwarzschild, Steven S. *The Pursuit of the Ideal: The Jewish Writings of Steven Schwarzschild*, edited by Menachem Kellner. Albany: State University of New York Press, 1990.

Seeskin, Kenneth. *No Other Gods: The Modern Struggle against Idolatry*. New York: Behrman House, 1995.

Shapira, Yizhak, and Yosef Elizur. *Torat ha-Melekh: Dinei Nefashot bein Yisrael le-'Amim* [in Hebrew]. Yizhar: Yeshivat Od Yosef Hai, 2010.

Shatz, David. "'From the Depths I Have Called to You': Jewish Reflections on September 11th and Contemporary Terrorism." In *Jewish Thought in Dialogue: Essays on Thinkers, Theologies, and Moral Theories*, edited by Shatz, 257–290. Boston: Academic Studies Press, 2009.

Socher, Abraham P. *The Radical Enlightenment of Solomon Maimon: Judaism, Heresy and Philosophy*. Stanford, Calif.: Stanford University Press, 2006.

Stern, Josef. "Maimonides on Amalek, Self-Corrective Mechanisms, and the War against Idolatry." In *Judaism and Modernity: The Religious Philosophy of David Hartman*, edited by Jonathan Malino, 359–392. London: Ashgate, 2004.

Yifrah, Yehudah. Op-Ed. *Makor Rishon, Sabbath Supplement*, September 3, 2010, 23.

7

Nahmanides on Law, Land, and Otherness
Joseph E. David

During the course of the past two millennia, the desire to resettle in the land of Israel never stopped being a vital ingredient of the Jewish religious mind. Sometimes, this desire was opposed by pro-exilic ideologies;[1] on other occasions, it remained a sentimental or eschatological phantasm. Beside that, various actual endeavors to immigrate and settle in Zion, motivated by religious ideas and purposes, are well documented and studied in contemporary historiography. Nevertheless, in discontinuation with the biblical narrative, according to which the unfortunate fate of the Canaanites is an inevitable outcome of the Israelites' attachment to the Promised Land, most of the Jewish medieval reflections did not associate these two states of affairs. As such, the fate of non-Israelites in the land of Israel was not a significant ingredient of the Jewish longing for the Holy Land. In that regard, the approach of R. Moses b. Nachman (1194–1270; hereafter, Nahmanides) is an exceptional one. For him, the fate of the biblical Canaanites illustrates a significant aspect of the very deep meaning of the Holy Land, though not an unavoidable result of the Israelites' existence on the land. Moreover, at the personal level, Nahmanides actually left the Iberian Peninsula, traveled to the Holy Land, and developed a strong theological motivation to resettle in the Holy Land. More interestingly, as we shall see, Nahmanides suggested, accordingly, a new perception of the law and an innovative meaning of otherness applied to the Canaanites.

In fact, Nahmanides' innovative approach could be fairly taken as a legal theology.[2] Accordingly, this chapter will articulate the fundamental pillars of his approach, which reformulate the traditional relation between law and land. Despite the fact that Nahmanides' theological novelty is well acknowledged both in the traditional and scholarly literature, my analysis will propose a new perspective about his conceptual and theological sources.[3] I will argue that, beside the mystical background, he also responded to legal and theological doctrines that pervaded in the European Christendom of his days. More precisely, I will show that Nahmanides introduces an innovative notion of the halakhah as divine law, according to which the divine law is derivative to the deity's association to his territory in terms of feudal lordship. Nahmanides introduces a spatial, or a territorial, notion of halakhah that stands against the traditional perceptions of halakhah as a direct prescription.[4] Consequently, my analysis will call for a reassessment of the components of his approach to the Holy Land[5] and of the motives behind his personal voyage to the Holy Land (around the year 1267).[6]

Law and Polycratic Lordship

Nahmanides' legal theology is encapsulated in his branding the fundamental notion of the divine law by the biblical idiom "the law of the land's Lord" (משפט אלהי הארץ). This term originated in the biblical tale about the fate of the Cuthim who were initially brought by Sargon II, the king of Assyria, to replace the exiled Israelites (2 Kgs 17:24–30). The Bible narrates that upon their arrival, the Cuthim were attacked by wild lions for their violation of "the law of the land's Lord," which they eventually acknowledged by the help of a priest of the Israelites, then observed, and thus survived. This miraculous episode provides Nahmanides with an opportunity to reveal the territorial dimensions of the halakhah, which is valid only within the land of Israel. Therefore, the biblical idiom משפט אלהי הארץ for Nahmanides not only stands for the local code of behavior, but also holds the fundamental rationale of the divine law as a territory-mediated law.[7] This articulation should not be taken lightly and in fact has no solid precedent in preceding mainstream rabbinic literature. In that respect, Nahmanides' legal theology can be fairly taken as a paradigm shift that affects the most fundamental concepts of every legal system—jurisdiction and sovereignty.

Nahmanides' legal imagination is deeply anchored in a heavenly political structure that includes astrological powers governed by heavenly constellations created, designed, and designated by God. As he notes, this should be understood against the backdrop of medieval astrology and the parallelism between heavenly and earthly political structures, which consequently generated the basileomorphic vocabulary of his legal theology.[8]

Indeed, among the various ancient representations of God, his image as a king is one of the most prominent ones. Nevertheless, even within biblical basileomorphic imagery, there is a clear distinction between two types, or two metaphors, of God as a king and ruler. The most common of them is the monocratic image according to which God is portrayed as imperial king, enjoying a centralized and universal control.[9] Nevertheless, the Bible also contains remnants of a polycratic image, according to which national gods subordinate to God, while each one administrates his own province. Within this metaphoric structure, divine domination upon earth is rather a distributive power, branching through inferior delegations that govern local domains or people. While the deity's power in the monocratic model is all encompassing, the polycratic image contains a structured hierarchy[10] and divine agency mediating between the supreme deity and his subjects.[11]

The tension between the monocratic and the polycratic images of God's kingship is perhaps best demonstrated in the two versions of Deuteronomy 32:8; while the Masoretic version stresses a monocratic representation of God and accordingly the idea that God divided the national boundaries according to his elected people, "the children of Israel," the versions of the Septuagint and one copy of Deuteronomy from Qumran state that the divine allocation was in accordance to the "angels of God" or "sons of God."[12] In fact, the theology of a polycratic heavenly structure in which divine power is distributed to secondary deities being in charge of particular nations or territories has Greek origins.[13] And the confrontation of the monocratic and the polycratic images stood for opposing theologies in the first centuries of Jewish-Christian[14] and Jewish-pagan[15] polemics and throughout the Middle Ages.[16]

Against the mainstream rabbinical tendency to overemphasize the monocracy of God's kingship, Nahmanides tends to view God's kingship as a polycracy, rather than an imperial monocracy. Interestingly, Nahmanides approves the polycratic image by reference to Deuteronomy 32:8. Being silent about the different versions of the last part of the verse, he is not favoring explicitly either version, though practically endorsing the polycratic reading of Deuteronomy 32:8:[17]

> But the secret of the matter is in the verse which states, When the Most High gave to the nations their inheritance, when He separated the children on men, He set people etc. For the portion of the Eternal is His people[18] etc. The meaning thereof is as follows: The glorious Name created everything and He placed the power of the lower creatures in the higher beings, giving over each and every nation in their lands, after their nations[19] some known star or constellation, as is known by means of astrological speculation.... He allotted to all nations constellations in the heavens, and higher above them the angels of the Supreme One whom He placed as lords over them.... Now the glorious name is God of gods, and Lord of lords.[20]

Nahmanides, like other medieval thinkers, used the esoteric method to solve tensions between widespread traditional perceptions and deeper truths. Here, too, he avoids the confrontation of the distinct meanings of Deuteronomy 32:8, but he reorganizes them vertically so the monocratic image is evident exoterically, while the "concealed truth" is a polycratic one; the pure monocracy of God is only an alleged representation, while genuinely divine controlling powers are distributive.

The polycratic image of God's kingship in fact paves the way for Nahmanides' reconstruction of the *God-land-law* matrix. It allows the corresponding individualization of the three components. Thus, in the same manner that the divine land is intimately related to God, so, too, the divine law is intimately connected with the divine land:[21]

> And the venerable God is the god of gods and the lord of lords over the whole world. But the Land of Israel, which is the *axis mundi*, is the inheritance of the Eternal designated to His name [מיוחדת לשמו]. He has placed none of the angels as chief, observer, or ruler over it, since He gave it as a heritage to His people who declare the Unity of His name [המייחד שמו]....
>
> Now He [also] sanctified the people who dwell in His Land with the sanctity of observing the laws against forbidden sexual relationships [קדושת העריות], and with the abundant commandments.... He has set us apart from all the nations over whom He appointed princes and other celestial powers, by giving us the Land so that He, blessed be He, will be our God, and we will be dedicated to His Name.

While the major streams of post-biblical Judaism celebrated the monocratic perception of God's sovereignty and rejected a polycratic theology, as is expressed ultimately in the Masoretic version, Nahmanides is much more sympathetic and consistent with the Christian scriptural version. In fact, it will not be excessive to view his stance as an attempt to revive the biblical option of polycratic theology. Nahmanides' construction of the *God-land-law* matrix, therefore, is not necessarily a direct outcome of kabbalistic or theurgic ideas.[22] Here, again, his views appear to be congenial with Christian traditional doctrines.[23] Against the enlightened (philosophical) ethos, according to which the religious consciousness has evolved from polytheism to monotheism, Nahmanides marks an opposite direction, according to which a monocratic deity is only the external cover for the "concealed truth" of a polycratic divine realm.

The preference for the polycratic model above the monocratic one should also be seen against the background of Nahmanides' contemporary legal and political imagination. More precisely, we might consider as relevant the decline of imperial structures in favor of feudal order. Through these changes, the claim for imperial supremacy of the Holy Roman Empire was challenged and replaced by secondary sovereignties in the form of local and territorial authorities.[24]

The dismissal of imperial lordship hence promoted a legal theory according to which the universe is a plural system of mutually independent territorial sovereignties.[25] Medieval jurists emphasized the distinction between a *de jure* overlordship (*dominus totius mundi*[26] or *rex universalis*) and a *de facto* independent kingship that rejects superior sovereignty (*principes superiores non recognoscentes*). The process of a change from imperial to feudal structures, from a unitary politics to localized and varied politics, might accelerate the polycratic imagination also in the theological realm. As such, we should not abandon the inspirational effects of feudalism and polycratic imagery upon

Nahmanides' construction of the *God-land-law* matrix and the identification of the Holy Land with the concept of "God's inheritance."

God's Inheritance

A cornerstone of Nahmanides' novel perception is his insistence on designating the Holy Land not as the "land of Israel" (ארץ ישראל) but rather as "the land of the Lord" ('ארץ ה) or alternatively, "God's inheritance" ('נחלת ה). Indeed, the term "God's inheritance" appears several times in the Bible. In most of the appearances it refers to the people of Israel; in fewer cases, it carries a territorial meaning, referring to a concrete piece of land.[27] Nahmanides, however, ignores the ethnic meaning and exclusively cleaves to the territorial meaning. Furthermore, the territorial meaning of "God's inheritance" becomes for him the fundamental pillar of the halakhah as territorial law. It illustrates the prioritization of the land's belonging to the deity rather than to the people of Israel.

As seen above, the idea of "God's inheritance" is consequential to the tension between the deity's totality and particularity. In Nahmanides' sermon of the New Year, given during his visit at Acre in 1269, the idea of "God's inheritance" demonstrates the independence of God's two images—as the creator and as a sovereign. These two images, Nahmanides insists, are not overlapping, and while God undeniably created the entire universe, his lordship is associated with a concrete territory:[28]

> And what is the meaning of [this phrase]: "The Land of the Lord"? Isn't the entire universe "The Land of the Lord"? [Behold] He created everything, He formed everything and everything is His... but the Land of Israel is the *axis mundi*, is God's inheritance peculiar to his name [מיוחדת לשמו]....He bestowed [the land] upon His people who proclaim the unity of His name (המיחד שמו).

Here Nahmanides organizes the *God-land-law* matrix in two phases. First, because of the singularity of the land as the center of the world and of the connection between heaven and earth, it is then God's special inheritance. Only at the second phase are those who proclaim the unity of God's name, the people of Israel, bestowed with His inheritance. The belonging of Israel to the Holy Land, therefore, stems from God's territorial lordship in feudal terms.[29]

Although the identification of the Holy Land and God's inheritance did not become a widespread concept within mainstream rabbinic thought, it was a vital component of the Crusades' propaganda and ideology. It articulated the legal and political justification of the Crusades and was used to encourage Christians to join the Crusades and to recover Christian control of Palestine.[30] The terminology of "God's inheritance" marks the Crusade writings from the early versions of Urban II's (late eleventh-century) sermon at Clermont.

Furthermore, after the crusaders' military defeat and the loss of control over Jerusalem and much of Palestine in the late twelfth century, Psalm 79, which opens with a reference to the violation of God's *haereditatem*, was introduced into the daily Mass for an extended period.[31] Equally, the rhetoric of the Second Crusade (1197–1192), such as the *Itinerarium Peregrinorum et Gesta Regis Ricardi*, includes increased references to the identification of the Holy Land as God's inheritance.[32] Accordingly, the believers' duty to support and join the Crusades was often conceptualized in terms of feudal responsibility for the lord's patrimony. Such an argumentation can be seen in the way that Jacques de Vitry (1160/1170–1240)[33] motivates potential crusaders by describing the duty to crusade as a test of vassalage loyalty:[34]

> The Lord has indeed suffered the loss of his patrimony and wants to test [his] friends and find out if you are his faithful vassals. He who holds a fief from a liege lord is rightfully deprived of his fief if he abandons him, when he is involved in a war and his inheritance is taken away from him [*hereditas sua illi aufertur*]. You hold your body and soul and all that you have from the highest emperor, who has you summoned today to come to his aid in battle, even if you are not bound by feudal law [*iure feodi*].
>
> I beseech you, brothers…that you come…to the aid of the Lord, who has been deprived of his inheritance, like faithful vassals and liege men, but also to your own aid, and that you may not receive such great grace in vain.[35]

The Holy Land is considered God's stolen patrimony of which He was also deprived. Therefore, the crusaders, as loyal vassals, are called upon to recover their lord's inheritance. Indeed, feudal imagination within Nahmanides' approach was not used to rationalize the establishment of political and armed powers or to encourage recruiting soldiers for a long journey. Nevertheless, the feudal conceptualizations did serve Nahmanides in articulating his legal theology and in accounting for its particular connection with the Holy Land.[36]

We have emphasized the extra-Jewish backdrop of Nahmanides' legal theology; now we turn to the intra-Jewish aspects. Perhaps the most dramatic point here is the fact that Nahmanides advocates the trope of divine sovereignty rather than the traditional image of God as the supreme legislator. As we shall see, the move from God the legislator to God the sovereign stands at the core of Nahmanides' reductive claim that the halakhah should be taken as territorial law.

Land Dependency

There (in the Holy Land) is the place for fulfilling the commandments and receiving upon oneself the Kingdom of Heaven. Our worship there is acceptable, for there is the House of our God and the Gates of Heaven.[37]

The candor of a thirteenth-century Spanish Jew who took a vow to emigrate to the Holy Land outlines the importance of physical attendance in a concrete place for a complete performance of religious duties. Indeed, the reference to Jacob's reaction to the revelation at Beth-el (בית-אל; literally, "God's residence"), in his escape to find refuge in *Aram*, encompasses the two features that Nahmanides' arguments above emphasized: the view of the Holy Land as God's residence and the venue at which heaven and earth meet up.[38] These features, he adds, make this place a vantage point in terms of religious worship.

The Nahmanidean reduction of the entire law to a territorial law, as well as the above popular desire to travel and reside in the Holy Land, could be understood by tracing the conceptual evolution of the talmudic category of *Mitzvot Hateluyot Bearetz* (מצוות התלויות בארץ; literally, "land-dependent commandments"). In fact, the categorization of the commandments according to their dependency on the land is to be understood in various ways due to the ambiguity of the term *land*, which might denote generally the earth or the ground, and particularly, the Holy Land, that is, the land of Israel. This dual meaning entails two notions of territorial dependency:

1. Laws whose practice is restricted to a designated territory, that is, the land of Israel (*Land-dependent commandments*);
2. Laws which apply to a land with no concrete territorial limits (*land-dependent commandments*).

In fact, these two notions originate in the talmudic literature in various contexts, and thus they produce different intersections between law and territory. The preeminence of the latter notion is well exemplified in the following midrash, which acknowledges both notions and subordinates the notion of Land-dependency to land-dependency:[39]

> *You shall utterly destroy all the places* [wherein the nations served their gods]: just as [the annihilation of] idolatry is singled out as being a corporal-duty[40] and not dependent on the land, and is obligatory both within and without the Land, so everything which is a corporal-duty and not dependent on the land is incumbent both within and without the Land.

Other talmudic sources, mainly those ascribed to the school of R. Shimeon b. Yohai, highlight the notion of *Land-dependency*:[41]

> R. Eleazar son of R. Shimeon said: All precept which the Israelites were commanded [to practice] before their entry into the Land are operative both within and without the Land; [Precepts which they were commanded] after their entry into the Land, are operative only within the Land.

The nomenclature of territorial-corporal duties echoes the typological contrast between territorial jurisdictions and personal jurisdictions.[42] However, against the talmudic legal tendency to view the corporal-territorial dichotomy as reflecting a reasonable taxonomy of the divine commandments, Nahmanides associates the dichotomy with rabbinic esotericism and the need to cover cryptic truths under unsuspected categorizations. Thus, the dichotomy does not reflect types of laws, but rather a covert truth that the halakhah is genuinely a territorial law, while its external appearance is as corporal law. The above doctrine of משפט אלהי הארץ is in fact the raison d'être of the divine law, an explosive truth that cannot be told to a wide audience and for this reason is presented as corporal law.

Commenting on the background of Abraham's blessings,[43] Nahmanides suggests viewing the corporal-territorial taxonomy as a constructed perplexity between the genuine essence of the law as territorial, concealed under an external image of corporal duties:[44]

> Although the commandments had been decreed to us as corporal duties [being valid] at any place, they are the *law of the god of the land*. And our rabbis hinted at this secret and I will explain it with God's help.

One can understand the urge to cover this explosive truth; it might dismantle the traditional conception of the divine law and hence contains a tangible risk of undermining the practical commitment to the halakhah. The antinomian aspects in Nahmanides' thought and writings have received attention in modern scholarship. As Halbertal has shown, Nahmanides' antinomian perception is strongly evident in his historiosophic picture and the notion of "the period of the Torah."[45] The antinomian prospect within the above account is even more intense and therefore more hazardous.[46]

Nahmanides' reference to the corporal-territorial taxonomy in other contexts carries an antinomian prospect as well. As such, the biblical restrictions imposed on sexual conducts listed in Leviticus 18 provides him with an opportunity to readdress the corporal-territorial taxonomy and fulfill his earlier promise to further explain this hinted secret. For Nahmanides, the scriptural narrative that ascribes the Canaanites' expulsion from the land to their illicit incestuous habits[47] supports viewing the entire body of the halakhah as territory-dependent and advocates the general doctrine of משפט אלהי הארץ. This scriptural statement, together with the midrashic idea about the nullity of the commandments in exilic circumstances, supplies Nahmanides a solid ground for his legal theology.

Nahmanides begins with a rhetorical questioning of the biblical consequential logic:[48]

> Scripture was very strict in forbidding these sexual relationships on account of the Land which becomes defiled by them, and which in turn will vomit out the people that do [these abominations]. Now, forbidden sexual relationships are matters [are in fact] corporal-duties, and do not depend on the Land [so why should the Land be affected by these personal immoral acts]?

Then Nahmanides further argues that the Canaanites' sexual misconducts are not considered corporal sins, but rather environmental vices that caused the removal of the Canaanites from the land. For the sake of grounding the unintuitive statement that even sexual behavior is seen as violating land-dependent commandments, Nahmanides embraces a midrashic account of the different meanings of obedience to the halakhah within the land and outside:[49]

> *And you perish quickly from off the good land.*[50] Although I banish you from the Land to outside the Land, make yourselves distinctive by the commandments, so that when you return they shall not be novelties to you. This can be compared to a master who was angry with his wife, and sent her back to her father's house and told her, "adorn yourself with precious things, so that when you come back they will not be novelties to you."

The midrash here introduces an optimistic sense of the exile by the comparison with a family crisis ending in divorce. Within this allegory, the recoverability of familial harmony is envisaged even during the darkest moments, when the couple separates and the wife is sent back to her father's household. The expulsion of the wife is accompanied by the husband's allusion to a possible reunion in the future. However, due to the long distance, the husband is still concerned about the prospect of reuniting with his beloved divorcée and therefore urges her to keep wearing her garments while separated from him.

The midrashic allegory outlines a rich imagery of relations between the divine law and the land under the metaphor of a household. The image of the commandments as garments is very significant and calls attention to the functionality of the law in the bond between God and Israel as husband and wife.[51] On the one hand, while living together at home, the garments are assigned to the husband and aim to keep the wife attractive to her husband. On the other hand, during their separation and her stay with her father, wearing the garments will remind her and make her ready to come back into relations with her husband. The divine law, therefore, has different roles within the divine space and the outer space: While the in-home purpose of the commandment is to maintain a living attraction between the two, outside the home it is designed to preserve a living memory of their coupling.

Clearly, Nahmanides finds the twofold aspects of the commandments coherent with the territorial image of the law. Accordingly, while at the home territory, the fulfillment of the divine laws is part of vital relations with the deity; in outside territories it is merely a reminder of such relations. Therefore, the corporal-territorial dichotomy does not reflect an essential typology within the halakhah, but rather two spatial contexts, or two legal modes—exile and homeland—in which the law has different ends. In the exilic circumstances, only corporal commandments that function as self-referential reminders are obligatory. Within the land, the commandments play a different role within the intimate relations with God in accordance with the doctrine of משפט אלהי הארץ:[52]

> Now the verses which state *and you perish quickly … and you shall lay up these my words* etc. make obligatory in the exile only corporal-commandments, such as the [wearing of] phylacteries and [placing of] mezuzah, and concerning them the rabbis explained [that we must observe them] so that they shall not be novelties to us when we return to the land, for the main [fulfillment] of the commandments is [to be kept] when dwelling in the Land of God.

The Nahmanidean reading of the midrash introduces a new apparatus of the halakhah as divine law, and accordingly, the concepts of sovereignty, legal authority, jurisdiction, and being subject to the law are redefined.

The Fate of the Canaanites: Between Identity and Otherness

> In the same city there are two peoples under the same king, and with the two people two ways of life, and with two ways of life two dominions, and with two dominions a double order of jurisdiction emerges [*duplex iurisdictionis ordo procedit*]. … The two dominions are the institutional Church and secular government; the double order of jurisdiction [*duplex iurisdictio*] is divine and human law. (Stephen of Tournai)[53]

The tension between territorial jurisdiction (i.e., laws that governed all relationships within a geographical area) and personal jurisdiction (applied to individuals based on their identity and belonging) is well apparent in late ancient times. Broadly speaking, these two types of jurisdiction should not be taken merely as principled implementations of the law but rather as formative factors in the shaping of cultural identities. Hence, for example, there was the ambivalence of early Christians who were identified with the Roman laws on certain occasions and alienated from the very same legal system on other occasions.[54] Likewise, the two types of jurisdictions exemplify the complex relations between religious *nomoi* based on an *ethnos*, or people, on the one hand, and imperial *nomos* that transcends these entities, on the other hand. Accordingly, Saint Paul escaped a scourging from the Jewish authorities of Jerusalem by claiming a personal jurisdiction, as being born a Roman citizen, which exempted him from the Judean territorial jurisdiction.[55] Moreover, as the religious message is taken to be universal and borderless, the jurisdiction of the divine law is expected not to be dependent on locality, but rather to be dependent on the person's status.[56]

For Stephen of Tourni (1128–1203), jurisdiction is indeed personal in its essence, and for this reason a *duplex iurisdictio*, or even multitude jurisdictions,

in the very same location is not impossible. Similarly, the mainstream of rabbinic thought cleaved to personal jurisdiction and approved the possibility of
a "double order of jurisdiction" for some people in one and the same place.
This is, perhaps, best demonstrated by the talmudic category of Noahide laws,
which are designated to the entire humankind against the comprehensive
halakhic commandments, by which only the Jews are addressed. Thus, while
Jews, as *Bnei Brith* (בני ברית; literally, "people of [the] covenant"), are obliged to
observe all the commandments for their covenantal relations, all humans, who
are *Bnei Noah* (בני נח; literally, "descendants of Noah"), are obliged to observe
only the few commandments defined as the Noahide laws.

Interestingly, Nahmanides' thick notion of territorial jurisdiction leads him
to challenge the talmudic division between the Noahide laws and the entire
body of halakhah. Being loyal to the rabbinic tradition, Nahmanides tiptoes
when criticizing the talmudic conception of Noahide laws by stating their
inconsistency with the plain biblical descriptions:[57]

> Now scripture mentions that the people of the land of Canaan were pun-
> ished on account of their immoral [sexual] deeds. And our rabbis have said
> that they were warned about these matters from the time of creation, when
> these laws were declared to Adam and Noah, for He does not punish unless
> He admonishes first.
>
> Scripture, however, did not state the admonition, but instead said that the
> Land would vomit them out, for the Land abhors *all these abominations.*[58]
> Now the Canaanites were not the only ones who were admonished about
> these matters, and the scriptural section mentions specifically, *After the
> doing of the land of Egypt, wherein you dwelt, shall you not do,*[59] which proves
> that the Egyptians also did all these abominations, and yet the land of Egypt
> did not vomit them out, nor did the lands of other nations vomit them out!
> Rather, this whole subject shows the distinction of the Land [of Israel] and
> its holiness [so that it alone is unable to retain sinners].

Nahmanides does not ignore the contrast between the talmudic construction
of Noahide laws and the scriptural descriptions. As a matter of fact, he even
stresses the gap between them as a way of criticizing the talmudic concept.
The presumptions of this concept are: (1) personal jurisdiction and (2) the
necessity of admonishment of the law[60]—two of which are inconsistent with
Nahmanides' doctrine of "the law of the land's Lord." In fact, his autonomist
approach leads him to acknowledge the universality of the divine law, as seen
above. Nevertheless, the universality of the law for Nahmanides is in the sense
of being non-tribal, but not in the sense of being valid and compulsory everywhere. His insistence on a territorial jurisdiction, in fact, saves him from holding a universal perception of the law in the latter sense.

The fate of the Canaanites, in the biblical narrative, indicates these two
aspects. First, Nahmanides accentuates the fact that the Canaanites were

punished even though they were never warned or notified about their wrong-doings. Second, he emphasizes that the law is considered obligatory, not only for the Israelites, but also for the Gentiles, who may commit sins in the land. Nahmanides brings to our attention the difference in retribution for the Egyptians' deeds and that of the Canaanites. This difference demonstrates the extent to which territoriality is indeed a crucial condition to the validity of the divine law. Thus, for the same transgressions of incest laws, the Canaanites and the Egyptians were treated differently. And while the Canaanites were severely punished and eventually vomited from the land, the Egyptians did not meet the same fate. So while the talmudic rabbis could endorse Stephen's hetero-geneous description, Nahmanides would reject it as a misconception of the divine law as a territorial law.

While difference is a matter of fact, otherness is a matter of discourse. More precisely, otherness is the result of a discursive process by which a dominant in-group (us/the self) constructs a dominated out-group (them/the other) by stigmatizing a difference—real or imagined—presented as a negation of iden-tity and thus as a motive for potential discrimination.

In the context of biblical tradition and post-biblical religious milieus, we can observe three meanings of otherness. The first meaning signifies the estrangement from God and the refusal to adhere to the order which he had given. It is something evil, something to be avoided at all costs. "Thou shalt not have strange gods [אלוהים אחרים; *deos alienos*] before me" (Exod 20:3).[61] Further on, terms of otherness such as ἀλλότριος, *alienus*, or [62]אחר, signify Satan and other competing gods.[63]

The second meaning is estrangement from the common worldly matters. Though the above meaning of otherness is charged with a negative value, otherness as disengagement from ordinary existential circumstances has an ambivalent value. A good example for this meaning can be seen in the Hebrew word *qodesh* (קודש), very much like the ancient Roman word *sacer*, which basically means anything that is "set apart" from ordinary life.[64] In fact, this meaning of otherness corresponds to the biblical idea of Israel as the elected son, or chosen people, distinguished from other peoples on earth.[65] Likewise Christian monasticism, and mainly desert monasticism, involved living as an other, in opposition to the world, in order to achieve an intimate and abid-ing knowledge of God. Being a monk, therefore, demanded renunciation and detachment, cutting one's ties to certain habitual ways of living, including cer-tain places, and withdrawing to a marginal existence in the desert. Later, the medieval ideal lacking any sense of belonging and implying landlessness, or a lack of connection with a particular land—*homo viator*—is perhaps another expression of otherness as estrangement from the world.[66]

The third meaning of otherness is a horizontal estrangement among human beings. In that sense, otherness and identity mutually define and exclude each other. Otherness in this meaning, as modern thinkers emphasize, signifies the estrangement from "us" or "ourselves." As Carl Schmitt and other thinkers have emphasized, "otherness" and "identity" are in fact two inseparable sides of the same coin, as the other exists in relation to the self and vice versa. Moreover, some argue that the creation of this type of otherness (i.e., othering) is deeply linked to asymmetrical power relationships and to the principle that allows individuals to be classified into two hierarchical groups: "them" and "us." In this way, the coherency of the out-group is a result of its opposition to the in-group's identity. In other words, only a dominant group is in a position to impose the value of its particularity (its identity) and to devalue the particularity of others (their otherness).

The biblical descriptions contain two distinct images of the Canaanites as others, which accordingly reflect two competing accounts of the Israelite identity.[67] The Canaanites in the book of Genesis are pictured as decent hosts who cause no threat at all to the identity of the ancestors. They are not described in opposition to the Israelites' existence or faith and therefore are not an object for polemical attacks. On the other hand, in other books, and mainly in Leviticus and Deuteronomy, the Canaanites as a group are stigmatized as horrendous sinners, justly dispossessed from the Promised Land. They are portrayed as sexually and religiously perverse. Later they are described as practicing child sacrifice, necromancy, resorting to soothsayers and diviners,[68] and worshipping images at hilltop fertility shrines.[69]

The Nahmanidean legal theology transcends the discourse of otherness. Because the law is compulsory for the residents of the Holy Land, with no exception for their religious or ethnic identity, the distinction between Jews and non-Jews in that regard is softened and even blurred to a large extent. Accordingly, the biblical fate of the Canaanites is not a result of their faith and religious status, nor an outcome of their otherness, but rather a direct consequence of their practical behavior. Nahmanides is more consistent with the image of the Canaanites in the book of Genesis, much more than their image as ultimate others. Against the image of the Canaanites as impure others or immoral others, Nahmanides revives the viewing of them as plausible residents under the divine law and hence natural inhabitants of the Promised Land.

This is another radical aspect of Nahmanides' legal theology based on the of *God-land-law* matrix: The Canaanites, in the sacred order of God's inheritance, are not strangers, and therefore are not essentially others. The territorialization of the divine law, together with the mystification of the Holy Land, in fact neutralizes the otherness of the Canaanites and cracks the implication of an "us-them" dichotomy within the jurisprudential perspective. In Nahmanides' eyes, the fate of the Canaanites is the same fate as that of the biblical Cuthim and Sodomites:[70] They were all vomited from the land because of their defiling conduct. The distressful fate of the Canaanites is not a result of the Israelite conquest, but rather of their violation of "the law of the land's Lord." In that respect, the fate of the Canaanites for Nahmanides illustrates the mechanism belonging to the land of Israel, and the Canaanite-Israelite coexistence under the laws of the God of the land is definitely conceivable.

Notes

This chapter is part of my article: "Dwelling within the Law: Nahmanides' Legal Theology," *Oxford Journal of Law and Religion*, (2013), pp. 1–21.

1. Pro-exilic ideologies are widespread in the talmudic literature. The self-perception of the Babylonian Geonim demonstrates the metaphoric displacement of Zion from being a geographical area to its being the scholastic institution of the yeshiva. See: Abraham Grossmann, "The Yeshivah of Eretz-Israel: Its Spiritual Activity and Standing in the Jewish World," in *Sefer Yerushalayim: Ha-Tekufah Ha-Muslemit Ha-Kedumah, 638–1099*, ed. Joshua Prawer (Jerusalem: Yad Yitshak Ben-Tsevi, 1987), 179–214. The Jewish Catalonian thinker Abraham bar Hiyya (1070–ca. 1140) claimed that the land of Israel would be stretched beyond the historical borderlines to include the entire world. In fact, Nahmanides' concurrent scholar, Ezra of Gerona (d. 1227), argued that the duty to settle in the land of Israel had been terminated and replaced by the "suffering of exile." On the analysis of these Catalonian scholars and their contexts, see Moshe Idel, "On the Land of Israel in Medieval Jewish Mystical Thought," in *The Land of Israel in Medieval Jewish Thought*, ed. Moshe Hallamish and Aviezer Ravitzky (Jerusalem: Yad Izhak Ben-Zvi, 1991), 193–214.

2. The term "legal theology" indicates an understanding of the law as it is driven from a theological picture. Put differently, it is a legal theory that cannot be described independently from theological perceptions. In that respect, much of the premodern legal theories can be fairly considered legal theologies.

3. Ravitzky views Nahmanides' perception as an evolutionary phase within a long-standing tradition around the idea of "Waymarks to Zion," an idea that originated in the *Sifre*, further developed within rabbinic and antinomian circles, and eventually merged into the Zionist theology as articulated by R. Abraham Isaac Kook (1865–1935). See Aviezer Ravitzky, " 'Waymarks to Zion': The History of Idea," in *The Land of Israel in Medieval Jewish Thought*, ed. Moshe Hallamish and Aviezer Ravitzky (Jerusalem: Yad Izhak Ben-Zvi, 1991), 1–39. Without denying Nahmanides' part within this tradition, I wish to portray his input as a radical proposal to modify the fundamental infrastructure of the halakhah, which eventually was not accepted as a plausible alternative. While Ravitzky distinguishes the halakhic aspect from the theological one, I propose to view them as ingredients of Nahmanides' legal theology.

4. Consider some prominent notions of divine law within the intellectual history of Jewish thought: Philo claims that the notion of divine law is consistent with and even overlaps natural law (John W. Martens, *One God, One Law: Philo of Alexandria on the Mosaic and Greco-Roman Law* [Boston: Brill Academic Publishers, 2003], 13–30). Maimonides views the divine law as exclusively originating in the monumental revelation at Sinai, and further extended and developed by human reasoning (Joseph E. David, "Maimonides, Nature, and Law: Refining the Framework," *Journal of Law Philosophy and Culture* 4, no. 1 [2010]: 85–100). Nissim Gerondi proposes to take the divine law as triggering divine plethora (Menachem Lorberbaum, *Politics and the Limits of Law: Secularizing the Political in Medieval Jewish Thought* [Stanford, Calif.: Stanford University Press, 2001], 93–149). Joseph Albo views the divine law as a universal vehicle to achieve spiritual success (Dror Ehrlich, "A Reassessment

of Natural Law in Rabbi Joseph Albo's 'Book of Principles,'" *Hebraic Political Studies* 1 [2006]: 413–439). A common denominator of these distinct notions is the embracing of a subject-addressed notion of the divine law.

5. Halbertal exposes the antinomian aspect of Nahmanides' halakhic thought through his anti-philosophical approaches to the problem of death and law. See Moshe Halbertal, *By Way of Truth: Nahmanides and the Creation of Tradition* (Jerusalem: Shalom Hartman Institute, 2006), 117–148.

6. For a challenge of the traditional narrative according to which Nahmanides' journey was an aftermath of the Barcelona debate see M. Kayserling, "The Jews of Spain," *JQR* 8, no. 3 (1896): 486–499. See also Idel, "Land of Israel," 205.

7. As we shall demonstrate in a forthcoming study, in order to explain this episode, in which the divine law was directed and demanded also for non-Jews, Nahmanides develops a theory of halakhah that transcends the division between Israel and the Gentiles.

8. Graetz coined the term *basileomorphism* for the representation of God by the imagery of kingship (Heinrich Graetz, "Die Mystische Literatur in Der Gaonaeischen Epoche," *Monatsschrift für Geschichte und Wissenschaft des Judentums* 8 [1859]: 67–78, 103–118, 40–53), probably by referring to the Byzantine court ritual. See Schäfer's critique on the usage of this term: Peter Schäfer, *The Origins of Jewish Mysticism* (Princeton, N.J.: Princeton University Press, 2009), 344. As Philip Alexander showed, probably imperial (Roman and Sasanian) court rituals stand at the background of *Heikhalot* royal imagery (Philip S. Alexander, "The Family of Caesar and the Family of God: The Image of the Emperor in the Heikhalot Literature," in *Images of Empire*, ed. Loveday Alexander [Sheffield, U.K.: JSOT Press, 1991], 276–297) and the perceptions of the heavenly entourage as *familia caelestis* (פמליה של מעלה) and *familia caesaris*. Also see Michael S. Heiser, "The Divine Council in Late Canonical and Non-Canonical Second Temple Jewish Literature" (PhD diss., University of Wisconsin-Madison, 2004).

9. "O clap your hands, all ye peoples; shout unto God with the voice of triumph. For God, Most-High, is terrible; He is a great king over all the earth.... For God is the king of all the earth.... God reigneth over the nations: God sitteth upon his holy throne." (Ps 47:2–3, 47:8–9).

10. On the principle of hierarchy in medieval legal thought, see Brian Tierney, "Origins of Jurisdiction: Hierarchy and Consent, 1250–1350," *Religion, Law, and the Growth of Constitutional Thought, 1150–1650* (Cambridge: Cambridge University Press, 1982), 29–53.

11. On the problem of divine agency in late ancient Judaism and Christianity, see Larry W. Hurtado, *One God, One Lord: Early Christian Devotion and Ancient Jewish Monotheism* (London: T & T Clark, 2005), 17–40. On the comparison of earthly and heavenly ideas of rulership in Christian texts of the third and fourth centuries C.E., see Sophie Lunn-Rockliffe, *Ambrosiaster's Political Theology* (Oxford: Oxford University Press, 2008), 127–145.

12. The interpretative phrase "angels of God" (ἀγγέλων θεοῦ) is found in nearly all the extant LXX manuscripts. However, several earlier manuscripts have instead "sons of God" (υἱῶν θεοῦ). This is a literal rendering of the Hebrew phrase בני אלוהים found in 4QDeut[j]. Most scholars agree that the Qumran reading has polytheistic overtones that later scribes found unacceptable. As a result, those scribes probably modified the verse to bring it more into line with Israel's monotheistic faith. On a possible Ugaritic background of this problem, see Jan Joosten, "A Note on the Text of Deuteronomy xxxii 8," *VT* 57, no. 4 (2007): 548–555.

13. For Plato the structure of distributed deities enables a stable and peaceful order of the universe: "Then, in the beginning, God ruled and supervised the whole revolution, and so

again, in the same way, all the parts of the universe were divided by regions among gods who ruled them, and, moreover, the animals were distributed by species and flocks among inferior deities as divine shepherds, each of whom was in all respects the independent guardian of the creatures under his own care, so that no creature was wild, nor did they eat one another, and there was no war among them, nor any strife whatsoever" (*Pol.* 271d–e).

14. The second-century church father Justin Martyr acknowledged the two different versions of Deut 32:8 and the preference of the monotheistic version by the Jews. See Dialogue of Justin, Philosopher and Martyr, with Trypho, a Jew, in *The Apostolic Fathers with Justin Martyr and Irenaeus*, ed. Alexander Roberts et al. (Christian Classics Ethereal Library), ch. 131, http://www.ccel.org/ccel/schaff/anf01.pdf, p. 706.

15. The Roman emperor Julian the Apostate (331–363) confronts the two kingly images by ascribing to Moses the image of God as exclusive sovereign and favoring the other image to the Romans: "If the immediate creator of the universe be he who is proclaimed by Moses, then we hold nobler beliefs concerning him, inasmuch as we consider him to be the master of all things in general, but that there are besides national gods who are subordinate to him and are like viceroys of a king, each administering separately his own province" (*Against the Galileans*).

16. See the discussion of St. Anselm of Canterbury: *Cur Deus Homo*, 1.18 in *A Scholastic Miscellany: Anselm to Ockham*, ed. Eugene Rathbone Fairweather (Philadelphia: Westminster Press, 1956), 132–134.

17. Nahmanides, *Commentary on the Torah*, trans. Charles Ber Chavel (New York: Shilo, 1971), Lev 18:25, p. 268.

18. Deut 32:8–9.

19. Gen 10:31.

20. Deut 10:17.

21. Nahmanides, *Commentary on the Torah*, Lev 18:25, pp. 268–269.

22. A polycratic theology that ascribes God's specialized sovereignty both to the people of Israel and the land of Israel appears in various post-biblical Jewish writings. See *Jub.* 15:31–32; *Targum Yerushalmi*, Gen 11:8, Deut 32:8–9; *Tanhuma*, Reeh 8; *Leqah Tov*, Gen 9:19; *Pirqei de-Rabbi Eli'ezer* 24. In Jewish medieval thought, this description appears in Zoharic passages, as the following: "Rabbi Ele'azar said, 'It is written: A land in which you will eat bread without scarcity, in which you will not lack anything (Deuteronomy 8:9). Why this repetition of in which? Because, as has been said, the blessed Holy One apportioned all nations and lands among deputies and envoys, while He has inherited the land of Israel, not granting it to any other envoy or deputy, rather ruling over it Himself alone. Similarly no other angel or deputy rules over the people of Israel, rather He alone. So He brought the people over whom no one else rules into the land over which no one else rules.'" (*Zohar*, VaYera, 108b). On the tension between Nahmanides' theological ideas and those of the Zohar, see Boaz Huss, "The Early Dissemination of Sefer Ha-Zohar," *Tarbiz* 70, no. 3–4 (2001): 507–542.

23. Funkenstein claimed that Nahmanides' typological hermeneutic was influenced by Christian theological hermeneutical methods. See Amos Funkenstein, "Nachmanides' Typological Reading of History," *Zion* 45, no. 1 (1980): 35–59. Halbertal pointed out that Nahmanides innovatively developed a rabbinic perception of the original sin, obviously under the inspiration of the Christian doctrine. See Halbertal, *By Way of Truth*, 121–126.

24. The breakdown of the unified concept of universal sovereignty was attributed to two powers. First, the strengthened position of the local kings backed by papal support (such as

the declaration of Pope Innocent III that the French kings need not recognize any higher authority). Second, the revival of the Aristotelian thought on the natural origin of the political society (thus the legitimization of the political life derived from its natural origin and not from its participation in a greater whole).

25. As some scholars have shown, this distinction founded the legal theory upon which later developed the sovereign territorial state of early modern times. See Wilhelm Georg Grewe, *The Epochs of International Law*, trans. Michael Byers (Berlin: Walter de Gruyter, 2000), 47; Walter Ullmann, "The Development of the Medieval Idea of Sovereignty," *English Historical Review* 64, no. 250 (1949): 1–33.

26. The statement "I am master of the world" (*dominus numdi*) made by the Roman Emperor Antoninus Pius (86–161) was later adopted to articulate the legal category of imperial sovereignty (*Dig.* 14.2.9).

27. This is explicitly the case with Jephthah's speech against the aggressive invasion by the Ammonites' king: "Will not you possess that which Chemosh your god gives you to possess? So whomsoever the LORD our God shall drive out from before us, them will we possess" (Judg 11:24). A similar case is David's pleading while being persecuted by Saul: "Cursed are [these men who stirred you up against me], for they have driven me out this day that I should not cleave to the inheritance of the Lord, saying: 'Go, serve other gods' " (1 Sam 26:19). The Talmud favors the territorial reading, as it supports the talmudic celebration of the duty to settle in the Holy Land: "Whoever lives in the Land of Israel may be considered to have a God, but whoever lives outside the Land may be regarded as one who has no God.... Similarly it was said in Scripture in [the story of] David" (*b. Ketub.*, 110b).

28. *Drashah for Rosh HaShanah*, in Nahmanides, *Writings of the Ramban*, trans. Charles Ber Chavel (New York: Shilo, 2009).

29. See Von Rad's statement on the independency of the idea of "promised land" and "God's land" in the Bible: "the promise of the land is a group of concepts which are completely independent of the concept of Jahweh as the owner of Canaan. Not in a single instance amongst the well-nigh innumerable passages where appeal is made to the promise of the land is this land described as the property of Jahweh—it is rather the land which formerly belonged to other nations, which Jahweh, in making his design in history effective, gave to Israel to possess" (Gerhard Von Rad, *Old Testament Theology* [New York: Harper, 1962], 2:300).

30. Norman Daniel, "The Legal and Political Theory of the Crusade," in *The Impact of the Crusades on Europe*, ed. Harry W. Hazard and Norman P. Zacour (Madison: University of Wisconsin Press, 1989), 3–38.

31. "O God, the heathen have come into your inheritance; your holy temple have they defiled; they have laid Jerusalem on heaps."

32. The announcement about the Islamic occupation sent by the archbishop of Tyre was about the occupation of God's inheritance by the Gentiles: "Fame had carried to the ears of all the kings, and of all the faithful, that the inheritance of Christ was occupied by the heathen" (*haereditatem Christi a gentibus occupatam*; p. 47). The Holy Land was given to Muslim hands due to the sins of the Christians so "the Lord seeing that the land...had sunk into an abyss of turpitude, treated with neglect his inheritance [*haereditatem Suam sprevit*], and suffered Saladin..." (p. 23). Accordingly the Christian defeat in the battle of Hittin (1187) is described as God's plan to hem "in his people with the sword" and to punish "the sins of men" by giving "over his inheritance [*haereditatem suam peccatis*] to slaughter and devastation" (p. 32). Likewise, Saladin's megalomaniac motive is described as an aspiration "to occupy the land

which is the inheritance of our Lord" (*haereditatem Domini totis viribus occupare conatur*) (pp. 28–29).

33. Jacques de Vitry toured France and Germany in recruiting crusaders and eventually became the Bishop of Acre (1216).

34. Christoph T. Maier, *Crusade Propaganda and Ideology: Model Sermons for the Preaching of the Cross* (Cambridge: Cambridge University Press, 2000), 98–99, 126–127.

35. This allegory was later adopted by Gilbert of Tournai. See Maier, *Crusade Propaganda and Ideology*, 186–187, 250–263.

36. Nahamanides' usage of the term "God's inheritance" vis-à-vis the Crusades' vocabulary might be seen as latent polemics with Christian self-identity as the true offspring of God and thus as the legitimized inheritors of God.

37. R. Asher b. Yehiel, *Responsa*, 8: 13, f. 13a.

38. The biblical association of God's residence with the gates of heaven appears to be among the motives of the Crusades, as can be seen in another sermon of Jacques de Vitry: "The cross is the key that opens the gates of paradise [*reserans portas paradise*]…as the house of God is recognized by the cross on top of it, so a man of the house of God [*homo dignoscitur domus Dei*] is recognized by the cross put on his shoulders (Maier, *Crusade Propaganda and Ideology*, 106–107).

39. *Sifre*, Reeh, 12:59.

40. "Corporal duty: i.e., not land-dependent. Not imposed on the ground and its fruits, but rather on individual's body. For instance: [wearing] phylacteries, [struggling against] idolatry…[practicing] circumcision, [avoiding] incest and so on" (Rashi, *t. Qidd.* 38a).

41. *t. Qidd.* 1:12.

42. Both above notions of territorial dependency can make sense of the territorial-personal (i.e., corporal) dichotomy.

43. "Because Abraham obeyed my voice, and kept my charge, my commandments, my statutes, and my laws" (Gen 26:5).

44. Nahmanides, *Commentary on the Torah*, Gen 26:5; Nahmanides, *Commentary on the Torah*, trans. Charles Ber Chavel (New York: Shilo, 1971).

45. The term "the period of the Torah" for Nahmanides illustrates the idea according to which the validity of the Torah is temporal and applicable only to the pre-messianic period in which there is a gap between human will and the divine law. In the future messianic period, by contrast, there will be no autonomous human will, no imposed law, and thus no individualization and human death. See Halbertal, *By Way of Truth*, 117–148.

46. See below.

47. "And the land is defiled: therefore I do visit the iniquity thereof upon it, and the land itself vomits out its inhabitants" (Lev 18:25).

48. Nahmanides, *Commentary on the Torah*, Lev 18:25, p. 268.

49. *Sifre*, ʿEqev, 43.

50. Deut 11:17.

51. While this perception is consistent with the spousal image of the relations to the deity, it stands in distance from traditional images of the divine law. A prominent image is built on the pharmacological metaphor originated in the Greek legal and political thought (Plato, *Pol.* 293b–c), the image of the divine law as light (see Thomas Aquinas, *The Summa Theologica of Saint Thomas Aquinas* [Chicago: William Benton, 1952], I:II, 91, 3, pp. 209–210), or as botanic organism (see Wael B. Hallaq, *A History of Islamic Legal Theories: An Introduction to Sunni Usul Al-Fiqh* [Cambridge: Cambridge University Press, 1997], 153).

52. Nahmanides, *Commentary on the Torah*, Lev 18:25, p. 272.

53. *Summa of Gratian's Decretum, in Studien Zur Summa Stephans Von Tournai: Ein Beitrag Zur Kanonistischen Wissenschaftsgeschichte Des Späten 12. Jahrhunderts*, ed. Herbert Kalb (Innsbruck: Universitätsverlag Wagner, 1983), 14.

54. See Andrew S. Jacobs, " 'Papian Commands One Thing, Our Paul Another': Roman Christians and Jewish Law in the Collatio Legum Mosaicarum Et Romanarum," in *Religion and Law in Classical and Christian Rome*, ed. Clifford Ando and Jörg Rüpke (Stuttgart: Steiner, 2006), 85–99.

55. Acts 22:25–29, 25:6–12, 26:32. It is accepted that since 1648 (Westphalia Treaty) the territorial law has been dominant. In modern times, it might reflect the confusion between the notions of the state and of the nation as decisive factors for determining persons' rights and responsibilities. See Simeon L. Guterman, *From Personal to Territorial Law: Aspects of the History and Structure of the Western Legal-Constitutional Tradition* (Metuchen, N.J.: Scarecrow Press, 1972), 11–29.

56. On the parallelism of the tribal-universal tension and the brother-other dichotomy in the Christian and Jewish background, see Marc Shell, "Tribal Brotherhood and Universal Otherhood," in *Children of the Earth: Literature, Politics, and Nationhood* (New York: Oxford University Press, 1993), 176–192.

57. Nahmanides, *Commentary on the Torah*, Lev 18:25, pp. 274–275.

58. Lev 18:27.

59. Lev 18:3.

60. The question of whether the compulsory dimension of the law is dependent on promulgation was a debated issue among medieval jurists. On the one hand, Gratian records that "a law is not really law until it has been made known" (*Leges instituuntur, cum promulgantur*) (Gratian, *Decretum Gratiani*, D.4.c.3.1.). On the other hand, naturalist jurists emphasized that "the natural law needs no promulgation" (*lex naturlais non indigent promulgatione*). (Thomas, *The Summa Theologica of Saint Thomas Aquinas*, I:II, 90, 4, pp. 207–208). On the incidences of these two principles in the Tannaitic literature, see Hirshman, *Torah for the Entire World*, 90–113.

61. See more: "It is I who have declared and saved and proclaimed, And there was no strange [god] among you" (Isa 43:12). Also one of the biblical meanings of otherness is fornication; see Judg 11:2.

62. In fact, the category of "otherness" (*alteritas*) versus "oneness" (*unitas*) did play a crucial role in medieval theologies; see Orrin F. Summerell, *The Otherness of God* (Charlottesville: University Press of Virginia, 1998). In late antiquity rabbinic literature, the Hebrew term for "other" (אחר; literally, "the other one") carries the meaning of the most foreign and thus the ultimate unacceptable. For example, the former rabbi Elisha b. Abuyah who was eventually considered heretical by the Tannaim (the sages of the Mishnah) was named "Other." See Alon Goshen-Gottstein, *The Sinner and the Amnesiac: The Rabbinic Invention of Elisha Ben Abuya and Eleazar Ben Arach* (Stanford, Calif.: Stanford University Press, 2000). Also, the pig's meat, which Torah prohibits eating (Lev 11:2–4, 11:7–8; Deut 14:8), is termed by the rabbis "other thing" (דבר אחר); see *b. Shabb.* 129b and *b. Ber.* 43b. For a survey of the "other" in Judaism in earlier scholarship, see John Joseph Collins and Daniel C. Harlow, *The "Other" in Second Temple Judaism: Essays in Honor of John J. Collins* (Grand Rapids, Mich.: Eerdmans).

63. See Mark S. Smith, *The Early History of God: Yahweh and the Other Deities in Ancient Israel* (Grand Rapids, Mich.: Eerdmans, 2002).

64. Though, the terms *qodesh* and *sacer* practically cover equally the meanings of "hallowed" and "cursed." See Giorgio Agamben and Daniel Heller-Roazen, *Homo Sacer: Sovereign Power and Bare Life* (Stanford, Calif.: Stanford University Press, 1998).

65. Accordingly, the Israelites are described as "a people who dwell apart, And will not be reckoned among the nations" (Num 23:9); their holiness is consequential to their being chosen by God: "For you are a holy people to the Lord your God, and the Lord has chosen you to be a people for His own possession out of all the peoples who are on the face of the earth" (Deut 14:2) and therefore they are to be sanctified like God: "You shall be holy, for I the Lord your God am holy" (Lev 19:2).

66. See Gerhart B. Ladner, "Homo Viator: Mediaeval Ideas on Alienation and Order," *Speculum* 42, no. 2 (1967): 233–259.

67. See Robert L. Cohn, "Before Israel: The Canaanites as Other in Biblical Traditions," in *The Other in Jewish Thought and History: Constructions of Jewish Culture and Identity*, ed. Laurence J. Silberstein and Robert L. Cohn (New York: New York University Press, 1995), 74–91.

68. Deut 18:9–14.

69. Deut 12:2–3.

70. Nahmanides, *Commentary on the Torah*, Gen 19:5.

Bibliography

Agamben, Giorgio, and Daniel Heller-Roazen. *Homo Sacer: Sovereign Power and Bare Life.* Stanford, Calif.: Stanford University Press, 1998.

Alexander, Philip S. "The Family of Caesar and the Family of God: The Image of the Emperor in the Heikhalot Literature." In *Images of Empire*, edited by Loveday Alexander, 276–297. Sheffield, U.K.: JSOT Press, 1991.

Anderson, Gary A. "The Status of the Torah before Sinai: The Retelling of the Bible in the Damascus Covenant and the Book of Jubilees." *Dead Sea Discoveries* 1, no. 1 (1994): 1–29.

Anselm of Canterbury. *Cur Deus Homo.* In *A Scholastic Miscellany: Anselm to Ockham*, edited by Eugene Rathbone Fairweather. Philadelphia: Westminster Press, 1956.

Aquinas, Thomas. *The Summa Theologica of Saint Thomas Aquinas.* Chicago: William Benton, 1952.

Asher b. Yehiel, *Responsa.* New York: Grossman Publishing House, 1954.

Cohn, Robert L. "Before Israel: The Canaanites as Other in Biblical Traditions." In *The Other in Jewish Thought and History: Constructions of Jewish Culture and Identity*, edited by Laurence J. Silberstein and Robert L. Cohn, 74–91. New York: New York University Press, 1995.

Collins, John Joseph, and Daniel C. Harlow. *The "Other" in Second Temple Judaism: Essays in Honor of John J. Collins.* Grand Rapids, Mich.: Eerdmans, 2011.

Daniel, Norman. "The Legal and Political Theory of the Crusade." In *The Impact of the Crusades on Europe*, edited by Harry W. Hazard and Norman P. Zacour, 3–38. Madison: University of Wisconsin Press, 1989.

David, Joseph E. "Maimonides, Nature, and Law: Refining the Framework." *Journal of Law Philosophy and Culture* 4, no. 1 (2010): 85–100.

Ehrlich, Dror. "A Reassessment of Natural Law in Rabbi Joseph Albo's 'Book of Principles.'" *Hebraic Political Studies* 1 (2006): 413–439.

Erder, Yoram. "Early Karaite Conceptions about Commandments Given before the Revelation of the Torah." *Proceedings of the American Academy for Jewish Research* 60 (1994): 101–140.

Funkenstein, Amos. "Nachmanides' Typological Reading of History." *Zion* 45, no. 1 (1980): 35–59.

Goshen-Gottstein, Alon. *The Sinner and the Amnesiac: The Rabbinic Invention of Elisha Ben Abuya and Eleazar Ben Arach*. Stanford, Calif.: Stanford University Press, 2000.

Graetz, Heinrich. "Die Mystische Literatur in Der Gaonaeischen Epoche." *Monatsschrift für Geschichte und Wissenschaft des Judentums* 8 (1859): 67–78, 103–118, 40–53.

Gratian. *Summa* of *Decretum*. In *Studien Zur Summa Stephans Von Tournai: Ein Beitrag Zur Kanonistischen Wissenschaftsgeschichte Des Späten 12. Jahrhunderts*, edited by Herbert Kalb. Innsbruck: Universitätsverlag Wagner, 1983.

Grewe, Wilhelm Georg. *The Epochs of International Law*. Translated by Michael Byers. Berlin: Walter de Gruyter, 2000.

Grossmann, Abraham. "The Yeshivah of Eretz-Israel: Its Spiritual Activity and Standing in the Jewish World." In *Sefer Yerushalayim: Ha-Tekufah Ha-Muslemit Ha-Kedumah, 638–1099*, edited by Joshua Prawer, 179–214. Jerusalem: Yad Yitshak Ben-Tsevi, 1987.

Guterman, Simeon L. *From Personal to Territorial Law: Aspects of the History and Structure of the Western Legal-Constitutional Tradition*. Metuchen, N.J.: Scarecrow Press, 1972.

Halbertal, Moshe. *By Way of Truth: Nahmanides and the Creation of Tradition*. Jerusalem: Shalom Hartman Institute, 2006.

Hallaq, Wael B. *A History of Islamic Legal Theories: An Introduction to Sunni Usul Al-Fiqh*. Cambridge: Cambridge University Press, 1997.

Heiser, Michael S. "The Divine Council in Late Canonical and Non-Canonical Second Temple Jewish Literature." PhD diss., University of Wisconsin-Madison, 2004.

Hirshman, Marc G. *Torah for the Entire World: A Universalist School of Rabbinic Thought*. Tel-Aviv: ha-Kibuts ha-meuhad, 1999.

Hurtado, Larry W. *One God, One Lord: Early Christian Devotion and Ancient Jewish Monotheism*. London: T & T Clark, 2005.

Huss, Boaz. "The Early Dissemination of Sefer Ha-Zohar." *Tarbiz* 70, no. 3–4 (2001): 507–542.

Idel, Moshe. "On the Land of Israel in Medieval Jewish Mystical Thought." In *The Land of Israel in Medieval Jewish Thought*, edited by Moshe Hallamish and Aviezer Ravitzky, 193–214. Jerusalem: Yad Izhak Ben-Zvi, 1991.

Jacobs, Andrew S. "'Papian Commands One Thing, Our Paul Another': Roman Christians and Jewish Law in the Collatio Legum Mosaicarum Et Romanarum." In *Religion and Law in Classical and Christian Rome*, edited by Clifford Ando and Jörg Rüpke, 85–99. Stuttgart: Steiner, 2006.

Joosten, Jan. "A Note on the Text of Deuteronomy xxxii 8." *VT* 57, no. 4 (2007): 548–555.

Justin Martyr. "*Dialogue of Justin, Philosopher and Martyr, with Trypho, a Jew*." In *The Apostolic Fathers with Justin Martyr and Irenaeus*, edited by Alexander Roberts et al. Christian Classics Ethereal Library. http://www.ccel.org/ccel/schaff/anf01.pdf.

Justinian. *The Digest of Justinian*. Edited by Theodor Mommsen and Paul Krueger. Translated by Alan Watson. Philadelphia: University of Pennsylvania Press, 1985.

Kayserling, M. "The Jews of Spain." *JQR* 8, no. 3 (1896): 486–499.

Ladner, Gerhart B. "Homo Viator: Mediaeval Ideas on Alienation and Order." *Speculum* 42, no. 2 (1967): 233–259.

Lorberbaum, Menachem. *Politics and the Limits of Law: Secularizing the Political in Medieval Jewish Thought*. Stanford, Calif.: Stanford University Press, 2001.

Lunn-Rockliffe, Sophie. *Ambrosiaster's Political Theology*. Oxford: Oxford University Press, 2008.

Maier, Christoph T. *Crusade Propaganda and Ideology: Model Sermons for the Preaching of the Cross*. Cambridge: Cambridge University Press, 2000.

Martens, John W. *One God, One Law: Philo of Alexandria on the Mosaic and Greco-Roman Law*. Boston: Brill Academic Publishers, 2003.

Nahmanides. *Commentary on the Torah*. Translated by Charles Ber Chavel. New York: Shilo, 1971.

Nahmanides. *Writings of the Ramban*. Translated by Charles Ber Chavel. New York: Shilo, 2009.

Ravitzky, Aviezer. "'Waymarks to Zion': The History of Idea." In *The Land of Israel in Medieval Jewish Thought*, edited by Moshe Hallamish and Aviezer Ravitzky, 1–39. Jerusalem: Yad Izhak Ben-Zvi, 1991.

Schäfer, Peter. *The Origins of Jewish Mysticism*. Princeton, N.J.: Princeton University Press, 2009.

Shell, Marc. "Tribal Brotherhood and Universal Otherhood." In *Children of the Earth: Literature, Politics, and Nationhood*, 176–192. New York: Oxford University Press, 1993.

Smith, Mark S. *The Early History of God: Yahweh and the Other Deities in Ancient Israel*. Grand Rapids, Mich.: Eerdmans, 2002.

Summerell, Orrin F. *The Otherness of God*. Charlottesville: University Press of Virginia, 1998.

Tierney, Brian. "Origins of Jurisdiction: Hierarchy and Consent, 1250–1350." In *Religion, Law, and the Growth of Constitutional Thought, 1150–1650*, 29–53. Cambridge: Cambridge University Press, 1982.

Ullmann, Walter. "The Development of the Medieval Idea of Sovereignty." *English Historical Review* 64, no. 250 (1949): 1–33.

Von Rad, Gerhard. *Old Testament Theology*. New York: Harper, 1962.

8

The Land of Israel and Canaan

A CASE STUDY OF THE SPIRITUAL WORLD OF GUR HASIDISM

Yoram Jacobson

This article intends to deal with one of the most important ideas, or rather, aspects, of the spiritual world of Gur Hasidism, as reflected in the relation between the land of Israel and Canaan. However, I would like to start with some comments concerning the historical-biographical background and literary heritage of this important school.

Gur Hasidism is named, as is customary in the world of Hasidism,[1] after the dwelling place of its rebbe and his court, Gora Kalwaria (known as Ger in Yiddish, and Gur in Hebrew), which lies only a short distance from Warsaw (about 30 km),[2] and in the early phase of its development this school was indeed an explicitly Warsaw Hasidism. Even in later generations, the dynasty of Gur was renowned for its close connections with the Warsaw community.[3] The founder of the dynasty, R. Isaac Meir Alter,[4] lived and had been active in Warsaw for decades before he began to serve as a rebbe in 1860, after he moved and settled in Gur. He is the faithful disciple, follower, and heir of his admired teacher, R. Menahem Mendel of Kotzk. Even before he became a rebbe, R. Isaac Meir was engaged, with much success, in disseminating Hasidism and strengthening its standing among the Jews of Warsaw. He crystallized Warsaw Hasidism as an organized force, and from an early stage shaped the character of the school, which, in the course of time, he came to lead as a learned and profound school of Hasidism, not merely as a popular one.

Let's take one step further: The seat of the court of Gur, which has been established for the past seventy years in Jerusalem, started in Warsaw, and shortly thereafter, for nearly eighty years, was located in Gora Kalwaria. By the turn of the nineteenth century, the school of Gur became the dominant Hasidism in Poland: the largest and most influential dynasty in Polish Hasidism. This decisive dominance found expression not only in the large number of its adherents and in the broad range of its social scope, which included ordinary Jews, scholars, and wealthy and powerful men of the world, but also in its influential position in Jewish public life in general, and within the Orthodox public in particular.[5] It is true that Gur Hasidism attained this stature primarily under the leadership of its third rebbe, R. Avraham Mordecai. But the period of his predecessor, R. Judah Aryeh Leib, the admired grandson of the founder and the second rebbe of Gur (1870–1905), was also of decisive importance, and the rebbe played a crucial role in establishing the path of the school's leadership and its social patterns and in setting its ideological system.[6] R. Judah Aryeh Leib[7] is the author of *Sefat Emet* (literally, The Language of Truth), which is the canonical text of Gur Hasidism and its most important composition up to the present day. As a huge collection of homiletical teachings, which follow both the weekly portions of the Torah and the Jewish festivals in their yearly cycle, *Sefat Emet* reflects to a large extent the influence of the author's grandfather and must be regarded as an amazingly profound text of Hasidic spirituality and a mature mystical composition of Hasidic thought as a whole.[8]

As I have mentioned, the inner circles of Gur represent basically a learned school of Hasidism. This description is not fully comprehensive. In its inner thought, the school of Gur should be characterized by an intense and penetrating, but not radical, spirituality. The characterization of the school of Gur as a movement of "householders," presented by M. Piekarz,[9] may perhaps be accepted to a certain degree of understanding in light of the social openness of this Hasidism, which was prepared to accept within its ranks anyone who was willing to accept the rule of the rebbe and submit to his authority, without insisting upon the strict and rigid criteria of Przysucha and Kotzk: intense spirituality, extreme intellectual honesty, and uncompromising adherence to the truth, first and foremost within the soul of the individual, who is immersed in his constant existential struggles. But upon a deeper reading of the homilies of *Sefat Emet*, whose thought directly continues that of the founder of the dynasty, this "householder-liness" evaporates, and in its stead there is revealed a demanding and consistent spirituality. This type of profound spirituality, which will be presented in this paper by analyzing some of its most important ideas, should be clearly distinguished from the radical and daring spirituality of early Hasidism, which was ready to confront the traditional patterns and values of Jewish life and thought.[10] The school of Gur, which was formed during the last third of the nineteenth century, belongs indeed to a very late phase of the development of Hasidism, but bearing in mind its canonical composition, one should reject its characterization as "householder-liness" as totally mistaken. The Hasidic world of Gur seeks to express its profound spiritual tendencies within the framework of the halakhah and the stable patterns of traditional Jewish existence. This type of spirituality is indeed more moderate in its concrete conclusions, but not less profound in its search of the true meaning of existence in a world in which the Divine dwells everywhere. The various leitmotifs appearing once and again in the homilies of *Sefat Emet* do not refer to concrete reality, and the repeated numerous references to the Sabbath, for example, are basically not intended to reinforce its shaky status as a result of the growing influence of the circles of Jewish secularism. Even if this description does express a certain truth, it must be regarded as only a very partial understanding of a far more complex whole, at whose root lies a serious and profound effort to uncover the spiritual layer of reality and to experience a mystical contact with it. The Sabbath, like the holy land of Israel, as we shall learn in the course of our discussions in this article, reflects the emphatic spirituality of this Hasidic movement and the mature mysticism developed in its inner circles.

Let us now gradually turn to our main subject, whose understanding requires a detailed and elaborate background.

The focal theoretical assumption of the homilies of *Sefat Emet* is that of the encompassing unity underlying all existence, whose source lies in the divine immanence: Divine vitality permeates everything, all the different and divergent phenomena of all the layers of reality and their manifold manifestations, in both the good and the bad, the right and the distorted, the true and the falsified therein. This assumption finds its expression in Gur's well-known doctrine of the holy or inner "point," whose significance I have elaborated in my first paper devoted to this school.[11] This doctrine, which in all its complexity lies beyond the scope of this article, is to be examined and analyzed within the framework of the immanentist tradition of Kabbalistic and Hasidic thought.

This "point," which is clearly the later Hasidic transformation of the divine spark in Lurianic Kabbalah, refers to the divine vitality that flows through and gives life to all things: the Archimedean point upon which reality rests and is based, all its manifestations being sustained by it. It is often described as the divine root, the center of all the peripheral circles, the beginning, the hidden fountain, the concealed divine light—many images already known to us from the Kabbalistic sources. But the main interest of *Sefat Emet* lies in the position of this "point" in the concrete world that is "below": In this world, called "Nature" (a term derived from the influential writings of the Maharal of Prague), the point of divine light is immersed in darkness, since the high and thick walls of "Nature" conceal it and prevent the appearance of its light. "Nature" in the system discussed does not refer to the physical as the object of the senses, or as a reality grasped by both empirical experience and theoretical analysis and study, but rather designates the law governing the world that separates itself from the Divine, denies its root, pushes it away to a remote and dark corner within it, and suppresses it to forgetfulness. This enclosure of "Nature" finds its expression first and foremost on the plane of human consciousness. "Nature" is a world that encloses itself within its own four walls, shrinks into its own realm, knows only itself and desires only the fulfillment of its needs and the satisfaction of its urges. "Nature" thus signifies the physical and especially psychological law or lawfulness governing one who, by closing himself within the narrow limits of his own autonomous existence, becomes, so to speak, separated and cut off from the divine root. In this sense, "Nature"—in which the divine life is hidden, remaining abandoned and forgotten behind the separating barriers of its matter, corporeality, and carnal needs and desires—is the contrast to and the complete opposite of holiness, which constitutes the ever flowing and expanding stream of unceasing life.[12] Whereas the course of events within "Nature" is an unchanging routine, in which there will never be any new manifestation, holiness appears in a constant renewal of the spirit.[13] At this point we witness a dialectical move, which we already know from much earlier Hasidic sources, based on Kabbalistic thought, namely, that God hid the "point," so that when its light is revealed—or, more precisely, when man engages in intense spiritual effort to reveal it—its light will shine more brightly and spread forth more powerfully into the entire world, even in the dark recesses where it had not previously been known.[14] Being the embodiment and both the starting point and the goal of the divine will, this "point" is also referred to as the cornerstone of "the Kingdom of Heaven," whose appearance is often identified with the uncovering of the hidden "point."[15] This appearance finds its most important expression in the emphatic demand of fulfilling the divine will as the only true will, while all other human wills should be pushed aside, ignored, and negated as false manifestations of "Nature."[16] The *Sefat Emet* thus comes to the conclusion that God gave man the free choice to establish within himself the reign of flesh and blood, in which he may arrogantly say: "I shall rule" (a well-known phrase that originates from the story of the conflict between King Solomon and his bitter rival Adoniyyah in 1 Kings 1:5 and is frequently cited in Hasidic sources in this context), or "it is I and there is none other than me"—in order that he may struggle with himself to defeat the imaginary kingdom that he has set up.[17] In this struggle he sets forth against his own nature, acting to nullify the kingdom of "Nature," which consists entirely of earthly desires and needs, and which has no true relation to the Divine. On the contrary, it is based upon the arrogant detachment from God, and this is its very essence. Man will then choose to negate his own free will, whose root lies in the distorted logic of "Nature" and whose purpose is to decide between its two falsified values, "good" and "evil," or, if you prefer, between what is mistakenly considered "good" and what is conceived as "evil" according to the principles of "Nature" and its law, which have nothing to do with holiness. Man is expected then to withdraw from himself and from his natural urges, to empty himself from his self, to enable the divine will to flow and be discovered as the focal point of everything within himself, and finally to reveal and establish the "Kingdom of Heaven." The departure from "Nature"— in the wake of the Maharal and under his influence[18]—is the central spiritual imperative of Gur Hasidism: Man must turn his back on his external matters, his life routine and fixed habits (all aspects of "Nature"). This externality, when cut off from innerness and uprooted from the immanent divine "point," which is the only source of a meaningful holy life, is defective and pointless. In this separation, the external things move in peripheral circles around themselves, without any activated base in holiness: a barren and chaotic reality, in the routine of whose existence no change will take place, and no redemption can be achieved.[19] This is a very important point in *Sefat Emet*: Being entirely enslaved by its unchangeable lawfulness, "Nature" cannot and will never be the realm of redemption, since redemption by its very essence is a renewed or rather new and totally different order in both the historical and the spiritual realms, whereas in "Nature" there is nothing new under the sun (Eccl 1:9), as already mentioned. The spiritual imperative means that man must ignore the barriers of his separated existence—and thereby bring about their negation. He needs to conduct a spiritual journey to seek the Divine within himself. Only when he discovers this point, namely when he connects himself to his divine self (the "point" within himself), when he accomplishes his own divine integration, does he leave "Nature" and is able to rise to the realm that lies beyond or above it, or in its depth—the realm of salvation.

This dialectical move appears repeatedly in *Sefat Emet* by means of the concepts of "exile" and "redemption." It is characteristic of the emphatic mystical spiritualism of Gur Hasidism, that the concrete historical significance of these concepts is at least of secondary importance to their understanding; their primary meaning is manifested in their spiritual interpretation. "Exile" means separation from the inner root. When man denies his divine root; ignores his "point" of holiness; rejects and forces it into a remote, dark, and forgotten corner of his heart; and submits to his own wills and urges as the desires of the falsified, distorted, and imaginary human kingdom of flesh and blood—he is in exile, thrown into a pointless movement of corporeality detached from holiness. But once he abandons this external and meaningless periphery and connects all his organs, deeds, interests, and emotions to the holy "point" and allows the concealed stream of divine light to burst forth and illuminate his existence, he frees himself from the dark prison of unchanging "Nature" and merits redemption, which starts with the very existential renewal brought about within himself.

At this point there appears a very intriguing dialectical idea concerning the relation between exile and redemption. As the aspect of the "point" that is destined to be revealed, but is still trapped in the thickness of "Nature," redemption is immersed in the depth of exile and hidden in its darkness. Moreover, redemption is the inner life of exile, which exists in "Nature" only, and is a phenomenon of the concrete world, covered and wrapped up in its corporeal garments. "Nature," "exile," and corporeal darkness are all ultimately the same, all existing for the sake of the revelation of the inner "point" and the appearance of its great divine light, redeemed from its concealment. Thus, exile is the necessary precondition of redemption, and redemption is the ultimate goal of exile and its innermost cause! There is no more an opposition here between the two, but a dialectical continuity, guided by the divine will from beginning to end, from exile to redemption.[20]

It is beyond the scope of this article to offer a detailed elucidation to the question of what the path toward this crucial discovery is. But three points should not be missed:

1. The Jewish person has an innate spiritual disposition, as inherited from his ancestors, to uncover the inner "point." Since the time of the patriarchs, the Jew alone has had a substantial relation with the Divine, which he alone can uncover. The patriarchs were diggers of wells, that is, their life within "Nature" was not one of conformance, but of refusal to surrender to corporeality and its temptations, and breaking through "Nature" and digging into its thick layers, they strove within it to uncover its hidden divine wells.[21] The author of *Sefat Emet* frequently uses Kabbalistic terminology in this context and relates to the gathering of the holy sparks, lifting them up from their concealment, which, as the opposite of sacred light, signifies the shells and the powers of evil.

2. The doctrine of the "openings of holiness" within the thick walls of "Nature," windows of spiritual illumination, is of great importance in this context. God sends man (the Jewish man, of course) into the exile of "Nature" so that even in its corporeal darkness, holiness may be revealed and made known. If opaque "Nature" were only enclosed and sealed within itself, man would fumble in total darkness and would be unable to find his way to redemption. Hence God tore open within "Nature" various openings of spiritual illumination, so that even when He again closed them, some light is able to penetrate through them, showing man the path of ascent and sanctification. From now on, he is commanded to find the locked gate and open it wide. There are two such gates within "Nature," which encompass all the manifestations of holiness that are found therein: the Sabbath, which is the gate of holiness within the category of time, and the land of Israel, which is the opening of holiness within the category of space.[22] The Sabbath in *Sefat Emet* is none other than the holy time that constantly flows as the divine life beneath the external wrappings of concrete and secular time of "Nature," whereas the land of Israel, like the Sabbath in the category of time, is none other than the holy space under the physical cover of the material world of "Nature." The land of Israel is nothing else but the concrete world in its innerness.[23]

3. The third point, regarding the status of the Torah and its commandments in the redemptive process, will serve us as a necessary preface to the understanding of the relationship between the land of Canaan and the land of Israel.

By the conduct of the Torah and its commandments, man frees himself from "Nature," transcending its bonds to uncover the Divine within its innermost hidden depth, or, if you prefer, to experience the transcendental within the concrete world. One may state, as I have already mentioned, that the author of *Sefat Emet* appears in this context as interested in fortifying the traditional Orthodox values against the strengthening streams of secularism within Polish Jewry. But it is clear that this is only the external aspect of his system, which seeks the spiritualization of life, including of course the practical aspects within the framework of halakhic worship, according to the divine imperative to uncover the ever-renewing spirit and set it free from the prison of "Nature." In certain inner circles of the school of Gur, this spiritualization happened undoubtedly to appear as a true mystical experience. In the most generalized formulation, the Torah designates the world in its ideal inwardness and spiritual structure, the divine "point" within "Nature," the Sabbath, or the sacred time, which flows as divine vitality under the cover of secular time. The performance of the commandments is the willing response to the transcendental call embodied in God's will, when man is delivered from his own private wills and empties himself to allow the divine will to be realized and revealed within himself: the Kingdom of Heaven instead of the imaginary human kingdom of flesh and blood.

Because of the crucial importance of these ideas for the understanding of our subject, it is necessary to elaborate on them in a more detailed discussion.

The Torah is conceived as the divine plan, the spiritual order and the inwardness of everything created.[24] The Torah is not just a structure, but must be regarded as divine substance underlying all created worlds. The Torah is indeed the root of existence and the sustaining vitality of all creatures, but in the concrete world the Torah has been wrapped up, and its light concealed within "Nature."[25] For those who move about and conduct their life only on the external layer of "Nature" and do not endeavor to discover the light of the Torah within it, "Nature" becomes a reality of exile. The spiritual light of the Torah within "Nature" is nothing but "the power of His works" (Ps 111:6), or deeds, namely, the divine power that sustains everything, including the material world, the one known by its Kabbalistic term as *Olam ha-'Asiyyah* (literally, the world of action),[26] which is interpreted in *Sefat Emet* as the realm of concrete and bodily acts.

Man's task—as a matter of fact, the task of the Jew, who is the true human being according to an ancient tradition, which has its origin in the world of the Sages[27]—is to correct "Nature," to purify it so thoroughly, that it will not conceal the Divine anymore, and finally, as the end of the spiritual path, to bring about the negation of exile. This task imposed on the Israelite nation is defined as its spiritual mission, which is basically a mission of testimony and clarification (through distinguishing and separating), to be performed and fulfilled in "Nature" and exile: to testify that everything that exists belongs to God, originating from and sustained by His life, and to uncover and bring clearly to light the divine immanent root underlying creation,[28] even the phenomena and powers that are seemingly opposed to Him. This mission is essentially one, but it is presented as directed toward different goals, which are none but different aspects of one process, and complement each other:

Exile is destined to uplift holy sparks from all places and add converts to the scattered people of Israel.[29]

Exile is destined to enable Israel to illuminate the whole world and to spread the glory of God's name, after being cleared and separated from any cover of doubt and concealment.[30]

Exile exists only in "Nature," which constitutes the external aspect of the created world garbed in corporeality. Inwardness, on the other hand, is beyond the access of alien powers. That is precisely why Israel was sent into exile: By their inner light and divine power, they can remove the corporeal garments, overcome darkness, bring the true reality to light, and correct everything.[31]

Exile is destined for testimony, which is needed precisely where existence is distorted and falsified and the truth is concealed, whereas lies and doubts increase everywhere. In order for the testimony, which signifies the spiritual effort to spread the clarified truth of the Divine and its sustaining power and rule everywhere, to be fully affirmed, Israel had to descend to the depth of the abyss and then ascend to heaven. The correction of this world is modeled on the process of creation: first darkness and thereafter light.[32]

The worship of the holy patriarchs, who are the prototypes of Israel in exile, was to correct "Nature" by clarifying that heaven and earth belong to God, the one and only source of life for the whole world.[33] By doing so, Israel negates the enclosed and autonomous standing of "Nature," and the divided world becomes one through its close connection with God. Exile is destined to bring the revelation of holiness in all the worlds, even in the corporeal one, to which Israel were sent, in spite of and precisely because of the much higher root of their souls. This material world of concrete action (*'Asiyyah*) is characterized by a mixture of good and evil, and there should the main spiritual effort of separating and clarifying be put forth. The correction of the world will be gradually completed by drawing the Shekhinah to dwell in the material world of *'Asiyyah*.[34] Man's worship—which takes place in exile only, since only there, within "Nature," is one forced to struggle to find the hidden way of the spirit—is destined to make clear that every human deed can be performed by the vitality of God only, since every dynamic manifestation expresses the activation of the divine vitality, the only one existing: There is no other vitality whatsoever! By connecting "Nature" to the power of the Maker (*koah ha-po'el*), "Nature" can no longer conceal holiness under its thick layers.[35] By going to Haran, Jacob entered the dark and dangerous places, to find there the illuminations, and to turn night into day. Jacob corrected all places from the depth of the abyss to the height of heaven.[36]

All these ideas are very frequent in *Sefat Emet*, connected time and again to the spiritual interpretation of the Sabbath and the land of Israel. But before reaching this surprising and intriguing interpretation, one further step is to be made, to answer a question of decisive importance: How are these goals expected to be achieved? What is man really expected to do?

The answer of *Sefat Emet* is based on the distinction often made between the conduct of pure speculative Torah, on the one hand, and that of deeds and commandments, on the other. Moses—and his generation as well—embody the inner conduct as the way of Torah and pure spirit. This way is entirely directed toward the spiritual elevation of man, who turns his back to the corporeal, ignores it and detaches himself from it, so as to negate it as an existing entity. The generation of the desert, whose highest level is embodied in the admired figure of Moses, its spiritual leader, has such a close and intimate relationship with God that it merits the level of His sons. Their way is that of Torah alone, and they embody the covenant of the tongue.[37] They knew the advantage of being spiritually protected under the Clouds of Glory that dwelled upon them, and preferred the spiritual "convenience" of this divine shelter to the difficulties, temptations, struggles, and agony entailed in the dangerous adventure of entering the land, which stands for the entire material world and its obstacles.[38]

As opposed to this entirely spiritual path of the Torah, the author of *Sefat Emet* introduces before his admiring adherents a second, totally different path: the conduct of both the patriarchs and those who entered the land, which is the conduct of concrete deeds and commandments performed in the world of action as bodily acts. They are completely prepared and ready for the spiritual endeavor to be made in the harsh and severe struggle with corporeality and "Nature," which they yearn to bring to a successful, redemptive end. Their covenant is that of flesh, meaning that they strive to find the way to the Divine precisely within "Nature,"[39] and not by separating themselves from it. As reflected in the behavior and determination of Caleb and Joshua, they are eagerly prepared to enter the land and conquer it for the revelation of holiness. This is a clear allusion to the relation between "Nature" and the land of Israel before its sanctification, namely, the relation between "Nature" and the land of Canaan: The land of Canaan is nothing but the land of Israel in its externality and corporeality, or, to put it differently, in its impure cover and "shells."[40] As opposed to the Written Torah, which denotes the pure spirit of holiness per se, there stands the Oral Torah, which seeks the revelation of the divine light in the created world and in all its corporeal manifestations. This Oral Torah is performed precisely by the conquerors of the land, whose most significant feature is expressed, as already mentioned, in their struggle with the corporeal world, so as to pave the way into its inwardness, to tear openings of spiritual illumination in its thick walls, to push away its darkness by letting the divine light in, and to purify its material reality.[41] This is the ultimate goal of human existence, and that is precisely why the author of *Sefat Emet* emphatically states that the generation of the wilderness and the acceptance of the Torah, both signifying the pure spiritual reality, necessarily preceded the entrance of the land, the aspect of concrete deeds (*'uvda* in Aramaic), as the preparation for it and its precondition.[42] Were we not taught that the pure speculative study leads to the practical performance?[43] The path of the Torah as a solely spiritual entity is indeed unique to Israel, but their ultimate goal is to correct precisely the corporeal reality, to uplift it and to give its ownership to God the Creator and to themselves as His chosen emissaries, so that eventually they merit the "heritage of the nations" (Ps 111:6), which is embodied in the land of Canaan.[44] In spite of the fact that one might detect a kind of contradiction between the unique spiritual essence of Israel and their goal in the concrete world, the latter derives from this essence and has its origin within it. The land of Canaan is nothing but "Nature."[45] The spies, who represent the generation of the wilderness, were expected to understand that the concealment of the Divine within "Nature" was imaginary, to stand up against it and to overcome its darkness by the power of their faith. Had their mission ended successfully, they would have brought the light of the Torah, the aspect of Moses, to the land of Israel, and exile would have ceased to exist.[46] The "heritage of the nations" would have then belonged to God alone as the only owner and ruler of earth. This would have been the very first moment of the last and final redemption.

As deeds to be performed in this world, the commandments serve as a shield against the danger of the encounter with the land of Canaan. It is through the performance of the commandments that one can survive in the swampy mud of the corporeal, whose characteristic feature is to swallow everything up. Thus one can maintain one's holiness even within the profane—on the condition that one's intent will be directed toward God alone.[47] The author of *Sefat Emet* underlines the element of struggle, by which only can the ultimate goal be achieved and the task fulfilled. God created the powers of evil for one purpose only: to serve as a strong rival to be fought by Israel and defeated.[48] One of the basic ideas of Moses Hayyim Luzzatto is echoed here as already mentioned: Evil was not created but for the sake of its total negation.[49] It thus becomes clear, according to *Sefat Emet*, that God could have given the land to Israel from the very beginning, but He gave it first to the Canaanites, who were the human embodiment of "Nature," in order that Israel would conquer it from them by the power of their spirit.[50]

The entrance to the land of Israel was difficult. It was difficult for Israel to abandon all the spiritual merits and qualities that were theirs in the wilderness, the realm of pure spirituality. But it was the task of that generation to turn their backs to their private needs, interests, and desires, and to place themselves in God's hands, so as to fulfill His will, embodied in the spiritual mission. This mission is to be carried out in this world precisely, namely, in the land of Canaan![51] There are two ideas to be pointed at here:

1. By his very definition, an emissary has to leave his primary and original place in order to perform his mission and complete it somewhere else, out of his place—namely, according to the system of *Sefat Emet*, in the outer and external layer of existence, in the land of Canaan! For a while, at least, the emissary must give up the convenience of his familiar place, arranged according to his taste and needs, which he has to leave.[52]

2. Only by stepping out of the spiritual shelter of the desert and acting as witnesses in the concrete world will Israel contribute to the manifestation of God's rule everywhere. God's kingdom will then spread out and become known everywhere, even in the concealed recesses and the dark, curved, and distorted side alleys of creation. The difficulty of the task originates from the seemingly striking contradiction between the spirituality of the desert and the corporeality and earthiness of the land, in which too God's rule is about to appear and His holiness to be manifested. The generation of the spies was indeed ready and fully prepared for the acceptance of the Torah, but they had serious difficulties to reach the degree of the land of Israel. They were repelled and discouraged by the fact that the land was under the rule of the Canaanites, and its holiness concealed by covering shells. That is precisely why it should have been clear that the entrance to the land of Israel (by then still Canaan), signifying the drawing of the divine Torah into the garbed primeval deed of God and its revelation therein, was destined to be the correction of the whole creation.[53] This entrance is the permanent task of the Jewish nation, and by it Israel is supposed to remove the shells, bear witness to God and His all encompassing vitality, and uplift earth unto heaven. The emphatic and repeated spiritual struggle entails the idea of faith: The land of Israel is presented as the aspect of faith and as the realm of its realization, since only by means of its strength can the true believer pave the path to the hidden divine truth within the darkness of "Nature," break through its barriers and reach the sacred inwardness. Faith is nothing but the intense and never ceasing attachment to the truth, which is still concealed and unknown; faith is thus man's path toward truth, and by its strength, or when strengthened by it, he is able to overcome all doubts and lies of corporeality. The correction achieved by faith is highly appreciated as the most elevated degree of worship, since it involves, of course, the element of struggle.[54] Precisely because of the fact, that in its external reality the land of

Israel—in fact, the land of Canaan—devours its inhabitants, were the spies expected to understand that the praise of the land and its glory were not recognizable from the outside, but the root of the whole creation was, and is, as an Archimedean point, hidden in its depth.[55] Is there not a kind of cognitive dissonance, which is so typical of the path of the spirit, to be traced here? The wicked Canaanites waged wars against Israel, to whose acts to sanctify "Nature" they were strongly opposed. But the Israelites were equipped with the "power of His acts" (Ps 111:6), that is to say, the aspect of the Torah as embodied in concrete and bodily acts, the commandments, and by performing them they were able to overcome "Nature" and the impurity of its wicked inhabitants, the Canaanites.[56]

And there is another aspect of the entrance to the land of Israel, which the author of *Sefat Emet* depicts as an act of extracting all the holy sparks from all the places to bring them together in the land of Israel.[57] This "togetherness" is the necessary outcome of their essence, since one of the most important features of holiness is that of its fertile and blessed unity, whereas impurity is characterized by its division, meaning both divided and dividing, its controversies and endless quarrels and barren fights. In a way, one may interpret this idea as connecting all lands together in their focal point, turning them all into one, the holy land of Israel. It is in this context that the land of Israel is repeatedly described as including all other lands: the entirety of them all and their root.[58] The extracted and purified sparks, whose purification lies in and derives from the fact that they are no more concealed and separated from each other, were not robbed or plundered by the Israeli nation. On the contrary, the new situation of the sparks signifies their restoration to their pure origin, bringing them to life, so to speak, again, or "opening" them as wells of flowing divine life, after they were garbed, hidden, scattered, and buried within "Nature."[59] In its deep meaning, the process described is the process of sanctification, which gradually comes into being by turning the impure land of Canaan into the holy land of Israel.[60] It thus becomes clear that only when the people of Israel enter their land, which as the aspect of holy acts and bodily worship, based on true effort and deep devotion, is more favored than the manna, the heavenly bread given by divine grace only,[61] only then is the inner form of the land fully completed and corrected.[62] The land of Israel is the spiritual center of the whole world. It signifies the possibility given to man to attach himself to the Divine, or, to put it differently, to live a spiritual life even and precisely in this corporeal world,[63] until this world too will be redeemed and elevated to holiness. The author of *Sefat Emet* clearly distinguishes between the two aspects of the land: According to the act of creation, wrapped up in the garments of "Nature," which is the law of the concrete world, the land was given to the Canaanites, but according to the Torah, which is the transcendental law of the spiritual world, the land has belonged to Israel ever since. In the framework of this spiritualized interpretation, one might add that the whole world belongs to Israel, since both in its entirety and in all of its individual details it was created by the power of the Torah, which is unique to them! The true entrance of Israel into their spiritual homeland is possible only by this power of the Torah, observed and practiced, whereas its neglect necessarily results in their expulsion, and the exiled nation is scattered in other lands, lands of matter and impurity.[64] In the beginning everything was spiritual, like Adam's garments of light and the status of Israel after crossing the sea and at Mount Sinai, but after the recurrent primordial fall there will be no recovery and redemption unless man is entirely engaged in the correction of corporeal deeds, or, if one prefers, in drawing the illuminating, purifying, and healing holiness into those deeds by connecting them to the "point," the inner source of divine energy.[65] Based on what has been explained at length in this article, we may also add: There will be no redemption unless Israel enters the land by the power of the commandments, turning the "heritage of the nations" into the sacred land of God and His people, the sanctified land. This land is the foretaste of the world to come. It transcends all other places and enables its true inhabitants to enter the gates of the world to come.[66] God showed His people the power of His creative deeds, which is garbed in "Nature." This frequently used verse means, according to the system discussed, that He taught them the way and imposed on them the spiritual imperative to open wide the locked gates of holiness, break through exile, and find the hidden land of Israel within it.

In my final conclusions, some of the ideas will be repeated in a slightly different way, while others will be presented in a new light with additional references.

Many of the notions depicted and discussed in this article have their homiletical origin in the famous verse of Psalms 111:6, already cited partially several times in the article.[67] The verse is frequently quoted together with some additional well-known homilies (like *Gen. Rab.* 1:2) by the Sages (used also in Rashi's commentary, which served as an important source of *Sefat Emet*). *Nahalat Goyim*, the land of all other nations, was destined, according to God's ideal plan and from the very beginning of creation, to be given to Israel. As the territories of those sunk in matter and its earthy lusts, the worldly nations, who do not know the path of holiness and will not merit the new order of redemption, "the heritage of the nations" signifies unredeemed "Nature," into which Israel was sent with the crucial task to sanctify it.

According to the doctrine of openings of holiness, one may state that every place in which holiness is revealed, and whose gates are open, is the land of Israel. And since holiness is meant to be revealed everywhere, and everywhere should its gates be opened, every place in the world, and each territory or "heritage" of the Gentiles, is the land of Israel. In this interpretation, the land of Israel is removed from its concrete and historical-geographical significance and given a new meaning as the possibility to live a spiritual life and worship God everywhere. Moreover, since holiness is meant to be revealed in the place of its concealment, as explained before, it is clear that only by the worship in exile can the land of Israel be revealed and made known.[68] Thus, the author of *Sefat Emet* says that the main merit of Israel is specifically in exile, and it is precisely there that their elevated quality as the witnesses and revealers of holiness is manifested.[69] Bearing this spiritualizing tendency in mind, the land of Israel is considered as the dwelling place of the blessings of holiness only in its inner sense,[70] while in the aspect of its external, concrete reality, it is in fact a land that devours its inhabitants,[71] and this is precisely what the spies failed to understand! The land of Israel is a unique and specially chosen place, the root of the whole world,[72] and it is often referred to as the "aspect of the world to come,"[73] which being concealed in the depth of this world, allows man to adhere to its spiritual or rather divine dimension even within the concrete reality, and in spite of all the temptations of "Nature." The uniqueness of the land of Israel means that it connects and ties together all other places, being the source of their divine abundance (the same applies, of course, to the Sabbath among all different times) and of holiness expanding "to all sides,"[74] including the remote, distorted, and dark "sides" of "Nature." The land of Israel is indeed God's chosen place, but as long as its holiness is not actualized but hidden and concealed within the thickness of its carnality, it is considered as the land of exile. The first name of the land, Canaan, alludes to the Aramaic ʿachna (almost the same letters), meaning the cursed snake[75] and the shells surrounding "Nature." The author adds that Canaan has to do with trade and goods that are imported from far away, meaning that being spiritually the most remote area in God's kingdom, Canaan precisely was destined to become the place of revelation, or the appearance of the illuminating holiness from far away, the depth of its "Nature."[76] The Canaanites never saw or experienced the true aspect of the land of Israel, the "inner land," which descended from heaven only when Israel entered the land and by their efforts transformed it.[77] The question of the land of Israel being originally the land of Canaan is raised again in another homily, and the answer is a daring and even a provocative one: It was the way of the Canaanites, who were traders, to show the defective and spoiled goods first![78] When first seen by the Canaanites—or even by the Jewish people—in its externality, in its aspect of "Nature," the land of Israel is defective, in spite of all the achievements of its civilization, and should be referred to as "waste," and only in its innerness, which can be seen, experienced, and manifested only by the people of Israel, is it holy! Their entering the land signifies the "correction of creation,"[79] separating good from evil and freeing the land from the Canaanites to become the dwelling place of God and His property,[80] instead of "the heritage of the nations" or the impure Gentiles. We have to conclude that, according to the very law of existence— both on the metaphysical plane and the human one—the land of Israel had to be Canaan's first, and only thereafter was destined to become God's holy territory, His recognized dwelling place and the embodiment of His absolute rule.[81] The origin of this surprising notion is to be found in the doctrine of evil developed by the Zohar, which points to a clear parallelism between the land of Israel and Bathsheba, one of the many symbols of the Shekhinah, who was necessarily Uriyyah the Hittite's wife first, and only thereafter could become David's spouse.[82] Is it not clear from these notions that the people of Israel must not behave like the Canaanites (signifying all the nations of the world), who try to build in the holy land with bricks and concrete as their main path?[83] Should one not see in these formulations the immanent ideological basis for the opposition of Gur Hasidism to the Zionist enterprise? Years ago I was told by one of the prominent figures in the court of Gur that he preferred the search of the true land of Israel in exile, where precisely it can be looked for and found, rather than bringing exile to the land of Israel, walking there in the footsteps of the Canaanites. Is not this attitude the direct outcome of the spiritual doctrines presented here?

Notes

1. On Hasidism in general, referred to here as a mystical system of thought, see G. Scholem, "Hasidism, The Latest Phase," in *Major Trends in Jewish Mysticism* (New York: Schocken Books, 1961), 325–350; I. Tishby, with J. Dan, "Hasidism" [in Hebrew], in *Encyclopaedia Hebraica*, 17 (Jerusalem and Tel Aviv: Encyclopaedia Publishing Company, 1965), 769–821; J. Weiss, "The Beginnings of the Hasidic Path" [in Hebrew], *Zion* 16 (1951), 46–105; R. Schatz Uffenheimer, *Hasidism as Mysticism* [in Hebrew] (Jerusalem: Magnes Press, 1968) (English translation by J. Chipman, Jerusalem: Princeton University Press / Magnes Press, 1993); Y. Jacobson, *Hasidic Thought* [in Hebrew] (Tel Aviv: Mod Books, 1985) (English translation, Tel Aviv: Mod Books, 1998); M. Idel, *Hasidism between Ecstasy and Magic* (New York: State University of New York Press, 1995) (Hebrew translation, Tel Aviv: Schocken Publishing House, 2000); R. Margolin, *The Human Temple* [in Hebrew] (Jerusalem: Magness Press, 2005); Ts. Kauffman, *In All Your Ways Know Him* [in Hebrew] (Jerusalem: Bar-Ilan University Press, 2009).

2. On Gora Kalwaria, see E. Bergman, "Gora Kalwaria: The Jewish Community and the Court of the Rebbe of Gur from the Beginning of the 19th Century to 1939" [in Hebrew], in *Hasidism in Poland*, ed. I. Bartal, R. Elior, and C. Shmeruk (Jerusalem: Bialik Institute, 1994), 111–117.

3. On the Hasidic school of Gur in Warsaw, see, for example, B. Levin, "Gur Hasidism Infiltrates into Warsaw" [in Hebrew], in *Encyclopaedia of the Jewish Diaspora, Poland Series, Warsaw*, vol. 2, ed. I. Gruenbaum (Tel Aviv: Encyclopaedia of the Jewish Diaspora, 1959), 219–228. See also N. Zohar, "'Agudath Israel' in Warsaw" [in Hebrew], *Encyclopaedia of the Jewish Diaspora*, 227–280.

4. On his life and spiritual world, see I. Alfasi, *Gur: The Founder, the Author of Hidushey haRim* [in Hebrew] (Tel Aviv: Sinai Publishing House, 1954). The second edition of this book (Tel Aviv 1978) is entirely identical to the first. However, it was published under a different title (*Gur: The History of Gur Hasidism*) due to an additional chapter on the following leaders of the dynasty, 203–222.

5. See, for example, A. Z. Aescoly, "Hasidism in Poland" [in Hebrew], in *Beit Yisrael bePolin*, ed. I. Halperin (Jerusalem: Youth Department of the Zionist Organisation, 1953), 2:125–128, 139–140.

6. On the first three prominent rebbes of Gur and their characterization according to their attitude toward the Hasidic leadership both in theory and in its actualization, see M. Piekarz, *The Hasidic Leadership* [in Hebrew], (Jerusalem: Bialik Institute, 1999), 288–292.

7. On his personal and spiritual development, see Y. Jacobson, "From Youth to Leadership and from Kabbalah to Hasidism: Stages of the Spiritual Development of the Author of *Sefat Emet*" [in Hebrew], in *R. Shatz-Uffenheimer Memorial Volume*, ed. R. Elior and J. Dan (Jerusalem: Jerusalem Studies in Jewish Thought, 1996), 2:429–446.

8. A selection of translated and interpreted homilies from *Sefat Emet*, including an introduction, was published by A. Green under the title: *The Language of Truth* (Philadelphia: Jewish Publication Society, 1998). A. Green dedicated part of his paper, "Three Warsaw Mystics," published in *R. Shatz-Uffenheimer Memorial Volume*, 6–21, to *Sefat Emet*. Two other interpreted selections from *Sefat Emet* were published by M. Shapira under the title: *Peiney Sefat Emet* [in Hebrew] (Ofrah: Shuva Institute, 2004–2005 [the year is mentioned only in two out of six volumes]) both in thematic order and according to the weekly portions of the Torah and some festivals. Another two-volume selection of *Sefat Emet* studies—also according to the weekly portions of the Torah—was recently published by S. Rosenberg under the title *Tikkon La'ad* [in Hebrew] (Alon Shevut: Yeshivat Har Etzion Publications, 2008).

9. See his paper: "'The Inner Point' of the Admorim of Gur and Alexander as a Reflection of their Ability to Adjust to Changing Times" [in Hebrew], in *Studies in Jewish Mysticism, Philosophy and Ethical Literature Presented to I. Tishby*, ed. J. Dan and J. Hacker (Jerusalem: Magnes Press, 1986), 636–637. He states that there are indeed no signs of concrete events, developments and processes of the period in *Sefat Emet* but maintains that its homilies testify indirectly to the social-spiritual reality of the period. The same formulation appears again in his later book *Ideological Trends of Hasidism in Poland during the Interwar Period and the Holocaust* [in Hebrew] (Jerusalem: Bialik Institute, 1990), 136–137. Piekarz claims that, in contrast to the trend of interiorization and spiritualization, which characterizes the early founders of Hasidism, the interest of the leaders of Gur is basically directed toward religious and social conservatism and the need to strengthen the Hasidic way of life (see his above mentioned paper, 629). Unfortunately, I cannot accept Piekarz's attitude, and *Sefat Emet* will be introduced below as a profound mystical system.

10. On the radical spirituality of early Hasidic sources, compared to the profound but moderate one in the doctrines of Gur, see J. Weiss, "Some Notes on the Social Background of Early Hasidism," in *Studies in East European Jewish Mysticism and Hasidism* (London: Littman Library of Jewish Civilization, 1997), 10–14; J. Weiss, "Torah Study in Early Hasidism," *Jewish Mysticism and Hasidism*, 56–68; J. Weiss, "The Beginnings of the Hasidic Path"; M. Piekarz, *The Beginning of Hasidism* [in Hebrew] (Jerusalem: Bialik Institute, 1978), 175–302; R. Shatz Uffenheimer, *Hasidism as Mysticism*, 41–77, 147–156; Ts. Kauffman, *In All Your Ways Know Him*, 523–571.

11. Y. Jacobson, "Exile and Redemption in Gur Hasidism" [in Hebrew], *Daat* 2–3 (1978–1979): 176–178. See also M. Piekarz's detailed discussion of the "inner point" in the schools of Gur and Alexander, "'The Inner Point,'" 617–660.

12. On "Nature" (Heb. "Tev'a"), which must be referred to as basically identical with the Habadic "Yesh" (literally, "Being"), see Y. Jacobson, "Exile and Redemption," 178–190. See also

the detailed discussion by Y. Jacobson, "Primordial Chaos and Creation in Gur Hasidism: The Sabbath That Preceded Creation," *Polin* 15 (2002): 221–240. Both "Nature" in the doctrine of Gur and "Being" in the system of Habad undergo the same dialectical change: They were both brought into existence in order to be eventually negated. The idea echoes one of Moses Hayyim Luzzatto's most significant notions concerning the power of evil, which was not created but to be nullified. See Y. Jacobson, "The Doctrine of Creation in the Thought of R. Shneour Zalman of Liadi" [in Hebrew], *Eshel Beer-Sheva* 1 (1976): esp. 359–361; Y. Jacobson, "Moses Hayyim Luzzatto's Doctrine of Divine Guidance and Its Relation to his Kabbalistic Teachings" [in Hebrew], *Italia Judaica* 3 (Tel Aviv–Rome, 1989): 30–35. On the origin of both the term "Nature" and the imperative of its negation in the writings of the Maharal of Prague, see my "Exile and Redemption," 180–181, n. 35. Numerous discussions on "Nature," matter, and corporeality are included in my paper: "The Order of Holiness and the Holiness of Order according to the Maharal of Prague" [in Hebrew] (in press).

13. "There is nothing new under the sun" (Eccl 1:9) of "Nature." See, for example, *Sefat Emet* (5 vols.), Jerusalem 1971 (later referred to as SE), vol. 1, Hanukkah, 100a–b. On the Hasidic imperative of constant spiritual renewal, see Y. Jacobson, *Hasidic Thought*, 81–88 (English translation, 107–117).

14. See Y. Jacobson, "Exile and Redemption," 189, 194–195. See also SE2, Shemot, 2b; Bo, 23b, 24a; Yitro, 49a; SE1, Hanukkah, 106a; Vayetze, 63b; and many more. The additional illumination is an idea already well-known in earlier Hasidic sources, especially in their discussions of the struggle with alien thoughts and its advantage. See, for example, Dov Baer of Meseritz, *Maggid Devarav Le-Ya'akov*, R. Schatz-Uffenheimer's critical edition (Jerusalem: Magnes Press, 1976), #50, p. 72; #167, p. 265.

15. On the proximity of the "point" and the divine kingdom or rather their identity, see my "Exile and Redemption," 184ff.

16. SE4, Shelah, 43b–44a, 53a. In another homily the author speaks about the destructive meaning of private wills. Man reaches his spiritual peace by negating himself as a private entity and dedicating all his powers to God and His worship alone. When doing this he has only one will, whereas in "Nature" a person's wills contradict each other. He who acts according to private interests might be captured by things that are against his own will. He will then be torn between contradicting wills, and peace will not reside in his soul. But he whose will is God's will only, has one encompassing will for everything, one will that directs him in all his acts. This is the meaning of true peace (SE1, Toledot, 52b, 52a).

17. Striving for the manifestation and realization of the divine truth both in the world as a whole and within his soul, man is requested to choose the negation of his seemingly free choice, which is illusive and not his, but essentially God's. Man's free choice is just a falsified and falsifying figment of imagination which conceals the one and only truth, that all human wills, reflected in one's choice, have their origin in God's vitality (SE2, Bo, 24a). All of man's chosen acts, tricks, and tactics are derived from the Creator's will, which is their inner source of power. And when man deciphers this secret, he will not anymore stand up and claim foolishly: "By the strength of my hand I have done" (Isa. 10:13). He then reaches the deep understanding, that God let the "other" wills and evil urges arouse within man's heart for one purpose only: to negate them (SE2, Bo, 32a). Free choice is man's path in the fallen and distorted world only, whereas in the pure beginning he had no choice whatsoever. See Y. Jacobson, "The Sanctity of the Profane in Gur Hasidism, Studies in the Concept of the Sabbath in *Sefat Emet*" [in Hebrew], in *Hasidism in Poland*, 274–275.

18. See above, n. 12.

19. As long as the world is disconnected from its inner root, the source of ever-flowing life, it will not have lasting offspring. As the keeper of the covenant, Noah the righteous is the best example for this frequently repeated idea (SE1, Noah, 11b).

20. Exile and redemption are of course the main subject of my "Exile and Redemption." Concerning "Nature" as a prison or a house of imprisoned slaves, see SE2, Yitro, 53b: It is true that God sustains everything. But this divine sustenance entails a process of separation: Separate powers, which have their origin in the Divine (and thus called "Elohim Aherim"), spread out to give life even to the heretics. "Nature" exists only by virtue of the Divine, which is immersed and sunk within it, sustaining each of its phenomena according to its contracted measure and unique form. This is the conduct of "the house of bondage" (Exod 13:3), since everything which is not in its place and is disconnected from its root should be referred to as an imprisoned slave, whereas true freedom is the attachment to the root.

As for the dialectical relationship between exile and redemption see, for example, SE1, Vayigash, 125a: "The root of exile is redemption, and exile cannot exist but by the power of redemption. Thus redemption is the vitality of exile." For the true believer "exile is a sign of redemption," and the harsher and more bitter exile is, the more it is a sign for the great redemption soon to come (SE2, Shemot, 4b, and see also SE1, Toledot, 58b). The descent of exile is for the sake of the redemptive rise (SE2, Shemot, 6a; Vaera, 19a). Exile is a preparation for redemption that follows (SE2, Shemot, 5b; SE4, Bemidbar, 8b).

21. The digging of the well signifies the intense endeavor, which involves struggles and wars against the disturbing powers of evil, which are active in "Nature" only, to find the Torah light concealed below, as opposed to the drawing of the Torah from above (SE4, Hukkat, 71b). On the patriarchs as diggers of wells, see SE1, Toledot, 53a, 57b. The patriarchs are the model and inner structure of their whole nation; see Y. Jacobson, "Exile and Redemption," 198. The inner point of Israel is the heritage implanted within them by their holy ancestors, and it will never fade away (SE3, Pesah, 51a). This emphatically repeated notion of Gur undoubtedly parallels the highly developed theory of Habad concerning the holy spark as the center of the "Divine Soul." See Y. Jacobson, "The Rectification of the Heart: Studies in the Psychic Teachings of R. Shneur Zalman of Liadi" [in Hebrew], in *Teudah* 10, Studies in Judaica, ed. M. A. Friedman (Tel Aviv: Tel Aviv University, Ramot Publishing, 1996), 365–381.

22. Time and space, שנה ועולם, according to the terminology of the "Book of Creation" (3:5–8), are presented as the two dimensions of matter and "Nature."

23. On this significant—I would rather say central—doctrine in *Sefat Emet*, see my comprehensive discussion in "Exile and Redemption," 203–208. The author speaks time and again—in the wake of the triple structure in the "Book of Creation"—about three openings: of time, space, and soul, which were given to Israel to open them wide. See, for example, SE1, Lekh Lekha, 29b. On the Sabbath, see Y. Jacobson, "The Sanctity of the Profane," 241–277; Y. Jacobson, "Primordial Chaos," 221–240.

24. SE4, Bemidbar, 7b. In the following lines, the author of *Sefat Emet* states that as the inwardness of the world, the Torah is unique to Israel represented by Moses, whereas the angels embody the aspect of external reality. As opposed to Moses there are the patriarchs: Being the Chariot or its carriers (*Gen. Rab.* 82:6), just as the angels, they acted on the external plane of existence and corrected it before the Torah was given as a pure spiritual entity. On this significant subject see below.

25. SE4, Bemidbar, 1b–2a. The Torah is the divine vitality within everything, and by its power the world was created. But this act of creation, by its very definition, involves the wrapping up of the sacred light and its concealment within "Nature," which is like the cover of a

garment or a name (since the name is not identical with the essence and serves only as its partial manifestation). That is why the author depicts creation as the name of the Torah. Since the name, as a name (Heb. *shem*), signifies the spreading of one's fame to far-lying districts, the study of Torah *lishmah* (namely, for its own sake, but literally, for its name) means the extending of the light of the Torah within the far-distanced territories of God, that is to say, in "Nature," which appears in this interpretation as God's name!

26. Contrary to Scholem's translation, *Major Trends*, 272.

27. See Yebamoth 61a, 103b; Sabbath 146a. The Kabbalah developed this notion along its historical path, but this lies beyond the scope of our discussion. The Hasidic world fully accepted this notion, although it did not have as much interest in historiosophical questions as the Kabbalah had.

28. This mission in all its complexity is discussed and interpreted at length in my "Exile and Redemption," 190–202. The basic assumption in this context is, that according to their very essence, the people of Israel belong to a spiritual or rather divine homeland, from which they came down to earth, but there is a split between their soul as a divine "portion" (Deut. 32:9) always attached to God, and their body, which as a created entity is under the rule of "Nature." One may also put it differently: There is a clear distinction between the divine aspect of their existence as embodied in the soul, and their bodily appearance on the stage of "Natural" history. This split is the necessary outcome of their mission. See SE4, Bemidbar, 3a. The significance of the missionary historical appearance is none but one: the existence of exile. As the embodiment of the divine will, the cosmic history takes place in "Nature" and becomes a history of exile, entailing only secretly the redemptive process.

29. SE2, Shemot, 5a.

30. SE2, Shemot, 6a. The mission in exile is presented at the end of the homily as a precondition for the acceptance of the Torah. The clarification of the glory of God's name signifies the establishing of the divine kingdom.

31. SE2, Shemot, 6b. In the following lines the author relates to the task of Israel to open the locked gates—the unique openings known to them alone. By fulfilling the request of Cant. 5:2 ("open to me") Israel merits the status of God's sister and beloved wife (including undoubtedly Kabbalistic allusions underlying the text).

32. SE2, Vaera, 18a; see also SE2, Bo, 26a. By the comprehensive testimony it will become evident that God is above and below, and there is none else beside Him. The same course is reflected in history: First Israel had to be under the enslavement and oppression of Pharaoh, and only then could they become God's worshippers. We shall encounter the same phases in the fate of the land of Israel.

33. SE2, Vaera, 15b.

34. SE2, Terumah, 72b, 73b.

35. SE1, Bereshit, 3a. The Hebrew term *Ma'aseh Bereshit*, meaning the act of creation, but literally "the act of the beginning," alludes to the fact that the power of the "beginning," which is frequently identified with the Torah, the Archimedean point of existence, dwells in every act and enables its occurrence. This power of the "beginning" is identical with "the power of His acts," God's power immersed in the concrete and corporeal world, which we shall encounter below.

36. SE1, Vayishlah, 71a, 75a.

37. Whereas the patriarchs were engaged in correcting the external layers of existence, the elevated rank of Moses found its expression in the inner conduct, in which no connection

with the concrete is sought, the path of the Torah as a pure spiritual entity (SE4, Bemidbar, 7b). The author of *Sefat Emet* repeatedly points in this context at the distinction between the manna, the heavenly bread, which like the Torah belongs to the purely spiritual realm, and the bread which is brought forth out of the land. The former embodies the generation of the wilderness whose deepest desire is to be totally detached from the concrete world, whereas the latter signifies those who entered the land of Israel. Since they abandoned their high spiritual level and descended to fulfill their mission and sanctify the land, they were given the possibility to elevate themselves again by the heave offering (SE4, Shelah, 47a). They were ready for the struggles and wars of their mission, whereas the generation that accepted the Torah, characterized by its comprehensive and profound metaphysical wisdom ("Dor De'ah"), is considered as the sons of the Lord (SE4, Shelah, 49a) who would apparently stay with their heavenly father. The distinction between the two is also reflected in Proverbs 6:23: While the generation of the wilderness embodies the Torah as a great and steady light, those who entered the land are symbolized by the commandment as a small flickering candle (SE4, Shelah, 49b, and see below). On the generation of the desert as the keepers of the covenant of the tongue, which signifies the correction of the soul, see SE4, Pinhas, 89a, 89b, 90a, etc. There is also another distinction that should be underlined: The generation of the desert drew the Torah from heaven to earth, while the conquerors of the land were engaged in uplifting earth to heaven (SE4, Shelah, 50a; see also SE4, Pinhas, 86b–87a, where the author adds that the former embodies the aspect of "we will hear" (Exod 24:7), whereas the latter signifies the aspect of "we will do": Hearing means the acceptance from the upper worlds, and doing signifies the readiness to act for the elevation of "Nature"). In the last referred to homily the author of *Sefat Emet* quite exceptionally connects these ideas to the concepts of "Being" and "Nothing": God created "Nature" as Being from Nothing, and man is commanded to negate Being and return it to Nothing (not on the ontological plane, of course, but on the religious-ethical one) by his arousal, directing his spiritual energy upward and pulling with himself the world that is below (SE4, Pinhas, 86b–87a. He attributes this dialectical move to "the wise," who probably allude to the writings of Habad, or even to earlier Hasidic thinkers. See also SE3, Behar, 98a; SE5, Rosh Hashanah, 76b. In this exciting homily the author states that creation of Being from Nothing is the contraction of the Divine within "Nature," under whose corporeal layers it is covered and dressed. This means that before creation no limited Being, confined within its borders, existed, and there was nothing but the Divine, whose glory filled everything, or, to put it differently, there was nothing but the Nothing. Being came into existence by the contraction of the divine light. The gradual expansion of the created entities involved and caused the appearance of death, since any descent of worlds should be regarded as death (as frequently mentioned in the Lurianic writings of Hayyim Vital): The contraction of the Divine signifies the limitation and reducing of life, and the appearance of death is its inevitable result. The creation of man as the latest and most important phase of God's creative act was destined for the opposite move of redrawing life from the divine origin. Presented as a "vessel" for returning the stream of life to the created and gradually "dying" worlds, man gave names to the created entities, and thus reconnected them to their root and brought them back to life. Concerning the famous declaration of Israel—"we will do and hear"—see SE3, Aharey Mot, 74a; SE2, Yitro, 48a, where another interpretation is introduced). The entirely spiritual essence of the generation of the wilderness becomes clear, beyond any doubt, according to these discussions, and many more. The formulation of uplifting earth and connecting it to heaven is repeated in many homilies. See, for example, SE3, Behar, 100b; SE4, Shelah, 50a; SE5, Haazinu, 89a.

38. Being always attached to the upper divine root (each one to his) and protected under the Clouds of Glory (see Rosh Hashanah, 3a), and all their acts performed "at the commandment of the Lord" (as quoted from Num. 9:18), the generation of the wilderness had difficulties in abandoning its "Sabbatical" level (SE4, Shelah, 47b; see also Y. Jacobson, "Exile and Redemption," 211–212) as opposed to workdays awaiting them in the land of Israel. The approach of the author of *Sefat Emet* toward the spies who represent the generation of the desert is sometimes very critical. Instead of a mission entirely dedicated to the fulfillment of God's will, intending to perform the commandments for Heaven's sake only and not as an expression of their own needs, too, they failed by letting their private wills and interests participate in their acts. They considered their self-correction as an important part of their path and did not negate themselves so as to totally obey God's word and carry out His command (SE4, Shelah, 53a). They were confused by the law of "Nature," according to which the time of entering the land had not yet come. Had they been fully attached to the inwardness and drawn by the unnatural conduct, or by the divine upper one, they would have been beyond any hesitation and would have entered the land by the power of the Torah, which is above "Nature," and is the divine law of corporeal reality (SE4, Shelah, 55b, 48a). According to another homily, their disastrous failure lies in the fact that they relied upon themselves, having the intention to conquer the land by their own power. They did not understand that the war of Canaan could not be waged by man's power, but by negating man's knowledge to God's will as the only guiding power of existence (SE4, Shelah, 51a. The homily points at Adam's sin as a parallel situation and considers it as the model of the sins of prominent figures). Only by such a decisive step, and as its result, can the divine power be activated to flow into the self-emptied human entity. The full analysis of the story of the spies lies beyond the scope of this article, and I intend to dedicate an elaborate discussion to this subject in the future.

39. Keeping the covenant is a prerequisite for winning the land, since by its very essence the covenant signifies the connection to the Divine, whose manifestation and activation are Israel's only way to gain the land. As opposed to the purely spiritual covenant of the tongue, the covenant of the flesh requires much more devotion and spiritual power, since it is carried out in the place of the foreskin, that is to say—in "Nature" and its covers (SE4, Pinhas, 89a). The distinction between the two covenants is the distinction between the correction of the soul by the Torah and the correction of the body by the commandments. Through circumcision, the covenant of the flesh, the body receives holiness. It becomes then clear that the body of a Jewish person has also a share in holiness. The covenant of the flesh draws illumination from the commandments to the bodily garment (SE4, Pinhas, 90a. See also SE3, Kedoshim, 82a–b).

40. The identity of the land of Canaan and "Nature" reappears time and again in many homilies. See, for example, SE4, Shelah, 44a. In this passage the author interprets the mission imposed on the spies to search (Heb. *veyaturu*) the land of Canaan (Num. 13:2) as an allusion to their task to draw the Torah (a pun on *veyaturu*) into "Nature." As long as the land was under the rule of Canaan, the shell was concealing its holiness, and the spies could not see its spiritual illuminating quality (SE4, Shelah, 48b).

41. The relationship between the Written Torah and the Oral one is marked by a kind of contradiction between the two, but at the same time they complement each other. The Oral Torah is nothing but the extension of the Written Torah into "Nature" so as to sanctify it by the commandments. In other words, by means of its oral aspect precisely, the Torah paves the way of correcting "Nature." As candles (Prov. 6:23) or vessels containing the light of the

Torah, the commandments are considered as a precondition for the bursting forth of the light and its steady appearance. Thus, by their obedient performance is the concrete attached to the Torah as the inwardness of the created world. Corresponding numerically to the organs of the human body, forming its inner structure, and being the expanding radiations of the Torah, the commandments enable the drawing of the light of the Torah into all human acts and activities. This is the true meaning of the Oral Torah: By the performance of its commandments it becomes clear that all creatures are none but vessels that are uniquely destined to hold the inner divine vitality that is within them and to uplift everything to its root (SE4, Behaalotekha, 34b–35a). The author of *Sefat Emet* distinguishes between the purely spiritual essence ("body") of the Torah, which is the Divine indeed, and the commandments, which are the emissaries for its manifestation in the concrete world (SE4, Shelah, 49b. As for the identity between the Holy One Blessed Be He and the Torah referred to in the text, see I. Tishby, *The Wisdom of the Zohar* [in Hebrew] (Jerusalem: Bialik Institute, 1961), 2:372; I. Tishby, *Studies in Kabbalah and Its Branches* [in Hebrew] (Jerusalem: Magnes Press, 1993), 3:941–960. See also *Zohar*, 2, 60a–b). The commandments are the aspect of the Torah as reflected and embodied in the concrete world (SE4, Hukkat, 71b). As opposed to the soul of the Torah, they embody its practical aspect by which the power of the Torah is drawn into all corporeal deeds in order to sanctify and correct them (SE5, Sukkot, 100a). By this expanding power of the Torah will the land of the Canaanites be conquered and elevated above "Nature." The conquest of the land by the commandments is the correction of corporeal deeds turned into divine commandments and attached to their root (SE5, Ekev, 22a), a decisive change that involves a lot of efforts to overcome the corporeal obstacles that block the path of man's worship. In that moment the corporeal will be subjugated to the sacred. Bearing in mind that the whole world is full of commandments, since God created everything for the sake of His honor (according to the well-known and frequently used statement of the Mishnah in *Abot* 6:11), which by its very essence vehemently seeks its expansion, it becomes clear that man's task is to perform the commandments all the time, everywhere and in everything. The light will then be manifested in the entire world, even in the lowest and most remote and forgotten districts of God's kingdom (which are symbolized by the heel [Heb. *'akev*] of the human body), His supreme honor known, and the final redemption achieved as the complete expansion of the divine light everywhere (SE5, Ekev, 25a). According to a very intriguing distinction, the Written Torah was brought down from its heavenly origin by Moses, whereas the Oral Torah as its commentary was intended specifically for the conquest of the land and the correction of "Nature." What does a commentary mean? The striking idea identifies the interpretation of the Torah with its expansion (the homiletically double meaning of the Heb. *mitpareshet*) in "Nature," and the flow of streams of life from the divine well to increase the blessing of holiness (SE5, Devarim, 5b). As the basic text of the Oral Torah, the Mishnah is referred to as the commentary on the Torah and its garbed extended appearance (SE5, Devarim, 6b–7a).

42. See SE4, Shelah, 50a; SE4, Balak, 79a: The generation of the wilderness was able to correct "Nature" only by entirely abandoning it first in order to enter the land afterward and rectify "Nature," thus elevating itself to the spiritual peak of its destination (*Yihud Shalem*, the complete and total unity in all its aspects). This explains the distinction between the two names of Jacob and Israel as embodying the two necessary phases: Fighting with Laban and Esau, Jacob signifies the correction of "Nature," whereas Israel points to the purely spiritual level unique to God's people. This distinction frequently appears in many Hasidic homiletical texts, especially the reference to the name Israel as *li rosh* (literally, mine is the head, or

I have reached the head), expressing a change in the order of the characters and meaning the achievement of the highest spiritual level.

43. *Qidd.* 40b, *Meg.* 27a.

44. SE4, Shavuot, 21b, and especially SE1, Vayeshev, 87b: The Torah was originally given to Israel for the sake of the innermost spiritual worship, like that of the ministering angels, but there was also "Nature" awaiting its redemptive process to be performed by Israel, that is to say, to gather and uplift all the holy sparks, or, as frequently formulated, to open the gates of inwardness and find the way to the hidden world to come (SE5, Ki Tetze, 47b), separate good from evil, connect all things to their root in holiness and bring them closer to each other (SE5, Ekev, 20b. All these are divergent aspects of one process: The separation of good from evil signifies its reconnection to the source of all things, the sacred meeting point where peace resides; only purified entities can adhere to the divine root, which is beyond the touch of evil, dross, and corporeal powers). Another formulation points at man's task to clarify the comprehensive and irresistible power of God's rule and to return everything to the root of unity, which is often depicted as the pure "Beginning" (SE2, Vaera, 18b; SE4, Balak, 80b), concealed within "Nature" and to be delivered free by Israel (SE3, Pesah, 41b). Israel's task is to separate and remove the waste of the "Beginning" so as to cause chaos (Heb. *tohu*), which as a mixture of good and evil does not enable any constructive and productive form of life to develop, to gradually fade away and disappear (SE3, Pesah, 45b; the homily refers to the phonetic proximity between the Hebrew *reshit* [literally, "beginning"] and *shirayim* [literally, the "residue" of waste]). The people of Israel were taught by their holy patriarchs that the correction of "Nature" involves the negation of its autonomous self-consciousness by giving the ownership of heaven and earth to their Creator (SE2, Vaera, 15b).

45. See, for example, SE4, Shelah, 44a.

46. SE4, Shelah, 46a, 48a: Had they entered the land by the power of Moses who was the source of their mission (as homiletically indicated by the phrase "send thou" in Num. 13:2), they would have been above "Nature," freed from its obstacles; in such an elevated situation, none of those could have stopped them from their spiritual journey. The entrance "by the power of Moses" signifies their total adherence to his most elevated spiritual level in spite of the apparent contradiction and dangerous collision between the concrete reality and their faith. Due to his spiritual radiation, Moses could not endure the concealment and the darkness of exile (SE2, Vaera, 15b, and below, n. 52).

47. SE4, Shelah, 46b.

48. SE4, Shelah, 47a. The powers of the "Other Side" lack any constructive structure and true existence and are nothing but a delusive imagination.

49. See Y. Jacobson, "Moses Hayyim Luzzatto's Doctrine of Divine Guidance and Its Relation to His Kabbalistic Teachings" [in Hebrew], 30–31, 41–42; Y. Jacobson, "The Divine Conduct and Its Reflection in the Suffering of the Righteous according to Ramhal" [in Hebrew], *Daat* 40 (1998): 58–63.

50. SE4, Shelah, 47a.

51. SE4, Shelah, 47b. Just as the perfection of the soul cannot be achieved but in this world precisely (in spite of the fact that its descent does not suit its own will), the Sabbath cannot be found but through worship within the profane (in the eschatological era only there will be a continuous time, a "day" of Sabbath only). The same is true concerning the land of Israel, which cannot be found but within the land of Canaan, which signifies "Nature" and exile.

52. He even must be somewhat contaminated by the corporeal waste, otherwise he would not be able to fulfill the task of correcting the spoiled reality! (SE2, Vaera, 19a. This daring

formulation might be interpreted as a slight hint to a cautious Kabbalistic or even Sabbatean tendency. The author explains, concerning Moses, that being prevented from entering the land was not just a punishment but a result of the fact that he could not endure any waste. See above, n. 46.)

53. SE4, Shelah, 48b.

54. As opposed to Israel's very essence embodied in the Torah, which is the purest divine truth, the glory of their elevated level in exile is recognizable precisely by the power of faith (SE2, Vaera, 18b) as the power of overcoming "Nature" and entering the land (SE4, Shelah, 46a). According to their purely spiritual essence rooted in the divine Torah, Israel is called "seed of truth" (Jer. 2:21), but after descending from their upper root to fulfill the holy mission, their conduct in this concrete world, which is frequently described as the "world of lie" and falsehood, must be one of faith. By faith only can this world, in which truth is entirely concealed, be gradually corrected and finally redeemed, and according to the increasing strength of faith the Divine is manifested without the garments of "Nature." This is precisely why the way of faith is estimated as the highest worship (SE4, Shelah, 50b). On this subject, see at length Y. Jacobson, "Truth and Faith in Gur Hasidic Thought" [in Hebrew], in *Studies in Jewish Mysticism, Philosophy and Ethical Literature Presented to I. Tishby*, ed. J. Dan and J. Hacker, (Jerusalem: Magnes Press, 1986), 593–616.

55. SE4, Shelah, 55a. Before the entrance to the land, its concealed spiritual treasure could not be seen. The entrance thus signifies, as already mentioned several times, the opening of the locked gates and the powerful march through them into the inner kingdom of the spirit.

56. SE4, Hukkat, 71b. Being rooted in the upper world, the people of Israel do not belong to the earthy and corporeal domain, and that is why they stimulate such a strong opposition within the inhabitants of the land, in which they strive, as the goal of their metaphysical mission within history and exile, "to arouse the power of holiness." These inhabitants are not able to reach and touch the heavenly root itself, but they do the utmost to keep earth as a corporeal entity, and to prevent its transformation by its connection to heaven. But being given the Torah, the people of Israel are bound to fulfill their mission to connect everything to its upper root, or to bring the Torah to its full actualization in concrete deeds.

57. SE4, Balak, 80b.

58. See, for example, SE1, Lekh Lekha, 26a; Vayetze, 69b (the land of Israel is frequently identified with the temple in this context, or most likely considered as its extension); Hanukkah, 115a; SE5, Ekev, 22a: The land of Israel is not one of many, distinguished among them by its own characteristics, but includes all the abundance coming down from heaven.

59. SE4, Balak, 80b. The idea is based on the famous homily by the Sages, *Gen. Rab.* 1:2.

60. The land of Israel was destined for the revelation of holiness, but the Canaanites concealed its light (SE3, Aharey Mot, 75a). Israel attained the merit of turning the land from curse to blessing, until it became the Holy Land (SE3, Kedoshim, 82a); they freed the land from the grasp of impurity and turned it into the domain of holiness (SE3, Metzora, 70a–b [the more corporeal a thing is, it conceals secretly more sparks of holiness], 72b). Holiness spreads everywhere, indeed, but on earth it is covered within the unpurified and dark mixture of "Nature," and only when Israel entered the land to uncover it, was the place renewed by abundance of holiness as a "vessel holding blessing" (*Uqtzim* 3:12; SE4, Maseey, 99b). The spiritual renewal is, of course, the opposite of the unchanging law of "Nature" and its constant routine.

61. See SE4, Maseey, 99b, and also SE4, Maseey, 101b; SE4, Shavuot, 12b. In all these homilies the author cites the well-known saying (*y. Orlah*, 1:3), discussed also in the beginning of Luzzatto's *Daat Tevunot*: "One who eats that which is not his is ashamed to look at his

benefactor." The fact that the people of Israel receive the abundance of holiness not as a divine gift, but through their own exertions and self-preparation to be the proper vessel for the holding of the heavenly blessings, is favored by God more than everything else. This is, of course, another aspect of the above mentioned significance of struggle and toil in the doctrines of *Sefat Emet*.

62. SE4, Maseey, 99a. The inner form of the land exists, of course, potentially from the very beginning of creation, and its actual completion signifies its comprehensive manifestation. The author explains that the land is destined for the dwelling of the Shekhinah only through the effort and devotion of Israel. He adds that by their entrance was the land of Israel below connected to its root above, thus causing the descent of its holy form and the immediate withdrawal of the directing angel below.

63. All the places spread out from the land of Israel, as the center of the world, which, in spite of its small size, is to be praised for its amazingly high quality, since inwardness is always the core and foundation of existence (SE4, Maseey, 101b). Only there can a person attach himself to his root, thus being integrated in the manifested spirituality (SE4, Maseey, 101a).

64. SE5, Devarim, 8a. The author expresses the hope of returning to the land of Israel quite excitingly. The fact that everything occurs by the power of the Torah only, including Israel's punishments and agony, might be a source of comfort for the tormented nation.

65. SE5, Vaethannan, 11b. According to a well-known Kabbalistic tradition, existing already in the Zohar, the author explains that the bright holy light drawn into the corporeal deeds blinds the wicked and the powers of the "Other Side", wards them off, and prevents them from using the divine vitality for undesirable intentions.

66. SE5, Ekev, 23b.

67. כח מעשיו הגיד לעמו לתת להם נחלת גוים (He showed His people the power of His works that He may give them the heritage of the nations).

68. See, for example, SE1, Hanukkah, 123a; SE4, Hukkat, 72b. See also Y. Jacobson, "Exile and Redemption," 208ff.

69. SE2, Vaera, 17a; SE4, Pinhas, 86b: The more clarification and testimony are needed (in the darkness of "Nature" and exile), the more the praise of Israel becomes apparent.

70. SE1, Vayishlah, 77b–78a: The Canaanites were familiar with the corporeal aspect of the land and knew how to turn it into an inhabited one. The people of Israel, on the other hand, know the secret of the inner settlement, and that is why they are known as "the dwellers of Thy house" (Ps. 84:5).

71. Under the rule of the Canaanites was the land of Israel the most spoiled place (SE4, Maseey, 100a).

72. SE2, Beshalah, 40a; SE2, Yitro, 48a.

73. SE1, Vayera, 35b. The covenant is depicted as the spiritual attachment of the righteous to the divine concealed secret, and it is to be achieved not by ignoring this world but precisely within it. The entrance of Israel into the land is a sign to the fact that they belong to the world to come(!) (SE4, Pinhas, 89b), since only those descending from the upper world, or from their innermost spiritual homeland, are able to transform the concrete reality; only by descending from the world to come as both their spiritual origin and destination, they had the power needed to enter their land and sanctify it. One can hear in some formulations a dull and distant erotic tone.

74. SE3, Pesah, 42a. The phrase might also be interpreted as an allusion to "the Other Side" of "Nature" as the Hasidic new significance of evil.

75. SE2, Vaera, 13a. The author adds that the surrounding snake has also a protective function: to protect the inwardness from being used improperly. This interesting notion is already known from the Zohar. See I. Tishby, *The Wisdom of the Zohar* [in Hebrew], vol. 1 (Jerusalem: Bialik Institute, 1957), 293. As for the Canaanites as traders or merchants, mentioned and discussed in the referred to homily, see Isa. 23:8 and Prov. 31:24. This identification is especially emphasized by the Sages: *Pesahim* 50a, *Tanhuma* Maseey, 9.

76. In the following lines of the homily, the author refers quite exceptionally to the alien thoughts and different kinds of the evil urge, but this is not within the scope of our discussion.

77. SE4, Maseey, 97b. Since this inner or upper land would not endure the Canaanites as its total opposite, the divine order was to exterminate them all. See also SE4, Maseey, 99a.

78. SE4, Maseey, 99b–100a, based on *Tanhuma* Shelah, 6. The author states in this context again, that as long as the wicked Canaanites were the rulers of the land, they did not see its spiritual hidden treasures at all and could only experience its external garment.

79. SE4, Shelah, 48b.

80. SE4, Shelah, 51a.

81. The same process applies to man's life, since in his early years he is subjugated under the rule of his evil urge, and only later, in adulthood, he frees himself from its influence to take upon himself the yoke of the divine kingdom (SE3, Behar, 95b).

82. *Zohar* 1, Noah, 73b. For the interpretation of this daring idea, see Y. Jacobson, "The Concept of Evil and Its Sanctification in Kabbalistic Thought," in *The Problem of Evil and Its Symbols in Jewish and Christian Tradition*, ed. H. Graf Reventlow and Y. Hoffman (London-New York: T & T Clark International, 2004), esp. 105.

83. Only Israel is able by the power of the Torah to turn the wilderness into a settled land and to correct the corporeal deeds (SE4, Maseey, 100a). There is a clear correlation between the two aspects. Under the rule of the Canaanites, the land of Israel was "a land that was not sown" (Jer. 2:2). See SE1, Lekh Lekha, 23b.

Bibliography

Aescoly, A. Z. "Hasidism in Poland" [in Hebrew]. In *Beit Yisrael bePolin*, edited by I. Halperin, 86–141. Jerusalem: Youth Department of the Zionist Organisation, 1953.

Alfasi, I. *Gur: The Founder, the Author of Hidushey haRim* [in Hebrew]. Tel Aviv: Sinai Publishing House, 1954. Second publication, *Gur: The History of Gur Hasidism* [in Hebrew]. Tel Aviv: Sinai Publishing House, 1978.

Bergman, E. "Gora Kalwaria: The Jewish Community and the Court of the Rebbe of Gur from the Beginning of the 19th Century to 1939" [in Hebrew]. In *Hasidism in Poland*, edited by I. Bartal, R. Elior, and C. Shmeruk, 111–117. Jerusalem: Bialik Institute, 1994.

Dov Baer of Meseritz. *Maggid Devarav Le-Yaakov*, edited by R. Schatz-Uffenheimer. Jerusalem: Magnes Press, 1976.

Green, A. *The Language of Truth*. Philadelphia: Jewish Publication Society, 1998.

——. "Three Warsaw Mystics." In *R. Shatz-Uffenheimer Memorial Volume*, vol. 2, edited by R. Elior and J. Dan, 1–58. Jerusalem: Jerusalem Studies in Jewish Thought, 1996.

Idel, M. *Hasidism between Ecstasy and Magic*. Albany: State University of New York Press, 1995. Hebrew translation, Tel Aviv: Schocken Publishing House, 2000.

Jacobson, Y. "The Order of Holiness and the Holiness of Order according to the Maharal of Prague" [in Hebrew]. In press.

——. "The Concept of Evil and Its Sanctification in Kabbalistic Thought." In *The Problem of Evil and Its Symbols in Jewish and Christian Tradition*, edited by H. Graf Reventlow and Y. Hoffman, 97–121. London-New York: T & T Clark International, 2004.

——. "Primordial Chaos and Creation in Gur Hasidism: The Sabbath That Preceded Creation." *Polin* 15 (2002): 221–240.

——. "The Divine Conduct and Its Reflection in the Suffering of the Righteous according to Ramhal" [in Hebrew]. *Daat* 40 (1998): 49–86.

——. *Hasidic Thought* [in Hebrew]. Tel Aviv: Mod Books, 1985. English translation, Tel Aviv: Mod Books, 1998.

——. "The Rectification of the Heart: Studies in the Psychic Teachings of R. Shneur Zalman of Liadi" [in Hebrew]. In *Teudah* 10, Studies in Judaica, edited by M. A. Friedman, 359–409. Tel Aviv: Tel Aviv University, Ramot Publishing, 1996.

——. "From Youth to Leadership and from Kabbalah to Hasidism: Stages of the Spiritual Development of the Author of Sefat Emet" [in Hebrew]. In *R. Shatz-Uffenheimer Memorial Volume*, vol. 2, edited by R. Elior and J. Dan, 429–446. Jerusalem: Jerusalem Studies in Jewish Thought, 1996.

——. "The Sanctity of the Profane in Gur Hasidism, Studies in the Concept of the Sabbath in Sefat Emet" [in Hebrew]. In *Hasidism in Poland*, edited by I. Bartal, R. Elior, and C. Shmeruk, 241–277. Jerusalem: Bialik Institute, 1994.

——. "Moses Hayyim Luzzatto's Doctrine of Divine Guidance and Its Relation to His Kabbalistic Teachings" [in Hebrew]. *Italia Judaica* 3 (1989): 27–46.

——. "Truth and Faith in Gur Hasidic Thought" [in Hebrew]. In *Studies in Jewish Mysticism, Philosophy and Ethical Literature Presented to I. Tishby*, edited by J. Dan and J. Hacker, 593–616. Jerusalem: Magnes Press, 1986.

——. "Exile and Redemption in Gur Hasidism" [in Hebrew]. *Daat* 2–3 (1978–1979): 175–215.

——. "The Doctrine of Creation in the Thought of R. Shneour Zalman of Liadi" [in Hebrew]. *Eshel Beer-Sheva* 1 (1976): 307–368.

Kauffman, Ts. *In All Your Ways Know Him* [in Hebrew]. Jerusalem: Bar Ilan University Press, 2009.

Levin, B. "Gur Hasidism Infiltrates into Warsaw" [in Hebrew]. In *Encyclopaedia of the Jewish Diaspora, Poland Series, Warsaw*, vol. 2, edited by I. Gruenbaum, 219–228. Tel Aviv: Encyclopaedia of the Jewish Diaspora Co., 1959.

Margolin, R. *The Human Temple* [in Hebrew]. Jerusalem: Magnes Press, 2005.

Piekarz, M. *The Hasidic Leadership* [in Hebrew]. Jerusalem: Bialik Institute, 1999.

——. *Ideological Trends of Hasidism in Poland during the Interwar Period and the Holocaust* [in Hebrew]. Jerusalem: Bialik Institute, 1990.

——. "'The Inner Point' of the Admorim of Gur and Alexander as a Reflection of Their Ability to Adjust to Changing Times" [in Hebrew]. In *Studies in Jewish Mysticism, Philosophy and Ethical Literature Presented to I. Tishby*, edited by J. Dan and J. Hacker, 617–660. Jerusalem: Magnes Press, 1986.

——. *The Beginning of Hasidism* [in Hebrew]. Jerusalem: Bialik Institute, 1978.

Rosenberg, S. *Tikkon La'ad* [in Hebrew]. Alon Shevut: Yeshivat Har Etzion Publications, 2008.

Schatz Uffenheimer, R. *Hasidism as Mysticism* [in Hebrew]. Jerusalem: Magnes Press, 1968. English translation by J. Chipman, Jerusalem: Princeton University Press / Magnes Press, 1993.

Scholem, G. *Major Trends in Jewish Mysticism*. New York: Schocken Books, 1961.

Shapira, M. *Peniney Sefat Emet* [in Hebrew]. Ofrah: Shuva Institute, 2004–2005.

Tishby, I. "'The Holy One Blessed Be He, the Torah and Israel Are All One': The Origin of the Phrase in the Commentary of Idra Raba by Ramhal" [in Hebrew]. In *Studies in Kabbalah and Its Branches*, vol. 3, 941–960. Jerusalem: Magnes Press, 1993.

——. *The Wisdom of the Zohar* [in Hebrew]. vol. 1. Jerusalem: Bialik Institute, 1957.

——. *The Wisdom of the Zohar* [in Hebrew]. vol. 2. Jerusalem: Bialik Insitute, 1961.

——. with J. Dan. "Hasidism" [in Hebrew]. *Encyclopaedia Hebraica*. Vol. 17, 769–821. Jerusalem and Tel Aviv: Encyclopaedia Publishing, 1965.

Weiss, J. "Some Notes on the Social Background of Early Hasidism." In *Studies in East European Jewish Mysticism and Hasidism*, edited by D. Goldstein with a new introduction by J. Dan, 3–26. London-Portland, Oregon: Littman Library of Jewish Civilization, 1997.

——. "Torah Study in Early Hasidism." In *Studies in East European Jewish Mysticism and Hasidism*, edited by D. Goldstein with a new introduction by J. Dan, 56–68. London-Portland, Oregon: Littman Library of Jewish Civilization, 1997.

——. "The Beginnings of the Hasidic Path" [in Hebrew]. *Zion* 16 (1951): 46–105.

Zohar, N. "'Agudath Israel' in Warsaw" [in Hebrew]. In *Encyclopaedia of the Jewish Diaspora, Poland Series, Warsaw*, vol. 2, edited by I. Gruenbaum, 227–280. Tel Aviv: Encyclopaedia of the Jewish Diaspora Co., 1959.

9

The Embarrassment of Joshua

STRATEGIES FOR INTERPRETING THE BIBLICAL ACCOUNT OF THE
CONQUEST OF CANAAN IN GERMAN-JEWISH NEO-ORTHODOXY IN
THE LATE NINETEENTH AND EARLY TWENTIETH CENTURIES

Matthias Morgenstern

"The Biblical tradition is unanimous in affirming that Israel was not native
to the land of Canaan but arrived there from abroad and conquered it."[1] The
canonical account of what has become known as the "conquest" of Canaan,
however, has been subjected to historical criticism since the nineteenth century. Modern scholarship, following Albrecht Alt's theory of transhumance,[2]
has suggested that "at least in its first phases, the occupation resulted from
peaceful settlement in the territories of the most extensive and least populated
city-states by groups grazing their herds there. The phenomenon could have
lasted for decades and perhaps centuries, and seems for the most part to have
had the approval of the local population. Only in the final stages could things
have become more violent."[3] Later research has moved the picture we have
today from the proto-history of the people of Israel even further away from a
plain historic understanding of the biblical account.[4] In his entry on the book
of Joshua in *WiBiLex*, the Internet encyclopedia on the Bible, Anton Cuffari
writes:

> The book of Joshua cannot be seen as a historical source for the so-called
> conquest of the land by the people of Israel. In all probability, such a bel-
> licose conquest as a military campaign by the twelve tribes people including
> the extermination of the original inhabitants of the land never happened.
> The decline in that era that can be determined historically and archaeologi-
> cally in the Canaanite city states including the destruction of some of these
> states cannot be regarded as the result of Israel's efforts.[5]

The modern Israeli archaeologist Israel Finkelstein is surprisingly in agreement with the Declaration of Independence of the modern State of Israel
made on May 14, 1948, which stated that "Eretz Israel was the birthplace of the
Jewish people." Finkelstein claims that early Hebrew culture did not develop

independently from Canaanite culture, but within this pagan culture, with probably only minor population influx from outside.[6] Accordingly, Richard Nelson sees the book of Joshua not as a historical witness to what may have happened in the twelfth to the tenth centuries B.C.E. but as a reflection of "what later generations believed had happened to their ancestors."[7]

When Rabbi Samson Raphael Hirsch (1808–1888), the Neo-Orthodox rabbi of the Jewish secessionist community (*Austrittsgemeinde*) in Frankfurt-am-Main, wrote his commentary on the Pentateuch, which was published between 1867 and 1878,[8] he could not have been aware of Julius Wellhausen's source critical analysis that was to appear some years later,[9] let alone Albrecht Alt's influential theory. On the other hand, Eichhorn's critical study on the Pentateuch, with its remarks concerning the questionable historicity and the dating of the biblical account, was already available.[10]

It is one of the striking features of Hirsch's entire oeuvre—not only of his exegetical texts—that he almost never refers to contemporary works. Thus, the critical discussion he *does* undertake with competing Jewish and non-Jewish scholars has to be reconstructed indirectly. In this case, we are lucky enough to have evidence that the question of biblical criticism of the earlier nineteenth century was indeed addressed in Frankfurt and in Hirsch's community. We know that this challenge was also taken up—at least partly—by Hirsch himself because his son-in-law, Joseph Gugenheimer (1831–1896)[11] (also Guggenheimer or Guggenheim), rabbi in Kolín (central Bohemia), wrote a series of articles on what he called the "hypotheses" of biblical criticism in the journal *Jeschurun* of which Hirsch was the editor.[12]

When dealing with the biblical account of the conquest of Canaan, Hirsch, like any Jewish Bible scholar or commentator in nineteenth-century Germany, was faced with a dilemma. On the one hand, the approach of biblical criticism was widely seen as a Christian—predominantly liberal Protestant—enterprise, often nourished by anti-Jewish feelings, that was undermining the historical foundations of the Jewish people.[13] Regarding the particular case of the book of Joshua, on the other hand, it seemed that the contents of this book were something to be embarrassed about. The results of Bible criticism—theoretically—might have been welcome from a Jewish point of view; in fact, the biblical account of the ban (*herem*) applied to the enemies of Israel in the land of Canaan, comprising the absolute destruction of these peoples including children and women, stood contrary to the cultural aspirations of German Judaism in at least two respects. First, the violence of the conquest narrative was contrary to the picture of Judaism as a tolerant, peaceful, and enlightened religion that German Jewish intellectuals, from the Right to the Left, wanted to paint—a picture that seemed to be a precondition of their acceptance into bourgeois German society and hence emancipation. Second, focusing on the biblical story seemed to imply that the Jews were not at home in Germany or in the respective countries of their Diaspora; their home was far away in the East, in a land now dominated by the Ottoman Empire. This means that, when dealing with the biblical account of the conquest of Canaan, there were three apologetic issues (the challenge of Bible criticism, the moral conflict of the "cruelty" of Joshua, and the question of the Jews being "strangers" in Germany) that every Jewish Bible scholar in nineteenth-century Germany willingly or unwillingly had to address. In this article, it will be shown that the different approaches of Jewish Bible scholars can be categorized according to the way they dealt with these partly contradicting issues.

Heinrich Graetz

Before discussing how Hirsch met this challenge and how two of his grand-sons, the Frankfurt attorney and philosopher Isaac Breuer and Rabbi Raphael Breuer of Aschaffenburg, continued the Hirschian approach in the twenti-eth century, some remarks on Heinrich Graetz (1817–1891), a former pupil of Hirsch, will help to set a framework for further investigation. Graetz's approach is of relevance here, because at the time of the early controversy between Orthodoxy and Reform Judaism, Graetz had begun his journalistic career on the Orthodox side; later he joined Zacharias Frankel's moderate conserva-tive wing, became professor for Jewish History at the Jüdisch-Theologisches Seminar (Jewish Theological Seminary) in Breslau (now Wrocław, Poland) in 1854, and developed his perspective on biblical criticism and on the account of the conquest of Canaan. When Hirsch was working on his commentary on the Pentateuch, Graetz's most influential studies on the history of the Jewish people had already started to appear.[14] Consequently, Graetz's history was dealt with critically in Hirsch's monthly *Jeschurun* by a number of (unsigned) arti-cles that were probably written by Hirsch himself.[15] The comparison of both may help to measure the extent to which each of them dealt with the apolo-getic issues above mentioned.

Graetz starts his historiographical overview of the earliest times (*die Vorgeschichte*) of the people of Israel with the crossing of the Jordan by the Israelite tribes for whom the heritage of Abraham, Isaac, and Jacob is but a far memory. He then determines a similarity between these tribes and the Canaanites that, in a way, seems to bring him close to the opinion that critical scholarship most unanimously agrees upon today, that Israel had its origins neither in Egypt nor in the desert of Sinai, but in Canaan:

> Viewed externally and superficially, the course of history from the entry of the Israelites into Canaan until well into the period of the kings can eas-ily be misleading. For the visible events have merely a political charac-ter.... Onstage are national leaders, heroes, kings, and generals. Alliances are made and broken. Any kind of spiritual activity in the background is

scarcely noticeable. The Judges who provide the earliest historical matter, heroes like Ehud, Gideon, his son Abimelech, and especially Jephthah and Samson, manifest so few Israelite traits that one could easily mistake them for Canaanites, Philistines, or Moabites.[16]

For Graetz, however, it is not warfare but spirituality that matters. Conceding that not all aspects of the biblical narrative bear the characteristics of historicity, he nevertheless aspires to an interpretation in accordance with the traits of Jewish history, as he perceives them. In Graetz's view this means, as a general rule, that Jewish history needs to be interpreted "spiritually," according to the norms of the moral law. In this particular case, this signifies the reduction of the violent features of the account as far as possible. The methodological devices that Graetz uses in this respect are typical of his time and of his historically conservative (but not orthodox) approach: a blending of historic reasoning that takes into account questions of probability with haggadic lore. He starts by declaring that "on crossing the Jordan and entering Canaan, the Israelites met with no resistance."[17] Minimizing the dimension of the atrocities perpetrated by the invaders, he then pursues that "the...inhabitants were now in such dread of the Israelites as to abandon their possessions without attempting to make any resistance."[18] In order to relativize the measures that Joshua took against the local population of Palestine, Graetz finally takes up a motif taken out of the rabbinic tradition and declares:

> There were three iniquities which the land was supposed to spurn as the most heinous. These were murder, licentiousness, and idolatry. The conviction was general that on account of such misdeeds the land had cast out its former inhabitants, and that it would not retain the Israelites if they indulged in similar crimes. These ideas took deep root amongst the people of Israel, and they regarded Palestine as surpassing in its precious qualities every other country.[19]

Graetz points to eight features of the biblical narrative and of post-biblical rabbinical tradition justifying Joshua's fight and minimizing the cruelty of his invasion. The way in which he highlights and sharpens these traditions clearly shows his moralizing and modern tendency:

1. Graetz points to the immoral behavior of the local population, especially of Jericho. The people of this city, he declares, "were sunk in lewdness and sexual aberrations."[20] When the Israelites entered the city, they met "with little resistance, they slew the population, which was enfeebled by depraved habits."[21]

2. After the defeat of the locals in Jericho, the Canaanites fled; according to Graetz this means that the ban upon them could not have been—and in fact was not—executed; Graetz affirms that a part of the Canaanite population fled as far away as Africa.[22]

3. Graetz then highlights the account of the agreement with resident populations of Canaan, an alliance between the local citizens and the invaders.

The Gibeonites, or Hivites, in the tract of land called Gibeon, freely submitted to Joshua and his people. They agreed that the Israelites should share with them the possession of their territory on the condition that their lives should be spared.... In this way the Israelites acquired possession of the whole mountain district from the borders of the great plain to the vicinity of Jerusalem.[23]

4. The Israelites then continued their fight not in order to conquer but in order to defend their allies, the Gibeonites, because those had been attacked by the remaining Canaanites.

The southern Canaanites now became more closely allied. The apprehension that their land might fall an easy prey to the invaders overcame their mutual jealousies and their love of feud; being thus brought into close union with each other they ventured to engage in aggressive warfare. Five kings, or rather chiefs of townships, those of Jebus (Jerusalem), Hebron, Jarmuth, Lachish and Eglon, joined together to punish the Gibeonites for submitting to the invaders, for whom they had opened the road, and whom they had helped to new conquests. The Gibeonites, in the face of this danger, implored the protection of Joshua, who forthwith led his victorious warriors against the allied troops of the five towns, and inflicted on them a crushing defeat near Gibeon.[24]

5. Graetz emphasizes that large parts of the country remained unoccupied, which implies that concerning these parts of the land no violent actions were taken: "The territories to the West of the Jordan had only partially been subjected and allotted. Large and important tracts of land were still in possession of the original inhabitants."[25]

6. He points to the fact that violence was applied not only toward the other but also internally because the Israelite tribes had started fighting among themselves and lost their former unity. This and the isolation of each tribe and its subsections, which were only concerned with their own affairs, prevented the tribes "from consolidating their forces against the original inhabitants of Canaan."[26]

7. Graetz then mentions the fact that the tribe of Judah avoided a war with the Jebusites, possibly even concluding a peace treaty with them, and they settled peacefully among the Canaanite population.[27]

8. Finally, he points to the fact that it was not the Canaanites alone who suffered violence and expulsion. The tribe of Dan was prevented by the Emorites from settling in the area that in today's Israel is called Gush Dan and had to flee to the mountains. Thus, a part of the Israelites had to wander around homeless in the land of Israel. Moreover, their homelessness was also due to intra-Israelite enmity:

> The sons of Ephraim and the Benjaminites refused them [i.e., the Danites] the possession of permanent dwelling-places. The Danites were therefore during a long time compelled to lead a camp-life, and at last one section of this tribe had to go in search of a settlement far away to the north.[28]

Graetz concludes:

> As in the lives of individuals, so in the lives of nations, the practical turn of events is liable to disappoint all anticipations. It is true the land of Canaan now belonged to the Israelites; but their conquests were of a precarious nature, and could again be wrested from them by a combined attack on the part of the dispossessed natives.[29]

Samson Raphael Hirsch

Hirsch did not write a commentary on the book of Joshua. Therefore, the biblical account of the Israelites taking possession of the land was not of direct interest to him. However, several passages in his commentary on the Pentateuch give the opportunity to draw a picture of his understanding of the biblical narrative.

In his comments on the story of Abraham having to leave his home (Gen 12:1), Hirsch explains that according to the Ramban (Nahmanides) the first movements of the Patriarch are "analogous to the later history of his people."[30] and "יציאת אור כשדים [the exodus of Ur Kashdim] would be a prototype of יציאת מצרים [the exodus of Egypt]."[31] It is remarkable, however, that Hirsch does not focus here on the land that the Patriarch is *promised* and that the Israelites were later *given* by God, but instead refers to the "land" that Abraham is *leaving*:

> ארץ מולדת, and בית [country, home land, and house] together form the soil out of which the personality of people grows. ארץ, the country, the nationality, with all the special bodily, mental and moral characteristics which it gives, (ארץ, as our country, is ארס, to which our whole being is "married," ערש, the cradle in which we grow to life... ארץ as the earth is our "cradle" and over it is שמים, our שם, there, our future).[32]

Though the reason for this shift of interest is only hinted at, it seems to be clear that Hirsch's decision not to focus on the Promised Land reflects his and his followers' relationship to the land where they are living, Germany:

> We have mentioned these thoughts innate in the Hebrew language to real-
> ize how deeply and intimately even our very language feels and values the
> worth of one's fatherland and birthplace. It is certainly not meant to be any
> belittling of this factor if the planting of the first Jewish germ demanded
> forsaking fatherland, birthplace and the paternal home. It is rather just
> the appreciation of these factors wherein lies the greatness of the isolation
> demanded here. This demand itself placed Abraham in the completest con-
> trast to the ruling tendency of his age.[33]

In his explanation of the words spoken by God to Abraham "(go) until the land which I shall show thee" (Gen 12:1), Hirsch then takes another step away from what later generations would call "Palestinocentrism."[34] According to Hirsch, it was not God but the Patriarch himself who opted for the land of Canaan as his permanent abode:

> One cannot say to somebody: "Go to the place to which I shall direct you,"
> he would then have to wait until he is at least told in which direction to
> go. Abraham would not have known, so to speak, "by which gate to leave
> Haran." Therefore the positive command could only have been, go away,
> never mind where, and wander about until you come to a place where I shall
> let you see by some visible sign, that there you are to remain. Abraham chose
> the way to Canaan by his own decision.[35]

This exegetical move, however, basically consists of an attempt to give an ethi-cal explanation of Abraham's choice. The land he fled was a land of corruption; the movement of his exodus was—according to Hirsch—a "mental movement towards the future."[36] The land Abraham went to was his closeness to God. "The hill of Moriah, the Mount of Zion," was "the last height of Lebanon in the south"; in the Bible "it is therefore called...ירכתי לבנון [the innermost part of Lebanon] to refer also to the moral meaning of 'white' as the refining and purifying colour (cf. Isa 1:18)."[37] In the context of this "moralized geography" Abraham remembered that Melkizedek was living in Canaan for whom "the recognition of God had been retained in its purest form," and "it was quite natural that he should wander in the direction towards where remembrance told of a time in which men stood in closer and nearer relationship to God." According to this "natural" explanation, Hirsch emphasizes that "the achieve-ment of 'nearness to God'" was "equally within the reach of the Lapp in Lapland as that of the Greek in Greece" and that "where Abraham lived...murderers, can also live."[38] On the other hand—obviously adding "supernatural" elements to his interpretation—Hirsch insists that the Patriarch was looking for a land where "men who live their lives in accordance with the Will of God *can* attain the fullest and highest degree of spiritual and moral consecration of their lives."[39] This meant, however, that on that same soil "at that time, and later too, men degenerated more and more until all they merited was extermination [*Vernichtungswürdigkeit*]."[40] "It was just that land which is so seductive that on it its inhabitants became so debauched in voluptuous luxury that the very land 'spewed them out,' just that land God chose to plant therein His people."[41]

In the following sections, I shall give a short outline of Hirsch's explanation of the narrative as reflected in his commentary on the Pentateuch. In comparison to Heinrich Graetz, we shall see a deepening and radicalization of the effort to minimize the violent features in this narrative and to moralize history. There is also an element of spiritualization—in the mold of Abraham's "mental movement towards the future"—but this spiritualization or allegorization that we encounter is only hinted at. It may be assumed that for Hirsch, because of his opposition to biblical criticism (though this issue is never openly raised), an explicit or even implicit dehistoricization of the events was not an option. At the same time, the remaining realistic features of the biblical account are exegetically counterbalanced: Time and again Hirsch emphasizes that the people of Israel would ultimately share and (when the Jerusalem Temple was destroyed) actually shared the same destiny as the Canaanites—extermination—when they rebelled against the will of God.

We find an explanation of Deuteronomy 7:1 ("the Lord clears away many nations before you") that takes the violence out of the picture:

> נשל is the specific term used for fruit being dropped from trees too early before they are ripe.... The land which up till now had borne the inhabitants denies them the use of its soil any longer, as God has judged them to have become unworthy of it. When you move in they will already be cast down by the land and you are only the gusty wind which has to clear the ground from what has fallen as waste on it, to make room for the planting of a more worthy pure growth.... "Planting" Israel in the land of the Canaanite population is a frequent conception in scripture.[42]

We read a commentary on Numbers 33:51–52 ("when you pass over the Jordan into the land of Canaan, then you shall drive out all the inhabitants of the land before you") that is complementary to Hirsch's "natural" explanation that takes the violence out of the picture and matches the etymological (or pseudo-etymological) interpretation we just encountered: "ירש—phonetically related to גרש, to drive away, from which we get further תירוש, the juice pressed out of the fruit."[43] In both explanations the conquest, the expropriation, and the destruction of the "aborigines" is painted in the colors of a natural, biological, agricultural process!

Nevertheless, in his commentary on Numbers 33:54, Hirsch adds the divine dimension of the conquest by underlining that the Israelites did not take action on their own initiative but by God's command. This implies that God was not only the master and sovereign of the world, but also the master and sovereign of the land of Israel and that "the Jewish people are not the owners of the Jewish land."[44]

> But inasmuch as the division of the land is to be made by a lot confirmed by God, just thereby the task is given to first render the land fit and prepared for those who are now to take it into possession by the removal of its inhabitants and their polytheistic memorials.[45]

In his explanation of Numbers 33:55 ("But if you do not drive out the inhabitants of the land from before you, then those of them whom you let remain shall be as pricks in your eyes and thorns in your sides, and they shall trouble you in the land where you dwell") Hirsch declares:

> By your tolerance towards the polytheistic inhabitants amongst you, you become tolerant to polytheism.... But by such authorized concession to the toleration of polytheism in the land of God, you forfeit the integrity of your own attachment to God, and with it, the justification for, and the protection of your existence in the land. And once you have forfeited the protection of God, those whom you tolerantly allowed in your land become your oppressors and enemies in your own land. The whole book of Judges is nothing but the history of the result of disregarding this warning.[46]

In this regard, the Frankfurt rabbi was in perfect harmony with biblical explanations from the left side of the religious spectrum of German Jewry. Even an outstanding liberal like the philosopher Hermann Cohen, in his masterwork *Religion of Reason out of the Sources of Judaism*, could declare with regard to the Canaanites:

> It is known how Scripture itself explicitly cautions against seduction by pagan customs and cults. This explains the harsh prescriptions for the destruction of idolatry and the idol worshipers. The cause for some laws...might have lain in the warding off of idolatry.[47]

For Hirsch, these high moral norms in relation to the land meant that the land would become, so to speak, metaphysically dangerous for the people of Israel if and when Israel failed to be obedient to the commandments from Sinai. "Finally you will become so unworthy of the land of God that He will drive you out of the land as His intention had been to let the nations be driven out by you."[48] In Hirsch's conception, the fundamental sanctity of the land of Israel found its expression even in topographical features and distinguishing marks such as "the appointment of the ערי מקלט (asylum cities) at the division of the Land" that were a "public expression of the fundamental principle of the dignity of human beings in the likeness of God."[49] Hirsch explains: "The land is only given on the condition of every human life being respected as being unassailably sacred to the Torah.... This holding human life to be sacred is to be made evident immediately on taking possession of the land."[50]

Isaac Breuer

The metaphysical danger of the land means, according to Hirsch's explanation, that the expulsion of the people of Israel from the land some hundred years later was ultimately a means of divine protection. Hirsch explains that the Israelites had to lose "their own country and national independence" in order not to "fall into the same degree of degeneration which brought about the destruction of the Canaanite inhabitants before them." He quotes a passage from the Babylonian Talmud (*Git.* 88a) that refers to the numerical value of the word ונושנתם ("when you have grown old in the land," Deut 4:25).

> The numerical value of the letters of the word add up to 852. But we only stayed in the land 850 years. 440 till the Temple was built and 410 years that the Temple existed. So that their fate of being driven out of the Land overtook them two years before the space of time indicated by ונושנתם . . . and this quick getting the people out of the land was a benevolent act of God for their salvation. The State and Temple went to ruin, but the people, with a remnant of their spiritual heritage that was still left in their hearts, went out to meet the solution of their great mission in the Dispersion.[51]

According to this explanation, God took them out of the country two years ahead of time because, had he waited for two more years, the total destruction of the people would have been the consequence.

While Hirsch compared the conquest and loss of the land to a natural, biological process, his grandson, the Frankfurt rabbi, attorney, novelist, and religious philosopher Isaac Breuer (1883–1946) made use of sources from the realm of contemporary political and social philosophy. In a comment on this biblical passage (Deut 4:25–26) and on Hirsch's talmudic interpretation, he hints at a kind of "Marxist" analysis of the historical development that lay behind this verse. In Breuer's paraphrase the biblical passage reads: "When you father children and grandchildren, and you become Philistines in the land . . . (then the Lord will scatter you among the peoples. . .)."[52] In this context, the word ונושנתם (when you have grown old), apart from its vague allusion to antiquity, is used to back up Breuer's critique of the bourgeoisie in general and especially the Jewish bourgeoisie. With some analogy to the Hegelian concept of history and the Marxist "laws" of historical materialism, the biblical text seemed to show that the bourgeoisie was doomed to failure; Breuer was waiting to see the "Philistine" world replaced one day by what he called "socialism of the Torah."[53]

Isaac Breuer did not elaborate on his understanding of the "embourgeoisement" of the biblical Canaanites (the "Philistines" at the time of Joshua) and 850 years later of the Israelites that resulted in their being scattered among the peoples. But he *did* comment on his understanding of the outline of historic events. Again, the plan of history would inevitably follow the sketch of the divine word in the Torah. Referring to God's promise in Leviticus 26:42 ("then I will remember my covenant with Jacob, and I will remember my covenant with Isaac, and I will remember my covenant with Abraham, and I will remember the land") and to Hirsch's explanation of this verse[54] and interpreting this sequence of biblical promises, where the order of the Patriarchs is chronologically reversed, Breuer foresaw a "dialectical" development of events in three steps. With the beginning of the Diaspora after the destruction of the Temple, the Jewish people entered into the "fate of Jacob." Later, after the pre-modern period had been overcome during the emancipation in the West in the nineteenth century, the Jews lived according to the "fate of Isaac." Breuer characterized this period as the time of the bourgeoisie (*Bürgertum*), the time of the social emancipation of the Jews, and the time of the educational slogan "Torah im Derekh Eretz."[55] This step in history, however, would be followed by the "Abraham period," the time of the national emancipation of the Jewish people in the twentieth century, the time when the return to Zion under the educational slogan "Torah im Derekh Eretz Israel"[56] would be close, at last the time to build up the socialism of the Torah in the land of the Torah, in Eretz Israel.[57]

Raphael Breuer

Raphael Breuer (1881–1932), rabbi (*Distriktsrabbiner*) in Aschaffenburg, northern Bavaria, and older brother of Isaac Breuer, took another direction. It must be mentioned that even before his commentary on the biblical book of Joshua came out in 1915, Raphael Breuer, who was known as a fervent anti-Zionist, had the reputation of being the *enfant terrible* of German-Jewish Orthodoxy.[58] In 1912 he published a provocative commentary on the biblical Song of Songs, an explanation according to the literary sense of this book as opposed to the traditionally accepted allegorical interpretation that understands this book as a metaphor of God's love toward the people of Israel.[59] This commentary had scandalized the Orthodox Jewish community in Germany to the effect that the founding conference of the Orthodox world organization, Agudat Israel, which had been planned to take place in Kattowitz (now Katowice) in May that year, had been in danger of being jeopardized. The new commentary on the book of Joshua, had it not been published during World War I (1915), could have had a scandalizing potential of the same degree.[60] It should be remarked that Raphael Breuer, together with his brother Rabbi Joseph Breuer (1882–1980), planned to write a series of biblical commentaries, first of all on the five Scrolls (*megillot*) and later on the earlier prophets. Although the authors of these commentaries wanted to write them in the spirit of Samson Raphael Hirsch, the grandfather of the Breuer brothers, who had published his explanations of the Torah and the Psalms,[61] this scholarly series dealing with "Nakh" literature ("Neviim" and "Ketuvim") was, by Orthodox measures, in itself an odd enterprise.

The commentary on Joshua makes an even stranger impression when we realize that Raphael Breuer, contrary to Graetz and Hirsch, chose to address the most salient apologetic issue in a quite different way. This becomes evident right at the beginning, in the preface of his book, when Breuer evokes the ethical problems of the biblical conquest of the land, connecting them directly with modern standards of human and international rights.[62] Breuer then goes on to explicitly enumerate the features of the book of Joshua that are contrary to these modern standards.

The rabbi of Aschaffenburg was, of course, aware of the fact that there were no people in the world who were conscious to the same degree of the necessity of human rights standards as the Jewish people, who had suffered so long in their history and desperately needed these standards to be applied. Should the book of Joshua have a *Jewish* origin, Breuer argues, this "Jewish author" would have had good reason to give an account of a history in which these human norms were met. The fact that the accounts in this book do not meet these standards leads to Breuer to the conclusion that this book, were it the history of mere human beings, would have a very doubtful ethical character.[63] But the book of Joshua, according to Breuer's commentary, is *not* a human book. As part of the biblical revelation, it is of divine origin, and Joshua's was not a profane war, but a liturgical action that can only be properly understood if one takes into account the holiness of the land of Israel. Breuer writes:

> Moderne Palästina-Liebe muß freilich die Ausrottung der heidnischen Völkerschaften als eine völkerrechtswidrige Grausamkeit empfinden, denn sie wird die gesamte Geschichte Palästinas unter dem Gesichtspunkte außerpalästinensischer Vorstellungen zu verstehen suchen.[64]

He goes on:

> It is a total misconception of the Jewish understanding of international law if we try to appreciate the judgments that were enacted to the original inhabitants of Palestine without connection to the concept of the holiness of the land.[65]

Whoever is able to appreciate this history in the spirit of the Torah, Breuer says, will understand that these events were nothing but a manifestation of the holiness of the seven commandments given to Noah. "In einem heiligen Lande haben Menschen keinen Platz, die noch nicht einmal die erste Stufe des Menschentums erklommen haben."[66] According to this conception, Joshua accomplished what Jews later than him—let alone secular Zionists—could and should never accomplish.

Accounts like Joshua 10:11 ("and as they [i.e., the enemies] fled before Israel, while they were going down the ascent of Beth Horon, the Lord threw down great stones from heaven upon them as far as Azeka, and they died. There were more who died because of the hailstones than the men of Israel killed with the sword") show that we are dealing here with a one-time event in the *Heilsgeschichte*, the divine history of salvation. In fact, the biblical narrative demonstrates that the Israelites had already tried to rationalize the events by explaining the miracles away. When the people saw simply big hailstones, not miraculous "great stones" thrown from heaven, Joshua asked God to make a miracle in order to prove to Israel that the Lord was fighting on the side of the Israelites (Josh 10:14).

According to Breuer, the book of Joshua is full of accounts that are contrary to military logic. In Joshua 10:24 ("Joshua summoned all the men of Israel to put their feet upon the necks of the five kings that had fought against Israel and the Gibeonites") we see a gesture that was, according to Breuer, in itself superfluous. It had only been necessary in order to convince the skeptics in the Israelite camp that God would keep his promises. Men, women, and animals were killed by Joshua's army—the same army that had spared the Gibeonite allies of Israel. Joshua's cruelty in his warfare had thus its reason in the lack of belief on behalf of the Israelites. Should Jews today on their own initiative—this is the implication of Breuer's commentary—try to act like Joshua did, these efforts would clearly contradict humanitarian law.

Although Breuer insists on the difference between biblical warfare and the war of his time, World War I, in the preface of his commentary we find an expression of support for the efforts of the central powers in Europe and for their attempt to bring down the Czarist regime in Russia. This inclination, however, is not motivated by an attempt to please the Germans; it is rooted in what Breuer sees as genuine Jewish interest—to defend their homeland against the "slavonic assault."[67] At the same time, we read sentences attenuating enthusiasm for warfare: "Kriege müssen geführt, sollten aber niemals verhimmelt werden."[68] Thus, Breuer draws a clear distinction between the present war and the holy wars in the Bible.

Needless to say, Breuer, with his reasoning regarding the literary character of the book of Joshua, is begging the question.[69] What is interesting here is that in the middle of World War I we find a text that is proudly Jewish and which, for that reason, ceases to argue apologetically. Paradoxically, this very argument of Breuer, which dispenses with rationalizations and moralizations of the biblical account, brings him closer to the modern understanding of the book of Joshua as expressed by contemporary scholars like Wolfgang Oswald and Ernst Axel Knauf (in the sense of modern literary and canon theory) than the apologetic endeavors of his predecessors. The book of Joshua should be seen as the narrative of the divine gift of the land to the people of Israel rather than the exposition of human efforts to conquer it, because attempts to find traces of a historical *Landnahme* arise from mistaken historical and apologetic assumptions that run contrary to the intention of the biblical text.

Conclusion

In the texts of Graetz, Hirsch, and Isaac Breuer we have seen—to different degrees, and partly between the lines—attempts to minimize the tensions between the biblical account of the conquest of Canaan and modern standards of understanding and judging human behavior in history. While Graetz and Hirsch preferred an implicit approach concerning the issue of biblical criticism,[70] both scholars made great efforts to deal with the ethical problems of the conquest in relativizing the atrocities committed by the conquerors, interpreting them as a consequence of the immoral behavior of the local population. In this sense, Hirsch added that, according to the Bible, the people of Israel ultimately shared the destiny of the Canaanites when they were unwilling to obey the will of God. In Hirsch's commentary there is also a clear apologetic tendency with regard to the German fatherland: For him, dealing with the history of the conquest of Canaan should not obscure the fact that ארץ (the country) and מולדת (the homeland), the "cradle" of German Jews, was in fact *Germany*. When Isaac Breuer replaces these motives with philosophical ideas of the late nineteenth century—class struggle and historical materialism—he seemingly conceals his apologetic interest. What he wants to underline is that the violence by the conquerors was in accordance with the general "laws of history"! It was only Isaac's brother Raphael Breuer who in this respect clearly abstained from apologetic tendencies. Writing in the middle of World War I, however, even *he* felt the urge, in the context of his commentary on the biblical book of Joshua, to underline the commitment of German Jews to Germany, the "soil where their cradle stood and where their ancestors are buried."[71]

Notes

1. Jan Alberto Soggin, *A History of Israel: From the Beginnings to the Bar Kochba Revolt AD 135*, trans. John Bowden (London: SCM Press, 1984), 138. I am grateful to my friend Wolfgang Oswald for his suggestions and remarks on an earlier version of this paper, particularly with regard to modern exegetic literature on the narrative of Israel's conquest of the land. Of special interest in connection with this topic is Oswald's study *Staatstheorie im Alten Israel: Der politische Diskurs im Pentateuch und in den Geschichtsbüchern des Alten Testaments* (Stuttgart: Kohlhammer, 2009), 102, 119–120. Wolfgang Oswald also emphasized to me that the biblical text, according to established exegetical terminology, should not be seen as a *Landnahme* (conquest of the land) but rather as a *Landgabe* (gift of the land) narrative, because according to the texts, the land was basically *given* to the Israelites rather then

conquered by them. Attempts to find literary traces of *Landnahme* features (that in some conceptions are seen as complementary to archaeological findings) arise from mistaken historical assumptions that run contrary to the intention of the biblical text that has to be read according to modern literary theory.

2. On Albrecht Alt's theory, see his article: "The Settlement of the Israelites in Palestine" (1925), in *Essays on Old Testament History and Religion*, trans. R. A. Wilson (Oxford: Doubleday, 1967).

3. Soggin, *History of Israel*, 152; see, on the other hand, Volkmar Fritz, *The Conquest in the Light of Archaeology*, in *Proceedings of the Eighth World Congress of Jewish Studies, Jerusalem 1981*, World Congress of Jewish Studies 1 (Jerusalem: World Union of Jewish Studies, 1982), 15–21. Fritz considers Alt's theory inadequate: "In fact we know little or nothing of the actual situation at the time of the 'conquest.'"

4. See, for example, Rainer Albertz, *A History of Israelite Religion in the Old Testament Period*, vol. 1, *From the Beginnings to the End of the Monarchy* (London: SCM Press, 1994) and Niels Peter Lemche, *Prelude to Israel's Past: Background and Beginnings of Israelite History and Identity* (Peabody, Mass.: Hendrickson, 1998).

5. Anton Cuffari, "Josua/Josuabuch," in *WiBiLex: Das wissenschaftliche Bibellexikon im Internet*, http://www.bibelwissenschaft.de/de/wibilex/das-bibellexikon/details/quelle/WIBI/zeichen/a/referenz/11717///cache/fd4e50b54b4c2805d8b2ccce45df6784/. "Das Josuabuch kann nicht als historische Quelle der sog. Landnahme des Volkes Israel angesehen werden. Aller Wahrscheinlichkeit nach hat es eine solche kriegerische Landnahme als Feldzug des Zwölf-Stämme-Volkes Israel samt der Vernichtung aller Bewohner des Landes nie gegeben. Der in jener Epoche historisch und archäologisch feststellbare Niedergang der kanaanäischen Stadtstaaten samt der Zerstörung einiger Städte ist nicht als das Werk Israels anzusehen."

6. See, for example, Israel Finkelstein, *The Archaeology of the Israelite Settlement* (Jerusalem: Israel Exploration Society, 1988).

7. Richard D. Nelson, *Joshua: A Commentary* (Louisville: Westminster John Knox Press, 1997), 4.

8. The volumes appeared as follows: Genesis, 1867; Exodus, 1869; Leviticus, 1873; Numbers, 1876; Deuteronomy, 1878. For an English edition of the commentary, see Samson Raphael Hirsch, *The Pentateuch Translated and Explained*, trans. Isaac Levy, 2nd ed. (New York: Judaica Press, 1971).

9. See, for example, Julius Wellhausen, *Prolegomena zur Geschichte Israels* (Berlin: Reimer, 1878); Julius Wellhausen, *Skizzen und Vorarbeiten 2: Die Composition des Hexateuchs* (Berlin: Reimer, 1885); Julius Welhausen, *Die Composition des Hexateuchs und der historischen Bücher des Alten Testaments* (Berlin: Reimer, 1889).

10. Johann Gottfried Eichhorn, *Einleitung ins Alte Testament* (Leipzig: Weidmann und Reich, 1780–1783); Heinrich Ewald, *Geschichte des Volkes Israel* (Göttingen: Dieterich, 1843–1859).

11. On Gugenheimer (also Guggenheimer or Gugenheim/Guggenheim), see Meir Hildesheimer and Matthias Morgenstern, "Rabbiner Samson Raphael Hirsch in der deutschsprachigen jüdischen Presse: Materialien zu einer bibliographischen Übersicht," *Jud.* 66 (2010): 414 and 430.

12. Joseph Gugenheimer, "Die Hypothesen der Bibelkritik und der Commentar zur Genesis von Herrn Rabbiner Hirsch," *Jeschurun* 13 (5627/1867): 293–313, 397–409; 14 (5628/1868): 1–18, 173–191, 312–325; 15 (5629/1869): 81–100, 179–192. Gugenheimer (*Jeschurun* 1867, p. 295) mentions Eichhorn's *Einleitung in das Alte Testament* and Ewald's *Geschichte des Volkes Israel*.

13. For the frequently quoted bon mot according to which "higher criticism is higher anti-semitism," see Josef Abrahams, *Jewish Interpretation of the Old Testament*, in *The People and the Book: Essays on the Old Testament*, ed. Arthur Samuel Peake (Oxford: Clarendon Press, 1925), 406, and M. Kapustin, "Biblical Criticism: A Traditionalist View," *Tradition* (Fall 1960): 29.

14. It is interesting to notice that Heinrich Graetz started his monumental work *Geschichte der Juden: Von den ältesten Zeiten bis auf die Gegenwart* (11 vols.) with vol. 4 (*Vom Untergang des jüdischen Staates bis zum Abschluß des Talmuds*) in Berlin, 1853 (2nd ed.: Leipzig 1866); vol. 1, *Geschichte der Israeliten von ihren Uranfängen (um 1500) bis zum Tode des Königs Salomo (um 977 vorchristlicher Zeit)* (Leipzig: Oskar Leiner, 1874), referring to the biblical period, was published as late as 1874, probably due to his embarrassment in dealing with the questions of biblical criticism. When Hirsch wrote his commentaries on Numbers (1876) and Deuteronomy (1878) he had probably read the first volume by Graetz. Hirsch's commentaries on Genesis, Exodus, and Leviticus appeared in 1867, 1869, and 1873.

15. "Geschichte der Juden von Dr. Grätz," *Jeschurun* 2 (5616/1856): 47–69, 89–103, 156–176, 188–214, 315–325, 424–442, 529–549 (see also www.compactmemory.de); Hirsch deals here critically with vol. 4 of the *Geschichte der Juden* (on the talmudic period), comparing it to a failed piece of art.

16. Heinrich Graetz, *The Structure of Jewish History and Other Essays*, trans. Ismar Schorsch (New York: Jewish Theological Seminary of America, 1975), 183f. For Graetz's extremely short coverage of the time of the Patriarchs, see *Geschichte der Juden*, vol. 1, 6–8. The first sentence of vol. 1 reads: "An einem sonnigen Frühlingstage drangen Hirtenstämme über den Jordan in ein Ländchen ein, das nur als ein etwas ausgedehnter Küstenstrich des Mittelmeeres gelten kann" (p. 3).

17. Heinrich Graetz, *History of the Jews: From the Earliest Times to the Present Day*, trans. Bella Löwy (London: David Nutt, 1891), 33.

18. Graetz, *History of the Jews*, 41.

19. Graetz, *History of the Jews*, 43.

20. Graetz, *Structure of Jewish History*, 179.

21. Graetz, *History of the Jews*, 34.

22. Graetz refers to Isa 17:9 in the LXX and to Procopius, *De Bello Vandalico*, 2.10; see also Hirsch on Deut 20:10–14 (with reference to *y. Shev.* 6:1, 36c, 57–58). On this rabbinic tradition, see Menahem Kister's article in the present volume.

23. Graetz, *History of the Jews*, 35.

24. Graetz, *History of the Jews*, 35f.

25. Graetz, *History of the Jews*, 52.

26. Graetz, *History of the Jews*, 52.

27. Graetz, *History of the Jews*, 39.

28. Graetz, *History of the Jews*, 40.

29. Graetz, *History of the Jews*, 53.

30. Samson Raphael Hirsch, *The Pentateuch: Translated and Explained*, vol. 1, *Genesis* (London, 1963), 235. German text: Samson Raphael Hirsch, *Der Pentateuch übersetzt und erläutert*, vol. 1, *Die Genesis* (reprint, Frankfurt am Main, 1986), 193.

31. Hirsch, *The Pentateuch*, vol. 1, 276 (German text: *Die Genesis*, 229).

32. Hirsch, *The Pentateuch*, vol. 1, 223 (on Gen 12:1; *Die Genesis*, 183); on the symbolism and the gender assignment of "the land" in this quote, see Matthias Morgenstern, "Fremde Mutter 'Erez Israel,'" *Jahrbuch für Biblische Theologie* 23 (2009): 195–210; Matthias

Morgenstern, "'Erez Israel,' madre straniera," *Concilium: Rivista internazionale di teologia* 43, no. 2 (2007): 87–98.

33. Hirsch, *The Pentateuch*, vol. 1, 224 (*Die Genesis*, 184).

34. On this term in the context of Jewish Orthodoxy, see Matthias Morgenstern, *From Frankfurt to Jerusalem: Isaac Breuer and the History of the Secession Dispute in Modern Jewish Orthodoxy* (Leiden: Brill, 2002), 214, 225.

35. Hirsch, *The Pentateuch*, vol. 1, 230 (*Die Genesis*, 189).

36. Hirsch, *The Pentateuch*, vol. 1, 230 (*Die Genesis*, 190: "eine geistige Hinbewegung, ein Hinstreben zu dem futuralen oder imperativen Begriffe").

37. Hirsch, *The Pentateuch*, vol. 5, *Deuteronomy* (London, 1966), 38 (on Deut 3:25); German text: *Der Pentateuch*, vol. 5, *Deuteronomium* (reprint, Frankfurt am Main, 1986), 31–32.

38. Hirsch, *The Pentateuch*, vol. 1, 233 (on Gen 12:6–7); *Die Genesis*, 191: "Das kann der Lappe in Lappland wie der Grieche in Griechenland erreichen."

39. Hirsch, *The Pentateuch*, vol. 1, 232 (on Gen 12:6–7).

40. Hirsch, *The Pentateuch*, vol. 1, 232 (*Die Genesis*, 191).

41. Hirsch, *The Pentateuch*, vol. 1, 233 (*Die Genesis*, 191).

42. Hirsch, *The Pentateuch*, vol. 5, *Deuteronomy*, 124 (*Deuteronomium*, p. 95).

43. Hirsch, *The Pentateuch*, vol. 4, *Numbers*, 544. German text: Samson Raphael Hirsch, *Der Pentateuch übersetzt und erläutert*, vol. 4, *Numeri* (reprint, Frankfurt am Main, 1986), 423.

44. Hirsch, *The Pentateuch*, vol. 3, *Leviticus*, 2nd. ed. (London, 1962), 732 (on Lev 25:4); see also Hirsch on Lev 25:2: Samson Raphael Hirsch, *Der Pentateuch übersetzt und erläutert*, vol. 3, *Leviticus* (reprint, Frankfurt am Main, 1986), 560–561.

45. Hirsch, *The Pentateuch*, vol. 4, 545 (*Numeri*, 424).

46. Hirsch, *The Pentateuch*, vol. 4, 546 (*Numeri*, 425: "Mit dieser dem Polytheismus im Gotteslande Berechtigung einräumenden Duldung büßt ihr aber selber die Integrität eurer Gotthörigkeit…").

47. Hermann Cohen, *Religion of Reason: Out of the Sources of Judaism*, trans. Simon Kaplan (Atlanta: Scholars Press, 1995), 340. Original German: *Religion der Vernunft aus den Quellen des Judentums* (Darmstadt, 1966, 395). In his chapter on image worship. Cohen writes: "Monotheism cannot permit any tolerance of polytheism. Idolatry has to be destroyed absolutely" (*Religion of Reason*, 52; *Religion der Vernunft*, 60). See also Cohen's comment on Exod 22:17 ("you shall not permit a sorceress to live!"): "If, however, monotheism is the only salvation for mankind, then there is no escape from the fact that idol worship and all kinds of magic must be destroyed. Tolerance is a principle that cannot be valid for the origin, setting up, and establishment of monotheism" (*Religion of Reason*, 233; *Religion der Vernunft*, 272). See also Matthias Morgenstern, "Hermann Cohen und seine Quellen des Judentums," in *Religion aus den Quellen der Vernunft: Hermann Cohen und das evangelische Christentum*, ed. Hans Martin Dober and Matthias Morgenstern (Tübingen: Mohr Siebeck, 2012), 3–27.

48. Hirsch, *The Pentateuch*, vol. 4, 546 (on Num 33:56); German text: *Numeri*, 425.

49. Hirsch, *The Pentateuch*, vol. 5, 74 (on Deut 4:41); German text: *Deuteronomium*, 59 ("Fundamentalgrundsatz von der gottebenbildlichen Menschendignität").

50. Hirsch, *The Pentateuch*, vol. 4, 554 (on Num 35:10); German text: *Numeri*, 431.

51.. Hirsch, *The Pentateuch*, vol. 5, 65 (on Deut 4:26); German text: *Deuteronomium*, 52.

52. Morgenstern, *From Frankfurt to Jerusalem*, 292. The French rendering of Charles Friedemann ("La loi dans la Pensée d'Isaac Breuer," *REJ* 131 [1972]: 127–157) is: "vous vous embourgeoiserez" (128). For the use of the term "philistine" see, for example; Samson

Raphael Hirsch, *Horeb: A Philosophy of Jewish Laws and Observations*, trans. Isidor Grunfeld (London: Soncino Press, 1962), 132ff. and Arthur Schopenhauer, *Parerga und Paralipomena: Kleine philosophische Schriften* (Berlin: Hayn, 1851), §123. On the concept of the "Philistines" in the context of German romantic critique of culture (*Kulturkritik*), see Morgenstern, *From Frankfurt to Jerusalem*, 212, 282, 290–294.

53. Isaac Breuer, *Die Welt als Schöpfung und Natur* (Frankfurt a. M.: Kauffmann, 1926), 12.

54. Hirsch, *The Pentateuch*, vol. 3, 804–807.

55. See, for example, Morgenstern, *From Frankfurt*, 168–187.

56. Morgenstern, *From Frankfurt*, 296–298.

57. On Breuer's "Marxism," see Morgenstern, *From Frankfurt*, 285–313; in his autobiography *Mein Weg* (posthumously published Jerusalem: Morascha-Verlag, 1988, p. 82) Breuer wrote: "Marx wurde mir eine Art Kant der Wirtschaft." He continued: "As Kant explained to me the relationship of self-conscious human beings to objective nature, so Marx explained the relationship of self-conscious human willing to economy.... Therefore, Proletarians of all countries, be united!" This last sentence, of course, refers to Marx's *Manifesto of the Communist Party* (1848).

58. On Raphael Breuer see: Morgenstern, *From Frankfurt*, 54–55 and 226–228.

59. Judging the Song of Songs according to the norms of rabbinic halakhah, Raphael Breuer maintained that this book (like Prov 7:6–23) gives a description of how—according to the literal sense of the text—men and women should *not* behave. Seen against the background of the traditional understanding of this biblical book (as a description of the most sublime love between God and Israel), this explanation was denounced as outrageous or even blasphemous by most of Breuer's contemporaries. For this commentary see: Matthias Morgenstern, "Von 'jüdischer Züchtigkeit' und 'sinnlichem Vergnügen': Die Kommentare zum Hohenlied von H. Graetz und R. Breuer," *Frankfurter Judaistische Beiträge* 28 (2001): 121–148; French translation: "'Pudeur juive' et 'jouissance sexuelle': Les commentaires du Cantique des Cantiques de H. Graetz et R. Breuer," *Tsafon: Revue d'études juives du Nord* 57 (printemps–été 2009): 27–58; Hebrew translation in *Revue européenne des études hébraïques* 9 (2003): 103–109.

60. Raphael Breuer, *Das Buch Josua: Übersetzt und erläutert* (Frankfurt a. M.: Sanger & Friedberg, 1915). In his preface (v), Breuer writes: "Dieses Buch lag schon seit langem im Manuskript druckfertig vor. Der Krieg hat sein Erscheinen verzögert. Wie es jetzt herauskommt, zeigt es sich mit einem Mal, daß es für sein Herauskommen keinen malerischeren Zeitpunkt hätte wählen können, als die Gegenwart. Das Buch Josua ist ein Kriegsbuch, das von Kämpfen und Siegen, von Landerwerb und Landverteilung redet. Welch eigenen Reiz mag es dem vom Lärm des Tages Ermüdeten bieten, beim Scheine der Weltkriegsflamme in einem Kriegsbuch aus verschollener Urzeit zu blättern!"

61. Samson Raphael Hirsch, *Die Psalmen: Übersetzt und erläutert* (Frankfurt a. M.: J. Kauffmann, 1882). Published as *The Psalms* (Jerusalem: Samson Raphael Hirsch Publications Society, 5737/1978).

62. Breuer, *Joshua*, ix.

63. In his commentary on the book of Joshua (*Josua* [Zürich: Theologischer Verlag Zürich, 2008]), Ernst Axel Knauf faces a similar question from a historical point of view and comes to quite a different conclusion. According to his explanation, the book of Joshua draws an obviously fictitious picture that matches and imitates the imperialist "theology" of the Assyrian Empire. In this understanding, the biblical narrative shows that the Israelites, according to the legal standards of the ancient Near East, had "rightly" conquered the land

and then "rightly" owned it because it was—absurd as it may sound to modern ears—in accordance with the legal and "moral" conceptions of that time, conceptions that the Assyrian army used later in its imperialistic enterprises.

64. Breuer, *Joshua*, ix: "Modern love for Palestine [Breuer of course hints at Zionism here—MM] will have the impression that the extermination of the pagan peoples was an atrocity contrary to humanitarian law, because this modern love will try to understand the history of Palestine from the perspective of extra-Palestinian conceptions."

65. Breuer, *Joshua*, ix.

66. Breuer, Joshua, ix: "In a holy country there is no place for human beings that have even not climbed to the first steps of humaneness."

67. Breuer, *Joshua*, xi: "Ein vom Krieg erfülltes und dem Krieg dienstbares Geschlecht wächst schon jetzt in unserer jüdischen Jugend heran. Das kann uns nicht Wunder nehmen. Wir deutschen Juden haben unser Vaterland immer geliebt. An der Einmütigkeit, mit welcher das ganze Deutschtum gegen den von West und Süd unterstützten Slavenüberfall sich erhebt, nehmen auch die deutschen Juden teil."

68. Breuer, *Joshua*, xi: "Wars should be led, they should not be worshipped."

69. Starting with the presupposition (the divine character of the book) that should be result of his enquiry is logically *petitio principii*.

70. For the attitude of Isaac Breuer to biblical criticism, see Matthias Morgenstern, "Jüdisch-orthodoxe Wege zur Bibelkritik," *Jud.* 56 (2000): 184–188.

71. Breuer, *Joshua*, xi: " Sie alle [i.e., all German Jews] fühlen, daß der Boden, auf dem ihre Wiege stand und auch die Gräber ihrer Ahnen liegen, ein heiliger Boden ist, den es gegen eine Welt von Feinden zu verteidigen gilt."

Bibliography

Abrahams, Josef. "Jewish Interpretation of the Old Testament." In *The People and the Book: Essays on the Old Testament*, edited by Arthur Samuel Peake, 403–431. Oxford: Clarendon Press, 1925.

Albertz, Rainer. *A History of Israelite Religion in the Old Testament Period*. Vol. 1. *From the Beginnings to the End of the Monarchy*. London: SCM Press, 1994.

Alt, Albrecht. *The Settlement of the Israelites in Palestine* (1925). In *Essays on Old Testament History and Religion*, translated by R. A. Wilson. Oxford: Doubleday, 1967.

Breuer, Isaac. *Mein Weg*. Jerusalem: Morascha-Verlag, 1988.

——. *Die Welt als Schöpfung und Natur*. Frankfurt a. M.: Kauffmann, 1926.

Breuer, Raphael. *Das Buch Josua: Übersetzt und erläutert*. Frankfurt a. M.: Sanger & Friedberg, 1915.

Cohen, Hermann. *Religion of Reason: Out of the Sources of Judaism*. Translated by Simon Kaplan. Atlanta: Scholars Press, 1995.

Cuffari, Anton. "Josua/Josuabuch." In *WiBiLex: Das wissenschaftliche Bibellexikon im Internet*. http://www.bibelwissenschaft.de/de/wibilex/das-bibellexikon/details/quelle/ WIBI/zeichen/a/referenz/11717///cache/fd4e50b54b4c2805d8b2ccce45df6784/.

Eichhorn, Johann Gottfried. *Einleitung ins Alte Testament*. Leipzig: Weidmann und Reich, 1780–1783.

Ewald, Heinrich. *Geschichte des Volkes Israel*. Göttingen: Dieterich, 1843–1859.

Finkelstein, Israel. *The Archaeology of the Israelite Settlement*. Jerusalem: Israel Exploration Society, 1988.

Friedmann, Charles. "La loi dans la pensée d'Isaac Breuer." *REJ* 131 (1972): 127–157.

Fritz, Volkmar. "The Conquest in the Light of Archaeology." In *Proceedings in the Eighth World Congress of Jewish Studies, Jerusalem 1981*, World Congress of Jewish Studies 1, 15–22. Jerusalem: World Union of Jewish Studies, 1982.

Graetz, Heinrich. *History of the Jews: From the Earliest Times to the Present Day*. Translated by Bella Löwy. London: David Nutt, 1891.

——. *Geschichte der Juden: Von den ältesten Zeiten bis auf die Gegenwart*. Vol. 1. *Geschichte der Israeliten von ihren Uranfängen (um 1500) bis zum Tode des Königs Salomo (um 977 vorchr. Zeit)*. Leipzig: Oskar Leiner, 1874.

——. *Geschichte der Juden: Von den ältesten Zeiten bis auf die Gegenwart*. Vol. 4. *Vom Untergang des jüdischen Staates bis zum Abschluß des Talmuds*. Leipzig: Oskar Leiner, 1866.

——. *Geschichte der Juden: Von den ältesten Zeiten bis auf die Gegenwart*. Vol. 4. *Vom Untergang des jüdischen Staates bis zum Abschluß des Talmuds*. Leipzig – Berlin: Oskar Leiner, 1853.

——. *The Structure of Jewish History and Other Essays*. Translated by Ismar Schorsch. New York: Jewish Theological Seminary of America. Distributed by Ktav, 1975.

Gugenheimer, Joseph. "Die Hypothesen der Bibelkritik und der Commentar zur Genesis von Herrn Rabbiner Hirsch." *Jeschurun* 15 (5629/1869): 81–100 and 179–192.

——. "Die Hypothesen der Bibelkritik und der Commentar zur Genesis von Herrn Rabbiner Hirsch." *Jeschurun* 14 (5628/1868): 1–18, 173–191, and 312–325.

——. "Die Hypothesen der Bibelkritik und der Commentar zur Genesis von Herrn Rabbiner Hirsch." *Jeschurun* 13 (5627/1867): 293–313 and 397–409.

Hildesheimer, Meir, and Matthias Morgenstern. "Rabbiner Samson Raphael Hirsch in der deutschsprachigen jüdischen Presse: Materialien zu einer bibliographischen Übersicht." *Judaica* 66 (2010): 162–185, 394–407, and 408–436.

Hirsch, Samson Raphael. *The Pentateuch Translated and Explained*. Translated by German Isaac Levy. London: Gateshead, 1963.

——. *Horeb: A Philosophy of Jewish Laws and Observations*. Translated by Isidor Grunfeld. London: Soncino Press, 1962.

——. *Die Psalmen: Übersetzt und erläutert*. Frankfurt a. M.: J. Kauffmann, 1882.

Kapustin, M. "Biblical Criticism: A Traditionalist View." *Tradition* 3, no.1 (Fall 1960): 25–33.

Knauf, Ernst Axel. *Josua*. Zürich: Theologischer Verlag Zürich, 2008.

Lemche, Niels Peter. *Prelude to Israel's Past: Background and Beginnings of Israelite History and Identity*. Peabody, Mass.: Hendrickson, 1998.

Morgenstern, Matthias, "'Erez Israel,' madre straniera." *Concilium: Rivista internazionale di teologia* 43, no. 2 (2007): 87–98.

——. "'Pudeur juive' et 'jouissance sexuelle': Les commentaires du Cantique des Cantiques de H. Graetz et R. Breuer." In *Tsafon: Revue d'études juives du Nord* 57 (printemps–été 2009): 27–58.

——. *From Frankfurt to Jerusalem: Isaac Breuer and the History of the Secession Dispute in Modern Jewish Orthodoxy*. Leiden: Brill, 2002.

——. "Von 'jüdischer Züchtigkeit' und 'sinnlichem Vergnügen': Die Kommentare zum Hohenlied von H. Graetz und R. Breuer." In *Frankfurter Judaistische Beiträge* 28 (2001): 121–148.

——. "Jüdisch-orthodoxe Wege zur Bibelkritik." *Jud.* 56 (2000): 184–188.

Matthias Morgenstern. "Hermann Cohen und seine Quellen des Judentums." In *Religion aus den Quellen der Vernunft: Hermann Cohen und das evangelische Christentum*, edited by Hans Martin Dober and Matthias Morgenstern, 3–27. Tübingen: Mohr Siebeck, 2012.

Nelson, Richard D. *Joshua: A Commentary.* Louisville: Westminster John Knox, 1997.

Oswald, Wolfgang. *Staatstheorie im Alten Israel: Der politische Diskurs im Pentateuch und in den Geschichtsbüchern des Alten Testaments.* Stuttgart: Kohlhammer, 2009.

Schopenhauer, Arthur. *Parerga und Paralipomena: Kleine philosophische Schriften.* Berlin: Hayn, 1851.

Soggin, Jan Alberto. *A History of Israel: From the Beginnings to the Bar Kochba Revolt AD 135.* Translated by John Bowden. London: SCM Press, 1984.

Wellhausen, Julius. *Die Composition des Hexateuchs und der historischen Bücher des Alten Testaments.* Berlin: Reimer, 1889.

——. *Skizzen und Vorarbeiten 2: Die Composition des Hexateuchs.* Berlin: Reimer, 1885.

——. *Prolegomena zur Geschichte Israels.* Berlin: Reimer, 1878.

PART II

The Changing Uses of the Category "Canaanites"

10

Where May Canaanites Be Found?

CANAANITES, PHOENICIANS, AND OTHERS IN JEWISH TEXTS FROM
THE HELLENISTIC AND ROMAN PERIOD

Katell Berthelot

When dealing with the Hellenistic and Roman period, one may wonder whether "Canaan" and "Canaanites" were names that still meant something concrete to anybody, beyond the memories from the biblical past. As a matter of fact, no pagan author of Greek or Roman literary texts seems to have used these names.[1] In Greek literature they first appear in the Septuagint; they are found in Jewish texts that rewrite Scriptures or refer to the biblical past (in most cases) and are then found in texts by Christian writers, mainly when the latter comment on biblical texts.

However, for some people, apparently, the Canaanites were not merely a people from the distant past. First, there is evidence that the name "Canaan" was sometimes used in Phoenicia itself as a self-designation.[2] Moreover, the fifth-century C.E. writer Augustinus mentions in passing that peasants in North Africa call themselves Canaanites.[3] Procopius of Caesarea, a Byzantine *rhetor* of the sixth century C.E. who wrote a history of the wars of the Emperor Justinian, affirms that the Moors in Libya have Canaanite origins and that they claim such ancestry themselves. Procopius first writes that it was Joshua "who led this people [the Hebrews] into Palestine [*Palaistinè*], and, by displaying a valour in war greater than that natural to a man, gained possession of the land."[4] Then he adds:

> Now at that time the whole country along the sea from Sidon as far as the boundaries of Egypt was called Phoenicia.... In that country there dwelt very populous tribes, the Gergesites and the Jebusites and some others with other names by which they are called in the history of the Hebrews. Now when these nations saw that the invading general was an irresistible prodigy, they emigrated from their ancestral homes and made their way to Egypt, which adjoined their country. And finding there no place sufficient for them to dwell in, since there has been a great population in Egypt from ancient times, they proceeded to Libya. And they established numerous cities and

took possession of the whole of Libya as far as the Pillars of Heracles, and there they have lived even up to my time, using the Phoenician tongue. They also built a fortress in Numidia, where now is the city called Tigisis. In that place are two columns made of white stones near by the great spring, having Phoenician letters cut in them which say in the Phoenician tongue: "We are they who fled from before the face of Joshua, the robber, the son of Nun."[5]

Finally, Procopius makes the interesting observation that when Phoenicians later settled in North Africa and founded Carthage, they were indeed considered kinsmen by the group that came from Canaan (now called the Moors), but that they remained different peoples, to the point that they even fought against each other at a later stage in history.

The connection between Canaanites and Phoenicians is a historical fact (at the linguistic, cultural, and religious levels).[6] Moreover, this connection is underlined in the Bible itself, starting with Genesis 10:15, "Canaan begat Sidon his firstborn." Pseudo-Eupolemus, thought to be a Samaritan author writing in Greek in the second century B.C.E., who is quoted by Alexander Polyhistor and then by Eusebius, writes in the same vein that Canaan was "the father of the Phoenicians."[7] Moreover, the names "Canaanite" and "Phoenician" are sometimes interchangeable (as in the Septuagint, which sometimes translates "Canaan" and "Canaanite" as "Phoenicia" and "Phoenician,"[8] and as in Procopius's excursus quoted above). Some Rabbinic texts allude to a migration of at least some Canaanite tribes from Canaan to Africa at the time of the conquest by Joshua[9] (Procopius's account is frequently mentioned in the discussion of those texts,[10] and the reverse is sometimes true as well[11]). All those elements have led some scholars to suggest that there may be a historical basis to the scenario according to which some Canaanite tribes settled in Africa.[12]

In this chapter, however, my purpose is not to disentangle those intricate historical issues, but rather to try to answer the following questions: In the Hellenistic and Roman period, did Jews consider that there were still "Canaanites" living in the land, or elsewhere? Were the categories "Canaan" and "Canaanites" relevant in any way to Jews at that time? In a more general way, which words did Jewish authors use to name the land and its non-Jewish inhabitants? And does the terminology teach us something about the way(s) Jews conceived of the relationship between Jews and non-Jews in the land? The necessarily brief answers proposed here are based on the analysis of Jewish literary works from the Hellenistic and Roman period, with the exception of rabbinic literature (which is much too vast to be dealt with in the framework of this chapter).

Three aspects of the topic will be addressed: first, Canaan and Canaanites as realities going back to a remote biblical past; second, contemporary names applied to biblical Canaan or to the Canaanites; third, contemporary places and people described as "Canaan" or "Canaanite."

1. Canaan and Canaanites as Realities Stemming from a Remote Biblical Past

In the vast majority of cases, the words "Canaan" and "Canaanites" occur in works or passages dealing with biblical stories and characters. This is quite apparent in compositions like the *Genesis Apocryphon* (XII 11), the *Visions of Amram* (4Q544 1 7, 4Q545 1a+b ii 18, 4Q547 9 9), the *Commentary on Genesis A* (4Q252 II 6, 10, 13), the *Apocryphon of the Pentateuch B* (4Q377 1 i 8), the *Apocryphon of Joshua B* (4Q379 12 6), the *Prophecy of Joshua* (4Q522 3 2; 9 ii 9) (considered by some as a third copy of the *Apocryphon of Joshua*), the *Temple Scroll* (LXII 14),[13] the book of *Jubilees* (12.15), *Exagogè* (v.1), the fragments of Demetrios the Chronographer quoted by Eusebius (2.6–8, 16, 18–19), *Joseph and Aseneth* (4.13; 6.5; 13.10), and so on. This is also the case in most of Philo's works and in Josephus' texts, though Josephus adds interesting information to the biblical account. But let us first get an overall view of the use of the words "Canaan" and "Canaanite" in Josephus' work.

Vita and *Contra Apionem* do not contain any occurrence of the terms. In Josephus' *Bellum judaicum*, they are found only three times, and always in connection with biblical data. In 4.459, when the Romans conquer Jericho, Josephus engages in an erudite digression in which he mentions that Jericho was the first town in the land of Canaan to be conquered by Joshua. Then, at the end of book 6, after the fall of Jerusalem, Josephus gives a short account of the history of the town and recalls that it was founded by a righteous Canaanite king (Melkizedek in Gen 14:18; the name is translated as "righteous king" in *B.J.* 6.438), and that David, the king of the Judeans/Jews, later expelled the Canaanite population and "settled there his own (people)" (κατοικίζει τὸν ἴδιον; *B.J.* 6.439).

In *Antiquitates judaicae*, references to the Canaanites are much more frequent, but appear only in books 1–9, and mostly in books 1–5. There are no more references to the Canaanites after the account of Sennacherib's campaign. Josephus' account of the division of the earth between Noah's descendants (Gen 10) in *Antiquitates judaicae* 1.138–139 is particularly interesting and helps us better understand the author's perception of the Canaanites:

> Chananaeus also had sons, of whom Sidonius built in Phoenicia a city named after him, still called Sidon by the Greeks, and Amathus [Hamathites] founded Amathus, which the inhabitants to this day call Amathè, though the Macedonians renamed it Epiphaneia after one of Alexander's successors. Arudaeus [Arvadites] occupied the island of Aradus, and Arucaeus [Arkites] Arkè in Lebanon. Of the seven others—Euaeus [Hivites], Chettaeus [Hittites], Jebuseus [Jebusites], Amorreus [Amorites], Gergesaeus [Girgashites], Seinaeus [Sinites], Samaraeus [Tsemarites]—we have no record in the sacred Scriptures beyond their names; for the Hebrews destroyed their cities, which owed this calamity to the following cause.[14]

Josephus then proceeds to tell the story of Noah's curse of Canaan in Genesis 9, explaining that the fate of the last seven Canaanite nations was caused by their ancestor's original curse.[15]

Although he mentions the descendants of Canaan in an order different from the one found in the Bible, Josephus gives the exact list from Genesis 10:15–19.[16] Noteworthy, however, is the distinction he draws between the Sidonians, Hamathites, Arvadites, and Arkites, on the one hand, and the seven remaining Canaanite nations, on the other. To a certain extent, Josephus may have been inspired by biblical data: The Hamathites, the Arvadites, and the Arkites are never mentioned in the Bible again, except for a passage in 1 Chronicles 1:16 that rewrites Genesis 10:15–19. Thus, they are never listed among the seven Canaanite peoples that are to be expelled or killed. However, if this is what Josephus had in mind, he lacked consistency, because the Sinites and the Tsemarites are also names that appear only in Genesis 10:15–19 and in 1 Chronicles 1:16. Moreover, the city of Sidon and the Sidonians are a different case altogether: True, they are generally not included in the lists of the Canaanite peoples that have to be expelled or killed; however, according to Joshua 13:5 and Judges 3:1–3, the Sidonians are included among the Canaanite populations who have to be dispossessed, even though, eventually, it did not happen (see Judg 3:1–3). Thus, the reason for Josephus' distinction between the two groups of peoples probably lies elsewhere.

Let us have a look at the geographical explanations provided by Josephus, which significantly differ from the biblical account and represent an innovation. The four peoples Josephus singles out are all connected with places in Phoenicia (or even Syria):[17] The latter are the famous cities of Sidon, Aradus or Arvad/Arwad (which once used to be a rival of Sidon), and Hamath,[18] as well as another town called Arce (Arkè), situated in northern Phoenicia near Tripolis, and whose location in Lebanon is highlighted by Josephus himself. A striking parallel is found in *Genesis Rabbah* 37.6, which states in its commentary on Genesis 10:15–18: "The Arkite: i.e. Arkas of the Lebanon."[19] Moreover, as in Josephus' *Antiquitates judaicae*, the Hellenistic name of Hamath, Epiphaneia, is mentioned in connection with the Hamathites. The midrash locates even more tribes in Phoenicia and Syria than Josephus does: "The Sinite: Orthosia. The Arvadite: Aradus. The Tsemarite: Hamats; and why is it called Tsemarite? Because wool is manufactured there. The Hamathite: Epiphania."[20] Orthosia is a Phoenician city located south of the Eleutherus River, in northern Phoenicia, and Hamats is identified by H. Freedman with Emesa in Syria.[21] By locating the Sinites and the Tsemarites in northern Phoenicia/Syria, like the other groups mentioned only in Genesis 10:15–19 and in 1 Chronicles 1:16, the midrash is more consistent than Josephus.[22]

However, both Josephus and the midrash contradict Genesis 10:19, which states that "the territory of the Canaanites extended from Sidon, in the direction of Gerar, as far as Gaza, and in the direction of Sodom, Gomorrah, Admah, and Tseboim, as far as Lasha." Now, Arwad, Arce, and Hamath are located in northern Phoenicia and in Syria,[23] far beyond the biblical northern border of Canaan as described in Genesis 10:19. What prompted Josephus to locate these tribes there was probably the similarity between the names of the peoples and those of the Phoenician cities, a similarity that does not exist in the case of the Sinites and of the Tsemarites. The reason that the Sidonians, Hamathites, Arvadites, and Arkites were singled out was their geographical location—but the relationship between their territories and the Promised Land where the children of Israel fought other Canaanite tribes needs to be examined more closely.

The issue of the borders of the land and of the fate of the "Phoenician Canaanites" is evoked again when Josephus rewrites the story of the Hebrew spies commanded by Moses to explore the land of Canaan. Numbers 13:21 (MT) states that the spies went "from the desert of Tzin until Rehov, near the entrance of Hamath" (ממדבר צן עד רחב לבא חמת). Other biblical texts, such as Joshua 13:5 and Judges 3:3, describe the northern border as extending from Mount Hermon until "the entrance of Hamath" or "Levo-Hamath." In Joshua 13:5-6, this area is included among the territories that still need to be con-quered, corresponding to "the land of the Giblites, and all Lebanon, from the sunrising, from Baal-Gad below Mount Hermon to the entrance of Hamath [MT: עד לבא חמת; LXX: ἕως τῆς εἰσόδου Εμαθ], all the inhabitants of the hill country from Lebanon to Misrephoth-Maim, all the Sidonians." God declares to Joshua that he will *dispossess* the inhabitants of the area, according to the Masoretic Text (Josh 13:6: אנכי אורישם מפני בני ישראל), or that he will *destroy* them, according to the Septuagint (ἐγὼ αὐτοὺς ἐξολεθρεύσω ἀπὸ προσώπου Ισραηλ). According to Numbers 13, the northern border of the Promised Land is thus defined in connection with a city called Hamath, probably the town located on the Orontes in Syria. However, the formula "Rehov at the entrance of Hamath" could designate a place much more southern than Hamath itself, so that the precise location of the northern border is still the subject of debate.[24] Moreover, according to Judges 3:1-3, God neither destroyed nor dispossessed "the Canaanites, the Sidonians, and the Hivites who dwelt in Mount Lebanon, from Mount Baal-Hermon until the entrance to Hamath" (v. 3),[25] in order to put Israel to the test and to teach the art of war to the Israelites who had not waged war so far.

In the Septuagint corresponding to Numbers 13:21 (22), the land is explored "from the desert of Sin until Rhaab, entering Hemath" (ἀπὸ τῆς ἐρήμου Σιν ἕως Ρααβ εἰσπορευομένων Ἐμάθ[26]). As for Josephus, he writes in *Antiquitates judaicae* 3.303: "(These), starting from the Egyptian border, traversed Canaan from end to end, reached the city of Amathè [Hamath] and Mount Libanus [οἳ διεξελθόντες ἀπὸ τῶν πρὸς Αἰγύπτῳ τὴν Χαναναίαν ἅπασαν ἐπί τε Ἀμάθην πόλιν καὶ Λίβανον ἀφικνοῦνται τὸ ὄρος], and after fully exploring the nature of the country and of its inhabitants, returned."[27] H. St. J. Thackeray comments

in a footnote: "Hamath on the Orontes in North Syria.²⁸ The Biblical phrase
(Num 13:21), 'the entering in of (entrance to) Hamath,' elsewhere named as the
northern boundary of Canaan, means a region far to the south of the city itself,
perhaps the depression between Lebanon and Hermon."²⁹ However, Josephus
does not speak about the "entrance of Hamath" or about a city south of Hamath,
but about Hamath itself. Louis H. Feldman notices Josephus' departure from
the biblical formulation, and expresses some surprise at the extent of the territory: "This is Hamath on the river Orontes in Syria. It is, nevertheless, hard to
suppose that the scouts went so far north, though it is apparently what Josephus
thought."³⁰ Undoubtedly, Josephus relied on the version of the Masoretic Text or
that of the Alexandrinus manuscript, and identified חמה in Numbers 13:21 with
Amathè, the town mentioned in *Antiquitates judaicae* 1.138. As a consequence,
the territory of the Hamathites was probably included in the land that was supposed to be conquered by the children of Israel. This means that, in accordance
with Joshua 13:5–6, Josephus considered the territories of the Sidonians, Arkites,
Arvadites, and Hamathites, or at least part of them, to have been included in
the land that was to be seized by Israel, even if these Canaanite tribes were not
mentioned among the seven nations doomed to be expelled or banned.

A passage from book 9 of *Antiquitates judaicae*, sections 206–207, corrobo-
rates this reading. It corresponds to 2 Kings 14:25, which states, concerning the
impious king of Israel Jeroboam II: "He was the one who restored the border
of Israel, from the entrance to Hamath (MT לבא חמת; LXX ἀπὸ εἰσόδου Αιμαθ)
until the sea of the Arava, according to the word which the Lord God of Israel
spoke through his servant Jonah the prophet." As to Josephus, he writes: "Now
a certain Jonah prophesied to him [Jeroboam II] that he should make war
on the Syrians and defeat their forces and extend his realm on the north as
far as the city of Amathè [ἕως Ἀμάθου πόλεως] and on the south as far as
lake Asphaltitis [Dead Sea]—for in ancient times these were the boundaries
of Canaan as the general Joshua had defined them. And so, having marched
against the Syrians, Jeroboam subdued their entire country, as Jonah had
prophesied" (9.206–207).³¹ Josephus' addition confirms that in his eyes, the
Promised Land (or Canaan) went as far north as Hamath in Syria. The other
notable fact is that Josephus attributes the delimitation of the borders not to
God but to "the general Joshua," in accordance with his tendency to enhance
the role of leaders such as Moses, Joshua, and so on.

However, according to Joshua 19:24–30, the territory of the sons of Asher
extended only until "the great Sidon" (v. 28). In *Antiquitates judaicae* 5.85,
Josephus seems to leave Sidon outside the Asherite territory, too. The reference to Arkè in 5.85 probably represents a scribal mistake, since the location
of this city does not fit into the borders of the Asherite territory as described
by both the biblical text and Josephus.³² After the description of the territories
of the children of Asher and Naphtali, Josephus adds a summary that does not
appear either in the Masoretic Text or in the Septuagint:

Thus did Joshua divide six of the nations that bore the names of the sons of Canaan and gave their land to the nine and a half tribes for their possession; for Amoritis, likewise so called after one of the children of Canaan, had already of yore been taken and apportioned by Moses to the two and a half tribes, as we have previously related. But the regions about Sidon, with those of the Arucaeans [Arkites], Amathaeans [Hamathites] and Aridaeans [Arvadites], remained unassigned [τὰ δὲ περὶ Σιδῶνα καὶ Ἀρουκαίους καὶ Ἀμαθαίους καὶ Ἀριδαίους ἀδιακόσμητα ἦν]. (5.88–89)

Moreover, "Joshua…charged each tribe to leave no remnant of the race of the Canaanites within their allotted territory, since their security and the maintenance of their ancestral institutions hung upon that alone: this Moses had already told them and of this he was himself persuaded" (5.90).[33] This passage makes clear that had the territories of the Sidonians, Arvadites, Hamathites, and Arkites been allotted, their inhabitants would probably have suffered the same fate as the other Canaanite tribes. But their territories were not conquered, and they were apparently left in peace.

What, according to Josephus, was the final fate of these "Phoenician Canaanites?" First, one must underline that concerning the other Canaanite nations listed in *Antiquitates judaicae* 1.139, Josephus' statement according to which "we have no record in the sacred Scriptures beyond their names" is at least partly inaccurate. Several biblical texts refer to the Amorites, the Jebusites, the Hittites, and so on, and tell us a lot more about them than just their names—be it only their resistance to the children of Israel and the fact that they remained in the land far beyond the period of the conquest, as it is reported in the second part of the book of Joshua and even more insistently in the book of Judges. In spite of his affirmation in *Antiquitates judaicae* 1.139 that the seven nations had disappeared, Josephus himself repeatedly echoes the biblical texts alluding to the continued presence of some Canaanite populations in the country until the period of the monarchy.[34] However, in *Antiquitates judaicae* 8.160–162, based on 1 Kings 9:20–23 (Solomon's decision to treat the remnant of the Canaanites as slaves), Josephus writes: "160. King Solomon also reduced to subjection those of the Canaanites who were still unsubmissive, that is, those who lived on Mount Libanos and as far as Amathè [τοὺς ἔτι τῶν Χαναναίων οὐχ ὑπακούοντας οἳ ἐν τῷ Λιβάνῳ διέτριβον ὄρει καὶ μέχρι πόλεως Ἀμάθης ὑποχειρίους], and imposed a tribute upon them and raised a yearly levy from them to be his serfs and perform menial tasks and till the soil."[35] In other words, contrary to the biblical text which clearly mentions "all the people who were left of the Amorites, Hittites, Perizzites, Hivites, and Jebusites…, their descendants who were left after them in the land, whom the people of Israel were unable to destroy utterly" (1 Kgs 9:20–21 MT),[36] Josephus argues that the people whom Solomon reduced to subjection were Phoenician Canaanites, belonging to the four groups listed in *Antiquitates judaicae* 1.138, not to the nations listed in section 139.

In conclusion, although Josephus mainly refers to the Canaanites as nations of the past banned by the Hebrews, he also distinguishes between the Canaanites in the territories where the children of Israel settled and the Canaanites in Phoenicia and Syria; on the other hand, his writings testify to the continued perception of a connection between Canaanites and Phoenicians down to his own time. The "Phoenician Canaanites" were not concerned by the commandments of expulsion or *herem*, because they dwelt in territories that were located on the fringes of the land promised by God to his people (inside it, according to the geographical descriptions provided in several biblical texts, but outside it in other cases), and above all in territories that, according to the biblical account itself, were not conquered. This explains the enduring existence of these Canaanite populations down through the ages until Solomon's time. Then, however, the curse against their ancestor was fulfilled, since they were subjected to slavery (according to Josephus' version of the story).

Finally, it must be underlined that nowhere does Josephus suggest that some non-Jewish population dwelling in the land in his own time may be identified with one of the seven nations of Canaan who were subjected to the ban.

2. Contemporary Names Applied to Biblical Canaan and to the Canaanites

Conversely, one must recall that some Jewish writers never use the terms "Canaan" and "Canaanites," even when dealing with biblical episodes. Thus, for instance, in the fragments preserved by Eusebius (who himself uses Polyhistor's account), Eupolemus deals at length with the reign of David and the construction of the Temple by Solomon, without mentioning the Canaanites as Josephus does in his *Antiquitates judaicae*. When he recalls the wars of David, Eupolemus uses names that were common in his own time and are not found in the Bible, such as "Itureans" and "Nabateans."[37] Apart from Eupolemus, in the Septuagint and the Pseudepigrapha in Greek, Itureans are mentioned only in 1 Chronicles 5:19, as a translation for the Hebrew name יטור (καὶ ἐποίουν πόλεμον μετὰ τῶν Αγαρηνῶν καὶ Ιτουραίων καὶ Ναφισαίων καὶ Ναδαβαίων), and Nabateans are evoked only in 1 Maccabees 5:25 and 9:35. Eupolemus mentions Nabdeans as well, but this reference is specific to him; the name has been explained either as a corrupt doublet of Nabateans, or as a scribal error for Zabadaious (1 Macc 12:31).[38] The use of the name Commagene, which designates a region in northern Syria, is also specific to Eupolemus; however, later it is found in Josephus, too. Another example of anachronism is Eupolemus' use of the name Scythopolis (the Greek name of Beth-Shean) for the period of the Babylonian conquest (Nebuchadnezzar).[39] To quote Carl Holladay: "The political and geographical situation envisioned here is Maccabean, not Davidic."[40]

To sum up, Eupolemus makes use of the terminology of his time and projects it in an anachronistic manner upon the events and the situations of the past, instead of looking at the present through the lenses of the past. "Canaan" does not seem to have been a useful geographical or ethnic category in his eyes.

However surprising it may seem at first glance, Philo, too, provides interesting examples of the tendency to refer to "Canaan" by using contemporary geographical or ethnic categories. We should bear in mind that in Philo's works, the names "Canaan" and "Canaanites" generally appear in the context of his interpretation of the Pentateuch. Now, in Philo's allegorical reading of the Exodus and of the conquest narrative, Egypt symbolizes the body and the passions,[41] Canaan the vices,[42] and the Promised Land (which, at the allegorical level, differs from Canaan) virtue.[43] Moreover, Egypt represents childhood, Canaan youth, and the Promised Land adulthood.[44] At that level, no past or contemporary *realia* are involved.

However, in several cases Philo also addresses the literal, "historical" meaning of the biblical text, and he sometimes uses contemporary names to describe biblical places and peoples. Thus, in *Hypothetica*, when it comes to the conquest of the land, Philo questions the reliability of a literal interpretation of the biblical narrative, asking whether it is reasonable to think that the Hebrews were able to attack a foreign country after forty years of wandering in the desert.[45] He asks the following rhetorical question: "Were they [the children of Israel] still superior in the number of their fighting men though they had fared so ill to the end, still strong and with weapons in their hand, and did they then take the land by force, defeating the combined Syrians and Phoenicians [Σύρους τε ὁμοῦ καὶ Φοίνικας] when fighting in their own country?"[46] Philo suggests that this scenario is highly unlikely, and that it is more plausible to suppose that the inhabitants of the land voluntarily surrendered it to the children of Israel, so that there was no war of conquest.[47] What I would like to emphasize here is the inaccurate and anachronistic use of the names "Syrians" and "Phoenicians" to designate the Canaanites. It shows that Philo was thinking in the geographical categories of his time. However, in the context of the conquest of the land, the identification of the Canaanites with Syrians and Phoenicians remains surprising.

Other examples of Philo's use of contemporary geographical and ethnic names in connection with biblical data may shed light on the surprising use of the names "Syrians" and "Phoenicians" in *Hypothetica*. In *De Iosepho* 230, in the context of the incident with Benjamin, when Judah speaks to Joseph and asks him to pity Jacob, the father of the child (Gen 44:18–34), he says:

> Take pity, then, on the old age of one who has spent all his years labouring in the arena of virtue. The cities of Syria he won over to receive and honour him, though his customs and usages were strange to them and very different, and those of the country alien to him in no small degree. But the nobility of

his life, and his acknowledged harmony of words with deeds and deeds with words, prevailed so that even those whom national feelings [or, rather: ancestral customs] prejudiced against him were brought over to his ways.[48]

Here Philo calls the land of Canaan "Syria." In *De vita Mosis* 1.214, when he recalls the attack of the Amalekites against the Hebrews (Exod 17:8–16), he refers to the former as "Phoenicians," a rather surprising designation for a people located in the Negev. In *De Abrahamo* 133, when he mentions the episode of Sodom, Philo writes that "the land of the Sodomites, a part of the land of Canaan afterwards called Palestinian Syria [or Syria-Palestine], was brimful of innumerable iniquities."[49] In *De vita Mosis* 1.163, Philo writes that Moses, "having received the authority which they [the children of Israel] willingly gave him, with the sanction and assent of God, proposed to lead them to settle in Phoenicia and Coelesyria and Palestine, then called (the land) of the Canaanites, the boundaries of which were three days' journey from Egypt."[50] The singular relative pronoun ἥ makes it clear that the place called the land of the Canaanites was *Palaistinè*, not the three areas taken together. Finally, later in *De vita Mosis* (1.237), Philo writes that the Hebrews could have "occupied the cities of Syria and their portions of land in the second year after leaving Egypt," but that they were condemned to err for forty years.[51] So for Philo the land of Canaan can be called either Syria, *Syria Palaistinè*, or *Palaistinè*.[52] The name Judaea appears in Philo's works as well, but, in contrast to Josephus,[53] Philo does not identify Canaan with Judaea. This is a chronological issue: The name *Judaea* is used by Philo only in connection with events from the Hellenistic and Roman period.

Herodotus, too, connected Syria and *Palaistinè*, and spoke about Syrians who were called *Palaistinoi* (3.5). As far as the inhabitants of the land are concerned, Philo may refer to them as Syrians and Phoenicians, but in contrast with Herodotus or later Josephus, Philo never uses the name *Palaistinoi* to designate a people, no matter the period. For instance, he presents Tamar as "a woman from *Palaistinè Syria*" (*Virt.* 221)—which, by the way, does not prevent her from becoming a righteous proselyte. He even speaks once about Judeans/ Jews who live in *Palaistinè Syria*, in *Probus* (75), at the very beginning of his account of the Essenes: "Palestinian Syria, too, has not failed to produce high moral excellence. In this country live a considerable part of the very populous nation of the Jews [or Judeans]."[54]

What these texts teach, in my view, is that Philo was rather imprecise in his use of geographical terms. The issue of the name of the land does not seem to have mattered much in his eyes. But it would be wrong to infer that the land, whatever its name, had no religious significance for him. Philo never uses the expression "Land of Israel," but he is one of the very few authors who use the expression "holy Land," which is quite rare both in biblical and in Second Temple literature.[55]

To sum up: Philo does not look at the land in his own time as "Canaan;" quite the opposite, he tends to use contemporary geographical or ethnic names when he writes about the literal, "historical" meaning of biblical stories. However, at least one passage from *Legatio ad Gaium* (202)[56] shows that even if the non-Jewish inhabitants of the land are not considered Canaanites in any way and may be authorized to live there, in Philo's view, the holiness of the Land by definition excludes idolatry.

3. Contemporary Places and People Described as "Canaan" or "Canaanite"

Finally, a third aspect of my inquiry pertains to the rare use of the term "Canaanite" to designate non-Jews in Jewish texts from the Hellenistic and Roman period. As a matter of fact, there is only one explicit case of this kind, in 1 Maccabees 9:37.[57]

It is well known that 1 Maccabees, which was originally written in Hebrew, contains biblical idioms, as well as many references or allusions to biblical events and characters.[58] To quote Uriel Rappaport, this book "follows the model of biblical historiography, especially that of the First Prophets,"[59] but it also minimizes the role of God in order to emphasize the role of the Hasmonean dynasty, thus departing from biblical historiography.[60]

In 1 Maccabees 9:37, the head of an apparently Nabatean tribe is designated as "one of the great nobles of Canaan" (ἑνὸς τῶν μεγάλων μεγιστάνων Χανααν).[61] What is the context of this passage? Judas Maccabeus is dead, and his brothers Jonathan and Simon flee to the desert to escape from Bacchides, a general in the army of Demetrius I. Jonathan then sends his brother John to the Nabateans[62] to ask them permission "to store with them the great amount of baggage which they had" (9:35). The story continues as follows: "36. But the sons of Jambri from Medeba[63] came out and seized John and all that he had, and departed with it. 37. After these things it was reported to Jonathan and Simon his brother, 'The sons of Jambri are celebrating a great wedding, and are conducting the bride, a daughter of one of the great nobles of Canaan, from Nadabath[64] with a large escort.' 38. And they remembered the blood of John their brother, and went up and hid under cover of the mountain." The end of the story is that Jonathan and Simon attacked the bridegroom and his friends: "Many were wounded and fell, and the rest fled to the mountain; and they took all their goods" (9:40).

This story tells us about an occasional punitive raid against a Nabatean or an Arab tribe (the precise identification of the "sons of Jambri" remains dubious) who had betrayed Jonathan and his brothers, and about a vengeance following the murder of John, not about an ideological religious war against Canaanites. Moreover, it must be underlined that the sons of Jambri, who committed the crime, are not the ones described as "one of the great nobles of Canaan"; it is rather the father of the bride, who apparently lives in Nadabath,[65] and not in Medeba, where the sons of Jambri come from. Although they may have been kinsmen, they are nevertheless distinct groups. It would therefore be far-fetched to look for an underlying ideological rationale behind this isolated use of the term "Canaan" in 1 Maccabees.[66] Rather, it is an additional example of the author's eclectic use of biblical expressions and vocabulary. Finally, in a book whose main reference is to David and his wars against the Philistines,[67] the exceptional use of the name "Canaan" in chapter 9 cannot be considered an indication that the author of 1 Maccabees saw the Hasmoneans as heirs to Joshua, who had to wage a new war against the "Canaanites" in order to reconquer the land.[68] Neither did "Canaanites" play a role as a category in the author's perception of the non-Jewish inhabitants of the land in his own time.

Conclusion

In most Jewish texts from the Hellenistic and Roman period, Canaan is the ancient name of the land known from the Bible, and the Canaanites are referred to as enemies or idolaters from the biblical past. There is no direct or explicit connection with the contemporary situation of the Jews in the land and with their non-Jewish neighbors. Phoenicians are often perceived as having Canaanite origins, but their geographical location grants them a status that differs from that of the "seven nations," even if they may be perceived as hostile to Judeans/Jews. In general, the names "Canaan" and "Canaanite" are not used to designate contemporary places and people; the reverse is actually more frequent: That is, contemporary terminology is used to refer to the land and its population in biblical times. There is only one case of non-Jews living on the fringe of Judaea in the Hellenistic and Roman period who are designated as "Canaanites," namely the reference to the father of the bride in 1 Maccabees 9:37, but this isolated use of the term in no way constitutes a paradigm of the way the Hasmoneans looked at the non-Jewish inhabitants of the land.

In that context, the reference to "a Canaanite woman" (γυνὴ Χαναναία) in Matthew 15:22, instead of a Greek, Syrophoenician woman in Mark 7:26, is all the more striking. It represents another example of the use of the term "Canaanite" to designate a person living on the fringes of the Land of Israel in the Hellenistic and Roman period. Since the encounter between Jesus and the woman takes place in the region of Tyre and Sidon, the use of the term "Canaanite" illustrates again the connection between Canaanites and Phoenicians repeatedly alluded to in ancient Jewish literature.[69] But the use of the term "Canaanite" instead of "Syrophoenician" is intentional: This name is chosen because the Canaanites represent the abominable idolaters par excellence.[70] As a consequence, Jesus' willingness to heal the woman's daughter has deep implications and becomes a paradigm for the integration of the Gentiles into the Jewish-Christian community. Although the gospel of Matthew makes use of the negative connotations of the term "Canaanite," which are supposed to be known to its readers, in the end, the category of the Canaanites itself is redeemed through the possibility to convert to Christianity.

Notes

1. One may object that Josephus quotes Nicolaus of Damascus in *Antiquities* 1.160, where the name "Chananaia" is used. The quotation is considered by M. Stern to be authentic; he writes in *GLAJJ* 2:234: "In Nicolaus Ἰουδαία is identical with the whole Χαναναία; here it has the broad meaning it assumed as a result of the Hasmonean conquests." One wonders how he reaches such a conclusion. Even if one cannot exclude that this represents an exception, it is sounder to consider that the use of the term "Canaan" in this passage is due to Josephus' rephrasing of Nicolaus' account.

2. Some coins from Berytus dated from the second century B.C.E. refer to Laodicea as the "mother/capital in Canaan," and the title of the city could be either "Laodicea in Canaan" or "Laodicea in Phoenicia," depending on which language was used ("Canaan" in Phoenician was translated as "Phoenicia" in Greek); see C. F. Hill, *A Catalogue of the Greek Coins in the British Museum: Phoenicia* (original ed. London 1910; Bologna: Arnaldo Forni, 1965), 1–2. See also J. B. Tsirkin, "Canaan. Phoenicia. Sidon," *Aula Orientalis* 19 (2001): 271–279.

3. *Exp. ad Rom.* 13 (PL 34–35, col. 2096) (*Chanani*). A Punic inscription also presents a man as the son of a Canaanite; see *KAI* 116 (line 3), as well as the commentary by H. Donner and W. Röllig, in *Kanaanäische und aramäische Inschriften*, 2nd ed. (Wiesbaden: Otto Harrassowitz Verlag, 1966–1969), 119–120.

4. *History of the Wars* 4.10.13, trans. H. B. Dewing, LCL, 287.

5. *History of the Wars* 4.10.15–22.

6. A. Lemaire speaks of a "Canaanite-Phoenician civilization" that lasted until the Hellenistic period in the east and until the Roman period in the west. See also G. Bunnens, "Canaan," in *Dictionnaire de la civilisation phénicienne et punique*, ed. E. Lipinski (Turnhout: Brepols, 1992), 87, who concludes: "La Bible n'a fait qu'adopter la terminologie égyptienne et si, au Iᵉʳ millénaire, une certaine affinité se décèle entre Canaan et Phénicie, c'est probablement que les Phéniciens sont les ultimes représentants des Cananéens du IIᵉ millénaire, mais même à cette époque, il n'y a pas assimilation complète des deux notions."

7. Eusebius, *Praep. ev.* 9.17.9. See also C. H. Holladay, *Fragments from Hellenistic Jewish Authors*, vol. 1, *Historians* (Chico: Scholars Press, 1983), 175.

8. The Hebrew names כנען and כנעני are translated as "Phoenicia" or "Phoenician" in Exod 6:15, 16:35; Josh 5:1, 5:12; and Job 40:30.

9. *Mekhilta de Rabbi Ishmael*, Pisha 18, ed. Horovitz-Rabin, 69–70; Tosefta *Shabbat* 7.25; Talmud Yerushalmi *Shevi'it* 6:1, 36c; *Lev. Rab.* 17.6 (and some later midrashim). On these texts, see K. Berthelot, "The Canaanites Who 'Trusted in God': An Original Interpretation of the Fate of the Canaanites in Rabbinic Literature," *JJS* 62, no. 2 (2011): 233–261; and Chapter 4 by Menahem Kister in the present volume.

10. See, in particular, the famous note by W. Bacher, "The Supposed Inscription upon 'Joshua the Robber,' Illustrated from Jewish Sources," *JQR* 3 (1891): 354–355; and H. Lewy, "Ein Rechtsstreit um Boden Palästinas im Altertum," *MGWJ*, no. 77 (1933): 84–99, 172–180.

11. See, for instance, A. H. Krappe, "Les Chananéens dans l'ancienne Afrique du Nord et en Espagne," *AJSL* 57, no. 3 (1940): 229–243 (on p. 233 he refers to the Palestinian Talmud).

12. On this issue see, among others, F.-C. Movers, *Die Phönizier. II/2. Geschichte der Colonien* (Berlin: Ferd. Dümmerl, 1850), 363ff; S. Gsell, *Histoire ancienne de l'Afrique du Nord* (Paris: Hachette, 1913), 1:340ss; A. H. Krappe, "Les Chananéens"; A. J. Frendo, "Two Long-lost Phoenician Inscriptions and the Emergence of Ancient Israel," *PEQ* 134 (2002): 37–43; Ph. C. Schmitz, "Procopius' Phoenician Inscriptions: Never Lost, not Found," *PEQ* 139, no. 2 (2007): 99–104 (a response to Frendo). For Krappe, for instance, the inscription "repose clairement sur les données de la version des Septante. En dernière analyse, elle semble devoir son origine aux préoccupations savantes de la société africaine du 1ᵉʳ siècle av. J.-C., et dont le roi Juba est un bon représentant. Cela n'empêche pas qu'elle repose sur une tradition ancienne touchant l'origine chananéenne de ces populations" ("Les Chananéens," 238).

13. The passage comes close to a quotation of the Deuteronomic prescription to put to the ban the seven nations of Canaan.

14. Trans. H. S. J. Thackeray, LCL, 67–69. Greek text: 138. ἐγένοντο δὲ καὶ Χαναναίου παῖδες Σιδώνιος ὃς καὶ πόλιν ἐπώνυμον ἔκτισεν ἐν τῇ Φοινίκῃ Σιδὼν δ᾽ ὑφ᾽ Ἑλλήνων καλεῖται Ἀμαθοῦς δὲ Ἀμάθουν κατῴκισεν ἥτις ἔστι καὶ νῦν ὑπὸ μὲν τῶν ἐπιχωρίων Ἀμάθη καλουμένη Μακεδόνες δ᾽ αὐτὴν Ἐπιφάνειαν ἀφ᾽ ἑνὸς τῶν ἐπιγόνων ἐπωνόμασαν Ἀρουδαῖος δὲ Ἄραδον τὴν νῆσον ἔσχεν Ἀρουκαῖος δὲ Ἄρκην τὴν ἐν τῷ Λιβάνῳ. 139. τῶν δὲ ἄλλων ἑπτὰ Εὐαίου Χετταίου Ἰεβουσαίου Ἀμορραίου Γεργεσαίου Σειναίου Σαμαραίου πλὴν τῶν ὀνομάτων ἐν ταῖς ἱεραῖς βίβλοις οὐδὲν ἔχομεν Ἑβραῖοι γὰρ αὐτῶν ἀνέστησαν τὰς πόλεις ἐκ τοιαύτης αἰτίας ἐν συμφορᾷ γενομένας.

15. On this causal link, see my analysis in "The Original Sin of the Canaanites," in *The 'Other' in Second Temple Judaism: Essays in Honor of John J. Collins*, ed. D. Harlow et al. (Grand Rapids: Eerdmans, 2011), 49–66.

16. Gen 10:15–19: "Χανααν δὲ ἐγέννησεν τὸν Σιδῶνα πρωτότοκον καὶ τὸν Χετταῖον, καὶ τὸν Ιεβουσαῖον καὶ τὸν Αμορραῖον καὶ τὸν Γεργεσαῖον καὶ τὸν Ευαῖον καὶ τὸν Αρουκαῖον καὶ τὸν Ασενναῖον καὶ τὸν Ἀράδιον καὶ τὸν Σαμαραῖον καὶ τὸν Αμαθι καὶ μετὰ τοῦτο διεσπάρησαν αἱ φυλαὶ τῶν Χαναναίων. καὶ ἐγένοντο τὰ ὅρια τῶν Χαναναίων ἀπὸ Σιδῶνος ἕως ἐλθεῖν εἰς Γεραρα καὶ Γάζαν ἕως ἐλθεῖν Σοδομων καὶ Γομορρας Αδαμα καὶ Σεβωιμ ἕως Λασα."

17. See Th. W. Franxman, *Genesis and the Jewish Antiquities of Flavius Josephus* (Rome: Pontifical Biblical Institute, 1979), 112.

18. Hamath on the Orontes, also called *Epiphanenses ad Orontem* by Plinius (*Hist. nat.* 5.82). See E. Nodet, *Les Antiquités juives. Livres I à III* (Paris: Cerf, 2000), 41 n. 4.

19. Ed. Theodor-Albeck, p. 348: את הערקי ארקס דליבנן.

20. *Gen. Rab.*: את הסיני ארתוסייה, את הארודי ארוד, את הצמרי חמץ, ולמה קורין אותו צמרי, שעושין בצמר, החמתי פיפניה. Trans. H. Freedman, *Midrash Rabbah*, 3rd ed. (London: Soncino Press, 1961), 298–299.

21. Theodor-Albeck locates it on the river Oronthes (*Midrash Rabbah*, 298–299).

22. The reason that the Hivites, identified with "the inhabitants of Hildin" (an unidentified city), are mentioned as well in *Genesis Rabbah* 37.6 (before the Arkites) may have to do with the fact that, according to Judg 3:1–3, at least part of the Hivites were living near Mount Lebanon, from Mount Hermon to the "entrance of Hamath" (see below), that is, in the same area. The rationale behind the explanations in *Genesis Rabbah* may to some extent be compared to that found in rabbinic texts dealing with the Girgashites, which argue that the latter

voluntarily left the land when they heard that the children of Israel were about to enter. This interesting story has been explained by the fact that, whereas the Girgashites appear on the lists of the peoples of Canaan in several verses, in Deut 20:17 (the chapter on the laws of warfare) and in subsequent passages such as Josh 9:1 and 12:8, the Girgashites are no longer mentioned, as if they had disappeared and were not involved any more in the wars waged by the children of Israel in Canaan. See W. Bacher, "The Supposed Inscription," 354–355. See also H. Lewy, "Ein Rechtsstreit um Boden Palästinas im Altertum," 178, who refers to *Deuteronomy Rabbah* 5.13 on Deut 20:10f.

23. See F.-M. Abel, *Géographie de la Palestine* (Paris: Gabalda, 1933), 1:256–257.

24. On the identification of Hamath and Levo-Hamath (which appears also in Num 34:8), see F.-M. Abel, *Géographie de la Palestine*, 1:299–301; M. Weinfeld, *The Promise of the Land: The Inheritance of the Land of Canaan by the Israelites* (Berkeley and Los Angeles: University of California Press, 1993), 52–56 (he writes on page 53, n.2 that "Lebo-hamath is Labweh, near the sources of the Orontes south of the city of Kadesh"); N. Wazana, כל גבולות ארץ [All the Boundaries of the Land; in Hebrew] (Jerusalem: Mossad Bialik, 2007), esp. 268–271 (an English translation is about to be published by Eisenbrauns, under the title *All the Boundaries of the Land: The Promised Land in Biblical Thought in Light of the Ancient Near East*). According to B. A. Levine, one should translate "to Rehov, at Lebo of Hamath," implying that Lebo is a village in the region of Hamath (*Numbers 1–20*, Anchor Bible 4A [New York: Doubleday, 1993], 350 and 354); he refers to B. Mazar, "*Lebô' Hamât*," in *Encyclopaedia Biblica*, vol. 4 [in Hebrew] (Jerusalem: Mossad Bialik, 1962), col. 416–418, who identifies Lebo with a place called Lab'u mentioned in the annals of Tiglath Pileser III, as well as with Libo, which is referred to in a Roman source. But even in that case, the exact location of Rehov with respect to Lebo remains uncertain.

25. Here the LXX transliterates the Hebrew name corresponding to "the entrance to Hamath": πάντα τὸν Χαναναῖον καὶ τὸν Σιδώνιον καὶ τὸν Εὐαῖον τὸν κατοικοῦντα τὸν Λίβανον ἀπὸ τοῦ ὄρους τοῦ Βαλαερμων ἕως Λοβωημαθ.

26. See J. W. Wevers (in collaboration with U. Quast), *Numeri: Septuaginta III/1* (Göttingen: Vandenhoeck & Ruprecht, 1982), 179. The Alexandrinus has Αιμαθ. A. Rahlfs chose Εφααθ. See also J. W. Wevers, "Text History of the Greek Numbers," *Abhandlungen der Akademie der Wissenschaften in Göttingen 125: Mitteilungen des Septuaginta-Unternehmens (MSU) XVI* (Göttingen: Vandenhoeck & Ruprecht, 1982), 7–139, who writes about Hamath: "Inexplicably, the tradition confused it with the Euphrates as is shown in the εφρααθ of *d n-75 t x-509* and *ephrath* of Arm. This apparently led to the error εφααθ attested in B 376 509 ᴸᵃᵗcod100 Saⁱ = Ra" (116).

27. Trans. H. St. J. Thackeray, LCL, 467.

28. Similarly, in connection with *Ant.* 7.107, H. St. J. Thackeray and R. Marcus identify Amathè with Hamath on the Orontes, in northern Syria (see *Ant.* 5–8, LCL, 61).

29. H. St. J. Thackeray, LCL, 466–467.

30. L. H. Feldman, *Flavius Josephus: Judean Antiquities 1–4* (Leiden: Brill, 2004), 324. On Josephus' understanding of biblical geography, see also B.-Z. Rosenfeld, "Flavius Josephus and His Portrayal of the Coast (Paralia) of Contemporary Roman Palestine: Geography and Ideology," *JQR* 91, no. 1–2 (2000): 143–183, esp. 170–175.

31. Trans. R. Marcus, LCL, 109. On this episode, see C. Begg, "Jeroboam II and Jonah (9,205–215)," in *Josephus' Story of the Later Monarchy (AJ 9,1–10,185)* (Leuven: Leuven University Press–Peeters, 2000), 251–272, esp. 252–254.

32. See E. Nodet, *Les Antiquités juives: Livres IV et V* (Paris: Cerf, 1995), 136.

33. Trans. H. St. J. Thackeray and R. Marcus, LCL, 201–203. See also C. Begg, *Flavius Josephus: Translation and Commentary*, vol. 4, *Judean Antiquities 5–7* (Leiden: Brill, 2005), 22.

34. See, for instance, *Ant.* 5.132–134, 5.140, 6.30, 7.61, 7.68.

35. Trans. R. Marcus, LCL, 303.

36. The LXX adds the Canaanites and the Girgashites to the list: πάντα τὸν λαὸν τὸν ὑπολελειμμένον ἀπὸ τοῦ Χετταίου καὶ τοῦ Ἀμορραίου καὶ τοῦ Φερεζαίου καὶ τοῦ Χαναναίου καὶ τοῦ Εὐαίου καὶ τοῦ Ιεβουσαίου καὶ τοῦ Γεργεσαίου τῶν μὴ ἐκ τῶν υἱῶν Ισραηλ ὄντων τὰ τέκνα αὐτῶν τὰ ὑπολελειμμένα μετ᾽ αὐτοὺς ἐν τῇ γῇ οὓς οὐκ ἐδύναντο οἱ υἱοὶ Ισραηλ ἐξολεθρεῦσαι αὐτούς…

37. See frag. 2, §3 (Eusebius, *Praep. ev.* 9.30.3): εἶτα Δαβὶδ τὸν τούτου υἱὸν δυναστεῦσαι, ὃν καταστρέψασθαι Σύρους τοὺς παρὰ τὸν Εὐφράτην οἰκοῦντας ποταμὸν καὶ τὴν Κομμαγηνὴν καὶ τοὺς ἐν Γαλαδηνῇ Ἀσσυρίους καὶ Φοίνικας. στρατεῦσαι δ᾽ αὐτὸν καὶ ἐπὶ Ἰδουμαίους καὶ Ἀμμανίτας καὶ Μωαβίτας καὶ Ἰτουραίους καὶ Ναβαταίους καὶ Ναβδαίους.

38. Cf. Holladay, *FHJA 1: Historians*, 140; Wacholder, *Eupolemus*, 131–139.

39. See frag. 4, §5 (Eusebius, *Praep. ev.* 9.39.5). "Scythopolis" is also found in 1 Maccabees and, of course, in Josephus.

40. Holladay, *FHJA 1: Historians*, 140.

41. On Philo's perception of Egypt, see the recent monograph by S. Pearce, *The Land of the Body* (Tübingen: Mohr Siebeck, 2007).

42. See *Congr.* 83: "the land of Canaan is the symbol of vices" (παθῶν μὲν Αἴγυπτος σύμβολόν ἐστι, κακιῶν δὲ ἡ Χαναναίων γῆ); *Sacr.* 90: "where reason is tossed to and fro, that is to the land of the Canaanites" (εἰς τὸν σαλεύοντα λόγον, τὴν τῶν Χαναναίων γῆν), *pace* A. Méasson in the French edition of *De Sacrificiis* (Paris: Cerf, 1966), 206, who thinks that the land of Canaan and the Promised Land are the same. It appears that the land of Canaan has to be *transformed* into the land of virtue, through the replacement of its inhabitants, or through the eradication of idolatry and the establishment of the proper cult.

43. See *Somn.* 2.76, in connection with Lev 23:10, "When you come into the land which I give you…". The entrance into the land is also said to be "an entry into philosophy" (*QE* 2.13). See B. Schaller, "Philon von Alexandreia und das 'Heilige Land,'" in *Fundamenta Judaica: Studien zum antiken Judentum and zum Neuen Testament*, ed. L. Doering and A. Steudel (Göttingen: Vandenhoeck & Ruprecht, 2001), 13–27, esp. 15.

44. See *Congr.* 83–86.

45. Before Philo, only Demetrius raises a similar question, asking about the origin of the weapons with which the Hebrews attacked Canaan. See Eusebius, *Praep. ev.* 9.29.16.

46. Eusebius, *Praep. ev.* 9.6.6; trans. F. H. Colson, LCL, 419.

47. On Philo's treatment of the conquest, see my article "Philo and the Conquest of Canaan," *JSJ* 38, no. 1 (2007): 39–56.

48. Transl. F. H. Colson, LCL, 251–253.

49. Cf. *Mos.* 2.56. Transl. F. H. Colson, LCL, 69.

50. ἐπειδὴ τοίνυν παρ᾽ ἑκόντων ἔλαβε τὴν ἀρχήν, βραβεύοντος καὶ ἐπινεύοντος θεοῦ, τὴν ἀποικίαν ἔστελλεν εἰς Φοινίκην καὶ Συρίαν τὴν κοίλην καὶ Παλαιστίνην, ἣ τότε προσηγορεύετο Χαναναίων, ἧς οἱ ὅροι τριῶν ἡμερῶν ὁδὸν διειστήκεσαν ἀπ᾽ Αἰγύπτου. Transl. F. H. Colson, LCL, 361.

51. See also *Mos.* 2.246 and *Spec.* 2.217.

52. From Herodotus onward, the name *Palaistinè* was frequent in Greek texts and generally designated the coastal part of biblical Canaan, rather than Canaan in the sense

of the whole area from the Jordan River until the Mediterranean Sea. In Herodotus' *Hist.* 4.39, it extends from Phoenicia until Egypt, but its oriental border is not indicated. See R. de Vaux, "Les Philistins dans la Septante," in *Wort, Liebe und Gottesspruch: Beiträge zur Septuaginta: Festschrift für Joseph Ziegler*, ed. J. Schreiner (Würzburg: Echter Verlag, 1972), 185–194; L. H. Feldman, "Some Observations on the Name of Palestine," in *Studies in Hellenistic Judaism* (Leiden: Brill, 1996), 553–576; J. M. Lieu, "Not Hellenes but Philistines? The Maccabees and Josephus Defining the 'Other,'" *JJS* 53, no. 2 (2002): 246–263.

53. See *Ant.* 1.134: "Chananeus, the fourth son of Ham, settled in the country now called Judaea and named it after himself Chananaea." See also *Ant.* 1.160, a quotation from Nicolaus of Damascus, which Josephus certainly rephrased to a great extent. As mentioned in the introduction, no Greek or Latin (non-Jewish, non-Christian) text uses the name *Canaan*.

54. Transl. F. H. Colson, LCL, 53–55.

55. See R. Wilken, *The Land Called Holy: Palestine in Christian History and Thought* (New Haven, Conn.: Yale University Press, 1992), 1–45.

56. "201. Hearing from travellers visiting them [the pagan inhabitants of Jamnia, which is described in §200 as "one of the most populous cities of Judaea," with an important Jewish population next to the pagan one] how earnestly Gaius was pressing his deification and the extreme hostility which he felt towards the whole Jewish race, they thought that a fit opportunity of attacking them had fallen in their way. Accordingly they erected an extemporized altar of the commonest material with the clay moulded into bricks, merely as a plan to injure their neighbours, for they knew that they would not allow their customs to be subverted, as indeed it turned out. 202. For, when they saw it and felt it intolerable that the sanctity which truly belongs to the holy Land should be destroyed, they met together and pulled it down." (trans. F. H. Colson, LCL, 105).

57. In the Theodotion version of Susanna 1:56, one of the wicked elders is accused by Daniel of being an "offspring of Canaan" (σπέρμα Χανααν) rather than a son of Judah, apparently to emphasize his wickedness. In any case, the elder is a Judean, not a Gentile. See *Susanna, Daniel, Bel et Draco*, ed. J. Ziegler, O. Munnich and D. Fraenkel, 2nd ed. (Göttingen: Vandenhoeck & Ruprecht, 1999), 230–231; D. M. Kay, *The Apocrypha and Pseudepigrapha of the Old Testament*, ed. R. H. Charles (London: Clarendon Press, 1913), 1:651; C. A. Moore, *Daniel, Esther and Jeremiah: The Additions*, Anchor Bible 44 (New York: Doubleday, 1977), 107, 111–112. The Septuagint has "Sidon" instead of "offspring of Canaan"; this variant shows how closely Sidonians and Canaanites were associated in Jewish texts (starting with Gen 10:15).

58. J. A. Goldstein, *1 Maccabees: A New Translation with Introduction and Commentary*, 2nd ed. (New York: Doubleday, 1984), 12–14, 21; D. Mendels, "An Inscribed Fragmented Memory from Palestine of the Hasmonean Period: The Case of 1 Maccabees," in *Memory in Jewish, Pagan and Christian Societies of the Graeco-Roman World* (London: T & T Clark, 2004), 81–88; U. Rappaport, *The First Book of Maccabees* [in Hebrew] (Jerusalem: Yad Ben Zvi Press, 2004), 34–35, 52–54.

59. "A Note on the Use of the Bible in 1 Maccabees," in *Biblical Perspectives: Early Use and Interpretation of the Bible in Light of the Dead Sea Scrolls*, ed. M. E. Stone and E. Chazon (Leiden: Brill, 1998), 175–179 (quotation 175). For J. C. Dancy, the balance between religious and political considerations changes gradually throughout the book, and the latter outweigh the former (*A Commentary on 1 Maccabees* [Oxford: Blackwell, 1954], 1).

60. On 1 Maccabees as an attempt to legitimize the Hasmonean dynasty, see Goldstein, *1 Maccabees*, 12, 33, 240–241; U. Rappaport, *The First Book of Maccabees*, 48–50; D. Mendels, "An Inscribed Fragmented Memory."

61. All the LXX mss have Χαναάν. In Josephus, *Ant.* 13.18, he is "one of the distinguished men among the Arabs, from the city of Nabatha" (ἀπὸ Ναβαθὰ πόλεως...τινὸς...τῶν ἐπιφανῶν παρὰ τοῖς Ἄραψιν).

62. Josephus speaks about "Nabatean Arabs" (τοὺς Ναβαταίους Ἄραβας) (*Ant.* 13.10).

63. In Josephus: "the sons of Amaraios lay in ambush for him outside the city of Medaba" (ἐνεδρεύσαντες ἐκ Μηδάβας πόλεως οἱ Ἀμαραίου παῖδες αὐτόν) (*Ant.* 13.11). R. Marcus recalls that already long ago, Clermont-Ganneau (*Recueil d'Archéologie Orientale* 2:185) suggested that the name Jambri came from Yaʿamrû, found on a Nabatean inscription near Medeba. Other scholars understand the form of the name in Josephus' *Ant.* as "Amorites"—which would have been the original term in the Hebrew version of 1 Macc—and point to the fact that Medeba is mentioned as an Amorite city in Num 21:29–31. Marcus, however, underlines that Medeba was generally known as a Moabite city; see *Jewish Antiquities Books XII–XIV*, LCL 4th ed. (Cambridge, Mass.: Harvard University Press, 1986), 233. For J. A. Goldstein, "they probably were Arabs" (*1 Maccabees*, 384). A. Kasher considers them an Arab tribe. See *Jews, Idumeans, and Ancient Arabs: Relations of the Jews in Eretz-Israel with the Nations of the Frontier and the Desert during the Hellenistic and Roman Era (332 BCE–70 CE)* (Tübingen: Mohr Siebeck, 1988), 34–35. Kasher stresses: "At all events they are not to be identified automatically with the Nabateans, as some scholars are inclined to do" (35 n. 35). See also G. W. Bowersock, *Roman Arabia* (Cambridge, Mass.: Harvard University Press, 1983), 20.

64. Some LXX manuscripts have other forms of the name: Ναβαδαθ in V 29-107 542, Ναβαθ in 71 19 55 340; Ναβατ in *L*-93 SyI. See W. Kappler, *Maccabaeorum libri I–IV* (Göttingen: Vandenhoek & Ruprecht, 1936), 103. Josephus has Nabatha (Ναβαθὰ) (*Ant.* 13.18). See the discussion in Goldstein, *1 Maccabees*, 384.

65. According to U. Rappaport, the town is not identified; see *First Book of Maccabees*, 239. A. Kasher locates it slightly southeast of Medeba (see *Jews, Idumeans, and Ancient Arabs*, 36).

66. *Pace* F.-M. Abel (*Les livres des Maccabées* [Paris: Gabalda, 1949], 168) and U. Rappaport (*First Book of Maccabees*, 239), for whom the name *Canaan* may imply an additional justification to the attack against the sons of Jambri, because of the biblical commandment of the *herem*. First, as mentioned above, the father of the bride is not a member of the "sons of Jambri." Second, although Jonathan and Simon kill several people, they do not exterminate them utterly, as would be expected had they wanted to conform to the *herem* prescription (Josephus, on the contrary, describes the massacre as total, and underlined that women and children perished as well, totaling four hundred persons; see *Ant.* 13.20–21). Third, there is only one occurrence of ἀναθεματίζειν (להחרים) in 1 Macc (5:5), and one cannot speak of a "*herem* ideology" in the book (see, however, the diverging interpretation by C. Batsch, *La guerre et les rites de guerre dans le judaïsme du deuxième Temple* [Leiden: Brill, 2005], 438–443; and also H. Dae Park, *Finding Herem? A Study of Luke-Acts in the Light of Herem* [London: T & T Clark, 2007], 53–66). Finally, the biblical texts pertaining to the Canaanites do not systematically prescribe to put them to the ban (*herem*).

   J. A. Goldstein considers that the name *Canaan* is actually a misreading for the Hebrew *Mâʿôn*, and points to the fact that Symmachus rendered *Mâʿôn* in Judg 10:12 as *Canaan*. See *1 Maccabees*, 385.

67. See S. von Dobbeler, *Die Bücher 1/2 Makkabäer*, Neuer Stuttgarter Kommentar, Altes Testament 11 (Stuttgart: Verlag Katholisches Bibelwerk, 1997), 44–46; H. Lichtenberger, "Geschichtsschreibung und Geschichtserzählung im 1. und 2. Makkabäerbuch," in *Die antike*

Historiographie und die Anfänge der christlichen Geschichtsschreibung, ed. E.-M. Becker (Berlin: de Gruyter, 2005), 197–212.

68. For a more detailed treatment of the question of whether the Hasmoneans referred to Joshua and the first conquest of the land as a model for their military campaigns, see D. Mendels, *The Land of Israel as a Political Concept in Hasmonean Literature* (Tübingen: Mohr Siebeck, 1987), 47, 51; Z. Safrai, "The Gentile Cities of Judea: Between the Hasmonean Occupation and the Roman Liberation," in *Studies in Historical Geography and Biblical Historiography presented to Zecharia Kallai*, ed. G. Galil and M. Weinfeld (Leiden: Brill, 2000), 63–90, esp. 77; K. Berthelot, "The Biblical Conquest of the Promised Land and the Hasmonean Wars according to 1 and 2 *Maccabees*," in *The Books of Maccabees: History, Theology, Ideology*, ed. G. Xeravits and J. Zsengeller (Leiden: Brill, 2007), 45–60.

69. Ulrich Luz, for instance, underlines this point: "'Canaanite' (Χαναναῖος) is not only a biblical expression for 'Gentile,' but presumably also the self-designation of the Phoenicians at the time of Matthew. The Syrian Matthew, who perhaps knew Aramaic, would then have replaced the typically 'western' designation 'Syro-Phoenician' (Συροφοινίκισσα) (Mark 7:26) with his own 'local' designation" (*Matthew 8–20: A Commentary*, Hermeneia [Minneapolis: Fortress Press, 2001], 338). However, "Canaanite" is not a biblical expression for Gentiles in general, and is not used in such a way in the first century C.E. In my view, Luz misses the pejorative meaning of the term "Canaanite."

70. For a survey of different explanations proposed for the change from "Syro-Phoenician" to "Canaanite," see W. D. Davies and D. C. Allison, *A Critical and Exegetical Commentary on the Gospel according to Saint Matthew* (Edinburgh: T & T Clark, 1991), 2:547; he concludes that the change most probably has to do with the negative connotations of the name "Canaanite" in the biblical tradition. F. W. Beare, *The Gospel According to Matthew* (Oxford: Basil Blackwell, 1981), 341, also emphasizes that the Canaanites are the traditional enemies of the children of Israel. J. M. C. Scott merely states: "What can be said with certainty is that, in the use of this word, intertextual echoes of a long tradition of bad blood between the original inhabitants of the land and their Jewish conquerors can be heard" ("Matthew 15.21–28: A Test-Case for Jesus' Manners," *JSNT* 63 [1996]: 21–44).

Bibliography

Abel, F.-M. *Les livres des Maccabées*. Paris: Gabalda, 1949.

——. *Géographie de la Palestine*. Paris: Gabalda, 1933.

Bacher, W. "The Supposed Inscription upon 'Joshua the Robber,' Illustrated from Jewish Sources." *JQR* 3 (1891): 354–355.

Batsch, C. *La guerre et les rites de guerre dans le judaïsme du deuxième Temple*. Leiden: Brill, 2005.

Beare, F. W. *The Gospel According to Matthew*. Oxford: Basil Blackwell, 1981.

Begg, C. *Flavius Josephus: Translation and Commentary*. Vol. 4. *Judean Antiquities 5–7*. Leiden: Brill, 2005.

——. "Jeroboam II and Jonah (9,205–215)." In *Josephus' Story of the Later Monarchy (AJ 9,1–10,185)*, 251–272. Leuven: Leuven University Press–Peeters, 2000.

Berthelot, K. "The Original Sin of the Canaanites." In *The 'Other' in Second Temple Judaism: Essays in Honor of John J. Collins*, edited by D. Harlow et al., 49–66. Grand Rapids, Mich.: Eerdmans, 2011.

——. "The Canaanites Who 'Trusted in God': An Original Interpretation of the Fate of the Canaanites in Rabbinic Literature." *JJS* 62, no. 2 (2011): 233–261.

——. "The Biblical Conquest of the Promised Land and the Hasmonean Wars according to *1* and *2 Maccabees*." In *The Books of Maccabees: History, Theology, Ideology*, edited by G. Xeravits and J. Zsengeller, 45–60. Leiden: Brill, 2007.

——. "Philo and the Conquest of Canaan." *JSJ* 38, no. 1 (2007): 39–56.

Bowersock, G. W. *Roman Arabia*. Cambridge, Mass.: Harvard University Press, 1983.

Bunnens, G. "Canaan." In *Dictionnaire de la civilisation phénicienne et punique*, edited by E. Lipinski, 87. Turnhout: Brepols, 1992.

Dancy, J. C. *A Commentary on 1 Maccabees*. Oxford: Blackwell, 1954.

Davies, W. D., and D. C. Allison. *A Critical and Exegetical Commentary on the Gospel according to Saint Matthew*. Edinburgh: T & T Clark, 1991.

Dobbeler, S. von. *Die Bücher 1/2 Makkabäer*. Neuer Stuttgarter Kommentar. Altes Testament 11. Stuttgart: Verlag Katholisches Bibelwerk, 1997.

Donner H., and W. Röllig. *Kanaanäische und aramäische Inschriften*, 2nd ed. Wiesbaden: Otto Harrassowitz Verlag, 1966–1969.

Feldman, L. H. *Flavius Josephus: Judean Antiquities 1–4*. Leiden: Brill, 2004.

——. "Some Observations on the Name of Palestine." In *Studies in Hellenistic Judaism*, 553–576. Leiden: Brill, 1996.

Franxman, Th. W. *Genesis and the Jewish Antiquities of Flavius Josephus*. Rome: Pontifical Biblical Institute, 1979.

Frendo, A. J. "Two Long-lost Phoenician Inscriptions and the Emergence of Ancient Israel." *PEQ* 134 (2002): 37–43.

Goldstein, J. A. *1 Maccabees: A New Translation with Introduction and Commentary*. 2nd ed. New York: Doubleday, 1984.

Gsell, S. *Histoire ancienne de l'Afrique du Nord*. Paris: Hachette, 1913.

Hill, C. F. *A Catalogue of the Greek Coins in the British Museum: Phoenicia*. First published London, 1910. Reprint, Bologna: Arnaldo Forni, 1965.

Holladay, C. H. *Fragments from Hellenistic Jewish Authors*. Vol. 1. *Historians*. Chico: Scholars Press, 1983.

Kappler, W. *Maccabaeorum libri I–IV*. Göttingen: Vandenhoek & Ruprecht, 1936.

Kasher, A. *Jews, Idumeans, and Ancient Arabs: Relations of the Jews in Eretz-Israel with the Nations of the Frontier and the Desert during the Hellenistic and Roman Era (332 BCE–70 CE)*. Tübingen: Mohr Siebeck, 1988.

Kay, D. M. *The Apocrypha and Pseudepigrapha of the Old Testament*. Edited by R. H. Charles. London: Clarendon Press, 1913.

Krappe, A. H. "Les Chananéens dans l'ancienne Afrique du Nord et en Espagne." *AJSL* 57, no. 3 (1940): 229–243.

Levine, B. A. *Numbers 1–20*. Anchor Bible 4A. New York: Doubleday, 1993.

Lewy, H. "Ein Rechtsstreit um Boden Palästinas im Altertum." *MGWJ* 77 (1933): 84–99, 172–180.

Lieu, J. M. "Not Hellenes but Philistines? The Maccabees and Josephus defining the 'Other'." *JJS* 53, no. 2 (2002): 246–263.

Lichtenberger, H. "Geschichtsschreibung und Geschichtserzählung im 1. und 2. Makkabäerbuch." In *Die antike Historiographie und die Anfänge der christlichen Geschichtsschreibung*, edited by E.-M. Becker, 197–212. Berlin: de Gruyter, 2005.

Luz, Ulrich. *Matthew 8–20: A Commentary*. Hermeneia. Minneapolis: Fortress Press, 2001.

Marcus, R. *Jewish Antiquities Books XII–XIV*. LCL. 4th ed. Cambridge, Mass.: Harvard University Press, 1986.

Mazar, B. "*Lebô' Hamât.*" In *Encyclopaedia Biblica*. Vol. 4 [in Hebrew], col. 416–418. Jerusalem: Mossad Bialik, 1962.

Mendels, D. "An Inscribed Fragmented Memory from Palestine of the Hasmonean Period: The Case of 1 Maccabees." In *Memory in Jewish, Pagan and Christian Societies of the Graeco-Roman World*, 81–88. London: T & T Clark, 2004.

——. *The Land of Israel as a Political Concept in Hasmonean Literature*. Tübingen: Mohr Siebeck, 1987.

Moore, C. A. *Daniel, Esther and Jeremiah: The Additions*. Anchor Bible 44. New York: Doubleday, 1977.

Movers, F.-C. *Die Phönizier. II/2. Geschichte der Colonien*. Berlin: Ferd, Dümmerl, 1850.

Nodet, E. *Les Antiquités juives: Livres I à III*. Paris: Cerf, 2000.

——. *Les Antiquités juives: Livres IV et V*. Paris: Cerf, 1995.

Park, H. Dae. *Finding Herem? A Study of Luke-Acts in the Light of Herem*. London: T & T Clark, 2007.

Rappaport, U. *The First Book of Maccabees* [in Hebrew]. Jerusalem: Yad Ben Zvi Press, 2004.

——. "A Note on the Use of the Bible in 1 *Maccabees.*" In *Biblical Perspectives: Early Use and Interpretation of the Bible in Light of the Dead Sea Scrolls*, edited by M. E. Stone and E. Chazon, 175–179. Leiden: Brill, 1998.

Rosenfeld, B.-Z. "Flavius Josephus and His Portrayal of the Coast (Paralia) of Contemporary Roman Palestine: Geography and Ideology." *JQR* 91, no. 1–2 (2000): 143–183.

Safrai, Z. "The Gentile Cities of Judea: Between the Hasmonean Occupation and the Roman Liberation." In *Studies in Historical Geography and Biblical Historiography Presented to Zecharia Kallai*, edited by G. Galil and M. Weinfeld, 63–90. Leiden: Brill, 2000.

Schaller, B. "Philon von Alexandreia und das 'Heilige Land.'" In *Fundamenta Judaica: Studien zum antiken Judentum und zum Neuen Testament*, edited by L. Doering and A. Steudel, 13–27. Göttingen: Vandenhoeck & Ruprecht, 2001.

Schmitz, Ph. C. "Procopius' Phoenician Inscriptions: Never Lost, not Found." *PEQ* 139, no. 2 (2007): 99–104.

Scott, J. M. C. "Matthew 15.21–28: A Test-Case for Jesus' Manners." *JSNT* 63 (1996): 21–44.

Tsirkin, J. B. "Canaan. Phoenicia. Sidon." *Aula Orientalis* 19 (2001): 271–279.

Vaux, R. de. "Les Philistins dans la Septante." In *Wort, Liebe und Gottesspruch: Beiträge zur Septuaginta: Festschrift für Joseph Ziegler*, edited by J. Schreiner, 185–194. Würzburg: Echter Verlag, 1972.

Weinfeld, M. *The Promise of the Land: The Inheritance of the Land of Canaan by the Israelites*. Berkeley and Los Angeles: University of California Press, 1993.

Wazana, N. כל גבולות ארץ [All the Boundaries of the Land; in Hebrew]. Jerusalem: Mossad Bialik, 2007.

Wevers, J. W. "Text History of the Greek Numbers." Abhandlungen der Akademie der Wissenschaften in Göttingen 125: Mitteilungen des Septuaginta-Unternehmens (MSU) XVI, 7–139. Göttingen: Vandenhoeck & Ruprecht, 1982.

Wevers, J. W., in collaboration with U. Quast. *Numeri: Septuaginta III/1*. Göttingen: Vandenhoeck & Ruprecht, 1982.

Wilken, R. *The Land Called Holy: Palestine in Christian History and Thought*. New Haven, Conn.: Yale University Press, 1992.

Ziegler, J., O. Munnich, and D. Fraenkel, eds. *Susanna, Daniel, Bel et Draco*, 2nd ed. Göttingen: Vandenhoeck & Ruprecht, 1999.

11

The Rabbinic Perception of the Presence of the Canaanites in the Land of Israel

Eyal Ben-Eliyahu

Introduction

What comes to mind when people visit local ancient sites or recall the ancient residents of a land? Do they deny the existence of previous possessors of the land, or do they recognize their existence? Let me illustrate my point by noting some examples, both current and historical. My personal impression from dozens of occasions is that, if asked, "From which period is that ancient building or structure?" most Arabs in Israel would answer: "the Roman period." A similar break in the historical continuum is found in the fourth-century *Itinerary of Bordeaux*. Its author attributed the remains of the Herodian Temple that he saw on the Temple Mount to the era of King Solomon.[1] In this case, he may have deliberately chosen to ignore Herod because of that figure's negative connotations in Christian tradition. A few centuries later, the anonymous guidebook to Jerusalem from the Cairo Genizah, which dates from the tenth or eleventh century, attributed the Christian churches on the slope of the Mount of Olives to King Solomon, identifying them with the *bamot* (cultic platforms) used in Solomon's day. Another identification by this traveler—of the house of Uzziah the King of Judah, on the summit of the Mount of Olives—apparently relates to the Byzantine Ascension Church. These surprising links were perhaps motivated by the traveler's wish to appropriate these Christian structures for his nation.[2]

In this chapter, I will examine the presence of the Canaanites in rabbinic literature, and will assert that rabbinic literature surprisingly makes no attempt to ignore the Canaanite presence in the history and the archaeology of the land. This is in direct opposition to what we would expect, given the biblical command to destroy and wipe out the Canaanites.[3] As we shall see, the Canaanites are present in rabbinic halakhic discourse and as part of the history and the archaeology of the land of Israel. Moreover, as shown by certain halakhic discussions, during the rabbinic period the descendants of the Canaanites were even considered to be actually present in the land of Israel.

The Appearances of the Canaanites in the Rabbinic Literature

The Canaanites appear in rabbinic literature in a number of different contexts and varied sources: Tannaitic and Amoraic, halakhic and midrashic. The first context is a legal one: In connection with a non-Jewish slave, rabbinic discourse uses the biblical term עבד כנעני ("Canaanite slave"). Through this term, rabbinic literature preserved the identity of the foreigner from biblical literature, based particularly on Noah's curse of Canaan: "Cursed be Canaan; the lowest of slaves shall he be to his brothers" (Gen 9:25).[4]

A second context is a cultural one. Rabbinic recognition of the cultural presence of the Canaanites is reflected in the term דרכי האמורי: "the ways of the Amorite," or "Amorite practices." The expression "the ways of the Amorite" relates to strange and foreign rituals, closer in nature to superstitions than to actual idolatry. The rabbis did not use expressions like "foreign customs," but rather the phrase "the ways of the Amorites," based on their perception that these strange, foreign customs had local, ancient roots.[5] For example:

> If a man slaughtered a beast and found therein an afterbirth, he whose appetite is robust may eat it.... It should not be buried at a cross-roads or hung on a tree, for such are the ways of the Amorite. (*m. Hul.* 4:7, Danby Edition)

The Mishna names three objects that people used to carry for healing purposes. The rabbis forbid carrying such objects. The rationale for the prohibition is that these practices are "the ways of the Amorite."

> Men may go out with a locust's egg or a jackal's tooth or with a nail of [the gallows of] one that was crucified, as a means of healing. So R. Meir. But the Sages say: Even on ordinary days this is forbidden as following in the ways of the Amorite. (*m. Shabb.* 6:10)

Both Talmuds distinguish between idolatrous practices and those of the Amorites.

> He who says, Be lucky, my luck [*gad gedi*] and tire not by day or night, is guilty of Amorite practices. R. Judah said: *Gad* is none other but an idolatrous term, for it is said: *You that prepare a table for Gad.* (*b. Shabbat* 67b)

R. Judah argues against the opinion that this is an Amorite practice. He regards the making of such a statement as idolatry; that is, Amorite practices are not seen as idolatrous. The same disagreement is repeated elsewhere.

The meaning of this distinction is that the rabbis did not identify the pagan worship with which they were familiar from the Greco-Roman world with the folkloristic practices and superstitions that they ascribed to the ancient traditions of the early, local residents: the Amorites. While Greco-Roman worship was considered "idolatry," the folkloristic practices and superstitions that they designated as "Amorite" were forbidden not as "idolatry," but because of "the ways of the Amorite." This prohibition seems to be softer than the one linked to idolatry. Accordingly, the use of the term "the ways of the Amorite" might be a way to distinguish between worship that was considered to be "idolatry" and foreign practices. The use of Canaanites and Amorites in these two halakhic definitions might be a designation for foreigners' slaves, or practices, but not necessarily for the ancient Canaanites and Amorites or their descendants.

A third realm in which we find the rabbis mentioning the Amorites goes beyond the halakhic definition of Canaanite slaves and references to cultural-superstitious practices. The Tannaim also recognize, and discuss, the possibility that objects found in old walls might be considered as having belonged to the Amorites. According to the Mishnah:

> [If] one found an object in a pile or in an old wall.
> lo, these things which he finds are his. (*m. Baba Metzia* 2:4)

The Tosefta explains why the finder can keep such objects: namely, because they apparently belonged to the Amorites. Thus, Tosefta *Baba Metzia* (2:12, ed. Lieberman) states: "For he can say to [any claimant], 'They come from the times of the Amorites.'" The Jerusalem Talmud (*Baba Metzia* 8c) as well states the same thing regarding objects found in an old wall: The finder may keep them.

In this context, the Babylonian Talmud asks if only Amorites hide objects, and answers that this ruling applies only when the object is rusty and therefore old:

> A Tanna taught: Because he [the finder] can say to him: They belonged to Amorites. Do then only Amorites hide objects, and not Israelites?—This holds good only if it [the find] is exceedingly rusty. (*b. Baba Metzia* 25b–26a)

This implies that the rabbis recognized that old objects hidden in walls and fences were the reflection of an actual Amorite presence in the land of Israel. This example shows that the rabbis were aware of the presence of the Canaanites as ancient residents in the land in the distant past, a presence that could still be perceived through the objects they left behind.

A fourth context relates to traces of Canaanite worship in the topography of the land itself, whose mountains and trees are seen as the sites of ancient cults. Thus, in Mishnah *Avodah Zarah* 3:5, we find the following statement by R. Akiba:

> Said R. Akiba: I shall explain and interpret the matter before you:

> In any place in which you find a high mountain, a lofty hill, or a green tree, you may take for granted that there is an idol there.

According to R. Akiba, every high mountain or lofty hill in the region is forbidden for use by Israelites because it was used by the Canaanites as a place of pagan worship.[6] The Jerusalem Talmud, *Avodah Zarah* 3:5 also reflects this notion:

> R. Boreqai taught before R. Mana, "This verse [Deut 7:28] teaches that the Canaanites did not leave a single mountain or valley on which they did not perform an act of idolatrous service."
>
> Now have we not reasoned and ruled, Something that is animate, even though it is not forbidden to an ordinary person, is forbidden to the Most High?
>
> [If so, how did they know] where the Chosen House [of the temple] was to be built?
>
> It was in accord with the instruction of the prophet: "So David went up at Gad's word, which he had spoken in the name of the Lord" (1 Chr 21:19).

In this discussion, the Jerusalem Talmud even goes so far as to state that the Temple Mount itself was a former site of pagan Canaanite worship and that it was nonetheless chosen through divine instruction revealed to the prophet Gad. This ascription of ancient Canaanite worship to the Temple Mount goes beyond the biblical notion that the Canaanites once possessed the land and worshipped their gods in it, by pointing specifically to the Temple Mount.

All the references discussed above are about the presence of Canaanites as inhabitants of the land in the past. Now I would like to assert that the rabbis were also acquainted with the notion that the descendants of the Canaanites survived, even during their period in the land of Israel.

The Descendants of the Canaanites in the Land of Israel at the Time of the Sages

The surprising acceptance of the idea that the descendants of Canaanites still inhabited the land of Israel at the time of the Sages can be deduced from the halakhic laws of agriculture. These sources are based on the principle that the land of Israel is obligated in the commandments relating to the land, only if this land is held by Jews. But if the only holders of the land are Gentiles, the commandments relating to the land do not apply.

One rabbinic opinion also sees the ancient Canaanites as the forefathers of the Samaritans (the "Kutim" in the terminology of the Sages), as Gedalyahu Alon and Shaul Lieberman have noted.[7] This would explain why the halakhah in the Rehov inscription holds that the region of Samaria is not obligated by the land of Israel–related commandments. According to the halakhah, any area that was once held by Jews is obligated by these commandments, even if it is now in Gentile hands. But if the Samaritans were the descendants of the Canaanites, this meant uninterrupted ownership of the Samaria region by non-Jews.

Perhaps the most surprising source concerning the presence of Canaanites, which reflects a rabbinic notion of a continuous Canaanite presence in the land of Israel, appears twice in the Jerusalem Talmud:

> Rabbi Joshua ben Levi would instruct his servant: "Buy no vegetables for me except from the garden of Sisera." (*y. Demai* 2:1, 22c)[8]

This was because he thought it had always been owned by Gentiles and was therefore never subject to tithing. But according to the following passage in the Jerusalem Talmud:

> Elijah, of blessed memory, met him [the servant]. He said to him, "Go tell your master that this is not the garden of Sisera. Rather it belonged to a Jew and they killed him and took it from him. If you wish to behave stringently, you should act like your fellows."

Rabbi Joshua ben Levi, a third-century C.E. Amora, asked that his vegetables be purchased only from the garden of Sisera because he thought that this garden belonged not to a Jew but to a Gentile named Sisera. I would like to assert that the name Sisera is not chosen by chance.[9] This name appears twice in the Bible. The first biblical Sisera is the captain of the guard of Yavin, the Canaanite king of Hatzor. The second one appears as part of the returnees from the Babylon community, in the list of the "the Netinim, and the children of Solomon's servants" [הנתינים ובני עבדי שלמה] in Ezra 2:43–58. There we find "the children of Sisera" (v. 3). According to 1 Kings 9:20–21 (and 2 Chr 8:7–8), "All the people that were left of the Amorites, the Hittites, the Perizzites, the Hivites, and the Jebusites, who were not of the children of Israel, even their children that were left after them in the land, whom the children of Israel were not able utterly to destroy, of them did Solomon raise a levy of bondservants [ויעלם שלמה למס עובד], unto this day." Ezra 2:43–58 refers to the descendants of Solomon's servants, who are therefore of Canaanite origin.

I suggest that the explanation for the surprising concept of "the garden of Sisera" must be sought in the second biblical appearance of the name Sisera among "the Netinim and the children of Solomon's servants." According to 1 Kings, these Netinim were regarded as Canaanites who paid taxes, hence the rabbinic name "taxpayers" to refer to this group. I further suggest that assigning the property in question to Sisera was intended to bypass the problem of the presence of Canaanites in the land of Israel. According to Deuteronomy 20:16, no Canaanites were to be left in the land ("In the towns of the latter peoples, however, which the Lord your God is giving you as a heritage, you shall not let a soul remain alive").

The precedent of the children of Sisera, who were mentioned in the book of Ezra as part of the returnees' community, enabled the rabbis to envision the existence of a garden owned by a descendant of the Canaanites: A garden that Joshua ben Levi thought had never been owned by a Jew. Nevertheless, because theoretically the existence of the descendants of the Canaanites in the land was forbidden, taking vegetables from their garden could not be a legitimate halakhic solution.

In accordance with 1 Kings and 2 Chronicles 8:7–8, in the rabbinic sources some regions are seen as settled by "taxpayers." The rabbinic acknowledgment that Canaanite taxpayers own parts of the land appears in several sources, including the Jerusalem Talmud and Midrash *Genesis Rabbah*. They reflect the debate regarding whether the presence of the Canaanites meant that these regions were obligated to observe the land of Israel–dependent commandments, such as the sabbatical year and the tithes, or not.

According to R. Joshua ben Levi, the regions settled by "taxpayers" (מעלי מסים) are not obligated to fulfill the "land-of-Israel dependent commandments."

> Rabbi Joshua ben Levi said it is written (Judg 11:13) "Jephtah fled because of his brothers and dwelled in the land Good [Tov]," that is Hippos. Why is it called "Good," because it frees from tithes. (*y. Shev.* 36c)

R. Joshua ben Levi is consistent in his viewpoint. This viewpoint postulates the continuous presence of Canaanites in the land of Israel from the time of Joshua until his day.

R. Immi, who disagrees with the ruling of R. Joshua ben Levi, does not debate the fact that these places were settled by Canaanites; he thinks, however, that the status of "taxpayers" does not exempt these regions from the land of Israel–dependent obligations:

> R. Immi asked: Are these not of the taxpayers? R. Immi is of the opinion that taxpayers count as if they were conquered.
>
> For R. Samuel bar Nahman said, Joshua sent three orders to the Land of Israel before they entered the Land: Those who want to evacuate should evacuate, those who want to make peace should make peace, and those who want to go to war should go to war. (*y. Shev.* 36c)

Taxpayers and their status are regarded similarly in Midrash *Genesis Rabbah* 98:12:

> R. Eleazar and R. Samuel b. Nahman disagree. R. Eleazar said: All the tribes left remnants [of the original inhabitants in that territory], but the tribe of Issachar did not leave a remnant. R. Samuel b. Nahman said: The tribe of Issachar too left a remnant, but they paid tribute. R. Assi observed: If they paid tribute, it is just as though they were made subject.

This status of taxpayers, which was created in line with the biblical precedent of King Solomon, represents a viewpoint that accepts a legitimate and continuous presence of Canaanites in the land of Israel,[10] despite the biblical commandment to expel or kill all the Canaanites. The Sages saw in the verses about the status of the Canaanites as taxpayers a halakhah that allowed the Canaanites to stay in the land, despite the explicit commandments found in the Pentateuch not to let them do so.

Conclusion

From this discussion, a picture emerges of rabbinic awareness of the presence of earlier residents—namely, the Canaanites—in the land of Israel. Thus we find references to this ancient nation in a legal category such as that of the "Canaanite slave," used to designate a Gentile slave. We also see that some strange rituals that had a foreign character were described as "the ways of the Amorite." Moreover, the rabbis also thought that some of the ancient and rusty objects that were hidden in the walls or in piles of stones might be physical remains of Amorite culture. According to R. Akiba, every high mountain, including the Temple Mount, was a place of Canaanite worship.

The Canaanites also appear in the discussion about what parts of the land of Israel are exempt from the land of Israel–dependent commandments, such as tithes. Here the rabbis refer to "the garden of Sisera" and to the status of "taxpayers," who are descendants of the local peoples who paid a levy to Solomon. I suggested that this status was based on the list of the Netinim and the children of Solomon's servants in Ezra 2:43–58, a passage that also names the sons of Sisera. The status of taxpayer enabled the rabbis to accept the presence of Canaanites in the land, in spite of the Pentateuchal prohibitions against letting them stay or live in the land of Israel.

The main reason that the rabbis had no difficulty with the presence of the Canaanites in the past or even in the present may be inferred from the beginning of Midrash *Genesis Rabbah* 1:3:

> R. Joshua of Skhnin quoted in R. Levi's name: "He has declared to his people the power of His work, in giving them the heritage of the nations" (Ps 111:6) Why did the Holy One, blessed be He, reveal to Israel what was created on the first day and on the second day, etc.? So that the nations of the world might not taunt Israel and say to them: Surely you are a nation of robbers: think of that! But Israel can report: And do you not hold yours as spoil? For surely "The Caphtorim, that came forth out of Caphtor destroyed them, and dwelt in their stead" (Deut 2:23). The world and the fullness thereof belong to God. When He wished, He gave it to you; and when He wished, He took it from you and gave it to us. Hence it is written, "In giving them the heritage of the nations, He hath declared to His people the power of His works." He declared the beginning to them.

The rabbis did not feel any necessity to blur or to diminish the Canaanite presence in the history of the land. They acknowledged it freely, referring to it in both halakhic and midrashic contexts, viewing it as one stage in the history of the land of Israel. Their confidence in Jewish possession of the land of Israel was grounded in their conception of the divine promise.

Notes

1. See O. Irshai, "The Christian Appropriation of Jerusalem in the Fourth Century: The Case of the Bordeaux Pilgrim," *JQR* 99 (2009): 465–486.

2. E. Ben Eliyahu, "Shlomo and Uziya-Kings of Judea in the 'Jerusalem Guide'" [in Hebrew], *New Studies on Jerusalem, Proceeding of the Sixth Conference* (Ramat-Gan: Merkaz Renert le-Limude Yerushalaim, 2000), 217–220.

3. Deut 12:3: "And you shall destroy their name out of that place."

4. We must note, however, that terms like *lost Canaanite belongings* (אבידה כנענית) and *Canaanite theft* (גזל כנעני) are the creations of censorship; in the printed versions, the words *foreigner* (גר) and *Gentile* (נכרי) found in the medieval manuscripts were changed to *Canaanite*, which carried no negative connotations. See M. Kahanah, "The Attitude to Foreigner at the Time of the Tannaim and Amoraim" [in Hebrew], *Et HaDaat* 3 (1999): 22–25.

5. We also find a reference in *Sifre Deut.* 306 to a biblical word (יערוף) as being a "Canaanite term."

6. Lately I claimed that in rabbinic literature, we can identify consistent polemic against the sanctity of "high mountains." See E. Ben Eliyahu, "The Role of the 'Holy Place' in Rabbinic Literature," *JSJ* 40 (2009): 260–280.

On the motif of a "high mountain" as an *axis mundi* connecting heaven and earth and serving as a site of revelation, see M. Eliade, "Sacred Places: Temple, Palace, 'Center of the World,'" in *Patterns in Comparative Religion* (London: Sheed & Ward, 1979); M. Eliade, "Axis Mundi," *Encyclopedia of Religion* (New York: Macmillan, 1982), 2:20–21; M. Eliade, "Mountains," *Encyclopedia of Religion* (New York: Macmillan, 1982), 10:130–134. See also the annotated bibliography there and the references to Eliade's extensive writings. R. L. Cohn used Eliade's models to interpret the role of the sacred place in the Bible, mainly the "high mountain." See R. L. Cohn, *The Shape of Sacred Space: Four Biblical Studies* (Chico, Calif.: Scholars Press, 1981). Regarding the "high mountain" as a holy place in Mediterranean society, see N. Purcell and P. Horden, *The Corrupting Sea: A Study of Mediterranean History* (Oxford: Blackwell, 2000), 413–414 and the revised bibliography there, p. 625.

7. Gedalyahu Alon claimed that sources from the Second Temple period and Christian writers from the fourth century C.E. and later suggest that the Samaritans are the descendants of the Canaanites. He and Lieberman found the same notion in several rabbinic sources. See Gedalyahu Alon, "The Origin of the Samaritans in Halakhic Tradition" [in Hebrew], *Tarbiz* 18 (1947): 146–156, also published in *Studies in Jewish History* (Tel-Aviv 1970), 2:1–10; Shaul Lieberman, "The Halakhic Inscription from the Bet-Shean Valley" [in Hebrew], *Tarbiz* 45 (1975–1976), 55–59; Itzhak Hamitovsky, "Talmudic Traditions Concerning the Distribution of the Samaritans in the Land of Israel during the Mishnah and Talmud Period in Light of Archeological Evidence," *Jerusalem and Eretz-Israel* 3 (2006): 72.

8. The same story with minor changes appears also in y. *Shev.* 9:9, 39a. See Shmuel Safrai, "The Practical Implementation of the Sabbatical Year after the Destruction of the

Second Temple" [in Hebrew], *Tarbiz* 36 (1966): 5–6; Yehuda Feliks, "Aftergrowths of the Sabbatical Year," *Jubilee Volume in Honor of Morieno Hagaon Rabbi Joseph B. Solovetchik* (Jerusalem: Mosad Harav Kook; New York: Yeshiva University, 1984) 1:384–386, also published in Yehuda Feliks, *Talmud Yerushalmi, Tractate Shevi'it, II* (Jerusalem: Rubin Mass, 1986), 430–431; Israel Rozenson, "Sisera in Shevi'it, Mitzvat Shevi'it: Land and Memory" [in Hebrew], *Siach-Sade* 6 (2000): 18–26, http://siach-sade.macam.ac.il/siach6/Rozenson.pdf.

9. According to Safrai, the name Sisera may be "only a literal nickname for an evil gentile" (Shmuel Safrai, "The Practical Implementation"). He also suggested that this garden was in Caesarea, the place that Rabbi Joshua ben Levi used to come to, while Feliks ("Aftergrowths of the Sabbatical Year") suggested Beit Guvrin. R. Shlomo Sirilio (sixteenth century) in his commentary to the Jerusalem Talmud concluded that it happened in Beth-shean.

10. In *m. Yad.* 4:5 and *t. Qiddushin* 5:4, one reads that Sennacherib, king of Assyria, "mixed up all the nations." As a consequence, the nations at the time of the Mishnah are not the biblical nations anymore. The Mishnah does not take into account the possibility that Ammon and Moab had descendants in the land or anywhere else, and the same is true in the Tosefta as far as Edomites are concerned. The Canaanites, however, were considered to have descendants in the land.

Israel Yuval, in oral conversion with me, suggested another connection to the haggadic phrase in *b. Git.* 57b: "Descendants of Sisera taught children in Jerusalem." Recently, Israel Rozenson ("Sisera in Shevi'it, Mitzvat Shevi'it") suggested that the choice of Sisera as holder of the garden symbolized the memory of the ancient presence of Canaanites in the land.

Bibliography

Alon, Gedalyahu. "The Origin of the Samaritans in Halakhic Tradition" [in Hebrew]. *Tarbiz* 18 (1947): 146–156. Also published in *Studies in Jewish History* (Tel-Aviv 1970), 2:1–10.

Ben Eliyahu, E. "The Role of the 'Holy Place' in Rabbinic Literature." *JSJ* 40 (2009): 260–280.

——. "Shlomo and Uziya-Kings of Judea in the 'Jerusalem Guide.'" *New Studies on Jerusalem, Proceeding of the Sixth Conference*, 217–220. Jerusalem: Merkaz Renert le-Limude, 2000.

Cohn, R. L. *The Shape of Sacred Space: Four Biblical Studies.* Chico, Calif.: Scholars Press, 1981.

Eliade, M. "Axis Mundi." *Encyclopedia of Religion.* Vol. 2, 20–21. New York: Macmillan, 1982.

——. "Mountains." *Encyclopedia of Religion.* Vol. 10, 130–134. New York: Macmillan, 1982.

——. "Sacred Places: Temple, Palace, 'Center of the World.'" In *Patterns in Comparative Religion.* London: Sheed & Ward, 1979.

Feliks, Yehuda. "Aftergrowths of the Sabbatical Year." *Jubilee Volume in Honor of Morieno Hagaon Rabbi Joseph B. Solovetchik.* Vol. 1, 384–386. Jerusalem: Mosad Harav Kook; New York: Yeshiva University, 1984. Also published in *Talmud Yerushalmi, Tractate Shevi'it.* Vol. 2, 430–431. Jerusalem: Rubin Mass, 1986.

Hamitovsky, Itzhak. "Talmudic Traditions Concerning the Distribution of the Samaritans in the Land of Israel during the Mishnah and Talmud Period in Light of Archeological Evidence." *Jerusalem and Eretz-Israel* 3 (2006): 72.

Irshai, O. "The Christian Appropriation of Jerusalem in the Fourth Century: The Case of the Bordeaux Pilgrim." *JQR* 99 (2009): 465–486.

Kahanah, M. "The Attitude to Foreigner at the Time of the Tannaim and Amoraim" [in Hebrew]. *Et HaDaat* 3 (1999): 22–25.

Lieberman, Shaul. "The Halakhic Inscription from the Bet-Shean Valley" [in Hebrew]. *Tarbiz* 45 (1975–1976): 55–59.

Purcell, N., and P. Horden, *The Corrupting Sea: A Study of Mediterranean History.* Oxford: Blackwell, 2000.

Rozenson, Israel. "Sisera in Shevi'it, Mitzvat Shevi'it: Land and Memory" [in Hebrew]. *Siach-Sade* 6 (2000): 18–26, http://siach-sade.macam.ac.il/siach6/Rozenson.pdf.

Safrai, Shmuel. "The Practical Implementation of the Sabbatical Year after the Destruction of the Second Temple" [in Hebrew]. *Tarbiz* 36 (1966): 5–6.

12

"Canaanites" in Medieval Jewish Households

Evyatar Marienberg

Most medieval Jews had never visited Canaan. Nevertheless, this fact did not prevent some of them from encountering Canaanites, or at least from perhaps believing that they had. The Bible declares in some verses that the Canaanites are to be exterminated; in others, it is held that they should be enslaved. Jews had, in different times and places, slaves and servants of non-Jewish origin. Often, Jewish sources referred to these slaves and servants as "Canaanites." Did these Jewish sources mean that these slaves and servants were direct descendants "in the flesh" of the original Canaanites, or rather that they were their descendants "in the spirit?" This chapter will discuss these issues.

European Slavery

In the first several centuries of the common era, both when the Roman Empire was still alive and relatively well, and in later centuries, slavery[1] was a major component of the European economy, Marc Bloch reminds us in one of his classic studies. "The slave was everywhere: in the fields, in shops, in workshops, in offices. The rich kept hundreds or thousands, and one had to be quite poor not to own at least one." Of course, the number and percentage of slaves were not always the same. "During the first century, a time of peace and prosperity, Pliny the Younger complained that slave manpower was so rare... in the third century, a slave was [still] quite expensive." Later on, though, in the fourth and fifth centuries, when the Roman Empire was declining due, among other things, to constant tribal attacks from within and from without, the number of people enslaved by victorious forces grew dramatically. Their market prices decreased accordingly. Ensuing wars between various European forces, before and after the fall of the Western Roman Empire in the sixth century, as well as the dramatic impoverishment of many groups that led them to sell themselves, or their children, as slaves, ensured a constant supply of slaves, even for those Europeans who had only moderate financial means.[2]

This situation started to change around the ninth century, when more and more slaves, *servi* in Latin (sing. *servus*), as well as "freemen," became *coloni* (sing. *colonus*), or what we commonly refer to as "serfs." Marc Bloch claimed decades ago that the main reason for this shift was economic. Changes in European economics made the maintenance of slaves simply too expensive, considering their productivity. Providing slaves with plots of land, in exchange for taxes payable to a landlord, proved to be a more sustainable method for large manorial estates.[3] Slaves in the older sense continued to exist, but their economic significance was notably lower in the second millennium C.E. than in the first.

Jews lived on the European continent as early as the second century B.C.E., but our actual knowledge about those early European Jews is meager. We know of some small communities or individuals here and there, mostly from Christian and royal sources, archaeological findings, graves, synagogues, and epigraphic material.[4] We also have different texts mentioning the various types of involvement that Jews had with slaves and the slave trade. In this chapter, we are not interested in the many attestations about Jews being slaves themselves, but rather in Jews on the other side of this sad relationship. Thus, for example, a Jewish slave trader from the sixth century is criticized by Pope Gregory the Great,[5] and in the eighth and ninth centuries, Emperors Charlemagne and Louis I the Pious granted some Jews the right to import and sell foreign slaves. Jewish involvement with slaves is mentioned in that century and in the following one by Agobard of Lyon, Arab sources, and records from the Danube area.[6] Despite all this, it is only around the tenth and eleventh centuries that we begin to have significant information, from Jewish sources, about Jewish life in Europe, in general, and Jewish sources that can reveal Jewish attitudes toward slavery, in particular. This opening of a window into European Jewish life coincides with the time in which slavery was less common in Europe, and serfdom, more.

That being said, the very definition of slavery is not clear. What, for example, was the exact difference between a servant and a slave? Often, we consider a servant to be a person fulfilling domestic tasks. However, whether that person was getting a real salary, or only what we might call pocket money, or nothing at all besides basic food and accommodation, is often unclear. As several scholars in different times and places have shown, the actual vocabulary used in the Middle Ages is often of little help. Similar terms are used to designate what seem to be different classes of people, and different terms refer at times to people who seem to have similar status. With regard to those working for Jews, the late Yaakov Katz said, with a clarity that is hard to surpass:

> The Jewish household in European countries, at least in the well-to-do class, was undoubtedly dependent upon "slaves and handmaids" to perform the major household tasks. The quotation marks framing the expression

"slaves and handmaids" are necessary because [the legal status of these people] includes a number of categories: bought slaves who were in every respect their owner's property, some having been circumcised and ritually immersed in water[7] and others who remained uncircumcised and without such immersion. The term "slaves and handmaids," however, is also applied to servants merely hired for their work, either for a fixed period of time or with no such limit. The meaning of the expression is not always clear, and it may be the case historically as well that the boundaries between these groups were also unclear, and that the involved parties themselves were unaware of the precise status of certain male and female servants. The important point [in the context of the current study] is that their place was in the household and they fulfilled their assigned roles within it.[8]

Indeed, the term most commonly used in Jewish literature to designate a person with limited freedom, *'eved* (עֶבֶד), is as ambiguous as similar terms in other languages. It may designate a person working in the fields from dawn until dusk and receiving no payment for that work. It may also designate a domestic servant who works for several years in someone else's household to save money for marriage or later life. And this term may also refer to many other economic and social categories, including, for example, serfs.

This short study does not deal with the involvement of Jews in the commercial aspects of slavery and the slave trade, a topic more suited scholars have dealt with, rather extensively, in recent years.[9] It concentrates on a specific semantic issue regarding the relations between Jews and people who worked for them, whether slaves, serfs, or servants. Those people had origins in many different places, but in medieval Jewish literature, and probably to some extent in daily life, they were almost always called "Canaanite slaves." It is this aspect of "the Canaanite question," at the center of this volume, which this chapter explores.

Biblical and Talmudic Origins

Slaves and slave owners are discussed in many places in the Pentateuch. Some texts distinguish between a slave who is "your brother"[10] or "Hebrew" (*'ivri*),[11] and a slave who is not, but is rather "from the people around you."[12]

In the talmudic literature, a new term appears: *'eved kena'ani*, a "Canaanite slave."[13] The term seems to have been coined in opposition to the biblical expression *'eved 'ivri*, "Hebrew slave." It is unquestionably shaped by the idea that Canaan and his descendants were cursed by Canaan's grandfather, Noah, to be a nation of slaves.[14] This "mythical" curse, though, is not the only possible biblical root of the idea. An explicit text in Leviticus explains, just after stating that the Israelites' compatriots should not be treated as slaves, where one can acquire real slaves:

Your male and female slaves are to come from the nations around you; from them you may buy slaves. You may also buy some of the temporary residents living among you and members of their clans born in your country, and they will become your property. You shall will them to your children as inherited property and enslave them forever.[15]

Clearly, according to the Pentateuch, when the Israelites arrived in the Promised Land, one of the "nations around them" was Canaan. Those who created many centuries later the term "Canaanite slave," and discussed it so often, had good reasons to believe that some of the first people the Israelites enslaved were, indeed, Canaanites.[16]

The Origins of Canaanite Slaves

In various Jewish medieval discussions of slaves and servants, both when the discussion seems theoretical and when it deals with actual enslaved people, the origins of these people and the implication of their designation as "Canaanite slaves" are questioned. One can identify two ways of thinking on the issue. The first explains the term as a generic one: All slaves, no matter where they come from, are called "Canaanites." Salomon ben Isaac (1040–1105), the famous French "Rashi," says, for example, in his commentary on the Talmud, that:

All idolaters[17] are like Canaanites when sold into slavery. Indeed, all slaves are called "Canaan" because it is written (Gen 9:25): "[Cursed be Canaan!] The lowest of slaves [will he be to his brothers]."[18]

In the same vein, the Spaniard Maimonides (1135–1204), in his legal magnum opus *Mishneh Torah*, explains in various places that any non-Jewish slave may be considered a "Canaanite slave." Thus, for example:

If an idolatrous king waged war and brought a bounty [of slaves] and sold it, and also if [that king] allowed whoever wanted to go and kidnap [people] from a nation fighting against him, and bring them and sell [them], and also if the king's laws said that whoever did not pay the tax would be sold [into slavery], or that whoever did this, or did not do that, should be sold [into slavery], [in all such cases], the laws of the king are binding, and a slave taken according to these laws is similar to a "Canaanite slave" in all matters.[19]

In addition to such statements, one can find in Jewish medieval literature another line of thought, which suggests that those people the Jews call "Canaanites," whether they are free or enslaved, are actual, biological descendants of the biblical Canaanites. The same Rashi—mentioned above as a supporter of the idea that the so-called "Canaanites" are not necessarily "real"

Canaanites—hints at this other possibility in his commentary on the Bible. The enslaved people are "real" Canaanites:

> Even when the descendants of Shem will be exiled, slaves from the descendants of Canaan will be sold to them.[20]

Obviously, in order to make such a claim, it was necessary to provide an explanation of the genealogical-historical connection between the ancient and the contemporary "Canaanites." Several texts do exactly that.

Various talmudic paragraphs discuss the fate of the Canaanites after the Israelites conquered the promised land. Several of them claim that the Canaanites fled to "Afrika" or "Afriki."[21] Thus, for example, we find in tractate *Sanhedrin* of the Babylonian Talmud that "when the people of Afrikia came to plead against Israel before Alexander of Macedon, they said, 'The land of Canaan belongs to us...Canaan was our ancestor.' "[22] Similarly, the *Mekhilta de-Rabbi Ishmael* provides us with a short related story:

> "After the Lord brings you into the land of the Canaanites" [Exod 13:11]: Canaan merited that the land would be called after him. What did the Canaanite do [to merit this]? When the Canaanite heard that Israel was coming to the land, [the Canaanite] evacuated it. God told the Canaanite, "You evacuated [the land] because of my sons; I will therefore call it after you, and will give you a land as beautiful as yours." And which one [was that]? Africa.[23]

The words Afrikia and Africa in these texts most probably meant the Roman province of Africa or *Ifriqiya*, the coastal regions of what are today western Libya, Tunisia, and eastern Algeria. Some of the texts cited in Chapter 10 by Katell Berthelot and Chapter 4 by Menahem Kister in this volume,[24] for example the one from Procopius and the one from the ninth chapter of Jubilees, hint to an even more western "Canaanite" occupation of North Africa. Both the mention of the "Pillars of Heracles" and the indication that the sea is the western border of their land point to the likelihood that their territory reached today's Strait of Gibraltar. Some Muslim traditions make the same claim, adding that the Berbers of North Africa are the descendants of the Canaanites.[25] There are also parallel Christian texts, for example by Augustine.

How did the idea that the Canaanites settled in Africa come to be? Evidently, it does have some grain of truth: The Phoenicians, closely related (if not identical) to the biblical Canaanites, were the founders of the major North African city of Carthage. The suggestion that there was some cultural connection between populations that reside(d) on the eastern shore of the Mediterranean and populations that reside on its southwestern shore, is based thus on certain reality. Moreover, groups that call themselves Amazigh, which others called Berbers, resided in this area for many centuries, and it is possible that some of the visible differences they have from other groups near them—relatively fair skin, for example—contributed to these theories.[26] The relatively new and fascinating field of DNA studies of world populations might provide us, maybe even in the near future, with clear(er) answers to such questions.

The tradition that the Canaanites relocated to Africa was not the only tradition about the issue among Jews. In some Jewish medieval sources, one can find the idea that the Canaanites moved not to Africa, but rather to Europe. Thus, for example, the famous itinerant Bible exegete Abraham Ibn Ezra of the twelfth century tells us that "We have heard from great [scholars] that the [people of the] land of Alemania are the Canaanites that fled from the Israelites when they arrived in the land [of Canaan]."[27]

A generation or two later, David Kimhi of Provence tells us, commenting on the same verse as Abraham Ibn Ezra, that:

> There is a tradition (קבלה) that the people of the land of Alemania were Canaanites. When the Canaanite left [the land] because of Joshua, like we explained in the book of Joshua, they went to the land of Alemania and Esclavonia, which is called the land of Ashkenaz. Still today, they are called "Canaanites."[28]

It is possible that the first mention in Jewish sources of the tradition that the Canaanites settled in Europe occurred in the book of *Yosifon*,[29] a work that medieval Jews generally believed to be penned by Josephus Flavius, or at least a summary of his historical work. Although we know today that *Yosifon* is an independent work from the tenth century, we must remember that medieval and early modern Jews considered it as one of their most reliable sources of historical information.

A long section describing the world's ethnic groups opens the book. At the very end of the first chapter of this description, the author provides a list of various nations, many of which we would describe today as Slavs. The book explains where these groups live:

> They reside on the coast from the border of Bulgar to Venice on the sea, and from there they continue to the border of Sachsony (or "the Saxons") [and] to the Great Sea. They are those who are called Esclavi, and some say they are descendants of Canaan.[30]

At that time, the Bulgars controlled, in addition to what is more or less current-day Bulgaria, southern parts of current day Romania, across the Danube, and continued to rule until the Carpathians pushed them out. The mention of the Saxons is appropriate as well: The Slavs indeed reached, at the time of the composition of *Yosifon*, the area of Lusatia (in German, *Lausitz*), which borders Saxony. Although the exact borders of the area described in this text might not be easy to ascertain,[31] they might include current-day Bulgaria, parts of Romania, former Yugoslav Republic of Macedonia, Albania, Serbia and Montenegro, Bosnia and Herzegovina, Croatia, Slovenia, and parts of the following modern states: Austria, Germany, the Czech Republic, Hungary, and Slovakia. It should be noted, though, that major parts of this vast area were very sparsely populated. But all this is of secondary importance for us here: Regardless of the exact borders of this area, we still have what might be the first mention in Jewish sources of the idea that the Canaanites' descendants were alive and well, and that they lived in a relative proximity to many of the European Jews.

Earlier in this chapter we posed the question of why the Canaanites were "sent" to Africa. Now we should ask the same question about their literary placement in Europe. In order to answer it, we might need to go back to the famous—or better, infamous—curse of Canaan in the book of Genesis:

> [Noah] said: "Cursed be Canaan! The lowest of slaves will he be to his broth-
> ers." He also said, "Blessed be the LORD, the God of Shem! May Canaan be
> the slave of Shem. May God extend Japheth's territory; may Japheth live in
> the tents of Shem, and may Canaan be the slave of Japheth."[32]

It might be suggested that in order to make it technically possible for the descendants of Canaan to be enslaved by both Shem and Japheth, the Canaanites had to be placed in relative proximity to both. The idea that Ham was the ancestor of some of the people of Africa, and Japheth of those of Europe, is common in both Jewish and Christian literature.[33] The presence of the descendants of Canaan, the son of Ham, in Africa, was explained already in different ways. In order to make the Canaanites also a possible source of slaves to Europeans, it is not surprising that they were "placed" on that continent as well.

Conclusion

What is the implication of the fact that Jews called enslaved people "Canaanites"? And what is the implication of a medieval European Jewish belief that the descendants of the Canaanites lived in what we would today call central and southeastern Europe? It seems that both ideas helped Jews to maintain a theological explanation for the enslavement of other humans. The first one, calling enslaved people "Canaanites" just because they were enslaved, helped to maintain the idea that enslavement was part of a natural order of things, by putting these people into an ancient, negative, category. The second concept, that the Canaanites lived in certain parts of Europe, particularly in Esclavonia, as Kimhi the Spaniard calls it, and in Esclavia, as the probably-Italian author of *Yosifon* hinted, was even more theologically useful. The very word "slaves," or in Latin, *sclavi*, came from the name of those nations from which, starting around the ninth century, many men, women, and children were enslaved by their own compatriots or by external forces. *Yosifon*'s assertion, written possibly only decades after a first correlation was made in some languages between the residents of that area and bound people,[34] made perfect sense: Those living there were not potential slaves because of their bad fortune. No, they were enslaved because this was a part of the divine plan. After all, they were descendants of Canaan.

Notes

1. The very question of the definition of slavery is an extremely complex one. Unfortunately, in such an article, we are not able to discuss the many issues involved. For a superb overview of the subject, see Ruth Mazo Karras, *Slavery and Society in Medieval Scandinavia* (New Haven, Conn.: Yale University Press, 1988), 5–39.

2. Marc Bloch, "How and Why Ancient Slavery Came to an End," in *Slavery and Serfdom in the Middle Ages: Selected Essays*, trans. William R. Beer (Berkeley and Los Angeles: University of California Press, 1975), 1–3.

3. For a review of this approach and comparing it with those of other important historians, see Pierre Bonnassie, "The Survival and Extinction of the Slave System in the Early Medieval West (Fourth to Eleventh Centuries)," in *From Slavery to Feudalism in South-Western Europe*, trans. Jean Birrell (Cambridge: Cambridge University Press, 1991), 1–59; Mazo Karras, *Slavery and Society*, 21–24. On the important differences regarding the existence of female and male slaves, see Susan Mosher Stuard, "Ancillary Evidence for the Decline of Medieval Slavery," *Past and Present* 149 (1995): 3–28.

4. See, for example, Mireille Hadas-Lebel, "Les Juifs en Europe dans l'Antiquité," *Tsafon* 50 (2005–2006): 15–22; Dan D. Y. Shapira, "Notes on Early Jewish History in Eastern and Central Europe," *Archivum Eurasiae Medii Aevi* 15 (2006–2007): 125–157.

5. See Adam Serfass, "Slavery and Pope Gregory the Great," *JECS* 14, no. 1 (2006): 97–102.

6. Toni Oelsner, Henry Wasserman, and Bertram Korn, "Slave Trade," *Encyclopaedia Judaica*, 2nd ed., vol. 18, edited by Michael Berenbaum and Fred Skolnik (Detroit: Macmillan Reference USA, 2007), 670–672.

7. Circumcision (for males) and immersion in a ritual bath (for both sexes) are a significant part (if not the central part) of the ritual of conversion to Judaism since the talmudic period.

8. Jacob Katz, *The "Shabbes Goy": A Study in Halakhic Flexibility*, trans. Yoel Lerner (Philadelphia: Jewish Publication Society, 1989), 49.

9. On these issues, see for example Eli Faber, *Jews, Slaves, and the Slave Trade: Setting the Record Straight* (New York: New York University Press, 1998); Saul S. Friedman, *Jews and the American Slave Trade* (New Brunswick, N.J.: Transaction Publishers, 1998); Michael Toch, "The European Jews of the High Middle Ages: Slave Traders?" [in Hebrew], *Zion* 64 (1999): 39–63.

10. Lev 25:39.

11. Exod 21:2; Deut 15:12.

12. Lev 25:44.

13. Examples: *m. B. Qam.* 8; *m. Qidd.* 1; *t. Ker.* 8; *'Avad.* 3; *Mekhilta de-Rabbi Ishmael*, Mishpatim 9; *Sifra*, Qedoshim 2; *Ketub.* 43a; *B. Qam.* 87a–88a; *B. Metzi'a* 71a, 99a; *Qidd.* 6b–7a, 22b–23b; *Ketub.* 58b; *Bek.* 13a; *Ker.* 11a; *y. 'Eruv.* 7:6; *y. Qidd.* 1:3; *y. Ma'as. S.* 4:3; *y. B. Qam.* 8:4–5.

14. Gen 9:25–27.

15. Lev 25:44–46a (NIV with modifications).

16. The term Canaanite has multiple meanings and connotations in the Bible. At times, it simply refers to one nation among others. At times, it seems it comes as a general title for all nations that inhabit the Promised Land. But there are also places in which, at least to some ancient and modern exegetes, it is a code name for merchants. This last meaning is especially intriguing because, although it appears in many translations of the Bible, it is, as far as I can say, far from obvious in the Hebrew text. Probably the most well-known example is in a verse from the hymn to the "Woman of Valor" in Prov 31. In verse 24, the MT reads "סָדִין עָשְׂתָה וַתִּמְכֹּר וַחֲגוֹר נָתְנָה לַכְּנַעֲנִי." Literally, this sentence should be translated as something like "She made linen garments and sold them, and girdles, she gave to the Canaanite." Nevertheless, most modern translations of the Bible, in those languages I was able to check, translate the word "Canaanite" as "merchant." Thus the New International Version reads "She makes linen garments and sells them, and supplies the merchants with sashes." The American Standard Version, following the King James Version, provides "And delivereth girdles unto the merchant." Luther had "einen Gürtel gibt sie dem Krämer," and the French Segond's translation provides "elle livre des ceintures au marchand." I was not able to locate where and when this nonliteral translation became the norm. Its origin is not in the LXX, which provides "Chananaiois" (χαναναίοις), nor in the Vulgate, which gives "Chananeo." All this is not to say that translating the word "Canaanite" as "merchant" is necessarily wrong. The Canaanites were known as merchants in certain periods. Tyre and Sidon, their famous cities, were major commercial centers. There are, in fact, biblical verses that may lead to such an identification of Canaanites with merchants or traders. In Ezek 17:4, we find the MT saying "אֵת רֹאשׁ יְנִיקוֹתָיו קָטָף וַיְבִיאֵהוּ אֶל־אֶרֶץ כְּנַעַן בְּעִיר רֹכְלִים שָׂמוֹ." A literal translation should be something like "he broke off its topmost shoot and carried it to the land of Canaan; he placed it in a city of traders." Here again, most translations omit the word "Canaan," and replace it by "traffick," "merchants," or "traders." But at least here we can understand that they do it in order to make the parallel between the two parts of the verse clear. Again, this does not happen yet in the LXX or in the Vulgate, both of which provide simply Canaan (χανααν/Chanaan). Another important verse is Isa 23:8. The MT is "מִי יָעַץ זֹאת עַל־צֹר הַמַּעֲטִירָה אֲשֶׁר סֹחֲרֶיה שָׂרִים כְּנַעֲנֶיהָ נִכְבַּדֵּי־אָרֶץ." Modern translations provide "merchants" or "traders" when they translate the word "Canaanites," something that happens also already in ancient translations. Thus, the Vulgate gives "institores," "peddlers." The LXX provides "τίς ταῦτα ἐβούλευσεν ἐπὶ Τύρον; μὴ ἥσσων ἐστὶν ἢ οὐκ ἰσχύει; οἱ ἔμποροι αὐτῆς ἔνδοξοι, ἄρχοντες τῆς γῆς." The only other place I found in which such a change already appears in the ancient translations of the Bible is in Job. The exact reference depends on the edition one uses. It can be 40:30, 40:25, or 41:6. The MT reads "יִכְרוּ עָלָיו חַבָּרִים יֶחֱצוּהוּ בֵּין כְּנַעֲנִים." A literal translation of the second half of the verse might be "[The Leviathan] will be divided among Canaanites." The word כנענים in the Hebrew becomes in the LXX "Phoenicians" (φοινίκων), which means indeed the same thing (according to linguists, both words, Canaanites and Phoenicians, have probably similar etymology). In the Vulgate, an additional step occurs, the one we looked for. These are not Canaanites anymore, nor Phoenicians. These are "negotiators," merchants.

17. In Rashi's terminology, as in the vast majority of medieval Jewish sources, this term often refers to all non-Jews. At times, it was used as an apologetic tool, enabling Jews to claim that they do not refer to Christians in their writings, but only to "idolaters."

18. Rashi on *Qidd.* 22b: "וכל עובדי כוכבים כנענים משנמכר לעבד אלא שכל עבדים נקראין על שם כנען משום דכתיב ביה עבד עבדים". This statement is often quoted without attributing it to Rashi (who I believe is its source). See, for example, Moses ben Joseph di Trani the Elder (1505–1585) in his

Kiryat Sefer (Venice 1551), "Laws of Slaves," ch. 5: "וכל אומות ככנענים משנמכר לעבד אלא שכל עבדים נקראים על שם כנען משום דכתיב ביה עבד עבדים".

19. Maimonides, *Mishneh Torah*, "Laws of Slaves" 9:4: "מלך עכו"ם שעשה מלחמה והביא שביה ומכרה וכן אם הרשה לכל מי שירצה שילך ויגנוב מאומה שהיא עושה עמו מלחמה שיביא וימכור לעצמו, וכן אם היו דיניו שכל מי שלא יתן המס ימכר, או מי שעשה כך וכך או לא יעשה ימכר הרי דיניו דין ועבד הנלקח בדינין אלו הרי הוא כעבד כנעני לכל דבר".

20. Rashi on Gen 9:27: "אף משיגלו בני שם ימכרו להם עבדים מבני כנען." I would like to thank Katell Berthelot for calling my attention to this text.

21. This issue is discussed also in other chapters in this volume. See especially Chapter 4 by Menahem Kister.

22. *Sanh.* 91a: "כשבאו בני אפריקיא לדון עם ישראל לפני אלכסנדרוס מוקדון, אמרו לו: ארץ כנען שלנו היא...וכנען אבוהון דהנהו אינשי הוה".

23. *Mekhilta de-Rabbi Ishmael, Bo*, 18: "והיה כי יביאך ה' אל ארץ הכנעני', זכה כנען שתקרא הארץ על שמו. וכי מה עשה כנען? אלא כיון ששמע כנען שישראל נכנסין לארץ, עמד ופינה מפניהם. אמר לו הקב"ה: אתה פנית מפני בני, אף אני אקרא הארץ על שמך, ואתן לך ארץ יפה כארצך. ואי זו זו? זו אפריקא." Parallel texts appear in many places, for example in *Num. Rab.* (Vilna), 17. In *Lev. Rab.* (Vilna/Margalios), 17, the nation in question is that of the Girgashites, not the Canaanites.

24. See Berthelot, Chapter 10 and Kister, Chapter 4, in this volume. See also Katell Berthelot, "The Canaanites Who 'Trusted in God': An Original Interpretation of the Fate of the Canaanites in Rabbinic Literature," *JJS* 62, no. 2 (2011): 233–261; David M. Goldenberg, "It is Permitted to Marry a Kushite," *AJS Review* 37, no. 1 (2013): 29–49.

25. On this issue, see the contribution of Paul Fenton in this volume, Chapter 13.

26. The term "Moors," formerly used in regard to populations of North Africa, has apparently, so tell us the ethnologists, no useful significance, as it puts together under one rubric many different groups.

27. Abraham Ibn Ezra (1089–c. 1164) on Obad 1:20: "שמענו מפי גדולים כי ארץ אלמני"ה הם הכנענים שברחו מפני בני ישראל בבאם אל הארץ".

28. David Kimhi (1160–1235) on Obad 1:20: "ואומרים בקבלה כי בני ארץ אלמני"א היו כנענים כי כשפנה כנעני מפני יהושע כמו שכתבנו בספר יהושע הלכו להם לארץ אלמני"א ואשקלוני"א שקורין ארץ אשכנז ועד היום קוראים אותם כנענים". It should be noted that Kimhi refers elsewhere to the rabbinic tradition that some members of the seven nations, perhaps the Canaanites, perhaps others, went to Africa. In his commentary of Isa 17:9 he says that "כי משבע' אומות רבים מהם ברחו ועזבו עריהם כשבאו ישראל לארץ, ובדרש אומר כי הכנעני פנה לפניהם והלך לאפריקי, ויש אומרים כי הפריזי פנה."

29. This claim is certainly not my own: It was suggested decades ago by several scholars, for example in a series of articles in *MGWJ*. See Hans Lewy, "Ein Rechtsstreit um dem Boden Palästinas im Altertum," *MGWJ* 2 (1933): 84–99; P. Rieger, "אשכנז=Deutschland," *MGWJ* 6 (1936): 455–459; Luitpold Israel Wallach, "Zur Etymologie אשכנז-Deutschland," *MGWJ* 1 (1939): 302–304.

30. David Flusser, *The Jossipon* (Jerusalem: Bialik Institute, 1981), 1:30–32: "והם חונים בחוף הים מגבול בולגר עד ביניטיקיא על הים ומשם מושכים עד גבול שקשני עד הים הגדול; הם הנקראים סקלאבי ואומרים אחרים כי הם מבני כנען". The word ביניטיקיא is clearly based on the Latin and Greek names for Venice: Veneti/Ouenetoi.

31. I would like to thank my colleague Zlatko Pleše for his help with issues related to the places mentioned in this text.

32. Gen 9:25–27 (NIV).

33. On this, see for example Benjamin Braude, "The Sons of Noah and the Construction of Ethnic and Geographical Identities in the Medieval and Early Modern Periods," *William and Mary Quarterly* 54, no. 1 (1997): 103–142.

34. On this issue, see the remarkable article of Roman Jakobson and Morris Halle, "The Term Canaan in Medieval Hebrew," *For Max Weinrich on His Seventieth Birthday: Studies in Jewish Languages, Literature, and Society* (The Hague: Mouton, 1964), 147–172, which I unfortunately discovered only after the completion of my own work.

Bibliography

Berthelot, Katell. "The Canaanites Who 'Trusted in God': An Original Interpretation of the Fate of the Canaanites in Rabbinic Literature." *JJS* 62, no. 2 (2011): 233–261.

Bloch, Marc. "How and Why Ancient Slavery Came to an End." In *Slavery and Serfdom in the Middle Ages: Selected Essays by Marc Bloch*, translated from the French William R. Beer, 1–31. Berkeley: University of California Press, 1975.

Bonnassie, Pierre. "The Survival and Extinction of the Slave System in the Early Medieval West (Fourth to Eleventh Centuries)." In *From Slavery to Feudalism in South-Western Europe*, translated by Jean Birrell, 1–59. Cambridge: Cambridge University Press, 1991.

Braude, Benjamin. "The Sons of Noah and the Construction of Ethnic and Geographical Identities in the Medieval and Early Modern Periods." *William and Mary Quarterly* 54, no. 1 (1997): 103–142.

Cross, Samuel H. *Slavic Civilization through the Ages*. New York: Russell, 1963.

Faber, Eli. *Jews, Slaves, and the Slave Trade: Setting the Record Straight*. New York: New York University Press, 1998.

Flusser, David. *The Jossipon*. Jerusalem: Bialik Institute, 1981.

Friedman, Saul S. *Jews and the American Slave Trade*. New Brunswick, N.J.: Transaction Publishers, 1998.

Goldenberg, David M. "It is Permitted to Marry a Kushite." *AJS Review* 37, no. 1 (2013): 29–49.

Hadas-Lebel, Mireille. "Les Juifs en Europe dans l'Antiquité." *Tsafon* 50 (2005–2006): 15–22.

Jakobson, Roman, and Morris Halle. "The Term Canaan in Medieval Hebrew." In *For Max Weinrich on His Seventieth Birthday: Studies in Jewish Languages, Literature, and Society*, 147–172. The Hague: Mouton, 1964.

Katz, Jacob. *The "Shabbes Goy": A Study in Halakhic Flexibility*. Translated by Yoel Lerner. Philadelphia: Jewish Publication Society, 1989.

Lewy, Hans. "Ein Rechtsstreit um dem Boden Palästinas im Altertum." *MGWJ* 2 (1933): 84–99.

Mazo Karras, Ruth. *Slavery and Society in Medieval Scandinavia*. New Haven, Conn.: Yale University Press, 1988.

Mosher Stuard, Susan. "Ancillary Evidence for the Decline of Medieval Slavery." *Past and Present* 149 (1995): 3–28.

Oelsner, Toni, Henry Wasserman, and Bertram Korn. "Slave Trade." *Encyclopaedia Judaica*, edited by Michael Berenbaum and Fred Skolnik. 2nd ed. Vol. 18, 670–672. Detroit: Macmillan Reference USA, 2007.

Rieger, P. "אשכנז=Deutschland." *MGWJ* 6 (1936): 455–459.

Serfass, Adam. "Slavery and Pope Gregory the Great." *JECS* 14, no. 1 (2006): 77–103.

Shapira, Dan D. Y. "Notes on Early Jewish History in Eastern and Central Europe." *Archivum Eurasiae Medii Aevi* 15 (2006–2007): 125–157.

Toch, Michael. "The European Jews of the High Middle Ages: Slave Traders?" [in Hebrew]. *Zion* 64 (1999): 39–63.

Wallach, Luitpold Israel. "Zur Etymologie אשכנז-Deutschland." *MGWJ* 1 (1939): 302–304.

13

The Canaanites of Africa

THE ORIGINS OF THE BERBERS ACCORDING TO MEDIEVAL MUSLIM AND JEWISH AUTHORS

Paul Fenton

This chapter proposes to retrace the absorption by Muslim sources of biblical and rabbinic traditions concerning the Canaanites and to examine whether there was any continuity between the religious, political, or ethical issues reflected in the Jewish sources and their Muslim sequels. An important element that has to be taken into account forthwith in considering this question is the curious fact that, by and large, the Arab historians identified the Middle Eastern Canaanites with the North African Berbers. The latter, spread over a vast territory from the Nile to the Atlantic, were known since ancient times. Not only the Arabs considered them to be of Canaanite descent; for as long ago as early antiquity, legends about the inhabitants of Africa circulated among scholars who traced their origins back to the Canaanites. One of the earliest testimonies to this affiliation is to be found in a letter by Saint Augustine (354–430). "Ask our peasants [*rustici*] who they are," he writes, "they will reply in Punic that they are Chenani. Does this form corrupted by their accent not correspond to Chananei [Canaanites]?"[1]

The fact that the North African peasants in the neighborhood of Hipponus still spoke Punic in the fifth century of the Christian era, more than a thousand years after the destruction of Carthage, has long been a subject of discussion. Some modern scholars, such as Ch. Courtois (1950), have wondered whether by the expression "*punice*" the Bishop of Hipponus was in fact referring to a Berber dialect, whereas others believed that he was indeed alluding to a Semitic dialect.[2] Though no text has been found to confirm this hypothesis, it is quite plausible that the Phoenicians had themselves introduced the name of Canaanites into Africa. Alternatively, the legendary connection between the Canaanites and North Africa was derived from biblical and rabbinic traditions, which were propagated by local Christian clerical and scholarly circles.

Another possible link may be the Jewish historian Flavius Josephus. Commenting on Genesis 10,[3] he calmly affirms that Euilas, one of the sons of

Kush, is the father of Euilaioi "who are called today Gaitouloi." The latter, obviously a reference to the Getules, were warlike nomads in Roman times belonging to a branch of the Zenete Berbers. However, his account is interspersed with other etymologies no less fantastic. Thus Ophren, Abraham's grandchild, made off to conquer Libya, where his descendants supposedly gave the name Africa to the country.

In the course of time the legend of the Canaanite origins of the North Africans was amplified and runs into several pages in the account given by Procopius of Caesarea. The latter had followed the Roman army, headed by the Byzantine general Belisarius, in 533 as a military chronicler. According to him, the impending conquest by Joshua of the land of Canaan induced the original inhabitants, the Girgashites, Jebusites, and other peoples mentioned in the "History of the Hebrews," to emigrate to Egypt. Having found that Egypt was already overpopulated they proceeded to Libya. Procopius goes on to explain that the Canaanites are the ancient inhabitants of Africa: "They still live there in our time and still speak the Phoenician tongue."[4]

He then proceeds to mention the stelae "in the Phoenician character" of Tigisis that bear the words: "We are the people who fled the face of Jesus (Joshua) the robber, son of Naus (Nun)." Wilhelm Bacher demonstrated long ago the antagonistic overtones of this supposed inscription reported by Procopius. Indeed, the Latin historian hailed from Caesarea, whose inhabitants had been traditionally hostile toward the Jews.[5]

Procopius may have been aware of the existence of Punic, or more exactly Libyan, stelae in the vicinity of Tingis, south of Cirta (Constantine), where the Roman army had fought. Even today, this region is extremely rich in large stelae, some of which are proper sculptured menhirs bearing Libyan dedications. These enormous stones (two examples of which can be seen in today's Museum of Constantine), were perhaps the origin of Procopius's "historical" account.[6] Alternatively, some scholars believe that his story was inspired by vague recollections of the remote Phoenician expansion westward, which long preceded the foundation of Carthage.

Rare are the peoples whose origins have been sought with so much constancy and imagination as the Berbers. One of the first legendary accounts of their origins, it too dating from antiquity, is provided by the Byzantine priest and chronicler Georgius Syncellus (died after 810). He also lived for many years in Palestine as a monk before emigrating to Constantinople in order to take up the important post of syncelle, or private secretary, of Tarasius, patriarch of Constantinople. Retiring to a monastery, he wrote his *Extract of Chronography* (*Ekloge chronographias*), which embraces world events from Adam and Eve to the reign of Diocletian.

According to his *Chronography* "The [Canaanites] fled from the face of the children of Israel and settled in Tripoli in Africa, for this country belonged to the portion of Ham."[7]

In his path-blazing article, Wilhelm Bacher had already noticed that these Greek and Latin accounts were probably indebted to certain rabbinical parallels that will be discussed presently. For his part, Hayyim Hirschberg, the great historian of North African Jewry, considered that these rabbinical legends about the Canaanite origins of the Africans had been circulated anew by the Latin authors at the time of the Roman Emperor Justinian (483–565) in order to discredit the increasing number of Jews in Africa in the eyes of the indigenous populations.[8] Since it will become clear that these texts had a considerable influence on later Muslim and Jewish legends, it will not be superfluous to outline some of them again in the framework of the present discussion.

In the book of Joshua (12:8, cf. 9.1) only six out of the seven Canaanite nations named in Deuteronomy 7:1 are mentioned as having been conquered, the Girgashites having been omitted. This omission created a historical fiction relating to their emigration to Africa.

> R. Samuel b. Nahman said: Joshua had sent to them [the Canaanites] three proclamations: "Whoever wishes to leave, let him leave; whoever wishes to make peace, let him make peace; whoever wishes to give battle, let him give battle." The Girgashites rose and left of their own accord, and as a reward there was given to them a land as good as their own land, as it is written [with regard to Israel] I shall come and take you away to a land like your own land, etc (Isa 36:17) namely [some place] in Africa.[9]

A similar account is supplied by the *Tosefta,* which, however, relates the incident to the Amorites:

> R. Simon b. Gamliel says: No nation is more peaceful than the Amorites, for we find that, trusting in God, they made their way to Africa, where God gave them a land as fair as their own, while the land of Israel was still called after their name (Canaan).[10]

The tradition is again given in the *Mekhilta,* on Exodus 13, where it relates directly to the Canaanites:

> "And it shall be when the Lord shall bring thee into the land of the Canaanite" (Exod 13:11).
>
> Canaan merited that the land should be called by his name. But what did Canaan do? Simply this: As soon as he heard that the Israelites were about to enter the land, he got up and moved away from before them. God then said to him: "You have moved away from before My children; I, in turn, will call the land by your name and will give you a goodly land in your own country." And which is it ? It is Africa.[11]

Historians have surmised that this midrash may be alluding to the settlement of Carthage by the Phoenicians or Canaanites.

To these accounts can be added a further noteworthy text from the Talmud, which relates how the Africans (*beney Afriqa*) appeal to Alexander the Great for their right of possessing Palestine, explaining that in the Bible it is referred to as "the land of Canaan," who was their ancestor.[12]

Medieval Legends about the Origins of the Berbers

Most interestingly, the foregoing legends were somehow transmitted to Muslim and Jewish authors of the Middle Ages, with, however, characteristic modifications. First, the early Muslim historians invented or repeated numerous biblical legends concerning the origins of the prophets. Closely attached to the patriarchal system, they were particularly fond of lengthy genealogies and relied heavily on the ancient oral traditions of the Arabs, but they also quoted writers who had access to biblical and Palmyrian sources. However, those concerning the Canaanites are particularly confused. Canaan, who according to Genesis 10:6 was the son of Ham and the grandson of Noah, is not mentioned in the Qur'an, but contradictory accounts of him are reported by the qur'anic commentators and traditionalists. He is generally equated with Yam, a fourth son of Noah, and is identified with the anonymous son referred to in sura 11:45, who perished in the flood on account of his disbelief. The classical commentator Abdallah b. Umar al-Baydawi (d. 1286) considers him to be the father of Nimrud, contrary to the biblical account that declares Kush, Canaan's brother, to be his father (Gen 10:7).[13]

According to the compiler of "prophetical legends" Ahmad Tha'labi (d. 1035), the Holy Land was inhabited by giant Canaanites who were the descendants of Noah. God had decreed to destroy them and make the land of Syria the residence of the children of Israel.[14] Another author of biblical legends, al-Kisa'i, relates how Joshua fought against these giants and made peace with the inhabitants of Ashqelon "and turned them away to their land."[15]

The belief that Kan'an was the father of the Canaanites who left the land of their own free will or fled before Joshua to Africa and became the ancestors of the Berbers is also known to later Arab historians. However, in the principal account, it is not just any descendant of Ham who becomes the ancestor of the Berbers but none other than Goliath, hero of the Philistines. According to the biblical texts, there is no connection between the Philistines and the Canaanites, but the fact that the Israelites had to wage wars against both peoples may have inspired the link. It is interesting to speculate to what degree these legends may also have been influenced either by the vague memories of the second century B.C. Numidian chief Jugurtha, mentioned by the Latin historian of Caesar's African campaign Sallust (86–34 B.C.), or by the term *Aguelid*, which means "king" in the northern Berber dialects, both of which terms are analogous to the name Goliath (Jalut).

One of the earliest Arab historians to echo this legend was Ibn al-Kalbi (737–819), who was born in Kufa, though he spent much of his life in Baghdad, where he collected information about the genealogies and history of the ancient Arabs. He indicates that according to one version, the Berbers had been expelled from Syria by Joshua son of Nun.[16]

'Abd ar-Rahman b. 'Abdallah Ibn 'Abd al-Hakam (803–871), a scholar of hadith who left an invaluable account of the Muslim conquest of North Africa and Spain, also believed the various Berber tribes to be of Canaanite origin. Although his *Futuh Ifriqiya wal-Andalus* is the earliest Arab account of the Islamic conquests of those countries, it was written about two centuries after the events it describes and mixes fact and fiction. This is what we read in the chapter of book 4 devoted to the conquest of Barqa:

> The Berber [*al-barbar*] had been in Palestine [*Falastin*]. When their king Jalut was slain by David, peace be upon him, they emigrated to the Maghreb until they eventually reached Libya [*Lubiya*] and Marmarica [*Maraqiya*]. The latter are two provinces situated in western Egypt which are not irrigated by the Nile, but rely upon rain from the heavens. There they divided up. The Zenata and Maghila continued their route towards the Maghreb and settled in the mountainous regions, whereas the Luwata penetrated into the Antabulus [Pentapolis] in the territory of Barqa, where they settled. They divided into factions and spread throughout this region of the Maghreb, until they reached Sus. The Hawwara settled in Kabda and the Nafusa in the territory of Sabrata. The Rums [indigenous population subjected to the Byzantines] who were to be found in these places had to evacuate the country, but the Afariq, who were in the service of the Rums, remained, and had to pay a tribute to all those who had conquered their land.[17]

In his *Muruj adh-dhahab*, written around 956, the great historian and geographer 'Ali b. Hasan al-Mas'udi (871–957), dubbed the "Herodotus of the Arabs," states: "Jalut the giant king of the Berbers, went out against them from the land of Filistin."[18]

Another historian, the Andalusian Abu 'Ubaydallah al-Bakri (1014–1094), composed an important source for the history of West Africa entitled *Kitab al-Masalik wa-al-Mamalik* (Book of Highways and of Kingdoms). He believed the Berbers to have been chased out of Syria by the Jews, after the death of Goliath. He agrees with al-Mas'udi that they sojourned for a time in Egypt. "They desired to remain in Egypt, but having been forced by the Copts to leave this country, they settled in Barka, in Ifriqiya, and in the Maghreb."[19]

In his *Kitab nuzhat al-mushtaq*, written in 1154, Muhammad al-Idrisi, who came about a century after al-Bakri, states that Jana, the forebear of all the Zenata, was the son of Dharis or Jalut (Goliath) who was slain by David.[20]

In the fourteenth century Ibn Khaldun (1332–1382), acclaimed as the greatest medieval Arab historian, devoted a whole chapter of his voluminous *History of the Berbers* to the multiple genealogies that previous Arabic writers, often of Berber origin, had concocted. All give an oriental origin to the different factions. The most frequent is similar to that related by Procopius. Ibn Khaldun explains that a branch of the Berbers, the Branes, descend from Mazigh. That certain inhabitants of ancient Africa had already placed some Mazigh or Madigh ancestor at the top of their genealogy need not surprise us since they have always called themselves by this name. Thus from this appellation derives that of the Medes (ancestors of the Moors), in the company of the Persians (equated with the Pharusians). Ibn Khaldun himself takes a firm position in favor of what he calls "the real fact, which allows to forgo all hypotheses":

> The Berbers are the children of Canaan, son of Ham, son of Noah, as we have already stated when dealing with the great divisions of the human species. Their ancestor was called Mazigh; their brothers were the Girgashites [Agrikesh]; the Philistines, children of Kasluhim, son of Misrayim, son of Ham, were their parents.[21] Their king bore the title Goliath [Jalut]. In Syria, wars raged between the Philistines and Israelites, which are related by history, during which the descendants of Canaan and the Girgashites supported the Philistines against the children of Israel. The latter circumstance probably led astray the person who represented Goliath as a Berber, whereas he belonged to the Philistines, relatives of the Berbers. No other opinion other than ours should be accepted; it is the only true one from which one should not turn aside.[22]

Despite Ibn Khaldun's reproach, we should nonetheless bear in mind another opinion, for it is not without consequence, which he reports with precision:

> All the Arab genealogists agree in considering the diverse Berber tribes of which I indicated the names, as really belonging to this race; only the origin of the Sanhaja and the Ketama are a subject of controversy for them. According to the generally accepted opinion, these two tribes belong to the Yemenites whom Ifricos established in Ifriqia when he invaded this country. On the other hand, the Berber genealogists claim that several of their tribes, such as the Luata, are Arabs descended from Himyar.[23]

The Canaanites in Later Muslim Sources

The present-day topography of Israel designates a hill opposite the modern city of Zfat/Safed as Har Kenaʿan, the mountain of Canaan. This, in fact, is the equivalent of Jabal Kenaʿan, which was the Arabic designation of this locality recorded by the medieval Arab geographers since at least the eleventh century. Under the entry "Kenaʿan," Yaqut b. ʿAbdallah (1179–1229) states in his encyclopaedic geographical dictionary *Muʾajam al-buldan*:

> [Kenaʿan] belongs to Syria. A certain [authority] says that between the place of Jacob in Kenaʿan and Joseph in Egypt there is a distance of a hundred

parasangs. Jacob's place of residence was in the territory of Nablus in which is to be found the pit [*jubb*] into which Joseph had been cast.[24] It is well known and is situated between Sijil and Nablus on the right hand side of the way. Now Jacob resided in the village known as Saylun,[25] whereas Abu Zayd says he was resident in Jordan, but all of these [localities] are near.

The name [Kena'an] is not of Arabic origin but it seems to me that it may derive from the Arabic expression *akna'*, i.e. "swear" or from the word *kunu'* which means "lowliness," or *kana'*, signifying "deficiency" or *kani'* which means that which flows *al-khadi*, or *al-kani'*, "he who turns aside" or *al-akna'* or *al-kani'*, i.e. that whose hand or similar member is mutilated.[26]

In his *Cosmography* (*Nukhbat al-dahar fi 'aja'ib al-barr wal-bahar*), the geographer Shams al-Din Abu 'Abdallah Muhammad al-Dimashqi (d. 1327), who died in Safed, provides the most detailed account of Kena'an, which he locates in the immediate vicinity of Safed:

> In the province of Safed are to be found Marj 'Ayun and the territory of Jarmuq. The latter is a regular ancient city whose inhabitants were a community of Hebrews who are connected to it and are called Jarmaqites. The Canaanites were to be found in the valley of Kena'an son of Noah. Mount Baqi' is counted among its provinces in which there is to be found a village called Baqi'a.[27] It contains running water, delicious quinces and abundant olives, fruit and vines. Mount Zabud looks out over Safed. [28]

The name of this locality is probably owed to the Muslim belief that this region was the original land of Canaan where the Hebrew patriarchs dwelled. Indeed, local traditions point out a number of sites, like Joseph's well, associated with biblical episodes. It has survived, too, in the toponymic surname Kanaan or Kena'ani, such as that of Dr. Tawfik Kanaan (1882–1964), the pioneer Palestinian anthropologist.

Incidentally, in modern Muslim political discourse, claims are made for the Arab origins of the Canaanites. Thus in the *Global Arabic Encyclopedia*, published in Saudi Arabia, the Canaanites and their affiliated tribe the Jebusites are said to be an Arab people who emigrated before the "Jews" around 2500 B.C.E. to Palestine from the Arabian Peninsula.[29] Conversely, Canaanite motifs have been adopted in modern Arabic literature, especially among the so-called Tammuzi poets.[30] This tendency forms an interesting parallel to the influential literary and artistic Israeli Canaanite movement.[31]

Later Jewish Sources

As we have seen, the rabbinic legends concerning the Canaanite origins of the Berbers, which had no doubt been transmitted initially by the Jews of the

North African diaspora, had influenced both Greek, Latin, and Arabic historians. That is not to say that they disappeared from later Jewish sources, where they indeed continued to survive, especially in the writings of the Jews in Muslim Spain and the Maghreb, where these traditions underwent a strange metamorphosis. Here the Berber peoples of the Maghreb become transformed into Philistines. In view of our above quotation from Ibn Khaldun, who states that the Philistines were related to the Canaanites, or even the much earlier claims of Procopius that the Canaanites were the ancestors of the Moors, one could speculate that a rebounding of Hellenistic and Arabic traditions back into Jewish literature took place. One of the oldest Jewish references to the Berbers as Philistines is to be found in a Ge'onic *responsum*, addressed in Hebrew by an enquirer from Andalusia to the scholars of Babylonia. Possibly dating from the tenth century, it relates the adventures of a merchant who narrowly escaped death when a caravan of Berbers (*pilishtim*) with whom he was traveling was waylayed by robbers.[32]

The identification of the Berbers with the Philistines was commonplace in medieval Muslim Spain[33] and is already to be found in the eleventh-century Hebrew poetry of Samuel ha-Nagid and Judah ha-Levi.[34] On the other hand, their Iberian contemporaries proposed a new geographical fate for the Canaanites, identified henceforth with the Franks! In his Hebrew commentary on the list of ancient nations in Obadiah 1:19–20, Abraham Ibn 'Ezra passes the Philistines without comment but remarks about the Canaanites in the verse "Thus they shall possess the Negeb and Mount Esau as well, the Shephelah and Philistia, the Canaanites until Zarphat, and that exiled force of Israelites [shall possess] what belongs to the Canaanites as far as Zarephath":

> I have heard from the mouth of great sages that the [inhabitants] of the land
> of Allemania are the Canaanites who fled from the Israelites when they came
> to the Holy Land and that Zarefat designates Franconia. [35]

When the Hebrew chronicler Abraham Ibn Da'ud of Toledo (d. 1180) refers to the Berber king of Grenada Habus b. Maksan, he calls him *melekh ha-pilishtim*, "King of the Philistines,"[36] and states, too, that the minister Joseph Ibn Naghrela was murdered by the Philistine, that is, Berber, chiefs.[37]

In his *Hygiene of the Souls*, written in Arabic around 1190, the philosopher and exegete Joseph Ibn Aqnin (d. 1220) describes the persecution of the Jews under the Almohads in Spain. When they traveled between cities, because of the distinctive attire imposed upon them, Jews were easy targets for the thieves and brigands of the Philistines—the Berbers who were rampant in the Andalusian countryside.[38]

The astronomer and Hebrew author Abraham Zacuto (1450–after 1510) of Salamanca wrote an account of Jewish genealogies from the earliest times, which contains much curious and valuable information. He subscribes to the myth that Sebta (Ceuta) was built by Shem, the son of Noah, and that

Joab ben Zeruya had reached its precincts.[39] We have here the oldest occurrence of a popular and long enduring legend that replaces Joshua with Joab son of Zeruya, King David's commander in chief, in the role of expeller of the Canaanites. According to the book of Samuel 2:10, the Israelite king sent Joab to wage war against the Ammonites. Indeed, Joab's supposed tomb is to be found in several places in North Africa where local Jewish legends, for example in Jerba and Morocco, tell of monuments inscribed with the words *Ad henah radafti ani Yoab b. Zeruya et ha-pilishtim* ("Up to this spot I, Joab son of Zeruyah, pursued the Philistines").

The physician and historian Joseph b. Joshua Ha-Kohen of Avignon (1496–after 1577), whose father was an exile from Spain authored *Emeq ha-bakha'*, an account of the persecution of the Jews. Discussing the rise of the Almohads in the year 1122, he names Ibn Tumert and the "rebels of the land of the Philistines."[40]

This appellation survived through pre-modern and modern times[41] and was even naturally adopted by Europeans visiting North Africa. Samuel Romanelli (1757–1814), a traveling scholar born in Mantova, Italy, visited Morocco from 1787 to 1790. He left a vivid account called *Massa ba-arab* in which he discusses the origins of the various races he encountered. He considers the Africans to be the descendants of Ham, and the rural Moors "that is the people of the Maghreb, as the descendants of the Philistines."[42]

In order to demonstrate the tenacity of the myth of the Philistine origins of the Berbers, I propose to terminate this survey with an illustration taken from two non-Jewish European sources. Charles Didier (1805–1864) was a Swiss author who visited Morocco in 1837.[43] Perhaps having misunderstood the information he gathered, he applies the term "Philistines" to the Jews who live among the Berbers:

> Cependant il y a dans les montagnes des tribus hébraïques dont l'établissement parait remonter à des temps antérieurs au christianisme. On les appelle et ils s'appellent eux-mêmes *Pilistins*, ou *Philistins*, et vivent confondus avec les Amazirgues [Berbers], qui les souffrent au milieu d'eux et ne les persécutent pas comme les Maures persécutent leurs coreligionnaires.[44]

Curiously, this identification is to be found a century later in the writings of an outstanding specialist of Moroccan affairs, Dr. Frederic Weisgerber (1868–1946). Hailing from Alsace, the latter was a physician and explorer who entered the service of the Makhzen in 1897 in order to treat the Grand Vizir. He subsequently became the correspondent of the Parisian newspaper *Le Temps*. Having survived the Fez massacre of 1912, he was appointed consultant of the French Protectorate in 1913. He published his memoirs, which first appeared in Rabat in 1947. The following passage, which applies the name "Philistines" to the indigenous Berberized Jews, is extracted therefrom:

> Les Israélites de Casablanca, comme ceux du Maroc en général, appartenaient à deux catégories distinctes: les *plichtim* (Palestiniens), qui sont

probablement un mélange de Juifs venus au Maroc lors des invasions arabes et de Berbères judaïsés, et les *sephardim* expulsés d'Espagne à la fin du XVème siècles. Les premiers habitaient principalement les villes et *kasbas* de l'intérieur et parlaient l'arabe ou le berbère suivant la region. Les seconds étaient fixés surtout à Tétuan et à Tanger et avaient conservé l'usage d'un espagnol caractérisé par une prononciation et certaines expressions archaïques. Dans les autres ports on trouvait un mélange des deux éléments.[45]

This paragraph aptly concludes this brief survey, which shows a continuous tradition of the legend ascribing Canaanite or Philistine origins to the inhabitants of North Africa, spread over more than a millennium. Paradoxically enough, a Jewish tradition attributing a Canaanite origin to the inhabitants of the western part of North Africa gave birth to a Muslim tradition identifying the Berbers as descendants of either the Canaanites or the Philistines, a tradition which itself finally led some modern observers to look at North African Jews as being of a Philistine stock!

As a more general conclusion and as an answer to our initial inquiry as to whether there was any continuity between the religious, political, or ethical issues reflected in the Jewish sources and their Islamic posterity, it must be said that the confusions that arose in the intermediate stages exclude such continuity. Indeed, from the outset the Arab sources did not have a clear idea of who the Canaanites were historically. Subsequent modifications due to the input of diverse traditions confused matters even more, and, as a result, the "Muslim" Canaanites came to be identified with a totally different ethnic entity with its own independent history and utterly foreign to the issues raised about them in Jewish sources.

Notes

1. Saint Augustine, *Epistolae ad Romanos inchoata expositio*, Patrologie Latine, vol. 34–35, ed. J.-P. Migne (Paris, 1864), p. 2096.

2. Ch. Courtois, "Saint Augustin et le problème de la survivance du punique," *Revue africaine* 94 (1950): 239–282.

3. On this text, see Chapter 10 by Katell Berthelot in the present volume.

4. Procopius, *History of the Wars*, Eng. trans. H. B. Dewing, *Bell. Vand.*, 2.10, (Cambridge, Mass.: Harvard University Press, 1992), 13–29. See also Hans Lewy, "Ein Rechtsstreit um den Boden Palästinas im Altertum," *MGWJ* 77 (1933): 84–99; W. Bacher, "The Supposed Inscription upon 'Joshua the Robber,'" *JQR* 3 (1890): 354–357. See also Menahem Kister's article in this volume.

5. Procopius, *History of the Wars*, 2.10.22.

6. See A. Berthier and R. Charlier, *Le sanctuaire punique d'El Hofra à Constantine* (Paris: Arts et métiers graphiques [Impr. nationale], 1955), 83–84. Charlier reads the dedicatory inscription of stele 102 as follows: "'Abdeshmun, son of Mudir, Kn'an [the Canaanite].'"

7. Georgius Syncellus and Niciphorus, *Chronologie*, vol. 1 (Bonn: E. Weber, 1829), 47.

8. H. Z. Hirschberg, *History of the Jews in North Africa*, vol. 1 (Leiden: Brill, 1974), 40–50. See also Hirschberg's "The Problems of the Judaized Berbers," *Journal of African History* 4 (1963): 313–339.

9. *Lev. Rab.* 17.6, trans. J. Israelstam (London: Soncino Press, 1939), 220–221. A similar text is to be found in *Deut. Rab.* 5.14, trans. J. Rabbinowitz (London: Soncino Press, 1939), 116 and *y. Shev.* 6:1, 36c.

10. *Tosephta, Based on the Erfurt and Vienna Codices with Parallels and Variants*, ed. M. S. Zuckermandel (Jerusalem: Wahrmann Books, 1963), *Shabb.* 7.25, p. 119. See W. Bacher, "The Supposed Inscription."

11. *Mekhilta*, Bo 18, ed. M. Friedman (Vienna, 1865), 21a; tractate Pisha, 18, *Mekhilta de-Rabbi Ishmael, a Critical Edition with an English Translation*, by Jacob Lauterbach, vol. 1 (Philadelphia: Jewish Publication Society of America, 2004), 107. An identical text is to be found in *Num. Rab.* 17.3, trans. J. Slotki (London: Soncino Press, 1939), 702. See also M. Mieses, "After the Destruction of Carthage" [in Hebrew], *Ha-Tequfah* 18 (1923): 229–230. On the problems in the manuscript transmission of the text from the *Mekhilta*, see Chapter 4 by Menahem Kister in this volume, as well as K. Berthelot, "The Canaanites Who 'Trusted in God': An Original Interpretation of the Fate of the Canaanites in Rabbinic Literature," *JJS* 62, no. 2 (2011): 233–261.

12. *b. Sanh.* 91a.

13. Beidhawii, *Commentarius in Coranum [Anwar at-Tanzil wa Asrar at-Ta'wil]*, ed. H. O. Fleischer (Lipsiae: F. C. Vogelii, I, 1846–1848), 513.

14. Tha'labi, *Qisas al-anbiya'* (Cairo: Halaby, AH 1356), 68.

15. Muhammed ben 'Abdallah al-Kisa'i, *Vita Prophetarum*, ed. Isaac Eisenberg, vol. 1 (Leiden: Brill, 1922), 96–97. See also Ibn Kathir, *Qisas al-anbiya'*, ed. A. al-Barudi and Kh. Sa'id (Cairo: Al Tawfikia Bookshop, 2008), 62.

16. His book *Jamharat al-Nasab* [The Abundance of Kinship], trans. W. Caskel, *Das genealogische Werk des Hisham ibn Muhammad al-Kalbi* (Leiden: Brill, 1966), 177.

17. Ibn 'Abd al-H'akam, *Conquête de l'Afrique du Nord et de l'Espagne [Futuh' Ifriqiya wa'l-Andalus]*, Arabic text with French translation, introduction, and notes by Albert Gateau (Algiers: Carbonel, 1948), 36 (Fr.), 35 (Ar.). See also Ibn Hawqal (*fl. c.* 950), ed. Kramers, 1:100, who also states that all the Berbers descend from the seed of Goliath.

18. Al-Mas'udi, *Muruj adh-dhahab*, ed. Ch. Pellat, vol. 1 (Beirut: Librairie orientale, 1965), 58.

19. El-Bekri, *Description de l'Afrique septentrionale*, ed. Baron de Slane (Paris: Imprimerie nationale, 1859).

20. Muhammad al-Idrisi, Description de l'Afrique septentrionale et saharienne: Texte arabe extrait du "Kitab Nuzhat al-muchtaq fi ikhtiraq al-afaq" (Algiers: La Maison des livres, 1957), 102, 88 (Fr.).

21. Interestingly, this is in conformity with the genealogies given in Gen 10:6, 10:13–14.

22. Ibn Khaldoun, *Histoire des Berbères*, trans. Baron de Slane, vol. 1 (Paris: Imprimerie nationale, 1968), 184. Ibn Khaldun is probably the source of late, local Muslim tradition which held the North Africans to be descended from Goliath. See the scholarly note by A. Cahen in L. Feraud, "Le Kitab el Adouani ou le Sahara de Constantine et de Tunis," *Recueil des notices et mémoires de la Société archéologique de la province de Constantine*, 12 (1868): 12–13 and 30.

23. Ibn Khaldoun, *Histoire des Berbères*, 185.

24. Known as Jubb Yusuf, the site of the well exists to this day northwest of the Lake of Tiberias in the vicinity of Kibbutz Amiad.

25. Saylun is the Arabic name for ancient Shilo, whose ruins are situated in Samaria in the vicinity of al-Lubban ash-Sharqiyya.

26. *Jacut's Geographisches Wörterbuch*, ed. F. Wüstenfeld (Leipzig: F. A. Brockhaus, 1869), 4:311–312. See also *Lexicon Geographicum, Marasid al-ittila'*, ed. T. G. Juynboll (Leiden: Brill, 1853), 2:511–512.

27. This is present-day Peqi'in in Upper Galilee.

28. *Cosmographie de Chems-ed-Din Abou Abdallah Mohammed ad-Dimichqui*, ed. A. F. Mehren (Saint Petersburg, 1866), 211. English translation in Guy LeStrange, *Palestine under the Moslems: A Description of Syria and the Holy Land from A.D. 650 to 1500* (London: Luzac, 1890).

29. *Al-mawsu'a al-'arabiyya al-'alamiyya*, vol. 20, 2nd ed. (Riyadh, 1999), 105.

30. On this tendancy, see N. El-Azama, "The Tammuzi Movement and the Influence of T. S. Eliot on Badr Shakir Al-Sayyab," in *Critical Perspectives on Modern Arabic Literature*, ed. Issa J. Boullata (Washington: Three Continents Press, 1980), 215–231.

31. On this movement, see Ron Kuzar, *Hebrew and Zionism: A Discourse Analytic Cultural Study* (Berlin: Mouton de Gruyter, 2001); and Chapter 14, "The Israeli Identity and the Canaanite Option," by David Ohana, in the present volume.

32. *Responsa Geonica [Teshuvot ha-Geonim]*, ed. S. Assaf (Jerusalem: Bialik, 1942), 83–84.

33. See the classical study by S. Kraus, "Die hebräischen Benennungen der modernen Völker," in *Jewish Studies in Memory of George A. Kohut*, ed. S. Baron and A. Marx (New York: Alexander Kohut Memorial Foundation, 1935), 379–412, 408–409, n. 67.

34. See D. Jarden (ed.), *Diwan Shemuel ha-Nagid* (Jerusalem: HUC Press, 1966), 17, 53, 97, and 112, and H. Schirmann, *Ha-Shirah ha-'ibrit bi-sefarad uve-frovans bi-ymay ha-baynayim* (Jerusalem: Bialik, 1954), 2:479.

35. On this issue, see Chapter 12 by Evyatar Marienberg in the present volume.

36. Abraham Ibn Da'ud, *The Book of Tradition [Sefer ha-Qabbalah]*, ed. and trans. G. Cohen (Philadelphia: Jewish Publication Society of America, 1967), 54 (Heb.), 72 (Eng.).

37. Abraham Ibn Da'ud, *The Book of Tradition*, 57 (Heb.), 77 (Eng.): *sarney ha-pilishtim*, expression derived from Josh 13:3.

38. Joseph Ibn 'Aqnin, *Tibb an-nufus* [Hygiene of the Souls], ch. 6, ms. (Oxford: Bodl. Neubauer 1273), fols. 143. French translation in P. Fenton and D. Littman, *L'Exil au Maghreb* (Paris: PUPS, 2010), 74.

39. Abraham Zacuto, *Liber Juchassin, Lexicon Biographicum et Historicum*, ed. H. Filipowski (London: J. Madden, 1857), fol. 225b–226b. This legend is also recorded by the traveler Joseph Sappir, *Even sappir*, vol. 2 (Lyck: Meqisey Nirdamim, 1874), 16.

40. Joseph Ha Cohen, *Emek habacha*, ed. M. Weiner (Leipzig: Leiner, 1858), anno 4092.

41. See Joseph Ben Naim, *Malkei rabbanan* (Jerusalem: Ha-Ma'arav, 1932), 44b; and Joseph Schwartz, *Tebu'at ha-aretz* (Jerusalem, 1900), 248.

42. Samuel Romanelli, *Massa ba-arab* (Berlin: Druckerei der Jüdischen Freischule, 1792), 2, Eng. trans. Norman and Yedidah Stillman, *Travail in an Arab Land* (Tuscaloosa: University of Alabama Press, 1989).

43. On Charles Didier, see Boussif Ouasti, "Charles Didier, premier romancier de Tanger," *Cahiers d'histoire culturelle* 3 (1997): 29–33.

44. Charles Didier, *Promenade au Maroc* (Paris: A. Dupon, 1844), 145.

45. F. Weisgerber, *Au seuil du Maroc moderne* (Rabat: Editions de la Porte, 2004), 24.

Bibliography

Al-mawsu'a al-'arabiyya al-'alamiyya. Vol. 20. 2nd ed. Riyadh, 1999 art. "Kana'an".

Assaf, S. *Responsa Geonica [Teshuvot ha-Geonim].* Jerusalem: Bialik, 1942.

Azama, N. el-. "The Tammuzi Movement and the Influence of T. S. Eliot on Badr Shakir Al-Sayyab." In *Critical Perspectives on Modern Arabic Literature*, edited by Issa J. Boullata, 215–231. Washington: Three Continents Press, 1980.

Bacher, W. "The Supposed Inscription upon 'Joshua the Robber.'" *JQR* 3 (1890): 354–357.

Beidhawii. *Commentarius in Coranum [Anwar at-Tanzil wa Asrar at-Ta'wil].* Edited by H. O. Fleischer. Lipsiae: F. C. Vogelii, I, 1846–1848.

Bekri, el-. *Description de l'Afrique septentrionale.* Edited by Baron de Slane. Paris: Imprimerie nationale, 1859.

Berthelot, K. "The Canaanites Who 'Trusted in God': An Original Interpretation of the Fate of the Canaanites in Rabbinic Literature." *JJS* 62, no. 2 (2011): 233–261.

Berthier, A., and R. Charlier. *Le sanctuaire punique d'El Hofra à Constantine.* Paris: Arts et métiers graphiques [Impr. nationale], 1955.

Cohen, Joseph Ha. *Emek habacha.* Edited by M. Weiner. Leipzig: Leiner, 1858.

Courtois, Ch. "Saint Augustin et le problème de la survivance du punique." *Revue africaine* 94 (1950): 239–282.

Didier, Charles. *Promenade au Maroc.* Paris: A. Dupon, 1844.

Georgius Syncellus and Niciphorus. *Chronologie.* Vol. 1. Bonn: E. Weber, 1829.

Hirschberg, H. Z. *History of the Jews in North Africa.* Vol. 1. Leiden: Brill, 1974.

——. "The Problems of the Judaized Berbers." *Journal of African History* 4 (1963): 313–339.

Ibn 'Abd al-H'akam. *Conquête de l'Afrique du Nord et de l'Espagne [Futuh' Ifriqiya wa'l-Andalus].* Arabic text with French translation, introduction, and notes by Albert Gateau. Algiers: Carbonel, 1948.

Ibn 'Aqnin, Joseph. *Tibb an-nufus* [Hygiene of the Souls]. Oxford: Bodl. Neubauer 1273. Translated into French by P. Fenton and D. Littman. *L'Exil au Maghreb.* Paris: PUPS, 2010.

Ibn Da'ud, Abraham. *The Book of Tradition [Sefer ha-Qabbalah].* Edited and translated by G. Cohen. Philadelphia: Jewish Publication Society of America, 1967.

Ibn Hawqal. Edited by Kramers. *Opus geographicum auctore Ibn Haukal sec. textum et imagines codicis constantinopolitani*, Leiden, E.J. Brill, 1938-9.

Ibn al-Kalbi. *Jamharat al-Nasab* [The Abundance of Kinship]. Translated by W. Caskel, *Das genealogische Werk des Hisham ibn Muhammad al-Kalbi.* Leiden: Brill, 1966.

Ibn Kathir. *Qisas al-anbiya'.* Edited by A. al-Barudi and Kh. Sa'id. Cairo: Al Tawfikia Bookshop, 2008.

Ibn Khaldoun. *Histoire des Berbères.* Translated by Baron de Slane. Vol. 1. Paris: Imprimerie nationale, 1968.

Idrisi, Muhammad al-. *Description de l'Afrique septentrionale et saharienne: Texte arabe extrait du "Kitab Nuzhat al-muchtaq fi ikhtiraq al-afaq."* Algiers: La Maison des livres, 1957.

Jarden, D., ed. *Diwan Shemuel ha-Nagid.* Jerusalem: HUC Press, 1966.

Juynboll, T. G., ed. *Lexicon Geographicum, Marasid al-ittila'.* Leiden: Brill, 1853.

Kisa'i, Muhammed ben 'Abdallah al-. *Vita Prophetarum.* Edited by Isaac Eisenberg. Vol. 1. Leiden: Brill, 1922.

Kraus, S. "Die hebräischen Benennungen der modernen Völker." In *Jewish Studies in Memory of George A. Kohut*, edited by S. Baron and A. Marx. New York: Alexander Kohut Memorial Foundation, 1935.

Kuzar, Ron. *Hebrew and Zionism: A Discourse Analytic Cultural Study*. Berlin: Mouton de Gruyter, 2001.

Lewy, Hans. "Ein Rechtsstreit um den Boden Palästinas im Altertum." *MGWJ* 77 (1933): 84–99.

Mas'udi, al-. *Muruj adh-dhahab*. Edited by Ch. Pellat. Vol. 1. Beirut: Librairie orientale, 1965.

Mehren, A. F., ed. *Cosmographie de Chems-ed-Din Abou Abdallah Mohammed ad-Dimichqui*. Saint Petersburg, 1866. Translated into English by Guy LeStrange. *Palestine under the Moslems: A Description of Syria and the Holy Land from A.D. 650 to 1500*. London: Luzac, 1890.

Mieses, M. "After the Destruction of Carthage" [in Hebrew]. *Ha-Tequfah* 18 (1923): 229–230.

Naim, Joseph Ben. *Malkei rabbanan*. Jerusalem: Ha-Ma'arav, 1932.

Ouasti, Boussif. "Charles Didier, premier romancier de Tanger." *Cahiers d'histoire culturelle* 3 (1997): 29–33.

Romanelli, Samuel. *Massa ba-arab*. Berlin: Druckerei der Jüdischen Freischule, 1792. Translated into English by Norman and Yedidah Stillman. *Travail in an Arab Land*. Tuscaloosa: University of Alabama Press, 1989.

Sappir, Joseph. *Even sappir*. Vol. 2. Lyck: Meqisey Nirdamim, 1874.

Schirmann, H. *Ha-Shirah ha-'ibrit bi-sefarad uve-frovans bi-ymay ha-baynayim*. Jerusalem: Bialik, 1954.

Schwartz, Joseph. *Tebu'at ha-aretz*. Jerusalem, A.M. Luncz, 1900.

Tha'labi, *Qisas al-anbiya'*. Cairo: Halaby, AH 1356.

Weisgerber, F. *Au seuil du Maroc moderne*. Rabat: Editions de la Porte, 2004.

Wüstenfeld, F., ed. *Jacut's Geographisches Wörterbuch*. Leipzig: F. A. Brockhaus, 1869.

Zacuto, Abraham. *Liber Juchassin, Lexicon Biographicum et Historicum*. Edited by H. Filipowski. London: J. Madden, 1857.

14

The Israeli Identity and the Canaanite Option
David Ohana

And the Canaanite (Discourse) Was Then in the Land

The Canaanite-Hebrew option has been an ever-continuous presence in Israeli discourse. Since the early 1940s, when the activities of the Committee for the Formation of Hebrew Youth began and the manifesto "Letter to Hebrew Youth" was published, this secular-radical option has formed part of the range of Israeli identity possibilities. The exploration of these identity possibilities, begun in the decade prior to the establishment of the State of Israel, has continued to the present. Canaanism was the boldest cultural challenge—at least in literary and intellectual circles—to Zionism, Judaism, and Israelism. The poet Yonatan Ratosh (1908–1981) was the founder of the "Canaanite Movement," which included about one hundred poets, writers, artists, and other intellectuals. The poet Avraham Shlonsky, literary editor of the newspaper Haaretz, coined the term "Canaanites" in condemnation of the group of "Young Hebrews." Nevertheless, the appellation stuck and was used to represent the movement. Ratosh offered a total alternative that would sever Israelism from Judaism and would adapt only the elements of nativist affiliation; the "place" (*makom*)—the physical, geographic space—would replace the "Place" (*Makom*), the metaphysical Jewish God. According to the "Canaanites," there would be a Hebraization of the peoples of the area who were "lacking nationality" and a complete severance from exilic Jewish history. Canaanism was an attempt at an Israelization, inspired by the French model that defines nationalism as a synthesis of territory and language.

The tree that was planted in the land of Canaan has branched in various ideologies and sprouted a diversity of commentaries. It would seem that all the possibilities of the Canaanite option have been exhausted in the discourse on Israeli identity: genuine Canaanism, native or acquired; metaphorical Canaanism; Zionist, post-Zionist, religious, and Palestinian Canaanism; Canaanism with a fascist-militarist-imperialist, or a civilian, flavor; universalist

Canaanism; Canaanism of the Right and Left; utopian Canaanism and biblical Canaanism; Canaanism with an affinity to the LEHI (Fighters for the Freedom of Israel) and Canaanism in the spirit of Ben-Gurion; Canaanism as a serious spatial-nationalist idea or as merely a generation's trend; an idea whose intellectual roots are in Europe and one whose footprints are to be found in the sands and shores of Canaan; an idea based on place or one dependent on time—time past, present, or future: *longue durée* or short-term time; "Semitic space," or the Greater Land of Israel, or the borders of the Green Line; a matter of ancient history and a cultural construction; an ideology or an aesthetic; an opposition to the Jewish "other" or the self-awareness of the native-born; immigrants' excessive repudiation of the country ("exile") from which they came, or the local inhabitant's normal sense of identity; and, at last, as the Canaanite Messianism that sanctifies geography to the point of a territory-centered fundamentalism.

The idea that there was a single language, the Canaanite tongue, in the "Semitic space" already had intellectual roots before Yonatan Ratosh founded the Canaanite group in Palestine at the beginning of the 1940s, and one can name some of the forerunners: Nachum Slouschz in his series of articles *Origins of the Hebrew* (1920); Itamar Ben-Avi, who was "like a Canaanite," in his book *Canaan Our Land, 5000 Years of Israel in Its Land* (1932);[1] Aharon Reuveni, the brother of Yitzhak Ben-Zvi, the second president of Israel, in his book *Shem, Ham and Japhet* (1932);[2] and Israel Belkind, in his study *The Arabs in Palestine—Where Are the Ten Tribes?* (1928).[3] Belkind saw the imposition of Hebrew on the Palestinian Arabs as an essential precondition for the establishment of the Hebrew nation and for the realization of Zionism. Of course, it was in particular Eliezer Ben-Yehuda, "the reviver of the Hebrew tongue on the Hebrew soil," who insisted that the revival of the language was integral to the revival of the nation: "We will resurrect the nation, and its language will be resurrected too!"[4]

Already in Europe at the turn of the twentieth century, the poet and translator Yaakov Klatzkin foretold that if the Zionist project of settling Palestine succeeded, the people would split into a territorial nation on the one hand and an extraterritorial religious community on the other.[5] In the Canaanite pantheon, the name is also inscribed by Absalom Feinberg, a member of the Nili espionage group, who wrote in a letter to his bride, "Don't be a Jewess, be a Hebrew!" and who wrote his address as "Jaffa, Land of the Hebrews."[6] In the history of the Yishuv (the Jewish community in Palestine), the figures of Ben-Gurion and Ben-Zvi, who in their research tried to locate the descendants of the Hebrews, stand out. More than anyone else, however, the writer and literary historian Haim Hazaz, with his story *Ha-drasha* (*The Sermon*; 1942), is known as formulating a precursor of the Canaanite idea, and it is not surprising that the perceptive Israeli literary scholar Dan Laor declared, "a clear line runs from Hazaz's work *Ha-drasha*, which is a powerful expression of the anti-exilic sentiments that exist in Zionist thought, to the ideology of the 'Young Hebrews' who call for the creation of a separate non-Jewish Hebrew nation on the soil of Palestine."[7]

Baruch Kurzweil, the Orthodox historian of Hebrew literature and cultural critic, seized on *Ha-drasha* as a treasure trove encapsulating "the conceptual principles of the whole of Hazaz's writings" that "can serve the Young Hebrews as the source of all their ideas on Judaism."[8] But Kurzweil was not able to disregard the challenging dialectical aspect of the story, a sort of "negative credo," unlike those who adopted the position of the Canaanites, who totally rejected Judaism. The "rejection of the exile" existed in various degrees from the founding fathers of Zionism to the generation of the sons in the Yishuv, but the "rejection of Judaism" had no place in the critical dialogue. Kurzweil claimed that "the rejection of Judaism as a spiritual phenomenon whose time had passed, and the necessity of seeing the national revival as something new and even opposed to Judaism are principles of the Berdichevsky school of thought." The barbs he directed at the literature of the national revival were ideological and relevant, but it should be pointed out that the promoters of the revival saw it not as a contradiction to Judaism but as an opportunity to give it a new, existential, and modern interpretation. At the same time, he revealed the Canaanite idea, whose early reverberations had been felt in the radical criticisms of Micha Yosef Berdichevsky, Shaul Tchernikovsky, and Yosef Haim Brenner, as having a real potential in the new secular culture.[9]

Kurzweil located the conceptual roots of the Canaanite idea in the culture of the secular awakening in eastern and central Europe at the turn of the twentieth century. His conservative outlook, which some describe as deterministic, and the uncompromising polarity he set between religion and secularism, prevented him from seeing the possibility that a dialectical Canaanism from his religious camp would arise and strike roots, and in the mid-twentieth century would cast secular Canaanism in the shade. In the words of the historian Anita Shapira, Kurzweil "denied the growth-potential of a new species of religious Canaanism which today is very actual among the settler communities."[10] The historian of education, known for her work on utopias, Rahel Alboim-Dror is of the opinion that Canaanism exposed the basic problems of Zionism, whose imprint can also be found in the national-religious movements, from the religious youth-movement Bnei Akiva to Gush Emunim, the national-religious movement for settlement in the occupied territories.[11]

A different view of the sources of Canaanism was expressed by the historian Yaakov Shavit. In his opinion, Canaanism developed an image of the past in which there was a supposed affinity to an ancient spatial civilization. This was based on an interpretation of the history of the ancient people of Israel, the main features of which were a national-territorial consciousness and an indigenous national experience. The Canaanite idea broke away from its radical Zionist ideological origins and became a radical anti-Zionist ideology. In

Ratosh's teachings, one may glimpse the post-Zionist idea: "There are even some who see [Ratosh] as the pioneer of the non-national vision of 'a state of all its citizens,' which he would have considered a nightmare."[12] Whether an image of the past or a non-national vision, the sources of the movement, according to Shavit, are to be found in maximalist Revisionism and people of the Right, such as Uri Zvi Greenberg and Abba Ahimeir, rather than figures of the Left.[13] Unlike him, however, the historian Israel Kolat finds the intellectual roots of Canaanism on the Left, and in left-wing figures such as Boaz Evron and Haim Gouri, and even Ben-Gurion and Moshe Dayan. In his opinion, Shavit's interpretation, which puts Canaanism on the Right, falsifies its image and significance.[14]

The 1938 meeting in Paris of Edya Horon and Ratosh, which signified the birth of the Canaanite group, resembles in its significance the meeting of Horon with Hillel Kook (a.k.a. Peter Bergson) and Shemuel Merlin, which introduced Canaanism to the heads of the Irgun Delegation, also known as the Bergson Group, in the United States. It was Horon who influenced the Hebrew Committee for the Liberation of the Nation, of which Kook and Merlin were members, to emphasize the designation "Hebrew" in its title and to differentiate it from the description "Jewish." In the pamphlet titled "The Time Has Come!" and written by the members of the committee after the Holocaust, it was stated that the foundation of their outlook and the basis of the recognition of historical truth was the fact that "the Hebrew nation is today an existing political entity."[15] In contrast to Ratosh's harsh statements about the Jews who perished in the Holocaust, the Hebrew revisionists in America declared that "the molten fire through which European Jewry passed," on the one hand, and "the courageousness, dedication and creative abilities which were revealed by our Yishuv," on the other, had formed the two parts of the nation into "a nation like all the nations, into the Hebrew nation in its own national territory." They asked for a political distinction to be made between the "Hebrew nation" and the "people of Israel" or "Jewish people." They opposed the partition scheme, supported a Hebrew state on both sides of the Jordan, and asked for a separation of religion and state. After the Yom Kippur War in 1973, they changed the designation "Hebrew nation" into the "modern Israeli nation" and supported the creation of a neighboring Palestinian state. Uri Avneri took the same path from Canaanite-Hebrew imperialism to a national compromise.

The Canaanite genealogy on the Israeli Right from Horon and Ratosh to Kook and Merlin continued with the Hebraic ideas of Shemuel Tamir and his faction, Lamerhav. Tamir, who was not a member of the Hebrew Committee for the Liberation of the Nation, befriended Merlin at the end of 1950 and founded the Lamerhav faction in rebellion against Menahem Begin and the leadership of the Herut Party. They urged a separation of religion and state, the nationalization of the Jewish National Fund, the dismantling of the Jewish Agency and the World Zionist Organization, and the upbuilding of Israel as a "Hebrew Mediterranean power" that would form a federation with its Arab neighbors and make alliances with the ethnic minorities in the Middle East.

With the Kastner affair, the Hebraic paths of Uri Avneri and Shemuel Tamir crossed. Avneri, who advocated the nativistic ideology of the "Semitic space," depicted Tamir in the journal *Ha-Olam ha-zeh*, which he edited, as the ideal type of the Sabra who blended into the space and opposed servile Judaism. The Kastner case was a golden opportunity to draw a contrast between the Sabra returning to his mythical-Canaanite roots and the mentality of people from "over there." The biographies of heroes in the weekly journal were one-dimensional constructions of the secular Hebrew Sabra versus the exile-Judenrat-Jewish Agency. According to that paper, "the archetype of the *stadtlan* [intermediary] was Mordechai the Jew. He never thought of rebelling; he relied on mediation. Mordechai the Jew was the complete opposite of Judah Maccabee, the man who arose, rebelled, fought and liberated."

Canaanism is a phenomenon distinct from both the Left and the Right. In the tensions it revealed in the collective identity, in the contradiction it pointed out between nationalism and religion and in the solutions it proposed, it served as a touchstone for the central dilemmas of Zionism. Boaz Evron identified the Canaanite idea as a radical and challenging extension of the Zionist movement, but also a contradiction of it; an expression of the consciousness of the native-born generation and their direct affinity with the homeland as against the acquired consciousness of the homeland of people like A. D. Gordon and David Ben-Gurion, an extension of Bible criticism, on the one hand, and a paradoxical involvement in Jewish messianic activities, on the other. The Canaanites' assumption that the annexation of a non-Jewish population in the territories conquered in the Six Day War would cause Israel to lose its Jewish character made them support the colonizing enterprise of the Greater Land of Israel and created a neo-Canaanite synthesis of religion and the Right: "The settlements of the religious Gush Emunim (Bloc of the Faithful) are a dialectical step towards the Hebrew 'Land of the East' that is above all ethnic, religious and community-related divisions and unites the entire population within the framework of a single nation, the Hebrew nation."[16]

The Canaanite challenge also exposed the secular and the ultra-Orthodox to the option of a "state of all its citizens." In a draft that Aharon Amir presented of the ideal state, he accepted the rightist neo-Canaanite principle of a Greater Land of Israel that has "an institutional-political structure that embraces the entire West Bank of the Jordan"[17] and annexes and Hebraicizes all the Palestinians within it, but he also accepted the secular leftist neo-Canaanite principle of the equality of all citizens: "I think it important that everyone will be a citizen and all will be considered sons of the land."[18] Margalit Shenar, the daughter of E. G. Horon, who joined Amir in founding another neo-Canaanite group, also believes there is no contradiction between occupation and liberalism: "The result must finally be a state of all its citizens.... We need the territories in order to realize a liberal ideology." At the opposite pole, the ultra-Orthodox member of Knesset Meir Porush thinks that most Israelis consider the Canaanites a strange group, but admits that one must recognize that their basic outlook has echoes, "and recently," he said, "we have witnessed the beginnings of a revival of the 'Canaanites' in a 2004 edition."[19] As an example, he pointed to Shulamit Aloni, the high priestess of human rights in Israel, who proposed that one's nationality should be defined as "Israeli" and not "Jewish." "It seems that the intention of today's 'Canaanites' is quite clear. They want to be a people like all others.... In their opinion, Israel should be 'a state of all its citizens' which gives all citizens equal rights, and not a Jewish state." That is how radically different ideological directions develop out of one idea.

The idea of a "state of all its citizens" is the jewel in the crown of post-Zionism. Post-Zionism, as a basic conception with many ramifications, sees the paradoxical formula of a "Jewish and democratic state" to be a contradiction that needs to be exposed, and holds that there has to be a separation not only of religion and state but also of state and nationality. Although the Zionist, Jewish-Israeli state is described by the conventional formula "nation-state," Uri Ram points out that this is only one possibility, and not a recommended one, of characterizing the mutual relationship of state and nation. There can also be a state that creates a nation, a state without a nation, a multinational state, or a nation without a state. Ram, who knows how the Canaanites and Uri Avneri have anticipated and contributed to the post-Zionist discourse, finds that the difference between them is that "a few Canaanites or Hebrews gave 'Hebraism' a national or even nationalistic interpretation, and the post-Zionists gave 'Israelism' a post-national and civil interpretation."[20] Avneri, like Horon and Ratosh, started out in the Revisionist movement but later gave a personal touch to Canaanite concepts by rejecting belligerent activism, territorial expansion, the myth of a glorious past, the glorification of youth, and spreading beyond "the two banks of the River Jordan." He also rejected the term "Middle East," which originated in Europe, as well as the term *eretz 'ever* (the land of 'Ever), which was of Canaanite origin; inspired by the German word *Raum*, he adopted the term "Semitic space." Unlike Ratosh, he did not expect the Arabs to become Hebrews but called for a recognition of their separate nationality and believed in sharing that space. The parallel between the Zionists and the crusaders led him to the conclusion that "only participation in the space, not territorial expansion, can save the Hebrews from the fate of the crusaders."[21] Nitza Harel thinks that Avneri proposed the model of an open Israel, "today called 'a state of all its citizens,'" combining the liberalism of human rights with Hebrew national romanticism.[22]

It was not in vain that the Canaanites went to America in search of an ideal model of a "state of all its citizens." The founding in the New World of a society of immigrants who became natives of a country without a history, who cut the umbilical cord binding them to their ancestors, who defined their nationality in terms of a common citizenship, separated religion from state and spoke a common language: All this lay behind the Canaanites' attraction to the American experience, and, as Dan Laor has said, explains the centrality of America in the Canaanite imagination.[23] As early as 1945, in envisaging a Canaanite utopia in his *Masa ha-petiha* (Opening Speech), Ratosh drew on the American precedent that was based, in his opinion, on a new indigenous national identity that negated one's previous identity. Some five years later, Amir published *Shirat eretz ha-ʿivrim* (*Song of the Land of the Hebrews*; 1949), inspired by Walt Whitman's *Leaves of Grass*, on the birth of a new people in a new land. The Canaanite group showed its awareness of the American experience by the translation of many classic works of American literature and poetry by Ratosh and Amir, by the promotion and publication of essays and articles on subjects relating to American culture in the journals *Aleph* and *Keshet*, and by devoting a special issue of *Keshet* to America (1971). In his introduction to that issue, Amir spoke of

> the idea of the essential parallel between the historical experience of the new American nation and the process of the formation or crystallisation of the nation in that country [. ..]. The formation of the American nation can be regarded as [. ..] an archetypical example and an archetypical model of the process of the growth of new nations, or even ones that are undergoing a renewal, from the beginning of the modern age.[24]

Three years later, Amir expressed his "American" ideal as follows: He said that he wished to "transform Israel into a society that is open—completely open—and that attracts immigration not specifically from Jewish sources."[25] Otherwise, he said, the Israelis will experience what would have been liable to happen to the Americans had they decided to accept only Anglo-Saxons and Protestants. However, the historian Yehoshua Arieli, a specialist in American history, saw things quite differently and maintained that the American experience was the antithesis of the Israeli experience. Arieli asked himself: What was it that united America, and what did it mean to be American? The State of Israel, in his opinion, is almost the archetype of organic, religious, and historical affiliation, unlike America, which is the archetype of the universal approach. In Puritan America and in the young republic, the Americans developed many allegories and metaphors identifying themselves with Israel and the Bible and felt themselves to be a kind of new Israel. The Americans, unlike the Canaanites, refused to cut themselves off from their Jewish heritage. In their Puritan tradition, there were many motifs derived from the Bible, such as the Exodus from slavery to freedom, the giving of the Law, and the chosen people. Jefferson proposed that the American seal should display the pillar of fire of the people of Israel. This motif of the Exodus from Egypt as a sacred analogy to the exodus from corrupt Europe to the land of liberty symbolized the consciousness of a new beginning.[26]

In addition to the parallel with the United States, there are some who see an analogy with the Palestinians. The Palestinian Canaanite idea also based itself on autochthonous/nativist ideology already having its starting point in the 1920s, and from then onward it never ceased to be present, in various doses, finding a place in the Palestinian historical consciousness and their national struggle. Paradoxically, whenever it was a matter of political compromise with the Israelis, the Palestinians started to delve into their historical roots. Yifrah Silverman, historian of the Middle East, claims that a comparison between the Canaanite founding myth developed by Ratosh and the Canaanites and that developed by the Palestinians shows that both are reflections in a mirror. Ratosh saw the Palestinians as descendants of the ancient Hebrews who came to the Fertile Crescent and from there penetrated the Arabian Peninsula, and the Palestinians think that the Canaanites originated in the Arabian Peninsula and from there spread to the desert and the Fertile Crescent. In Ratosh's opinion, the Canaanite tongue was a proto-Hebrew, and the Palestinians see it as a proto-Arabic language. The Israeli Canaanite founding myth expands the Hebrew identity into that of the entire territory of ancient 'Ever (the whole Middle East), while the Palestinian myth is one of contraction, and limits their mythical-historical claims solely to their own society. That is the secret of its power in the Palestinian context and perhaps also the explanation of the acceptability and popularity of the myth among the Palestinians. The core of Palestinian national identity is territory. The Arabic language is secondary.[27]

The Israeli-Palestinian Druze poet Samih al-Qasim contributed to the glorification of the Palestinian Canaanite founding myth with his essay "The Jerusalem Covenant," published on the eve of the El-Aksa intifada.[28] The year was 1400 B.C.E., and out of the recesses of time burst forth an ancient Arab voice, the voice of the Jebusite king Zedek, king of the city of Jerusalem that was then called "Ayel Baal," who turned to the Palestinians and Arabs of today to tell them about the history of Jerusalem. In the battle between the Jewish army and the Jebusite-Canaanite-Arab army, Joshua Bin Nun threatened to set fire to Jerusalem, which had been founded by the king of Salem four hundred years earlier. Despite an initial success in pushing back the invaders, the city was finally conquered by David the Hebrew. From that time onward, the chronicles of Jerusalem were filled with foreign kings who invaded it again and again. The crusader invaders who hid behind the cross and its symbols at first defeated the Muslims and Jews who were besieged in the city, "but later a brave commander appeared upon the stage of history. His name was Salah ad-Din al-Ayyubi, and in the battle of Hittin in 1187 he gave the invaders their just deserts." In modern history as well, the role of the invaders from Europe was not neglected. Napoleon led repeated slaughters, and General Allenby "was scornful of the hero of Hittin when he stood before his tomb in Damascus, and did not feel in the depths of his heart any fear of the sword of revenge. But his despicable tongue will be cut off. And the Muslim Arabs will say: the

Roman shall not enter the Temple." From the beginning of Zionism, there have never ceased to be "generations of mass-corruption, piercing barbed wire and heroes bearing from head to foot the torments of the revolt of the year 1937, the catastrophe of 1948, the dreams of the blessed revolt of the year 1960, the sorrow of the defeat of 1967 and the groans of the Palestinian fighters." Would it be correct to see the poet-ideologist Samih al-Qasim, who persists in relating in his writings and appearances to the Canaanite and crusader myths, as the Palestinian counterpart of the poet-ideologist Ratosh?

Here the Canaanite challenge has become a weapon in the hands of promoters of identity fighting against the creation of the collective Israeli portrait. There are some who have seen the challenge as a central feature in the spectrum of ideas put forward by Zionism, an attractive alternative possibility for the founding of a Hebrew culture.[29] There are some who have pointed to it as a scalpel exposing basic problems, such as the mutual relationship of Israeli sovereignty and the Jewish Diaspora, the continuity of the history of the people of Israel, the way it integrates into the area, and the problem of finding its place in the region.[30] There are some who depict it as a Uganda-like mutation of the "Jewish state" whose imagined Canaanite identity is based on a "mystical view of the soil."[31] There are some for whom the Canaanite idea is one of the three myths contending for the soul of the Israeli, together with the Jewish myth and the Zionist myth.[32] There are some who warn that "Ratosh's pan-Hebraism was latent with a not inconsiderable degree of nihilism. The Hebrew vision implies the self-destruction of the small Jewish community for the sake of an imperialist merger....Moreover, beyond the epic of the Hebrew conquest there is nothing except annihilation."[33] There are some who are not alarmed by the Canaanite idea, which they view as a secular attempt to justify Zionism. Even so, they reject the theological basis of Zionism as exilic. The Canaanites interpreted normalization as a return to ancient roots, to that which preceded the Oral Law and thus were ready to accept the Palestinian Arabs, as well, beneath the cover of the new identity.[34] Concerning this, there are some who are surprised that the founders of the Labour movement preferred the religious myths of the chosen people and the land chosen by God to the alternative Canaanite myth without the metaphysical connotations. It would seem to be correct to describe the presence of the Canaanite idea in the Israeli discourse "as an inseparable part of the continual and continuing cultural war over the nature of Israeli society."[35]

Yonatan Ratosh: A Prophet in His Own Country

The assertive figure of Yonatan Ratosh, the personification of the "Young Hebrews" movement, emanated ideological decisiveness and cultivated an avant-garde image, surrounded by a body of ancient texts and archaic-modern poetry imbued with a philosophy of history with a single, exclusive utopian direction.[36] Shlonsky received poems by Ratosh signed with the pen-name A. L. Haran. Did the proliferation of names and pseudonyms—Uriel Halperin, who was Yonatan Ratosh, but also A. L. Haran and Uriel Shelah as well as A. Paran and Mar Sasson—not indicate a constant identity-deficiency that gave rise to a tendency to despise the traditions handed down from the forefathers, a sort of Freudian patricide, in the absence of which it was difficult to create a "new" identity and a "new" culture that was connected with a continuous historical memory?

In Ratosh's later personal testimony, written not long before his death, the introduction to the book *Reshit ha-yamim* (*The Beginning of Days*; 1982), published after his death, he guided his readers candidly, stage by stage, through the vicissitudes of his identity. At first he was preoccupied with two sides of the trinity that made up mandatory Palestine: the British and the Arabs. The Jewish problem did not concern him in his youth: He thought it would not be long before the people of Mea Shearim, the "black Jews" as he called them, would disappear. He was quite certain that their grandchildren would be like himself. But neither the ultra-Orthodox nor the (neo-)Canaanites vanished: Both of them remained with us as rival twins.

Ratosh recalled the years of his youth, after he finished high school:

> One Sabbath morning I was sitting with two boys my age on a bench on Allenby Street smoking. A Jewish fellow came over to us, I don't remember if he was from the ultra-Orthodox or simply a traditionalist, and he reminded us about [the prohibition of] smoking on the Sabbath. My friends extinguished their cigarettes. I refused saying, "But I am not a Jew." The man didn't know what to make of what I said. Perhaps it was unclear even to me. I only know that I wasn't at all religious.[37]

He was as yet only dimly aware of the revolutionary distinction between "Jews" and "Hebrews," and his awakening to it often took place in an unconscious way. Ratosh went to France in his early twenties: "And again, the question arose: Who am I? Who are we? At home, in our country, I was not concerned with the question of identity." He had lived in the first Hebrew city, the *moshavot* (smallholders' cooperative settlements) were Hebrew, his school was *Ha-gymnasia ha-'ivrit* (the Hebrew High School). He understood that to be called a "Hebrew" in French was as if someone introduced himself as a "Sanskrit," the term for the ancient Indian sacred language. If he had introduced himself that way in the United States, they would immediately have asked him if he was an Orthodox, Reform, or Conservative Hebrew, for in America "Hebrew" was a respectful term for a Jew, just as in France the term *Israélite* served that purpose. Ratosh makes us share in the crystallization of his self-awareness, in the ever-increasing polarization that took place between the landscape of his "Hebrew" homeland and the distant, alien world of Jewish concepts, history, family:

> As for me, it was clear to me that there was a significant difference between myself and Trotsky and his Jewish friends in the Bolshevik Politbureau in Russia, and between Walter Rathenau, the Jewish foreign minister of Germany and the Jews Léon Blum and Georges Mendel, the left-wing and right-wing politicians in France, and between the British Jew Lord Reading and the American Jews Bernard Baruch and Henry Morgenthau, not to speak of all those who spoke different foreign languages, who were assimilated to their countries, their languages and their hierarchies; and, needless to say, all the peddlers and artisans who spoke Yiddish and the black-coated ones with their communities and rabbis.[38]

In their wish to get rid of the Jews, Ratosh continued, the anti-Semites in Europe would shout at them, "Go to Palestine!" That was a good enough reason for him to identify himself as a "Palestinian," from the word *Palestine*, the accepted European term for his country, which was simply a translation. In the ordinary usage of people in Europe, in the language of the Zionists of Russia and Germany, people like him were "Palestinians." This was at most a local description, like *Halili* (someone from Hebron) or *Nablusi* (someone from Nablus). Ratosh was drawn into the traditional Jewish snare of creating an association between the identities Hebrew-Jew-Israeli, and, in his own words, "I did not have the capacity, I did not have the tools, to stand up to the Jewish brainwashing." He rejected Judaism as a religion and as an emotional identification with a community dispersed throughout the world, but he could not entirely liberate himself from the biblical tales and the Zionism he grew up with, like all members of his generation. He was unable as yet to discern the essential difference between the Hebrew era, known anachronistically, in his opinion, as the "First Temple period," and the Jewish era called the "Second Temple period." He came to believe that Jewish historiography tried to blur the differences between the two periods, the two realities: between a people living in its homeland and "a scattered and divided people," a community defined by its founders. This historiography was in his eyes a form of ideological propaganda that sought to create an identity between two different things.

Until 1937, the year when Ratosh was dismissed from the editorship of the Revisionist journal *Ha-Yarden*, his views were eminently Zionist, although his natural feelings were ill-adapted to a systematic theoretical doctrine. In a series of articles entitled "We Want to Rule," he demanded the departure of the British Mandate, which was not in accordance with the Revisionist Ten-Year Plan and prevented the emergence of the leadership of a "colonizing" regime for the encouragement of Jewish settlement in Palestine until there was a "Hebrew" majority in the country.[39] If a Jewish state were declared immediately, he thought, it would automatically achieve a Jewish majority, as there

already existed a national society with a distinct cultural character. Despite
his linguistic distinction between the "Palestinian Hebrew" and the "Jew" who
lived abroad, he claimed that every Jew in the Diaspora could, through a declaration, be made a citizen of the land of Canaan.

The year of his journey to Paris, 1938, was a turning point in his life, a
dividing of the waters in which he was transformed from a "Hebrew" into a
"Canaanite." At the beginning of the year he still wrote essays from the point
of view of a Jewish national historian, which he intended to publish in the
future under the title *The Jerusalem Government: Essays on the History of the
Hebrews*. In the first essay, "Over the Jordan," he explained how history could
be a mobilizing myth. In his essay "Introduction to Hebrew History," he said
he preferred writing national history, that is to say "Hebrew" history, to writing universal history, because the history of the past is a history of nations.
"Hebrew" history is the history of the people of Israel as a nation-state localized in a specific territory, whereas Jewish history is a history of the people of
Israel without a geography.[40]

It was clear to Ratosh before he met Edya Horon, the historian of the ancient
East, that Judaism was not really accepted by the people and kings before the
Babylonian exile, and the "idol-worshippers" were his ancestors, not only on
the other side of the Euphrates. He was quite convinced that "Hebrew" tribes
dwelled in the land long before any date that could be ascertained, but all this
did not subvert the very core of Judaism: the identity of the "Hebrews" with
Judaism, the belief that the "Jews" came out of Egypt, that the "Hebrews" were
their elite, and that those who returned from exile in Babylon and Persia, and
in particular Ezra and Nehemiah, were religious and ethnic extremists like
the ultra-Orthodox sects. After meeting Horon, however, his attitude changed.
He now believed that the classical "Hebrew" period of the judges and kings
revealed the mendacious tendencies of Jewish historiography: He regarded the
Exodus from Egypt as a Jewish legend, and Israel no longer appeared to be
a small and harassed state, a ball between the two major powers on the Nile
and the Euphrates. On the contrary, Israel was the cornerstone of the land
of 'Ever, of which Israelite and Sidonian Canaan was the heart. The removal
of the "Zionist brainwashing exposed the body of religious and ethnic interpretation by Jewish tradition," and when Ratosh came to write his collection
The Walker in Darkness (1965), and *Sword Poems* (1969), he abandoned Jewish
symbols and concepts, and began to praise war:

> And every loyal heart and true
> Will mark his brow with blood
> With blood mark his right hand
> And with heart's blood say Amen
> And consecrated for day of battle
> And consecrated in blood and soul

> In communion with all his brethren
> Brother to brother will show forth
> Brother to brother will speak out
> A pact of brethren each will vow.[41]

Essentially, Ratosh acquired most of his new outlook from Horon, who continued in his book *Eretz ha-Kedem* (*The Land of Kedem*) to develop the view that tied history to geography.[42] Israel, said Horon, is not a Jewish state but a stage in the national revival of Canaan, the land of 'Ever, the common home of the Hebrew-speaking peoples before Judaism was born. There was no truth, in his opinion, in the claims of the Arabs or the claims of the Zionists. There is no Arab nation, for the simple reason that it is dispersed in its different diasporas and is not amenable to crystallization into a single nation. Hence, there is no Palestinian people either. The Arab world (or the so-called Arab world) has only a linguistic significance, and it exists only in the sense that "Latin Europe" existed in the Middle Ages. The only true Arabs are the Bedouins. Pan-Arabism is thus a nationalism without a nation. The "Hebraization" of the Arabs would make them equal citizens of a secular and democratic state. The Hebrew movement supports a secular state and its aim is really the transformation of the whole "land of the Euphrates." Because modern national societies consider community and religion to be of minor importance, there must be a total separation of religion and state. The regime in Israel is undemocratic because of the "Jewish Zionist consciousness" that it tries to impose on the inhabitants of the land, a consciousness connected with its concept of the nation. The conclusion is that Jewish history cannot be represented as the history of the Hebrew nation. A distinction must be made between Jewish literature written in Hebrew and authentic Hebrew literature, both ancient and contemporary.

Horon's views were well-received by the heads of Beitar (the Revisionist Youth Movement), and he was asked to write *Toldot ha-umma ha-'ivrit* (*The History of the Hebrew Nation*). Discoveries of a connection between the Phoenician settlements in North Africa and the people of Israel added a Mediterranean seafaring dimension to the history of the Jews. Jabotinsky understood the potential of what Yaakov Shavit called "the image of the historical past of the people of Israel" presented by Horon.[43] The people of Israel, as a conglomeration of peoples, created Israel as a separate entity in the time of the United Kingdom. In the time of the kings, the Jebusite, the Hittite, and the Phoenician were swallowed up in Judah and Israel, and thus the first Hebrew emerged as a citizen of the Mediterranean. This discovery was very important: Jabotinsky wished to distinguish Hebraism from Arabism, but when he read Horon's *Canaan and the Arabs* in 1939, he expressed his disappointment to Horon: "This is my advice as an author: don't give way to a tendency to demean Israel in order to glorify the Arabs, or demean monotheism in order to affirm idolatry."[44] What attracted

Ratosh to Horon—a non-Jewish Hebrew authenticity with Canaanite roots—
was precisely what distanced Jabotinsky from him. Ratosh, for his part, was
disappointed in the revisionists who drew closer to the national-religious, and
this "Zionist" alliance completely distanced the Canaanites from the national
Right and finally made possible the transition from "Hebraism" to "Canaanism"
divorcing itself completely from Judaism.

After his dramatic and fateful meeting with Horon, Ratosh returned to
Palestine and began to organize an intellectual group as the basis for a political movement. At the same time, Haim Hazaz's *The Sermon* was published in
a supplement of *Haaretz*. It was a heretical piece, the main point of which was
that "the land of Israel is already not Judaism,"[45] and Baruch Kurzweil correctly
concluded that Yudke's words in Hazaz's story were "the source of all their
(i.e., the Canaanites) ideas on Judaism."[46] The Canaanite founding manifesto,
"Epistle to Hebrew Youth," which was published in 1943 by the Committee
for the Consolidation of Hebrew Youth, was expanded about a year later
into the "Opening Speech" intended for the first sitting of the Meeting of the
Committee with Representatives of the Cells. This "written declaration" was
addressed to the young people, the people of tomorrow, bearers of the Hebrew
revolution, in a terse and declamatory language, in the spirit of the European
manifestos of that period. The call to detach Hebraism from Judaism, and,
more than that, the call to detach oneself from the Jews—the year was 1943!—
reached its climax here:

> The Committee for the Formation of Hebrew Youth summons you to
> reflect on the depth of the chasm and alienation that separates you, the
> Hebrew youth, from all those Jews in the Diaspora.... The Committee for
> the Formation of Hebrew Youth turns to you because you are the strength
> of tomorrow in this land.... The Committee for the Formation of Hebrew
> Youth is not afraid for you because of the scorn and admonishment that will
> be poured out upon you...but...is in fear...that you will become accus-
> tomed to the manners of the Jewish Diaspora, lest your heart go astray after
> its outlook and criteria,...lest you learn its ways and...forget who you are,
> a part of a normal nation, a part of the ascendant Hebrew nation.... And we
> do not promise you pleasure, neither personal nor social. We promise all
> who follow us the full misunderstanding of the public at large.... We prom-
> ise the full force of the clash with Zionism, from its deepest roots to...its
> fullest power and corruption, and we promise the fullness of the blind, ava-
> ricious and vicious hatred from all the various bureaucracies—to the bitter
> end....] But we know the power of the illumination of Hebrew conscious-
> ness. This consciousness, when it will come upon you, will totally purify
> [you] of the vestiges of your reprehensible education.... The tie that binds
> the generations of Judaism cannot be loosened; it can only be severed. And
> you, child of the native land, can cut it.[47]

The Hebrew youth, he said, was not "one that escaped from the sword," "a persecuted Jew"; he did not represent "a mixed multitude of refugees" or a "pilgrim," but "a normal people," "a healthy youth, at home in its country" that "despises the manifestations of Jewish senility." Ratosh was contemptuous of scattered Jewry, its great men and activists, its sages and leaders, its rabbis and scholars, its martyrs and Messiahs, its Zionists and ghetto fighters. He did not find anything to admire in the wretched so-called glorious Second Temple period, in the heroes and rebels and kings and zealots or those who sacrificed their lives at Massada. They were merely proof that no personal heroism or goodwill could help the Jews in dispersion; every rebellion is foredoomed to failure and every revival to degeneration. The imbroglio of the centuries of Judaism cannot be disentangled: It can only be severed. A new world awaits the new Hebrew! This new world is the primeval world, a Hebrew golden age as against the fog of dispersion, which stands between the homeland and the people's past. The removal of the "Jewish" cobwebs would clear the way to the vision of a great Hebrew future, and hidden forces stifled by Judaism and Zionism would rise up.

In *Masa hapetihah* (*The Opening Discourse*), a year later, Ratosh's anti-Jewish venom reached new heights. A year before the end of the Second World War, when the facts of the Holocaust had been revealed and were known in Palestine as everywhere else, Ratosh called Judaism "the inebriation of the Jewish poison." Of Judaism, he said that "this enemy will devour us voraciously...and if we do not root it out, we are lost. This country cannot be both Hebrew and Jewish, for if we do not trample underfoot that whole sick culture of the immigrants and pilgrims, that leprosy will infect us all." Moreover, "the poison that destroys all that is good in them [the Jews] is the very poison from which we have arisen to disinfect ourselves, and we protect our souls from it, for no one knows its power as we do." In place of the "Jewish poison," Ratosh proposed:

> There is no Hebrew other than the child of the land of 'Ever, the land of the Hebrews'—no one else. And whoever is not a native of this land, the land of the Hebrews, cannot become a Hebrew, is not a Hebrew, and never was. And whoever comes from the Jewish dispersion, its times and its places, is, from the beginning to the end of days, a Jew, not a Hebrew, and he can be nothing but a Jew—good or bad, proud or lowly, but still a Jew. And a Jew and a Hebrew can never be the same. Whoever is a Hebrew cannot be a Jew, and whoever is a Jew cannot be a Hebrew. [48]

Ratosh now unfurled the blue and purple flag: "Many bodies and factions have sprung up in the Yishuv, but none of them has produced a new flag." He already answered his future critics: "Whoever is imbued with the Jewish poison...will be afraid to raise a flag....That rag and that pole belong to the foolish, vain beliefs of the *goyim* and their world. Many people need a flag. Wise and intelligent Jews know that one does not raise and does not lower that coloured rag and pole." The flag was turned against both the Right and Left, who in his opinion were lying to themselves when they spoke of a new Hebrew: Hashomer Hatzair, who spoke of a new Hebrew type but really meant their version of the Jewish type; the Fighters for the Freedom of Israel (LEHI), who were careful to write *Hebrew* on their pamphlets but also meant the Jew, and even Ben-Gurion, who made flowery speeches on Hebrew and Hebrew independence, hoped for a Jewish state. The Canaanite radical nationalism was beyond the ideological camps of both the Left and Right.

In the article "The Land of the Euphrates," which he wrote after the Six Day War, Ratosh summed up his views concerning Hebraism.[49] In this country, as in other lands of immigration, a new nation arose at the turn of the twentieth century. It came into being within the geographical and linguistic framework of the classical Hebrew nation before Judaism was created. At the same time, a process of national resurrection occurred, as had happened several times to the ancient nation as it renewed itself. The Israeli territory is a natural and inseparable part of the land of the Euphrates, which is the classical Hebrew land that extends from the Egyptian border to the Tigris. In an interview given in 1981, Ratosh again asserted that the Hebrews are the pioneers and nucleus of the resurrection of the Land of the Euphrates on a secular, national basis and not on the basis of a religious community. This resurrection is based on the classical Hebrew roots common to all the inhabitants of the land before Judaism came into existence.[50]

As Kutzweil said, "The Young Hebrews were not the first to put their faith in a revival of myth." The taste for myth was very prevalent in Europe in the 1930s and was a fashionable field of research in France with the research of Georges Dumézil and Claude Lévi-Strauss.[51] Yonatan Ratosh was exposed to this mental atmosphere during his stay in Paris in the thirties, and he felt that his meeting in Paris with Horon was a "liberating shock" and the moment of birth of the anti-Zionist, secular, radical "Canaanite" outlook. Horon had opened his eyes. He smashed the religious, community-centered Jewish spectacles through which "ancient Jewish history and existence" appeared to be "a sort of divine exception in the history of mankind. It was no longer a nation of priests, a Messiah under the orders of God, sent to fulfill a divine mission outside its country."[52] The scholars' discovery of myth, together with the uncovering of archaeological finds from the ancient East, encouraged the perception that the Canaanites who lived in Ugarit shared the same culture as the Israelites, a culture expressed in a common mythological literature.

Ratosh saw the revival of Hebrew-Canaanite myth as a conceptual symbol and an aesthetic and political tool for the creation of the new Hebrew culture. The Hebrew myths were intended to form part of the national culture, just as the Greek myths formed part of European culture. Leading researchers of Hebrew culture have attached great importance to Ratosh's use of myth. For the literary scholar Dan Miron, it is a world of images and metaphors expressing a personal point of view;[53] the historian Yaakov Shavit sees it as a multipurpose construction, a rich world that expresses the experiences and consciousness of the modern Hebrew;[54] the literary scholar Nurit Graetz finds a correlation between the poetic structure and the choice of the myth of Tammuz and Ratosh's national ideology;[55] Yehuda Libes, a scholar of the Kabbalah, sees Ratosh as the creator of a new religious myth, and he was therefore in his opinion more religious than many religious people when he spoke of the resurrection of a god.[56] Whatever the case, the myth of ancient Hebraism deviated in its radicalism from the crystallizing Israeli consciousness that always moved upon the axis of Judaism and Zionism.[57]

However, the Canaanite myth was not confined only to the Hebrew culture. Ratosh's national vision was wholly secular, but politically he was very much to the Right. Canaanism was not satisfied with the "Hebraization" of the Jewish homeland but demanded the Hebraization of the entire Middle East. Finally, after 1967, the religious-Zionist settlers adopted Ratosh's Canaanite order of priorities, which placed the land before anything else. In this connection, it is interesting to note that Rabbi Zvi Yehuda Kook, head of the Merkav HaZav Yeshiva, was the first person to offer a financial contribution to Aharon Amir in his attempt to recreate the Canaanite group after the Six Day War. The cunning of history joined the Young Hebrews to the hills of Judea and Samaria, and the Canaanite was then in the Greater Land of Israel! A prediction was made at an early stage by three Orthodox intellectuals, the most eminent sons of religious Zionism, and also by Gershom Scholem, that Hebraism would conquer Judaism. They correctly saw that the Canaanite challenge was the dialectical opposite of the challenge of religion. After the Six Day War, Canaanism came in by the back door, and the blue and purple flag was wrapped in a prayer-shawl.

Gershom Scholem: Neither Canaanism, nor Messianism

A discussion of Gush Emunim (Bloc of the Faithful) as a unique case of the Canaanization of Sabbataianism requires one to go to the starting point of Gershom Scholem's views on Zionism. In a conversation with the writer Ehud Ben Ezer, Scholem distinguished two trends that from the beginning preserved the special quality of Zionism: the trend of persistence and continuity and the trend to rebellion. Zionism was preserved by the interplay of these two principles. The question was: "Is Zionism a movement that seeks a continuation of what has been the Jewish tradition throughout the generations, or had it come to introduce a change into the historic phenomenon called Judaism?"[58] One branch saw Zionism as the fulfillment of traditional Judaism, while the activist branch favored rebellion and spiritual renewal: "They said, we are sick to death of the exilic mentality, but they were not Canaanites. They said, change, but not a new beginning." The centrifugal trend favored adaptation and assimilation, and the centripetal trend favored internal Jewish strengthening: "Here in Israel we may enumerate all the Canaanite manifestations as part of the centrifugal trend." As against this, the other trend wanted Jewish renewal in Israel. Zionism, in his opinion, cultivated the essence of the Jewish people because it did not support one trend exclusively. A dialectical process requires the dynamic of two principles, a conflict of continuity and rebellion.

The trouble with the Canaanite movement, thought Scholem, was that it sought to annul the dialectical tension that nourished Judaism, Zionism, and Israelism. He claimed that there was no contradiction between continuity and rebellion, but simply this fruitful tension: "We obviously all seek continuation, except for the Canaanites." This dialectic, according to Scholem, and also according to his friend Walter Benjamin, not only applied to the future, but also to the past. There were utopian elements in Judaism that looked back to the past: elevated, hidden things that had not yet been rediscovered. The subversive history of Judaism of these two scholars sought to undermine the supremacy of the rabbinical version and to present a different version, a history of others. Benjamin wanted to reconstruct utopian elements in the past, to pass over the successful and celebrate the oppressed, and Scholem wished to revive the memory of individuals and movements in Judaism that had incurred disapproval.[59] With their refreshing treatment of history, Benjamin and Scholem went against accepted opinion and bestowed legitimacy on the subversive episodes in Judaism.

Canaanism, according to Scholem, could not be considered a utopian element in the Jewish historical development: "In my opinion, cutting the living tie with the heritage of the generations is educational murder. I admit it. I am downright anti-Canaanite."[60] Even from its own point of view, Canaanism clearly did not regard itself as part of the Jewish dialectic. Its representatives denied the continuity of history: "They want to 'leap' over the exile," he said, as if there were some kind of internal bridge to biblical times, but the leap to the Bible was fictitious, as the reality in the Bible was one that no longer existed. Like Kurzweil, Scholem saw that "this Canaanitism has deep roots with Berdichevsky: a process of centrifugality is taking place among us: young fellows dream of cutting their ties with the entire past and of national existence without a tradition—cutting ties with recent past." In Scholem's opinion, Ben-Gurion was one of the main people responsible for the Canaanite outlook:

> Ben-Gurion encouraged the Canaanites because he skipped directly to the Bible and rejected all exile. But he leapt into the moral Bible, while they turned to the pagan Bible. Ben-Gurion has today forgotten the fact that he alienated himself. He thought then that we were returning to a Biblical historical continuity. But such a continuity exists only in books, and not in history. The continuity of the Biblical period existed within a religious reality

and within a historical reality. Ben-Gurion encouraged movements towards cutting off their ties with Judaism here in Israel. But it is impossible to strike roots right into the Bible.[61]

And indeed, Ben-Gurion placed the emphasis in his refurbished biblical commentary on the land rather than religion, the mother country rather than Judaism, the homeland rather than the "wanderings" of exile. Ben-Gurion compared the achievements of the Israel Defense Forces to the conquest of the land by Joshua; archaeology, in his opinion, had replaced the Talmud; he preferred Berdichevsky to Ahad Ha-Am; and the "rejection of the exile" was the bridge that connected the biblical Hebrew to the "new Hebrew."[62] Although Scholem saw a difference between Ben-Gurion's "moral" Bible and the "idolatrous Bible" of the Canaanites, he felt that cutting off the connection with the legacy of the generations was educational murder, and he consequently described himself as a violent anti-Canaanite. Although he did not consider atheism to be taboo and thought it even quite legitimate, he believed that the secular Canaanite interpretation of the history of the Jews did not have a solid foundation. He said that if the Canaanites had triumphed, all they would have done would be to create a small sect and not a new Hebrew nation. Their victory would have canceled out the dialectical relationship of Israel and the Diaspora and led to a total polarization with the Jews and a dissolution into the Semitic space. Scholem's views on the Canaanites—"this 'new people,' this sect of Jews"[63]—recall Christianity, which cut itself off from Judaism, more than Sabbataianism, which Scholem claimed was a legitimate dialectical link in the chain of Jewish history, for it hastened the modernization of Judaism. The State of Israel forms part of the historical continuum, unlike the Canaanites, who wanted to create a new national identity based on a leap back to the ancient history of Israel.

Scholem wished to expose the fictitious nature of the basic Canaanite conceptions. Their idea of a "new Hebrew nation" that would arise in the "land of the Euphrates," as if a people could cut itself off from its roots, was unrealistic. The Canaanites, in negating the "essence" that united the Jewish people, would "bring the whole Yishuv to assimilation, destruction or emigration." Their conceptions concerning the past and future were basically untenable:

> They, the Canaanites, would bring the entire Jewish settlement to total assimilation, to oblivion or to emigration. The Canaanites have fictitious concepts as regards the past, the period of the Bible, and the future, too. The fact that we have not been carried away in the tempests of history happens to be a result of anti-Canaanitism. I am not interested in a State of Canaan. It is an empty game of fictions, a sectarian game of a small irresponsible and unserious group. And all of this arises from their unwillingness to admit that Judaism can be a living, growing, developing body. If it is impossible to the People of Israel to exist in the Land of Israel as a body possessing

historical vitality, responsible for itself—then what did we come here for? Why do I have to live in a country with a Canaanite government, when the only thing we have in common is that we have both learned Hebrew? The fact of speaking Hebrew is not in itself a redeeming fact.[64]

To the idea that underlying the Canaanite outlook there was a desire to bring about a secular and democratic revolution in the whole "land of the Euphrates," among all the Arabs, Scholem replied by drawing an analogy with Trotsky's effrontery in carrying out a secular revolution among an alien people, the Russians. He had previously had a similar dispute with the Jewish Marxists: "We have had our fill of the theory that we must be oil on the wheels of the revolution—that is not what we came to this country for! Not in order to be that kind of revolutionaries. And I am telling you—the Canaanite outlook will fail here just as the Jewish Communists failed in Russia."[65] Scholem also rejected another analogy, that with the United States,[66] for there was no comparison between the conditions of settlement in the two places: "What are the Canaanites to do if the Arabs are not Indians? Perhaps only a few thousand of the Arabs will be able to join the Canaanite scheme of creating a new Levantine nation."[67]

Scholem attacked the idea from two directions: To the assertion that Yeshayahu Leibowitz would describe his views on Judaism and secular nation-hood as essentially Canaanite, he answered that, unlike Leibowitz, who saw Judaism as something circumscribed, Judaism to him was a living and dynamic phenomenon. To another assertion, that the Canaanites thought he had a particularly Jewish outlook, he replied: "I am in the middle of a process, or of a path. I believe that if something is alive, it is in the middle. What has brought me here is no different from what brought other Zionist Jews here. Anyone who denies that like the Canaanites—then there is no reason why his sect should withstand the tempest of history and the Arab world."[68] An exclusive emphasis on the Canaanite polarity misses the point somewhat, but an overemphasis on the messianic polarity reveals a lack of understanding of the principle of continuity in history. Scholem tried, together with his warning about the challenge of Canaanism, to warn against the practice of Messianism in the historical reality.

On two occasions, Scholem dwelled on this price of Messianism: In his introduction to his monumental work *Sabbatai Sevi* (1957), he wrote: "Jewish historiography has generally chosen to ignore the fact that the Jewish people have paid a very high price for the messianic idea."[69] In 1972 Scholem con-tinued, in his essay "The Messianic Idea in Judaism," to speak of the price of Messianism: "What I have in mind is the price demanded by Messianism, the price which the Jewish people has to pay out of its own substance for this idea which it handed over to the world. . . . For the Messianic idea is not only con-solation and hope. Every attempt to realize it tears open the chasms that lead each of its manifestations *ad absurdum*."[70]

Scholem considered "the beginning of redemption"—a phrase coined by Rabbi Abraham Kook—to be a "dangerous formula." Rabbi Kook understood the secularity of the Jews in Eretz Israel as part of the process of setting up a modern nation. In a lecture to the intellectual circle at Kibbutz Oranim in 1975, Scholem said about Rabbi Kook: "He created a confusion of concepts by authorizing a mixture of the ideal of building a society and state with contemporary Messianism."[71] However, Scholem was frightened of the nationalization of concepts: "Ben-Gurion used the term 'Messianism' no less than the people of the religious camp, who perhaps really believed in 'the beginning of redemption.'"[72] In Scholem's opinion, Ben-Gurion's Messianism was directed toward the State of Israel, whereas the Messianism of Gush Emunim focused on the land of Canaan. He saw Gush Emunim as a modern version of the Sabbatian movement as follows: "Like the Sabbatians, their messianic program can only lead to disaster.... Today, the consequences of such Messianism are also political, and that is the great danger."[73]

According to Scholem, Gush Emunim overturned the historical basis of Zionism by combining the mythical with the historical and the metaphysical with the concrete. To the question of whether Messianism was still a Zionist enterprise, Scholem answered: "Today we have the Gush Emunim, which is definitely a Messianic group. They use biblical verses for political purposes."[74] Scholem expressed his fears of "the extremists in Gush Emunim," who "use religious sanctions in order to justify their activities in the territories."[75]

There is half a century between Rabbi Kook and the actions of Gush Emunim, but what they have in common is the mixture of one thing (religion) with another thing of a different kind (nationalism). The messianic yearning became a practical Messianism when the secularity of the land of Israel was sanctified. The messianic form of Canaanite yearning is the concretization of an idea, the process by which the Ten Commandments are translated into the sphere of action, so that a metaphorical Messianism becomes an actual Messianism. Scholem's fears concerned the Sabbatean dynamic as revealed in three syntheses of land-of-Israel Zionism: the pioneer-messianic synthesis of Rabbi Kook, the state-messianic synthesis of Ben-Gurion, and the Canaanite-messianic synthesis of Gush Emunim. Canaanite Messianism developed the moment when the messianic yearning for the land took precedence over all other aspects of observance. The symbol became a reality and the idea became a fetish.

Are the Israelis Already Canaanites?

Three years after the foundation of the Israeli state, some of the outstanding Israeli intellectuals of that period, including Joseph Klausner, Natan Rotenstreich, and Yeshayahu Leibowitz, met to discuss the question that Ernst

Simon had raised a few months earlier in his lecture titled "Are We Still Jews?" In the lecture Simon had said: "Very, very many of the young people who have grown up in this country feel themselves to be solely Hebrews, Israelis, even if they do not define themselves as 'Canaanites.' Their national sentiment is very strong, and an Arab who has been born in the country is closer to them than a Jew who has come to the country from nearby or than a Jew who lives in New York."[76] More than sixty years ago, Simon clearly recognized the radical option available to Israeli Jews at the time when some of them were forging themselves a state: the Canaanite option that favors geography over history, an enlarged identity over cultural or religious continuity.

Simon developed a typology of two religious states of mind: the "Catholic," which sanctifies the profane as well as the sacred, and the "Protestant," which differentiates the sacred from the profane.[77] Simon felt that "Catholic" Judaism is liable to lead to a frozen orthodoxy, to withdrawal, to factionalism, to ultra-Orthodox mentality. "Protestant" Judaism, on the other hand, is liable to lead to a negation of the sacred, and in place of God one gets the homeland, and in place of a future-oriented transcendental Messianism one gets a "Canaanite" Messianism that stresses the concrete, the here-and-now. "Protestant" Judaism encourages secularity, denies transcendence, and sanctions Canaanism. "Catholic" Judaism is liable to lead to ultra-Orthodoxy, to the alienation of religion, and to the ascription of Messianism to the state.

In Rabbi Kook, Simon saw a mixture of "concrete Messianism," as he called it, and an original approach to the relationship between the sacred and the profane. Through the dialectic of the people of Israel and the land of Israel, the "concrete" Messianism was shown to be present in the Yishuv, and the secular pioneers in the land of Canaan were "*tzaddiqim* despite themselves." Rabbi Kook did not believe that the pioneers' good deed of redeeming the land could come about through a sin. Simon's conclusion was: "The tragic outcome of this Messianic-religious-actual doctrine is manifest in its new secular metamorphosis: the generation of the birth of the State of Israel is crowned as 'the days of the Messiah.' There is a great danger in this political-actual Messianism."[78] Simon criticized those who were so convinced that the founding of the state was the manifestation of he who "records the generations" and "orders the cycles of time" that it was seen as the approach of the "days of the Messiah," when the distinction between sacred and profane no longer exists. In his opinion, the vitality of historical Judaism was shown by its rejection of every contemporary call for redemption, whether from Christianity, Islam, Sabbatai Tzvi, communism, or Canaanite Messianism.

Like Simon, the question that never ceased to preoccupy Baruch Kurzweil was, are we still Jews (without Judaism), or are we already Canaanites? Would the universal Messianism of historical Judaism become a "Canaanite Messianism" of modern Jewish nationalism? Kurzweil had already examined these Canaanite tendencies of modern Jewish nationalism and their cultural roots at the turn of the twentieth century. He showed that, from the ideological point of view, the "Young Hebrews" of the Yonatan Ratosh variety were an Israeli version of an exilic Jewish manifestation—a logical conclusion of intellectual and aesthetic tendencies that had existed in Hebrew literature for a hundred years.[79] In the writings of Berdichevsky, Shneur, and Tchernikovsky, one can already see a rejection of the Jewish exilic past and an affirmation of archaic and mystical pre-Israelite and Canaanite elements, but in Kurzweil's opinion this theoretical aesthetic trend in the literature of the Hebrew revival had now become the daily reality of the Israeli children in their own country. The Canaanite movement was a radical and conclusive stage in the process of secularization and in practice brought the tendencies in modern Jewish nationalism to a paradoxical outcome.

The problem that troubled Kurzweil was the change that had taken place in modern times from "abstract Jews" to "Hebrew Jews," a development that went from Berdichevsky to romantic Zionism and Hebrew culture.[80] In this "godless theology," myth had a place of decisive importance: "Intellectual play with myth without religious faith, and, no less important, the mobilization of myth for political ends, are especially negative phenomena because they remove the restraints of rational criticism and throw the gates of the irrational wide open."[81] The mixing of the theological and the secular reached its climax in the transformation of the messianic idea into a political reality: "Israel knows this . . . and yet it hitches Messianic-apocalyptic horses onto the wagon of State. The religious-Messianic dream is its credentials for its appearance on the stage of history! Like it or not, the religious-Messianic eschatology is the metaphysical basis of the State, and this eschatology is given a secular interpretation. The State declares its very existence, its living immanence, to be the presence and realization of transcendentality."[82]

The Six Day War placed the overlapping of the sacred and the profane, the theological and the political, the messianic and the territorial in a fascinating perspective. One could say that the ironic, scathing comments made by Kurzweil in 1970 are a good exposition of his critique of "territorial Messianism":

The year 1967 placed practical Zionism, which could only be a political-*mamlachti* Zionism, at its most fateful crossroads. The conquest of the entire country in the Six-Day War was a most powerful and dangerous challenge, a kind of touchstone of the truth and authenticity of the historiosophical interpretation that Zionism gave to Judaism. The national-secular redemption was complete. The territorial Messianism had achieved its aims. The heavenly Messianism had come down to earth. It was almost a proof of the complete legitimacy of Zionism's claim to be the continuation and the living and life-giving actualization of Judaism. The ancient myths at the heart of Judaism—and in the form of their rational reworking as well—had become a historical actuality. The soldiers who captured the Wall were truly like dreamers. Breaking into the Old City and conquering it were extra-temporal manifestations. The "now" was also the past; the past was identical with the future. A synoptic vision united them all. Divine historicity, which is meta-historical, and normal, secular historicity, the product of time, seemed to melt into one another and become as one, and there were consequently many who spoke of a religious revival. There was clearly a blurring of distinctions.... The distinction between sacred and profane was obliterated. From now on, everything was sacred or could be sacred.

Zionism and its daughter, the State of Israel, which had reached the Wall through military conquest as the realization of the earthly Messianism, could never forsake the Wall and abandon the conquered areas of the Land of Israel without estranging itself from its historiosophical understanding of Judaism. Practical Zionism was caught in the web of its achievements. Abandoning them would be to admit its failure as the representative and agent of the historical continuity of Judaism.... It could not be that the gallop of the Messianic apocalypse could be held up in order to permit the passengers to get out and look at the spectacular scenery of the Day of the Lord.... The blowing of the ram's horn by all the Chief Rabbis next to the Wall will not change anything and from now on it will simply be a magical rite. Similarly, there cannot be a beginning of redemption at a time when full redemption is achieved and abandoned.[83]

Kurzweil claimed that in 1967 religious Zionism faced its moment of truth. The conquest of the West Bank (Judea and Samaria) was its greatest challenge because then, in his opinion, a philosophy of history came into existence that saw the State of Israel as the fulfillment and essence of Judaism. The national-secular redemption reached its culmination with the conquest of parts of the homeland: Thus, Messianism, on the one hand, and Canaanism, on the other, came together in what Kurzweil called "territorial Messianism," whose origins were influenced by the pretension of "new Hebrews" to give birth to themselves and to base their claims on the territorial "place" and not on the metaphysical "Place" (i.e., God).

Isaiah Leibowitz, as Simon and Kurzweil, saw that in the process of making nationhood a supreme value, "Rabbi Kook had a heavy responsibility, because he raised Jewish nationhood to the level of something sacred."[84] Leibowitz summarized Rabbi Kook's political theology as follows: "What happens to the people of Israel today reflects processes taking place in the sacred sphere and not in human history." According to Leibowitz, the theologization of the political and the politicization of the theological gave birth to Gush Emunim, which was "nationalism in a wrapping of religious sanctity supplied by Rabbi Kook." The source of inspiration for Gush Emunim was in fact Rabbi Kook, in whose work the universal element and the national element were united: "The physical upbuilding of the nation and the manifestation of its spirit are one and the same, and all of it is part of the upbuilding of the world."[85]

In the deterministic Messianism of Gush Emunim, which combined the religious and the political Messianism, there was a radicalization, represented by the shift from Rabbi Kook's "historical necessity" to the activation and anticipation of the end of his son, Rabbi Tzvi Yehuda Kook. This radicalization marked a change from the universal, cosmic-universal dimension of Messianism to the particular national-Israeli dimension. Where the nationalistic and Canaanitic Gush Emunim version of Messianism was concerned, Leibowitz saw that "when it becomes clear that the State has no splendour, eternity or glory, everything will explode. This is exactly what happened to the disciples of Sabbatai Tzvi, who suddenly had nothing left. The people of Gush Emunim likewise have no knowledge of plain Judaism without the Messianic gleam."[86] Leibowitz's comparison of Gush Emunim to Sabbataianism and Christianity was not simply an extreme way of expressing himself but was an attempt to expose, once again, the radical significance, as he saw it, of this national-religious movement that explained the sanctity of the land in messianic terms: "As soon as the Messianic idea began to have practical consequences, it almost destroyed the Jewish people. It gave birth to Christianity and Sabbataianism, and—in our days—to Gush Emunim."[87]

What was new and original in Leibowitz's criticism is the claim—made by a Zionist and not a post-Zionist—that the occupation was destroying Zionism. That was a radical charge, and he also made it against religious Zionism, which he felt had largely become a neo-Canaanite ideology with its sanctification of the trees, stones, and graves of Judea and Samaria. Leibowitz's fear of Canaanism was shown in the concern he expressed in 1968 that "the state [would] no longer be a Jewish State but a Canaanite State" and that the land would take precedence over the Torah.[88] Four years later, in his review of a book by Eliezer Livne, Leibowitz declared that for young people, "the main idea is that 'Israeliness' is the antithesis of 'Judaism', which is alien to it," and he added:

> If the outstanding literary expression of anti-Jewish Zionism was Hazaz's "Sermon," the "Canaanite" movement was a caricatural expression of it. The adherents of that school of thought even described themselves as anti-Jewish because of Zionism's declared connection with the Jewish people and its history. Although a doctrinal, belligerent Canaanism has been confined to a small minority and is regarded as a marginal phenomenon, this current has in fact left its imprint on the society and culture of the state created by Zionism, and expresses the unconscious and sometimes conscious feelings of many sections of the public, and especially of the youth and intellectuals.[89]

The attempt to ascribe sanctity to the Greater Land of Israel, according to Leibowitz, was idolatry, a mythological interpretation that tried to turn a philosophy of history into an ideology.[90] Leibowitz wished to expose the philosophy of history of Gush Emunim as a messianic ideology that sought to turn politics into myth and myth into a reality. His great fear was that the messianic myth of the Greater Land of Israel would become a genetic mutation of Zionism. He exposes the process of Canaanization as paradoxically resulting from the domination of the land of Israel by the Jewish Torah. This surprising dialectical development to which Leibowitz drew attention represented a penetration of the Canaanite ideology to a central position in the State of Israel. This was not due to the pressure of the secular Canaanite movement on the center but precisely to the annexation of the historical homeland by religious Zionism: "The people has replaced God, the land has replaced the Torah and nationalism has replaced faith."[91]

Leibowitz believed that the period between the War of Independence and the Six Day War was the most "normal" period in the history of Israel, and therefore perhaps the most Zionist: Others did not rule over the Israelis, and the Israelis did not rule over others. Until his death, Leibowitz waged an all-out war against the mythologization of the Greater Land of Israel, and called for a return to the Zionist rationale as he saw it: A free people cannot be an occupying people. Zionism, in his opinion, had been conquered from within and had lost its humanistic character. The Leibowitzian philosophy aiming at clarifying concepts and distinguishing between sacred and secular fused with his political thinking, calling for a withdrawal from the occupied territories. His main conclusions were: "The claim that the idea of the Greater Land of Israel is the essence of Zionism is a total lie; this is because it is nationalism dressed up as holiness."[92] Underlying Leibowitz's thinking was a fear of two things: a political theology such as one finds in Carl Schmitt and a political mythology such as Ernst Cassirer warned about.[93] The theology and the mythology were liable to become Janus-faced: the transcendental face glancing towards the Shekhinah and the idolatrous face looking towards the tangible. Leibowitz was afraid that the policy of Gush Emunim, the concretization of the land, which was becoming a form of neo-Canaanism, and the concretization of the state would lead to fascism.

The combination of what Simon, Kurzweil, and Leibowitz called a "concrete Messianism" and the old-new Canaanism was in their opinion disastrous. They feared a messianic "anticipation of the end," a fetishization of the state, a neutralization of Jewish life in the era of secular Jewish nationalism. Through this separation of spheres, they sought to make the secular world rational in that it would be open to investigation and criticism. As followers of the neo-Kantian tradition, they wanted a Judaism free from the restrictions of matter and materiality. This was the Protestant conception of a religion free from myths: If we cleanse the land from the fetishes of symbolism, we shall be left with practical questions alone. The land ceases to be the ancestral heritage, a relic of Canaanism combined with a kind of fetishistic Judaism.

Conclusions

What in fact was the Canaanite idea? Its main point was nativistic Israeli nationhood, the geographical conception that it was the plot of land that defined the national identity of a country's inhabitants. It was not the collective memory, the cultural heritage, ethnics, or biology that created a nation, but the physical space and the language that obliterated differences and formed a national melting-pot. It was the space that gave national significance: For example, Arabs and crusaders were assimilated into the Sidonian space, and that is how Lebanese nationhood came into being. This view was, of course, in contradiction to the classical Arab or Muslim viewpoint, as it explained the Sidonian civilization as a geopolitical product of the crusader and Arab conquests. Among the Arabs, however, there were similar views, like the pharaonic conception in Egypt and the Syrian nationalism of Anton Sa'ada.[94] Here, the nativism in the Arab territorial nationalism ignored the invaders.

Unlike this nativistic variety, Zionism was a historical nationalism. Canaanism subverted it in seeing the present and not the past as the decisive time factor, making "nowness" the guiding principle of identity.[95] The significance of nativism as a metaphor is that it is not only a matter of being born in a place but an identity gained through a cultural concept that turns the immigrant into a native. The imagined Canaanite community is defined in the terms of Benedict Anderson's formulation: collective time—the present—a territory, and a common language. Many people call for economic migrants or non-Jews living in Israel to be not only citizens of the State of Israel but full partners in the Hebrew nation. Yaron London has praised Israel for "granting citizenship to useful immigrants," explaining that "love of a country is not conveyed through a heritage but through a creative culture, and Israel is a most effective producer of culture."[96]

There have been many and varied expressions of the Canaanite idea (which is not necessarily identical with Yonatan Ratosh's "Canaanite group") in the Israeli public sphere. The sociological and demographic changes that have taken place in Israel and the Jewish Diaspora have lowered the tone of the debate on the Canaanite option. The shrinking of the Jewish people in the Diaspora, the impressive demographic growth of the Israelis and especially of the "Sabras," the immigration to Israel of over a million former citizens of the Soviet Union (a large part of whom are not of Jewish origin), the globalization that has brought in its wake a large number of foreign workers, some of whom have children who were born in Israel: All this and more shows that the Canaanite idea is no longer the property of a closed sect and is likely to be realized not as a deliberate plan and not as the fulfillment of a utopian vision, but through the force of events, without any ideological intention.

Secular intellectuals in Israel have always been attracted by the Canaanite idea. They wished to eliminate the contradictions and tensions inherent in the process of the secularization of the Jewish identity within the national framework. In the "Canaanite hour," as the poet Haim Gouri called the window of Hebrew opportunity in Eretz Israel (Palestine), many young people in the Yishuv (Jewish community) were enraptured by the possibility of acquiring a native identity free of remnants of the past, of the burden of history, and of the imposition of the remains of exilic Judaism: a new identity that embodied self-construction and local autonomy. In describing the encounter with the Canaanite proposition as a "change of religion" and a "true religious experience," Gouri recognized the nativistic idea as an existential or even religious awakening.[97] It was a kind of revelation, the possibility of acquiring a new identity on the lines of the Freudian "Oedipus complex," a sort of rebellion against the parents who came from *there*, from the inauthentic place, from exile.

The radical innovation of Ratosh and his group was their total rebellion against Judaism as a religious, cultural, and ethnic entity, and its replacement by a nativistic and linguistic experience. Ahad Ha-Am understood its revolutionary potential when he saw the native-born "Hebrews" as Canaanites on his visit to the country: "Here you are bringing up ancient Jews. You want to obliterate two thousand years of exile and go back to the culture of ancient Canaan." This was an observation about a subconscious Canaanism that sought to overcome a lack felt by the native-born by reverting to an ancient, primeval identity. The term "Hebraism" was the war-cry of the Hebrew pioneers of the early twentieth century, a flag by which they wished to demarcate the watershed between themselves, the native-born Hebrew-speakers with their Hebrew homeland, and the Jews in foreign countries who spoke a thousand languages. Hebraism was the nativistic consciousness that saw the motherland as the source of identity; and Canaanism was an ideological outlook that came out of it and transcended it by setting itself in opposition to the Jewish religion, history, and Diaspora.[98]

The founders of Zionism did not accept the Canaanite claim, which of course was formulated much later, but its territorial logic was understood by all. They saw the Hebrew "nation" as umbilically connected to the Jewish community. Zionism sought to link Jewish history in all its metamorphoses to the place where it all began: The Israelite place was the "metaphorical womb" of Jewish history; hence the belief that exile was the absence, the negation of Jewish autonomy, an autonomy that could only exist in Eretz Israel.[99] Exile was seen as a sickness and the native Hebrew identity as the cure. A. B. Yehoshua sees Zionism as "the name of the cure for a certain kind of Jewish sickness called exile," with its various victims—the religious, the liberal, the socialist, the nationalist, the bourgeois, and the anarchist.[100] In his opinion, exile was not imposed on the Jewish people but was a situation that was chosen by the Jews in order to escape from the basic conflict of Jewish identity: the one between Jewish nationhood and the Jewish religion.

Some, however, have seen the exile in a positive light. In their opinion, the shift from fidelity to the place itself to that of the memory of the place after the defeat of Bar Kochba was necessary in order to make the loss of the land surmountable.[101] Retaining the memory of the place helped the Pharisaic rabbis to overcome that loss. Not everyone has seen the exile as a punishment, and for some major Jewish thinkers the text was the most important factor. Hermann Cohen saw Jewish history as a progress from the national condition to the exilic condition.[102] Franz Rosenzweig, who saw the soil as a "fetter" and the Jew as "a travelling, wandering eminence," thought that "a place where the nation loves its native soil more than it loves its life is always in danger."[103] Hannah Arendt pointed out the special value of the Jew as a "pariah,"[104] and Bernard Lazare called him a "wanderer by choice."[105] Edmond Jabès preferred the text as a homeland,[106] and, where George Steiner was concerned, the Jewish intellectual always lived on his suitcases and spread avant-garde, universalistic ideas.[107] Hebrew independence is the end of Judaism, an idea that the brothers Daniel and Jonathan Boyarin expressed as follows: "The exile, not monotheism, is the major contribution of Judaism to the world."[108]

As against these ideas, major Israeli intellectuals began to develop an anti-exilic ideology very close to the Canaanite outlook. The historian Yigael Elam distinguishes between Jewish nationhood, which exists only in Israel, and the Jewish religion, describing historical Judaism as a nation/religion that can exist only in exile. The nation-state of Israel is, in the final analysis, always the community of the Jewish religion.[109] The playwright Yehoshua Sobol continues this line of thought and warns of "the Jewish reaction that raises its head and threatens to engulf the Hebrew identity and the Hebrew spirit that made possible the creation of the Yishuv and its transformation from a state-in-the-making to a state like any other."[110] The philosopher Yosef Agassi also thinks that "if Israel is a nation-state, its theocratic clothing must be removed," and, like Hillel Kook, he proposes separating the Jewish religion from the Israeli nation, making Israel into a liberal, democratic, Western nation-state.[111] Without Ratosh-like noises, Canaanite tom-toms, and the mythological aesthetics of Baal and Ashterot, the call for a Hebrew state is being heard once again, but this time not from the fringes of the cultural establishment but through the front door of an Israelism defined in terms of territory and language alone.

It is no wonder that even the Sabra Haim Gouri recoiled from these Canaanite ideas. He, too, was unable to separate Ratosh the wonderful poet of *The Black Canopy* from Ratosh the ideologist. Canaanism worried him in its denial of the duality of the Israeli identity in the context of the return to Zion: "This challenge had a great fascination, but I knew that the denial of any connection or affinity between the Jew and the Hebrew and placing them in opposition with such relentless hostility invalidated any possible explanation of our existence here and destroyed lofty cultural values which we saw as our property. We have committed ourselves to the Hebrew, land-of-Israel alternative, not to cutting the Gordian knot. Making Zionism an enemy of the Hebrew renaissance makes Hebraism into a shallow spiritual salon, something meta-historical, a false romanticism in the name of the distant past."[112]

In the short history of the crystallization of the Israeli identity, from the "Hebrew," the "pioneer," and the "Sabra" to the itemization of the Hebrew image through an ever-increasing cleavage, who can guarantee us that the Canaanite option has completely disappeared? Perhaps its ultimate conclusion—separation between Israeli citizenship and the Jewish religion—is becoming so relevant that a complete split between the homeland (the Hebrew or Israeli) and the people (the assimilated Jew) will finally succeed? Perhaps this process will take place not as a deliberate act and not in the hope of realizing a utopian vision but simply through the force of reality, without any ideological factor.[113]

Is post-Zionism a secular, leftist neo-Canaanism? Post-Zionism as a guiding principle—going over from history to geography—is a nativistic conception that turns its back on the continuity of the history of the people, part of whom have returned to realize its nationhood in its land, and only recognizes those who reside here and now.[114] Underlying the post-Zionist ideology is the assumption of the existence of a local society based on a civil rather than a national definition: the state belongs to its citizens, not to history.[115] Because Zionism completed its task in founding the state, one should remove its protective covering—that is, cancel the Law of Return—effect a de-Zionization of Israel, and from that moment see the resulting secular democratic state as a "state of all its citizens." According to the nativistic conceptions of the new identity, which places at its heart the geographical factor and not the Jewish surplus value, the Israelis are formalistically defined as a collection of citizens living under a single roof. It is the *place* that defines the Israelis in this way. Some would say that the true significance of post-Zionism is thus the severing of the umbilical cord between the Israeli homeland and the Jewish people and culture, between the landscape of the country and its history, between the language and its sources. In the words of one of those responsible for this phenomenon: "Post-Zionism means the denial of all hidden threads binding together separate phenomena, of a special connection between the people of Israel today and yesterday whether in the country or in the Diaspora, between the Israeli culture and its sources or between the Hebrew language and its history."[116]

Is Gush Emunim a religious, right-wing neo-Canaanism? In the messianic model proposed by the trinity of Torah, land, and people, the earthly locality is given first place. If post-Zionism makes connection with the place the sole identity-card, Gush Emunim raises place to a sanctified level and settlement to the status of myth, enshrining return to the land as a supreme principle. In its settlement-political activities, Gush Emunim sought to restore the true model of the Greater Land of Israel. The frontiers of political compromise were replaced by the frontiers of the Promise. This movement, which blended political theology with the myth of settlement, was based on the precedence of the ancient Jews over the country's Arab inhabitants.[117]

The two most daring and heretical assaults on Israeli-Jewish identity, which are umbilically connected to Zionism, are the Canaanite and the crusader narratives. On the one hand, the mythological construction of Zionism as a modern crusade describes Israel as a Western colonial enterprise planted in the heart of the East, alien to the area, its logic and its peoples, whose end must be degeneration and defeat. On the other hand, the nativist construction of Israel as neo-Canaanitic, which defines the nation in purely geographical terms as an imagined native community, demands breaking away from the chain of historical continuity. Those are the two greatest anxieties that Zionism and Israel need to encounter and answer forcefully.

Notes

1. Ittamar Ben-Avi, *Canaan Our Land: 5000 Years of Israel in Its Land* [in Hebrew] (Jerusalem: Zion, 1932).

2. Aharon Reuveni, *Shem, Ham and Japhet* [in Hebrew] (Tel Aviv: Saadia Shoshani Press, 1932).

3. Israel Belkind, *The Arabs in Palestine: Where Are the Ten Tribes?* [in Hebrew] (Tel Aviv: Hermon: 1928).

4. Aharon Amir, "Undress Shulamit—The Hebrew Renaissance: Option or Destiny?" [in Hebrew], *Nativ 3* (2000): 50–51; see also also Eliezer Ben Yehuda, *Hamagid* [in Hebrew] (1881), 35–37.

5. Ya'akov Klatzkin, "The Galut Cannot Survive" [in Hebrew], in *Essays*, introduction by Yosef Shechter (Tel Aviv 1965), 19–31.

6. Aharon Amir, "Hebrew Renaissance," 50.

7. Dan Laor, "From 'Hadrasha' to Epistle to the Hebrew Youth" [in Hebrew], *Alpayim 21* (2001): 185.

8. Baruch Kurzweil, "The Nature and Origins of the 'Young Hebrews' (Canaanites)," in *Our New Literature: Continuity or Revolution?* [in Hebrew] (Tel Aviv: Schocken, 1971), 287.

9. Dan Laor, "Kurzweil and the Canaanites: Between Insight and Struggle" [in Hebrew], in *Keshet: After 40 Years* (1998), 32–45.

10. Shapira, "'Denial of the Exile,'" 22.

11. Danny Jacoby, ed., *One Land, Two Peoples* [in Hebrew] (Jerusalem: Magnes Press, 1999), 104.

12. Yaakov Shavit, "With Vision, Fire and Sword" [in Hebrew], *Haaretz: Cultural and Literary Supplement*, special issue on the tenth anniversary of the death of the poet Yonatan Ratosh, April 6, 2001.

13. Yaakov Shavit, *The New Hebrew Nation: A Study in Israeli Heresy and Fantasy* (London: Frank Cass, 1987).

14. Israel Kolat, "The Permutations of Hebrew Canaanism" [in Hebrew], in Jacoby, *One Land, Two Peoples*, 93–95.

15. Hillel Kook, Shemuel Merlin, et al., *The Time Has Come! A Clarification of the Principles and a Political Declaration by the Hebrew Committee of National Liberation* [in Hebrew] (Washington: Hanukkah, 1944).

16. Boaz Evron, *National Reckoning*, 351–373.

17. Aharon Amir, "The Second Republic" [in Hebrew], *Haaretz*, October 19, 2006.

18. Vered Kellner, "How Lovely Were the Nights!" [in Hebrew], *Kol Ha-Ir*, October 12, 2001.

19. Meir Porush, "Canaanites, 2004 Model" [in Hebrew], *Haaretz*, 20 January 2004.

20. Uri Ram, *Time of the "Post": Nationalism and the Politics of Knowledge in Israel* [in Hebrew] (Tel Aviv: Resling, 2006), 162.

21. Nitza Erel,*"Without Fear and Prejudice": Uri Avnery and Ha'olam Ha'ze* [in Hebrew] (Jerusalem: Magnes Press, 2006), 33.

22. Erel,*"Without Fear and Prejudice,"* 21–36.

23. Dan Laor, "American Literature and Israeli Culture: The Case of the Canaanites," *Israel Studies* 5, no. 1 (Spring 2000): 287–300.

24. Aharon Amir, "The Shock of Proximity" [in Hebrew], *Keshet* 4 (1971): 6–7.

25. Aharon Amir, in the symposium "Seeking Roots" [in Hebrew], *Keshet* 62 (1974): 29.

26. David Ohana, "Yehoshua Arieli and the Responsibility of the Historian," in *The Rage of the Intellectuals: Political Radicalism and Social Criticism in Europe and Israel* (Tel Aviv 2005), 109–128.

27. Ifrach Zilberman, *The Canaanite Founding Myth of the Palestinian Society* [in Hebrew] (Jerusalem: Jerusalem Institute, 1993); Yehoshua Porath, "Hebrew Canaanism and Arabic Canaanism" [in Hebrew], in Jacoby, *One Land, Two Peoples,* 83–92.

28. Samich El-Kassem, "The Jerusalem Covenant," *Kul El-Arab*, 14 May 1999.

29. Elboim-Dror, ibid., 103.

30. Kolat, "Permutations of Hebrew Canaanism," 93–96, 110.

31. Ella Belfer, *A Split Identity: The Conflict between the Sacred and the Secular in the Jewish World* (Ramat-Gan: Bar Ilan University Press, 2004), 103–106.

32. Ishai Cordoba, "Not a Jew From Yavne but a Hebrew from Samaria!" [in Hebrew], *Haaretz Literary Supplement*, September 27, 2000.

33. Sasson Sofer, "Canaanites and Semites" [in Hebrew], in *The Beginnings of Political Thought in Israel* (Tel Aviv: Schocken, 2001), 381.

34. Amitzur Ilan, in Jacoby, *One Land, Two Peoples,* 104–107.

35. Dan Laor, "Kurzweil and the Canaanites," in Jacoby, *One Land, Two Peoples,* 44.

36. Yehoshua Porath, *The Life of Uriel Shelah* (Yonatan Ratosh) (Tel Aviv: Mahbarot Le Sifrut, 1989).

37. Yonatan Ratosh, *The First Days: Hebrew Overtures* (Tel Aviv: Hadar, 1982), 9 cited in James S. Diamond, *Homeland or Holy Land: The "Canaanite" Critic of Israel* (Indianapolis: Indiana University Press 1986), 27.

38. Ratosh, *First Days*, 27.

39. Yaakov Shavit, *From Majority to a State: The Revisionist Movement; The Plan for a Colonisatory Regime and Social Ideas 1925–1935* [in Hebrew] (Tel Aviv: Hadar, 1978), 137–151.

40. Shavit, *New Hebrew Nation*, 25–36.

41. Yonatan Ratosh, *The Walker in Darkness: Poems* [in Hebrew] (Tel Aviv: Hadar, 1965); Yonatan Ratosh, *Sword Poems* [in Hebrew] (Tel Aviv 1969).

42. Adyah Gurevitch Gor Horon, *East and West: A History of Canaan and the Land of the Hebrews* [in Hebrew] (Tel Aviv: Hermon Press, 2000).

43. Shavit, *New Hebrew Nation*, 73–103.

44. Ari Jabotinsky, *My Father, Ze'ev Jabotinsky* [in Hebrew] (Tel Aviv: Steimatzky Press, 1981), 134–135.

45. Shavit, *New Hebrew Nation*, 58.

46. Kurzweil, "The Nature and Origins of the 'Young Hebrews' (Canaanites)," in *Our New Literature: Continuity or Revolution?* 60.

47. Yonatan Ratosh, "Epistle to the Hebrew Youth" [in Hebrew], in *First Days* (Tel Aviv: Ratosh, 1982), 32–37.

48. Ratosh, "Epistle to the Hebrew Youth," 32–37.

49. Yonatan Ratosh, *The Opening Discourse: In Executive Session with the Agents of the Cells* [First Meeting] [in Hebrew] (Tel Aviv: Ratosh, 1944), 149–203.

50. Yonatan Ratosh, "Euphrates Land" [in Hebrew], *From Victory to Collapse: An Alef* (Tel Aviv: Ratosh, 1976), 37–38.

51. Marcel Mauss, "Compte-rendu de G. Dumézil, *Le Festin d'immortalité*," *L'Année sociologique*, n.s. 1 (1925); David Pace, *Claude Levi-Strauss: The Bearer of Ashes* (London: Routledge, 1983).

52. Ratosh, *First Days*, 14.

53. Dan Meron, "Yonatan Ratosh as a Literary Hero," *Haaretz*, April 9, 1990, April 15, 1990.

54. Shavit, *New Hebrew Nation*, 131–159.

55. Nurit Graetz, "The Myth of Tammuz, Modernism, Nationalism and Canaanism in the Poetry of Ratosh," in *The Canaanite Group: Literature and Ideology*, ed. Yaakov Shavit (Tel Aviv: Open University, 1987), 112–126.

56. Yehuda Liebes, "The Tikkun of the Godhead: The Zohar and Yonatan Ratosh" [in Hebrew] *Alpayim* 7 (1993): 26–28.

57. "Twenty Years after the Death of the Poet Yonatan Ratosh, Founder of the 'Young Hebrews Movement'" [in Hebrew], special issue, *Haaretz Cultural and Literary Supplement*, 6 April 2001.

58. Ehud Ben Ezer, ed., *Unease in Zion*, foreword by Robert Alter (New York: Quadrangle, 1974), 273.

59. Susan A. Handelman, *Fragments of Redemption: Jewish Thought and Literary Theory in Benjamin Scholem and Levinas* (Bloomington: Indiana University Press, 1971).

60. Ben Ezer, *Unease in Zion*, 277.

61. Ben Ezer, *Unease in Zion*, 278.

62. David Ohana, *Political Theologies in the Holy Land: Israeli Messianism and Its Critics* (London: Routledge, 2009), 17–53.

63. Ben Ezer, *Unease in Zion*, 288–289.

64. Ben Ezer, *Unease in Zion*, 289.

65. Ben Ezer, *Unease in Zion*, 290.

66. Dan Laor, "American Literature and Israeli Culture."

67. Ben Ezer, *Unease in Zion*, 290

68. Ben Ezer, *Unease in Zion*, 291.

69. Scholem, *Sabbati Sevi: The Mystical Messiah 1626–1676*, rev. ed., trans. Zvi R. Werblowsky (Princeton, N.J.: Princeton University Press, 1973), xii.

70. Scholem, "The Messianic Idea in Judaism," in *The Messianic Idea in Judaism and Other Essays on Jewish Spirituality* (New York: Knopf, 1995), 35–36. Scholem repeated these words in his concluding remarks at a study conference on the subject of "The Messianic

Idea in Jewish Thought," held in honor of his birthday at the Israel Academy of Sciences and Humanities on December 4–5, 1977. See Scholem, "Messianism: A Never Ending Quest," in *On the Possibility of Jewish Mysticism in Our Time and Other Essays* (Philadelphia: Jewish Publication Society of America, 1997), 102–113.

71. Avraham Shapira, "Introduction: Heritage as a Source to Renaissance; the Spiritual Identity of Gershom Scholem" [in Hebrew], in *Explication and Implications: Writings on Jewish Heritage and Renaissance*, ed. Scholem (Tel Aviv: Am Oved, 1982), ii, 15.

72. "Ze'ev Galili Interviews Gersom Scholem: Messianism, Zionism and Anarchy in the Language" [in Hebrew], in *Continuity and Rebellion*, ed. Scholem (Tel Aviv: Am Oved, 1994), 56–64.

73. David Biale, "The Threat of Messianism: An Interview with Gershom Scholem," *New York Review of Books*, August 14, 1980.

74. Biale, "The Threat of Messianism."

75. Gershom Scholem, interview by Irving Howe, "The Only Thing in My Life I Have Never Doubted Is the Existence of God," *Present Tense* 8, no. 1 (Autumn 1980): 53–57.

76. "Debate between Authors: Are We Still Jews?" *Aleph* (January 1952); also published in *Haaretz*, December 6, 1951.

77. Akiva Ernst Simon, *Are We Still Jews?* (Sifriat Poalim, Tel Aviv, 1983), 9–46.

78. Yehoyada Amir, *Bridges: Akibah Ernst Simon and the "Hope of the Lines"* [in Hebrew] (Jerusalem: Am Oved, 1996), 42.

79. Kurzweil, "The Nature and Origins of the 'Young Hebrews' (Canaanites)."

80. Baruch Kurzweil, *Our New Literature: Continuity or Revolution* [in Hebrew] (Tel Aviv 1971), 270–300.

81. Baruch Kurzweil, *Struggling for the Principles of Judaism* [in Hebrew] (Jerusalem: Schocken, 1969).

82. Baruch Kurzweil, "On the Usefulness and the Danger of the Science of Judaism," cited in David Ohana, *Messianism and Mamlachtiut: Ben-Gurion and the Intellectuals, between Political Vision and Political Theology* [in Hebrew] (Sede Boker: The Ben Gurion Research Institute for the Study of Israel and Zionism, 2003), 373.

83. Kurzweil, "Israel and the Diaspora" [in Hebrew], *Struggling for the Principles of Judaism*, 273.

84. Michael Shashar, *Why are People Afraid of Yeshajahu Leibowitz* [in Hebrew] (Jerusalem: Shashar, 1995), 48.

85. Shashar, *Yeshajahu Leibowitz*, 29.

86. David Ohana, "El sionismo de Yeshayahu Leibowitz," *Kivunim: Revista de Sionismo y Judaismo* (1997), 37–52.

87. Shashar, *Yeshajahu Leibowitz*, 128.

88. Leibowitz, *Judaism, Human Values and the Jewish State*, trans. Eliezer Goldman, et al. (Cambridge, Mass.: Harvard University Press, 1992), 156.

89. Leibowitz, *Judaism, Jewish People and the State of Israel* [in Hebrew] (Jerusalem: Schocken Books, 1976), 287–288.

90. Avishai Margalit and Moshe Halbertal, *Idolatry* (Cambridge, Mass.: Harvard University Press, 1992).

91. David Ohana, "Every Government Is Evil: Interview with Leibowitz" [in Hebrew], *Maariv*, 22 January 1993.

82. David Ohana, "Yeshayahu Leibowitz: The Radical Intellectual and the Critic of 'the Canaanite Messianism'" [in Hebrew], in *Yeshayahu Leibowitz: Between Conservatism and Radicalism; Reflections on His Philosophy*, ed. Aviezer Ravitzky (Jerusalem 2007), 155–177.

93. Ernst Cassirer, *The Philosophy of Symbolic Forms*, trans. R. Manheim, vol. 2 (New Haven, Conn.: Yale University Press, 1954); Carl Schmitt, *Political Theology: Four Chapters on the Concept of Sovereignty*, trans. G. Schwab (Cambridge, Mass.: MIT Press, 1996).

94. Albert Hourani, *Arabic Thought in the Liberal Age 1798–1939* (Oxford: Oxford University Press, 1962), 319–323.

95. Hannan Hever, "An Imagined Native Community: 'Canaanite Literature' in Israeli Culture" [in Hebrew], *Israeli Sociology* 2, no. 1 (1999): 148.

96. Yaron London, "Toto Tamuz and the Law of Return," *Yediot Aharonot*, July 9, 2007.

97. Haim Gouri, "The Canaanite Hour" [in Hebrew], *Maariv*, 26 December 1975.

98. Yonatan Ratosh, "Birth of the Nation" [in Hebrew], *Reshit Yamim, Ptihot Ivriot* (Tel Aviv: Ratosh, 1982), 38.

99 Avi Sagi, *The Jewish-Israeli Voyage: Culture and Identity* [in Hebrew] (Jerusalem: Shalom Hartman Institute, 2006), 235.

100. Ruvik Rosenthal, ed., *The Heart of the Matter: Redefining Social and National Issues* [in Hebrew] (Jerusalem: Keter, 2005), 59.

101. Harry Berger, "The Lie of the Land: The Text beyond Canaan," *Representations* 25 (1989); William David Davies, *The Gospel and the Land: Early Christianity and Jewish Territorial Doctrine* (Berkeley: Scholars Press, 1974); Regina M. Schwartz, "Nations and Nationalism: Adultery in the House of David," *Critical Inquiry* 19, no. 1 (Autumn 1992).

102. Eva Jospe, ed., *Reason and Hope: Selections from the Jewish Writings of Hermann Cohen* (Cincinnati: Hebrew Union College Press 1971).

103. Franz Rosenzweig, *The Star of Redemption* [in Hebrew] (Jerusalem: Mossad Bialik, 1970), 324.

104. Hanna Arendt, *The Jew as Pariah: Jewish Identity and Politics in the Modern Age* (New York: Grove Press, 1978).

105. Bernand Lazare, *Job's Dungheap* (New York: Schocken Books, 1949).

106. See also chapter 7: "Mediteranean Option." David Ohana, *The Origins of Israeli Mythology: Neither Canaanites Nor Crusaders*, Cambridge University Press, Cambridge and New York, 2012.

107. George Steiner, "The Wandering Jew," *Ptahim* 1 (1969): 17–23; George Steiner, "The Exile Jew" [in Hebrew], *Haaretz*, Galeria, November 7, 1999.

108. Daniel and Yonatan Boyarin, "No Homeland to Israel: On the Place of the Jews" [in Hebrew], *Theory and Criticism* 5 (1994): 100.

109. Igal Elam, *End of Judaism: Religion-Nation* [in Hebrew] (Tel Aviv: Yediot Aharonot, 2000), 253.

110. Yehoshua Sobol, "Not a People of Masters" [in Hebrew], *Haaretz*, May 11, 2005.

111. Yosef Agasi, *Between Religion and Nation: Towards Israeli National Identity* [in Hebrew] (Tel Aviv: Papyrus, 1984), 165; Yosef Agasi, Yehudit Buber Agasi, and Moshe Berant, *Who Is Israeli?* [in Hebrew] (Tel Aviv: Kivunim, 1991).

112. Haim Gouri, "A Call to the Hebrews" [in Hebrew], *Davar*, August 12, 1983.

113. David Ohana, "The Meaning of Jewish-Israeli Identity," in *Contemporary Jewries, Convergence and Divergence*, ed. Eliezer Ben-Rafael, Yosef Gorny, and Ya'akov Ro'i (Boston: Brill, 2003), 65–78.

114. Adriana Kemp, David Newman, Uri Ram, and Oren Yiftachel, eds., *Israelis in Conflict: Hegemonies, Identities and Challenges* (Brighton: Sussex Academic Press, 2004); Ephraim Nimni, ed., *The Challenge of Post-Zionism: Alternatives to Fundamentalist Politics in Israel* (London: Zed Books, 2003); Tom Segev, *Elvis in Jerusalem: Post-Zionism and the Americanization of Israel* (New York: Henry Holt. 2003); Hagit Boger, "Post-Zionism Discourse and the Israeli National Consensus: What Has Changed?" *Response* 66 (1996): 28–44; Herbert Kelman, "Israel in Transition from Zionism to Post-Zionism," *Annals of the American Academy* 555 (1998): 46–61; Deborah Wheeler, "Does Post-Zionism Has a Future?" in *Traditions and Transitions in Israel Studies: Books on Israel 4*, ed. Laura Zitttrain Eisenberg (New York: University of New York Press, 2003), 159–180.

115. Laurence J. Silberstein, *The Postzionism Debates: Knowledge and Power in Israeli Culture* (New York: Routledge, 1999).

116. Yosef Dan, "On Post-Zionism, Oral Hebrew, and Futile Messianism" [in Hebrew], *Haaretz*, March 25, 1995.

117. Michael Feige, *Settling in the Hearts: Jewish Fundamentalism in the Occupied Territories* (Detroit: Wayne State University Press, 2008); Janet Aviad, "The Messianism of Gush Emunim," *Studies in Contemporary Jewry* 7 (1991): 197–213; David Newman and Tamar Hermann, "A Comparative Study of Gush Emunim and Peace Now," *Middle-Eastern Studies* 28 (1992): 509–530; Ian Lustick, *For the Land and the Lord: Jewish Fundamentalism in Israel* (New York: Council on Foreign Relations, 1991); Ehud Sprinzak "Gush Emunim: The Iceberg Model of Political Extremism," *Jerusalem Quarterly* 21 (1981): 28–47; David Weisburd and Vered Vinitzky, "Vigilantism as Rational Social Control: The Case of the Gush Emunim Settlers," in *Cross Current in Israeli Culture and Politics*, ed. Myron Aronoff (New Brunswick: Transaction Publishers, 1984); L.Weisburd and E. Waring, "Settlement Motivations in Gush Emunim Movement: Comparing Bonds of Altruism and Self-Interest," in *The Impact of Gush Emunim* (London: Palgrave Macmillan, 1985), 183–199.

Bibliography

Agasi, Yosef. *Between Religion and Nation: Towards Israeli National Identity* [in Hebrew]. Tel Aviv: Papyrus, 1984.

Agasi, Yosef, Yehudit Buber Agasi, and Moshe Berant. *Who Is Israeli?* [in Hebrew]. Tel Aviv: Kivunim, 1991.

Amir, Aharon. "The Second Republic" [in Hebrew]. *Haaretz*, October 19, 2006.

——. "Undress Shulamit—The Hebrew Renaissance: Option or Destiny?" [in Hebrew]. *Nativ* 3 (2000): 50–51.

——. In the symposium "Seeking Roots" [in Hebrew]. *Keshet* 62 (1974): 29.

——. "The Shock of Proximity" [in Hebrew]. *Keshet* 4 (1971): 6–7.

Amir, Yehoyada. *Bridges: Akibah Ernst Simon and the "Hope of the Lines"* [in Hebrew]. Jerusalem: Am Oved, 2004.

Arendt, Hanna. *The Jew as Pariah: Jewish Identity and Politics in the Modern Age.* New York: Grove Press, 1978.

Aviad, Janet. "The Messianism of Gush Emunim." *Studies in Contemporary Jewry* 7 (1991): 197–213.

Belfer, Ella. *A Split Identity: The Conflict between the Sacred and the Secular in the Jewish World* [in Hebrew]. Ramat-Gan: Bar Ilan University Press, 2004.

Belkind, Israel. *The Arabs in Palestine: Where Are the Ten Tribes?* [in Hebrew]. Tel Aviv: Hermon, 1928.

Ben-Avi, Ittamar. *Canaan Our Land: 5000 Years of Israel in Its Land* [in Hebrew]. Jerusalem: Zion, 1932.

Ben Ezer, Ehud, ed. *Unease in Zion*. Foreword by Robert Alter. New York: Quadrangle, 1974.

Ben Yehuda, Eliezer. *Hamagid* [in Hebrew]. 1881.

Berger, Harry. "The Lie of the Land: The Text beyond Canaan." *Representations* 25 (1989): 119–138.

Biale, David. "The Threat of Messianism: An Interview with Gershom Scholem." *New York Review of Books*, August 14, 1980.

Boger, Hagit. "Post-Zionism Discourse and the Israeli National Consensus: What Has Changed?" *Response* 66 (1996): 28–44.

Boyarin, Daniel, and Yonatan Boyarin. "No Homeland to Israel: On the Place of the Jews" [in Hebrew]. *Theory and Criticism* 5 (1994): 79–104.

Cassirer, Ernst. *The Philosophy of Symbolic Forms*. Translated by R. Manheim. Vol. 2. New Haven, Conn.: Yale University Press, 1954.

Cordoba, Ishai. "Not a Jew From Yavne but a Hebrew from Samaria!" [in Hebrew]. *Haaretz Literary Supplement*, September 27, 2000.

Dan, Yosef. "On Post-Zionism, Oral Hebrew, and Futile Messianism" [in Hebrew]. *Haaretz*, March 25, 1995.

Davies, William David. *The Gospel and the Land: Early Christianity and Jewish Territorial Doctrine*. Berkeley: Scholars Press, 1974.

"Debate between Authors: Are We still Jews?" [in Hebrew]. *Aleph* (January 1952) also published in *Haaretz*, December 6, 1951.

Diamond, S. James. *Homeland or Holy Land: The "Canaanite" Critic of Israel*. Indianapolis: Indiana University Press, 1986.

Elam, Igal. *End of Judaism: Religion-Nation* [in Hebrew]. Tel Aviv: Yediot Aharonot, 2000.

El-Kassem, Samich. "The Jerusalem Covenant." *Kul El-Arab*. May 14, 1999.

Erel, Nitza. *"Without Fear and Prejudice": Uri Avnery and Ha'olam Ha'ze* [in Hebrew]. Jerusalem: Magnes Press, 2006.

Feige, Michael. *Settling in the Hearts: Jewish Fundamentalism in the Occupied Territories*. Detroit: Wayne State University Press, 2008.

Galili, Zeev. Interview with Gershom Scholem. "Messianism, Zionism and Anarchy in the Language" [in Hebrew]. In *Continuity and Rebellion*, edited by Gershom Scholem, 56–64. Tel Aviv: Am Oved, 1994.

Gouri, Haim. "A Call to the Hebrews" [in Hebrew]. *Davar*, August 12, 1983.

———. "The Canaanite Hour" [in Hebrew]. *Maariv*, December 26, 1975.

Graetz, Nurit. "The Myth of Tammuz, Modernism, Nationalism and Canaanism in the Poetry of Ratosh." In *The Canaanite Group: Literature and Ideology* [in Hebrew], edited by Yaakov Shavit, 112–126. Tel Aviv: Open University, 1987.

Handelman, Susan A. *Fragments of Redemption: Jewish Thought and Literary Theory in Benjamin Scholem and Levinas*. Bloomington: Indiana University Press, 1971.

Hever, Hannan. "An Imagined Native Community: 'Canaanite Literature' in Israeli Culture" [in Hebrew]. *Israeli Sociology* 2, no. 1 (1999): 147–199.

Horon, Adyah Gurevitch Gor. *East and West: A History of Canaan and the Land of the Hebrews* [in Hebrew]. Tel Aviv: Hermon Press, 2000.

Hourani, Albert. *Arabic Thought in the Liberal Age 1798–1939.* Oxford: Oxford University Press, 1962.

Jabotinsky, Ari. *My Father, Ze'ev Jabotinsky* [in Hebrew]. Tel Aviv: Steimatzky Press, 1981.

Jacoby, Danny, ed. *One Land, Two Peoples* [in Hebrew]. Jerusalem: Magnes Press, 1999.

Jospe, Eva, ed. *Reason and Hope: Selections from the Jewish Writings of Hermann Cohen.* Cincinnati: Hebrew Union College Press, 1971.

Kelman, Herbert. "Israel in Transition from Zionism to Post-Zionism." *Annals of the American Academy* 555 (1998): 46–61.

Kellner, Vered. "How Lovely Were the Nights!" [in Hebrew]. *Kol Ha-Ir*, October 12, 2001.

Kemp, Adriana, David Newman, Uri Ram, and Oren Yiftachel, eds. *Israelis in Conflict: Hegemonies, Identities and Challenges.* Brighton: Sussex Academic Press, 2004.

Klatzkin, Ya'akov. "The Galut Cannot Survive" [in Hebrew]. In *Essays*, introduction by Yosef Shechter, 19–31. Tel Aviv: Dvir, 1965.

Kolat, Israel. "The Permutations of Hebrew Canaanism" [in Hebrew]. In Jacoby, *One Land, Two Peoples*. Jerusalem: Magnes Press, 93–95.

Kook, Hillel, Shemuel Merlin, et al., *The Time Has Come! A Clarification of the Principles and a Political Declaration by the Hebrew Committee of National Liberation* [in Hebrew]. Washington: Hanukkah, 1944.

Kurzweil, Baruch. "On the Usefulness and the Danger of the Science of Judaism." Cited in David Ohana, *Messianism and Mamlachtiut: Ben-Gurion and the Intellectuals, between Political Vision and Political Theology* [in Hebrew]. Sede Boker: Ben Gurion Research Institute for the Study of Israel and Zionism, 2003.

——. "The Nature and Origins of the 'Young Hebrews' (Canaanites)" [in Hebrew]. In *Our New Literature: Continuity or Revolution?* pp. 270–300. Tel Aviv: Schocken, 1971.

——. *Struggling for the Principles of Judaism* [in Hebrew]. Jerusalem: Schocken, 1969.

Laor, Dan. "From 'Hadrasha' to Epistle to the Hebrew Youth" [in Hebrew]. *Alpayim* 21 (2001): 171–186.

——. "American Literature and Israeli Culture: The Case of the Canaanites" *Israel Studies* 5, no. 1 (Spring 2000): 287–300.

——. "Kurzweil and the Canaanites: Between Insight and Struggle" [in Hebrew]. In *Keshet: After 40 Years* (1998): 32–45.

Lazare, Bernand. *Job's Dungheap.* New York: Schocken Books, 1949.

Leibowitz, Yeshayahu. *Judaism, Human Values and the Jewish State.* Translated by Eliezer Goldman, et al. Cambridge, Mass.: Harvard University Press, 1992.

——. *Judaism, Jewish People and the State of Israel* [in Hebrew]. Jerusalem: Schocken Books, 1976.

Liebes, Yehuda. "The Tikkun of the Godhead: The Zohar and Yonatan Ratosh" [in Hebrew]. *Alpayim* 7 (1993): 26–28.

London, Yaron. "Toto Tamuz and the Law of Return" [in Hebrew]. *Yediot Aharonot*, July 9, 2007.

Lustick, Ian. *For the Land and the Lord: Jewish Fundamentalism in Israel.* New York: Council on Foreign Relations, 1991.

Margalit, Avishai, and Moshe Halbertal. *Idolatry.* Cambridge, Mass.: Harvard University Press, 1992.

Mauss, Marcel. *Compte rendu de G. Dumezil: Le Festin d'immortalité. L'Année sociologique.* n.s. 1. 1925.

Meron, Dan. "Yonatan Ratosh as a Literary Hero" [in Hebrew]. *Haaretz*, April 9, 1990, April 15, 1990.

Newman, David, and Tamar Hermann. "A Comparative Study of Gush Emunim and Peace Now." *Middle-Eastern Studies* 28 (1992): 509–530.

Nimni, Ephraim, ed. *The Challenge of Post-Zionism: Alternatives to Fundamentalist Politics in Israel.* London: Zed Books, 2003.

Ohana, David. *Political Theologies in the Holy Land: Israeli Messianism and Its Critics.* London: Routledge, 2009.

——. "Yeshayahu Leibowitz: The Radical Intellectual and the Critic of 'the Canaanite Messianism'" [in Hebrew]. In *Yeshayahu Leibowitz: Between Conservatism and Radicalism; Reflections on His Philosophy*, edited by Aviezer Ravitzky, 155–177. Jerusalem 2007.

——. "Yehoshua Arieli and the Responsibility of the Historian" [in Hebrew]. In *The Rage of the Intellectuals: Political Radicalism and Social Criticism in Europe and Israel*, 109–128. Tel Aviv 2005.

——. "The Meaning of Jewish-Israeli Identity." In *Contemporary Jewries, Convergence and Divergence*, edited by Eliezer Ben-Rafael, Yosef Gorny, and Yaacov Ro'i, 65–78. Boston: Brill, 2003.

——. "El sionismo de Yeshayahu Leibowitz," *Kivunim: Revista de Sionismo y Judaismo* (1997): 37–52.

——. "Every Government Is Evil: Interview with Leibowitz" [in Hebrew]. *Maariv*, January 22, 1993.

Pace, David. *Claude Levi-Strauss: The Bearer of Ashes.* London: Routledge, 1983.

Porush, Meir. "Canaanites, 2004 Model" [in Hebrew]. *Haaretz*, January 20, 2004.

Porath, Yehoshua. "Hebrew Canaanism and Arabic Canaanism" [in Hebrew]. In Jacoby, *One Land, Two Peoples*, 83–92.

——. *The Life of Uriel Shelah* (Yonatan Ratosh) [in Hebrew]. Tel Aviv: Mahbarot Le Sifrut, 1989.

Ram, Uri. *Time of the "Post": Nationalism and the Politics of Knowledge in Israel* [in Hebrew]. Tel Aviv: Resling, 2006.

Ratosh, Yonatan. *The First Days: Hebrew Overtures* [in Hebrew]. Tel Aviv: Hadar, 1982.

——. "Euphrates Land." In *From Victory to Collapse* [in Hebrew], 37–38. Tel Aviv: Hadar, 1976.

——. *Sword Poems* [in Hebrew]. Tel Aviv: Hadar, 1969.

——. *The Walker in Darkness: Poems* [in Hebrew]. Tel Aviv: Hadar, 1965.

——. *The Opening Discourse: In Executive Session with the Agents of the Cells* [First Meeting] [in Hebrew]. Tel Aviv: Hadar, 1944.

Reuveni, Aharon. *Shem, Ham and Japhet* [in Hebrew]. Tel Aviv: Saadia Shoshani Press, 1932.

Rosenthal, Ruvik, ed. *The Heart of the Matter: Redefining Social and National Issues* [in Hebrew]. Jerusalem: Keter, 2005.

Rosenzweig, Franz. *The Star of Redemption* [in Hebrew]. Jerusalem: Mossad Bialik, 1970.

Sagi, Avi. *The Jewish-Israeli Voyage: Culture and Identity* [in Hebrew]. Jerusalem: Shalom Hartman Institute, 2006.

Schmitt, Carl. *Political Theology: Four Chapters on the Concept of Sovereignty.* Translated by G. Schwab. Cambridge, Mass.: MIT Press, 1996.

Scholem, Gershom. "Messianism: A Never Ending Quest." In *On the Possibility of Jewish Mysticism in Our Time and Other Essays*, 102–113. Philadelphia: Jewish Publication Society of America, 1997.

———. "The Messianic Idea in Judaism." In *The Messianic Idea in Judaism and Other Essays on Jewish Spirituality*, 35–36. New York: Knopf, 1995.

———. Interview by Irving Howe. "The Only Thing in My Life I Have Never Doubted Is the Existence of God," *Present Tense* 8, no. 1 (Autumn 1980): 53–57.

———. "The Messianic Idea in Jewish Thought," held in honor of his birthday at the Israel Academy of Sciences and Humanities on December 4–5, 1977.

———. *Sabbati Sevi: The Mystical Messiah 1626–1676*. Revised edition. Translated by Zvi R. Werblowsky. Princeton: Princeton University Press, 1973.

Schwartz, Regina M. "Nations and Nationalism: Adultery in the House of David." *Critical Inquiry* 19, no. 1 (Autumn 1992).

Shapira, Avraham. "Introduction: Heritage as a Source to Renaissance; the Spiritual Identity of Gershom Scholem" [in Hebrew]. In *Explication and Implications: Writings on Jewish Heritage and Renaissance*, edited by Gershom Scholem. Tel Aviv: Am Oved, 1982.

Shashar, Michael. *Why Are People Afraid of Yeshajahu Leibwitz* [in Hebrew]. Jerusalem: Shashar, 1995.

Shavit, Yaakov. "With Vision, Fire and Sword" [in Hebrew]. *Haaretz: Cultural and Literary Supplement*, special issue on the tenth anniversary of the death of the poet Yonatan Ratosh, April 6, 2001.

———. *The New Hebrew Nation: A Study in Israeli Heresy and Fantasy*. London: Frank Cass, 1987.

———. *From Majority to a State: The Revisionist Movement; The Plan for a Colonisatory Regime and Social Ideas 1925–1935* [in Hebrew]. Tel Aviv: Hadar, 1978.

Silberstein, Laurence J. *The Postzionism Debates: Knowledge and Power in Israeli Culture*. New York: Routledge, 1999.

Sprinzak, Ehud. "Gush Emunim: The Iceberg Model of Political Extremism." *Jerusalem Quarterly* 21 (1981): 28–47.

Steiner, George. "The Exile Jew" [in Hebrew]. *Haaretz, Galeria*, November 7, 1999.

———. "The Wandering Jew" [in Hebrew]. *Ptahim* 1 (1969): 17–23.

Sobol, Yehoshua. "Not a People of Masters" [in Hebrew]. *Haaretz*, May 11, 2005.

Sofer, Sasson. "Canaanite and Semites" [in Hebrew]. In *The Beginnings of Political Thought in Israel*. Tel Aviv: Schocken, 2001.

Segev, Tom. *Elvis in Jerusalem: Post-Zionism and the Americanization of Israel*. New York: Henry Holt, 2003.

———. "Twenty Years after the Death of the Poet Yonatan Ratosh, Founder of the 'Young Hebrews Movement'" [in Hebrew]. Special issue. *Haaretz Cultural and Literary Supplement*, April 6, 2001.

Weisburd, David, and Vered Vinitzky. "Vigilantism as Rational Social Control: The Case of the Gush Emunim Settlers." In *Cross Current in Israeli Culture and Politics*, edited by Myron Aronoff, 69–88. New Brunswick: Transaction Publishers, 1984.

Weisburd, L., and E. Waring. "Settlement Motivations in Gush Emunim Movement: Comparing Bonds of Altruism and Self-Interest." In *The Impact of Gush Emunim*, edited by David Newman, 183–199. London: Palgrave Macmillan, 1985.

Wheeler, Deborah. "Does Post-Zionism Has a Future?" In *Traditions and Transitions in Israel Studies: Books on Israel 4*, edited by Laura Zitttrain Eisenberg, 159–180. New York: University of New York Press, 2003.

Zilberman, Ifrach. *The Canaanite Founding Myth of the Palestinian Society* [in Hebrew]. Jerusalem: Jerusalem Institute, 1993.

PART III

Modern Jewish Thinkers on The Gift of the Land and the Fate of the Canaanites

15

The Conquest of Eretz Israel and the Seven Nations in Religious-Zionist Thought*

Dov Schwartz

The biblical command in Leviticus 18:3 and elsewhere prescribes complete detachment from Canaanite laws and from the Canaanites (prohibiting marriage, pacts, and any other form of cultural and religious influence). At the same time, it orders the destruction and eradication of the Canaanite peoples: "You shall save alive nothing that breathes" (Deut 20:16). Scripture, however, opened up options for a broad interpretation of the destruction command:

1. Immediately after the formulation of these prohibitions, the Bible explains the reason for them: "That they teach you not to do after all their abominations" (Deut 20:17). Scripture, then, fears the negative spiritual influence of the local nations on the people of Israel and, should this influence be removed, the destruction command would be canceled. Rabbinic writings indeed state that, when the Torah was engraved in stone upon entering Eretz Israel, the following words were added: "Had they [the local nations] done penitence, they would have been accepted."[1]

2. Concerning the seven nations, Scripture states: "They shall not dwell in your land" (Exod 23:33), and previous verses note that the intention in this wording was expulsion ("Little by little I will drive them out from before you" [Exod 23:30, and elsewhere]). The Babylonian Talmud notes that the reference here is to those who had refused to relinquish idolatry.[2] The Bible itself, then, did not consider destruction the only possible option.

Some ancient talmudic and midrashic sources even explicitly claimed that Joshua allowed the seven nations to escape without waging war at all.[3] The reasons for a war against these nations are thus not ethnic but distinctly religious and educational, warranting the following conclusions:

1. The destruction of the seven nations is a function of their idolatry.
2. The duty to eradicate idolatry follows from its negative influence on the Jewish people.

3. These nations' relinquishment of idolatry, or even their expulsion,[4] can therefore substitute for their destruction.

These issues are connected to other matters, such as the command to destroy Amalek, which will not concern me here. Two readings have evolved concerning the seven nations, which eventually turned into two halakhic approaches:

1. *The textual reading, which implies these nations' destruction*: The halakhic outlook that unfolded from this reading pins their destruction on the nations themselves. According to this view, they have no right to exist, and they should be pursued wherever they are found. Their destruction is not context-bound. The law that applies to them, then, is close to that applied to Amalek, which must be hounded everywhere at all times. Both are manifestations of absolute evil, which should be eradicated. This is the view supported by the author of *Sefer haHinukh*, as shown below.

2. *The contextual reading, which implies the purification of the chosen land from these nations*: The halakhic outlook derived from it pins the nations' destruction on their persistent adherence to their idolatrous, immoral ways and on their negation of the people of Israel's right to their land. When the nations change their ways, then, the command to destroy them is, by default, no longer valid. The distinction between the seven nations and Amalek is thus essential. The nations are pursued since they are physically in Eretz Israel, and support for this view in Scripture and in the talmudic literature was noted above. The contextual approach was supported by Nahmanides, as shown below.[5]

The return to Eretz Israel at the end of the nineteenth and in the course of the twentieth centuries reopened the question of the attitude toward the ancient local nations in its connection to the Arab problem. The modern awakening involves a moral dimension, and the confrontation with the problem of the seven nations occurred along two dimensions:

1. The ostensibly indiscriminate destruction of an entire nation.
2. The fact that these nations had lived in Eretz Israel prior to the people of Israel, which seemingly grants them some rights.

The focus of the following discussion is on the modes that religious Zionism adopted in its concern with the issue of the seven nations and the attitude toward them at the time of Joshua's conquest of the land. The discussion will be divided into three parts:

1. General and doctrinal aspects of the religious-Zionist attitude toward Eretz Israel and its foreign inhabitants;
2. Specific halakhic approaches bearing on the seven nations;

3. Conceptual and metaphysical approaches bearing on the seven nations.

The approaches of religious Zionism presented here cover several periods and appear in the writings of various thinkers. The central assumption is that most religious-Zionist views, be they militant or moderate, endorsed the contextual approach, meaning that the destruction command is context-bound rather than absolute.

Basic Assumptions

The tie linking religious Zionism to the seven nations question is predicated on a number of factors, including distinctions between the conditions that had characterized the attitude toward the nations in the past and the present nations, the reactions of religious Zionism to the aggressiveness that characterizes the "new Jew," and the different perceptions of Eretz Israel in religious-Zionist thought. These factors are presented briefly below.

PAST AND PRESENT

The biblical attitude toward the Canaanites and to the other nations dwelling in Eretz Israel has concerned religious-Zionist thought to some extent, but not as obsessively as might have been expected. As a result of the distinctions between biblical and current circumstances, and specifically between the seven nations and Palestinian Arabs, this issue has not played an essential, existential role in Zionist thought in general or in religious Zionism in particular. The distinctions are the following:

1. *A religious distinction*: In the biblical period, there was a command to destroy the seven nations; in the present, no such command has been issued. The reason is not merely the disappearance of the ancient nations, but essential changes in the historical, political, and theological surroundings. Religiously, the monotheistic faith of Islam has eliminated the theological risk. The presence of Arabs in Eretz Israel is a fact and, were it not for the prevalent state of war, hostility toward them would be unjustified.

2. *A historical distinction*: In the biblical period, there was apparently a possibility of removing non-Jewish dwellers from Eretz Israel; in the present, this option is simply nonexistent, even after the State of Israel gained control over most of the biblical territory.

3. *A moral distinction*: In the biblical period, the religious norm prevailed, and universal moral criteria were virtually meaningless; in

the present, added to the religious norm are norms accepted by the community of nations.

The attitude to the seven nations, therefore, was not a high priority in religious-Zionist philosophy, which derived its attitude toward them from the attitude to the stranger and from the attachment to Eretz Israel. Nonetheless, several interesting approaches on this matter evolved in this philosophy.

POWER

Religious Zionism emerged as a faction within the Zionist movement. Zionism was a political movement, and its aim was to obtain a "charter," that is, to settle Eretz Israel following international recognition of the right of the Jewish people to their land. The aims that the Zionist movement set itself, at least at the start, did not include an armed struggle with the surrounding nations. Zionist ideology as such, then, was not marked *ab initio* by violence and force. Aggressiveness is indeed a sign of the national honor, but the use of force was almost invariably perceived as a "last resort."[6] Religious Zionism, by contrast, acknowledged by its very definition the authority of the sacred texts, which included "holy" wars to gain control of the land. The conquest of the land from the nations dwelling in it is presented as an ancestral divine command. Religious-Zionist thought, therefore, does relate to the biblical inheritance of the land in the course of a war with the seven nations and to the command to obliterate them.

The moral attitude of religious Zionism to the seven biblical nations is derived directly from the attitude toward biblical and talmudic texts. The thinkers and leaders of religious Zionism tended to be learned men, well-versed in the sources. The moral attitude, however, was also indirectly determined by the movement's attitude regarding force and war. Religious Zionism became acquainted with force and with the use of violence in its early years,[7] but maintained a reserved and qualified attitude toward force until the Six Day War and the Yom Kippur War. Two caveats to this statement are in place:

1. Central trends within religious Zionism had supported the use of force in the pre-state underground movements and in the reprisal operations in Israel's early years. The views of the movement's leaders, R. Meir Berlin (Bar-Ilan) and R. Yehuda Leib Hacohen Fischman (Maimon), offer reliable evidence of such trends.[8]
2. The very aspiration to create a "normal" national and political entity in Eretz Israel dictates the establishment of a defensive army. Recourse to force is thus inevitable, given the Zionist vision in general and the religious-Zionist one in particular.[9]

The next stage occurred after the Six Day War and the Yom Kippur War, and the ensuing changes in Israeli society and politics. Henceforth, the association of religious Zionism with force would proceed without remorse. Gush Emunim, which would serve religious Zionism as a compensation mechanism for its having missed out on the pioneering myth, would also serve as compensation for its removal from the foci of military power. The growth and strengthening of the Gush has been discussed at length in the research literature and will not be considered directly here.[10] An additional sign of the process of increasing familiarity with force is the current integration of religious Zionists in the army leadership and the emergence of militaristic literature written by young religious Zionists.[11]

This chapter deals with the connection of religious Zionism to the biblical sources and with the interpretation of these sources as mirroring the movement's attitude to the nations dwelling in the Promised Land. I do not intend to deal directly with the attitude toward the Arabs—either with the ideological and operational approaches formulated in the context of the dispute over the right to Eretz Israel, or with the attitude toward its resident aliens in the present. My concern is with the question of whether acquaintance with force changed the attitude to the seven nations in religious-Zionist thought.

ERETZ ISRAEL

The attitude toward the nations dwelling in the land derives directly from the role of Eretz Israel in the national philosophy. Some, as noted, pin the war against the seven nations on their residence in the land, contrary to the case of Amalek, which should be pursued everywhere. Religious-Zionist thought fluctuates between three approaches:[12]

1. *A national secular approach*: According to this view, the association between a people and its land can be assessed on the basis of secular criteria—concrete or spiritual-symbolic. According to the concrete-material criterion stressed, for instance, in the writings of several Labor-Zionist thinkers, the national land plays a role as (a) a locus of refuge and survival; (b) a locus of material, agricultural, and industrial development; and (c) a locus of cultural development. According to the spiritual-symbolic criterion—as in the "spiritual center" conception of Ahad-Ha-Am—the land is perceived as the cultural cradle that enriches the Diaspora, as a national symbol, and as an expression of the nation's historical legacy.[13] Furthermore, Eretz Israel occupies a different place and has a different value in rational and romantic outlooks, which deny the validity of religious authority and of the religious establishment, and present the nation's connection to its land without relying on them. Although no specific formulation of this approach appears in religious-Zionist writings, its contents did influence the apologetic philosophy of R. Yitzhak Yaakov Reines and the views of other Mizrahi founders.[14]

2. *A halakhic-religious approach*: This approach measures a people's attachment to their land in legal-halakhic categories. It rests on a practical, "earthly" assumption, whereby the Torah can be fully observed only in the Holy Land (land-bound commandments, judicial instances such as the Sanhedrin, and so forth). Since observance of the Torah is a necessary component in the national perfection of the Jewish people, the settlement of Eretz Israel becomes a basic national need. I refer to this approach as "practical and earthly" because, by nature, halakhah is observed in the material world and relates to the legal aspects of the "lowest" material circumstances. The halakhic realm per se does not in any way require recognition of metaphysical or spiritual layers beyond its practical obligations. An approach of this type has shaped the philosophy of many Zionist thinkers, including R. Joseph B. Soloveitchik and his circle.

3. *A religious-spiritual approach*: This approach views Eretz Israel as a concrete expression of spiritual and metaphysical dimensions. Earthly clods are merely the external wrap of dynamic and turbulent spiritual entities, which have personal feelings, yearnings, and preferences. The encounter between the people and the land now becomes a combination of two independent factors, which together create a powerful, irrational divine perfection. This approach gathered enormous impetus in the views of kabbalists and religious Zionists with mystical tendencies, who saw Eretz Israel as a reflection of hidden divine *sefirot*. The halakhic approach may engage in a dialogue with the secular one in an attempt to shape a shared "normal life" through adaptation and flexibility within certain limits. By contrast, the spiritual approach rests on mystical terms that are specific to mystics and their groups and are not a basis for mutual exchanges. This is also a total approach, which explains events fully according to its perspective and leaves no room for other interpretations. This approach was the foundation for the philosophy of R. Abraham Ha-Kohen Kook and his ideological circle, and also left its mark in the thinking of the HaPo'el HaMizrahi movement.

When confronting the secular-national approach, religious Zionism has fluctuated between the religious-halakhic and the religious-spiritual approaches.

Halakhic Approaches

Following is an account of attitudes toward the seven nations that reflect different ways of confronting this matter in religious-Zionist thought, from discussions that are halakhic in character or involve halakhic-legal implications to discussions that are distinctly aggadic or ideological. The halakhic material will be discussed in the following order:

1. *The contextual approach*: The attitude toward the Canaanites is context-bound.
2. *The radicalization of the contextual approach*: The Torah command is disregarded.
3. *The textual approach*: The attitude toward the Canaanites is absolute.

THE DISCOVERY OF THE NAHMANIDEAN METHOD[15]

Religious Zionism had restorative models—models from the remote and recent past that it sought to reapply to the awakening nationalism. One such model was the Golden Age of Spain, which saw an outburst of innovation and creativity.[16] A personal paragon that religious Zionism set up was Maimonides, a leader of variegated talents whose creativity extended over and united many areas.[17] Nahmanides was not an uncommon figure in the pantheon of religious-Zionist thought, except for his *aliyah* to Eretz Israel, which the movement's ideologues considered a religious-Zionist act.[18] Nahmanides can hardly be claimed to be an ideal model of a religious Zionist. One of his rulings, however, proved decisive for the movement and turned him into no less than "the father of all Israel."[19] His ruling on inheriting the land appears in Nahmanides' glosses to Maimonides' *Book of Commandments*. R. Yitzhak Yaakov Reines, the founder of the Mizrahi, cites Nahmanides in full in part 4 of his book *Or Hadash 'al Tzion* (A New Light on Zion):

> The fourth commandment [which Maimonides did not enumerate in his *Book of Commandments*] that we have been commanded is to inherit the land that God gave us, and not to abandon it to other nations or to desolation,[20] as we have been told, "And you shall dispossess the inhabitants of the land, and dwell in it; for I have given you the land to possess it" (Num 33:53), and you shall settle the land that I have sworn to your fathers (according to Deut 1:8).[21]

R. Reines then proceeded to quote Nahmanides' reference to the seven nations who were then dwelling in Eretz Israel:

> Do not confuse this with the commandment on the war against the seven nations that they were told to lay waste to, as it is said, "you shall utterly destroy them" (Deut 20:17). It is not the case that we were ordered to kill those idolaters[22] in their war against us. Should they seek peace, we shall make peace with them and, under certain conditions, let them be, but we will not leave the land to them or to any other idolatrous nation at any time. The same applies should those nations flee and leave, as it is said (*Deut. Rab.*,

Shofetim) about the Girgashites that they turned away and left, and the Holy
One, blessed be He, gave them a good land, which is Africa. As for us, we
have been commanded to come to the land, to conquer it, and to settle our
tribes in it.[23]

Or Hadash 'al Tzion is the most important book of propaganda written at
the time the Mizrahi was created, and R. Reines thought it appropriate to
cite Nahmanides in full and analyze his statements. He seems to have viewed
Nahmanides' approach as conclusive proof of the diplomatic approach adopted
by Zionism. He emphasizes that, when Nahmanides writes "we will not abandon the land to them," what he means is "we will redeem it from strangers
and bring it into Israel's possession," as well as "we will remove it from their
possession and bring it into ours."[24] In other words, the Torah affirmed the
legal legitimacy of Eretz Israel belonging to the people of Israel and the option
of a war against the seven nations as merely a last resort, to be chosen only if
they choose to struggle against the Jewish people's rule over its land. R. Reines
stresses that Nahmanides' approach does not consider the destruction of the
nations as necessarily included in the commandment to inherit the land. In
his view, "the commandment is the conquest, so that the war of conquest is
necessarily a Torah-commanded [*mitzvah*] or obligatory [*hovah*] war, but not
for the purpose of destroying these nations."[25]

R. Reines is also willing to accept the non-Zionist Orthodox view that forbids
the people of Israel to conquer Eretz Israel by force, as specified in the prohibition of "revolt" (*aliyah bahomah*), probably implying that only a future messiah
can adopt military means to conquer the land. Yet, conquest through persuasion, meaning diplomatic activity in pursuit of the Zionist ideal, has never been
forbidden. "Moreover, he [Nahmanides] obviously never intended to say that
conquest through war is a commandment, since the people of Israel have been
sworn to keep away throughout their exile from rebellion and trespass, God forbid. Unquestionably, then, what he intended is a voluntary taking."[26] R. Reines
thus created a clear division: Conquest is a means, and legal possession and
settlement of the land are the end. He admitted that, in the Bible, conquest
implies military action, but since it is only a means, diplomacy can replace it.
In sum: "The voluntary taking replaces belligerent conquest."[27] R. Reines set up
an equation in which conquest equals acquiring legal rights equals persuasion.

R. Reines's interpretation of Nahmanides and its adaptation to the present
can be summed up in the following principles:

1. If the seven nations (or the local Arabs) will accept that the Jewish
   people are the legal owners of Eretz Israel, there is no difference
   between past and present, and the rule is:

   a. There is no obligation to destroy the nations dwelling in Eretz Israel.
   b. There is no obligation to expel the nations from Eretz Israel.

2. If the seven nations do not accept this ownership, there is a distinction between the remote past and the present.

   a. In biblical times, both persuasion and war were options.
   b. Today, only persuasion is an option.

Several years after the creation of the State of Israel, R. Shaul Israeli, who was the leading figure in the rabbinical council of HaPo'el HaMizrahi and would later become a teacher at the Merkaz haRav Yeshiva, wrote a scholarly article entitled "The Status of the Gentile in Israel in the Light of the Torah."[28] In this article, R. Israeli clarified that, according to Nahmanides, reconciliation with the seven nations is indeed possible "under certain conditions," referring to compliance with the Noahide laws. By contrast, regarding other nations (and in particular the Arabs), not even this condition is necessary. Nahmanides and his faction (Rashi, R. Abraham of Posquières) had applied the prohibition of "they shall not dwell in your land" only to the seven nations, contrary to views that expanded it to include all the nations whose members do not fit the definition of *ger toshav* (settler stranger), referring to those who have accepted the seven Noahide laws.[29] R. Israeli also indicated elsewhere another implication of Nahmanides' method, whereby "the commandment of conquest is not necessarily through war,"[30] and thereby endorsed some of R. Reines's distinctions. R. Israeli fully explored all aspects of Nahmanides' method and emphasized its different aspects.

Nahmanides' glosses to the *Book of the Commandments* became established as the metaphysical and practical-performative foundation of R. Tzvi Yehuda Ha-Kohen Kook's endeavor. Metaphysically, R. Tzvi Yehuda relied on Nahmanides for his conception of Eretz Israel as a spiritual entity, of which the concrete earth is merely a thin cover.[31] Practically, he relied on this approach to justify his relentless struggle against any territorial concessions. Some brief remarks on the metaphysical aspect follow. In 1959, R. Tzvi Yehuda wrote:

> The progression of ten sayings in the order of the creation of heaven and earth [begins] through the revelation of God's spirit, which hovers over the surface of the deep water of unformed void and darkness and, through it, reaches its commandments on the being of light. So it is in the process of climbing from rung to rung in Israel's renaissance. In the beginning [of] the end, we observed the divine rule of the King of the universe, the Creator of man and the Giver of the Torah that this, our land, will be ruled and settled by us and in our possession.[32]

In a note, R. Tzvi Yehuda refers to the above quote from Nahmanides, implying that Nahmanides demanded Jewish rule over Eretz Israel in order to preserve the cosmic order. R. Tzvi Yehuda draws a parallel between creation *ex nihilo* and the resettlement of Eretz Israel, and compares the various waves of immigration to the re-creation of the land. Both occur in a gradual, step-by-step process. Without the rule of the Jewish people, the metaphysical union between the people of Israel and Eretz Israel does not prevail, so that, as it were, the land substantially disappears. The renewal of Jewish rule, therefore, leads to the reunion of the people and the land. Jewish settlement and the establishment of Jewish rule involve "concrete divine holiness." This is a holiness of action, that is, of fulfilling the prescription formulated by Nahmanides: "We have been commanded to inherit the land that God gave us, and not to abandon it to other nations."[33] In R. Tzvi Yehuda's teachings, Nahmanides' call became synonymous with metaphysical and cosmic order, the most important issue of all, and he had no hesitations about disparaging and questioning the authority of those who disputed this decision.[34]

R. Tzvi Yehuda did not relate explicitly to Nahmanides' reference to the seven nations, but clearly implied that his most essential demand from the nations dwelling in Eretz Israel is the recognition of the Jewish people's rule:

> Hence, we command like Nahmanides to all generations, in the words of our God, King of the universe, that not they will rule here, in Jerusalem, in Judea and Samaria, in the Golan and in Jericho, but we will rule here in our land over all the thousands of our people, the House of Israel... a clear definition of Nahmanides' "land in the nation's hands" means, in simple Hebrew: rule, government, state.[35]

Although he is referring to Arabs, R. Tzvi Yehuda has obviously endorsed Nahmanides' position concerning Canaanites and other biblical nations too. Indeed, in his lectures, R. Tzvi Yehuda specifically said:

> [Eretz Israel] is the special land that belongs to Abraham, our forefather, who knew his Maker, and his seed must be wrapped in it in the purity of holiness. Therefore, Eretz Israel must be cleansed of idolatry. The war against the seven nations came about because they are idol worshippers, and it is not an absolute war. If they abandon their idolatry, and cause no harm to our rule and to our ownership of this land (as a divine gift to Abraham)—it is possible for them to live in our midst as minorities.[36]

The presence of other nations in Eretz Israel is thus contingent on two conditions: their absolute rejection of idolatry and their acknowledgment of Jewish rule as legitimate. Unlike his predecessors, R. Tzvi Yehuda placed particular emphasis on the recognition of Jewish rule, which is thought to convey the centrality of *mamlakhtiut* in his thought.[37] This principle operates to the detriment of other nations. A largely paradoxical phenomenon is evident in R. Tzvi Yehuda's thought: Adopting an extreme view concerning the importance of the land and its metaphysical and mystical aspects led to a tolerant approach toward the Canaanites. Recognizing the significance of the land and of its metaphysical connection to the chosen people makes the destruction of the seven nations redundant.

R. Tzvi Yehuda's disciples insisted on the tolerance marking Nahmanides' approach concerning the seven nations. R. Shlomo Aviner notes:

> True, we and the Arabs are presently involved in a territorial dispute; they have arguments, and we have arguments. This is not a personal dispute, and there is no personal rancor but rather a defined national conflict at this time, over this land, and this is the source of all the troubles.... Nahmanides stresses that the starting point is that we must settle this land, even if for this purpose we become entangled in war. We have no interest in a war with the seven nations, unless they attack us. The Talmud calls these "the wars waged by Joshua to conquer" (*b. Sotah* 44b), and this war in no way resembles that with Amalek.[38]

R. Aviner places the Arabs and the seven nations in the same category, as Nahmanides' approach indeed allows. He expresses fear lest the "national sense" should blunt the "moral sense," and he therefore demands fairness toward the non-Jewish residents of the land. He justifies this approach by claiming that "Joshua too, at the time of the conquest and the settlement, allowed the nations dwelling in the land the possibility of staying."[39] The *mamlakhti* condition for such moral behavior is unequivocal: unquestioned recognition of Jewish authority over Eretz Israel.

THE EXPULSION OF THE NATIONS

R. Yitzhak Nussenbaum was a "preacher of Zion" and a member of the Zionist movement, and he eventually became active in the Mizrahi in Poland. He interpreted the command to destroy the seven nations as implying their expulsion from Eretz Israel.

Nussenbaum was critical of the dispersed pattern of Jewish settlement. Following a visit to Eretz Israel in 1905, he published his impressions in his autobiography (*Alei Heldi*) and embedded them in his preaching. In his view, this dispersal creates problems mainly regarding defense from the surrounding Arabs, but also entails negative social and educational implications. He therefore highlighted the centralized pattern of settlement in biblical times. Nussenbaum tended to use homiletics to clarify his ideas, and he discussed centralization in a homily on the weekly Torah reading of *Mattot* (Num 30–32). His homily discusses the request of the tribes of Reuben and Gad to settle on the Eastern bank of the Jordan and Moses' harsh response to them. Nussenbaum explained Moses' opposition to the immediate settlement of the eastern bank as due to the centralization principle. In his view, Moses argued that had these tribes settled in the eastern bank of the Jordan upon arrival, they would have created isolated communities in the midst of a vast area. This dispersal would have exposed them to the destructive influence of the surrounding nations:

What the Torah wants is that, where the children of Israel settle, no trace should remain of the original nations. "They should not dwell in your land, lest they make you sin against me: for if you serve their gods, it will surely be a snare to you" (Exod 23:33). On the other hand, however, "I will not drive them out before you in one year; lest the land become desolate and the wild beasts multiply against you. Little by little I will drive them out from before you, until you be increased, and inherit the land" (Exod 23:29–30). Hence, the plan for the conquest called for settling all the Jews only in the center of the land at this stage, yet without being surrounded by their enemies on all sides—from the sea to the Jordan and from the brook of Egypt to the entrance to Hamath.[40] Thus, only the children of Israel would settle in these places and all the Gentiles would be expelled from them without the land becoming desolate. The number of Jews at the time sufficed for this, and slowly, according to the increase of the people, they would spread on all three sides and press their neighbors further and further from the border of their areas toward the Red Sea southwards, to the Arabian desert in the East, and to Mesopotamia northwards. In this way, the nucleus, the center, would always be solid, populated only by the children of Israel developing according to their own spirit, without foreign influence from outside and without ensnarement inside. Slowly, not only would they spread their rule throughout the land but also their spiritual influence, and the land would truly become "Eretz Israel," a land that Israel also rules spiritually![41]

The presence of other nations was feared both as an existential threat and as a spiritual influence. Nussenbaum drew a distinction between *conquest* and *hold*. *Conquest* refers to the general plan, that is, to the entire Land of Israel; *hold* refers to a defined place from within the range. The divine plan demanded the conquest of the entire Land of Israel and at the same time demanded centralized settlement at the initial stage. That is, the biblical people of Israel were meant to settle only in the center and, with natural increase, gradually push out the local nations eastward, northward, and southward. The Bible, as it were, conceived a demographic ploy for the full conquest of the land.

Following R. Reines, Nussenbaum included the purchase of lands in the category of conquest. He therefore called for purchasing lands throughout Eretz Israel ("this conquest must take place wherever possible"),[42] but he also required that the settlement remain centralized in its initial stages. Nussenbaum thus held that, *ab initio*, the Torah had intended the nations to be expelled. Only in the case of an armed struggle does the command call for destruction.

FROM EXPULSION TO EMPATHY

Nussenbaum related to this command in various articles, as discussed below. His approach, substituting expulsion for destruction, was adopted by other thinkers. One of them is R. Hayyim Hirschensohn, who stated that the command of conquering Eretz Israel means "to expel the seven nations."[43] In any event, he claimed, the command applies only at the time of the conquest of the land, when these nations posed a spiritual and existential threat. After the conquest, however, the picture changes radically in two ways:

1. The command of destruction is no longer valid and is replaced by the prohibition of "shedding innocent blood."[44]
2. International law applies to the behavior toward the nations, and requires the endorsement of moral norms vis-à-vis the seven nations as well.[45]

On this question, too, R. Hirschensohn stands out as a thinker who combines realistic and humanistic aspects in his rulings. Hirschensohn fluctuated between extremes, replacing expulsion within norms of respect and concern.

TRANSGRESSING TORAH COMMANDMENTS?

Religious-Zionist preaching sought to moderate the destruction command on the one hand and, on the other, to grant Joshua, who had conducted the war against the seven nations, extraordinary powers as the leader of the people in the settlement of Eretz Israel. This trend is evident in the preaching of Yitzhak Nussenbaum and Zeev Gold.

In Nussenbaum's later discussions, the seven nations dwelling in Canaan reflect an alternative culture. The cultural war is not necessarily between idolatry and monotheism, but between a local culture radiating charm, on the one hand, and a superior divine culture, on the other. In his view, the returning spies had claimed as follows: "All the people we saw there are virtuous,[46] polite, and cultured, graced with appealing qualities. Their cultural attainments inspire one to surrender to them spiritually and morally."[47] Through this clearly anachronistic claim, the preacher endeavors to make the distant past relevant to the present.

In an article he wrote two years later, at the beginning of 1933, Nussenbaum presented an interesting halakhic innovation. He claimed that, at the time of the war, Joshua had been commanded to destroy the seven nations but had never intended to obey this order. Joshua understood the command of destruction as a command to wage war against the nations, that is, to bring the people of Israel to military maturity. The destruction of the nations was not perceived in its literal meaning, given that the text describes at length the seven nations' settlements and enclaves. And God indeed accepted Joshua's interpretation. "Scripture agrees with this interpretation, as it were, and finds room to praise it."[48] Nussenbaum added his own innovation, as follows:

> We do not find that, in peaceful times, the children of Israel oppressed these
> inhabitants to expel them from their land, to prevent them from working

and earning a living, or to avoid negotiating with them. Quite the contrary! We must think that our forefathers, who followed Moses' law, abided by the many warnings of "you shall neither vex a stranger, nor oppress him," culminating in "the stranger that dwells with you shall be to you as one born among you, and you shall love him as yourself" (Lev 19:34).[49]

Nussenbaum drew a distinction between the command to destroy the nations at times of war and their status during peace. His interpretation of the attitude toward the nations creates an interesting halakhic construction:

1. At times of war, the prescriptive command is to destroy the nations ("leaving no trace in it [Eretz Israel] of the seven nations dwelling in it"). The prescriptive command was interpreted as a war against these nations, leading to their expulsion, but not to their destruction.
2. At times of peace, the command of destruction becomes invalid, to be replaced by a proscriptive command that forbids vexing the stranger. The status of the inhabitants shifts from that of enemy nations to that of strangers.[50]

Nussenbaum created a pseudo-halakhic move here, although he did not rely on a halakhic ruling. Moreover, he claimed that Joshua had changed the biblical command of destruction and turned it into a command to wage war. R. Zeev Gold, a leading activist of religious Zionism in the United States and in Eretz Israel, supported this approach. R. Gold preached at length on the superiority of heroism of the spirit over heroism in battle, in the context of the call to peace before war: "When you come near to a city to fight against it, then proclaim peace to it" (Deut 20:10). He then expanded this claim and argued: "Most of the wars fought by the Jewish people have been defensive wars."[51] This claim applies also to the seven nations:

And even the obligatory, prescribed war [*milhemet hovah*] against the seven nations, of which the Torah says "you shall save alive nothing that breathes," was a defensive war. When the Holy One, blessed be He, saw that no honest generation would ever come from them until the end of times and that they might poison the entire world with their cravings and corruption, He assigned the people of Israel the task of performing this operation and fight the thirty-one kings to save the world from wrongdoing. Nevertheless, Joshua sent three messages before entering Eretz Israel. In the first, he sent a message saying that whoever wishes to flee should flee. In the second—that whoever wishes to make peace, should make peace. In the third—whoever wishes to wage war, should wage war. Only one whose corruption overwhelms him to the point that he does not wish to conclude a full peace—only against him will he fight. (*y. Shev.* 6)[52]

R. Tzvi Yehuda had used the term *operation* concerning the Holocaust, which he interpreted as a deliberate separation that was imposed on the people of

Israel to lead them to abandon the exile and move to Eretz Israel.[53] By contrast, R. Gold used this term to denote the destruction of the seven nations. R. Gold, then, did not renounce the apocalyptic dimension of destroying cosmic evil as a mission incumbent on the people of Israel. These nations are destroyed because their potential damage extends to the entire world. And yet, R. Gold emphasized that the destruction relates only to those who insist on waging war against the people of Israel. The seeds of aggression within them compel their utter destruction. Furthermore, R. Gold emphasized the midrashic motif of Joshua's initiative, who exhausted all the possibilities before going out to battle. He redirected the readers' attention to the midrash stating that an entire nation (the Girgashites) preferred not to fight and left.[54]

Both R. Nussenbaum and R. Gold stressed Joshua's daring in changing an explicit scriptural command or in adding to it by calling for peace with the seven nations. This was also the view of R. Simon Federbusch, a Mizrahi activist in the United States and in Israel. Federbusch viewed the call for peace as an explicit stance that is also relevant to the war with the seven nations. Rather than considering this call an innovation introduced by Joshua, however, he held that the call for peace is anchored in religious law: "According to the Torah, it is forbidden to attack a people suddenly without first proposing peace. Only if they reject the proposal are belligerent activities against them allowed. This is an instance of a last warning, the ultimatum that is now binding on all nations according to international law."[55]

For R. Federbusch, it is clear that the law follows Maimonides and his faction, who ruled that the call for peace applies also during the conquest of Eretz Israel. Hence, the "spiritual mission" of the Jewish people, which is "to bring the surrendering idolatrous people under the wings of moral humanity,"[56] relates also to the Canaanites and to the other nations who resided in Eretz Israel. This explicit view emerged despite the express biblical command to destroy the seven nations. "Talmudic sages emphasized that the Torah command to destroy the seven nations when conquering the land had not been carried out—Joshua had called on them to make peace, and had fought only against those that had refused."[57] R. Federbusch emphasized the midrashic tradition stating that God accepted, as it were, the decision of Moses and Joshua not to carry out the destruction order.[58] Between the lines, R. Federbusch found merit in the fact that King Saul and the people had shown compassion to the king of Amalek. In his view, the feeling of compassion inspires the law.

UNBENDING VIEWS

R. Eliezer Waldenberg influenced religious-Zionist discourse, although he was not openly affiliated with the movement. His three-volume work, *Sefer Hilkhot Medinah*, was published a few years after the creation of the State of Israel. It reflects the thrust of his views, which generally support the Jewish national renaissance. In this work, R. Waldenberg offered a series of clarifications on the halakhic conduct of the state. He deliberately refrained from clear-cut rulings and merely traced the course of the discussions, from which the reader is meant to understand the drift of the decision. R. Waldenberg showed that the war with the seven nations appears under two different categories in a Tannaitic dispute. According to R. Yehuda, this war is defined as an "obligatory war" or, according to the rabbinic term, a "Torah-commanded [*mitzvah*] war."[59] Yet, the Sages are not in conflict concerning the content of the law: No one is exempt from such a war ("not even a bridegroom from his chamber and a bride from her canopy"). The dispute concerns preventive wars, that is, wars initiated deliberately lest an idolatrous enemy should attack. The question is whether such a war is in the category of "one performing a commandment is exempt from others."

In the course of R. Waldenberg's discussions, the war against the seven nations emerges as the paradigm of a war compelling everyone's participation, without any exceptions. The discussions focus on the question of what other kind of war is coextensive with, or similar to, this paradigm (for instance, a preventive war, a war to help Jews attacked elsewhere, and so forth). R. Waldenberg cites Rashi's Talmud commentary on *b. Sanhedrin* 2a, who "issued an unequivocal ruling" and stated that any war unrelated to Joshua's conquest of the land is considered a voluntary war:

> In my humble opinion, Rashi's method appears to require further explanation. Rashi holds that, since we had been commanded from Sinai by the Torah to conquer our land whenever we can do so, this war does not require permission from the court. But any other war of conquest beyond the borders of our land, since it is not commanded by the Torah, does require the court's permission. Hence, a war that is like Joshua's war and aims to conquer the land, be it a war against the seven nations or against Amalek, and mainly because its aim is to conquer the land, will be in the category of a Torah-commanded war and will not require the court's permission. Any war whose purpose is not to conquer the land, however, even if the war itself is in the category of a Torah-commanded war, such as the destruction of Amalek or of the seven nations found beyond the borders of the land [see *Sefer haHinukh*, commandment 604, which commands they should be obliterated wherever they are] does require court permission. Waging an open war against them in order to conquer their dwelling places and take away their wealth requires permission. The reason is that, although the Torah commands us to erase their memory and obliterate them wherever they are, this command can be performed without an open war of conquest by individuals or by organized groups engaging in guerrilla warfare. Waging

an official war of conquest, therefore, requires permission from a court of seventy-one.[60]

R. Waldenberg's ruling is clear and unequivocal. In his view, the destruction of the seven nations is an unambiguous command that leaves no room for leniency. Clearly, he endorses the view of the *Sefer haHinukh*, which is inconsistent with that of Nahmanides. The author of *Sefer haHinukh* enumerates two commandments concerning the seven nations:

1. *A prescriptive commandment*: "To kill the seven nations that held our land before we conquered it from them...and to eradicate them from wherever they are."[61]
2. A proscriptive commandment: "We have been warned not to allow any one of the seven nations to survive, wherever they might be."[62] This commandment must be observed, even in the absence of life-endangering circumstances.

The author of *Sefer haHinukh* emphasized that these commandments are valid forever and not only for the time of the biblical conquest and settlement of the land. His explanation is that nations, like individuals, are given free choice, and since these nations chose the path of moral corruption they are doomed to be destroyed. R. Waldenberg, as noted, supports this approach and qualifies it only with one caveat: Initiating a war against the seven nations beyond the borders of the land requires the court's permission. "After they have received permission from the court to wage a war, this war assumes the validity of a Torah-commanded war,"[63] but within the borders of Eretz Israel, no permission is required to wage war against the nations. He also endorses the approach of *Sefer haHinukh* that the obligation is to pursue the members of the seven nations even after conquering the land, and holds that such pursuit is in the category of "a Torah-commanded war," which takes precedence over a voluntary war.[64]

R. Waldenberg never retreated from this position. R. Yitzhak Kulitz asked R. Waldenberg concerning these issues in 1992, and he simply sent a copy of the relevant chapter in *Sefer Hilkhot Medinah*. The question and the responsum were printed in his *Responsa Tzitz Eliezer* (part 20, number 43). According to R. Waldenberg, the commandment to destroy the nations relates also to their remnants and, in principle, is valid today as well, even though they cannot be identified.

R. Shlomo Goren, chief rabbi of the Israel Defense Forces (IDF) and later of the State of Israel, also supported the view of *Sefer haHinukh*, whereby the obligation to destroy the seven nations is not confined to the time of war. He relates specifically to the discussion in *Sefer haHinukh* and wonders why the destruction of members of the seven nations applies only when no risk is involved. R. Goren notes that this question appears already in *Minhat Hinukh*.

The solution that R. Goren suggested draws a distinction between the individual and the collective. Incumbent on the collective is a commandment of
destruction, even if Canaanite resistance poses a danger, but for the individual,
the commandment is binding only if it is not life-endangering.[65]

Conceptual and Symbolic Approaches

Whereas halakhah moves along clearly set methodological and inferential
paths, aggadah roams freely over a broad and limitless domain. The discussion
below deals with the moral justification for destroying the Canaanite nations
as formulated in aggadic sources and in ideological discussions about these
nations' current manifestations.

COSMIC ANCHORING

The disciples of R. Abraham Yitzhak Ha-Kohen Kook, as noted, "necessarily" adopted a tolerant attitude, meaning that, having endorsed Nahmanides'
approach requiring Jewish rule over Eretz Israel, they had to accept the shift
from obligatory destruction to (compelled) recognition of the Jewish people's
rule over their land. R. Kook presented the theosophical and cosmic basis for
his circle's views. First, he stated that Eretz Israel is called "the Land of Canaan"
because of its qualities: It is in its powers to transform the depth of impurity
into the height of purity. In the spirit of "collecting the sparks" postulated in
Lurianic Kabbalah, R. Kook claimed that "a sublime treasure of life is hidden
in it [the Land of Canaan], a treasure of light within the troves of darkness."[66]
Yet, contrary to the kabbalistic approach that supports the disappearance of
the husk and its melting as the sparks are collected, R. Kook emphasized that
the nature of evil would itself change into good through the merit of the land.
Second, it is because of its uniqueness that the chosen land is taken away from
the seven nations and given to the people of Israel as its inheritance.[67]

Starting from these assumptions, R. Kook shifted to the cosmic basis of the
seven nations:

> Were it not for the sin of the golden calf, the nations dwelling in Eretz Israel
> would have made peace with the people of Israel and would have acknowl-
> edged their rule because the name of God after which they are called would
> have evoked in them the fear of glory, no war would have been waged, and
> influence would have proceeded peacefully, as in messianic times.[68]

This passage points to two issues. First, what is demanded from the nations
is recognition ("acknowledgment") of Jewish rule. Nahmanides' approach
emerges between the lines. Second, the sin of the golden calf caused the state
of war. R. Kook adopted the cosmic meanings of the sin of the golden calf

according to mystical literature ("apostasy," damage to the divine chariot, and so forth). To some extent, the people of Israel are held to be indirectly responsible for the war against the seven nations. Had they refrained from sin, the land's dwellers would have been influenced by them and would have abandoned the path of war.

R. Tzvi Yehuda generally endorsed a tolerant attitude, as noted, but interpreted the cosmic anchoring in other ways. He commented on R. Federbusch's stance discussed above, stating that Joshua had deliberately breached the destruction order. Cited below is R. Federbusch's position and R. Tzvi Yehuda's comments on it.

R. Federbusch:

> The Torah law on the destruction of the Canaanite nations was formulated at a time of anger at the cruelty of these nations toward the wandering and persecuted people of Israel, to which many point as opposed to the principle of love for one's fellow creatures. Thus, this law has become for midrash writers a source for invoking the value of peace and the feeling of compassion, even when this feeling prevents observance of the Torah laws.[69]

R. Tzvi Yehuda:

> The Torah is not a matter of that time and its anger, but of eternity and of the very essence and value of the people of Israel and of these nations in the order of the world and of humanity.[70]

Contrary to R. Kook's approach, whereby evil turns into good in the Holy Land, R. Tzvi Yehuda negated any transformation in the world's order—the Gentile nations are at their level and the people of Israel are at theirs. Every stage of reality is engraved in the cosmic order. The ontological distinction between Israel and the nations, not a given historical situation (the period of the conquest), is the reason for the persecution of the seven nations.

This argument appears to bolster the claim proposed above, stating that the tolerant approach of R. Tzvi Yehuda and his circle derives from their adoption of Nahmanides' view. R. Tzvi Yehuda had claimed that recognition of Jewish rule rescinds the command of pursuing the nations, and this is an eternal rather than a temporary matter. Nahmanides' view was the basis for the *mamlakhti* approach, that is, for the recognition of Jewish rule in Eretz Israel. Since the principle of *mamlakhtiut* is so essential, this recognition denies the basis for destroying these nations if they have indeed acknowledged Jewish rule.

Philosophically and metaphysically, R. Tzvi Yehuda and his disciples continued the cosmic stance of R. Kook's circle. In their view, the distinction between Israel and the nations is essential and substantial. R. Tzvi Yehuda, as noted, argued that Israel and the seven nations reflect different stages in the scale of reality. R. Kook and his disciple R. Harlap[71] had excelled at formulating this approach, which rests on a demonic perception of these nations. The halakhic "compromise" retains this metaphysical distinction.

A DISCOURSE OF RIGHTS

Many have relied on Rashi's exegesis of the first verse of the Bible, where he explained the cosmogonic opening of the Torah by reference to the Jewish people's right to their land. Since God as Creator owns all the lands in the universe, the divine decision to grant the Land of Canaan to the Jewish people is a moral decision. R. Judah Leib Maimon (Fishman), a prominent leader of religious Zionism, tried to find additional dimensions of the Jewish people's moral claim to their land. He found the theological argument insufficient, and his extensive aggadic erudition helped him to find a moral-historical argument as well. R. Maimon relied on a tradition in *Sefer haYovlim* (the *Book of Jubilees*) to argue that the Land of Canaan had been meant *ab initio* for the people of Israel, and Canaan took it by force.[72] "And Canaan saw that the land of Lebanon up to the brook of Egypt was excellent, and did not go to the land that was its heritage, westward from the sea" (*Jub.* 10:41). Despite the rebuke of his father, Ham, and of his brothers, Kush and Egypt, Canaan would not relax his hold on the land, and the *Book of Jubilees* presents his destruction as a prophecy of his father and his brothers, "because through the sword you have gained hold, and through the sword will your children fall and you will forever be wiped out" (*Jub.* 10:45). R. Maimon also found parallel versions of this tradition in the midrash literature.[73] In his view, "the children of Shem and 'Eber who saw God's hand in this [the fact that the flood did not affect Eretz Israel], chose to come and settle on that land and establish there the center for spreading the faith in the one God."[74] And he summed up: "Hence, this land has been the land of the Hebrews and the center of Shem's children, who are the bearers of pure faith since ancestral times."[75] The presence of the seven nations in Eretz Israel, therefore, results from theft, and this land had been meant from the start for the Jewish people.

A similar approach, though formulated in different terms, appears in the thought of R. Hayyim Tchernowitz (Rav Tsa'ir). Tchernowitz was a rabbi and a Talmud researcher, but his starting point in the discourse of rights about the land was actually national, in a romantic and mystical style.[76] In an article he wrote in 1939, Tchernowitz ascribed to the Bible the approach assuming "a mysterious-spiritual tie between the people and their land."[77] His evidence for a natural link between the people of Israel and their land and for their right to it is twofold:

1. Abraham was promised the land in the covenant, when he was explicitly told that the land would be given to his seed "for ever" (Gen 13:15).

2. Prophecy (at least at the start) emerges in Eretz Israel. Yehuda Halevi's approach in *The Book of the Kuzari* becomes the basis for the nation's right to its land.

The seven nations, then, dwelt in a land that is not natural to them. Rav Tsaʻir relies on the fact that the nations had illegally stolen Eretz Israel from other nations:

> And therefore, because a nation can fully develop its creativity only in its native land, the break-in of strangers into the land was considered a forced entry and a transgression of universal law.... Although the children of Israel conquered the land by sword, in this war they relied on the promise and the mission of the covenant. Furthermore, Jewish tradition, now confirmed by the discoveries of archeological excavations, knew that the Canaanites who had dwelt on the land before the children of Israel had captured it by force from other nations that had dwelt in it previously, and therefore obtained it during Joshua's conquest. Commenting on the verse "and the Avvim who dwelt in Hatserim" (Deut 2:23), Rashi says: "Because the Caphtorim destroyed them and replaced them, you are now allowed to take it from them." That is, because they had gained hold of the land through fraud, not through law and justice.[78]

Tchernowitz, as noted, relies on the discourse of legal rights that follow directly from a people's natural association with their land. He does not resort to the midrashic traditions of R. Maimon because romantic nationalism provides him with an adequate foundation for his claims. He does refer to hermeneutical traditions through Rashi's commentary, but his conceptual foundation is the national discourse. Tchernowitz emphasizes that, although the people of Israel realized their right to their land by way of war, their claim is strictly legal. He uses the halakhic claim that the holiness of the land is acquired by settling it rather than by conquering it by military force.[79] This argument clarifies that the seven nations stole lands that did not belong to them, so that the people of Israel had a national and moral right to wage war against them. Natural law (in the national sense) and international law coalesce in Tchernowitz's discourse.

In the article *"Zo ha-Derekh"* ["This Is the Way"], written in 1929, Tchernowitz enlisted the fact that, the biblical command notwithstanding, Joshua allowed many from these nations to remain in Eretz Israel in order to establish the rights claim: "In the first conquest, many of these nations remained in the land and Joshua did not inherit them."[80] The presence of many from the seven nations in Eretz Israel did not violate the right of the people of Israel to their land. Eretz Israel was ruled by a chosen people, and the ancient world accepted this. Hence, although the number of Jews residing in Eretz Israel is now negligible (about one hundred and fifty thousand), this should not constitute an objection to Jews ruling over their land. Tchernowitz called for mobilizing international recognition ("the League of Nations and America")[81] of the Jewish people's right to their land. The seven nations serve him as the moral basis in positive terms and as evidence for international law in negative terms.

MODERN CANAANITES

This discussion about conceptual aspects of the connection to the local nations would be incomplete without considering the attitude to Canaanism.[82] David Tzvi Pinkas, the minister of transport representing the Mizrahi in the early years of the State of Israel, enacted an ordinance immobilizing private cars on the Sabbath in order to save on fuel. On June 20, 1952, a bomb was planted at his home, but it failed to detonate. Another bomb was planted the next day and caused serious damage to the minister's apartment.[83] Amos Kenan, a writer and columnist who had targeted religious coercion in his writings, was the suspect in these attacks. Kenan belonged to the "Canaanites" group. The contemporary discourse in the press reflected different attitudes toward the seven nations, and I discuss several of its aspects below.

Shlomo Zalman Shragai, an eminent ideologue of HaPoʻel HaMizrahi, explained the attack as a struggle unfolding at the classic theological level: heresy versus faith. The struggle over religious coercion turned into the struggle of idolatry versus monotheism, Canaanism versus Judaism. But Shragai held that Canaanism is merely the inevitable result of the secularism that characterizes public life in the developing State of Israel: secularism engendered Canaanism. Those who struggled against the Sabbath in the name of modernity ultimately led to a struggle against the Sabbath in the name of Canaanism. In an article he devoted to this issue, he wrote:

> The true bomber, the original source of defilement in this bomb, is the atheist who wishes to eradicate the essence of the Sabbath ... who seeks a Sabbath of Gentiles and in his search arrives at a Sabbath of Canaanites, at ... Baal.[84]
>
> Modern freethinking citizens have traced the countenance of this country, which has engendered "Canaanites" in their image. They have created its soul, as it were. And this is its image ... Baal worshippers.[85]

Baal is obviously the central Canaanite god. For Shragai, the danger of modern Canaanism is moral nihilism. He who denies the God of Israel and abolishes the commandment of the Sabbath will eventually abolish the moral commandments as well. Antinomianism leads to moral libertinage. Canaanism follows directly from the secularization process of the young state. In some sense, Canaanism turns into a symbol of secularization.

Shragai entered into a controversy with secular press columnists who expressed concern about the attack and about the sympathy for Kenan among young people present at Kenan's trial. In his view, what required attention was the source of the problem—secularization. Another article that Shragai wrote on the subject ends as follows:

> The abyss that has opened up in light of the bomb thrown at the Sabbath and at ... the government compels all those in whose heart the spark of love for their people, for their land, and for original Jewish culture still burns. All of them should raise their voice in the ancient call: "Put away the strange gods that are among us!"[86]

The ideological and political struggle for the religious status of the young state turned into the theological struggle of the Jewish people against the idolatry that had taken hold in Eretz Israel from antiquity and until the national renaissance. This approach reflects the religious-Zionist reaction to the encounter between radical secularization and the conservative-innovative ideology that seeks to contend with modernity.

Conclusion

The discourse about the seven nations and about their destiny in religious Zionism exposes a built-in apologetic facet. In various ways, most religious-Zionist thinkers replaced the destruction with expulsion or with an even more radically tolerant attitude. The movement's acquaintance with power and belligerence did not change the apologetic orientation on the issue of the seven nations. The example of R. Waldenberg represents an exception. The tolerant attitude that relies on Nahmanides was not part of the repertoire for a classic, positivist halakhist like R. Waldenberg. He accepted unequivocally the stance of the *Sefer haHinukh*, whereby these nations should be destroyed at all times and in all circumstances. But R. Waldenberg was not a member of the Mizrahi, though he strongly identified with religious-Zionist views.

R. Waldenberg's stance also exposes a potential tension between the positions of a conservative halakhist, who relates positively to the foundation of the state as such, and the attitudes of spiritual leaders and men of action such as R. Nussenbaum and R. Tzvi Yehuda Kook, who were aware of the public and moral dimensions involved in the commands to destroy the nations. This tension prevails also among halakhists who accept modernity, such as R. Hirschensohn and Rav Tsa'ir, who assigned great weight to international law and to political recognition by the League of Nations, and among conservative halakhists.

It bears emphasis that the discourse about the seven nations in religious Zionism had a distinctly halakhic dimension. The reference to Nahmanides' glosses on Maimonides' *Book of Commandments* conveys deep seriousness. Both R. Reines and R. Tzvi Yehuda Kook presented an apologetic discourse, confronting the foreign presence in biblical Eretz Israel with tools that are definitely halakhic. The interlocutors they would have wished for were the eastern European rabbis (R. Reines) and the non-Zionist Orthodoxy in Eretz Israel (R. Tzvi Yehuda Kook). The wound of religious Zionism, which opened up with the creation of the movement in eastern Europe, continued to bleed: The most prominent leaders of religious Jewry refused to grant halakhic sanction to the Zionist movement and strongly rejected those who were attracted to it.[87] Due to their apologetic approach, rabbis like Reines and Kook were not ready to focus the discussion on the existence of values that cannot be framed solely within halakhic parameters. The discourse on the borders of Eretz Israel in R. Kook's circle was also committed to reliance on halakhic evidence. This type of thinking is increasingly less frequent among thinkers who operate in the United States, for instance. Among many of them—Rabbis Joseph B. Soloveitchik, Aharon and Moshe Lichtenstein, and others—the discourse on inheriting the land does not address halakhic concerns, and the attitude toward the nations dwelling on the land is derived from halakhic discourse.

Various thinkers subverted the literal biblical command of destroying the seven nations and replaced it with an approach widespread in the sources, whereby a call for peace precedes the war. R. Nussenbaum replaced the command of destruction with expulsion. Methodologically, different thinkers adopted the model of replacing the command with a prohibition.[88]

Notes

* This article has been translated by Batya Stein.

1. b. Sotah 35b. See also t. Sotah 8:7; Sifrei on Deuteronomy 202, 18. Note that, in this article, the term Canaanites refers at times to the seven nations dwelling in Eretz Israel and at times only to the Canaanite nation, a particular one among the seven.

2. b. Git. 45a. See also Mekhilta de-Rashbi, where the reference is extended to include every idolatrous nation and not only these seven. This is also the ruling in texts that enumerate the commandments (Maimonides, The Book of Commandments, Proscriptive Commandments, 51; Sefer haHinukh, commandment 94). The literal reading relates to the seven nations.

3. y. Shev. 6:1 (36c); Lev. Rab. 17:6. See also the wording of Maimonides in the Mishneh Torah, "Laws of Kings" 6:5: "Joshua sent three written messages before he entered the Land of Israel. The first one said 'Whoever wants to flee, flee.' The second one said 'Whoever wants to make peace, make peace.' Then he sent another one that said, 'Whoever wants to make war, make war.'"

4. In this context, note that some halakhic approaches claim that the obligation to eliminate idolatry applies only in Eretz Israel.

5. In formal terms, these approaches could be referred to as gavra (textual) and heftsa (contextual). Nahmanides pins his outlook on a view that has no bearing to this discussion, which identifies wisdom with magic and with astral magic. This view is somewhat tolerant of idolatry in other countries, since it is perceived as a legitimate magic way of drawing down the divine emanation by means of images. By contrast, Eretz Israel spews out idol worshippers.

6. See, for instance, Anita Shapira, *Land and Power: The Zionist Resort to Force 1881–1948*, trans. William Templer (New York: Oxford University Press, 1992).

7. See Dror Greenblum, "From the Bravery of the Spirit to the Sanctification of Power: Power and Bravery in Religious-Zionism 1948–1967" [in Hebrew], (PhD diss., Haifa University, 2009).

8. See Hilda Schatzberger, *Resistance and Tradition in Mandatory Palestine* [in Hebrew] (Ramat-Gan: Bar-Ilan University, 1985).

9. A collection of testimonies on the volunteering of religious soldiers in the Second World War is included in the two volumes of *Be-Hitnadev Am: Religious Volunteers in the Second World War* [in Hebrew], vol. 1, ed. Dov Knohl (Tel Aviv: Moreshet, 1989); vol. 2, ed. Yosef Shapira (Tel Aviv: Moreshet, 1991). On their involvement at the initial stages of the Haganah and the Israel Defense Force (IDF), see Yehiel A. Eliash, *Maʿaseh ha-Ba be-Hazon* (Tel Aviv: Merkaz Elitzur, 1999); Mordechai Friedman, *The Religious Units in the Haganah and the Palmah* [in Hebrew] (Ramat-Gan: Bar-Ilan University 2005). The heroic legacy is also preserved in Dov Knohl, ed., *Siege in the Hills of Hevron*, trans. Isaac Halevy-Levin (Jerusalem: Kfar Etzion Educational Center, 1973), and Yohanan Ben-Yaakov, ed., *Gush Etzion: Fifty Years of Struggle and Endeavor* [in Hebrew] (Kfar Etzion: Field School, 1978).

10. For sources, see Dov Schwartz, *Religious Zionism: History and Ideology*, trans. Batya Stein (Boston: Academic Studies Press, 2009).

11. See Haim Sabato, *Adjusting Sights*, trans. Hillel Halkin (New Milford, CT: Toby Press, 2003); Michael Schonfeld, *Back from Lebanon and Wherever They May Be* [in Hebrew] (Tel Aviv: Miskal, 2007); Asael Lubotsky, *From the Wilderness and Lebanon* [in Hebrew] (Tel Aviv: Miskal, 2008); Yair Ansbacher, *A Shadow of a Bird* [in Hebrew] (Tel Aviv: Miskal, 2009). The novel of Haim Beer, *A Time for Trimming* [in Hebrew] (Tel Aviv: Am Oved, 1987) may be seen as anticipating this genre.

12. On these approaches, see Dov Schwartz, *The Land of Israel in Religious-Zionist Thought* [in Hebrew] (Tel Aviv: Am Oved, 1997).

13. Note that the balance between the anti-Semitic drive for the appearance of Zionism and the symbolic-legacy drive that perceives Eretz Israel in somewhat mystical terms still awaits independent research. See Walter Lacqueur, *A History of Zionism* (London: Tauris Parke, 2003), 589–591.

14. On R. Reines, see also the contribution of Warren Zeev Harvey (Chapter 16) in the present volume [Note of the editors].

15. On Nahmanides and his original contribution to the Jewish reflection on the issues dealt with in this book, see Chapter 7 by Joseph David in the present volume [Note of the editors].

16. See Dov Schwartz, *Faith at the Crossroads: A Theological Profile of Religious-Zionism*, trans. Batya Stein (Leiden: Brill, 2002), 150–151.

17. Schwartz, *Faith at the Crossroads*, 171.

18. Schwartz, *Faith at the Crossroads*, 134–135.

19. This is how R. Tzvi Yehuda Kook refers to him in *Lintivot Israel* (Jerusalem: Hoshen Lev, 1997), 308 ff. See below.

20. Some religious-Zionist rabbis have concluded that, according to Nahmanides, planting trees (on the fifteenth of Shvat, for instance) is in the category of a personal commandment. See, for instance, Yehuda Shaviv, "Planting (2)" [in Hebrew], Circular of Yeshivat Har-Etzion, *Alon Shevut* 122 (January 1988); Elisha Aviner, "Agriculture—Value or Livelihood? Labor vs.

Easy Money" [in Hebrew], *Emunat Itekha*, no. 14, (January–February 1997), www.daat.ac.il/daat/kitveyet/emunat/14/01402.htm. I do not discuss this aspect of Nahmanides' claims here.

21. Maimonides, *The Book of Commandments, with Nahmanides' Glosses*, ed. Hayyim Dov Chavell [in Hebrew] (Jerusalem: Mosad Harav Kook, 1981), 244; Yitzhak Yaakov Reines, *Or Hadash 'al Tzion* [*A New Light on Zion*] [in Hebrew] (Vilnius: Rom, 1902), 17b.

22. In Chavell's edition, "the nations," and so henceforth. The version that R. Reines used did not suggest an association between the nations and idolatry.

23. Maimonides, *The Book of Commandments*, 245; Reines, *Or Hadash 'al Tzion*, 17b. The view that the destruction of the seven nations is not compulsory was not introduced by Nahmanides. Maimonides, as noted, stated in the "Laws of Kings" that the call for peace before waging war is to be issued in a Torah-commanded war as well (see note 2 above), and if the nations have taken upon themselves to abide by the seven Noahide laws, war is avoided. But Nahmanides is often cited because he claims that the settlement of the land is one of the prescribed commandments. See Schwartz, *Land of Israel*, 28; Warren Zeev Harvey, "Rabbi Reines on the Commandment to Dwell in Eretz Israel," in *The Land of Israel in 20th Century Jewish Thought*, ed. Aviezer Ravitzky (Jerusalem: Yad Yitzhak Ben Zvi, 2004), 303–314. The above noted options regarding the seven nations were destruction, expulsion, and penitence. Nahmanides added peace ("if they want to make peace, we will make peace"). Possibly, the distinction between penitence and peace, if it exists, hinges on abandoning idolatry or also on adopting the seven Noahide laws.

24. Reines, *Or Hadash 'al Tzion*, 18a.

25. Reines, *Or Hadash 'al Tzion*, 18b.

26. Reines, *Or Hadash 'al Tzion*, 18b. See also Aviezer Ravitzky, *Messianism, Zionism, and Jewish Religious Radicalism*, trans. Michael Swirsky and Jonathan Chipman (Chicago: University of Chicago Press, 1996), 218–219.

27. Reines, *Or Hadash 'al Tzion*, 19a.

28. The article appeared in *Ha-Torah ve-ha-Medinah* 7–8 (1955–1956): 96–120. A brief summary of the article appeared in Uri Dassberg and Assaf Cohen, "Jewish-Gentile Relationships: A Bibliographical Survey" [in Hebrew], in *Benei Israel u-Benei Noah* [*Jews and Aliens*], ed. Ben-Zion Krieger and Uri Dassberg (Elkana: Orot Israel, 1988), 96.

29. R. Israeli noted that, in any event, this prohibition does not presently apply for various reasons (the jubilee year is no longer customary, and the definition of "the Jews are powerful" has not been realized). Eliav Schochetman qualified this approach on several grounds and argued that "the prohibition of 'they will not dwell in your land' has not been rescinded at all, yet the current reality does not enable its fulfillment." See Eliav Schochetman, *And He Confirmed It for Jacob as a Law* [in Hebrew] (Jerusalem: n.p. 1995), 18. On another perspective on the attitude to Gentiles, see Jacob Blidstein, "The State of Israel in the Halakic Thought of R. Shaul Israeli" [in Hebrew], in *On Both Sides of the Bridge: Religion and State in the Early Years of Israel*, ed. Mordechai Bar-On and Zvi Tsameret (Jerusalem: Yad Yitzhak Ben-Zvi, 2002), 356–358.

30. Citing R. Shlomo b. Simeon Duran. See Shaul Israeli, *Eretz Hemdah* [in Hebrew] (Jerusalem: Mosad Harav Kook, 1999), 17.

31. See above.

32. Kook, *Lintivot Israel*, 1:222.

33. Kook, *Lintivot Israel*, 3:89.

34. Kook, *Lintivot Israel*, 3:308.

35. Tzvi Yehuda Kook, *Land of the Hart* [in Hebrew], ed. Harel Cohen (Beth El: Netivei Or, 2003), 24–25.

36. Shlomo Aviner, ed. *Conversations with R. Zvi Yehuda* [in Hebrew] (Beth-El: Sifriyat Havah, 2008), 170.

37. According to the *mamlakhti* approach, the State of Israel is a holy entity. Consequently, its government and institutions are also endowed with spiritual and religious value.

38. Shlomo Aviner, *East of Beth-El: Halakhic and Eretz Israeli Inquiries* [in Hebrew] (Jerusalem: n.p., 1990), 202.

39. Aviner, *East of Beth-El*, 244. Elsewhere, R. Aviner wonders why Eretz Israel was given to the seven nations before it was given to the people of Israel. His answer is unequivocal: "[Eretz Israel] had always been meant for us, and the Canaanites were then its keepers." See *be-Ahavah u-be-Emunah* (Beth-El: Sifriyat Havah, 2000), 244. The Jewish people, then, had forever been the legal rulers in Eretz Israel, even if other nations dwelt in it at times.

40. See 1 Kgs 8:65; 2 Chr 7:8.

41. Yitzhak Nussenbaum, *Sermons for the Sabbaths and the Festivals* [in Hebrew] (Vilnius: L. Eppel, 1908), 219–220.

42. Nussenbaum, *Sermons for the Sabbaths*, 222.

43. Hayyim Hirschensohn, *Responsa Malki ba-Kodesh* [in Hebrew], vol. 1, ed. David Zohar (Jerusalem: Shalom Hartman Institute, 2006), 144. The book was originally published in 1929.

44. Hayyim Hirschensohn, *These Are the Words of the Covenant* [in Hebrew], vol. 1 (Jerusalem: Ha-Ivri, 1926), 70–71. Cited in David Zohar, *Jewish Commitment in a Modern World: R. Hayyim Hirschensohn and His Attitude to Modernity* [in Hebrew] (Jerusalem and Ramat-Gan: Shalom Hartman Institute and Bar-Ilan University, 2003), 234.

45. See Eliezer Schweid, *Democracy and Halakhah: Studies in the Thought of R. Hayyim Hirschensohn* [in Hebrew], 2nd ed. (Jerusalem: Magnes Press, 1998), 34. On the influence of international law on R. Herzog's attitude to Gentiles, see Yosef Ahituv, "Halakhic Vacillations of the Chief Rabbi Isaac Halevi Herzog during the Early Years of the State of Israel" [in Hebrew], in *The Challenge of Independence: Ideological and Cultural Aspects of Israel's First Decade*, ed. Mordechai Bar-On (Jerusalem: Yad Yitzhak Ben-Zvi, 1999), 206–207.

46. In the original, *anshei middot*, according to Numbers 13:32. The term *middah* in the denotation of virtue does not appear in the Bible, and is first used in Tannaitic literature.

47. Yitzhak Nussenbaum, *Ancient Heritage* [*Kiniyanei Kedem*] [in Hebrew] (Warsaw: Grafia, 1931), 89.

48. Yitzhak Nussenbaum, "At Times of Conquest, of Defense, and of Peace" [in Hebrew], in *Selected Writings* (Tel Aviv: Levin Epstein, 1948), 89.

49. Nussenbaum, "Times of Conquest, of Defense, and of Peace," 244–245.

50. A minimal requirement from a resident stranger (according to certain views) is to abandon idolatry.

51. Zeev Gold, *Nivei Zahav* [*Golden Sayings*] [in Hebrew] (Jerusalem: Mosad Ha-Rav Kook, 1949), 509.

52. Gold, *Nivei Zahav*, 509–510.

53. Ravitzky, *Religious Radicalism*, 126–127; Dov Schwartz, *Challenge and Crisis in Rabbi Kook's Circle* [in Hebrew] (Tel Aviv: Am Oved, 2001), ch. 1.

54. Gold, *Golden Sayings*, according to *Mekhilta de R. Ishmael*, Bo, Masekhta de-Pisha 18, s.v. "*ve-hayah*"; *Sifrei on Deuteronomy*, 37; *Lev. Rab.* 17: 6, and more. See also Chapter 4 by Menahem Kister in the present volume [Note of the editors].

55. Simon Federbusch, *The Torah and Kingdom: The State in Judaism* [in Hebrew] (Jerusalem: Mosad Ha-Rav Kook, 1973), 205.

56. Federbusch, *Torah and Kingdom*, 206.

57. Federbusch, *Torah and Kingdom*, 218–219.

58. Federbusch, *Torah and Kingdom*, 219; *Tanh*. 96.

59. *m. Sotah* 8:7; *b. Sotah* 44b.

60. Eliezer Waldenberg, *Sefer Hilkhot Medinah* [in Hebrew], (Jerusalem: Itah, 1952), 2:104–105. The book was reprinted in 2007, thirty days after R. Waldenberg's death. Its reappearance evoked a storm in *Haredi* circles. On R. Waldenberg's views, see Asher Cohen, *The Prayer Shawl and the Flag: Religious-Zionism and the Vision of a Torah State in Israel's Early Years* [in Hebrew] (Jerusalem: Yad Yitzhak Ben Zvi, 1998), 73–80; Yosef Ahituv, "From Bible to Sword: The Torah Image of the Israel Defense Forces during Israel's Early Years" [in Hebrew], in *On Both Sides of the Bridge: Religion and State in the Early Years of Israel*, ed. Mordechai Bar-On and Zvi Tsameret (Jerusalem: Yad Yitzhak Ben-Zvi, 2002), 425–432.

61. Hayyim Dov Chavell, ed., *Sefer haHinukh* [in Hebrew], no. 423 (Jerusalem: Mosad Ha-Rav Kook, 1974), p. 540.

62. *Sefer haHinukh*, 529, p. 547.

63. Waldenberg, *Sefer Hilkhot Medinah*, 105.

64. Waldenberg, *Sefer Hilkhot Medinah*, 107.

65. Shlomo Goren, "The Holy Land and Saving Human Life" [in Hebrew], *Tehumin* 15 (1995): 15.

66. *'Olat ha-Reayah* [prayer book with the *Olat haReayah*, commentary by R. Abraham Yitzhak Hacohen Kook; in Hebrew], vol. 1 (Jerusalem: Mosad Ha-Rav Kook, 1963), 40.

67. *'Olat ha-Reayah*, vol. 2, 83.

68. Abraham Hacohen Kook, *Lights* [in Hebrew] (Jerusalem: Mosad Ha-Rav Kook, 1963), 14 in reference to *Shmona Qevatzim*, 6, 123.

69. Federbusch, *Torah and Kingdom*, 219.

70. Federbusch, *Torah and Kingdom*, 242.

71. See Schwartz, *Challenge and Crisis*, ch. 11.

72. On this tradition in the *Book of Jubilees*, see Chapter 4 by Menahem Kister in the present volume [Note of the editors].

73. For instance *Sifra*, Qedoshim, parashah 10, 15, 17; *Yalkut Shimoni*, Qedoshim, 626. In these sources, the Canaanites are called "the keepers of the place" until the Jewish people's settlement.

74. Judah Leib Hacohen Maimon, *Religious-Zionism and Its Development: Chapters in the History of the People of Israel and the Land of Israel* [in Hebrew] (Jerusalem: WZO, 1937), 15. On R. Maimon's connection to aggada on the issue of Eretz Israel and the right of the Jewish people to it, see Schwartz, *Land of Israel*, ch. 9.

75. Maimon, *Religious-Zionism and Its Development*, 16.

76. This type of nationalism took shape in the thought of Herder, Fichte, and Savigny. See, for instance, J. L. Talmon, *The Origins of Totalitarian Democracy* (London: Secker and Warburg, 1952), 38–42. On this approach in Tchernowitz's thought, see Schwartz, *Land of Israel*, 38.

77. Rav Tsa'ir, *At the Gates of Zion: Collected Articles on Eretz Israel and Zionism* [in Hebrew] (New York: Schulzinger, 1937), 212.

78. Rav Tsa'ir, *At the Gates of Zion*, 212–213.

79. "Although they did have a legal right to the land, since in Joshua's time they resorted to force and the sword, the land could not absorb the holiness of its mission forever. Only at the

beginning of the Second Temple era, in Cyrus' times, when they returned to the deserted land and did not need to conquer it by force, the land became holy forever after" (Rav Tsaʻir, *At the Gates of Zion*, 213). Tchernowitz emphasized the legitimacy of settlement, an approach consistent with his support for political Zionism. This pattern of thought recurs in the philosophy of R. Joseph B. Soloveitchik. See Schwartz, *Land of Israel*, 191. See also Abraham Hacohen Kook, *Epistles* [in Hebrew], vol. 4 (Jerusalem: Mosad Ha-Rav Kook, 1961), 57.

80. Rav Tsaʻir, *At the Gates of Zion*, 232.

81. Rav Tsaʻir, *At the Gates of Zion*, 242. On the international legal authority, see Tsaʻir, *At the Gates of Zion*, 261.

82. On Canaanism, see David Ohana's article in the present volume [Note of the editors].

83. About two months later, Pinkas suffered a heart attack and died, and some thought this was a result of the incident. Columnist Yonah Cohen, for instance, wrote: "When he [Pinkas] was Minister of Transport and at the height of his powers, wicked men came to hurt him and put out the spark of his life." See Yonah Cohen, *"The Ledger Lies Open and the Hand Writes": Fifty Years of Journalism 1938-1988* [in Hebrew] (Jerusalem: Moreshet, 1995), 211.

84. Shlomo Zalman Shragai, *An Hour and an Eternity: Inquiries into Issues of Religion, Zionism, and the State* [in Hebrew] (Jerusalem: Mosad Ha-Rav Kook, 1960), 263 (first published in *Ha-Tsofeh*, 22 August 1952). Shragai called the Canaanites "new Baal worshippers" and "Baal servants."

85. Shragai, *An Hour and an Eternity*, 269.

86. Shragai, *An Hour and an Eternity*, 277. According to Gen 35:2, Josh 24:23, and elsewhere.

87. See Schwartz, *Faith at the Crossroads*, 137–140.

88. For a similar move in rabbinic literature concerning objects that are defined as *herem*, see Chapter 3 by Ishay Rosen-Zvi in the present volume [Note of the editors].

Bibliography

Ahituv, Yosef. "From Bible to Sword: The Torah Image of the Israel Defense Forces during Israel's Early Years" [in Hebrew]. In *On Both Sides of the Bridge: Religion and State in the Early Years of Israel*, edited by Mordechai Bar-On and Zvi Tsameret, 425–432. Jerusalem: Yad Yitzhak Ben-Zvi, 2002.

——. "Halakhic Vacillations of the Chief Rabbi Isaac Halevi Herzog during the Early Years of the State of Israel" [in Hebrew], in *The Challenge of Independence: Ideological and Cultural Aspects of Israel's First Decade*, edited by Mordechai Bar-On, 206–207. Jerusalem: Yad Yitzhak Ben-Zvi, 1999.

Ansbacher, Yaʼir. *A Shadow of a Bird* [in Hebrew]. Tel Aviv: Miskal, 2009.

Aviner, Elisha. "Agriculture—Value or Livelihood? Labor vs. Easy Money" [in Hebrew], *Emunat Itekha*, no. 14, January–February 1997, 7–10.

Aviner, Shlomo, ed. *Conversations with R. Zvi Yehuda* [in Hebrew]. Beth-El: Sifriyat Havah, 2008.

——. *Be-Ahavah u-be-Emunah*. Beth-El: Sifriyat Havah, 2000.

——. *East of Beth-El: Halakhic and Eretz Israeli Inquiries* [in Hebrew]. Jerusalem: n.p., 1990.

Beʼer, Haim. *A Time for Trimming* [in Hebrew]. Tel Aviv: Am Oved, 1987.

Ben-Yaakov, Yohanan, ed. *Gush Etzion: Fifty Years of Struggle and Endeavour* [in Hebrew]. Kfar Etzion: Field School, 1978.

Blidstein, Jacob. "The State of Israel in the Halakhic Thought of R. Shaul Israeli" [in Hebrew]. In *On Both Sides of the Bridge: Religion and State in the Early Years of Israel*, edited by Mordechai Bar-On and Zvi Tsameret, 356–358. Jerusalem: Yad Yitzhak Ben-Zvi, 2002.

Chavell, Hayyim Dov, ed., *Sefer haHinukh* [in Hebrew]. Jerusalem: Mosad Ha-Rav Kook, 1974.

Cohen, Asher. *The Prayer Shawl and the Flag: Religious-Zionism and the Vision of a Torah State in Israel's Early Years* [in Hebrew]. Jerusalem: Yad Yitzhak Ben Zvi, 1998.

Cohen, Yonah. *"The Ledger Lies Open and the Hand Writes": Fifty Years of Journalism 1938–1988* [in Hebrew]. Jerusalem: Moreshet, 1995.

Dassberg, Uri, and Assaf Cohen. "Jewish-Gentile Relationships: A Bibliographical Survey" [in Hebrew]. In *Benei Israel u-Benei Noah* [*Jews and Aliens*], edited by Ben-Zion Krieger and Uri Dassberg. Elkana: Orot Israel, 1988.

Eliash, Yehiel A. *Ma'aseh ha-Ba be-Hazon*. Tel Aviv: Merkaz Elitzur, 1999.

Federbusch, Simon. *The Torah and Kingdom: The State in Judaism* [in Hebrew]. Jerusalem: Mosad Ha-Rav Kook, 1973.

Friedman, Mordechai. *The Religious Units in the Haganah and the Palmah* [in Hebrew]. Ramat-Gan: Bar-Ilan University, 2005.

Gold, Zeev. *Nivei Zahav* [*Golden Sayings*; in Hebrew]. Jerusalem: Mosad Ha-Rav Kook, 1949.

Goren, Shlomo. "The Holy Land and Saving Human Life" [in Hebrew]. *Tehumin* 15 (1995): 11–22.

Harvey, Warren Zev. "Rabbi Reines on the Commandment to Dwell in Eretz Israel." In *The Land of Israel in 20th Century Jewish Thought* [in Hebrew], edited by Aviezer Ravitzky, 303–314. Jerusalem: Yad Yitzhak Ben Zvi, 2004.

Hirschensohn, Hayyim. *These Are the Words of the Covenant* [in Hebrew]. Vol. 1. Jerusalem: Ha-Ivri, 1926.

——. *Responsa Malki ba-Kodesh* [in Hebrew]. Vol. 1. Edited by David Zohar. Jerusalem: Shalom Hartman Institute, [1906] 2006.

Israeli, Shaul. *Eretz Hemdah* [in Hebrew]. Jerusalem: Mosad Harav Kook, 1999.

——. "The Status of the Gentile in Israel in the Light of the Torah." *Ha-Torah ve-ha-Medinah* 7–8 (1955–1956): 96–120.

Knohl, Dov, ed. *Be-Hitnadev Am: Religious Volunteers in the Second World War* [in Hebrew]. Vol. 1. Tel Aviv: Moreshet, 1989.

——, ed. *Siege in the Hills of Hevron*. Translated by Isaac Halevy-Levin. Jerusalem: Kfar Etzion Educational Centre, 1973.

Kook, Abraham Hacohen. *Lights* [in Hebrew]. Jerusalem: Mosad Ha-Rav Kook, 1963.

——. *Epistles* [in Hebrew]. Vol. 4. Jerusalem: Mosad Ha-Rav Kook, 1961.

Kook, Tzvi Yehuda. *Land of the Hart* [in Hebrew]. Edited by Zalman Baruch Melamed. Beth El: Netivei Or, 2003.

——. *Lintivot Israel*. Jerusalem: Hoshen Lev, [1966] 1997.

Lacqueur, Walter. *A History of Zionism*. London: Tauris Parke, 2003.

Lubotsky, Asael. *From the Wilderness and Lebanon* [in Hebrew]. Tel Aviv: Miskal, 2008.

Maimon, Judah Leib Hacohen. *Religious-Zionism and Its Development: Chapters in the History of the People of Israel and the Land of Israel* [in Hebrew]. Jerusalem: WZO, 1937.

Maimonides, *The Book of Commandments, with Nahmanides' Glosses.* Edited by Hayyim Dov Chavell [in Hebrew]. Jerusalem: Mosad Harav Kook, 1981.

Nussenbaum, Yitzhak. "At Times of Conquest, of Defense, and of Peace" [in Hebrew]. In *Selected Writings,* 244–248. Tel Aviv: Levin Epstein, 1948.

———. *Ancient Heritage* [*Kiniyanei Kedem;* in Hebrew]. Warsaw: Grafia, 1931.

———. *Sermons for the Sabbaths and the Festivals* [in Hebrew]. Vilnius: L. Eppel, 1908.

Olat ha-Reayah. [Prayer book with the *Olat haReayah,* commentary by R. Abraham Yitzhak Hacohen Kook; in Hebrew]. Vol. 1. Jerusalem: Mosad Ha-Rav Kook, 1963.

Ravitzky, Aviezer. *Messianism, Zionism, and Jewish Religious Radicalism.* Translated by Michael Swirsky and Jonathan Chipman. Chicago: University of Chicago Press, 1996.

Reines, Yitzhak Yaakov. *Or Hadash 'al Tzion* [A New Light on Zion; in Hebrew]. Vilnius: Rom, 1902.

Sabato, Haim. *Adjusting Sights.* Translated by Hillel Halkin. New Milford, CT: Toby Press, 2003.

Schatzberger, Hilda. *Resistance and Tradition in Mandatory Palestine* [in Hebrew]. Ramat-Gan: Bar-Ilan University, 1985.

Schochetman, Eliav. *And He Confirmed It for Jacob as a Law* [in Hebrew]. Jerusalem: n.p. 1995.

Schonfeld, Michael. *Back from Lebanon and Wherever They May Be* [in Hebrew]. Tel Aviv: Miskal, 2007.

Schwartz, Dov. *Religious Zionism: History and Ideology.* Translated by Batya Stein. Boston: Academic Studies Press, 2009.

———. *Challenge and Crisis in Rabbi Kook's Circle* [in Hebrew]. Tel Aviv: Am Oved, 2001.

———. *Faith at the Crossroads: A Theological Profile of Religious-Zionism.* Translated by Batya Stein. Leiden: Brill, 2001.

———. *The Land of Israel in Religious-Zionist Thought* [in Hebrew]. Tel Aviv: Am Oved, 1997.

Schweid, Eliezer. *Democracy and Halakhah: Studies in the Thought of R. Hayyim Hirschensohn* [in Hebrew]. 2nd ed. Jerusalem: Magnes Press, 1998.

Shapira, Anita. *Land and Power: The Zionist Resort to Force 1881–1948.* Translated by William Templer. New York: Oxford University Press, 1992.

Shapira, Yosef, ed. *Be-Hitnadev Am: Religious Volunteers in the Second World War* [in Hebrew]. Vol. 2. Tel Aviv: Moreshet, 1991.

Shaviv, Yehuda. "Planting (2)" [in Hebrew]. Circular of Yeshivat Har-Etzion, *Alon Shevut* 122 (January 1988).

Shragai, Shlomo Zalman. *An Hour and an Eternity: Inquiries into Issues of Religion, Zionism, and the State* [in Hebrew]. Jerusalem: Mosad Ha-Rav Kook, 1960. First published in *Ha-Tsofeh,* August 22, 1952.

Talmon, J. L. *The Origins of Totalitarian Democracy.* London: Secker and Warburg, 1952.

Rav Tsa'ir, *At the Gates of Zion: Collected Articles on Eretz Israel and Zionism* [in Hebrew]. New York: Schulzinger, 1937.

Waldenberg, Eliezer. *Sefer Hilkhot Medinah* [in Hebrew]. Vol. 2. Jerusalem: Itah, 1952.

Zohar, David. *Jewish Commitment in a Modern World: R. Hayyim Hirschensohn and His Attitude to Modernity* [in Hebrew]. Jerusalem and Ramat-Gan: Shalom Hartman Institute and Bar-Ilan University, 2003.

16

Rabbi Reines on the Conquest of
Canaan and Zionism

Warren Zeev Harvey

In our post-post-modern era, we all know very well that there is no objective history, and what we call "history" depends on who tells the story. Everyone has his or her narrative. Many sundry factors are responsible for determining which one eventually becomes most popular, most accepted, most respectable, or—as the scholars say—"canonic."

What really happened during the Israeli War of Independence? We Israelis have a noble and heartwarming narrative. The Palestinian Arabs, however, have a completely different one that flatly contradicts ours. Each side tries hard to get its narrative accepted by as many people as possible.

What really happened during the American Revolution? Bred and born in New York, I learned the American narrative with my ABCs and never realized there was another one until, as a young man, I moved to Montreal to take up a teaching position at McGill University. There I was exposed to the British-Canadian narrative. The British-Canadian narrative of the Colonies' Revolt differs from the American narrative of the American Revolution no less than the Palestinian narrative of *al-nakbah* differs from the Israeli narrative of *milhemet ha-komemiyyut.*

What about the ancient conquest of Canaan by the Israelite tribes? What really happened *then*? Well, we all are familiar with the Israelite narrative as recorded in the most widely read book of all, the Bible, but what about the Canaanite narrative? David Hartman wrote so well:

> It is crucial to understand that in the Bible there is only one people's story. Where in the Book of Joshua do we find how the Canaanites or the Jebusites felt when the Children of Israel came into the Land? Who ever spoke about what it meant to be a Canaanite?[1]

What *was* the Canaanite narrative? We don't have their story, their narrative. Our understanding of the Israelite conquest of Canaan is thus unavoidably one-sided and one-dimensional.

Given its unilateral nature, the biblical narrative of the conquest of Canaan is potentially dangerous if we try to use it as a model for our own Zionism. If we do so, we risk turning our Zionism into a holy militarism that disregards the rights of others and sanctifies the blessing of our father Isaac, "And by the sword shall you live" (Gen 27:40). In other words, we risk turning our Zionism into an ideology stereotypical of the children of Esau, that is, something down-right un-Jewish. Critics of Israel even now sometimes turn to us with words to the effect: "What you people are doing to the Palestinians is what you did to the Canaanites!"[2]

The danger that the model of the conquest of Canaan poses to our Jewish values was absolutely clear to the great founders of religious Zionism, Rabbi Samuel Mohilever (1824–1898) and Rabbi Isaac Jacob Reines (1839–1915), although admittedly it may not be so clear to many today who deem themselves their spiritual descendants.

In this chapter, I should like to examine briefly Rabbi Reines's views on Zionism, the commandment to dwell in the land of Israel, and the Canaanites. We shall see how, in setting down the foundations of religious Zionism, Reines worked hard to sever all connections between modern political Zionism and the ancient Israelites' war of conquest against the Canaanites. Zionism, for him, was all about fulfilling the grand divine commandment of settling the land of Israel, but he insisted that this precious commandment must never be interpreted through the model of the Israelite war on Canaan.

Reines was able to sever all connections between modern political Zionism and the ancient Israelite conquest of Canaan because he was both a wise political leader and a magisterial halakhist. His Zionism was built on pragmatic political wisdom and on hard-nosed halakhah, not on European nationalism—that is, not on the ideology of the children of Esau. Halakhah is by its nature anti-fundamentalist. For example, the text says "an eye for an eye" (Exod 21:24 and parallels), but the halakhah says: It is written "eye" but it doesn't mean that at all, it means monetary compensation (*b. B. Qam.* 84a). Reines's argument on behalf of Zionism begins with halakhah. His main discussion of the subject is found in his 1901 classic, *Or Hadash 'al Tzion* (A New Light on Zion).[3]

Medieval Background

The primary medieval halakhic source regarding the commandment to live in the land of Israel was the preeminent thirteenth-century Catalonian scholar, Rabbi Moses ben Nahman, known as Nahmanides or, by acronym, Ramban.[4] In his commentary on Maimonides' *Book of the Commandments*, he added an appendix, "Commandments That the Master Forgot to List." The fourth positive commandment that Maimonides "forgot" is the commandment to live in the land of Israel. Nahmanides defined it as follows:

> We were commanded to inherit the Land...and not to abandon it into the hands of other nations or to let it lay desolate.... "And you shall drive out the inhabitants of the Land and dwell therein, for unto you have I given the Land to possess it, and you shall settle the Land" [Num 33:53–54; cf. v. 52].... Thus, we have been commanded concerning the conquest [of the Land] throughout all generations.... "Dwelling in the Land of Israel is equal to all the commandments" [*Sifre Deuteronomy*, 80].[5]

Nahmanides thus rules explicitly that there is a commandment to inherit the land, which is a commandment of conquest, a commandment of war, and it pertains in every generation, including today, right now. God allotted us the land and commanded us to possess it, which means to drive out all its alien inhabitants; and this is not only a commandment binding on all Jews today, but it is equal to all the other commandments! It sounds as if this might mean that the most important divine commandment in the Bible is to drive the Palestinians out of the land!

Fortunately, this commandment was interpreted by the renowned fourteenth-century Catalonian—and later Algerian—rabbinic authority, Rabbi Isaac ben Sheshet, known by acronym as Ribash, who was a student of students of Nahmanides. Ribash redefined Nahmanides commandment as follows:

> There is no doubt that immigration [i.e., "going up," *ha-ʿaliyyah*] to the Land of Israel is a commandment [in all times]. [However, those who returned from the Babylonian Captivity did so] only by the license of Cyrus [Ezra 1:1–4]. So too now, there obtains one of the Three Oaths that the Holy One, blessed be He, adjured Israel, "not to storm the wall" [literally, not to "go up" on the wall, *she-lo yaʿalu ba-homah*] [*b. Ketub.* 111a; cf. *Song Rab.* 2:7].[6]

According to Ribash, following Nahmanides, there is a commandment of ʿaliyyah, that is, "going up" or immigrating to the land of Israel, and it is binding on every Jew today as always. However, Ribash explains, this commandment may no longer be fulfilled by war or violence because of the oath that God adjured the Jewish people after the destruction of the First Temple "not to storm the wall," that is, not to try to conquer the land by force (cf. Joel 2:7). This oath is one of the Three Oaths (or Six Oaths) that, according to the rabbinic exposition, are encrypted poetically in the recurring verse in Song of Songs: "I adjure you, O daughters of Jerusalem, by the gazelles, and by the hinds of the field, that you awaken not, nor stir up love, until it please" (2:7, 3:5, cf. 8:4). Thus, the return to Zion after the Babylonian Captivity and the building of the Second Temple were not achieved by means of war or violence but peacefully by means of the license duly granted by King Cyrus of Persia.

The antimilitaristic sentiment reflected in Ribash's amendment of Nahmanides' halakhic position is found two generations earlier in a comment by Rabbi Bahya ben Asher of Saragossa, a student of a student of Nahmanides. According to an old rabbinic exegesis of Genesis 32:8–15, Jacob prepared himself for three things before his encounter with Esau: "Prayer, gifts, war."[7] Nahmanides, in his *Commentary on Genesis*, added that Jacob's behavior is a model for his descendants in their own encounters with the children of Esau in future generations: "And it is meet for us to hold fast to the ways of Jacob, who prepared himself for three things."[8] Bahya, commenting on this same biblical text, repeats Nahmanides' moral but substantially revises it: "So too we must follow the ways of the Patriarchs and prepare ourselves to greet [the children of Esau] with gifts and a soft tongue, and with prayer before God, may He be exalted, but war is impossible, as it is said, 'I adjure you, O daughters of Jerusalem,' etc. He adjured them not to provoke war with the nations."[9] Bahya amended Nahmanides' homily, and Ribash subsequently amended his law. Both modified Nahmanides on the basis of the talmudic teaching that God adjured Israel not to conquer the land by force. Bahya's opinion regarding Jacob's three preparations appears to be part of his general moralizing attitude. As Menachem Kellner has shown, Bahya was conflicted about the unjust violence (*hamas*) involved in the conquest of Canaan.[10] It seems that the moral problem of the conquest of Canaan was discussed in the Aragonite and Catalonian talmudic academies in the thirteenth and fourteenth centuries by rabbis who grew up on the teachings of Nahmanides. These rabbis made a moralizing use of the talmudic exposition of Song of Songs, according to which God adjured Israel not to storm the wall.

Rabbi Mohilever's Position

Writing in 1890, Rabbi Samuel Mohilever, a founder of the Hibbat Zion movement and an early supporter of Theodor Herzl's political Zionism, resourcefully applied the ruling of Ribash to the modern efforts to settle the land of Israel:

> Now, with regard to what Nahmanides wrote, that there is a commandment for all generations, even in our time, to inherit the Land and dwell therein, his intention is clearly that the inheritance is not by means of war; for we are neither able nor permitted to wage war in our time, as has been explained in *Ketubot* 111a. For the Holy One, blessed be He, adjured us not to rebel against the nations..., and not to "storm the wall." Rashi interpreted this expression as meaning "with a strong hand" [Commentary on *Ketubot, ad loc.*]. Therefore, the positive commandment of inheritance, which obtains also in our day, is only that we endeavor to purchase the Land from its owners.

With every piece of land that we purchase, we fulfill the commandment of inheritance....However, by merely purchasing land we have not fulfilled the commandment in a perfect way, for this commandment includes two things: "And you shall *inherit* the Land and *dwell* therein" [Num 33:53].[11]

Here we see the principled position of the early religious Zionists, based on Nahmanides and Ribash: It is a divine commandment to settle the land, but the settlement must be done only by peaceful means, such as purchasing land, for God has forbidden conquest of the land "with a strong hand."

Rabbi Reines's Analysis

Rabbi Reines, the founder in 1902 of Mizrahi, the religious faction of Herzl's Zionist movement, developed in detail the halakhic position of Rabbi Mohilever. He began by examining the prooftext cited by Nahmanides, "And you shall inherit the Land and dwell therein" [Num 33:53]. On the face of it, he reasoned, this verse seems to comprise two distinct commandments: the first, to inherit, conquer, or seize the land, which one could do without thereupon dwelling in it; the second, to dwell in the land, which one could do without having conquered it.[12] Reines explains that in fact there is only one commandment: to dwell in the land. Dwelling in the land is the essence and goal of the commandment, while conquering the land is merely a means to that end. It is the nature of means that they change from time to time and from situation to situation: In the days of Joshua and David, the accepted means of inheriting the land was war, but today only peaceful means are acceptable. Thus, the essence and goal of the commandment is dwelling in the land, which includes "the required work of an inhabited land, like sowing, planting, and the like," and it is dwelling in the land that is, according to the rabbis, "equal to all the other commandments."[13]

Nahmanides, continues Rabbi Reines, "beyond all doubt" could *not* have meant that there is today a commandment to conquer the land by war, for "have not the children of Israel been effectively adjured...to keep far away from any plots of rebellion or treachery?" Rather, he concludes, Nahmanides evidently meant that the commandment today to settle the land is to be fulfilled by means of "voluntary acquisition" (*ha-lekihah ha-retzonit*).[14] Like Ribash and Rabbi Mohilever, Reines avails himself of the talmudic teaching about the oath "not to storm the wall" in order to turn Nahmanides' potentially militant commandment into a thoroughly peaceful one.

In order to prove that from a halakhic point of view voluntary acquisition is equal to military conquest as a means of "inheriting the land," Rabbi Reines analyzes two discussions in the Jerusalem Talmud: *Mo'ed Qatan* 2:4, 81b (one may buy houses in the land of Israel from a non-Jew on the Sabbath) and

Shabbat 1:8, 4a–b (Joshua's conquest of Jericho defers the Sabbath). From the analogy between these two texts, Reines concludes that from a halakhic point of view there is no essential difference between conquering the land by force or acquiring it by voluntary means: The only practical difference is that war was a legitimate means in the past, but today only peaceful means are permitted.[15]

According to Rabbi Reines's exposition, God may thus be said to have had an ethical motivation when He adjured Israel to "awaken not, nor stir up love, until it please." He explains further: God understood the great passion (*teshukah*) Israel had for the land of Israel and knew they would strive to return to the land, therefore He adjured them "not to hurry the end [of the Exile] by means that are forbidden to enter into the assembly of Israel."[16] The divine adjuration was all about *means*. Recognizing Israel's mighty and abundant love for their land, God adjured them in the Exile to restrain themselves and never to use improper means in seeking to return to it. Love does not justify violence.

The oath "not to storm the wall" is thus in the eyes of Rabbi Reines not merely a technical legal clause or a quaint homily, but a poetic expression of an ethical teaching. Reines's comments about the divine adjuration should probably be understood against the background of his views on the prophetic teachings concerning war and peace. He writes, for example:

> Our holy visionaries set down for us the highest end: "Nation shall not lift up sword against nation" [Isa 2:4], "the wolf shall dwell with the lamb" [Isa 11:6], "for the earth shall be full of the knowledge of the Lord" [Isa 11:9]. All this is the result of human progress [*hishtalmut*], for humanity will so progress until there shall be no willful destruction.... There is no doubt that humanity will arrive at the level of "nation shall not lift up sword against nation," and then it will consider its past an enormous insanity [*shigga'on atzum*].[17]

The oath "not to storm the wall" may thus be understood to reflect "the highest end" preached by the Hebrew prophets. Isaiah taught: War must be stopped; nation shall not lift up sword against nation! The prophets heralded a new age for humanity, teaching that war is immoral, inhuman, and enormously insane. In light of these teachings of the Hebrew prophets, it seems to follow that the land of Israel may not be acquired by war but only by peaceful means. The boldly progressive Isaianic vision of world peace would appear to find an immediate practical expression in the talmudic text concerning the oath "not to storm the wall." Although Reines does not say so explicitly, it seems clear that his interpretation of the oath "not to storm the wall" is related closely to his understanding of the prophetic teachings concerning war and peace.

War, Rabbi Reines wrote, is "the disgrace of the human species."[18] It came to be in ancient times, caused by "exaggerated lust and a wild will."[19] It contradicts all the moral values of the Torah: "The house of study and weapons of war are two contraries that have no middle ground" for "the house of study is an open protest against war and those who make war...and you have no greater desecration of the holy than the introduction of instruments of destruction into the house of Torah and wisdom" (see *b. Sanh.* 82a).[20]

In ancient days, it was permissible to conquer the Canaanites by war and violence, and Joshua did so. However, the great prophets of Israel forbade this atavistic practice. The biblical conquest of the Canaanites thus cannot be a paradigm for us today. We are not permitted to imitate the Israelite conquerors of the land of Canaan. We are forbidden to confuse today's Palestinians with yesterday's Canaanites. One who violates the oath not to "storm the wall" does not merely violate an enigmatic or marginal aggadah, but violates a central moral teaching of the Hebrew prophets: "Nation shall not lift up sword against nation for the earth shall be full of the knowledge of the Lord!"

In sum, according to the teachings of Rabbi Reines, we may not do to our Arab neighbors *hic et nunc* what the Israelites were long ago commanded to do to the Canaanites. The political and economic program of Zionism, settling the land in peace through legitimate and recognized agreements with the nations, is today the only way permitted by Jewish Law to fulfill the great commandment of dwelling in the land of Israel. If war was the accepted means of fulfilling the commandment in the days of Joshua and David, Zionism is the only halakhically lawful way to fulfill it today.

The Maccabees

What about the Maccabees and their victorious war against the Seleucid occupiers, commemorated on the holiday of Hanukkah? Although Rabbi Reines was profoundly antimilitaristic, he was not a pacifist, and he recognized the legitimacy of defensive wars and wars of national liberation against occupying powers, such as that of the Maccabees against the Seleucids. He praises the Maccabees for having fought "to throw the yoke of Greece from off their neck."[21] The Maccabees were not the conquerors but the conquered. They were in rebellion against the conquerors. Clearly, the divine oath that forbade wars of conquest or aggression does not forbid defensive wars or wars of national liberation against occupying powers.

Nonetheless, Rabbi Reines asks, in an inspirational sermon delivered on the holiday of Hanukkah, what can we learn today from the battles of the Maccabees? If we are forbidden to wage war to conquer the land, how is Hanukkah relevant to us? His response is as follows:

> The fundamental thing is to learn from this event to uphold the sense of dignity of our nation and of our religion...to strive to raise up the horn of Israel and settle them on their land....This may be done by means that

are legitimate and permitted even today, namely, by means of voluntary acquisition.[22]

Hanukkah teaches us to be firm in our commitment to Judaism and to the independence of the Jewish people in the land of Israel, which may be achieved only by "voluntary acquisition." It teaches us, in other words, to be good Zionists.

Be that as it may, Rabbi Reines is careful not to draw any parallels between the Maccabees and the conquering army of Joshua. Indeed, one is almost tempted to say that if there is any parallel at all here, it is between the Maccabees and the Canaanites.

The Oath Not to Storm the Wall: A Moral Imperative

As we have seen, Rabbi Reines's interpretation of the oath "not to storm the wall" is characterized by its antimilitaristic and moral tenor. God has adjured us "not to storm the wall," that is, not to try to conquer the land of Israel by force, because wars of conquest, like all wars of aggression, are immoral. Reines emphasized the Isaianic vision of world peace: "Nation shall not lift up sword against nation" (Isa 2:4).

In giving an antimilitaristic and moral explanation to the oath "not to storm the wall," Rabbi Reines was—as noted above—continuing an interpretative direction evidenced by the medieval Catalonian rabbis Bahya ben Asher and Isaac ben Sheshet. However, it is striking that the antimilitaristic and moral interpretation of the oath "not to storm the wall" was not adopted by most commentators, who preferred instead theological or mystical interpretations. A detailed analysis of medieval and modern discussions of the oath "not to storm the wall" is found in Aviezer Ravitzky's important essay, "The Impact of the Three Oaths in Jewish History."[23]

A famous early use of the oath "not to storm the wall" is that of Rabbi Isaac Leon ben Eliezer Ibn Zur, rabbi in Ancona in the first half of the sixteenth century, who wrote *Criticisms* on Nahmanides' Commentary on Maimonides' *Book of the Commandments*. When Nahmanides rules that there is a commandment to live in the land of Israel, Ibn Zur replies: "The commandment to inherit the Land and to inhabit it obtained only during the days of Moses, Joshua, and David . . . but since [the Israelites] were exiled from their land this commandment does not obtain . . . until the time of the coming of the Messiah; for indeed we have been commanded [*b. Ketub.* 111a] . . . not to rebel against the nations in order to conquer the land by force." Ibn Zur's point is not moral but theological: God has decreed the exile of the Jewish people until "the coming of the Messiah," and until that time there is no commandment to dwell in the land.[24]

Another well-known use of the oath is that of Moses Mendelssohn. Countering the argument by some Christians that Jews should not be given civil rights in European states because their true allegiance is to the land of Israel, he wrote in 1781: "Our Talmudic sages had the foresight to emphasize again and again the prohibition to return to Palestine on our own. They made it unmistakably clear that we must not take even a single step preparatory to a return to Palestine, and a subsequent restoration of our nation there, unless and until the great miracles and extraordinary signs promised us in Scripture were to occur. And they substantiated that prohibition by citing the somewhat mystical yet truly captivating verses of the Song of Songs: *I adjure you, O daughters of Jerusalem, by the gazelles, and by the hinds of the field, that you awaken not, nor stir up love, until it please* [2:7; 3:5]."[25] Presumably influenced by Ibn Zur, Mendelssohn argues here that the divine oath prohibits us from returning to the land of Israel until God shows us "great miracles and extraordinary signs." Like Ibn Zur, his explanation is theological or mystical, not moral.

The most controversial twentieth-century use of the oath is that of Rabbi Joel Teitelbaum (1887–1979), leader of the Satmar Hasidic sect, in his anti-Zionist polemical book *Va-Yoel Mosheh* (1959). Teitelbaum holds that the oath "not to storm the wall" forbids "the majority" of Jews from living in Israel until the coming of the Messiah. Moreover, he claims that the distinction between settlement by force and settlement by license is irrelevant, for all significant settlement is prohibited. God, for whatever uncanny reason, has decreed that the Jews must remain in exile until the coming of the Messiah, and therefore the Jews must "not storm the wall."[26] Like Ibn Zur and Mendelssohn, his explanation of the oath is theological or mystical, not moral.

One important authority who did follow Rabbi Reines's moral interpretation of the oath "not to storm the wall" was Rabbi Abraham Isaac Ha-Kohen Kook, the first Ashkenazi chief rabbi of Mandatory Palestine. He writes that the return to Zion in our days must be "according to the way of the Torah, in love and peace, and not by storming the wall or by rebelling against the nations of the world," and he cites the words of the prophet regarding the building of the Second Temple, "Not by might, nor by power, but by My spirit, saith the Lord of hosts" (Zech 4:6).[27] Elsewhere, in explaining the oath "not to storm the wall," he explains that war is "an abomination to us" (*piggul lanu*).[28]

However, in religious Zionist circles today, the oath "not to storm the wall" is not usually understood according to the moral interpretation of Rabbi Reines and Rabbi Kook, but according to a theopolitical approach. According to this approach, the oath "not to storm the wall" is anachronistic, irrelevant, and nonexistent; for since the nations have endorsed Jewish sovereignty in the land of Israel (e.g., the Balfour Declaration, the San Remo Conference, and the United Nations General Assembly Resolution 181), Jewish settlement in the land can no longer be considered "storming the wall." As Rabbi Avraham

Elkanah Kahana Shapira (1914–2007), Ashkenazi chief rabbi of the State of Israel (1983–1993), put it, the oath is simply "not applicable in our days."[29] This theopolitical approach is often said to be based on the opinions of two distinguished Eastern European authorities, Rabbi Abraham Bornstein (1838–1885) of Sochochov and Rabbi Meir Simcha Ha-Kohen of Dvinsk (1843–1926).[30]

According to Rabbis Ibn Zur, Moses of Dessau, and Teitelbaum, the oath "not to storm the wall" forbids the establishment of a Jewish state in the land of Israel until the coming of the Messiah or the appearance of "great miracles and extraordinary signs." According to Rabbi Reines, on the contrary, the oath represents, in our own time, the messianic value of peace.

According to Rabbi Shapira and most other contemporary religious Zionist rabbis, the oath "not to storm the wall" forbids nothing today because it is no longer applicable. According to Rabbis Mohilever, Reines, and Kook, on the contrary, it is emphatically applicable and requires us to settle the land of Israel only by peaceful means, and it thereby forbids us to treat the Palestinian Arabs in the same way that our ancestors treated the Canaanites.

While most religious Zionists in recent years have seen the talmudic discussion of the oath "not to storm the wall" as an uncomfortable and embarrassing text that must somehow be neutralized or explained away, Rabbi Reines understood it to teach an exalted moral imperative.

Notes

1. David Hartman, *Conflicting Visions* (New York: Schocken Books, 1990), 232.

2. Cf. Richard Dawkins' comment to Menachem Kellner: "The Books of Joshua and Judges are among the most chillingly racist and genocidal documents ever written.... [T]hey should...not be used to justify turning Palestinians in our time off their land and installing new Jewish settlers" (e-mail from Dawkins to Kellner, April 20, 2002).

3. Isaac Jacob Reines, *Or Hadash 'al Tzion* (Vilnius: Widow and Brothers Romm, 1901), 4, 1–10, pp. 14b–32b; see also his *Sefer ha-'Arakhim* [*Lexicon of Homiletics*], ed. A. B. Reines (New York: Reines Publication Society, 1926), s.v. *kibbush ha-aretz*, pp. 298–300. See my Hebrew essay, "Rabbi Reines on the Commandment to Dwell in the Land of Israel," in *Eretz Yisrael ba-Hagut ha-Yehudit ba-Me'ah ha-20*, ed. Aviezer Ravitzky (Jerusalem: Yad Ben-Zvi, 2004), 303–314. See also Elie Holzer, *Herev Pifiyyot be-Yadam* (Jerusalem: Keter Books, 2009), 19–60.

4. On Nahmanides, see the contribution of Joseph David (Chapter 7) in the present volume.

5. Maimonides, *Sefer ha-Mitzvot*, with commentaries of Nahmanides, Rabbi Isaac Leon ben Eliezer Ibn Zur ("Megillat Esther"), et al., Warsaw: Isaac Goldman, 1883, 2:21b.

6. Ribash, *Responsa* (Vilnius: L. L. Matz, 1878), 19b n. 101. See also the similar ruling by Rabbi Solomon ben Simeon Duran, who was rabbi of Algiers a generation after Ribash: Rashbash, *Responsa* (Leghorn: Abraham Meldola, 1742), 2b–3a n. 2. Regarding *b. Ketub.* 111a, some texts read *ke-homah* (as a wall) not *ba-homah* (on the wall). See also *b. Yoma* 9b and *Song Rab.* 2:18 and 8:11 on Song 8:9–10 ("If she be a wall...I am a wall, and my breasts like the towers thereof, then was I in His eyes as one that found peace"). If one reads *ke-homah*, the oath would seem to forbid immigration to the land *en masse* or by a majority of

the people (see Rashi, Commentary on *b. Yoma* 9b). According to *b. Kebub.* 111a, God adjured Israel *inter alia* not to storm the wall, not to rebel against the nations, and not to hurry the end (of the Exile).

7. *Tanhuma*, ed. S. Buber, Genesis, p. 83a. See also Rashi, *Commentary on Genesis* 32:8.

8. Nahmanides, *Commentary on Pentateuch*, ed. C. D. Chavel (Jerusalem: Mosad Ha-Rav Kook, 1962), introduction to pericope Va-yishlah, p. 180; see also his commentary on Gen 32:9, p. 182.

9. Bahya, *Commentary on Pentateuch*, ed. Chavel (Jerusalem: Mosad Ha-Rav Kook, 1971), on Genesis 32:8, p. 278.

10. Bahya, *Commentary on Pentateuch*, on Deuteronomy 20:10, pp. 371–372, "If your heart hesitates, saying that we thus do unjust violence," etc. Bahya's basic justification of the cruel actions committed during the conquest is theological, not moral—a sort of Kierkegaardian "suspension of the ethical." On Bahya's position, see Menachem Kellner, "And Yet, the Texts Remain: The Problem of the Command to Destroy the Canaanites" (Chapter 6 in this volume).

11. Abraham Jacob Slotzki, *Shivat Tzion* (Warsaw: 1898), 9–10; new ed., ed. Y. Salmon (Jerusalem and Beersheba: Dinur Center, 1998), 73–74. In the passage from Nahmanides' quoted previously, Num 33:53 was translated: "And you *shall drive out the inhabitants of the Land* and dwell therein." However, this translation would be incorrect for Rabbis Mohilever or Reines.

12. Reines, *Or Hadash*, 4, 3, pp. 17b–18a.

13. Reines, *Or Hadash*, 4, 3, pp. 18a–b.

14. Reines, *Or Hadash*, 4, 3, p. 18b. See also Reines, *Sefer ha-'Arakhim*, 299: "It must be understood correctly what it means to say we have a commandment to inherit the empire of Ishmael [i.e., the Ottoman Empire]; for we have been effectively adjured 'not to storm the wall' [*b. Ketub.* 111a]....However, Nahmanides' intent [when he ruled that there is a commandment to conquer the land] is conquest by means of purchase, that is, the commandment is to buy land in the Land of Israel and to settle on the soil."

15. Reines, *Or Hadash*, 4, 4, p. 19a; see also Reines, *Sefer ha-'Arakhim*, 298.

16. Reines, *Sefer ha-'Arakhim*, s.v. *hitbolelut*, p. 152. Regarding the expression "forbidden to enter into the assembly of Israel," see, e.g., Deut 23:2–4, 23:9. The assembly of Israel has a sacred vocation, and violence has no place in it.

17. Reines, *Sefer ha-'Arakhim*, s.v. *kishsharon ha-umah ve-te'udato*, p. 330.

18. Reines, *Or le-Arba'ah 'Asar* (Piotrków: Solomon Belchatovsky, 1913), 4, 2, p. 49a.

19. Reines, *Or le-Arba'ah 'Asar*, 51a.

20. Reines, *Orah va-Simhah* (Vilnius: Widow and Brothers Romm, 1898), ch. 3, pp. 22a–b.

21. Reines, *Or Hadash*, 8, 3, p. 119b.

22. Reines, *Or Hadash*, 8, 3, p. 120b.

23. Aviezer Ravitzky, *Messianism, Zionism, and Jewish Religious Radicalism*, trans. M. Swirsky and J. Chipman (Chicago: University of Chicago Press, 1996), 211–234.

24. Ibn Zur, *Megillat Esther*, in Maimonides, *Sefer ha-Mitzvot*, vol. 2, *Commandments That the Master Forgot to List*, pos. com. 4, p. 21b.

25. Moses Mendelssohn, *Selections from His Writings*, trans. E. Jospe (New York: Viking, 1975), 85.

26. Joel Teitelbaum, *Va-Yoel Mosheh* (Brooklyn: Sender Deutch, 1961), 1, 9–17, pp. 42–51. His rejection of the relevance of the distinction between settlement by force and settlement by

license depends largely on his prolix deconstruction of Rashi's comment defining "to storm the wall" as "with a strong hand" (Rashi, Commentary on *b. Ketub.* 111a; see above, n. 10).

27. Abraham Isaac Kook, *'Olat Re'iyyah* (Jerusalem: Mosad Ha-Rav Kook, 1985), 1:376–377.

28. Abraham Isaac Kook, "On Zionism," [in Hebrew], *Ha-Devir* 7–9 (1930): 29.

29. Avraham Shapira, "On Returning Territories of the Land of Israel" [in Hebrew], *Morashah* 9 (1975): 15–21.

30. Ibid. Rabbi Bornstein argued that if the Jews are granted permission to dwell in the land of Israel, then dwelling there cannot involve "storming the wall" (see Bornstein, *Avne Nezer* [Piotrków: Henoch Folman, 1912–1934], nn. 454, 456). Rabbi Meir Simcha wrote in 1922 that after the San Remo Conference (1920), where the "enlightened governments" confirmed the Balfour Declaration, "the fear of the oaths has departed" (Hebrew text in Simon Federbush, *Torah u-Melukhah* [Jerusalem: Mosad Ha-Rav Kook, 1961], 91–92). See also Rabbi Tzvi Yehuda Ha-Kohen Kook, *Le-Netivot Yisrael* (Jerusalem: Tzur-Ot, 1979), 2:167, and Rabbi Shlomo Aviner, *Berurim be-'Inyan she-lo Ya'alu ke-Homah* (Jerusalem: private, 1980). See my "Rabbi Reines on the Commandment to Dwell in the Land of Israel," 313 n. 39.

Bibliography

Aviner, Shlomo. *Berurim be-'Inyan she-lo Ya'alu ke-Homah.* Jerusalem: private, 1980.

Bahya. *Commentary on Pentateuch.* Edited by C. D. Chavel. Jerusalem: Mosad Ha-Rav Kook, 1971.

Bornstein, Abraham. *Avne Nezer.* Piotrków: Henoch Folman, 1912–1934.

Federbush, Simon. *Torah u-Melukhah.* Jerusalem: Mosad Ha-Rav Kook, 1961.

Hartman, David. *Conflicting Visions.* New York: Schocken Books, 1990.

Harvey, Warren Zev. "Rabbi Reines on the Commandment to Dwell in the Land of Israel" [in Hebrew]. In *Eretz Yisrael ba-Hagut ha-Yehudit ba-Me'ah ha-20,* edited by Aviezer Ravitzky, 303–314. Jerusalem: Yad Ben-Zvi, 2004.

Holzer, Eli. *Herev Pifiyyot be-Yadam.* Jerusalem: Keter Books, 2009.

Kellner, Menachem. "And Yet, the Texts Remain: The Problem of the Command to Destroy the Canaanites" (Chapter 6 in this volume).

Kook, Abraham Isaac. *'Olat Re'iyyah.* Jerusalem: Mosad Ha-Rav Kook, 1985.

——. "On Zionism" [in Hebrew]. *Ha-Devir* 7–9 (1930): 28–33.

Kook, Tzvi Yehuda. *Le-Netivot Yisrael.* Jerusalem: Tzur-Ot, 1979.

Maimonides. *Sefer ha-Mitzvot, with Commentaries of Nahmanides,* Rabbi Isaac Leon ben Eliezer Ibn Zur et al. Warsaw: Isaac Goldman, 1883.

Mendelssohn, Moses. *Selections from His Writings.* Translated by E. Jospe. New York: Viking, 1975.

Nahmanides. *Commentary on Pentateuch.* Edited by C. D. Chavel. Jerusalem: Mosad Ha-Rav Kook, 1962.

Rashbash. *Responsa.* Leghorn: Abraham Meldola, 1742.

Ravitzky, Aviezer. *Messianism, Zionism, and Jewish Religious Radicalism.* Translated by M. Swirsky and J. Chipman. Chicago: University of Chicago Press, 1996.

Reines, Isaac Jacob. *Sefer ha-'Arakhim [Lexicon of Homiletics].* Edited by A. B. Reines. New York: Reines Publication Society, 1926.

——. *Or le-Arba'ah 'Asar.* Piotrków: Solomon Belchatovsky, 1913.

——. *Or Hadash 'al Tzion*. Vilnius: Widow and Brothers Romm, 1901.

——. *Orah va-Simhah*. Vilnius: Widow and Brothers Romm, 1898.

Ribash. *Responsa*. Vilnius: Matz, 1878.

Shapira, Avraham. "On Returning Territories of the Land of Israel" [in Hebrew]. *Morashah* 9 (1975): 15–21.

Slotzki, Abraham Jacob. *Shivat Tzion*. Warsaw: 1898. New edition edited by Y. Salmon. Jerusalem and Beersheba: Dinur Center, 1998.

Teitelbaum, Joel. *Va-Yoel Mosheh*. Brooklyn: Sender Deutch, 1961.

17

The Conquest of the Land of Israel and Associated Moral Questions in the Teachings of Rabbi Kook and His Disciples

THOUGHTS IN LIGHT OF THE BOOK HEREV PIPIYOT BE-YADAM

Avinoam Rosenak

Introduction

Not infrequently, the study of modern Jewish thought generates a challenging conflation of theoretical scholarship and political and cultural discourse. Aviezer Ravitzky's book *Messianism, Zionism, and Jewish Religious Radicalism* (originally published in Hebrew [1993] as *Ha-qetz ha-meguleh u-medinat ha-yehudim*) offers an instructive example of that sort of admixture, having resonated both in the scholarly world and in cultural discourse, and it is far from the only such example. Works of this sort pose the question—to self-conscious writer and critical reader alike—of whether the scholar is presenting only the results of "pure" scholarship or whether his personal agenda might be part of his scholarly analysis. That question, in turn, gives rise to others: What exactly do we mean when we speak of "pure scholarship"? What assumptions underlie that term? Can those assumptions withstand hermeneutic criticism? And, finally, might it not be the case that every scholarly study reflects some agenda? In an analogous way, and in light of the many studies in this area, it becomes clear that political discourse likewise is not free of underlying ideological and religious assumptions. It follows that anyone who wants to understand cultural and political discourse in depth must carefully and deliberately examine the theoretical and intellectual roots of that discourse, which might otherwise be taken—wrongly—as nothing more than empty political posturing.

In this chapter, I want to explore a theoretical matter concerning Rabbi Abraham Isaac Ha-Kohen Kook's complex attitude with regard to the inhabitants of biblical Canaan; the conquest of the land of Israel, past and present; and the potentially troublesome moral questions thereby raised. The article will examine these issues on a number of levels.

First, I will examine the critical comments of several scholars regarding the affinity between Rabbi Kook and his disciples (an affinity and a critique that serve as the background for this inquiry). Second, I will examine Rabbi Kook's writings on the conquest of ancient Canaan from its inhabitants, his assessment of the morality of that action, and his view of the connection between the biblical conquest and contemporary historical events. In the third part of the chapter, I will consider Elie Holzer's recent book *Herev pipiyot be-yadam* [*Double-Edged Sword: Military Activism in the Thought of Religious Zionism*]*, a work that deals with, among other things, the matters at issue here. I will describe some of Holzer's conclusions regarding the ties between Rabbi Kook and his disciples, offer some critical arguments, and suggest alternative explanations.

In the course of this inquiry, I will also try to clarify how the concept of "unity of opposites" bears on our understanding of the linkage between Rabbi Kook's students and their teacher and how that concept can explain and illuminate, in a slightly different fashion, the nature of the relationships between the master and his disciples.

The article will note two reactions on Rabbi Kook's part to the morality of war and the conquest of the land of Israel. His attitude with respect to the issue in the biblical period appears to be the polar opposite of his totally nonviolent attitude in modern times. The gap between these reactions is evident and might well be taken as an internal inconsistency. What I want to do here is trace Rabbi Kook's dialectical logic, consider the complex attitude of academic scholarship toward these issues, and probe the ways in which Rabbi Kook's disciples have tried to apply his logic in the here and now—a context that Rabbi Kook did not know and could never have imagined.

Rabbi A. I. H. Kook: Perceptions of the Man and His Disciples

Rabbi Abraham Isaac Ha-Kohen Kook (1865–1935) played a central role in shaping religious Zionist thought in the twentieth century. He was appointed rabbi of Jaffa and its surroundings in 1904, and served as rabbi of Jerusalem and the first chief rabbi of Israel from 1921 until 1935. In 1923, he established the yeshiva that later came to be known as Merkaz haRav. His son, Rabbi Tzvi Yehuda Kook (1891–1982), who prepared most of his father's writings for publication, became head of Yeshivat Merkaz haRav in 1952, following the death of Rabbi Harlap, who had succeeded the elder Rabbi Kook in that position. In that capacity, he was the principal spokesman for his father's teachings. He also served as rabbi of the Gush Emunim settlement movement.

The connection between Rabbi Kook *père* and Rabbi Kook *fils*, and between the elder Rabbi Kook and his son's students—who saw themselves as continuing in the path he had set—is a matter of fraught, long-standing, and turbulent debate to which many pages have been devoted in both scholarly and polemical publications. It is that debate that underlies the present inquiry.

Some scholars see a substantive gap between the elder Rabbi Kook, on the one hand, and his son and his son's students, on the other—a gap that demonstrates the abandonment of the master's open and complex teachings by his radical and fundamentalist disciples. Others, however, find a profound affinity between Rabbi Kook and his disciples, maintaining that the characteristics that seem to divide the students from their teacher in fact grow from seeds sown by the teacher's ideas. Aviezer Ravitzky noted both the linkage and the gap between master and disciples in his *Messianism, Zionism, and Jewish Religious Radicalism*, referred to earlier, and his essay on determinism and free will.[1] He described Rabbi Kook's teachings as having a deterministic-redemptive dimension—a determinism that underlies both his concept of history and politics and his hope for and belief in a conscious moral and spiritual revolution that is destined to take place, albeit through the exercise of free will. In other words, Ravitzky argues that Rabbi Kook emphasized the deterministic certainty of material redemption, for "there is no [further] exile...after the redemption."[2] With regard to the spiritual realm, however, Rabbi Kook identified a "deficit" in the attitude "of the Zionist movement...to the sanctity of Israel and the Torah and to the commandments that are our life and length of days overall."[3] In Rabbi Kook's view, as Ravitzky puts it, "Israel's distinctive character" ensured that the nation as a whole would not collapse entirely, but the conclusion of the process and its redemptive fulfillment "are a matter for each individual—his efforts and his personal presence in the 'assembly of the righteous.' Here, free will is granted and a decision is required."[4]

Ravitzky argues that this deterministic certainty became more pronounced among Rabbi Kook's disciples. Rabbi Harlap emphasized that "it is as clear as the noonday sun that there will not be a third destruction and that the State of Israel that has arisen will never be shaken."[5] That principle came to be regarded as true both on the physical plane and on the still-to-be-realized spiritual plane. As its spiritual fulfillment was delayed, the belief in its certainty grew stronger, and ubiquitous indications of repentance and return were identified.[6] The gradual approach of "the revealed and the concealed, the external and the internal, the soon-to-be-realized consolidation of terrestrial, historical salvation with conscious, voluntary religious awareness"[7] was converted into a midrash that blunts "the sting of recalcitrant reality" and lends it "the optimistic aspect of the vision."[8]

Ravitzky set up freedom and determinism as polar opposites, and his analyses therefore rely on models taken from the field of political science. They regularly address the tension between utopian programs that offer total solutions and human freedom that relies on "reading the tea leaves of the times"—analyses that explicate "the direction of the forces of history" and ascertain the meaning of events.[9]

Against the background of these analyses, some have reached the conclusion that Gush Emunim is a movement utterly unconnected to reality, motivated exclusively by messianic principles. In that spirit, some have compared it to Sabbateanism. Avraham Shapira, for example, argued that their transgressions against the dictates of morality and the laws of the state partook, in their view, of "holy sin" (mitzvah ha-baah be-aveirah, literally, a commandment performed through the mechanism of a transgression). "Like the Sabbateans before them, they dwell in a universe that lies beyond the obligations of law and morality that mark the reality in which all other Jews—those outside their community—are situated."[10] According to Shapira, Gershom Scholem's discussion of Sabbateanism can, "with names changed, fairly be applied to the situation emerging in the wake of Gush Emunim's settlement activity. Blindly following the revelations and directives of their teacher, they open the way to positions, opinions, and actions that annul the principles of morality, the laws of our state, and the social dictates that underlie Judaism; and they consider their transgressions to be holy."[11] The movement is described as involving "mystical fervor," "a sense of being swept away," and "a readiness to take extreme actions"; according to Shapira, "it inevitably gives rise to unsavory associations from the past, both for us and for others."[12]

Similar in tone are the writings of Uriel Tal, a researcher of the Nazi movement and its theology[13] who was among the first to study Gush Emunim. He conceptualizes (and judges) Rabbi Kook and his movement as a "stream of political messianism" (a negative) in contrast to "political restraint"[14] (a positive). "Political messianism" sees politics as a sacred process of raising the Shekhinah (God's presence, personified in the mystical literature) from the dust;[15] sees victory as "a divine miracle"; regards our time as "the era of eschatological redemption"; and equates the returning of Israeli land to the Arabs with the returning of God's presence to the forces of evil.[16] This movement is to its (better) counterpart as the totalitarian and the zealous are to the moral and the realistic;[17] as zealousness, mystification, and ecstasy are to sound restraint, rationalism, enlightenment, moderation, forbearance, and support for compromise.[18]

According to Tal, what we see here is the establishment of a "political theology" or a "political religion," whose consequences can be understood "from the historical experience of the Third Reich,"[19] and whose characteristics resemble those of twentieth-century fascist, nationalist, and racist movements.[20]

Against this turbulent background, I want to take another look at the teachings of Rabbi Kook and his disciples regarding the past and present conquest of the land.

Rabbi A. I. H. Kook on War and Peace

As noted, we can identify two different ways in which Rabbi Kook treated the nature of war in general and the conquest of the land of Israel in particular. The question of morality is central to both of them.[21]

ON THE RIGHT TO WAR

Rabbi Kook's observations on the right to conquer the land of Israel from the Canaanites and on fulfilling the biblical commandments related thereto (reviewed below) grow out of the conceptual scheme and the moral vision he sets for Israel.

The biblical account of how the patriarchs and Joshua struggled against the inhabitants of the land and fulfilled the divine command to wage "obligatory war" can be understood in a positive way, given the background of the time and place in which the actions took place. As Rabbi Kook says in *Orot*: "We look at the early generations, those whose stories are recounted in the Torah, the Prophets, and the Writings, those who were engaged in war—and [we see that] they were great men whom we relate to amicably and view as holy. We understand that the spark within the soul is the foundation...and those mighty souls return to live among us as in the past."[22] War, then, is a form of expression that reveals—in the time and place under discussion—the full might of the souls that established the nation and fought God's war. The spirit that must move it now is the spirit that moved it then. This is the war of good against evil, light against darkness. Israel's war against the seven Canaanite nations is not merely a war for the conquest of land; it is a moral and spiritual war. Avoiding or delaying that war invites disaster.

In a letter written in 1900 to Dr. Benjamin Menasheh Levin, who had expressed discomfort over the moral implications of the biblical accounts of conquest and of the obligation to wage war to the end against Amalek, Rabbi Kook clarifies his attitude toward the biblical story and the duty to conquer and destroy. According to Rabbi Kook, all Israelite conduct, past and present, must be understood as manifesting a natural yearning "for godly self-identity." Prophecy sets forth the proper way to actualize that yearning. Set against that positive drive is an opposing culture of wickedness and folly, replete with promiscuity, murder, and idolatry.[23] Israelite culture, in contract, is depicted as one that labors in Torah, manifests upright character, and attains spiritual exaltation through sacred song, prayer, and virtuous actions. The negative culture, in Rabbi Kook's account, devastates the world and fouls the pure air that is suffused with divine idealism.[24]

War, then, is necessary, for there is an imperative to bring about the victory of morality and to free "the wretched world" from the grasp of the "wickedness and folly" that regards "the wild animal in humanity…as the purpose of its life." The war that must be declared is neither personal nor national; it is, rather, an ideological and educational "war…against the evil" in man and "against the vileness within him." It is a war of "the mighty and the holy," and those dedicated to it are willing to die on its altar.

As already noted, prophecy transformed this abstract idea into something concrete and identified its specific goals. It "declared the race of Amalek" to be a race whose opposition to Israel was absolute and "irremediable" except by "erasing its memory."[25] In the spirit of Maharal,[26] Rabbi Kook explains the dichotomy between Amalek and Israel in terms of a tension between nature (Amalekite) and miracle (Israelite).[27] Rabbi Kook even makes it clear that Amalek's hatred for Israel is unique in that it is directed not against the nation as a whole but against every individual.[28] Amalek despises Israel's sanctity as a matter of principle.[29] It strives to destroy every Israelite soul, and its hatred for Israel is absolute, "in the manner of the hatred of evil for good, because it is its opposite." It follows that this hatred requires a response different from one governed by the otherwise applicable laws of war.[30] King Saul erred, according to Rabbi Kook, when he spared the life of Agag, the Amalekite king, and thereby applied to him the general notion that kings consider captivity to be more demeaning than death. Israel is required to destroy Amalek absolutely because of Amalek's desire to destroy Israel absolutely. Amalek is the "essence of impurity" whose very existence defiles all and "crowds out holiness"; accordingly, "extirpating it is a commandment."[31] Its evil is so great, Rabbi Kook maintains, and the clash between Israel and Amalek so frontal,[32] that when Israel warred against Amalek in the wilderness, Moses took pains to avert his gaze from "the filthy place" and not to look at "the evil image of the man of wickedness" embodied in Amalek; hence it is said of him that "his hands remained steady" (literally, "faithful"; Exod 17:12).[33]

Prophecy, as noted, leads a person to "the happiness of peace and the pleasure of love,"[34] heralding a vision of the future in which "humanity will have no need for any enterprise based on hatred." That ideal situation will come about with the extirpation of Amalek and the seven Canaanite nations. Any doubt or hesitation in the war against them will stand in the way of Israel's—and the entire world's—attainment of that end. In the past, a hesitant operation against Amalek and the Canaanite nations brought about "all those material and spiritual woes." Their remnant, allowed to survive, "taught us to do all their despicable deeds: consigning sons and daughters to the flames and all the [other] abominations of the Amorites." Against that background, Rabbi Kook responds to Levin, we can respond to the moral question of "why we treated them cruelly": "We cannot envisage how dismal and base the world would be but for that cruelty of ours." So, too, "we cannot envisage how evil and vile" the world would be "but for the pure illumination of God's light and ways"[35] that are conveyed in his revelation in history through Israel.

According to Rabbi Kook, it is Christianity that "strives to extirpate the attribute of hatred,"[36] and hopes to attain the ideal life without first engaging in a genuine confrontation with evil. That effort is unrealistic, however, and nothing has ever come of it; on the contrary, Christianity has spilled more blood than any other religion "and had increased loathing through its extirpation of hatred." On the basis of this psycho-cultural logic, Rabbi Kook accounts for the horrors of the First World War. In his wartime notebook, he explains that the outbreak of violence—despite what he regarded as its inevitability, as we shall see—resulted from the unnatural repression of hatred, which then erupted in an unrestrained, universally destructive manner.[37] The desire to hasten the end in an unnatural way, to erase "hatred...prematurely," creates a divide between "the light of divine faith" and "the routines of life in society," and that, in turn, caused "the nations under its wing...to glory in idolatrous traits."[38]

All that said, Rabbi Kook does not deny that our ancestors at times may have acted wrongly. "We are not responsible for all the acts done by the nation's heroes," he says, and the prophets indeed protested some of those actions. Maimonides taught[39] that no one is flawless and that "some actions taken by the greatest of the great are deserving of criticism." Everyone sins—but that sin does not negate what is primary.[40]

ANTIVIOLENCE

In contrast to the foregoing observations about the biblical period, Rabbi Kook explains the unique nature of his own time, marked by the return to Zion, and expresses the hope that in this messianic era, Israel will be able to return to political activity and do so in a context free of violence and war. His comments, however, are made in a broader context in which he considers the importance of the First World War and takes a positive view of its role in actualizing the nation's unique potential.[41] But in contrast to the natural process of war (carried out through the warlike conduct of the nations), Rabbi Kook foresees for Israel a supernatural present free of all violence.[42] The process is clearly set out in *Orot*. "When there is a great war in the world, the power of the Messiah is awakened. The time of singing has come,[43] the pruning of the despots. The wicked are annihilated from the world and the world becomes purged; the voice of the turtledove is heard in our land."[44] Positing a symbiotic relationship between Israel and the nations, he argues that Israel is the seed of humanity,[45] and Israel's ability to attain its purpose depends on the other nations' ability to achieve self-fulfillment. The nations' unhealthy moral state breaks out amid the storms of war, and the war will likely punish them, refine them,[46] and shape them anew.[47] Accordingly, "whenever there is a nation in the world that has not been fully actualized through its actions, there is a corresponding darkness in the absorbed light of the community of Israel. And so, when governments skirmish against one another, forms related to the perfection of nations are actualized, and a complementary force emerges within the community of Israel that anticipates the footsteps of the Messiah, may he come and appear speedily and in our days."[48] For that reason, the First World War is a positive and essential event for Israel. Once the battles subside, the footsteps of the Messiah will appear; the more intense the war, the greater the messianic expectation. As he saw it, the purpose of the First World War was to prepare the ground for the revelation of the End, which will make possible Israel's return to its land. Israel must prepare itself to do so,[49] but these days of redemption differ from the past in that Israel will be able to carry out its political operations without violence and war.[50] This utopian state of affairs, which Rabbi Kook believed was truly at hand, had been implicit from the outset in the establishment of the Israelite nation. It is a privilege conditioned on self-awareness and on Israel having clean hands with regard to its spiritual obligations. As part of his idealistic historiosophy, Rabbi Kook assumed that as soon as the nations recognized Israel's inner strength and dedication to it,[51] any need for war would evaporate. All the struggles of the past resulted from the sin of the golden calf, which prevented the nations from making peace with and acknowledging Israel.[52] The developmental process of doing so is something that applies to all humankind, which is destined, in Rabbi Kook's vision, to be united "as one family, at which time all conflicts, and the all evil traits that result from divisions and borders between nations, will come to an end."[53]

The Importance of the Physical and of National and Political Instrumentalities

The process by which universal peace emerges is closely tied to Israel's particularistic process of physical and spiritual self-perfection. All components of reality are interconnected and affect one another, and Israel is the nucleus around which the nations of the world function.[54] An important part of Israel's process of self-perfection in the time of redemption, according to Rabbi Kook, is its return to the domain of the physical: "The Holy One blessed be He instructed us regarding the sanctity of the body"; the body is termed "holy flesh," in parallel to the "holy spirit."[55] This linkage is conveyed both by his philosophical writings[56] and his halakhic writings.[57] Rabbi Kook attacked asceticism and "droopy piety." He foresaw a spiritual return, accompanied by a "physical return creating healthy blood, healthy flesh, well-built and powerful bodies, an intense spirit shining on strong muscles";[58] and he well understood the feelings of the Zionist pioneers who disparagingly rejected "the bent back, the sad, drawn faces exuding fear and cowardice...along with the despair of poverty."[59]

In discussing the importance of the return to the physical, Rabbi Kook made use of kabbalistic and messianic concepts. Augmenting the sanctity of the spirit is bound up with augmenting the sanctity of the body. The spirit refines bodily might;[60] in turn, the strengthening of the body is a necessary condition for the continued strengthening of the spirit.[61] Emergence from exile is embodied in the strengthening of the body, along with the spiritual, psychological, and sociological consequences of that process. And so, for Rabbi Kook, bodily and spiritual developments affect each other. Exile, as a depressed and abnormal physical state, exerted, and continues to exert, an influence on Israel's depressed spiritual power.[62] Psychophysical duality is a source of strength, not a limiting factor. The interdependence of the binary forces serves as a moral and religious defensive barrier. The spirit must function as a gatekeeper, excluding any negative use of the physical. Israel's glory does not arise out of its might,[63] and we must "be wary of [physical] extremism." Physical power must be filtered and preserved from "all the negativity associated with it."[64] The return to the body does not mean imitation of the practices of the nations;[65] it must serve, rather, as a base on which Israel's distinctive spiritual powers can be augmented.

At the same time, Jewish nationalism acquires a political body. With the strengthening of its physical-political instrumentalities, it regains wisdom, might, uprightness, and "inner purity." The recognition that "it possesses a land, possesses a language, a literature, an army" is vital to its national development.[66] Israel will be unable to actualize its spiritual strength without "a political and social state, a seat of national government, situated at the height of human culture." But these instrumentalities will be of no use unless "the absolute divine idea reigns there, vivifying the nation and the Land with the light of its life."[67]

THE VISION OF PEACE AND THE UNITY OF OPPOSITES

Before immigrating to the land of Israel, Rabbi Kook spoke of **faithfulness to the Torah** as the source from which peace and love would flow and as a necessary condition for developing a sense of purity and of human brotherhood based on the recognition that we were created by the "Master of all the World." Only if Israel recognizes as much will the way be cleared to recognition on the part of all other nations, "and then the blessings of peace will begin to dwell within the world."[68] The quest for peace appears in Rabbi Kook's letters and his other writings.[69]

In Rabbi Kook's vision, faithfulness to the Torah is the necessary condition for freeing Israel from the cycle of war. Elie Holzer provides an extensive description of this strain of Rabbi Kook's thought, and his comprehensive book *Herev pipiyot be-yadam* gathers a wealth of insights and sources related to our subject.[70] According to Rabbi Kook, Israel lacks the inner drive for physical warfare, "for we were not commanded to bear the sword of war." Israel is commanded, rather, to call on God's name. Only after Israel internalizes and disseminates this idea will the nations come to recognize "the majesty, the sacred glory, and the universal peace that will follow" from these ideas. At that point, the nations will "rush to seek the Lord God of Israel."[71] Israel's spiritual flourishing—the reversal of the sin of the golden calf that opened the cycle of violence—turns out to be the basis on which Rabbi Kook envisions the establishment of the State of Israel.[72]

This antiwar tendency is a manifestation of Rabbi Kook's doctrine of the unity of opposites.[73] In the context of our discussion, that doctrine would argue for the importance of opposing strains in the relationship between Israel and the other nations of the world. On the one hand, logic requires a hostile and warlike relationship that facilitates preservation of distinctions and withdrawal of the particular from the universal. Every group must define itself vis-à-vis its opposite and must fight for the purity of its principles and spirit, defeating every threat that might arise to challenge its separate existence (as was the case in the biblical period, described earlier). At the same time, however, a unity-of-opposites perspective, like monotheism itself, believes that all opposites derive from a common source and, accordingly, that all opposites embody and express the all-embracing divine source. It follows that each of the opposites in any given dichotomy plays—and exists to play—a vital and necessary role. In light of that stance, logic allows for—requires, even—the avoidance of war and the maintenance of peaceful relations, for there is some element of truth to be derived from every nation. Despite the moral differences among nations, we must attain a consciousness that allows us to see how "every nation imparts...some mark on the understanding that is drawn from the light of the Torah, on the basis of its own natural and historical decisions."[74] In that spirit, one can speak well of Christianity, "which truly sought to extirpate the quality of hatred," even though it erred in how it weighed that goal in relation to reality.[75] That approach can find the positive even in nations and personalities seen as negative, such as Pharaoh and Egypt, Haman, Sisera, and Sennacherib.[76] Rabbi Kook raises the banner of Jewish justice—as distinct from Western liberalism—which manages to come up with "a spark of hope" for even "the least of nations." "The rabbis regarded the actions of the Canaanites as more vile than those of any other nation, yet they allowed for Job to live among them."[77] This dialectic approach also blurs the Western binary between "material" and "spiritual," between "body" and "soul," and it emphasizes the importance of the flesh and the material alongside the spiritual and the abstract.[78] Eating kosher meat is a means for elevating and accepting the crude, beastly, material dimension into the domain of the sacred. The joining strives to raise everything to the level at which the dross is removed and only the pure remains.

Only a select few have the capacity to navigate the paradoxical logic of the unity of opposites. Not everyone is able to extract the sparks from within the husks and, even more difficult, to see within the husks themselves an element of spark, to see the light within the dark. Rabbi Kook saw himself as standing on the front lines of that effort with reference to his secular surroundings. The process is all-embracing and is available to be applied to the alien and the evil, to the nations of the world and to violence.

The capacity to contain opposites of this sort, Rabbi Kook argues, is a unique cognitive quality linked to the spiritual nature of the land of Israel. It is the quality of "unitary" cognition, as distinct from cognition of "a segmented world." It differs from the sort of cognition to be found in other lands, where "it is impossible for the unitary view of the world to be revealed, and the segmented world reigns mightily."[79]

This unitary approach, however, is not an imposed harmony that denies the range of differences. Together with its premise of an all-pervasive unity, it reiterates the call to clarify the distinctiveness of the various counterposed positions and their opposition to one another. Rabbi Kook identifies the common root shared by religious and secular Jews and the profound positive quality of the secular "other,"[80] but in the same breath he condemns Sabbath desecration in the Zionist settlements, which he regards as capable of ruining the entire Zionist enterprise in the same manner as the golden calf in its day.[81] He calls for "a civil war" (literally, "a fraternal war") over it: "We today are approaching a war, a commanded war, and we approach it in great pain. When all is said and done, however, I must proclaim that it is a fraternal war; it is a war against our brothers, not our enemies. Not Israel against the Canaanite or the Amalekite, but Judah against Simeon and Simeon against Benjamin."[82]

Rabbi Kook and His Students: Schism or Continuity?

As noted, the most comprehensive and up-to-date study of the question at hand is that of Elie Holzer, and I will analyze and react to his position as I explain my own. In considering Rabbi Kook's writings, Holzer takes pains to differentiate between his treatment of the biblical period, when war became essential following the sin of the golden calf, and of the present, a period of hoped-for redemption, which requires a politics grounded in faith, consistent with a time when it will be possible for a state to exist without "wickedness and barbarity."[83] Holzer even shows how Rabbi Kook reframed the principle of the "Three Oaths"[84]—a midrashic and normative platform on which opponents of Zionism and of active settlement of the land based much of their argument[85]— and transformed them into moral limitations on the innovative, contemporary process of conquering the land. In contrast to the passivity implied by the conventional understanding of the oaths, Rabbi Kook enlisted the first two oaths (that Israel would not "ascend the wall," that is, engage in large-scale immigration to the land, and would not rebel against the nations of the world)[86] in his cause, interpreting them as moral directives that limit and forbid the use of military force against the nations of the world—a position derived from the nature of the messianic destiny described earlier.[87] Holzer nicely points out the complexity of Rabbi Kook's position that affirms the body but simultaneously has reservations about the cult of force—a cult that runs counter to Israel's sanctity.[88]

As for Rabbi Tzvi Yehuda Kook, Holzer writes that the son, in his youth, was entirely under the influence of his father[89] and maintained a utopian and idealized view of Israeli politics.[90] He considered the basic justification for the Israeli polity to lie in its idealized, spiritual dimension,[91] and he saw in Israeli politics an alternative to the politics of the world at large. The first change identified by Holzer in Rabbi Tzvi Yehuda's position appears in articles he wrote during the early 1940s, in which he conveyed his sense that the nations of the world did not understand the significance of Israel's national revival.[92] He developed a rhetoric of belief in Israel's might as something flowing from God's presence,[93] and that concept took center stage in his statements and those of his students. His students went on to lose the elder Rabbi Kook's harmonious idealism regarding the nations of the world and came to see them as an impediment that had to be kept from interfering with the process of redemption.[94] After the Six Day War, the perception of Israeli military prowess as an expression of divine election and favor becomes prominent among these students.[95] The use of force comes to be seen as embodying the enhanced Jewish image[96] and as a marker of the desired transition between exile and redemption,[97] between degradation and pride.[98] The army and its might are seen as something holy,[99] an expression of God's name.[100] Weapons become sanctified,[101] transformed into a means for restoring God's presence to the land of Israel.[102]

The commandment to conquer the land of Israel also acquires a changed status. It is no longer one commandment among many; it is, rather, a "meta-commandment" that necessarily embodies a desirable war. In Rabbi Tzvi Yehuda Kook's words:

> We were commanded to conquer the Land. Conquest is war, and war is self-sacrifice.... By virtue of the commandment to conquer the Land we are duty-bound, we are commanded, to enter into a state of warfare even if we are killed. This is a unique commandment of the Torah, and, as such, its weight is equal to that of the entire Torah.... When we had no army, it was impossible to fulfill the commandment of conquest, even though the commandment itself applied in all generations, as Nahmanides said. But now, He who brings things to pass and foresees all from the beginning has arranged for us to possess the instrumentalities that allow us to fulfill the commandment; we have, God be praised, an army.... Now, God be praised, the time has come when the eternal, divine, spiritual oath joins with conquest by the descendants and their progeny: "We will not leave it desolate or in the

hands of some other nation"—not American, not European, not Arab; it will be only in our hands, the hand of the divine nation. We have reached this stage of maturity in our time, political maturity associated with fulfilling this overall commandment; and, in that sense, how fortunate are we, how good our lot, that we have merited this.[103]

The elder Rabbi Kook's vision of peace was shifted by his son's disciples to the distant future;[104] for the present, the ability to wage war became a privilege. That was true even of an optional war,[105] the waging of which acquired metaphysical implications. The approach becomes even more forceful when "the commandment to conquer the Land" makes the use of military force something that **should be initiated**.[106] "Military aggressiveness" becomes an "a priori halakhic duty," as Holzer puts it.[107] In Rabbi Aviner's words, "We must dwell in the Land even at the cost of war. More than that, even if there is peace, we must initiate a war of liberation to conquer it. Without this Land, we are not the people of Israel."[108]

FROM UTOPIAN "UNITY OF OPPOSITES" TO REAL-WORLD MESSIANISM

Holzer's interpretation is reasonable, and he is right in noting Rabbi Kook's disciples' emphasis on the role of force. My purpose here is not to attack his position but only to add some incidental remarks that may alter the overall picture a bit.

We are dealing here with a utopian vision that foretold the nature of our own time, and it therefore would seem to be a simple matter to examine its validity. But the death of the vision's author—Rabbi Kook—makes it impossible to assess his reaction to the vision's collapse. As noted, Rabbi Kook described, throughout his writings, his utopian hope for the absence of violence, depicting present and future as a sort of transnatural history. I am inclined to believe that Rabbi Kook truly hoped and believed that things would turn out that way. But I believe as well that during the final decade of his life, in his role as chief rabbi, Rabbi Kook came to believe that his vision was indeed a utopian one and that reality might not follow the course it dictated. That was the case in his struggle for the Western Wall, where he ran into fervent Arab opposition[109] that his vision could not account for, and even worse were the Arab riots of 1929, which took place against the background of that dispute. He did not expect the outbreak of violence that engulfed Jerusalem and made the city into a battlefield. He was alarmed as well by the measured reaction of the British, who initially refused to get involved—a refusal at odds with the historiosophic role that Rabbi Kook had assigned to the British Empire[110] and following which his attitude toward Britain changed.[111] When news of the victims of the Hebron Massacre reached

Jerusalem, Rabbi Kook was terribly upset, and legend has it that he fainted when the saw the Hebron refugees.

Following the riots (in October 1929) and in reaction to the mufti's statements blaming them on the Jews, Rabbi Kook published a sharp reaction in the newspaper *Netivah*. But he was careful to distinguish between the extremists in the Muslim world and the moderates who feel "sorrow and shame over the evil acts of a minority among them." His comments reveal that he remained hopeful about the continuation of "that same tradition of peace and mutuality directed toward building the land of Israel together with all its inhabitants . . . and making it into a Garden of Eden."[112]

We see, then, that Rabbi Kook's vision of peace knew its share of challenges. He was not totally unaware of the complexities of reality—though he could not have imagined the events of the Holocaust or of Israel's wars.

It is important to recognize that though Rabbi Kook's vision was one of hope and faith in future harmony, it was not built on foundations of harmonious tranquility. Quite the contrary: The foundations of his teachings are dialectic, encompassing opposites. When Rabbi Kook, during the course of his life, encountered factors inconsistent with his vision, he did not hesitate to emphasize, and even amplify, the conflict—though here, too, he did so out of faith that emphasizing the opposition was a necessary condition to future dialectical peacemaking. Examples include his uncompromising struggle against the New Yishuv's desecration of the Sabbath and his positions on such issues as the controversy over the sabbatical year, the obligation of agricultural settlements to observe the commandments that pertain to the land, kashrut, and milking cows on the Sabbath.[113] He did not hesitate, as we have seen, to declare a "fraternal war," yet he also spoke of the exalted status of the secularists as prophets[114] and as people who "stand within the area defined by the ministering angels"[115] and whose sanctity is so great that the world cannot bear it.[116] These dialectical comments grow out of Rabbi Kook's efforts to deal with the complexities of reality. Still, he hoped the political reality would be different, and he therefore constructed a utopian vision. The riots of 1929 were a harsh and disturbing lesson regarding the fact that politics, too, comprises "light and darkness in confused concert," but it was too late for him to update his practical teachings, and he died from cancer about six years after the riots.

One can think of various possible reactions on the part of his students to the breach between the vision and the reality. They could have decided, first, to rescind the messianic vision, to end the idealized view of reality, and to adopt the alternative view that employed the force of arms (in the manner of the historiosophy adopted by Mapai and the Revisionists). Second, they might have decided to withdraw from activism within history and to await the Messiah (as did various Haredi groups). Finally, they might have decided that Rabbi Kook's vision, taken literally, remained valid, and that they should refrain from the use of force without regard to the political and military events that the Yishuv was dealing with.

The first possibility requires conversion to a secular view of history; the second requires conversion to an anti-Zionist position; and the third requires a messianic perspective totally severed from reality. But there remained a fourth possibility that Rabbi Kook's followers could adopt: that of continuing to maintain the messianic vision as a goal and a historiosophic framework, while treating complex, conflicted reality as something that must be dealt with through other means. Faithful to Rabbi Kook's writings, they chose to treat the biblical instructions—which those writings adopted and justified—as instructions that were in force in the reality of the present day but were nevertheless a part of the messianic doctrine of unity of opposites. As we saw earlier, an insistent and uncompromising struggle was not something that Rabbi Kook considered to be at odds with the unity of opposites. On the contrary, it is firmly rooted in his teachings. His students applied that construct to political and military reality in the face of a history that turned out to be inconsistent with his vision. Their writings show how Rabbi Kook's arguments based on the sin of the golden calf became an explanation for why warfare remained a necessity, albeit a disfavored one, in the here and now, given that reality remained flawed and the nation of Israel had not yet attained the hoped-for degree of faith that could persuade the nations of the justice of its cause. For example, Rabbi Izak (the head of the Bet Orot Yeshiva) argues that "given the state of the world today, one must wage war to have the privilege of settling in the land of Israel, serving God fully, and thereby meriting the good. That is because Israel has not yet attained its own state of perfection." In this regard he quotes a statement by Rabbi Kook whose context we saw earlier in connection with the biblical world: "But for the sin of the Golden Calf, the nations dwelling in the land of Israel would have made peace with Israel and acknowledged [their authority] (*Orot*, 14)".[117]

According to Holzer, "imposing limits on political-messianic activism" is required by the "unique character" of the nation, on the basis of "the essential nature of its messianic destiny," and in light of "its assessments and interpretation of the historical reality of the age."[118] But we must remember that the biblical narrative reflects unlimited historical activism, demonstrating that neither the messianic destiny nor the nation's distinctive quality is impaired by it. The disagreement is over how to interpret historical reality and the extent to which it corresponds to a utopia that is free of the violence found hitherto in every known political construct.

MORAL WAR AND FUNDAMENTALISM

As an outgrowth of this understanding of the world and of Rabbi Kook's writings about the Bible described earlier, Rabbi Kook's disciples returned to the biblical sources, which serve as a bright thread linking many of their writings on morality and warfare. Let me cite some examples from the writings of Rabbi

Danny Izak and Amos Cohen, which clearly manifest a literary link between the new understanding of contemporary political reality and the references to Rabbi Kook's writings on the biblical context. Izak offers a classic example of an account that finds a clear affinity between the biblical situation and the Israeli here-and-now, doing so in a manner anchored in Rabbi Kook's interpretation of Scripture. Izak begins with an account of the normative and ethical framework that ought to govern relations with the inhabitants of the land. In that account, he makes straightforward use of the verses in Deuteronomy[119] that command the Israelites to observe the commandments and speak of the associated reward; he thereby teaches us about the duty to observe the commandments in the land ("a land which the LORD your God looks after"[120]), the reward for fulfilling them, and the punishment for transgressing them. In his understanding—influenced by Rabbi Judah Halevi and Rabbi Kook— Abraham journeyed to the land because only there was it possible to find "true life."[121] The war for the land requires overcoming fear[122] and having faith that God is the master of war,[123] the redeemer,[124] and the One who bestows title to the land.[125] "Just wars" are those that bear God's mark; as supporting authority for that, he cites Rabbi Kook, who "writes of the wars fought by the heroes of the nation in early times."[126] To ensure that the war is just, Israel is obligated "to walk in God's path" and avoid the influence of "the Land's inhabitants";[127] they do so by distancing themselves from idolatry.[128] The "morality of war," Izak teaches, is determined not by how it is conducted but by its goals (namely, the extirpation of evil and revelation of God's light in the world). On that basis, Izak propounds his critique of contemporary warfare:

> If we follow our own true path, then war is for the purpose of extirpating evil from the world, removing the disturbances that prevent God's light from being revealed. That war is true and moral, even if some of its military operations appears immoral to one regarding them in a superficial, external manner. (In our present war we find people who, out of good motives, prevent the army from undertaking certain operations. On occasion, that results in casualties to our soldiers. If those people understood the essence of the people of Israel's war, it would be clear to them that the war was just and moral, for it is waged against those who curse God's name. With that understanding, we would act with force and might against our enemies. It is true that this perspective flows from an intense and profound faith in the Eternal One of Israel, something not yet attained by all; but there is no doubt that the more we advance in the process of redemption, the more our faith advances and deepens.)
>
> It is as the Torah writes: "You shall destroy all the peoples that the Lord your God delivers to you, *showing them no* pity..." (7:16). "He will deliver their kings into your hand and *you shall obliterate* their name from under the heavens; no man shall stand up to you *until you have wiped them out*"

(v. 24). We do not rejoice in battle, but when there is a true need, we fight firmly and decisively until the final victory, through which God's name will be exalted in the world.[129]

Joshua built an altar upon entering the land, from which Izak infers that his war was one that extends life and advances the world. Joshua's operation—in which he pursues five Amorite kings hiding in a cave, directs his officers to put the kings' legs over the heads, smites them, kills them, and hangs them from a tree until evening[130]—serves Izak as an example of "a true and moral operation, for it contributes to the diminution of the forces of evil in the world."[131]

Broad use of biblical verses to illuminate the here-and-now in a fundamentalist manner also characterizes Amos Cohen's article "*Musar be-milhemet kena'an*" ("Morality in the War for Canaan"),[132] which adopts those verses as contemporary halakhic guidance. Through a comparison between the books of Deuteronomy and Exodus, Cohen distinguishes between the conduct of "commanded war" (*milhemet mitzvah*) and of optional war (*milhemet reshut*). A commanded war is a blitzkrieg having no economic purpose; accordingly, men, women, and children alike are to be killed. An optional war is meant to enrich the coffers of the state, so women and children are to be spared. In light of the biblical text, he describes the extent to which one may offer peace in the war against the seven nations and to which the members of those nations may continue to reside in the land of Israel as individuals. He infers from Scripture that those who are conquered may be allowed to live as long as the local population does not "raise its head"; but with their changed attitude, "it became necessary to reinstate the original commandment of total annihilation." "Sadly," Cohen argues in a relevant theme, "the [Israelite] tribes who settled in the Land were 'enlightened' and did not carry out [the commandment]";[133] their exercise of restraint led to the empowerment of the Jebusites.[134] The prophet bemoans the execution of a treaty with "the inhabitants of the Land"[135] and the moral degradation it entailed. The episode of the "Givah concubine,"[136] with its obvious affinities to Sodom, was the result of that sin,[137] as were sins related to illicit sexuality,[138] child sacrifice to Moloch,[139] and, ultimately, the expulsion of the sinners from the land.[140] In the course of this account, Rabbi Kook's words are cited as supporting authority.[141] From the Bible, Cohen learns that Amalek's opposition to Israel and the resulting obligation to destroy it[142] is associated with its proximity[143] and its cruelty.[144] While Israel is committed to the law of war that forbids destruction of the land's vegetation, Amalek, the Midianites, and the Kedemites destroy everything in their encampment.[145] Though the doctrine of unity of opposites might incline us to go easier on them, Cohen argues—following Rabbi Kook—that "they are comparable to the foreskin that must be removed in order to perfect a man. As long as Amalek exists in the world, God's name is lacking in the world."[146] Here, too, "moral war" requires the proper intention.[147] Cohen infers the nature of "Jewish morality" from Saul being considered to have sinned in taking mercy on Agag, the Amalekite king, and from the battle waged by the Jews of Susa against Haman and his support-ers. Noting that the Jews of Susa took none of the spoils,[148] even though they were permitted to do so,[149] Cohen concludes that

> Judaism is not a religion of wars. In contrast to Christianity and Islam, with their missionary aspects, it is the only religion that does not presume to seek physical dominion over the world. To be a Jew is a great privilege but also entails substantial duties and responsibilities, and one who wants to enter the community of Israel must prove that he is indeed worthy to do so and desires with all his heart to join the nation of Israel and undertake the duties thereby entailed. Our aspiration is for worldwide peace. The messianic era will be characterized by worldwide acceptance of the yoke of the kingdom of heaven—"all flesh will call on Your name"—and by the nations' acceptance of the fact that the Jewish nation is the bearer of God's name in the world. As the "kingdom of priests and holy nation," it is the spiritual force among the nations; from it, justice and righteousness will spread throughout the world, as Isaiah prophesied: "And it shall come to pass in the end of days, that the mountain of the LORD's house shall be established as the top of the mountains, and shall be exalted above the hills; and all nations shall flow unto it. And many peoples shall go and say: 'Come you, and let us go up to the mountain of the Lord...'" (Isa 2:2–4).[150]

Rabbi Kook's disciples have been tarred more than once with the brush of fundamentalism,[151] and this sort of writing is indeed fundamentalist[152] in the sense that it takes canonical sources from the past and applies them directly as instructions for action in the present, manifesting no sensitivity to the tempo-ral gap and its many implications. Cohen's comments also negate our power to judge the divine command and the acts of our ancestors; in that sense, he deviates from the spirit of Rabbi Kook's writings.[153]

Still, the content of these articles entails a certain application of the unity of opposites doctrine in the sense that this "real-world messianism" is grounded both in the pacifist messianic vision and in an understanding of the "real-world" and the "biblical" reality. These opposites complement each other. Rabbi Kook's historiosophic vision, on the one hand, and his biblical exegesis, on the other, become a reality in which opposites continue to war with each other and an inner tension is maintained between ideal and real. For these disciples, Rabbi Kook's writings about the biblical past become a contemporary instruction manual, and his writings about what he took to be the here-and-now become a part of the vision of the end of days to which we are to aspire.

In light of this understanding, Ravitzky's criticism of Rabbi Kook's disciples, described earlier, is dampened a bit. The claim that the disciples created an a priori midrash that blunts "the sting of recalcitrant reality" and gave here "an encouraging aspect of the vision"[154] is not an inevitable interpretation. On the contrary, it is precisely the disciples who would seem to have saved Rabbi Kook by freeing his doctrines from a messianic pacifism partaking of an a priori midrash that declines to recognize the sting of reality and offers encouragement that is severed from reality. Instead of associating his doctrines with those qualities, it restores to it the dialectic tension of unity of opposites derived from Rabbi Kook's own biblical exegesis.

Avraham Shapira's comments cited earlier likewise are called into question. The disciples produced a novel interpretation of their teacher's' words, and they do not demonstrate a tendency to "blindly follow the... directives of their teacher." The articles discussed above also make extensive use of the term "morality" as a relevant concept, though it differs in content and logic from that of Shapira.

Conclusion

Let me end with a few critical remarks arising in the wake of a conversation with Elie Holzer about his book and this chapter.

One can certainly find the principle of unity of opposites in the statements of Rabbi Kook's disciples, and I have tried to point to its presence. One vital component of the doctrine, however, is missing from *some* of them in the context at hand: the principle of humility, expressed in sensitivity and attentiveness to the claims of the "other." In the unity of opposites, Rabbi Kook was fully aware of the opposition of the "other" to one's own position in the dispute over one's claims, but he nevertheless regarded the "other" as a subject worthy of study, whose source of vitality should be examined—a divine vitality, requiring study and internalization. Rabbi Kook faced the "other" in the form of Brenner and Berdichevsky, and his attitude toward them comprised powerful opposition and powerful love in equal part. But the "other" faced by his disciples is in the typological mode of the Canaanite and the Amalekite— hence the midrashic burden heaped upon these concepts—along with elements of the Jewish Left. Current events and the intense polemics prevalent in Israeli society brought about a blurring of boundaries between Jewish and non-Jewish sides, and the conflict became harsh and existential. The principle of "humility" that requires attentiveness to the claims of the "other" became ever more eroded.

In our conversation, Holzer argued that an important impetus to his writing lies in the consciousness of a child of Holocaust survivors, born and raised in the Diaspora, for whom the existence of the State of Israel was not self-evident. In this worldview, the State of Israel remains a fragile entity requiring care and protection, and he therefore reacts with horror to the arrogance of settlers presuming to trample on the institutions of its government. Moreover, he is

troubled by the continued discourse about an all-encompassing divine presence that transforms history into a litmus test for God's continually revealed
will; as he sees it, continued adherence to that position—which can be found in
Rabbi Kook himself and in his disciples[155]—represents a failure to internalize the
Holocaust's theological implications. He believes it impossible to carry on the
rhetoric of divine immanence popular in these circles without accounting for
the events of the Holocaust and its implications. To his mind, the discussions
carried on in Merkaz Harav circles and the supposedly post-Holocaust thinking
that developed there[156] simply make no sense. It seems to me that these comments allow for a more profound understanding of Holzer's important study.

But in light of what I said earlier, I think it is possible to appreciate the mag-
nitude of the difficult demand that Holzer makes of Kook's disciples; it is, in
effect, a request for conversion—something beyond their capacity and hence
unjustified. Acting against the institutions of the state is certainly problematic
and certainly inconsistent with a sense that the state's existence is fragile—
a sense I share. But to renounce, on account of the Holocaust, a position of
immanence that asserts God's presence in history—replacing it with some
other approach—seems to me an excessive demand. Individuals may be able
to do so, but the majority need to have an immanent historiosophic midrash—
and that midrash will not please one who, like Holzer, does not adopt an
immanent stand.

At the same time, the demand for post-Holocaust thinking strikes me as an
important demand that cannot be ignored. A post-Holocaust ear finds it hard
to bear a call for the destruction of a population because a prophecy concretely
labels one nation or another a "race" that must be destroyed because "there is
no remedy for it" other than "extirpating its memory," since it represents the
"essence of impurity" and therefore "destroying it is a commandment."[157] A religious discourse that can include such statements after the Holocaust and lacks
all sensitivity to their twentieth-century historiosophic context is a problematic
sort of discourse, even if there is no comparison between the practices of the Jews
making the statements and the practices sadly familiar to us from the Holocaust.

Notes

* Jerusalem: Shalom Hartman Institute, et al., 2009.

1. Aviezer Ravitzky, "It Is Foreseen Yet Free Will Is Given: Messianism, Zionism, and the
Future of Israel in the Varied Religious Perspectives in Israel" [in Hebrew], in *Israel Facing
the Twenty-First Century* [in Hebrew], ed. A. Har-Even (Jerusalem: Van Leer Institute, 1984),
135–197.

2. A. I. H. Kook, *Orot ha-tehiyah* (Jerusalem: Mosad Harav Kook, 1982), 26.

3. A. I. H. Kook, *Maamarei ha-reayah*, part 2 (Speeches before Mizrahi committees and
conventions), 484–485.

4. Ravitzky, "It Is Foreseen," 157–158.

5. R. Harlap, *Ma'ayanei ha-yeshu'ah* (Jerusalem: Midrash Gavohah Letalmud Beit Zevul, 1982), 127. See also Ravitzky, "It Is Foreseen," 158 n. 62.

6. R. Shlomo Aviner, "Return and Redemption" [in Hebrew], *'Amudim* 376 [Shevat 5737] (1977): 150–153.

7. Ravitzky, "It Is Foreseen," 161.

8. Ravitzky, "It Is Foreseen," 162.

9. Ravitzky, "It Is Foreseen," 162; Jacob Talmon, *Political Messianism* [in Hebrew] (Tel-Aviv: Am Oved and Dvir, 1965), 1; Jacob Talmon, *The Origins of Totalitarian Democracy* [in Hebrew] (Tel-Aviv: Dvir, 1955), 15–20. See also the bibliography in Ravitzky, "It Is Foreseen," 165 n. 78.

10. Avraham Shapira, "Gush Emunim: False Messianism?" [in Hebrew], *Shedeimot* 56 (Winter 1974–1975): 142.

11. Shapira, "Gush Emunim," 143.

12. Shapira, "Gush Emunim," 145.

13. Uriel Tal, *Anti-Semitism in the Second German Reich, 1871–1914* [in Hebrew] (PhD diss., Hebrew University, 1962); Uriel Tal, *Political Theology and the Third Reich* [in Hebrew], ed. Paul Mendes-Flohr (Tel-Aviv: Sifriyat Hapo'alim, 1991).

14. Uriel Tal, "Messianism vs. Political Restraint in Religious Zionism" [in Hebrew], in *Myth and Reason in Contemporary Judaism* [in Hebrew], ed. Uriel Tal (Tel-Aviv, Sifriyat Hapo'alim, 1987), 98–114.

15. Uriel Tal, "Foundations of Political Messianism in Israel" [in Hebrew], in *Myth and Reason*, ed. Uriel Tal, 115.

16. Uriel Tal, *Myth and Reason*, 98–99.

17. Uriel Tal, *Myth and Reason*, 99–100.

18. Uriel Tal, *Myth and Reason*, 105.

19. Uriel Tal, *Myth and Reason*, 114. See also Ehud Luz's discussion of Tal in Luz's *Wrestling with an Angel: Power, Morality, and Jewish Identity*, trans. Michael Swirsky (New Haven, Conn.: Yale University Press, 2003), 167–169.

20. There is an extensive polemical and scholarly literature regarding (and opposing) Gush Emunim and the ties between Rabbi Kook's disciples who make up the movement and their master. See Dov Schwartz, *Etgar u-mashber be-hug ha-Rav Kook* [*Challenge and Crisis in Rabbi Kook's Circle*] (Tel-Aviv: Am Oved, 2005); Ehud Sprintzak, *Ish ha-yashar be-'einav: I-legalizm be-hevrah ha-yisraelit* [*Antinomianism in Israeli Society*] (Tel-Aviv: Sifriyat Hapo'alim, 1986); 'Akiva Eldar and Idit Zertal, *Adonei ha-aretz: Ha-mitnahelim u-medinat Yisrael, 1967–2004* [*Lords of the Land: The Settlers and the State of Israel, 1967–2004*] (Tel-Aviv: Dvir, 2004); Anat Rot, *Sod ha-koah: Mo'ezet yesha' u-ma'avaqeka be-gader ha-hafradah u-ve-tokhnit ha-hitnatqut* [*Secret of Its Strength: The Yesha Council and Its Campaign against the Security Fence and the Disengagement Plan*] (Jerusalem: Israel Democracy Institute, 2005); Shelomo Fischer, *Self-Expression and Democracy in Radical Religious Zionist Ideology* (PhD diss., Hebrew University, 2007); Gidon Aran, "Jewish Zionist Fundamentalism: The Bloc of the Faithful (Gush Emunim) in Israel," in *Fundamentalism Observed*, ed. Martin Marty and Scott Appelby (Chicago: University of Chicago Press, 1991), 265–344; Ian Lustick, *For the Land of the Lord: Jewish Fundamentalism in Israel* (New York: Council on Foreign Relations, 1988); Martin Marty and Scott Appelby, eds. *The Fundamentalism Project*, 5 vols. (Chicago: University of Chicago Press, 1991–1995); Gershom Gorenberg, *The Accidental Empire: Israel and the Birth of Settlements, 1967–1977* (New York: New York Times Books, 2006).

21. The term "morality" (*musar*) plays a central role in Rabbi Kook's doctrines (see A. I. H. Kook, *Orot ha-torah* [Jerusalem: Mosad Harav Kook, 1982], chap. 12, par. 4), and Rabbi Kook forcefully argued that "piety must not displace a person's natural morality"; see, in that regard, A. I. H. Kook, *Orot ha-qodesh* (Jerusalem: Mosad Harav Kook, 1985), Introduction, 27. Nevertheless, Elie Holzer correctly emphasizes that for Rabbi Kook, the term we are translating as "morality" is not limited to ethics in the conventional sense. It is not morality that is primary; it is the holiness that encompasses it: "It therefore is utterly impossible to demand that there be a moral nation in the world; there can only be a holy nation" (Kook, *Orot ha-qodesh* 3, 13 and see passim). See also Shalom Rosenberg, "Introduction to Rabbi Kook's Thought" [in Hebrew], in *Yovel orot: The Thought of Rabbi Abraham Isaac Ha-Kohen Kook, of Blessed Memory* [in Hebrew], ed. Benjamin Ish-Shalom and Shalom Rosenberg (Jerusalem: Sifriyat Eliner, 2008), 52–63; Yosef Ben-Shlomo, *Studies in the Teachings of Rabbi Kook* [in Hebrew] (Tel-Aviv: Ministry of Defense, 1989), 51–60. On morality as an internal quality rather than merely an external attitude, see A. I. H. Kook, *Orot* (Jerusalem: Mosad Harav Kook, 1982), 136.

22. Kook, *Orot, Ha-milhamah*, 2, pp. 14–15.

23. A. I. H. Kook, "*Al da'at ha-shem u-milhamot ha-shem*" ["On Knowledge of God and God's wars"], *Maamarei ha-reayah* 2, p. 508.

24. A. I. H. Kook, "*Al da'at ha-shem u-milhamot ha-shem*."

25. A. I. H. Kook, "*Al da'at ha-shem u-milhamot ha-shem*," 509.

26. See Tamar Ross, "Miracle as Another Dimension in the Thought of Maharal of Prague" [in Hebrew], *Da'at* 17 (1986): 81–97.

27. A. I. H. Kook, *Shemoneh Qevatzim* [*Eight Files*] (Hebron, Kiryat-Arba, and Jerusalem, 1999), par. 251, p. 95; see also Kook, *Orot, Yisrael u-tehiyato*, 2, regarding the distinction between causational understanding and moral understanding.

28. Kook, *Ginzei reayah*, ed. R. Ben-Zion Shapira [there is no publication data], 26.

29. Kook, *Maamarei ha-reayah*, 2, p. 508; Kook, *Shemoneh Qevatzim*, *qovetz* 6, pars. 251–252; *Beit orot, Be-shalah* (2007), http://www.beitorot.org/content.asp?pageid=98.

30. See also R. Tzvi Yehuda Kook's Torah discussions, Series 1, *Huqqat* (1974), "'*Amaleq*," par. 8. See also Tzvi Yehuda Kook, *Reeh*, "*Mehiyat 'Amaleq*" ["Extirpation of Amalek"], par. 11. See also R. Harlap, *Ha-nishqefah kemo shahar* (Jerusalem: Mekhon Halakhah Berurah u-Beirur Halakhah, 2003), Derashot, "*Mehiqat 'Amaleq*."

31. A. I. H. Kook, *Ginzei ha-reayah*, 26.

32. Kook, *Orot, Orot ha-tehiyah* 9, p. 63; Kook, *Shemoneh Qevatzim*, *qovetz* 6, secs. 251–252; *'Ayin ayeh, Berakhot* 2, chap. 9—*Ha-roeh*, 310. *Berakhot* 58a, p. 379. *'Ayin ayeh* 2, *Berakhot* 9, 10; Kook, *Olat reayah* 1, p. 232; Kook, *'Arpelei tohar* (Jerusalem: R. Zvi Yehuda Kook Institute, 1983), 110.

33. *Meorot ha-reayah le-hanuqah, arba parshiyot, u-purim* (Jerusalem: R. Zvi Yehuda Kook Institute, 1995), Parashat Zakhor.

34. A. I. H. Kook, "*Al da'at ha-shem u-milhamot ha-shem*," 509.

35. A. I. H. Kook, "*Al da'at ha-shem u-milhamot ha-shem*," 509.

36. A. I. H. Kook, "*Al da'at ha-shem u-milhamot ha-shem*," 509.

37. A. I. H. Kook, *Orot, Ha-milhamah* 5, p. 16.

38. A. I. H. Kook, "*Al da'at ha-shem u-milhamot ha-shem*," 509.

39. Maimonides, *Shemoneh peraqim*, chap. 7.

40. A. I. H. Kook, "*Al da'at ha-shem u-milhamot ha-shem*," 509–510: "Light clouds do not darken the appearance of the sun glowing in the heavens, and white teeth do not lighten the face of the Ethiopian."

41. Kook, *Orot, Ha-milhamah*, 6, p. 16.

42. This idea, too, is associated with Maharal; see below, n. 55.

43. The words are quoted from Song 2:12. The Hebrew (*et ha-zamir higiʿa*) can also mean "the time of pruning has come"; hence the next clause.—Translator's note.

44. Kook, *Orot* 1, *Ha-milhamah*, p. 14.

45. "The community of Israel is the quintessence of existence overall" (Kook, *ʾArpelei tohar*, 56; Kook, *Shemoneh Qevatzim*, qovetz 2, par. 15; Kook, *Orot* 1, 1, p. 129); see also Yoel Bin-Nun, "Nationalism and Humanism in Israel" [in Hebrew], in *Yovel orot*, 174–175; Avinoam Rosenak, *Prophetic Halakhah: The Philosophy of Halakhah in the Teachings of Rabbi A. I. H. Kook* [in Hebrew] (Jerusalem: Magnes Press, 2007), 58–87.

46. Below, n. 67 (repression in the name of morality).

47. Kook, *Orot, Ha-milhamah*, 8, p. 16.

48. Kook, *Orot, Ha-milhamah*, 6, p. 16.

49. Kook, *Orot, Ha-milhamah*, 1, p. 14; Kook, *Orot, Ha-milhamah*, 9, p. 17.

50. Kook, *Orot, Ha-milhamah*, 3, p. 15.

51. Kook, *Orot, Ha-milhamah*, 9, p. 18.

52. *Exod. Rab.* (Vilna), Mishpatim, 32:1. See also Aaron Moses ben Mordecai, *Commentary on R. Moses Hayyim Lutzatto's Sefer hoqer u-meqabbel* [in Hebrew] (Johannesburg, 1953), chap. 9, sec. 5; Kook, *Orot, Ha-milhamah*, 3, p. 154, p. 15.

53. Kook, *Orot, Orot yisrael*, chap. 5, sec. 11, p. 157.

54 Rosenak, *Prophetic Halakhah*.

55. "Holy flesh, not less so than holy spirit" (Kook, *Shmoneh Qevatzim*, qovetz 3, sec. 273, p. 100).

56. Kook, *ʾArpelei tohar*, 2–3; Kook, *Shmoneh Qevatzim*, qovetz 2, sec. 6, pp. 294–295; Kook, *Orot ha-qodesh* 2, pp. 290–291; Kook, *ʿOlat reayah* 1, p. 39; Kook, *Iggerot ha-reayah* (Jerusalem: Mosad Harav Kook, 1981), 3, p. 58 (1917); "and on everything we impress the glory of the sacred"; Kook, *Maamarei ha-reayah*, 94–99, 234–235, 404–411, et al.

57. For example, the obligation to maintain bodily cleanliness (Kook, *Mizvot reayah* [Jerusalem: Mosad Harav Kook, 1985], Kook, *Orah hahyim* 2:6, p. 17, col. b); and the recognition of the profound link between physical health and the ability to serve and know God (Kook, *Orah hahyim* 6:1, 33a). See also Maimonides, *Guide*, 3.27. In this context, see Avraham Bik, "The Guide of the Perplexed in His Teachings," in *Zikhron ha-reayah*, ed. Y. Raphael (Jerusalem, 1986), 92–106. Attributing sanctity to the body is consistent with burying fetuses that look like amnions as long as their human form is complete (Kook, *Mizvot reayah*, *Orah hahyim*, 526:10, 81a). All of this is to avoid shaming the body (Kook, *Mizvot reayah*, *Orah hahyim*, 526:10, 81b). Following a person's death, the importance of the body becomes a halakhic symbol expressed through the duty to tend to its burial, an action that is important for living and dead alike. In Rabbi Kook's words: "For all activities and ways of life are connected, even after a person's death" (*ʿAyin ayah, Berakhot* 1, p. 89, chap. 3, par. 3).

58. Kook, *Orot*, sec. 33, p. 80.

59. Kook, *Iggerot*, 1:185.

60. See: "The great need for holiness" (Kook, *Iggerot* 4, p. 89, et passim).

61. Kook, *Orot, Orot ha-tehiyah*, sec. 34, p. 81.

62. Kook, *Orot, Orot ha-tehiyah*, sec. 19, p. 74, s.v. "*ha-galut lo hayetah yekholah lehotzi.*"

63. Kook, Orot, *ʿEder ha-yaqar—ʿiqvei ha-tzon*, pp. 52–53, s.v. "*anu tzerikhim lehavin ve-ladaʿat.*"

64. Kook, *Orot*, *'Eder ha-yaqar*—*'iqvei ha-tzon*.

65. Kook, *Orot*, *'Eder ha-yaqar*—*'iqvei ha-tzon*, pp. 53–56, s.v. *"lo lishkoah she-'aleinu hovah."*

66. Kook, *Orot*, *Ha-milhamah*, sec. 7, p. 16.

67. Kook, *Orot*, *"Ha-ideial be-Yisrael*," sec. 2, p. 104.

68. Kook, *Otzerot ha-reayah* [Collected articles by Rabbi Abraham Isaac Ha-Kohen Kook], vol. 2, ed. Moshe Yehiel Tzuriel (Tel-Aviv, 1988), Kook, *"Te'udat Yisrael u-leumiyato"* ["Israel's Destiny and Nationalism"], 709.

69. Kook, *Iggerot* 2, 667 [Adar 5674] (1914), pp. 288–289; Kook, *Hazon ha-geulah* (Jerusalem, 1941), 290, s.v. *"anahnu hayyavim lehakhnis."*

70. Elie Holzer, *Herev pipiyot*, 63–87.

71. Kook, *'Olat reayah* 1 (Jerusalem, 1985), p. 233.

72. "Israel will make its way not through raging turbulence, for the Lord is not in the earthquake but in the still, small voice [cf. 1 Kgs 19:11–12]....When we shape the path that leads to overall perfection,...even if we encounter the noise and turbulence of war, in the manner of military heroes, it will remain to foster the divine sanctity emitted by the light of Israel as it makes its way step-by-step, calmly and with moderation" (Kook, *'Olat reayah*, 315–316).

73. For a broader treatment of this doctrine, see Rosenak, *Prophetic Halakhah*, 44–56; Avinoam Rosenak, *Rabbi Kook* [in Hebrew] (Jerusalem: Zalman Shazar Center, 2007), 54–57.

74. *'Ayin ayeh*, *Shabbat* 1 (Jerusalem: 1994), chap. 2, par. 44, p. 30a; Kook, *'Olat reayah* 1, p. 316; A. I. H. Kook, *Meorot ha-reayah*, *Shevu'ot*, (Jerusalem: Rabbi Zvi Yehudah Ha-Kohen Kook Institute, 1994), 296.

75. A. I. H. *"Al da'at ha-shem u-milhamot ha-shem,"* *Maamarei ha-reayah*, 2, p. 509. So, too, in his comments on Christianity, Kook, *Iggerot*, 1, pp. 51–52, s.v. *"ve-lamah zeh yitmah kevodo."*

76. A. I. H. Kook, *Maamarei ha-reayah*, 2, p. 510, s.v. *"eineinu tovah lehabit al ha-kol."*

77. A. I. H. Kook, *Iggerot*, 1, p. 52.

78. A. I. H. Kook, *ShmonehQevatzim*, vol. 3, *qovetz* 7, sec. 103, pp. 181–182. On the implications of this stance and its contrast to Rabbi Kook's "vision of vegetarianism," see Rosenak, *Prophetic Halakhah*, 358–364.

79. Kook, *Orot ha-qodesh*, 2, pp. 423–424; Kook, *Shmoneh Qevatzim*, vol. 3, *qovetz* 7, sec. 62, pp. 154–155.

80. Rabbi Kook's statements on this are very forceful. See Rosenak, *Rabbi Kook*, 34–42.

81. See below, nn. 82–83.

82. Kook, *Otzrot ha-reayah*, 4, p. 94.

83. Kook, *Orot*, *Ha-milhamah*, 3, p. 15.

84. *b. Ketub*. 111a.

85. Ravitzky, "It Is Foreseen," 139–146; Ravitzky, *Messianism Zionism, and Jewish Religious Radicalism* [in Hebrew] (Tel-Aviv: Am Oved, 1993), 211–234.

86. Rabbi Kook considered the third oath—not to hasten the End—to have been canceled; from his perspective, it no longer applies now that the era of redemption has begun. See also R. Shlomo Aviner, *A People and Its Land: The Revival of the Nation on Its Land* [in Hebrew] (Bet-El: Sifriyat Havvah, 1999), part 3, question 7: *"Be-'inyan shalosh ha-shevu'ot"* (from *'Itturei kohanim*, Iyyar 5753 [1993]).

87. Kook, *'Olat reayah* 1, pp. 376–377, s.v. *"u-mitokh ha-hozeq ha-homri yavo hozeq nafshi ruhani."* See also his articles: Kook, "On the Basis of the Sanhedrin" [in Hebrew] and "On Zionism" [in Hebrew], *Otzrot ha-reayah*, p. 929.

88. See, more broadly, Holzer, *Herev pipiyot be-yadam*, 77–79; Holzer, "Evolution of the Idea of the 'Three Oaths' in Religious Zionism" [in Hebrew], *Da'at* 47 (2001): 129–145.

89. This is evident, for example, in a letter written in 1913, in which he adopted his father's harmonious messianic vision and argued that because Zionism was the beginning of the redemptive process, it would eventually arouse the sympathy of the Arab leadership, who would embrace it with open arms: Tzvi Yehuda Kook, "'Al ha-pereq" [On the Agenda], *Le-netivot Yisrael*, Menorah (Tel-Aviv, 1967), 15; quoted in the original Hebrew in Holzer, *Herev pipiyot*, 204.

90. Tzvi Yehuda Kook, *Le-netivot Yisrael*, 15; Holzer, *Herev pipiyot*, 204–205.

91. Tzvi Yehuda Kook, *Le-netivot Yisrael*, 15; Holzer, *Herev pipiyot*, 204–205.

92. Holzer, *Herev pipiyot*, 205–206.

93. Tzvi Yehuda Kook, "*Netzah emunateinu*," *Le-netivot Yisrael*, 84; Holzer, *Herev pipiyot*, 205–206.

94. Tzvi Yehuda Kook, "*Netzah emunateinu*," *Le-netivot Yisrael*, 82–83; Holzer, *Herev pipiyot*, 205–206.

95. Tzvi Yehuda Kook, "Guarding the Israeli nation" [in Hebrew], *Le-netivot Yisrael*, 106; Holzer, *Herev pipiyot*, 208.

96. Tzvi Yehuda Kook, *Le-netivot Yisrael*, 108.

97. Holzer, *Herev pipiyot*, 209.

98. Tzvi Yehuda Kook, *Le-netivot Yisrael*, 70; Holzer, *Herev pipiyot*, 209.

99. "The state requires an army and so the army is holy" (Tzvi Yehuda Kook, "The Land of Israel and the Full Redemption" [in Hebrew], in *Be-ma'arakhah ha-tzibburit*, 120). See also Tzvi Yehuda Kook, "The Sanctity of the Holy People on the Holy Ground," in *Religious Zionism and the State* [in Hebrew], ed. Yosef and Avraham Tirosh (Jerusalem, 1978), 122; Tzvi Yehuda Kook, "The Land of Israel: We Shall Not Move from Here!" *Sihot Ha-ratziyah 'al eretz Yisrael*, [in Hebrew], par. 21.

100. "From the name of God, which reveals itself in the army's might, its power and pride, there will be revealed more and more of the way to act in God's name" (Tzvi Yehuda Kook, *Mitokh Ha-Torah Ha-Goelet* [From the Redeeming Torah], Haim Avihu Schwartz (Au. & ed.), A. Schwartz publication, Jerusalem 1983, Vol. 1, "Israel's Sanctuary and the Festivals: Independence Day 1975," 47).

101. "For when we recall that it is God who gives us the strength to act mightily, it is no longer 'by my strength and the might of my hand' in the negative sense; it is rather, the study and fulfillment of the Torah. We learn that we must carry out the commandment imposed on us with this strength—that is, conquest of the Land" (*Eretz ha-tzevi, Mizmor yom tov shel medinat Yisrael*, par. 5: "*'ain be-miz'ad yom ha-'atzmaut mi-shum 'kohi ve-'ozem yadi'*" ["An Independence Day parade does not assert 'by my strength and the might of my hand'"], p. 4; Holzer, *Herev pipiyot*, 224). Holzer notes the resemblance of these comments to the spirit of the *Lehi* [Lohamei herut Yisrael; "fighters for the freedom of Israel," known as the Stern Gang, a radical paramilitary group during the time of the Mandate]. On the source cited by Holzer, see Gerald Krummer, "*Lehitpallel be-rovah, motivim datiyyim be-ta'amulah shel ha-lehi*," in *Dat u-mahteret be-eretz Yisrael bi-tequfat ha-mandat* [*Religion and Underground in the Land of Israel under the Mandate*], ed. Hayyim Genizi (undated), 60.

102. Tzvi Yehuda Kook, *Sihot Ha-raziyah 'al eretz Yisrael*, "*Eretz Yisrael—lo nazuz mi-kan*" [*The Land of Israel: We Shall Not Move from Here!*], par. 10; Tzvi Yehuda Kook, "To Be a Good Jew Is First and Foremost to Live in the Land of Israel" [in Hebrew], in *The State in Jewish Thought: Sources and Articles* [in Hebrew], ed. Aryeh Strikovsky (Jerusalem, 1982),

212. Holzer notes the change in wording between "every additional soldier" and "every additional gun" (4 n. 59).

103. Tzvi Yehuda Kook, *Ha-torah ha-goelet* [*The Redemptive Torah*], chap. 6; "*Mitzvat kibbush ha-aretz*" ["The Commandment to Conquer the Land"], p. 31. See also Tzvi Yehuda Kook, "*Bein 'am le-artzo,*" *Artzi* 2 (1982): 17; Holzer, *Herev pipiyot*, 230.

104. See Zalman Barukh Melamed (head of Yeshivat Bet-El), "*'Inyanei milhamah*" ["On Warfare"], *Iyyar* 12 [5767] (2007).

105. Zalman Barukh Melamed, section headed "*Milhamah yezumah*" [initiated war].

106. Gideon Aran, *Mi-tziyonut datit le-dat tziyonit: Shoreshei gush emunim ve-tarbuto* [*From Religious Zionism to Zionist Religion: The Roots and Culture of Gush Emunim*] (PhD diss., Hebrew University, 1987); Aviezer Ravitzky, *Messianism, Zionism, and Jewish Religious Radicalism* (Chicago: University of Chicago Press, 1996), 129–130.

107. Holzer, *Herev pipiyot*, 232.

108. Shlomo Aviner, "*Yerushat ha-aretz ve-ha-be'ayah ha-musarit*" ["Acquiring the Land: The Moral Problem"], *Arzi* 2 [Iyyar-Sivan 5742] (1982): 11; R. Waldman, *Zevi ra'anan* (Tel-Aviv: Gush Emunim, 1980): 195; Holzer, *Herev pipiyot*, 232.

109. See Rosenak, *Rabbi Kook*, 259–265.

110. Rosenak, *Rabbi Kook*, 170–176.

111. Rosenak, *Rabbi Kook*, 267.

112. Kook, *Otzrot ha-reayah*, 2, *Maamarei eretz Yisrael*: "*Teshuvat ha-rav le-mufti ha-'aravi*" ["The Rabbi's Response to the Arab Mufti"], 1047–1049.

113. Rosenak, *Prophetic Halakhah*, 270–281.

114. Kook, *'Arpelei tohar*, 15.

115. Kook, *Orot ha-qodesh*, 1, p. 298; Kook, *'Arpelei tohar*, 15–16.

116. Kook, *Iggerot*, 4, p. 217; Rosenak, *Rabbi Kook*, 36–42.

117. R. Danny Izak, *Milhamah musarit* [*Moral War*] [16 Av 5766] (2006), http://www.kipa.co.il/pash/show.asp?id=14010.

118. Holzer, *Herev pipiyot*, 87.

119. Deut 7:12–13, 11:13.

120. Deut 11:12.

121. Izak, *Milhamah musarit*.

122. Deut 7:17–18.

123. Deut 7:21.

124. Deut 9:3.

125. Deut 11:23.

126. "'A war for their existence, the existence of the nation, recognized inwardly as God's war' (*Orot*, p. 14)" (Izak, *Milhamah musarit*).

127. Izak, *Milhamah musarit*.

128. "You shall burn the statues of their gods in fire…so as not to bring an abomination into your house, making you as accursed as it; you shall utterly detest it and utterly abhor it, for it is accursed" (Deut 7:25–26). "I forewarn you this day that you shall surely perish" (Deut 8:19). "Lest your heart be deceived and you turn aside and serve other gods and bow to them" (Deut 11:16).

129. Izak, *Milhamah musarit*.

130. Josh 10:18, 10:24, 10:26.

131. Izak, *Milhamah musarit*.

132. Amos Cohen, *Musar be-milhemet kena'an*, http://tora.us.fm/tnk1/kma/qjrim2/musr_hmlxma.html.

133. Cohen, *Musar be-milhemet kena'an.*

134. Judg 1:21; 2 Sam 5:6–9.

135. Judg 2:1–2.

136. Judg 2:19–21.

137. Judg 1:21.

138. "They engaged in idolatry only to allow themselves to engage in illicit sexuality" (*t. Sanh.* 63b).

139. Jer 32:35; Deut 9:4–5, 12:29–31, 18:9–14.

140. "And the land was defiled, therefore I did visit its iniquity upon it, and the land vomited out her inhabitants" (Lev 18:24–30).

141. See: "Rabbi Kook considers the force of the Canaanite influence to this day…Cush, and Mitzraim, and Put, and Canaan (Gen 10:6)" (Cohen, *Musar be-milhemet kena'an*).

142. Deut 25:17–19.

143. "The Amalekite and the Canaanite dwell in the valley" (Num 14:25); Num 14:43–45.

144. Cohen, *Musar be-milhemet kena'an*, text at n. 6.

145. Judg 6:1–5. Cohen cites additional proof; Cohen, *Musar be-milhemet kena'an*, text at n. 6.

146. Cohen grounds his comments in Rashi; see Rashi on Exod 17:16.

147. Cohen, *Musar be-milhemet kena'an.*

148. Esth 9:15.

149. Esth 8:10.

150. Cohen, *Musar be-milhemet kena'an.*

151. Shlomo Fischer, "*Fundamentalizm ve-heqer ha-tziyonut ha-datit*" ["Fundamentalism and the Study of Religious Zionism"], *Teioriyah u-biqqoret* 31 (2007): 263–273.

152. Fischer, "*Fundamentalizm ve-heqer ha-tziyonut ha-datit*," 265.

153. Kook, *Orot ha-qodesh*, 3, p. 27; Tamar Ross, "The Cognitive Value of Religious Truth Statements: Rabbi A. I. Kook and Postmodernism", Yaakov Elman and Jeffrey Gorock (eds.), Hazon Nahum: Studies in Jewish Law and History ro Dr. Norman Lamm, Yeshivah University, New York 1997, pp. 479–528.

154. Ravitzky, "It Is Foreseen," 162.

155. Shlomo Hayyim Aviner, *Mishbarayikh ve-galayikh 'averu 'alai: 'Al ha-shoah* [On the Holocaust] (Jerusalem: Sifriyat Havvah, 2000), 31–39 et passim.

156. See, for example, Tzvi Yehuda Kook, "*Ha-shoah, sihah* 1 (5727)" ["The Holocaust, Discussion 1, 1967"]; Eliyahu Bazak, *Medabber bi-tzedaqah* [*Speaking Righteousness*], ed. Roni Nisinowitz (Eilat, 2000), 13; see also Avinoam Rosenak, "Faith, Crisis, and Silence in Post-Holocaust Jewish Thought and in the Teachings of André Neher" [in Hebrew], in *Eternity in Times of Change: André Neher and Post-Holocaust Franco-Jewish Thought* [in Hebrew], ed. Yehoyada Amir (Tel-Aviv: Hakibbutz Hameuhad and the Van Leer Institute, 2005), 157–158.

157. Above p. 404.

Bibliography

Aran, Gidon. "Jewish Zionist Fundamentalism: The Bloc of the Faithful (Gush Emunim) in Israel." In *Fundamentalism Observed*, edited by Martin Marty and Scott Appelby, 265–344. Chicago: University of Chicago Press, 1991.

——. *Mi-tziyonut datit le-dat tziyonit: Shoreshei gush emunim ve-tarbuto* [*From Religious Zionism to Zionist Religion: The Roots and Culture of Gush Emunim*]. PhD diss., Hebrew University, 1987.

Aviner, Shlomo Hayyim. *Mishbarayikh ve-galayikh 'averu 'alai: 'Al ha-shoah* [*On the Holocaust*]. Jerusalem: Sifriyat Havvah, 2000.

——. *A People and Its Land: The Revival of the Nation on Its Land* [in Hebrew]. Bet-El: Sifriyat Havvah, 1999.

——. "*Yerushat ha-aretz ve-ha-be'ayah ha-musarit*" ["Acquiring the Land: The Moral Problem"]. *Artzi* 2 [Iyyar-Sivan 5742] (1982): 4–13.

——. "Return and Redemption" [in Hebrew]. *'Amudim* 376 [Shevat 5737] (1977): 150–153.

Bazak, Eliyahu. *Medabber bi-tzedaqah* [*Speaking Righteousness*]. Edited by Roni Nisinowitz. Eilat: Yeshivat Ayelet Ha-Shachar, 2000.

Ben Mordecai, Aaron Moses. *Commentary on R. Moses Hayyim Lutzzatto's Sefer hoqer u-meqabbel* [in Hebrew]. Johannesburg, 1953.

Ben-Shlomo, Yosef. *Studies in the Teachings of Rabbi Kook* [in Hebrew]. Tel-Aviv: Ministry of Defense, 1989.

Bik, Avraham. "The Guide of the Perplexed in His Teachings." [in Hebrew] In *Zikhron ha-reayah*, edited by Yitzhak Raphael. Jerusalem: Mosad Ha-Rav Kook, 1986.

Bin-Nun, Yoel. "Nationalism and Humanism in Israel" [in Hebrew]. In *Yovel orot*, edited by B. Ish Shalom and S. Rosenberg, 169–208. Jerusalem: Elinor, 1988.

Eldar, 'Akiva, and Idit Zertal. *Adonei ha-aretz: Ha-mitnahelim u-medinat Yisrael, 1967–2004* [*Lords of the Land: The Settlers and the State of Israel, 1967–2004*]. Tel-Aviv: Dvir, 2004.

Fischer, Shlomo. "*Fundamentalizm ve-heqer ha-tziyonut ha-datit*" ["Fundamentalism and the Study of Religious Zionism"]. *Teioriyah u-biqqoret* 31 (2007): 263–273.

——. *Self-Expression and Democracy in Radical Religious Zionist Ideology*. PhD diss., Hebrew University, 2007.

Gorenberg, Gershom. *The Accidental Empire: Israel and the Birth of Settlements, 1967–1977*. New York: New York Times Books, 2006.

Harlap, Yaakov Moshe. *Ha-nishqefah kemo shahar*. Jerusalem: Mekhon Halakhah Berurah u-Beirur Halakhah, 2003.

——. *Ma'ayanei ha-yeshu'ah*. Jerusalem: Midrash Gavohah Letalmud Beit Zevul, 1982.

Holzer, Elie. *Herev pipiyot.* [*A Double Edged Sword: Military Activism in the Thought of Religious Zionism*]. Jerusalem and Ramat Gan: Shalom Hartman Institute The Faculty of Law, Bar Ilan University and Keter Books, 2009.

Holzer, Elie. "Evolution of the Idea of the 'Three Oaths' in Religious Zionism" [in Hebrew]. *Da'at* 47 (2001): 129–145.

Kook, A. I. H. *Shemoneh Qevatzim* [*Eight Files*]. Hebron, Kiryat-Arba, and Jerusalem, 1999.

——. *Meorot ha-reayah le-hanuqah, arba parshiyot, u-purim*. Jerusalem: R. Zvi Yehuda Kook Institute, 1995.

——. *'Ayin ayeh, Shabbat* 1. Jerusalem: Ha-Machon Al Shem Rabbi Zvi Y. Kook, 1994.

——. *Otzerot ha-reayah* [Collected articles by Rabbi Abraham Isaac Ha-Kohen Kook]. Vol. 2. Edited by Moshe Yehiel Tzuriel. Tel-Aviv: Yeshivat Sha'labim, 1988.

——. *Mitzvot reayah*. Jerusalem: Mosad Harav Kook, 1985.

——. *'Olat reayah* 1. Jerusalem: Mosad Ha-Rav Kook, 1985.

——. *Orot ha-qodesh*. Jerusalem: Mosad Harav Kook, 1985.

——. *'Arpelei tohar*. Jerusalem: R. Zvi Yehuda Kook Institute, 1983.

——. *Orot ha-tehiyah*. Jerusalem: Mosad Harav Kook, 1982.

——. *Orot ha-torah*. Jerusalem: Mosad Harav Kook, 1982.

——. *Orot*, Jerusalem: Mosad Harav Kook, 1982

——. *Iggerot ha-reayah*. Jerusalem: Mosad Harav Kook, 1981.

——. *Hatzon ha-geulah*. Jerusalem: Rabbi Kook's Friends Publication Society, 1941.

——. *"Te'udat Yisrael u-leumiyato"* ["Israel's Destiny and Nationalism"]. In *Otzerot ha-reayah* [Collected Articles by Rabbi Abraham Isaac Ha-Kohen Kook], vol. 2, edited by Moshe Yehiel Zuriel, 706. Tel-Aviv: Segal publication, 1988.

——. *Ginzei reayah*. Edited by R. Ben-Zion Shapira. (No publication data).

——. *Maamarei ha-reayah*. [Speeches before Mizrahi committees and conventions]. Part 2. Jerusalem: Goldah Katz Foundation, 1984, 484–485.

Kook, Tzvi Yehuda. *"Bein 'am le-artzo."* *Artzi* 2 (1982): 15–23.

——. "To Be a Good Jew Is First and Foremost to Live in the Land of Israel" [in Hebrew]. In *The State in Jewish Thought: Sources and Articles* [in Hebrew], edited by Aryeh Strikovsky, 211–213. Jerusalem: Torah Culture Department, Ministry of Education and Culture, 1982.

——. "The Sanctity of the Holy People on the Holy Ground." In *Religious Zionism and the State* [in Hebrew], edited by Yosef and Avraham Tirosh, 140–146. Jerusalem: Ministry of Education, 1978.

——. *"'Al ha-pereq"* ["On the Agenda"]. *Le-netivot Yisrael*. Menorah. Tel-Aviv, 1967.

——. "Ha-shoah, sihah 1 (5727)" ["The Holocaust, Discussion 1, 1967"].

Krummer, Gerald. *"Lehitpallel be-rovah, motivim datiyyim be-ta'amulah shel ha-lehi."* In *Dat u-mahteret be-eretz Yisrael bi-tequfat ha-mandat* [*Religion and Underground in the Land of Israel under the Mandate*], edited by Hayyim Genizi, 68–57. Tel Aviv: Moreshem publication, 1995.

Lustick, Ian. *For the Land of the Lord: Jewish Fundamentalism in Israel*. New York: Council on Foreign Relations, 1988.

Luz, Ehud. *Wrestling with an Angel: Power, Morality, and Jewish Identity*. Translated by Michael Swirsky. New Haven, Conn.: Yale University Press, 2003.

Marty, Martin, and Scott Appelby, eds. *The Fundamentalism Project*. 5 vols. Chicago: University of Chicago Press, 1991–1995.

Melamed, Zalman Barukh. *"'Inyanei milhamah"* ["On Warfare"]. *Iyyar* 12 [5767] (2007) (in http://www.yeshiva.org.il/midrash/doc/doc17/ki-tetze63.doc).

Ravitzky, Aviezer. *Messianism, Zionism, and Jewish Religious Radicalism* [in Hebrew]. Tel-Aviv: Am Oved, 1993. English translation, Chicago: University of Chicago Press, 1996.

——. "It Is Foreseen Yet Free Will Is Given: Messianism, Zionism, and the Future of Israel in the Varied Religious Perspectives in Israel" [in Hebrew]. In *Israel Facing the Twenty-First Century* [in Hebrew], edited by A. Har-Even, 135–197. Jerusalem: Van Leer Institute, 1984.

Rosenak, Avinoam. *Prophetic Halakhah: The Philosophy of Halakhah in the Teachings of Rabbi A. I. H. Kook* [in Hebrew]. Jerusalem: Magnes Press, 2007.

——. *Rabbi Kook* [in Hebrew]. Jerusalem: Zalman Shazar Center, 2007.

——. "Faith, Crisis, and Silence in Post-Holocaust Jewish Thought and in the Teachings of André Neher" [in Hebrew]. In *Eternity in Times of Change: André Neher and Post-Holocaust Franco-Jewish Thought* [in Hebrew], edited by Yehoyada Amir, 153–192. Tel-Aviv: Hakibbutz Hameuhad and the Van Leer Institute, 2005.

Rosenberg, Shalom. "Introduction to Rabbi Kook's Thought" [in Hebrew]. In *Yovel orot: The Thought of Rabbi Abraham Isaac Ha-Kohen Kook, of Blessed Memory* [in Hebrew], edited by Benjamin Ish-Shalom and Shalom Rosenberg, 27–105. Jerusalem: Sifriyat Eliner, 2008.

Ross, Tamar. "Miracle as Another Dimension in the Thought of Maharal of Prague" [in Hebrew]. *Da'at* 17 (1986): 81–97.

Rot, Anat. *Sod ha-koah: Mo'etzet yesha' u-maavaqeka be-gader ha-hafradah u-ve-tokhnit ha-hitnatqut* [*Secret of Its Strength: The Yesha Council and Its Campaign against the Security Fence and the Disengagement Plan*]. Jerusalem: Israel Democracy Institute, 2005.

Schwartz, Dov. *Etgar u-mashber be-hug ha-Rav Kook* [*Challenge and Crisis in Rabbi Kook's Circle*]. Tel-Aviv: Am Oved, 2005.

Shapira, Avraham. "Gush Emunim: False Messianism?" [in Hebrew]. *Shedeimot* 56 (Winter 1974–1975): 142–145.

Sprintzak, Ehud. *Ish ha-yashar be-'einav: I-legalizm be-hevrah ha-yisraelit* [*Antinomianism in Israeli Society*]. Tel-Aviv: Sifriyat Hapo'alim, 1986.

Tal, Uriel. *Political Theology and the Third Reich* [in Hebrew]. Edited by Paul Mendes-Flohr. Tel-Aviv: Sifriyat Hapo'alim, 1991.

——. "Messianism vs. Political Restraint in Religious Zionism" [in Hebrew]. In *Myth and Reason in Contemporary Judaism* [in Hebrew], edited by Uriel Tal, 98–114. Tel-Aviv: Sifriyat Hapo'alim, 1987.

——. "Foundations of Political Messianism in Israel" [in Hebrew]. In *Myth and Reason in Contemporary Judaism* [in Hebrew], edited by Uriel Tal, 115–132. Tel-Aviv: Sifriyat Hapo'alim, 1987.

——. *Anti-Semitism in the Second German Reich, 1871–1914* [in Hebrew]. PhD diss., Hebrew University, 1962.

Talmon, Jacob. *Political Messianism* [in Hebrew]. Tel-Aviv: Am Oved and Dvir, 1965.

——. *The Origins of Totalitarian Democracy* [in Hebrew]. Tel-Aviv: Dvir, 1955.

Waldman, R. *Zevi ra'anan*. Tel-Aviv: Gush Emunim, 1980.

{ 18 }

R. Moshe Feinstein on *Milhemet Mitzvah*

HALAKHAH, MORALITY, AND EXEGESIS

Baruch Alster

R. Moshe Feinstein (Uzda, Belarus, 1895–New York, 1986) is widely recognized as one of the foremost halakhic decisors of the late twentieth century, and an outstanding leader of post-Holocaust American Orthodoxy. His magnum opus, *Iggerot Moshe* (*IgM*), is a collection of responsa on various topics in halakhah.[1] R. Feinstein is best known for his almost total independence in deciding halakhah, his pioneering responsa on medical issues, and his relative leniency in many issues relevant to the viability of Orthodox Jewish life in America.[2] However, as has been noted by various scholars, Feinstein's outlook was all but modern. True, he tended to accept the physical realities of contemporary American life, and he was grateful for America's ideals of equality and freedom that enabled Orthodox Jews to practice their religion unhindered by outside coercion.[3] But he was unwilling to compromise on any matter he thought would create the slightest change in Judaism itself, such as many issues pertaining to the role of women in Judaism and the status of Conservative and Reform Jews, and he was wary of any substantial integration by Orthodox Jews into general American society.[4] According to Feinstein, Jews must submit their own will to that of God, as is expressed in the halakhic system,[5] and not try to distort the divine will by Americanizing halakhah.

For this reason, his responsum dealing with the laws of "obligatory war" (מלחמת מצוה), that is, a war against the seven Canaanite nations and Amalek, seems anomalous. The moral problem in killing innocents as commanded in such wars (Deut 20:16–17, 25:19) is well-known and has been dealt with by traditional Judaism since ancient times, as can be seen throughout the present volume.[6] Throughout history, many rabbis have struggled with this issue, devising various solutions to the problem, some of which we will discuss later. But among Orthodox thinkers, I believe Feinstein's solution is by far the boldest.

The Responsum

In September 1978, Israeli prime minister Menahem Begin and Egyptian president Anwar Sadat signed the Camp David Accords, in which Israel agreed to withdraw from the Sinai Peninsula, and in principle also from other territories it had administered since the Six Day War.[7] While most Israelis supported this agreement, others opposed it for ideological reasons.[8] One such group was the Habad-Lubavitch Hasidic sect, led by the Brooklyn-based Lubavitcher rebbe, Menahem Mendel Schneersohn (1902–1994). According to R. Schneersohn, any land ceded by Israel would embolden Israel's enemies and inevitably bring war rather than peace, thus causing more loss of Jewish life. Therefore, he concluded, it is halakhically forbidden to trade Israeli-controlled land for a peace agreement.[9]

In order to rally support for his position, Schneersohn contacted a number of prominent rabbis, among them Feinstein, to sign a petition opposing the agreements with Egypt. For this purpose, he sent one of his prominent Israel-based Hasidim, Nochum Trebnick, chief rabbi of the Lubavitch town of Kefar-Habad, to contact Feinstein. His answer, dated October 26, 1978, appears in *Iggerot Moshe*, vol. 7, *Hoshen Mishpat*, responsum 78.[10] I present in this chapter a discussion of the responsum's content based on my own English translation, with the original Hebrew appearing in the notes.

> I believe you are aware that I do not usually respond promptly even when asked. But regarding matters I have not been asked about, it is not my place to respond, even if it is a private question regarding ritual law.[11]

Feinstein begins by explaining why he had not previously responded to Schneersohn's call to sign the petition: He himself had not been asked personally to sign, and it is not his custom to give halakhic rulings—in our case, regarding the permissibility of ceding territory to Egypt—without first being asked his opinion.[12] Besides, even if he had been asked, he claims that he usually takes his time responding.[13] So before Trebnick turned to him specifically, there was no way he would even discuss this issue. But there are other reasons as well that he has not responded, as he hints at the end of this last sentence: Feinstein sees his expertise as being in "private question[s] regarding ritual law." Schneersohn's petition, of course, does not come under this category. As Feinstein continues:

> Even when asked, I have responded only to private inquiries on matters pertaining to the questioner himself, and then only when my answer would not insult another rabbi. As to public questions, I have never responded to them, neither in writing nor orally.[14]

Even now, after Schneersohn sent Trebnick to contact him, Feinstein is unwilling to sign the petition, citing no less than three reasons for his refusal. First, the questioner, in this case Trebnick, is not personally involved in the decision to sign the Camp David Accords. Second, in what may imply criticism of the proposed petition, Feinstein is unwilling to "insult another rabbi," that is, to infringe another rabbi's jurisdiction. As this question is a matter of Israeli foreign policy, one must turn to Israeli, not American, rabbis for guidance. And finally, as he already hinted, Feinstein does not view public policy as his field of expertise.[15]

However, there seems to be a more basic reason for R. Feinstein's refusal to sign the petition—he understands halakhah itself as effectively forbidding any current Jewish government to wage war, implying that the prevention of war accomplished by the agreement is a worthy goal in and of itself.[16] As the responsum continues:

> You may have heard what I have told my students. I think that in war, as it is a matter of life and death, one needs a special command, the Urim and Thummim,[17] and the Sanhedrin,[18] even in an obligatory war like the war against Amalek.[19]

According to Feinstein, waging war without explicit divine approval, through both a specific prophetic command and the priestly Urim and Thummim, is forbidden. This is true even regarding those known as "obligatory wars" (מלחמת מצוה), defined halakhically as those against the seven nations or Amalek,[20] and *a fortiori* regarding other so-called optional wars (מלחמת רשות). So in our era, when all three institutions mentioned by Feinstein do not exist, war is simply forbidden.

As Feinstein seemingly contradicts himself here, a comment is in order. At the end of the previous paragraph, he mentioned that he has never ruled on a public matter. Now, he says he has an opinion on the halakhic propriety of war. However, we should pay attention to his exact wording here. R. Feinstein did not say in this paragraph that he gave a ruling regarding war, but rather that this is what he taught his students. As opposed to public rulings, subjects taught at Lithuanian-style *yeshivot*—Feinstein headed the New York–based Mesivta Tiferes Jerusalem[21]—are not chosen by their applicability to practical halakhah, but by their surfacing in whichever talmudic tractate the yeshiva happens to be learning in a given term. In other words, Feinstein may have had theoretical opinions on many issues of public halakhah, but he would not formulate them as a practical ruling, as many other factors must then be taken into account.

R. Feinstein now proceeds to base his opinion on biblical and post-biblical history:

> This must be so, as David and Solomon and all the righteous kings did not initiate war against Amalek, and this is so clearly obvious that it is indisputable. Only when the idolaters, such as Greek King Antiochus, attacked

Israel, did they wage war in the Second Commonwealth, as this was for defensive purposes.[22]

Here we see that the only way a Jewish government may wage war according to halakhah, sans prophets and priests, is by way of self-defense. Only when the enemy attacks may the Jews respond.[23] Again, in context, this implies that a peace agreement is a worthy goal for a Jewish state, at least in theory.

Now that he has completed his theoretical discussion, R. Feinstein returns to the matter at hand:

> I have never discussed, nor even thought, about how to resolve this issue, because those in charge in the ruling government in *Eretz Israel*[24] would never ask me such matters. Therefore, any discussion would only be a waste of time. Also, it is unclear to me how to decide, so most definitely there is no way I would rule on this.[25]

Feinstein realizes, of course, that his theoretical opinion does not constitute a formal ruling and that likely as not he would rule against the agreement if he had all relevant information. But, as he has already stated, there is no way he would have been asked his opinion by the Israeli government—even had the government consulted rabbis, he would not be the one involved, as he is not Israeli, and such matters are inconclusive halakhically by definition, or at least Feinstein does not deem himself competent to decide on these matters.[26]

The responsum then concludes with a prayer for redemption, especially apt in situations like this:

> Therefore, we trust only God, as everything is in His power. We pray to Him to have mercy on us and all of Israel so that everything should be for the best and that He should send our righteous Messiah soon.[27]

Now that I have explained the responsum in its historical context, I turn to analyze it to determine how R. Feinstein confronts the legal, theological, and moral problems inherent in the biblical laws and narratives regarding "obligatory war."

Halakhic Perspectives

Let us begin with the legal issue. Normative halakhah generally follows the understanding that the wars against Amalek and the seven nations come under the rubric of "obligatory war,"[28] which constitute a "biblical commandment" (מצוה דאורייתא). This is derived explicitly from Deuteronomy (20:16–18 regarding the seven nations and 25:19 regarding Amalek). And as the commandment has already been given, there is no need for the king to request permission from anyone to carry out these commandments, as opposed to "optional wars," in which permission must be granted by the High Court. As Maimonides says:[29]

> For an obligatory war, the king need not obtain the permission of the court, but rather may go forth of his own initiative at any time and compel the people to go with him. But for an optional war, he may not lead forth the people without the permission of the court of seventy-one.

But Feinstein effectively denies in his responsum any lasting practical significance to the laws of obligatory war, as he requires a "special command" (ציווי מיוחד) for each case of their implementation. Not only is the High Court required to give its permission, and not only are the Urim and Thummim to be consulted, as many authorities require for any war,[30] but it is also necessary to have an additional prophetic injunction (impossible today) that the law is to be implemented at a specific point in time. The Torah's commandment itself is not enough. The only likely significance of the verses in Deuteronomy, then, is to confer the legal status of biblical law on such wars.[31] Thus, R. Feinstein virtually cancels a biblical (and thus divine) commandment, but without of course formally annulling it.

Feinstein's explicit halakhic reasoning here builds on two concepts. First, it cites the importance of preserving life (פיקוח נפש). I am assuming that he means preserving the life of the Jewish (in this case, Israeli) soldiers, who would be risking their lives by going to war.[32] In general, it is accepted that only three commandments may override the principle of preserving life: the prohibitions on murder, idolatry, and adultery and incest (*t. Shabb.* 16:14). However, according to many authorities, as even optional war is permitted by Jewish law, even such a war must somehow override this principle, as warfare by definition involves danger.[33] R. Feinstein proposes almost the exact opposite, claiming that preserving life overrides even obligatory war, unless there is a "special command" by a contemporary prophet. While the principle of preserving life had already been used to limit the possibility of warfare,[34] it is extremely rare to find an opinion requiring a specific prophecy in order to be able to fulfill what should have been a biblical commandment.[35]

The second concept brought by Feinstein is the use of biblical narratives to determine halakhah. Feinstein uses these narratives as case law: As biblical characters known to be righteous behaved in a certain way, so must we. If "David and Solomon and all the righteous kings did not initiate war against Amalek," then we shouldn't either, unless there is no choice, either because of a direct prophecy or, God forbid, an enemy attack. Although the Bible is generally not used as a legal source in halakhic discourse, many decisors take exception to this rule when there is no alternative source or, in other words, in cases where "it is unclear...how to decide."[36] The lack of traditional halakhic sources forces R. Feinstein to look back to the Bible for guidance.

Both these halakhic mechanisms serve to tell us that we are dealing here with a remarkable decision. But precisely because this is not the standard reading of the relevant sources, we should be aware that there may be other factors influencing the decision—specifically, a desire to see Jewish law as moral.

Moral Perspectives

I turn now to the moral aspects of the responsum. In a 1994 article,[37] Avi Sagi distinguished between two moral responses to the command to annihilate Amalek common in halakhic writings: the "practical" response, according to which all commands pertaining to ancient nations are moot, as "Long ago Sennacherib, King of Assyria, came up and confused all the nations [beyond recognition],"[38] and the "theoretical" response, according to which the entire commandment is limited by certain moral considerations.[39] Maimonides is the main proponent of this approach, as he applies the biblical requirement to call for peace before attacking, even in an obligatory war, as he says:[40]

> No war, whether optional or obligatory, is to be declared against anyone before first offering terms of peace, as it says (Deut 20:10): "When you come near to a city to fight against it, then proclaim peace to it." If the inhabitants make peace and accept the seven commandments enjoined upon the Noahides, none of them may be slain, but they become tributary, as it says (v. 11): "[all the people to be found in it] shall be tributaries to you, and they shall serve you."

What kind of morality do we see here? In one sense, R. Feinstein's responsum is closer to the practical model, as he does not explicitly discuss any moral principle—the concept of preserving life, as I have already mentioned, most likely refers to the danger to Jewish soldiers.[41] However, the broad nature of the limitations that Feinstein places on obligatory war puts him closer to Maimonides' theoretical approach, whereby full annihilation of Amalek and the seven nations was never meant unconditionally. For Maimonides, the condition is these nations' refusal to accept the Israelites' terms for peace;[42] while for Feinstein, the condition is an explicit divine command mandating the immediate application of the annihilation laws.[43]

In addition, Feinstein's responsum may be understood in terms of what Sagi and Daniel Statman view as a common Jewish attitude toward the relationship of morality and religion.[44] According to this approach, termed the "weak dependence" approach, morality exists independently of God, but its application is dependent on divine command. In other words, God's command does not determine what is moral, but rather shows us proper moral behavior, as God himself is morally perfect.[45]

In this case, we are dealing with commandments that are at first glance morally reprehensible. True, they are divine commands, and thus by definition must be moral, even if we do not understand how. But these particular commandments are so problematic morally that even the Torah's legislation is not enough by itself. God must intervene and prove beyond doubt that this is his will. Anything less will leave us unsure of whether our application of the *mitzvah* is correct and therefore moral, or incorrect and therefore immoral. Feinstein's responsum seems to represent a belief that only express divine intervention can overcome our moral reservations about this issue.

Exegetical Perspectives

Let us turn now to the exegetical aspects of the responsum. As I have already stated, the use of biblical prooftexts is fairly uncommon in halakhic decision making and is most likely used here because Feinstein could not find alternative sources. However, his interpretive remark is interesting in and of itself, as I believe it can cast light on at least one exegetical problem in the Former Prophets.

R. Feinstein does not quote a specific verse in the responsum but rather offers a broad generalization: "David and Solomon and all the righteous kings did not initiate war against Amalek." This statement is, at first glance, inaccurate, as David fought Amalek while still a fugitive from King Saul, as I will discuss shortly. However, in general, Feinstein's observation is correct, not only with regard to Amalek but even more so with regard to the seven nations.

After the initial conquest of the Promised Land, many cities still remained under Canaanite control, as is well established in the second half of the book of Joshua and the first chapters of Judges.[46] But the seven nations are mentioned as remaining in the land in much later periods, and the Bible does not seem to have a problem with this. Thus, in the story of David's census in 2 Samuel 24, the royal messengers visit Canaanite and Hivite cities (verse 7), and David himself buys the Temple Mount in Jerusalem from the Jebusite king Araunah (verses 18–25).[47] Two other Canaanite peoples, the Hittites and the Amorites, are also mentioned in Samuel.[48]

Indeed, it is only Solomon who, in 1 Kings 9:20–21 (paralleled in 2 Chr 8:7–8), manages to subjugate the remnants of the seven nations:

> As for all the people who were left of the Hittites, and the Amorites, and the Perizzites, and the Hivites, and the Jebusites...of their children, who were left after them in the land, whom the children of Israel did not wipe out, Solomon raised a levy of them until this day.

However, even he did not fulfill the commandment to annihilate them, as correctly pointed out by R. Feinstein. The only post-conquest full-fledged war against the Canaanites mentioned in the Bible is the defensive war fought by Deborah and Barak in Judges 4, according to an express divine command.

But while the seven nations seem to blend in with Israel as time goes by, Amalek remains one of Israel's tormentors throughout the book of Judges.[49] During this period, the only Israelite leader to combat Amalek directly is Gideon, but the text is clear that this is a defensive war (see Judg 6:3, 6:33, 7:12), and thus does not undermine Feinstein's thesis.

Later, of course, King Saul is specifically called upon to annihilate Amalek. Basically, he succeeds in his task (1 Sam 14:48), the delay in killing his Amalekite counterpart Agag (15:7–9, 15:32–33) notwithstanding. But it seems that even after this success, Amalek somehow survives and is still active later in Saul's reign. It is then that David fought with them while still a fugitive—first initiating an attack in 1 Samuel 27:8 and then responding when the Amalekites destroyed Ziklag in 1 Samuel 30.

The first case refers to an episode from the time when David received asylum from King Achish of Gath. In order to retain favor with his host, David would pretend to bring him Israelite spoils, so Achish would think he had crossed the lines and was no longer loyal to his own people. But David actually had fought the Amalekites and other enemies of Israel.

David's second battle with Amalek came not much later, while Saul was fighting his last battle. After being sent away from the Philistine camp, David and his battalion returned to their hometown of Ziklag only to find the city burned to the ground by the Amalekites, all women and children therein taken captive. David then proceeded to attack his enemies, rescue the women and children, and send part of the spoils to various Judean chieftains.

These two battles pose an exegetical problem. In 1 Samuel 15:3, Saul is explicitly forbidden to take any spoils from Amalek, as he is commanded to annihilate even "ox and sheep, camel and ass." David, on the other hand, had no compunction in either of his battles about taking spoils from Amalek and using them for his own purposes.

However, when Feinstein says that David did not fight Amalek, he means that he did not fight an obligatory war against them, as that is the only kind of war he is speaking of. In both cases where David fought the Amalekites, he really had no choice: in chapter 27, he had to either keep up his charade with Achish or place himself and his men in mortal danger; in chapter 30, the war was clearly defensive, as David's goal was to rescue his and his men's wives and children. David was not bound then by the laws of obligatory war and did not have to conform to their limitations.[50]

So the only real obligatory wars to be fought in ancient Israel, according to R. Feinstein, were those of Joshua and Saul, and possibly Deborah, all of whom received an explicit divine command to commence hostilities. Few other battles were fought against the relevant nations, and even they were matters of necessity, in which case Feinstein is clear that the restrictions on obligatory war do not apply.[51] So his claim that "all the righteous kings did not initiate" obligatory war remains true and may serve as a basis for his novel halakhic ruling.

Conclusion

In conclusion, Feinstein's responsum proposes a revolutionary halakhic thesis that seems tenuous on legal grounds. However, if we look at it from a moral perspective, it conforms to the kind of morality typically found in rabbinic writings, and from an exegetical perspective, it is based on a sound reading of the history of the Israelites' relationship with the seven nations and Amalek.

Notes

1. See Moshe Feinstein, *Iggerot Moshe* [in Hebrew], 9 vols. (New York: [self-published], 1959–2011). For scholarship on Feinstein and his halakhic oeuvre, the most comprehensive study is Harel Gordin, "*Halacha* and *Halachic* Decisions in a Changing World: An Interdisciplinary Approach to Examining the *Halachic* Decisions of Rabbbi Moshe Feinstein" [Hebrew with English abstract] (PhD diss., Tel Aviv University, 2007). For general biographical information on Feinstein in English, see Norma Baumel Joseph, "Feinstein, Moses," *American National Biography* (New York: Oxford University Press, 1999), 7:794–795.

2. See Gordin, "*Halacha* and *Halachic* Decisions," 16–17, who contrasts Feinstein's approach in America to that of R. Avraham Yeshayahu Karelitz ("the Hazon Ish") in Israel.

3. See especially his homily for the 150th anniversary of the establishment of the U.S. federal government in 1939: Moshe Feinstein, *Darash Moshe* [in Hebrew] (Bene Beraq, 1988), 1:415–416. On this homily, see also Gordin, "*Halacha* and *Halachic* Decisions," 34; below, footnote 43.

4. In general, see Gordin, "*Halacha* and *Halachic* Decisions," 34–37. For a list of "modern" issues on which Feinstein ruled strictly, see Angel's contrast of Feinstein with R. Hayyim David Halevy: Marc D. Angel, "A Study of the Halakhic Approaches of Two Modern *Posekim,*" *Tradition* 23, no. 3 (1988): 41–52. For a discussion of Feinstein's positions on women's issues, see Norma Baumel Joseph, "Feinstein, Rabbi Moses," in *Jewish Women: A Comprehensive Historical Encyclopedia*, ed. Paula E. Hyman and Dalia Ofer (Jerusalem: Shalvi, 2006), electronic resource, and references therein; Gordin, "*Halacha* and *Halachic* Decisions," 185–212, and references therein. On his attitude toward non-Orthodox Jews, see Michael Stanislawski, "Paradoxes of 'Leniency': Rabbi Moshe Feinstein on Conservative Marriages and Divorces" [in English], in *Let the Old Make Way for the New: Studies in the Social and Cultural History of Eastern European Jewry Presented to Immanuel Etkes* [predominantly in Hebrew], ed. David Assaf and Ada Rapoport-Albert (Jerusalem: Shazar Center, 2009), 2:261–279; Gordin, "*Halacha* and *Halachic* Decisions," 91–104, and references therein.

5. On the importance of submitting one's will to that of God in Feinstein's worldview, see Menashe Binenfeld, "R. Moshe Feinstein's Educational Approach" [in Hebrew], *Bisde Hemed* 42, no. 4 (1999): 32–33.

6. See the following chapters in this volume: Menahem Kister, "The Fate of the Canaanites and the Despoliation of the Egyptians: Polemics among Jews, Pagans, Christians

and Gnostics; Motifs and Motives"; Meira Polliack and Marzena Zawanowska, "'God Would Not Give the Land, but to the Obedient': Medieval Karaite Responses to the Curse of Canaan (Genesis 9:25)"; Menachem Kellner, "And Yet, the Texts Remain: The Problem of Genocidal Biblical Texts"; Joseph David, "Nahmanides on Law, Land, and Otherness"; and Matthias Morgenstern, "The Embarrassment of Joshua: Strategies for Interpreting the Biblical Account of the Conquest of Canaan in German-Jewish Neo-Orthodoxy in the Late Nineteenth and Early Twentieth Centuries."

7. For a copy of the accords, see "Camp David Accords," Israeli Foreign Ministry, September 17, 1978, http://www.mfa.gov.il/MFA/Peace+Process/Guide+to+the+Peace+Process/Camp+David+Accords.htm. For a survey of the events surrounding the Accords, see Kenneth W. Stein, *Heroic Diplomacy: Sadat, Kissinger, Carter, Begin, and the Quest for Arab-Israeli Peace* (New York: Routledge, 1999).

8. For a brief survey of many of these opposition groups, see Ehud Sprinzak, "The Response of the Radical Right to the 1978 Camp David Accords" [in Hebrew], in *The Camp David Process: Lectures* (Jerusalem: Begin Heritage Center, 2002), 28–31.

9. Schneersohn's pronouncements on the land-for-peace issue from 1968 on were collected by Levi Groner in his two-volume *When I Called, None Did Answer: The Lubavitcher Rebbe's Lectures on the Integrity of the Land [of Israel]* [in Hebrew] (Jerusalem: M.L., 2004).

10. I would like to thank R. Shabtai Rappoport, who witnessed the writing of this responsum, for sharing his firsthand knowledge as to the nature of R. Trebnick's question (personal communication, 24 Nov. 2009).

11. Original Hebrew text: הנה כמדומני שידוע דרכי לכתר"ה אשר איני ממהר להשיב אף להשואלים אותי ולדברים שלא נשאלתי לא שייך כלל שאשיב אף שהיה זה שאלה פרטית בדיני איסור והיתר.

12. In general, even when dealing with broader issues, Feinstein's responsa are worded as solutions to the specific problem posed by the questioner. A good example of this may be found in his responsum on displaying national flags in the synagogue (*IgM*, vol. 1, *Orah Hayyim*, responsum 46). For an analysis of this passage, see Mark Washofsky, "Responsa and the Art of Writing: Three Examples from the *Teshuvot* of Rabbi Moshe Feinstein," in *An American Rabbinate: A Festschrift for Walter Jacob*, Peter S. Knobel and Mark N. Staitman (Pittsburgh: Rodef Shalom, 2000), 181–186. In this responsum, Feinstein's answer is focused on the question that was actually presented to him—not whether such a display in the synagogue is acceptable (it is not), but whether one may establish a competing synagogue in order to counter such behavior (one may not).

13. This statement is not necessarily true, and is likely an exaggeration, stemming from both Feinstein's modesty and from what seems to be his lack of enthusiasm in responding to Trebnick. See below, note 15.

14. Original Hebrew text: וכל תשובותי אף להשואלים אותי היו רק בעניינים פרטיים שנוגע להיחיד ששאל אותי ודוקא כשלא כשלא היתה פגיעה לאיזה רב, ושאלה כללית לא השבתי מעולם לא בכתב ולא בעל פה.

15. This statement, as the one regarding his tardiness in responding (see above, note 13) seems to be an exaggeration. Although Feinstein indeed dealt mainly with private matters in his responsa, he also served in leadership positions in American *haredi* (ultra-Orthodox) rabbinical and educational organizations, most notably as chairman of Agudath Israel of America's Council of Torah Sages from 1963 on. Although this organization was not involved at the time with public affairs as much as in recent years, there were always public issues to be dealt with. On the issues dealt with during Feinstein's lifetime, see Daniel Gutenmacher, "Agudath Israel of America and the State of Israel: The Case of the Jewish Observer," in

Israel and Diaspora Jewry: Ideological and Political Perspectives, ed. Eliezer Don-Yehiya (Ramat-Gan: Bar-Ilan University Press, 1991), 109–126. On the trend toward more involvement in public affairs in recent years, see Nosson Scherman, "Spokesman in the Halls of Government: Agudath Israel's Evolving Public Role in Shtadlonus and Advocacy," *Jewish Observer* 25, no. 4 (1992): 28–37.

16. This does not seem to me an appropriate answer to the Lubavitch opposition to the Camp David Accords, as it stemmed from Schneersohn's belief that the accords would not actually save lives, but rather endanger them (see the section above, titled "The Responsum"). In any case, Feinstein's basic antiwar stance seems to be well-grounded in the writings of other rabbis from the Lithuanian yeshiva tradition. See Yitzhak Avi Roness, "On the Morality of War in Twentieth Century Halachic Literature: Morality, Halacha and Nationalism" [in Hebrew], in *The Kipa and the Helmet*, ed. Moshe Rachimi (Elkana: Orot Israel College Press, 2009), 196–200.

17. The Urim and Tummim are a means of divination mentioned occasionally in the Bible. According to the laws of the Tabernacle, the Urim and Tummim are to be placed on the High Priest's breastplate (Exod 28:30). Their use in public matters, presumably warfare, is mandated in the Pentateuch as well, when Joshua is commanded to obey Eleazar's instructions received via the Urim and Tummim (Num 27:21). For an analysis of the relevant biblical passages and the various theories as to what the Urim and Tummim actually were and how they were used, see Cornelis van Dam, *The Urim and Thummim: A Means of Revelation in Ancient Israel* (Winona Lake: Eisenbrauns, 1997). For a survey of their role according to rabbinic tradition, see Meir Berlin and Shlomo Yosef Zevin (eds.), "Urim and Thummim" [in Hebrew], *Talmudic Encyclopedia*, vol. 1 (Jerusalem: Talmudic Encyclopedia, 1947), 182–185.

18. The Sanhedrin (High Court) was a Jewish leadership body during the Second Temple period. On its history and various functions, see most recently Lester L. Grabbe, "Sanhedrin, Sanhedriyyot, or Mere Invention?" *JSJ* 39 (2008): 1–19. Rabbinic tradition sees this institution as dating back to the time of Moses himself.

19. Original Hebrew text: ואולי שמעו ממני מה שאמרתי לתלמידי מה שאני סובר שענין מלחמה כיון שנוגע לפקוח נפש צריך ציוי מיוחד ואורים ותומים וסנהדרין אף במלחמת מצוה כמלחמת עמלק.

20. See Maimonides, *Mishneh Torah*, "Laws of Kings and Wars," 5:1. Note that Maimonides includes defensive wars in this category as well, while Feinstein, later on in this responsum, places defensive wars in a category of their own.

21. On Feinstein's role in the American yeshiva world, see Yehuda Susman, "The Halakhic Methodology of R. Moshe Feinstein as Reflected through a Comparison of the 'Dibrot Moshe' and the 'Igrot Moshe'" [in Hebrew] (MA thesis, Bar Ilan University, 2007), 9–10.

22. Original Hebrew text: ומוכרח זה מהא דדוד ושלמה וכל מלכים הצדיקים לא יצאו להלחם בעמלק, וזה דבר ברור ומוכרח שלא שייך לפלוג ע"ז, ורק כשנפלו העכו"ם על ישראל כהא דאנטיוכוס מלך יון וכדומה דהוא להצלה עשו מלחמה בבית שני.

23. There has been much discussion in contemporary halakhic literature concerning exactly which military acts may be included in the "self-defense" category. See Stuart Cohen, "The Re-Discovery of Orthodox Jewish Laws Relating to the Military and War ('Hilkhot Tzavah u-Milchamah') in Contemporary Israel: Trends and Implications," *Israel Studies* 12, no. 2 (2007): 15–17, and references therein.

24. It is common among *haredim* not to refer to the State of Israel as just "Israel," but rather to use "Eretz Israel" (the Land of Israel) or "Medinat Israel" (the State of Israel). Even some Zionist rabbis have adopted this practice, following the lead of R. Joseph B. Soloveitchik,

"On the Love of Torah and the Redemption of the Generation's Soul" [in Hebrew], in *In Aloneness, in Togetherness: A Selection of Hebrew Writings* (Jerusalem: Orot, 1976), 405. As to R. Feinstein's less-than-positive attitude toward Zionism and the State of Israel, note his referring to the founders of the state as "evildoers" (רשעים) in the responsum on flags in the synagogue mentioned above, note 12.

25. Original Hebrew text: ולא דנתי כלום אף לא במחשבה איך להכריע כי לא שייך שישאלו ממני מי שבידם במלכות השולטת בא"י ענינים אלו והיה עצם הנידון לפני בזה רק לבטלה וגם לא ברור לפני איך לדון וכ"ש שלא שייך לפני להשיב.

26. Feinstein's stance here is to be expected, as it is standard both for *haredim* and for non-Israeli rabbis. See Chaim Burgansky, "More about Halakhic Rulings and Political Issues," *Democratic Culture* 7 (2003): 49–51 [in Hebrew]. Throughout most of the article (52–72), Burgansky attempts to prove that this stance has substance to it, as halakhic discourse regarding political matters is, in his opinion, fundamentally different from standard halakhic discourse. Regarding Feinstein's own involvement in political issues, see above, note 15.

27. Original Hebrew text: שלכן אנו בטוחים רק על השי"ת שהכל הוא רק בידו ומתפללים אליו שירחם עלינו ועל כל ישראל ויהיה הכל לטובה וגם ישלח לנו בקרוב משיח צדקנו.

28. See above, note 20.

29. Maimonides, *Mishneh Torah*, "Laws of Kings and Wars," 5:2. All translations of Maimonides in this article are my own.

30. See Yehudah Zoldan, "Waging Obligatory and Optional Wars Today" [in Hebrew], in *The Kingdom of Judah and Israel* (Merkaz Shapira: Or Etzyon Torah Institute, 2002), 271–283, for a summary of rabbinic opinions on the halakhic requirements for going to war.

31. For the legal implications of the distinction between biblical and rabbinic commandments, see Joel Roth, *The Halakhic Process: A Systemic Analysis* (New York: Jewish Theological Seminary of America, 1986), 24–45.

32. Regarding the possibility that he is referring to the danger to enemy civilians, see the section below, titled "Moral Perspectives," including note 41. According to Roness, "On the Morality of War," 197 n. 8, R. Avraham Yeshayahu Karelitz (the "Hazon Ish") explicitly opposed war for this reason, but most other rabbis did not concur with him on this matter.

33. See Roness, "On the Morality of War," 200–210, for a survey of rabbinic opinions as to how to reconcile the permissibility of war with the principle of preserving life.

34. See sources cited by Roness, "On the Morality of War."

35. The only possible source I found for this is not even in a halakhic work per se, but rather a collection of novellae on the Torah based on oral teachings of Feinstein's older contemporary, R. Isaac Zeev Soloveichik (1886–1959), compiled by his students. See *Hiddushe Rabbenu haGRaZ Soloveichik mippi haShemu'a 'al Hatorah* (Jerusalem: [n.p.], 1958), 62. However, Soloveichik limits this analysis to war against Amalek, and does not apply it to war against the Canaanites, probably for exegetical reasons alone.

36. In general, the use of the Bible for halakhic purposes began its decline during the Amoraic period. After the redaction of the Talmud, such use became even scarcer. See Yitschak D. Gilat, "Halakhic Interpretations (*Midrash*) of Scripture in Post-Talmudic Periods" [Hebrew, English summary on p. xxxvi], in *Michtam Le-David: Rabbi David Ochs Memorial Volume (1905–1975)*, ed. Yitschak D. Gilat and Eliezer Stern (Ramat-Gan: Bar-Ilan University, 1978), 210–231. For a list of such post-Talmudic use of the Bible, see most recently Haim Sabato, "Can *Halakhot* Be Derived from *Derashot* Not Found in the Talmud?" [in Hebrew], in *Teshurah Le-'Amos: Collected Studies in Biblical Exegesis Presented to 'Amos Hakham*, ed. Moshe Bar-Asher et al. (Alon Shevut: Tevunot, 2007), 499–519.

37. Avi Sagi, "The Punishment of Amalek in Jewish Tradition: Coping with the Moral Problem," *HTR* 87 (1994): 323–346.

38. *m. Yad.* 4:4 (trans. Philip Blackman [London: Mishna Press, 1955], 6:769). The Mishna itself does not discuss Amalekites or Canaanites, but rather Ammonites and Moabites, in light of the prohibition against marrying their descendants (see Deut 23:4). For the application to Amalek in halakhic literature, see Sagi, "Punishment of Amalek," 338–339.

39. On the theoretical response, see Sagi, "Punishment of Amalek," 340–345. In addition, Sagi ("Punishment of Amalek," 337) points out that even non-moral "literal" responses to the annihilation law are likely based on some sort of moral justification.

40. Maimonides, *Mishneh Torah*, "Laws of Kings and Wars," 6:1. Biblical quotations here and throughout this article are based on the Koren edition (trans. Harold Fisch, Jerusalem: Koren, 1989), with proper names modified to fit the standard English spelling.

41. See above, the section titled "Halakhic Perspectives," including note 32. In addition, in his posthumous collection of homilies, *Darash Moshe*, Feinstein mentions in passing that it is currently forbidden to observe the commandment to annihilate Amalek, commenting that this is inherent to the Jews' current pre-redemptive state (*galut*). See Feinstein, *Darash Moshe*, 1:159.

42. To appreciate the extent of Maimonides' originality on this issue vis-à-vis his biblical and rabbinic sources, see Sagi, "Punishment of Amalek," 341–342.

43. In his homilies, Feinstein does not limit this commandment (other than his statement regarding *galut*—see above, note 41), but rather stresses Amalek's wickedness, including its moral wickedness (contrasted especially with the United States) as the basis for this commandment; and that the way to combat Amalek is by setting a good example for others with good deeds. See Feinstein, *Darash Moshe*, 1:415–416; vol. 2 (New York: 1999), 33. On the former responsum, see above, note 3.

44. See Avi Sagi and Daniel Statman, "Divine Command Morality and the Jewish Tradition," *JRE* 23 (1995): 39–67.

45. For a full analysis of the weak dependence approach in religion in general (not necessarily Judaism), see Avi Sagi and Daniel Statman, *Religion and Morality*, trans. Batya Stein (Amsterdam: Rodopi, 1995), 79–113.

46. See discussion in Nili Wazana's " 'Everything Was Fulfilled' versus 'The Land That Yet Remains': Contrasting Conceptions of the Fulfillment of the Promise in the Book of Joshua," Chapter 1 of the present volume.

47. In the parallel story in 1 Chr 21, the episode involving Araunah (there called Ornan and not referred to as "king") appears in an expanded form (verses 18–30), but the messengers' route is not given in detail, only "So Joab departed, and went throughout all Israel, and came to Jerusalem" (verse 4), omitting the Canaanite and Hivite cities. If Araunah's royal status in 2 Sam 24:23 is not a scribal error, it is possible that these two differences between Samuel and Chronicles represent an attempt by the Chronicler to downplay the seven nations' presence in Davidic Israel. Regarding Araunah's being called "king," see P. Kyle McCarter, *II Samuel* (New York: Doubleday, 1984; AB), 508; Sara Japhet, *I & II Chronicles* (OTL) (Louisville: Westminster John Knox, 1993), 386–387. McCarter sees the word "king" in Samuel as a scribal error (or possibly as referring to David), while Japhet sees the MT as correct, with the word "king" referring to Araunah.

48. In 1 Sam 7:14, peace between Israel and the Amorites is mentioned, although the term there may refer to non-Israelite nations in general. See J. Andrew Dearman, "Amorites," *The New Interpreter's Dictionary of the Bible* (Nashville: Abingdon, 2006), 1:134. Also, Hittites

served in David's court (1 Sam 26:6; 2 Sam 23:39), and Solomon loved Hittite women (1 Kgs 11:1), although these may be from the neo-Hittite states in Asia Minor. For the distinction between various groups called "Hittites" in the Bible, see Gregory McMahon, "Hittites in the OT," *ABD* (New York: Doubleday, 1992), 3:232–233.

49. See Judg 3:13 and 10:12. The mention of Amalek in the Song of Deborah (5:14) is problematic, with many interpretations and emendations offered, some of which also portray Amalek as an enemy of the Israelites. See Yairah Amit, *Judges* [in Hebrew], Miqra leYisrael (Tel Aviv: Am Oved and Jerusalem: Magnes, 1999), 102.

50. Amalek is also listed as one of the nations from whom David took spoils in 2 Sam 8:12 (1 Chr 18:11). It is unclear which battles are referred to here, or to what extent David conformed to the rules of obligatory war.

51. The only real exception in biblical narrative is the brief comment regarding the Simeonites' private war against Amalek, presumably during the reign of Hezekiah, in 1 Chr 4:43.

Bibliography

Amit, Yairah. *Judges* [in Hebrew]. Miqra leYisrael. Tel Aviv: Am Oved, and Jerusalem: Magnes, 1999.

Angel, Marc D. "A Study of the Halakhic Approaches of Two Modern *Posekim*." *Tradition* 23, no. 3 (1988): 41–52.

Berlin, Meir, and Shlomo Yosef Zevin, eds. "Urim and Thummim" [in Hebrew]. *Talmudic Encyclopedia*. Jerusalem: Talmudic Encyclopedia, 1947. 1:182–185.

Binenfeld, Menashe. "R. Moshe Feinstein's Educational Approach" [in Hebrew]. *Bisde Hemed* 42, no. 4 (1999): 31–59.

Burgansky, Chaim. "More about Halakhic Rulings and Political Issues" [in Hebrew]. *Democratic Culture* 7 (2003): 49–72.

Cohen, Stuart. "The Re-Discovery of Orthodox Jewish Laws Relating to the Military and War ('Hilkhot Tzavah u-Milchamah') in Contemporary Israel: Trends and Implications." *Israel Studies* 12, no. 2 (2007): 1–28.

Dam, Cornelis van. *The Urim and Thummim: A Means of Revelation in Ancient Israel*. Winona Lake, Ind.: Eisenbrauns, 1997.

Dearman, J. Andrew. "Amorites." *New Interpreter's Dictionary of the Bible*. Nashville: Abingdon, 2006, 1:134.

Feinstein, Moshe. *Iggerot Moshe* [in Hebrew]. 8 vols. New York: self-published, 1959–1996.

Feinstein, Moshe. *Darash Moshe*. Vol. 1. Bene Beraq: Ohel Yosef, 1988. Vol. 2. New York: Mesorah, 1999.

Gilat, Yitschak D. "Halakhic Interpretations (*Midrash*) of Scripture in Post-Talmudic Periods" [in Hebrew; English summary on p. xxxvi]. In *Michtam Le-David: Rabbi David Ochs Memorial Volume (1905–1975)*, edited by Yitschak D. Gilat and Eliezer Stern, 210–231. Ramat-Gan: Bar-Ilan University, 1978.

Gordin, Harel. "*Halacha* and *Halachic* Decisions in a Changing World: An Interdisciplinary Approach to Examining the *Halachic* Decisions of Rabbbi Moshe Feinstein" [in Hebrew with English abstract]. PhD diss. Tel Aviv University, 2007.

Grabbe, Lester L. "Sanhedrin, Sanhedriyyot, or Mere Invention?" *JSJ* 39 (2008): 1–19.

Groner, Levi. *When I Called, None Did Answer: The Lubavitcher Rebbe's Lectures on the Integrity of the Land [of Israel]* [in Hebrew]. Jerusalem: M.L., 2004.

Gutenmacher, Daniel. "Agudath Israel of America and the State of Israel: The Case of the Jewish Observer." In *Israel and Diaspora Jewry: Ideological and Political Perspectives*, edited by Eliezer Don-Yehiya, 109–126. Ramat-Gan: Bar-Ilan University Press, 1991.

Japhet, Sara. *I & II Chronicles* (OTL). Louisville: Westminster John Knox, 1993.

Joseph, Norma Baumel. "Feinstein, Moses." *American National Biography*. New York: Oxford University Press, 1999, 7:794–795.

Joseph, Norma Baumel. "Feinstein, Rabbi Moses." In *Jewish Women: A Comprehensive Historical Encyclopedia*, edited by Paula E. Hyman and Dalia Ofer. Jerusalem: Shalvi, 2006, electronic resource.

McCarter, P. Kyle. *II Samuel*. AB. New York: Doubleday, 1984.

McMahon, Gregory. "Hittites in the OT." *ABD*. New York: Doubleday, 1992, 3:231–233.

Roness, Yitzchak Avi. "On the Morality of War in Twentieth Century Halachic Literature: Morality, Halacha and Nationalism." In *The Kipa and the Helmet*, edited by Moshe Rachimi, 193–213. Elkana: Orot Israel College Press, 2009.

Roth, Joel. *The Halakhic Process: A Systemic Analysis*. New York: Jewish Theological Seminary of America, 1986.

Sabato, Haim. "Can *Halakhot* Be Derived from *Derashot* Not Found in the Talmud?" [in Hebrew]. In *Teshurah Le-ʿAmos: Collected Studies in Biblical Exegesis Presented to ʿAmos Hakham*, edited by Moshe Bar-Asher et al., 499–519. Alon Shevut: Tevunot, 2007.

Sagi, Avi. "The Punishment of Amalek in Jewish Tradition: Coping with the Moral Problem." *HTR* 87 (1994): 323–346.

Sagi, Avi, and Daniel Statman. "Divine Command Morality and the Jewish Tradition." *JRE* 23 (1995): 39–67.

Sagi, Avi, and Daniel Statman. *Religion and Morality*. Translated by Batya Stein, 79–113. Amsterdam: Rodopi, 1995.

Scherman, Nosson. "Spokesman in the Halls of Government: Agudath Israel's Evolving Public Role in Shtadlonus and Advocacy." *Jewish Observer* 25, no. 4 (1992): 28–37.

Soloveichik, Isaac Zeev. *Hiddushe Rabbenu haGRaZ Soloveichik mippi haShemuʿa ʿal Hatora*. Jerusalem: [n.p.], 1958.

Soloveitchik, Joseph B. "On the Love of Torah and the Redemption of the Generation's Soul." In *In Aloneness, in Togetherness: A Selection of Hebrew Writings* [in Hebrew], edited by Pinchas H. Peli, 401–432. Jerusalem: Orot, 1976.

Sprinzak, Ehud. "The Response of the Radical Right to the 1978 Camp David Accords." In *The Camp David Process: Lectures* [in Hebrew], 28–31. Jerusalem: Begin Heritage Center, 2002.

Stanislawski, Michael. "Paradoxes of 'Leniency': Rabbi Moshe Feinstein on Conservative Marriages and Divorces" [in English]. In *Let the Old Make Way for the New: Studies in the Social and Cultural History of Eastern European Jewry Presented to Immanuel Etkes* [predominantly in Hebrew], edited by David Assaf and Ada Rapoport-Albert. Jerusalem: Shazar Center, 2009, 2:261–279.

Stein, Kenneth W. *Heroic Diplomacy: Sadat, Kissinger, Carter, Begin, and the Quest for Arab-Israeli Peace*. New York: Routledge, 1999.

Susman, Yehuda. "The Halakhic Methodology of R. Moshe Feinstein as Reflected Through a Comparison of the 'Dibrot Moshe' and the 'Igrot Moshe' " [in Hebrew]. MA thesis. Bar Ilan University, 2007.

Washofsky, Mark. "Responsa and the Art of Writing: Three Examples from the *Teshuvot* of Rabbi Moshe Feinstein." In *An American Rabbinate: A Festschrift for Walter Jacob*, edited by Peter S. Knobel and Mark N. Staitman, 149–204. Pittsburgh: Rodef Shalom, 2000.

Zoldan, Yehudah. "Waging Obligatory and Optional Wars Today" [in Hebrew]. In *The Kingdom of Judah and Israel*, 271–283. Merkaz Shapira: Or Etzyon Torah Institute, 2002.

The Fate of the Canaanites and the State of Israel in the Philosophy of Emmanuel Levinas

Annabel Herzog

As a Jew and as a philosopher dedicated to ethical and political questions, Levinas wrote a lot about the State of Israel. Nonetheless, to speak about the State of Israel in Levinas's work raises a problem: His philosophy is fundamentally an "ethical" philosophy, which, as he used this word, meant a harsh critique and almost a rejection of politics—of *all* politics. Inevitably, this meant a harsh critique *also* of the State of Israel. I am not speaking here of mere criticism of a particular Israeli policy. Levinas's ethics entails a criticism and sometimes a rejection of politics per se, of politics *in general*.[1] As such, his ethics would be expected to have a deep problem with the very existence of the State of Israel—as it does, in fact, have with the existence of all other states.

However, even a superficial reading of Levinas's works reveals that he praised the State of Israel. His talmudic readings, in particular, include many statements in favor of the existence of a Jewish state. Since his ethics involves a harsh critique of the very existence of the political, and since he praised the State of Israel, the State of Israel seems to play a problematic role in his philosophy. Perhaps its exceptionally positive treatment in Levinas's philosophy constitutes some kind of paradox, or some kind of contradiction.[2] From a philosophical point of view, it is important to determine whether Levinas contradicted himself when he praised the State of Israel, or if he praised the State of Israel for reasons that would explain or even overcome that apparent contradiction, namely, which would be philosophically enlightening and legitimate. I would like to understand what was worthy of praise for Levinas in the State of Israel in spite of his general criticism of the political.

I will start by explaining why the State of Israel per se is a problematic topic in the philosophy of Emmanuel Levinas. I will then recount Levinas's contradictory position toward the State of Israel in analyzing his reading of tractate *Sotah* 34b–35a, "Promised Land or Permitted Land?" which focuses on the reactions of the spies sent out by Moses to scout the land of Canaan in Numbers 13–14. Finally, I will show that Levinas's position on the State of Israel allows us to understand better his philosophy in general, and to grasp more firmly the political challenges of renewed Jewish sovereignty in the Middle East.

Ethics versus Politics

Levinas's philosophy is fundamentally an ethics. For many philosophers, "ethics" and "morals" are the same thing. The word "ethics" comes from the Greek *ethos*. The word "morals" comes from the Latin *mores*. Like *ethos*, *mores* means "customs" or "manners." Therefore, etymologically, "ethics" and "morals" are synonyms and refer to proper behavior according to social norms or conventions. In philosophy, too, the words "ethics" and "morals" are often used synonymously, but not to express proper behavior according to customs and manners. For many philosophers, they instead express a universal idea or concept of proper behavior—that is, according to a divine, natural, or rational definition of the Good. For Levinas, however, "ethics" and "morals" are not synonyms. Indeed, they have nothing in common. For him, "morals" refers to any *set of rules* of proper, right, or good behavior. It does not make any difference if these rules supposedly derive from God or nature, or from any particular society. What counts is that they can be enunciated, comprehended, and conceptualized. One can reflect upon them; one can explain them. One can give *reasons* for them. One can offer *arguments* on their behalf. As such, morals belong to the group of things, events, and attitudes that can be thought, explained, and defined—namely, things that consist of conceptual rules and follow rules. These things, events, or attitudes are the topics of practices and domains of study such as history, science, or politics. Levinas uses the word "ontology" to designate the things, events, and attitudes that can be understood by means of concepts. "Ontology" means literally "the study of being." It concerns all things that are, and, as such, can be thought and taught.

As opposed to "morals," "ethics" designates not a set of rules of behavior but rather the *encounter* with another person—an encounter that precedes all rules. When we meet another person, says Levinas, even before we know who that person is—or is not—before we think of how to behave with that person, before we start to behave in a good or bad way, we meet his or her absolute difference, his or her absolute *otherness*. A person whom we meet is, like us, a human being. Like us, he or she has a body, opinions, a personal story, family, friends, attributes, and so on. But before we think about all these things or do anything, when we meet the other person we *first* meet the fact that he or she is *other*, namely, is something that we cannot know or understand at all.[3] The fact that the other is not us and that therefore there is something in him or her that we cannot know at all is called by Levinas "the face of the other." Accordingly, ethics is the encounter with the face of the other.

But, says Levinas, it often happens that when I meet the face of the other my impulse is not to accept it as such. Instead of accepting the face of the other as other, I try to recognize something that I know, something that is *not* other, but similar to me: For instance, I think, "this is a human being." In so doing, I try to understand the other's otherness, that is, I try to explain away the other's otherness, to "reduce" it to something that is similar to me—in Levinas's terms, to sameness. The attempt to reduce otherness to *sameness* is the very essence of ontology. Ever since Parmenides, ontology has sought uncompromisingly to turn everything into sameness. All ontological attitudes—scientific, political, moral, and so on—try to understand, categorize, order, submit, and control the world by reducing otherness to sameness.

Thus, the ethical encounter with the face of the other is often accompanied by the ontological effort to reduce the face of the other to sameness, thereby destroying it; for when I transform something that is different from me into something that is similar to me, I destroy its difference, its otherness, and its distinctiveness. I try to remake the other in my own image. In a very emphatic and dramatic way, Levinas says that to reduce the otherness of the other to sameness is to murder the other. The spectrum of such murder is very broad. It starts from an apparently insignificant indifference to the face of the other: I do not pay attention to the fact that the other is different from me. It ends in wars and conquests in which people try to submit other people to their own rules, to the way they want things to be, to their sameness.

Therefore, according to Levinas, otherness is always in danger of being destroyed. When I meet the face of the other, he or she begs me, "Please do not kill me, protect me!" It is because I have the ability to murder the other that I am absolutely *responsible* for him or her.[4] Levinas also says these things in another way. Ethics, he argues, is the encounter with the Voice of God who, in the face of the other, utters his commands: Thou shalt not murder! Love thy neighbor as thyself! The command of God in the face of the other cannot be "known," "understood," or "categorized." It is not a thing upon which one can reflect. It is unquestionable and infinite; it is not a concept; it comes without explanation. It gives no reasons. When I see the other, I hear God commanding my absolute responsibility in his or her face.

However, as I have already said, there are many different sets of rules that belong to ontology—morals, politics, science, aesthetics, and so on. Politics and the state—all states—belong to ontology. They belong to the incessantly renewed attempt at destroying otherness. They are, in other words, on the side of murder. Politics and the state—all states, every state, including Israel when Israel deals with political leadership and conquest—all are on the side of murder.[5] In Levinas's philosophy, the relationship between ethics and politics, between "Thou shalt not murder" and "Thou shalt murder," is a central and profound problem, and nowhere is this problem sharper, keener, or more acute than in his writings on the State of Israel.

Good Spies and Bad Spies

Levinas focused on the question of the State of Israel in many texts, and in particular in his talmudic reading called "Promised Land or Permitted Land?" (1965).[6] He therein analyzes the reactions of the spies (*ha-meraglim*) sent out by Moses to scout the land of Canaan in Numbers 13–14. As we recall, Moses sent out twelve spies to get information about the land of Canaan. When they returned, ten of them said: "But the people are strong that dwelleth in the land, and the cities are walled, and very great: and moreover we saw the children of Anak there" (Num 13:28). Only two of the spies, Caleb the son of Jephunneh and Joshua the son of Nun, said, "We can conquer the Land."

The first idea that emerges from Levinas's reading of the talmudic text is that the ten "bad" spies, the ones who warned the people about the dangers of the land, were in fact righteous and pure. With some irony, Levinas underlines the rabbis' own irony. Indeed, the Talmud mentions that the names of the twelve spies sent to Canaan reflected their acts—and hence, reflected the bad acts of ten of them. But the signification of these names, says the Talmud, has been lost except for two of them. Levinas says: The rabbis cannot be serious about this! The signification of the spies' names in Numbers 13 is very easy to understand. They—the bad spies!—all have names with beautiful significations: for example, "Shammua ben Zaccur," he who listens, son of he who remembers; "Shaphat ben Hori," he who judges, son of he who is free; "Palti ben Raphu," he who spares, son of he who was healed. If these names reflect acts, the acts were very pure! As Levinas remarks, only people who wanted to convince us that the spies were bad people would be able to "forget" the signification of their names![7]

What was the bad spies' sin? According to Levinas, they wanted to prevent the Israelite people from making the land into an object of adoration. Continuing the rabbis' line of thought, Levinas writes that the bad spies were motivated by a desire to "shame the worshippers of Land." Levinas makes his allusion crystal clear: The bad spies' report of what they saw was intended to shame those he calls "the Zionists of that time."[8] To express this with a play on words, I would say that the bad spies told the people *to cultivate (la'avod)* the promised land but not to *make a cult of (la'avod)* of it. In Latin, as in Hebrew, cultivation (*cultus, avodah*) and worship (*cultus, avodah*) are designated by the same word.

Levinas notes that, according to the Talmud, both Caleb and Joshua, the two good spies, were tempted to follow the ten bad spies. But they were not tempted by evil; they were tempted by the bad spies' concern for justice. The bad spies were concerned about justice! According to Levinas, the meaning of that justice is given a bit later in the Talmud, when the rabbis interpret the bad spies' repeated statement that the inhabitants of Canaan were "giants" or "children of Anak" (Num 13:28, 13:32, 13:33: *yelidey ha-anak, anshey middot, beney anak*). Reading the talmudic discussion, Levinas asks, What did the spies fear? He gives three possible answers.

The first is an easy one: The spies saw the big and strong Canaanites and were scared. These just-freed slaves made a quick comparison between the obvious strength of the Canaanite giants and their own obvious weakness—only made worse by the dubious behavior of a God who never shows Himself. The result of the comparison was clear: The Canaanites were much stronger and thus very frightening.[9]

The second answer is quite different. Levinas suggests that when they saw the Canaanites, the spies saw the future of Israel. They saw what would become of their children and grandchildren in the land of Canaan. They saw powerful people who—according to the talmudic interpretation—built awesome cities and dug deep holes wherever they put their feet. They saw Zionists, modern Israelis. Strong, healthy, robust *sabras*. And they said, "No, we do not want that! These people—these giants, these builders, these construction workers, these Zionists—are the end of the Jewish people."[10]

The third answer is that when they saw the land so beautifully built and cultivated by the Canaanites, the spies thought: We do not have the right to conquer what has been made by others. Even if that land is the land in which Abraham, Isaac, and Jacob are buried, even if that land is the land of our ancestors, we do not have such a right. The ancestry of Abraham, Isaac, and Jacob—ancestors who spoke with God and received His promise—cannot give us the right to expropriate other people, no matter what these people are, no matter what they did or do.[11]

We have here a clear example of Levinas's criticism of the very existence of the state through the biblical metaphor of the conquest of Canaan. The State of Israel puts Jewish existence in physical and spiritual danger because it means the choice of ontology over ethics. The children of Israel are going to meet the other—the local inhabitants of the land. But that meeting is not planned to be an ethical meeting. It is planned to be an event of death and destruction of all existing difference. The ten bad spies said, "No, we will not do that." The ten bad spies were very ethical people.

Is this exactly what Levinas meant? Did he not think like everybody else that the ten bad spies were bad? But how could they be bad if they cared so much for ethics?

Levinas gives a first answer at the end of his talmudic reading. He reinterprets the Talmud's interpretation of Caleb's reassuring words to the people of Israel (Num 14:7–9), and says: The conquest of the land of Israel was not going to be like other conquests. It was not going to be an imperialist act—or, at least, it was not *planned* to be an imperialist act. It was not to be a conquest like all conquests, *ke-khol ha-goyim*. According to Caleb's words, the land was to be conquered in order to build a society that respects a universal conception of justice—a society based on equality, freedom, and peace for *all*. That universal conception of justice was and is higher than the local, nationalist, historical conception of justice for one people alone—for the people who arrived first to the land, or for those who were physically stronger, or for those who had famous ancestors buried in that land. Giving again a contemporary twist to his reading of the Bible and of the Talmud, Levinas adds: "This universal conception of justice was the goal of the first kibbutzim."[12]

In another text, called "Jewish Thought Today" (1961), he writes:

The State of Israel is [after many centuries] the first opportunity [for the Jewish people] to move into history by bringing about a just world. It is therefore a search for the absolute and for purity. The sacrifices and works which the realization of this justice invites men to make give a body once more to the spirit that animated the prophets and the Talmud.... We must not lose sight of the universal meaning that this work assumes in the eyes of the Israelis themselves, who believe they are working for humanity.[13]

When the people who inherited the vision of universal justice of the Prophets and the Talmud set up a state, it must not be a state like every other state.

In a third text, called "The State of Israel and the Religion of Israel" (1951), Levinas makes an important distinction. He writes: "The contrast is between those who seek to have a State in order to have justice and those who seek justice in order to ensure the survival of the State."[14] What counts is justice, not the state. Therefore one could say that the good spies understood that no political society is ever so important in and of itself. Hence, the Canaanite state is not that important, either. Levinas says that the state in itself is never intrinsically or ultimately important. What is important is justice for all. The ultimate goal is a society of justice and equality. Political existence is not an end, but a means; and justice is not a means, but an end. The real purpose of the conquest was not a state; it was the Torah, namely, universal justice.

The bad spies were against the idolatry of the land, but they had no universal goal. For Levinas, it is not enough to be against idolatry. One must also recognize the supreme goal, which is universal justice. In his talmudic readings, Levinas often develops the idea that not to sin is not enough: One cannot just refuse to do bad things and do nothing. To do nothing is bad. One must refuse to do bad things and at the same time build a just world. In "Judaism and Revolution" (1969), he writes: "Man must build the universe: the universe is built through work and study. Everything else is distraction. Distraction is evil."[15] Therefore the people of Israel *had to conquer the land in order to build a society of justice for all.*

Still, we are left with a serious problem regarding the Canaanites and their buildings. And, hence, I do not know if Levinas's thesis is completely convincing. I am not sure that the best way to convince people of one's good intentions and universal principles of justice is to conquer their land and proclaim that "universal justice" is ultimately more important. Is Levinas saying that the goal of Torah is above everything else, that the end of Torah justifies all means—even murder? Is he not therefore simply contradicting himself? Can he seriously mean that the ten spies were ethically pure, but were *wrong*[16] because they did not understand the universal justice of a Torah that, in the meantime, commanded an ontological destruction, a destruction contrary to the divine command "Thou shalt not murder" heard in the face of the other, of the Canaanite other?

Can a philosopher seriously defend such an idea? Can an *ethical* philosophy seriously defend it? Can we accept it?

The Goal of the State of Israel

On the one hand, there is no doubt that, for Levinas, the ten bad spies missed the point of the Torah. They refused to worship the land, but they did not trust God. On the other hand, how could a Voice that commands "Thou shalt not murder" also command the violent and bloody conquest of the land—even if that conquest would eventually establish a so-called society of universal justice?

According to what I have said until now, Levinas had to deal with three ideas.

The first idea is that political action consists of conquest and murder. Political action is sameness—love of oneself. Levinas once wrote that the state is "the ultimate refuge of idolatry"[17] and condemned the "commonplace mystique of the earth as native soil."[18] Accordingly, the highest danger is to worship the land and the state, as the ten spies rightly understood.

The second idea is that ethics is above the land and the state, and the Torah expresses the basic command of ethical responsibility. Its "Thou shalt not murder" is the first and foremost ethical injunction.

The third idea is that political action is necessary to establish a society of Torah, that is, a society of universal justice. Political action—and therefore the *risk* of murder—is necessary to establish universal justice.[19]

The combination of these three apparently incompatible ideas constitutes the philosophy of Emmanuel Levinas. However, this philosophy is not a dialectic, that is, an attempt at resolving the contradiction.[20] The contradiction remains. The three contradictory ideas coexist—*one*, politics is murder; *two*, God commands "Thou shalt not murder"; *three*, we need politics to establish a society that does not murder.

According to Levinas, politics is war and murder,[21] and this is *why* ethical responsibility is of the utmost importance and has the utmost authority. Ethics comes first and is above *everything* related to the land and to the state. The highest values—namely, the prohibition to kill and the injunction of responsibility—must be above everything else. However, ethical responsibility alone does not build anything. The care for the other may lead only to *self-sacrifice* or to *doing nothing*. Perhaps self-sacrifice is the best behavior—Levinas sometimes says that it is—but it is not a livable behavior.[22] As to doing nothing, as I said earlier, it *is* evil. Life consists not only of caring for the other but also of *doing things with the other*. Doing things with the other means a sociopolitical life and involvement in historical processes. It means sameness. But this sameness entails the risk of murder: This is why we need ethics and the prohibition of murder!

It never ends. There is no resolution of the contradiction of politics and ethics but an incessant back-and-forth between them. Jacques Derrida called this a "double-bind."[23] Ethics comes to stop politics when politics becomes too violent. Politics and moral rules come to realize the ethical care for life that would not be realized otherwise. One must take the risk of politics in order to achieve the higher goal of ethics, because something must be done. As Levinas writes in "The State of Caesar and the State of David" (1971):

> Talmudic wisdom is aware of the internal contradiction of the State subordi-
> nating some men to others in order to liberate them, whatever the principles
> embodied by those who hold power. It is a contradiction against which the
> very person who refuses the political order is not protected, since in abstain-
> ing from all collaboration with the ruling power, he collaborates with the
> dark powers that the State represses.[24]

Does this mean, again, that the end—the Torah—justifies the means? No, because, as I just said, there is an endless back-and-forth between politics and ethics. The state is needed, but it is not self-justified, and it can *never* do whatever it pleases. Ethics is always there. The prohibition of murder is always there, and it has the highest value. At each step of political action, ethics comes and disturbs that action. Universal justice remains the goal precisely because ethics is always there and violent means are never justified. Is the final upshot, then, that the state simply should be subjugated to laws that prevent it from violence? Did we need Levinas to learn that trivial truth? Did we need his philosophy to know that a state should be regulated by the higher power of good laws?

Let us insist: Levinas does not merely say that a state should be regulated by good laws. He says and repeats, again and again, that the state is not the higher goal. The state must never be allowed to be more than a means. It must never be taken as an end in itself. The bad spies understood this, even if they forgot what the higher goal was about. And what *is* the higher goal about? Not a comfortable or selfish private life, a life of care for *my own individual rights*, as in the liberal state.[25] The higher goal, for Levinas, is universal and altruistic justice, namely, *care and responsibility for the other*. Therefore—and this is the extremely original side of Levinas's philosophy—the state should be established not only for the sake of those who build it and fight for it, but also for the sake of the other—those who are not part of the political enterprise, those who lost everything, those who are defeated. Levinas aims at a "reversal of the order of things": For him, the important part of politics is precisely to deal with what is not politics itself, namely, what is beyond the rights of the state's members—responsibility for the poor and the aliens.[26]

This is how Levinas understands the Jewish presence on the land of Israel. It is, or it should be, a political entity that uses political means and rules but which, beyond these means and rules, looks for something else. It is a state that is, or should be, searching for Torah, that is, a state that realizes the command of responsibility for the other—who, by definition, is beyond all definitions, is never like us, is never part of us. Levinas does not say it in those terms, but I will conclude by being more Levinassian than Levinas and say: The Israelite conquest of the land can be justified only if it eventually makes room for the Canaanites—against the will of the God who said, in Deuteronomy 20:16–17, "You shall not let a soul remain alive. No, you must proscribe them—the Hittites and the Amorites, the Canaanites and the Perizzites, the Hivites and the Jebusites, as the Lord your God has commanded you"—but obeying the God who said, "Thou shalt not murder."

Notes

1. See Emmanuel Levinas, *Totality and Infinity*, trans. Alphonso Lingis (Pittsburgh: Duquesne University Press, 1969), 21–30.

2. Simon Critchley speaks about the "vexed question of Israel." See his "Introduction," *Parallax* 8, no. 3 (2002):2.

3. As Levinas metaphorically writes, "The best way of encountering the Other is not even to notice the color of his eyes." *Ethics and Infinity*, trans. Richard A. Cohen (Pittsburgh: Duquesne University Press, 1985), 85.

4. See Emmanuel Levinas, *Otherwise Than Being or Beyond Essence*, trans. Alphonso Lingis (Pittsburgh: Duquesne University Press, 1998), esp. ch. 4, pp. 99–131.

5. According to Levinas, politics is "the art of foreseeing war and of winning it by every means." *Totality and Infinity*, 21.

6. A reading of *Sotah* 34b–35a. Emmanuel Levinas, *Nine Talmudic Readings*, trans. Annette Aronowicz (Bloomington: Indiana University Press, 1990), 51–69.

7. Levinas, *Nine Talmudic Readings*, 58.

8. Levinas, *Nine Talmudic Readings*, 56.

9. Levinas, *Nine Talmudic Readings*, 60.

10. Levinas, *Nine Talmudic Readings*, 61.

11. Levinas, *Nine Talmudic Readings*, 61.

12. Levinas, Nine Talmudic Readings, 66.

13. Emmanuel Levinas, *Difficult Freedom*, trans. Seán Hand (Baltimore: The John Hopkins University Press, 1990) 164.

14. Levinas, *Difficult Freedom*, 218.

15. Levinas, *Nine Talmudic Readings*, 111.

16. Levinas, *Nine Talmudic Readings*, 69.

17. Emmanuel Levinas, *Beyond the Verse*, trans. Gary D. Mole (Bloomington: Indiana University Press, 1994), 183.

18. Emmanuel Levinas, "Ethics and Politics," in *The Levinas Reader*, ed. Seán Hand (Oxford: Basil Blackwell, 1989), 296.

19. See Levinas, *Beyond the Verse*, 186–187.

20. There is no synthesis of ethics and politics, but politics is superimposed on ethics: "To the extravagant generosity of the for-the-other is superimposed a reasonable order, ancillary or angelic, of justice through knowledge, and philosophy here is a measure brought to the infinity of the being-for-the-other of peace and proximity, and is like the wisdom of love." Emmanuel Levinas, "Peace and Proximity," in *Basic Philosophical Writings*, ed. Adriaan T. Peperzak, Simon Critchley, and Robert Bernasconi (Bloomington: Indiana University Press, 1996), 169.

21. Levinas, *Totality and Infinity*, 21–22.

22. See Hilary Putnam, "Levinas and Judaism," in *The Cambridge Companion to Levinas*, ed. Simon Critchley and Robert Bernasconi (New York: Cambridge University Press, 2002), 56–57. Putman's main criticism against Levinas is that his radical statements about ethical responsibility are often followed by vague statements, which reduce all radicalism and stipulate that in concrete life the ethical demands cannot be realized.

23. Jacques Derrida, *Adieu to Emmanuel Levinas*, trans. P.-A. Brault and M. Naas (Stanford, Calif.: Stanford University Press, 1999), 20, 33.

24. Levinas, *Beyond the Verse*, 184. Translation modified.

25. See my "Is Liberalism 'All We Need'? Levinas's Politics of Surplus," *Political Theory* 30 (2002).

26. Emmanuel Levinas, *At the Time of the Nations*, trans. M. B. Smith (Bloomington: Indiana University Press, 1994), 61.

Bibliography

Critchley, Simon. "Introduction." *Parallax* 8, no. 3 (2002): 1–4.

Derrida, Jacques. *Adieu to Emmanuel Levinas*. Translated by P.-A. Brault and M. Naas. Stanford, Calif.: Stanford University Press, 1999.

Herzog, Annabel. "Is Liberalism 'All We Need'? Levinas's Politics of Surplus." *Political Theory* 30 (2002): 204–227.

Levinas, Emmanuel. *Otherwise Than Being or Beyond Essence*. Translated by Alphonso Lingis. Pittsburgh: Duquesne University Press, 1998.

Levinas, Emmanuel. "Peace and Proximity." In *Basic Philosophical Writings*, edited by Adriaan T. Peperzak, Simon Critchley, and Robert Bernasconi, 161–170. Bloomington: Indiana University Press, 1996.

Levinas, Emmanuel. *At the Time of the Nations*. Translated by M. B. Smith. Bloomington: Indiana University Press, 1994.

Levinas, Emmanuel. *Beyond the Verse*. Translated by Gary D. Mole. Bloomington: Indiana University Press, 1994.

Levinas, Emmanuel. *Nine Talmudic Readings*. Translated by Annette Aronowicz. Bloomington: Indiana University Press, 1990.

Levinas, Emmanuel. "Ethics and Politics." In *The Levinas Reader*, edited by Seán Hand, 289–297. Oxford: Basil Blackwell, 1989.

Levinas, Emmanuel. *Ethics and Infinity*. Translated by Richard A. Cohen. Pittsburgh: Duquesne University Press, 1985.

Levinas, Emmanuel. *Totality and Infinity*. Translated by Alphonso Lingis. Pittsburgh: Duquesne University Press, 1969.

Putnam, Hilary. "Levinas and Judaism." In *The Cambridge Companion to Levinas*, edited by Simon Critchley and Robert Bernasconi, 33–62. New York: Cambridge University Press, 2002.

The Institute for the Research of
Eretz Israel Its People and Cultures

מכון ון ליר בירושלים
THE VAN LEER JERUSALEM INSTITUTE
معهد فان لير في القدس

Centre de recherche
français à Jérusalem

{ APPENDIX }

The Gift of the Land and the Fate of the Canaanites in Jewish Thought, from Antiquity to the Modern Period

JERUSALEM, 8–10 DECEMBER 2009

Program

TUESDAY, 8 DECEMBER 2009, AT THE FRENCH RESEARCH CENTER, 3 SHIMSHON ST., BAKA

14:00–14:30
Welcome Remarks: Sophie Kessler-Mesguich, Director, CRFJ
General Introduction: Katell Berthelot

14:30–16:00: *Biblical Texts and Jewish Literature from the Second Temple Period*
Chair: James Kugel

- Nili Wazana: 'Everything was fulfilled' *versus* 'the Land that still remains:' Contrasting Conceptions of the Fulfillment of the Promise in the Book of Joshua
- Katell Berthelot: Where May Canaanites Be Found? Canaanites, Phoenicians and Others in Jewish Texts from the Hellenistic and Roman Period

16:00–16:30 Coffee Break
16:30–19:00 ***Biblical Texts and Jewish Literature from the Second Temple Period*** (Con.)
Chair: James Kugel

- Michael Avioz: Land Theology in Josephus: A Reappraisal
- Menahem Kister: The Emergence of the Polemic Concerning the Fate of the Canaanites: Motives and Motifs

19:00 Dinner

WEDNESDAY, 9 DECEMBER 2009, AT THE VAN LEER JERUSALEM INSTITUTE, 43 JABOTINSKY ST.

9:15: Opening Remarks: Gabriel Motzkin, Director, The Van Leer Jerusalem Institute
9:30–11:00 ***Rabbinic Literature***
Chair: Marc Hirshman

- Ishay Rosen-Zvi: Idolatry and the Biblical Concept of *Herem* in Tannaitic Midrash
- Eyal Ben Eliyahu: The Rabbinic Perception of the Presence of the Canaanites in the Land of Israel

11:00–11:30 Coffee Break
11:30–12:30 ***Biblical Texts, Jewish Literature from the Second Temple Period and Rabbinic Literature*** (Cont.)

- Marc Hirshman: discussion of the preceding papers, general discussion

12:30–14:00 Lunch Break
14:00–15:30: ***Medieval Jewish Thought***
Chair: Israel Yuval

- Menachem Kellner: *Milhemet Mitzvah* (Obligatory War) and the Seven Canaanite Nations
- Evyatar Marienberg: *The Canaanite was then in the Land*: 'Canaanites' in Jewish European Medieval Households

15:30–16:00 Coffee Break
16:00–18:00 ***Medieval Jewish Thought*** (Cont.)
Chair: Joseph David

- Haggai Ben Shammai: Theological Consideration of the Radical Treatment of the 'Seven Nations' in Medieval Judaeo-Arabic Exegesis

- Paul Fenton: Canaan and the Fate of the Canaanites according to Muslim Writers
- General discussion

18:00: Cocktail

19:15–21:30 (מושב ערב ביד יצחק בן-צבי (פתוח לציבור הרחב /הכניסה חופשית
יו"ר: פרופ' דניאל שוורץ
הרצאות:
פרופ' ישראל קנוהל, הוויכוח בין מקורות התורה בשאלת היחס לעמי כנען
פרופ' דב שוורץ, כיבוש הארץ והיחס לאומות היושבות עליה בהגות הציונית הדתית

19:15–21:30 *Evening Session at the Yad Ben-Zvi* (open to the public; in Hebrew)
Chair: Daniel Schwartz

Lectures by:

Prof. Israel Knohl: The Debate between Biblical Sources about the Issue of the Peoples of Canaan

Prof. Dov Schwartz: Religious Zionism on the Seven Nations and the Conquest of the Land of Israel

THURSDAY, 10 DECEMBER 2009, AT THE VAN LEER JERUSALEM INSTITUTE

9:30–11:00 *Modern and Contemporary Jewish Thought*
Chair: Edward Breuer

- Matthias Morgenstern: The Biblical Conquest of Canaan in the Eyes of German-Jewish Orthodoxy
- Yoram Jacobson: The Relation between the Land of Canaan and the Land of Israel according to the Hasidic School of Gur

11:00–11:30 Coffee Break
11:30–13:00
Chair: Avinoam Rosenak

- Joseph David: Between the Canaanites and the Israelites – A Land of Crimes and Laws of its Own
- Baruch Alster: R. Moshe Feinstein on *Milchemet Mitsvah*: Halakhah, Morality, and Exegesis

13:00–14:30 Lunch Break
14:30–16:00 *Modern and Contemporary Jewish Thought* (Con.)
Chair: Jonathan Cohen

- Steven Kepnes: Herman Cohen on Canaanites and *gerim*
- Annabel Herzog: Emmanuel Levinas on Canaanites and Zionism

16:00–16:30 Coffee Break
16:30–18:00

- Zeev Harvey: Rabbi Reines on the Conquest of Canaan and Zionism
- General discussion and conclusion

19:00: Dinner

LIST OF PARTICIPANTS

- Baruch Alster (Bar-Ilan University)
- Michael Avioz (Bar-Ilan University)
- Eyal Ben Elyahu (The Hebrew University of Jerusalem)
- Haggai Ben Shammai (The Hebrew University of Jerusalem)
- Katell Berthelot (CNRS – French Research Center in Jerusalem)
- Joseph David (The Hebrew University of Jerusalem)
- Paul Fenton (Paris IV-Sorbonne University)
- Zeev Harvey (The Hebrew University of Jerusalem)
- Annabel Herzog (Haifa University)
- Marc Hirshman (The Hebrew University of Jerusalem)
- Yoram Jacobson (Tel-Aviv University)
- Menachem Kellner (Haifa University)
- Steve Kepnes (Colgate University)
- Menahem Kister (The Hebrew University of Jerusalem)
- Israel Knohl (The Hebrew University of Jerusalem)
- Evyatar Marienberg (University of North Carolina)
- Matthias Morgenstern (Tübingen University)
- Gabriel Motzkin (The Van Leer Jerusalem Institute)
- Ishay Rosen-Zvi (Tel-Aviv University)
- Daniel Schwartz (The Hebrew University of Jerusalem)
- Dov Schwartz (Bar-Ilan University)
- Nili Wazana (The Hebrew University of Jerusalem)

{ INDEX OF ANCIENT SOURCES }

Rabbinic Literature